ACADEMIC READING

Fifth Edition

Kathleen T. McWhorter

Niagara County Community College

PEARSON
Longman

New York • San Francisco • Boston
London • Toronto • Sydney • Tokyo • Singapore • Madrid
Mexico City • Munich • Paris • Cape Town • Hong Kong • Montreal

Vice President and Editor in Chief: Joseph Terry
Senior Acquisitions Editor: Steven Rigolosi
Deveopment Manager: Janet Lanphier
Development Editor: Leslie Taggart
Senior Marketing Manager: Melanie Craig
Senior Supplements Editor: Donna Campion
Media Supplements Editor: Nancy Garcia
Production Manager: Joseph Vella
Project Coordination, Text Design, and Electronic Page Makeup: Thompson Steele, Inc.
Cover Design Manager: John Callahan
Cover Designer: Kay Petronio
Cover Photos: Courtesy of PhotoDisc, Inc.
Manufacturing Buyer: Roy L. Pickering, Jr.
Printer and Binder: The Hamilton Printing Co.
Cover Printer: Phoenix Color Corp.

Library of Congress Cataloging-in-Publication Data

McWhorter, Kathleen T.
    Academic reading / Kathleen T. McWhorter.—5th ed.
      p. cm.
    Includes bibliographical references (p.) and index.
    ISBN 0-321-10425-0 (alk. paper)
    1. Reading (Higher education) 2. Study skills. 3. Reading comprehension. I. Title.

 LB2395.3.M37 2003
 428.4'071'l—dc21   2003048268

Please visit our Website at www.ablongman.com/mcwhorter

ISBN 0-321-10424-2

    3 4 5 6 7 8 9 10—HT—06 05 04

CONTENTS

PREFACE

Each academic discipline has its own subject matter, approach, and methodology. Consequently, reading assignments in each discipline require unique sets of reading skills and strategies. Many students who possess adequate general reading skills have not learned to adapt them to the demands of different academic disciplines. *Academic Reading* is a unique text that focuses on these important discipline-specific reading skills.

APPROACH

Although many texts teach general reading skills, few show students how to apply, modify, and adapt their skills to accommodate the unique features and requirements of various academic disciplines. This text provides a complete review of comprehension and vocabulary skills and general textbook reading strategies; then it discusses ways to apply these strategies to six major academic disciplines.

Academic Reading uses several current, effective methodologies to develop reading skills.

- **Active Reading** For many students, reading is a passive assimilation process: their goal is to acquire as many facts and as much information as possible. The active reading approach used in *Academic Reading* encourages students to interact with the text by predicting, questioning, and evaluating ideas.
- **Levels of Thinking** Using Bloom's taxonomy of cognitive skills as a framework, this book shows students how to apply higher-order thinking skills to their course work.
- **Metacomprehension** Metacomprehension is the reader's awareness of his or her own comprehension processes. Mature and proficient readers exert a great deal of cognitive control over their reading: they analyze reading tasks, select appropriate reading strategies, and monitor the effectiveness of those strategies. This text guides students in developing these metacomprehensive strategies.
- **Academic Thought Patterns** The text describes six common academic thought patterns that are used in various disciplines to organize and structure ideas. Four additional patterns are also discussed. These patterns, presented as organizing schemata, are used to establish order, consistency, and predictability within academic disciplines.

- **Writing As Learning**   Although most students regard writing as a means of communication, few are accustomed to using it as a reading aid to help them organize information, focus ideas, recognize relationships, or generate new ideas. This text introduces writing as a vehicle for learning. Techniques such as underlining, outlining, note taking, and cognitive mapping are approached as learning strategies.
- **Learning Style**   Not all students learn in the same way. To help students discover their unique learning preferences, the text includes a Learning Style Questionnaire and offers students suggestions for adapting their study methods to suit learning style characteristics.

DISCIPLINE-SPECIFIC READING SKILLS

With the fundamental skills in place, college students are able to develop a diverse repertoire of reading strategies and to select and alternate among them. Some of the discipline-specific reading skills they will develop include the following:

In Social Sciences
- understanding theories in the social sciences
- reading reports of research
- making comparisons and applications

In Business
- reading models
- reviewing case studies
- studying organization charts and flowcharts
- approaching supplemental readings

In Humanities and the Arts
- understanding figurative language
- reading poetry and short stories
- working with literary criticism
- studying visual elements in art

In Mathematics
- understanding mathematical language
- reading sample problems
- verbalizing processes
- reading graphics
- approaching word problems

In Natural Sciences
- previewing before reading
- understanding scientific approaches

- studying sample problems
- learning terminology and notation

In Technical and Applied Fields
- reading illustrations and drawings
- using visualization
- reading technical manuals
- employing problem-solving strategies

Each chapter in Part Four includes a list of Web sites important to the discipline. These lists will help students find reliable academic sources to consult for research and reading in the field.

CONTENT OVERVIEW

Academic Reading is organized into four units. Chapters within each unit are interchangeable, allowing the instructor to adapt the material to a variety of instructional sequences.

Part 1, Fundamental Reading Strategies, presents fundamental reading strategies that provide the foundation for the remainder of the text. Chapter 1 introduces the key concepts of active reading and comprehension monitoring, and includes a learning style analysis. Chapter 2 presents fundamental comprehension skills and integrates the concept of adjusting rate to meet comprehension demands. Chapter 3 discusses vocabulary: contextual aids, structural analysis, and specialized terminology.

Part 2, Critical Reading Strategies, teaches students to interpret and evaluate what they read. Chapter 4 concentrates on evaluating the author's message and includes topics such as making inferences, distinguishing between fact and opinion, and analyzing the writer's tone. In Chapter 5 students are shown how to analyze the author's technique; topics include evaluating generalizations and assumptions, understanding connotative meanings, and recognizing manipulative language. Reading and evaluating arguments, both inductive and deductive, and identifying errors in logical reasoning are the focus of Chapter 6.

Part 3, Academic Reading Strategies, is concerned with recognizing patterns of general academic thought, learning from textbooks, reading graphics, reading online sources, using writing to learn, and approaching research, reference, and collateral assignments.

Part 4, Strategies for Specific Disciplines, consists of six chapters, each of which focuses on reading strategies for a specific discipline: social sciences, business, humanities and arts, mathematics, natural sciences, and technical fields. Each chapter describes unique characteristics of the discipline, specialized reading techniques, predominant thought patterns, and methods for adapting study techniques.

SPECIAL FEATURES

The following features enhance the text's effectiveness.

- **Learning Objectives** Each chapter begins with a brief list of objectives that establishes its focus and provides students with purposes for reading. The objectives can also be used as a way to review and check retention after reading the chapter.
- **Discipline Overviews** The text provides an introduction to six major academic disciplines. It acquaints the student with the basic subject matter and the basic approach used in those disciplines. For example, the text explains and discusses
  - why social science is a "science"
  - how business focuses on organization and management
  - literature as a focus on ideas
  - why mathematics is a sequential thinking process
  - how the sciences focus on explanations of natural phenomena
  - the importance of application and performance in technical fields
  - The text gives suggestions for adapting study techniques to meet the requirements of each academic discipline.

- **Multimedia Activities** Each chapter contains two Web activities that reinforce the skills taught in the chapter.
- **Chapter Summaries** Each chapter includes a summary intended to help students review and consolidate chapter content.
- **Reading Selections** Each chapter concludes with one or more reading selections from a college textbook or related academic source to reinforce the skills and strategies presented in the chapter. Each reading is accompanied by a vocabulary review exercise, comprehension questions, critical thinking questions, and an exercise on applying learning/study strategies.
- **Paired Readings** Nine sets of paired readings are included in the text. Each pair provides two viewpoints on a given topic and encourages students to integrate ideas and synthesize sources. Questions are included to guide students in applying critical thinking skills to make connections between the ideas and approaches of the readings.
- **Academic Applications** Exercises labeled "Academic Application" require students to apply their reading skills to textbook or course materials from their other college courses.

- **Exercises for Collaborative Learning**   Additional exercises designated "Learning Collaboratively" have been added to provide structured activities in which students can learn from one another as they analyze and apply skills introduced in the chapter.

CHANGES IN THE FIFTH EDITION

Numerous changes and additions have been made in the fifth edition.

- **NEW Chapter 5 on Critical Reading**   Chapter 5, "Evaluating the Author's Techniques," encourages students to analyze how an author achieves his or her purpose. The chapter discusses connotative and figurative language, bias, missing information, generalizations, and assumptions. The chapter also shows students how to recognize and evaluate manipulative language, including using clichés, jargon, allusions, euphemisms, doublespeak, and hyperbole. Chapters 4, 5, and 6 now form a new Part Two of the book, "Critical Reading Strategies."
- **NEW Mulitmedia Applications**   Each chapter now includes two Web-based activities that reinforce the skills taught in the chapter and enable students to see academic applications of chapter content.
- **Curriculum-Specific Web Sites**   Each chapter in Part Four contains a list of useful academic Web sites that students can visit to initiate reading or research within a discipline. The list is divided into four categories: Directories/Web Guides, Journals/Indexes/Databases, References, and Government Resources.
- **Revised Chapter 10, Reading Online**   This chapter has been refocused to emphasize the evaluation of electronic sources. The chapter discusses the differences between reading online and print sources and shows students how to develop new ways of thinking and learning when reading electronic sources.
- **Expanded Coverage of Academic Thought Patterns**   Three exercises have been added for each pattern, allowing students to grasp how the patterns work in a variety of textbook excerpts. Four new patterns have been added—statement-clarification, summary, generalization-example, and addition—along with practice exercises.
- **New Readings**   Twelve new end-of-chapter reading selections have been chosen to provide current, up-to-date coverage of a wide range of academic fields. Numerous in-chapter textbook excerpts have also been replaced or updated.
- **Academic Success Appendix**   The study tips, previously dispersed throughout Parts 1 and 2, have been moved to an appendix, allowing students to access them more easily.

BOOK-SPECIFIC ANCILLARY MATERIALS

The Instructor's Manual   The Instructor's Manual provides numerous suggestions for using the text, including how to structure the course and how to
approach each section of the book. The Instructor's Manual also contains a
complete answer key for the text, and a set of overhead projection transparency
masters (0-321-10426-9).

Assessment Package/Test Bank   An assessment package/test bank accompanies the text. It contains two sets of multiple-choice chapter review quizzes that
measure students' knowledge of chapter content. It also contains a set of mastery tests that measure students' ability to apply concepts, principles, and techniques taught in the chapter. The mastery tests simulate actual academic
situations, assignments, and course materials and are designed to be self-
scoring if the instructor so desires (0-321-10427-7).

PowerPoint Slides   A series of PowerPoint slides for each chapter can be
downloaded free from the Longman Web site at http://www.awlonline.com/
basicskills/mcwhorter.

McWhorter Companion Website   A dedicated Web site to accompany the
McWhorter reading and study skills series is available to instructors and students. This Web site includes study tips, electronically scored quizzes and tests,
Internet activities and links, a bulletin board, and more. Please visit the site at
http://www.ablongman.com/mcwhorter.

THE LONGMAN DEVELOPMENTAL READING PACKAGE

In addition to the book-specific supplements discussed above, a series of other
skills-based supplements is available for both instructors and students. All of
these supplements are available either free or at greatly reduced prices.

For Additional Reading and Reference

The Dictionary Deal   Two dictionaries can be shrink-wrapped with this text for a
nominal fee. *The New American Webster Handy College Dictionary* is a paperback
reference text with more than 100,000 entries. *Merriam Webster's Collegiate
Dictionary,* tenth edition, is a hardback reference with a citation file of more than
14.5 million examples of English words drawn from actual use. Contact your
local Addison Wesley Longman sales consultant for information on how to order.

Penguin Quality Paperback Titles   A series of Penguin paperbacks is available
at a significant discount when shrink-wrapped with this title. Some titles avail-

able are: Toni Morrison's *Beloved,* Julia Alvarez's *How the Garcia Girls Lost Their Accents,* Mark Twain's *The Adventures of Huckleberry Finn, Narrative of the Life of Frederick Douglass,* Harriet Beecher Stowe's *Uncle Tom's Cabin,* Dr. Martin Luther King Jr.'s *Why We Can't Wait,* and plays by Shakespeare, Miller, and Albee. For a complete list of titles or more information on how to order Penguin titles at a discount, please contact your Addison Wesley Longman sales consultant.

The Longman Textbook Reader   This supplement, for use in developmental reading courses, offers five complete chapters from AWL textbooks: computer science, biology, psychology, communications, and business. Each chapter includes additional comprehension quizzes, critical thinking questions, and group activities. Available FREE when packaged with *Academic Reading.* Contact your local Longman sales consultant for information on how to order this special package.

The Pocket Reader, First Edition, and The Brief Pocket Reader, First Edition These inexpensive volumes contain 80 and 50 brief readings respectively (1–3 pages each) on a variety of themes: writers on writing, nature, women and men, customs and habits, politics, rights and obligations, and coming of age. Also included is an alternate rhetorical table of contents (*The Pocket Reader:* 0-321-07668-0; *The Brief Pocket Reader:* 0-321-07699-9).

Newsweek Alliance   Instructors may choose to shrink-wrap a 12-week subscription to *Newsweek* with any Longman text. The price of the subscription is 57 cents per issue (a total of $6.84 for the subscription). Available with the subscription is a free "Interactive Guide to *Newsweek*"—a workbook for students who are using the text. In addition, *Newsweek* provides a wide variety of instructor supplements free to teachers, including maps, Skills Builders, and weekly quizzes. Contact your local Addison Wesley Longman sales consultant for information on how to order *Newsweek* packaged with *Academic Reading.*

Electronic and Online Offerings

Longman Reading Road Trip Multimedia Software, Version 2.0   This innovative and exciting multimedia reading software is available either in CD-ROM format or as a site license. The package takes students on a tour of 15 cities and landmarks throughout the United States. Each of the 15 modules corresponds to a reading or study skill (for example, finding the main idea, understanding patterns of organization, and thinking critically). All modules contain a tour of the location, instruction and tutorial, exercises, interactive feedback, and mastery tests. This second release includes more streamlined and flexible navigation, along with hundreds of new readings, exercises, and tests. Use ISBN number 0-201-71565-1 to order *Academic Reading* packaged with Free Reading Road Trip 2.0 for your students.

***Researching Online,* Fifth Edition**   A perfect companion for a new age, this indispensable new supplement helps students navigate the Internet. Adapted from *Teaching Online,* the instructor's Internet guide, *Researching Online* speaks directly to students, giving them detailed, step-by-step instructions for performing electronic searches. Available free when shrink-wrapped with this text. Contact your local Addison Wesley Longman sales consultant for information on how to order.

Research Navigator*™ *Guide for English.   Designed to teach students how to conduct high-quality online research and to document it properly, Research Navigator guides provide discipline-specific academic resources, in addition to helpful tips on the writing process, online research, and finding and citing valid sources. Free when packaged with any Allyn & Bacon/Longman text, Research Navigator guides include an access code to Research Navigator™ — providing access to thousands of academic journals and periodicals, the NY Times Search by Subject Archive, Link Library, Library Guides, and more.

The Longman English Pages Web Site   Both students and instructors can visit our free content-rich Web site for additional reading selections and writing exercises. From the Longman English pages, visitors can conduct a simulated Web search, learn how to write a résumé and cover letter, or try their hand at poetry writing. Stop by and visit us at http://www.ablongman.com/englishpages.

The Longman Electronic Newsletter   Twice a month during the spring and fall, instructors who have subscribed receive a free copy of the Longman Basic Skills Newsletter in their e-mailbox. Written by experienced classroom instructors, the newsletter offers teaching tips, classroom activities, book reviews, and more. To subscribe, visit the Longman Basic Skills Web Site at http://www.ablongman.com/basicskills, or send an e-mail to Basic Skills@ablongman.com.

For Instructors

Electronic Test Bank for Reading   This electronic test bank offers more than 3,000 questions in all areas of reading, including vocabulary, main idea, supporting details, patterns of organization, language, critical thinking, analytical reasoning, inference, point of view, visual aids, and textbook reading. With this easy-to-use CD-ROM, instructors simply choose questions from the electronic test bank, then print out the completed test for distribution (0-321-08179-X).

CLAST Test Package, Fourth Edition   These two 40-item objective tests evaluate students' readiness for the CLAST exams. Strategies for teaching CLAST preparedness are included. Free with any Longman English title (Reproducible sheets: 0-321-01950-4; Computerized IBM version: 0-321-01982-2; Computerized Mac version: 0-321-01983-0).

TASP Test Package, Third Edition   These 12 practice pre-tests and post-tests assess the same reading and writing skills covered in the TASP examination. Free with any Longman English title (Reproducible sheets: 0-321-01959-8; Computerized IBM version: 0-321-01985-7; Computerized Mac version: 0-321-01984-9).

***Teaching Online: Internet Research, Conversation, and Composition,* Second Edition**   Ideal for instructors who have never surfed the Net, this easy-to-follow guide offers basic definitions, numerous examples, and step-by-step information about finding and using Internet sources. Free to adopters (0-321-01957-1).

ACKNOWLEDGMENTS

I wish to acknowledge the contributions of my colleagues and reviewers who have provided valuable advice and suggestions for this and previous editions of *Academic Reading:* Betty Andrews-Tobias, Suffolk Community College; Thomas Athey, California State Technical College; Pamela Bourgeois, California State University, Northridge; Janice Buchner, Suffolk County Community College; Terry Bullock, University of Cincinnati; Marilyn Burke, Austin Community College; Steve Cohen, Norwalk Community Technical College; Diane Cole, Pensacola Junior College; Janet Curtis, Fullerton College; Pat D'Allessio, Dutchess Community College; Susan Deese, University of New Mexico; Cathlene Denny, St. Johns River Community College; J. Ross Eshleman, Wayne State University; Helen Gilbart, St. Petersburg Junior College; Ed Gill, Indiana Vocational Technical College; Brian Holmes, San Jose State University; Jenny Joczik, College of Charleston; Sandra Keith, St. Cloud State University; Kathleen Kiefer, Colorado State University; Terry Kozek, Housatonic Community College; Linda W. Larou, Dutchess Community College; Beverly Lipper, Dutchess Community College; Alice Mackey, Missouri Western State College; Gail Moore, York Technical College; David Murphy, Waubonsee Community College; Karen Nelson, Craven Community College; Michael Newman, Hunter College; Jan Pechenek, Tufts University; Paul Perdew, University of Scranton; Michelle Peterson, Santa Barbara City College; Karen Samson, Chicago State University; Nancy E. Smith, Florida Community College at Jacksonville; Andrew Szilagyi, University of Houston; Betsy Tobias, Suffolk County Community College; Katherine Wellington, Metropolitan State University; Michaeline Wideman, University of Cincinnati; Mary Wolting, Indiana University–Purdue University; Lawrence Ziewaz, Michigan State University.

I am particularly indebted to Leslie Taggart, my developmental editor, for her most valuable advice and guidance. She has contributed knowledge, creativity, and energy, as well as practicality. I also wish to thank Steven Rigolosi, Senior Acquisitions Editor, for his active and enthusiastic role in developing the revision plan and overseeing its implementation.

KATHLEEN T. MCWHORTER

THE MCWHORTER READING AND STUDY SKILLS SERIES

Kathleen McWhorter has written numerous textbooks for reading and study skills courses. All the McWhorter books emphasize research-proven techniques for active learning, critical thinking and metacognition, writing to learn, and learning styles, as well as providing detailed coverage of new online contexts for reading.

Academic Reading combines six chapters on reading in the disciplines—the social sciences, business, the humanities and literature, mathematics, the natural sciences, and the technical and applied fields—with coverage of reading comprehension and critical thinking. Fundamental reading strategies, including how to read arguments, and academic reading strategies, such as how to read research and collateral assignments, provide a strong basis for the discipline-specific reading strategies. This text is designed for use in the third reading course, or in a college-level reading course.

College Reading and Study Skills presents the basic techniques for college success, including time management, analysis of learning style, active reading, and notetaking. The text offers strategies for strengthening literal and critical comprehension, improving vocabulary skills, and developing reading flexibility. Students also discover methods for reading and learning from textbook assignments, including outlining and summarizing, and for taking exams.

Efficient and Flexible Reading teaches students how to vary their approach to written texts based on the material and their purpose for reading. In addition to instruction in literal and critical comprehension skills, vocabulary, and study skills, *Efficient and Flexible Reading* teaches students how to identify text structures and thought patterns for more efficient learning. Emphasizing reading as an active thinking process, the text (designed for use in the second reading course) presents systems for monitoring concentration, comprehension, and recall.

Essential Reading Skills, designed for use in the first reading course, is the most basic of the McWhorter texts. Focusing on the essential reading skills of vocabulary development, main idea, details, and patterns of organization (with a brief introduction to critical reading), this text features a programmed approach of instruction, example, and practice, followed by a series of review and mastery tests on each reading skill.

Guide to College Reading is designed for use in the first reading course, focusing on the key areas of reading comprehension, vocabulary improvement, and textbook reading. Guide to College Reading provides instruction in the basics—main idea, vocabulary building, supporting details, and patterns of organization. Extensive skill practice and four mastery tests in each chapter provide ample practice in the basic reading skills. Additional readings at the end of the text provide more exercises and applications.

Reading Across the Disciplines improves college students' reading and thinking skills through brief skill instruction and extensive practice structured around readings in various academic disciplines. *Reading Across the Disciplines* is organized into three parts. Part One, "Reading and Thinking in College," presents a brief skill introduction (in handbook format) introducing students to essential vocabulary, comprehension, critical reading, and reading rate skills. Part Two, "Selections from Academic Disciplines," has twelve chapters, each containing four readings representative of a different academic discipline. Part Three, "Textbook Chapter Readings," contains two complete textbook chapters that enable students to practice skills on longer pieces of writing.

Study and Critical Thinking Skills in College integrates the study and critical thinking skills students need to achieve college success. Active learning strategies and techniques that develop students' proficiency in interacting with text and lecture material are presented, along with three chapters on test taking strategies. Students learn how they can take charge of their college careers, establish goals, and manage their time, in addition to how to take notes in class, study specialized vocabulary, and organize and synthesize content from lectures and reading. For use in study skills, freshman orientation, or academic success courses.

CHAPTER 1

STRATEGIES FOR ACTIVE READING

LEARNING OBJECTIVES

✦ To understand how reading contributes to college success
✦ To assess your learning style
✦ To build your concentration skills
✦ To develop multilevel thinking skills
✦ To learn to preview and predict before reading
✦ To develop questions to guide your reading
✦ To check your comprehension

Ask college students to name the ingredients of success in college, and they are likely to say:

"Knowing how to study."

"You have to like school."

"Hard work!"

"Time to study!"

"Motivation!"

Students seldom mention reading as an essential skill, and yet reading is a hidden factor in college success. When you think of college, you may think of attending classes and labs, completing assignments, studying for and taking exams, and writing papers. A closer look, however, reveals that reading is an important part of each of these activities.

Reading stays "behind the scenes" because instructors rarely evaluate it directly. Grades are based on outcomes: that is, how well you express your ideas in papers or how well you do on exams. Yet reading is the primary means by which you acquire your ideas and gather information.

Throughout this text, you will learn numerous ways to use reading as a tool for college success.

READING AND ACADEMIC SUCCESS

Reading involves much more than moving your eyes across lines of print, more than recognizing words, and more than reading sentences. **Reading is thinking.** It is an active process of identifying important ideas and comparing, evaluating, and applying them.

Have you ever gone to a ballgame and watched the fans? Most do not sit and watch passively. Instead, they direct the plays, criticize the calls, encourage the players, and reprimand the coach. They care enough to get actively engaged with the game. Just like interested fans, active readers get involved. They question, challenge, and criticize, as well as understand. Table 1–1 contrasts the active strategies of successful readers with the passive ones of less successful readers.

Throughout the remainder of this chapter, you will discover specific strategies for becoming a more active learner. Not all strategies will work for everyone. Experiment to discover those that work for you.

EXERCISE 1–1	*Consider each of the following reading assignments. Discuss different ways in which you could get actively involved with them.*

1. Reading two poems by e.e. cummings for a literature class.
2. Reviewing procedures for your next biology lab.
3. Taking notes on an article in *Time* magazine assigned by your political science instructor.

TABLE 1–1   ACTIVE VERSUS PASSIVE READING

Active Readers . . .	Passive Readers . . .
Tailor their reading to suit each assignment.	Read all assignments the same way.
Analyze the purpose of an assignment.	Read an assignment *because* it was assigned.
Adjust their speed to suit their purpose.	Read everything at the same speed.
Question ideas in the assignment.	Accept whatever is in print as true.
Compare and connect textbook material with lecture content.	Study lecture notes and textbook separately.
Skim headings to find out what an assignment is about before beginning to read.	Check the length of an assignment and then begin reading.
Make sure they understand what they are reading as they go along.	Read until the assignment is completed.
Read with pencil in hand, highlighting, jotting notes, and marking key vocabulary.	Simply read.
Develop personalized strategies that are particularly effective.	Follow routine, standard methods.

EXERCISE 1–2

Write a list of active reading strategies you already use. Add to your list several new strategies that you intend to begin using. Compare your list with a classmate's.

_____

_____

_____

ASSESSING YOUR LEARNING STYLE

Textbook reading assignments are central to many college classes. Your instructors make daily or weekly assignments and expect you to read the material, learn it, and pass tests on it. Textbook assignments often form the basis of class lectures and discussions. An important part of many college classes, then, consists of completing reading assignments.

Reading and understanding an assignment, however, does not mean you have learned the material. You need to do more than read to learn the content. What else should you do? The answer is not simple.

People differ in how they learn and the methods and strategies they use to learn. These differences can be explained by what is known as *learning style.* Your learning style can begin to explain why some courses are easier for you than others and why you learn better from one instructor than another. Learning style also can explain why certain assignments are easy for you and other learning tasks are difficult.

The following brief Learning Style Questionnaire will help you analyze how you learn and show you how to develop an action plan for learning what you read. Complete and score the questionnaire before continuing with this section.

Learning Style Questionnaire

DIRECTIONS: Each item presents two choices. Select the alternative that best describes you. In cases in which neither choice suits you, select the one that is closer to your preference. Write the letter of your choice in the blank to the left of each item.

Part One

_____ 1. I would prefer to follow a set of
a. oral directions.
b. written directions.

_____ 2. I would prefer to
a. attend a lecture given by a famous psychologist.
b. read an article written by the psychologist.

_____ 3. When I am introduced to someone, it is easier for me to remember the person's
a. name.
b. face.

_____ 4. I find it easier to learn new information using
a. language (words).
b. images (pictures).

_____ 5. I prefer classes in which the instructor
   a. lectures and answers questions.
   b. uses films and videos.

_____ 6. To follow current events, I would prefer to
   a. listen to the news on the radio.
   b. read the newspaper.

_____ 7. To learn how to operate a fax machine, I would prefer to
   a. listen to a friend's explanation.
   b. watch a demonstration.

Part Two

_____ 8. I prefer to
   a. work with facts and details.
   b. construct theories and ideas.

_____ 9. I would prefer a job involving
   a. following specific instructions.
   b. reading, writing, and analyzing.

_____ 10. I prefer to
   a. solve math problems using a formula.
   b. discover why the formula works.

_____ 11. I would prefer to write a term paper explaining
   a. how a process works.
   b. a theory.

_____ 12. I prefer tasks that require me to
   a. follow careful, detailed instructions.
   b. use reasoning and critical analysis.

_____ 13. For a criminal justice course, I would prefer to
   a. discover how and when a law can be used.
   b. learn how and why it became law.

_____ 14. To learn more about the operation of a high-speed computer printer, I would prefer to
   a. work with several types of printers.
   b. understand the principles on which they operate.

Part Three

_____ 15. To solve a math problem, I would prefer to
   a. draw or visualize the problem.
   b. study a sample problem and use it as a model.

_____ 16. To best remember something, I
   a. create a mental picture.
   b. write it down.

_____ 17. Assembling a bicycle from a diagram would be
   a. easy.
   b. challenging.

_____ 18. I prefer classes in which I
   a. handle equipment or work with models.
   b. participate in a class discussion.

_____ 19. To understand and remember
how a machine works, I would
a. draw a diagram.
b. write notes.

_____ 20. I enjoy
a. drawing or working with
my hands.
b. speaking, writing, and
listening.

_____ 21. If I were trying to locate an office
on an unfamiliar campus,
I would prefer
a. a map.
b. written directions.

Part Four

_____ 22. For a grade in biology lab,
I would prefer to
a. work with a lab partner.
b. work alone.

_____ 23. When faced with a difficult
personal problem, I prefer to
a. discuss it with others.
b. resolve it myself.

_____ 24. Many instructors could improve
their classes by
a. including more discussion and
group activities.
b. allowing students to work on
their own more frequently.

_____ 25. When listening to a lecturer or
speaker, I respond more to the
a. person presenting the idea.
b. ideas themselves.

_____ 26. When on a team project, I prefer
to
a. work with several team
members.
b. divide the tasks and complete
those assigned to me.

_____ 27. I prefer to shop and do errands
a. with friends.
b. by myself.

_____ 28. A job in a busy office is
a. more appealing than working
alone.
b. less appealing than working
alone.

Part Five

_____ 29. To make decisions, I rely on
a. my experiences and gut
feelings.
b. facts and objective data.

_____ 30. To complete a task, I
a. can use whatever is available
to get the job done.
b. must have everything I need
at hand.

_____ 31. I prefer to express my ideas and
feelings through
a. music, song, or poetry.
b. direct, concise language.

_____ 32. I prefer instructors who
a. allow students to be guided
by their own interests.
b. make their expectations clear
and explicit.

_____ 33. I tend to
    a. challenge and question what
       I hear and read.
    b. accept what I hear and read.

_____ 34. I prefer
    a. essay exams.
    b. objective exams.

_____ 35. In completing an assignment,
    I prefer to
    a. figure out my own approach.
    b. be told exactly what to do.

To score your questionnaire, record the total number of a's you selected and the total number of b's for each part of the questionnaire. Record your totals in the scoring grid provided below.

SCORING GRID

Part	Total # of Choice "a"	Total # of Choice "b"
One	_____ Auditory	_____ Visual
Two	_____ Applied	_____ Conceptual
Three	_____ Spatial	_____ Verbal
Four	_____ Social	_____ Independent
Five	_____ Creative	_____ Pragmatic

Now, circle your higher score for each part of the questionnaire. The word below the score you circled indicates a strength in your learning style. The next section explains how to interpret your scores.

Interpreting Your Scores

Each of the five parts of the questionnaire identifies one aspect of your learning style. These five aspects are explained below.

Part One: Auditory or Visual Learners   This score indicates whether you learn more effectively by listening (auditory) or by seeing (visual). If your auditory score is higher than your visual score, you tend to learn more easily by hearing than by reading. A higher visual score suggests strengths with visual modes of learning such as reading, studying pictures, reading diagrams, and so forth.

Part Two: Applied or Conceptual Learners   This score describes the types of learning tasks and learning situations you instinctively prefer and find easiest to handle. If you are an applied learner, you prefer tasks that involve real objects and situations. Therefore, practical, real-life examples are ideal for you. If you are a conceptual learner, you prefer to work with language and ideas; you tend to rely less on practical applications for understanding than applied learners.

Part Three: Spatial or Verbal Learners   This score reveals your ability to work with spatial relationships. Spatial learners can visualize or mentally "see" how things work or how they are positioned in space. Their strengths may include drawing, assembling, or repairing things. Verbal or nonspatial learners lack skills in positioning things in space. Instead, they rely on verbal or language skills.

Part Four: Social or Independent Learners   This score reveals whether you like to work alone or with others. If you are a social learner, you prefer to work with others—such as classmates and instructors—closely and directly. You tend to be people-oriented and enjoy personal interaction. If you are an independent learner, you tend to be self-directed or self-motivated as well as goal-oriented.

Part Five: Creative or Pragmatic Learners   This score describes the approach you prefer to take toward learning tasks. Creative learners are imaginative and innovative. They prefer to learn through discovery or experimentation. They are comfortable taking risks and following hunches. Pragmatic learners are practical, logical, and systematic. They seek order and are comfortable following rules.

If you disagree with any part of the Learning Style Questionnaire, go with your own instincts, rather than the questionnaire results. Think of the questionnaire as just a quick assessment, but trust your self-knowledge.

Using Learning Style Effectively

Now that you have completed the Learning Style Questionnaire and know more about *how* you learn, you are ready to develop an action plan for learning what you read. Suppose you have discovered that you are an auditory learner. You still have to read your assignments, which is a visual task. To learn the assignment, however, you should translate the material into an auditory form. For example, you could repeat aloud, using your own words, information that you want to remember, or you could tape-record key information and play it back. If you are a social learner, you could work with a classmate, the two of you testing each other out loud. Such activities not only shift the presentation of ideas from visual to auditory form but also give you practice in using internal dialogue (see p. 26).

Table 1–2 on page 8 lists the different types of learning styles and offers suggestions for how students who exhibit each style might learn most effectively from a reading assignment. You can use this table to build an action plan for more effective learning.

1. Circle the five aspects of learning style in which you received the highest scores on the Learning Style Questionnaire. Disregard the others.

2. Read through the suggestions that apply to you.

3. Place a checkmark in front of suggestions that you think will work for you. Choose at least one for each of your five learning styles.

TABLE 1–2   LEARNING STYLES AND READING/LEARNING STRATEGIES

If your learning style is . . .	Then the reading/learning strategies to use are . . .	If your learning style is . . .	Then the reading/learning strategies to use are . . .
Auditory	• Discuss/study with friends. • Talk aloud when studying. • Tape-record self-testing questions and answers.	Verbal	• Translate diagrams and drawings into language. • Record steps, processes, and procedures in words. • Write summaries. • Write your interpretation next to textbook drawings, maps, and graphics.
Visual	• Draw diagrams, charts, and/or tables. • Try to visualize events. • Use films and videos. • Use computer-assisted instruction when available.	Social	• Form study groups. • Find a study partner. • Interact with the instructor. • Work with a tutor.
Applied	• Think of practical situations to which learning applies. • Associate ideas with their application. • Use case studies, examples, and applications to cue your learning.	Independent	• Use computer-assisted instruction. • Purchase review workbooks or study guides when available.
Conceptual	• Organize materials. • Use outlining. • Focus on organizational patterns.	Creative	• Ask and answer questions. • Record your own ideas in the margins of textbooks.
Spatial	• Use mapping. • Use outlining. • Draw diagrams; make charts and sketches. • Use visualization.	Pragmatic	• Study in an organized environment. • Write lists of steps, procedures, and processes. • Paraphrase difficult materials.

4. List the suggestions that you chose below.

   a. _____

   b. _____

   c. _____

   d. _____

   e. _____

The next step is to experiment with these techniques, one at a time. Use one technique for a while, and then move to the next. Continue using the techniques that seem to work, and work on revising or modifying those that do not. Do not hesitate to experiment with other techniques listed in the table. You may find other techniques that work well for you.

Overcoming Limitations

You should also work on developing learning styles in which you are weak because your learning style is not fixed or unchanging. You can improve areas in which you scored lower. Even though you may be weak in auditory learning, for example, many of your professors will lecture and expect you to take notes. If you work on improving your listening and note-taking skills, you can learn to handle lectures more effectively. Make a conscious effort at improving areas of weakness as well as taking advantage of your strengths.

BUILDING YOUR CONCENTRATION

Concentration is the ability to focus on the task at hand. Most students find that by improving their concentration, they can reduce their reading time. Building your concentration is a three-part process: eliminating distractions, focusing your attention, and assessing your concentration.

Eliminating Distractions

Activities going on around you can break your concentration. A dog barking, a radio playing, and an overheard conversation are examples of distractions. The first step in improving your concentration is to eliminate distractions. Use the following suggestions in eliminating distractions.

1. *Choose a place conducive to reading.* The spot you select should be as free of distractions and interruptions as possible. If your home or dorm is too busy or noisy, you will be distracted. Study in a quiet place such as student lounge areas or library study areas. Find a place you can associate with studying so that you are ready to concentrate as soon as you sit down. Although your TV chair or your bed may look like a perfect place to study, you already associate them with relaxation and sleep. If you read and work at the same desk or study carrel regularly, you will find that when you sit down you will feel ready to concentrate, and distractions will be less bothersome.

2. *Notice your physical state.* If you are tired, you will have trouble concentrating. If you are hungry, your thoughts will drift toward food. If you feel sluggish and inactive, you may not be able to focus on your work. Try to schedule reading or studying at times when your physical needs are not likely to interfere. If you find that you are hungry, tired, or sluggish while reading, stop and take a break, have a snack, or get up and walk around. If you are physically or mentally exhausted, you may need to stop and find a better time to complete the assignment.

3. *Have necessary materials available.* When you sit down to work, be sure that you have all the needed materials. Surrounding yourself with these tools helps to create a psychological readiness for reading and eliminates the distraction created by breaking off your work to find a book or pen.

4. *Choose your peak periods of attention.* The time of day or night when you read also influences how easy or difficult it is to shut out distractions. You have a natural time limit for how long you can successfully attend to a task; this is your **attention span.** People experience peaks and valleys in their attention spans. Some people are very alert in the early morning, whereas others find they are most focused at midday or in the early evening. To make concentration easier, try to read during the peaks of your attention span. Choose the times of day when you are most alert and when it is easiest to keep your mind on what you are doing. If you are not aware of your own peaks of attention, analyze your reading effectiveness. Over a period of several days, keep track of when you read and study and how much you accomplish each time. Then look for a pattern.

5. *Keep a list of distractions.* Often, as you are reading or studying, you will be distracted by thoughts of something you must remember to do. If you have a dental appointment scheduled for the next afternoon, you will find that a reminder occasionally flashes through your mind. To help overcome these distractions, keep a list of them. Use a sheet of paper to jot down these mental reminders as they occur. You will find that writing them down on paper temporarily eliminates reminders from your conscious memory.

Focusing Your Attention

Focusing your attention means directing all mental activity to what you are reading. To help focus your attention on the material you are reading, try the following.

1. *Set goals.* Achieving your goals is positive and rewarding; it feels good to accomplish what you set out to do. Before each study or reading session, set specific goals and time limits. Divide large assignments into smaller parts to give yourself the best chance to achieve your goals. Concentrating on these goals and time limits will help you avoid distractions; your attention will remain on your reading. One student set the following reading goals for herself for one evening of study.

Reread Psych lecture notes	15 min.
Read first half Chapter 10—Psych	90 min.
Review Chapter 9—Accounting	30 min.
Read short story—English	30 min.

2. *Reward yourself.* Meeting goals within a time limit is a reward in itself. Other rewards could include watching TV, snacking, or making phone calls. Use these activities as rewards by arranging them to follow periods of reading and studying. For example, you might call a friend after you finish your math problems, or you could plan to rewrite your English composition before watching a favorite TV program.

3. *Begin by reviewing previously read material.* Reviewing the preceding assignment will direct your attention to today's work and help you make the "mental switch" from your preceding activity to what you are doing now.

4. *Write and underline as you read.* It is easy to let your mind wander while reading, especially if you find the material dull or boring. One way to solve this problem is to involve yourself in your reading by writing or underlining the important ideas in each section. Make marginal notes, and jot down questions. These activities force you to think: to identify important ideas, to see how they are related, and to evaluate their worth and importance. Refer to Chapters 2 and 4–6 for specific suggestions on each of these techniques.

5. *Approach assignments critically.* Be an active reader. Instead of simply trying to take in large amounts of information, read critically. Seek ideas you question or disagree with. Look for points of view, opinions, and unsupported statements. Try to predict how the author's train of thought is developing. Make connections with what you already know about the subject, with what you have read before, and with what the instructor has said in class. If you can maintain an active, critical point of view, you will minimize distractions.

Assessing Your Concentration

Once you are aware of your concentration level and can recognize when your focus is fading, you can take action to control and improve your concentration. Begin by keeping track, for a half-hour or so, of how many times your mind wanders. Use a piece of paper to make a tally of distractions as they occur. Each time you think about something other than what you are reading, make a mark on the paper. You probably will be surprised at how many times your concentration was broken during the time you were keeping count. Work on decreasing the tally; use this method once a week or so as a check on your concentration. After reading, analyze your performance. Why did you lose your concentration? Was it an external distraction? Did an idea in the text trigger your memory of a related idea? Look for patterns: At what time of day are you most easily distracted? Where are you studying when many distractions occur? What are you studying? Adjust your reading habits to decrease distractions and improve concentration.

EXERCISE 1-3

Make a list of common distractions and problems that interfere with your concentration. Next to each item, note how you can overcome it. Discuss with classmates or your instructor any items for which you have no remedy.

_____

_____

_____

_____

EXERCISE 1–4	*Discuss how each student might improve his or her concentration in the following situations.*

1. A student cannot concentrate because of frequent interruptions by his two preschool children.
2. A student says she cannot concentrate because she is obsessed with a conflict she is having with her parents.
3. A student says he cannot read sociology for longer than a half-hour because he becomes restless and bored.

DEVELOPING LEVELS OF THINKING

Throughout your educational career, your primary task is to **understand** and **recall** information. Consequently, you may not be prepared when your instructors ask you to **apply**, **analyze**, **synthesize**, and **evaluate** information.

Table 1–3 describes a hierarchy, or progression, of thinking skills. It was developed by Benjamin Bloom in 1956 and remains widely used among educators in many academic disciplines. You will notice that the progression moves from basic literal understanding to more complex skills that involve synthesis and evaluation.

When they write exams, most college instructors assume that you can operate at each of these levels. Table 1–4 shows a few items from an exam for a course in interpersonal communication. Note how the items demand different levels of thinking. You do not need to identify the level of thinking that a particular assignment or test item requires. However, you should be able to think and work at each of these levels.

TABLE 1–3   LEVELS OF THINKING

Level	Examples
Knowledge: recalling information; repeating information with no changes	Recalling dates; memorizing definitions
Comprehension: understanding ideas; using rules and following directions	Explaining a law; recognizing what is important
Application: applying knowledge to a new situation	Using knowledge of formulas to solve a new physics problem
Analysis: seeing relationships; breaking information into parts; analyzing how things work	Comparing two poems by the same author
Synthesis: putting ideas and information together in a unique way; creating something new	Designing a new computer program
Evaluation: making judgments; assessing the worth of information	Evaluating the effectiveness or value of an argument opposing the death penalty

TABLE 1–4 **LEVEL OF THINKING REQUIRED**	
Test Item	Level of Thinking Required
Define nonverbal communication.	Knowledge
Explain how nonverbal communication works.	Comprehension
Describe three instances in which you have observed nonverbal communication.	Application
Study the two pictures projected on the screen in the front of the classroom, and compare the nonverbal messages sent in each.	Analysis
Construct, for an international student visiting your home town, a set of guidelines that will enable him or her to understand local nonverbal communication.	Synthesis
Evaluate an essay whose major premise is "Nonverbal communication skills should be taught formally as part of the educational process."	Evaluation

The following passage is taken from a psychology textbook chapter on memory and learning. Read the passage, and study the list that follows.

Some of the oldest data in psychology tell us that retrieval will be improved if practice (encoding) is spread out over time, with rest intervals spaced in between. . . . In fact, this experiment, first performed in 1946, provides such reliable results that it is commonly used as a student project in psychology classes. The task is to write the letters of the alphabet, upside down and from right to left. (If you think that sounds easy, give it a try.)

Subjects are given the opportunity to practice the task under four conditions. The *massed-practice* group works with no breaks between trials. The three *distributed-practice* groups receive the same amount of practice, but get rest intervals interspersed between each 1-minute trial. One group gets a 3- to 5-second break between trials, a second group receives a 30-second rest, and a third group gets a 45-second break between trials.

. . . Subjects in all four groups begin at about the same (poor) level of performance. After 20 minutes of practice, the performance of all the groups shows improvement, but by far, the massed practice (no rest) group does the poorest, and the 45-second rest group does the best.

The conclusion from years of research is that almost without exception, *distributed practice is superior to massed practice.* There are exceptions, however. Some tasks may suffer from having rest intervals inserted in practice time. In general, whenever you must keep track of many things at the same time, you should mass your practice until you have finished whatever you are working on. If, for example, you are working on a complex math problem, you should work it through until you find a solution, whether it's time for a rest break or not. And of course, you should not break up your practice in such a way as to disrupt the meaningfulness of the material you are studying.

—Gerow, *Psychology: An Introduction,* pp. 217–18

Below you can see how you might use each level of thinking to understand and evaluate this passage on memory and learning.

Knowledge	How was the experiment designed?
Comprehension	What did the experiment show about learning?
Application	How can I use distributed practice to plan my study time tonight?
Analysis	Why is distributed practice more effective?
Synthesis	What kind of experiment could I design to test what types of tasks benefit most (and which least) from distributed practice?
Evaluation	How effective is distributed practice?

As mentioned earlier, professors use these levels of thinking in writing exams. An effective way to prepare for an exam, then, is to be sure you have thought about the test material at each level. Do this by predicting possible test questions at each level.

EXERCISE 1–5

Read the following excerpt from an interpersonal communications textbook. Demonstrate your ability to think at various levels by answering the following questions.

A **friendship relationship** is one marked by very close association, contact, or familiarity. Usually a warm friendship has developed as a result of a long association, but this is not always the case. Sometimes friendship develops suddenly. Friendship relationships are very personal or private, and they are often characterized by different types of communication.

People seek friendship relationships for many reasons. These reasons may operate singly or in conjunction with each other. Many overlap. In some situations, with some people, one of these reasons may sustain a relationship, whereas in others, several are likely to operate. The more needs that are fulfilled in a relationship, the more solid the foundation upon which the relationship rests. You seek friendship relationships to fulfill six basic needs: for enjoyment, security, affection, self-esteem, freedom, and equality. They are not necessarily ranked here in order of importance.

Enjoyment is an important, perhaps the most important, need that friendships fulfill. Simply put, friends enjoy each other's company. The "What do you want to do?" syndrome ("I don't know, what do you want to do?") often occurs because neither friend really cares. Just enjoying being together is enough; *doing* something (anything!) is secondary. . . .

Affection relates to a sense of belonging. This could encompass sexual gratification, but does not need to. Affection suggests a moderate feeling toward or emotional attachment to another person. When you feel tender attachment for others or pleasure in being with them, you are experiencing affection. Abraham Maslow labels this "belonging and love needs," placing this need among the basic or essential needs after "psychological" and "safety" needs.

Self-esteem is felt when you are recognized or appreciated by others. Sometimes being with someone enhances your status. Also, if other people attribute a joint identity to your relationship with another person, this may also increase your self-esteem. Self-esteem is affected because such a high premium is often placed on dating and "going steady." Maslow places self-esteem needs only one step higher than affection—as slightly less essential and more optional.

—Weaver, *Understanding Interpersonal Communication,* pp. 423–26

Knowledge and Comprehension

1. Define a friendship relationship.

2. List the six basic needs that friendship relationships fulfill.

3. Explain the meaning of the term *self-esteem.*

Application

4. Name a person with whom you have a friendship that fulfills your need for self-esteem.

Analysis

5. Think of a long-standing friendship. Analyze that friendship by identifying the needs it fulfills.

Synthesis

6. The author states that the six basic needs are not necessarily ranked in order of importance. On the basis of your experience with friendships, list these needs in order of importance to you.

Evaluation

7. Do you agree with the author's statement that a high premium often is placed on dating? Why or why not?

EXERCISE 1–6

Academic Application

Select a one- or two-page section from one of your textbooks. Read the section, and then write questions that might be asked to test your thinking at each level.

_____

_____

_____

_____

_____

_____

_____

PREVIEWING AND PREDICTING

Previewing and predicting are skills that will help you to think beyond the basic levels of knowledge and comprehension. **Previewing** is a means of familiarizing yourself with the content and organization of an assignment *before* you read it. Think of previewing as getting a "sneak preview" of what a chapter or reading will be about. You can then read the material more easily and more rapidly.

How to Preview Textbook Assignments

Use the following steps to become familiar with a textbook chapter's content and organization.

1. *Read the chapter title.* The title indicates the topic of the article or chapter; the subtitle suggests the specific focus of, or approach to, the topic.

2. *Read the introduction or the first paragraph.* The introduction or first paragraph serves as a lead-in to the chapter by establishing the overall subject and suggesting how it will be developed.

3. *Read each boldface (dark print) heading.* Headings label the contents of each section and announce the major topic of the section.

4. *Read the first sentence under each major heading.* The first sentence often states the central thought of the section. If the first sentence seems introductory, read the last sentence; often, this sentence states or restates the central thought.

5. *Note any typographical aids.* Italics are used to emphasize important terminology and definitions by distinguishing them from the rest of the passage. Material that is numbered 1, 2, 3; lettered a, b, c; or presented in list form is also of special importance.

6. *Note any graphic aids.* Graphs, charts, photographs, and tables often suggest what is important in the chapter. Be sure to read the captions of photographs and the legends on graphs, charts, or tables.

7. *Read the last paragraph or summary.* This provides a condensed view of the chapter by outlining its key points.

8. *Quickly read any end-of-article or end-of-chapter material.* This might include references, study questions, discussion questions, chapter outlines, or vocabulary lists. If there are study questions, read them through quickly because they tell you what is important to remember in the chapter. If a vocabulary list is included, skim through it to identify the terms you will be learning as you read.

A section of a speech communication textbook chapter discussing purposes of listening is reprinted here to illustrate how previewing is done. The portions to focus on when previewing are shaded. Read only those portions. After you have finished, test how well your previewing worked by answering the questions in Exercise 1–7.

PURPOSES OF LISTENING

Speakers' motivations for speechmaking vary from situation to situation just as listeners' purposes for paying attention vary. Researchers have identified five types of listening (each serving a different purpose): (a) appreciative, (b) discriminative, (c) therapeutic, (d) comprehension, and (e) critical.

Appreciative Listening

Appreciative listening focuses on something other than the primary message. People who are principally concerned with participating in the experience are appreciative listeners. Some listeners enjoy seeing a famous speaker. Other listeners enjoy the art of good public speaking, pleasing vocal modulation, clever uses of language, impressive phraseology, and the skillful use of supporting materials. Still other listeners simply like to attend special occasions such as inaugurations, dedications, and graduations.

Discriminative Listening

Discriminative listening requires listeners to draw conclusions from the way a message is presented rather than from what is said. In discriminative listening, people seek to understand what the speaker really thinks, believes, or feels. You're engaging in discriminative listening when you draw conclusions about how angry your parents are with you, based not on what they say, but on how they say it. Journalists listening to the way that a message is presented often second-guess the attitudes of national leaders on foreign policy. Performers, of course, can convey emotions such as anger or exhilaration to audiences through their delivery alone. In each of these examples, an important dimension of listening is based on relatively sophisticated inferences drawn from—rather than found in—messages.

Therapeutic Listening

Therapeutic listening is intended to provide emotional support to the speaker. It is more typical of interpersonal than public communication—the therapeutic listener acts as a sounding board for a speaker attempting to talk through a problem, work out a difficult situation, or express deep emotions. Sometimes, however, therapeutic listening occurs in public speaking situations such as when a sports star apologizes for unprofessional behavior, a religious convert describes a soul-saving experience, or a classmate reviews a personal problem and thanks friends for their help in solving it. In therapeutic listening, special social bonding occurs between speaker and listener. Consider the communication of joy that occurs when listeners react to someone who wants to tell others about a new relationship, a new baby, a promotion at work, or an award at school.

Listening for Comprehension

Listening for comprehension occurs when the listener wants to gain additional information or insights provided by the speaker. This is probably the form of listening with which you are most familiar. When you listen to radio or TV news programs, to classroom lectures on the four principal causes of World War II, or to an orientation official previewing your school's new registration process, you're listening to understand—to comprehend information, ideas, and processes.

Critical Listening

Critical listening requires listeners to both interpret and evaluate the message. The most sophisticated kind of listening is critical listening. It demands that auditors go beyond understanding the message to interpreting it, judging its strengths and weaknesses, and assigning it some value. You'll practice this sort of listening in your class. You may also use critical listening as you evaluate commercials, political campaign speeches, advice from career counselors, or arguments offered by controversial talk show guests. When you listen critically, you decide to accept or reject ideas. You may also resolve to act or delay action on the message. . . .

The variety of listening purposes has serious implications for both listeners and speakers. Appreciative listeners are highly selective, watching for metaphors, responding to speaking tones, and searching out memorable phrasings. At the other extreme, critical listeners work hard to catch relevant details, to judge the soundness of competing arguments and to rationally decide whether to accept ideas. Therapeutic listeners decide when to positively reinforce speakers through applause or other signs of approval, and those listening for comprehension distinguish between important and unimportant information. Finally, discriminative listeners search for clues to unspoken ideas or feelings that are relevant to themselves. As you think about your own listening purposes, you'll find yourself adapting your listening behavior to the speaking situation more carefully.

—Gronbeck et al., *Principles of Speech Communication,* pp. 38–39

EXERCISE 1–7 | *Without referring to the passage, answer each of the following true-false questions.*

_____ 1. Discriminative listening requires listeners to pay attention to how the message is presented rather than to the message itself.

_____ 2. The purpose of therapeutic listening is to provide support for the speaker.

_____ 3. The purpose of listening for comprehension is to acquire information.

_____ 4. In appreciative listening, the listener focuses on the primary message.

_____ 5. Depending on their purpose, listeners pay attention to different parts of a message.

You probably were able to answer all (or most) of the questions correctly. Previewing, then, does provide you with a great deal of information. If you were to return to the passage from the speech communication textbook and read the entire section, you would find it easier to do than if you had not previewed.

When you preview an assignment, use the following hints to get the most out of it.

- Assess the difficulty of the material.
- Discover how it is organized.
- Identify the overall subject.
- Establish what type of material it is (for example, practical, research report, historical background, or case study).
- Look for logical breaking points where you might divide the assignment into portions, perhaps reserving a portion for a later study session.
- Identify points at which you might stop and review.
- Look for connections between the assignment and class lectures.

Previewing Nontextbook Material

With nontextbook material, you may have to make changes in how you preview. Many articles, essays, and reference books do not have the same features as textbook chapters. They may lack headings or clearly identifiable introductions and summaries. The following hints will help you to preview materials of this sort.

- *Pay close attention to the title;* it may make a statement about the theme or key focus of the article.
- *Identify the author and source of the material.* This information may provide clues about the article's content or focus.
- *Read the first paragraph carefully, searching for a statement of purpose or theme.*
- *If there are no headings, read the first sentence of each paragraph.* The first sentence of the paragraph is often the topic sentence that states the main idea of the paragraph. By reading first sentences, you will encounter most of the key ideas in the article.
- *Pay close attention to the last paragraph.* It probably will not provide a summary, but it usually serves as a conclusion to the article.

Why Previewing Is Effective

Previewing helps you to make decisions about how you will approach the material. On the basis of what you discover about the assignment's organization and content, you can select the reading and study strategies that will be most effective.

Previewing puts your mind in gear and helps you start thinking about the subject.

Also, previewing gives you a mental outline of the chapter's content. It enables you to see how ideas are connected, and, since you know where the author is headed, your reading will be easier than if you had not previewed. Previewing, however, is never a substitute for careful, thorough reading.

EXERCISE 1–8   *Select a textbook chapter that you have not read and preview it using the procedure described in this section. When you have finished, answer the following questions.*

1. What is its overall subject?
2. What topics (aspects of the subject) does the chapter discuss? List as many as you can recall.
3. How difficult do you expect the chapter to be?
4. How is the subject approached? In other words, is the material practical, theoretical, historical, research oriented, or procedural?
5. How can you apply this material in your class?

Activating Background Knowledge

After previewing your assignment, you should take a moment to think about what you already know about the topic. Whatever the topic, you probably know *something* about it: this is your background knowledge. For example, a student was about to read an article titled "Growing Urban Problems" for a sociology class. His first thought was that he knew very little about urban problems because he lived in a rural area. But when he thought of a recent trip to a nearby city, he remembered seeing the homeless people and crowded conditions. This recollection helped him remember reading about drug problems, drive-by shootings, and muggings.

Activating your background knowledge aids your reading in three ways. First, it makes reading easier because you have already thought about the topic. Second, the material is easier to remember because you can connect the new information with what you already know. Third, topics become more interesting if you can link them to your own experiences. Here are some techniques to help you activate your background knowledge.

- *Ask questions, and try to answer them.* If a chapter in your biology textbook titled "Human Diseases" contains headings such as "Infectious diseases," "Sexually transmitted diseases," "Cancer," and "Vascular diseases," you might ask and try to answer such questions as the following: What kinds of infectious diseases have I seen? What caused them? What do I know about preventing cancer and other diseases?
- *Draw on your own experience.* If a chapter in your business textbook is titled "Advertising: Its Purpose and Design," you might think of several ads you have seen and analyze the purpose of each and how it was constructed.
- *Brainstorm.* Write down everything that comes to mind about the topic. Suppose you're about to read a chapter in your sociology textbook on domestic violence. You might list types of violence—child abuse, rape, and so on. You might write questions such as "What causes child abuse?" and "How can it be prevented?" Alternatively, you might list incidents of domestic violence you have heard or read about. Any of these approaches will help to make the topic interesting.

EXERCISE 1–9   *Assume you have just previewed a chapter in your psychology text on psychological disorders. Discover what you already know about psychological disorders by using each of the techniques suggested previously. Then answer the questions that follow.*

1. Did you discover you knew more about psychological disorders than you initially thought?
2. Which technique worked best? Why?

Making Predictions

We make predictions about many tasks before we undertake them. We predict how long it will take to drive to a shopping mall, how much dinner will cost at a new restaurant, how long a party will last, or how difficult an exam will be. Prediction helps us organize our time and cope with new situations.

Prediction is an important part of active reading as well. It enables you to approach the material systematically. Also, it helps you read actively because you continually accept or reject your predictions. As you preview, you can predict the development of ideas, the organization of the material, and the author's conclusions. For example, for her philosophy class, a student began to preview an essay titled "Do Computers Have a Right to Life?" From the title, she predicted that the essay would discuss the topic of artificial intelligence: whether computers can "think." Then, as she read the essay, she discovered that this prediction was correct.

When you make predictions, you draw on your background knowledge and experience, making connections between what you already know about the subject and the clues you pick up through previewing. Now, predict the topic and/or point of view of each of the following articles.

"Dangerous Myths about Nuclear Energy"

"Where Darwin Went Wrong on Evolution"

"Why I Am Not a Christian"

Did you predict that the first article would favor the use of nuclear energy, that the second would hold that evolutionary theory is incorrect, and that the third would be concerned with religious beliefs?

In textbook chapters, the boldface headings serve as section "titles" and also are helpful in predicting content and organization. Considered together, chapter headings often suggest the development of ideas through the chapter. For instance, the following headings appeared in a sociology text chapter titled "Energy and the Environment."

The Limits of Fossil Fuels

Nuclear Power: High Promises, Grave Dangers

Conservation: The Hidden "Energy Source"

Solar Power: An Emerging Role

These headings reveal the author's approach to energy resources. We can predict that the chapter will describe the supply of fossil fuels as finite and nuclear power as dangerous; conservation and solar energy will be offered as viable alternatives.

EXERCISE 1–10 | *Predict the subject and/or point of view of each of the following essays or articles.*

1. "Reality as Presented by Television News"
2. "TV Violence—The Shocking New Threat to Society"
3. "Professional Sports: Necessary Violence"

EXERCISE 1–11 | *Turn to the table of contents in one of your textbooks. Study the headings for two or three chapters you have not read. Predict the organization or focus of each chapter. Explain which words in the headings helped you make your prediction.*

_____

_____

_____

DEVELOPING GUIDE QUESTIONS

Have you ever read an entire page or more and forgotten everything you read? Have you found yourself going from paragraph to paragraph without really thinking about what the writer is saying? Because you are not looking for anything in particular as you read, you do not notice or remember anything specific.

Reading should be a purposeful activity. You should have a reason for reading each piece of material that you pick up. Before you begin reading any article, selection, or chapter, you should know what you want to find out. Your purpose will vary with the situation. For example, you might read a magazine article on child abuse for the purpose of learning more about the general nature and extent of the problem. On the other hand, if you were doing a research paper for a sociology course on the topic of child abuse, your purpose might be quite specific. You would be looking for facts and figures about the causes, effects, and extent of child abuse so you could use this information in your paper.

The easiest way to make certain you are reading purposefully is to use guide questions. These are specific questions that guide or direct your attention to what is important in each chapter section you are reading. Guide questions are most useful in developing the knowledge and comprehension levels of thinking.

One of the easiest ways to make up guide questions is to turn the chapter title and headings into questions that you will try to answer as you read. Jot them down in the margin of your text, next to each heading, until you get in the habit of forming them. Later, you can form the questions mentally. For instance, for a chapter from a sociology text titled "Methods of Studying

Society," you could ask, "What are the methods of studying society?" Then, as you read the chapter, you could look for and underline the answer. Here are three other examples of questions you might ask.

Chapter Title:	"Nine Principles of Communication"
Question:	What are the nine principles of communication?
Essay Title:	"The Real Way to Prevent Nuclear War"
Questions:	How does the essayist think nuclear war can be prevented?
	Are these preventive measures realistic and practical?
Chapter Heading:	"Theories of Color Vision"
Questions:	What are the theories of color vision?
	How do they differ?

Avoid asking guide questions that have one-word answers or that require recall of details. "How," "what," and "why" questions generally are more useful than those beginning with "who," "when," and "where."

EXERCISE 1–12

Write at least one guide question for each of the following headings that appeared in a criminology textbook.

Headings	Questions
Technology and Criminal Justice	_____
Criminalistics: Past, Present, and Future	_____
Justice System Today	_____
Cybercrime: The New White-Collar Crime	_____
Rules of Terrorism	_____
Controlling Terrorism	_____
Technology and Individual Rights	_____

EXERCISE 1–13

Select a chapter from one of your textbooks, and write guide questions for each major heading.

_____

_____

_____

_____

CHECKING YOUR COMPREHENSION

You maintain an awareness or "check" on how well you are performing many of your daily activities. In sports such as racquetball, tennis, and bowling, you know if you are playing a poor game; you actually keep score and deliberately try to correct errors and improve your performance. When preparing a favorite food, you often taste as you cook to be sure the recipe will taste the way you want it. When you wash your car, you check to be sure that you have not missed any spots.

A similar type of checking should occur as you read. You need to "keep score" of how effectively you are comprehending and reacting to content. Because reading is a mental process, it is more difficult to check than is bowling or cooking. You may understand certain ideas you read and be confused by others.

Recognizing Comprehension Signals

What happens when you read material you can understand easily? Does it seem that everything "clicks"? Do ideas seem to fit together and make sense? Is that "click" noticeably absent at other times?

Read each of the following excerpts. As you read, be alert to how well you understand each one.

Excerpt 1

As you well know, all you have to do to reveal anger is change the way you talk: you may talk louder, faster, and more articulately than usual. You can say exactly the same thing in a fit of anger as in a state of delight and change your meaning by how you say it. You can say "I hate you" to sound angry, teasing, or cruel. Vocal cues are what is lost when your words are written down. The term often used to refer to this quality is paralanguage. As noted before, it includes all the nonlanguage means of vocal expression, such as rate, pitch, and tone. It includes, therefore, what occurs beyond or in addition to the words you speak.

—Weaver, *Understanding Interpersonal Communication,* pp. 226–27

Excerpt 2

Large-quantity waste generators and SQGs must comply with the RCRA regulations, including obtaining an EPA identification (EPA ID) number, proper handling of the waste transport, manifesting the waste (discussed in the next section), and proper record keeping and reporting. Conditionally exempt SQGs do not require EPA ID numbers. Appropriate transport handling requires suitable packaging to prevent leakage and labeling of the packaged waste to identify its characteristics and dangers.

—Nathanson, *Basic Environmental Technology,* p. 351

Did you feel comfortable and confident as you read Excerpt 1? Did the ideas seem to lead from one to another and make sense? How did you feel while reading Excerpt 2? Probably you found it difficult and felt confused. Unfamiliar

TABLE 1–5   COMPREHENSION SIGNALS

Positive Signals	Negative Signals
You feel comfortable and have some knowledge about the topic.	The topic is unfamiliar, yet the author assumes you understand it.
You recognize most words or can figure them out from context.	Many words are unfamiliar.
You can express the main ideas in your own words.	You must reread the main ideas and use the author's language to explain them.
You understand why the material was assigned.	You do not know why the material was assigned and cannot explain why it is important.
You read at a regular, comfortable pace.	You often slow down or reread.
You are able to make connections between ideas.	You are unable to detect relationships; the organization is not apparent.
You are able to see where the author is leading.	You feel as if you are struggling to stay with the author and are unable to predict what will follow.
You understand what is important.	Nothing (or everything) seems important.

terms were used, and you could not follow the flow of ideas, so the whole passage did not make sense.

Table 1–5 lists and compares common signals to assist you in checking your comprehension. Not all the signals appear at the same time, and not all the signals work for everyone. As you study the list, identify those positive signals you sensed as you read the first excerpt about paralanguage. Then identify the negative signals you sensed when reading the excerpt about waste generators.

EXERCISE 1–14

Academic Application

Select and read a three- to four-page section of a chapter in one of your textbooks. Be alert for positive and negative comprehension signals as you read. After reading the section, answer the following questions.

1. How would you rate your overall comprehension? What positive signals did you sense? Did you feel any negative signals?
2. Where was your comprehension strongest?
3. Did you feel at any time that you had lost, or were about to lose, comprehension? If so, go back to that part now. What made it difficult to read?

Checking Techniques

At times, signals of poor comprehension do not come through clearly enough. In fact, you may think you understand what you have read until you are questioned in class or take an exam. Only then do you discover that your comprehension is incomplete. Alternatively, you may find that you comprehend material on a factual level, but you cannot apply, analyze, synthesize, or evaluate what you read. Use the following checking techniques to determine whether you really understand what you read.

1. *Use your guide questions.* Earlier in this chapter, you learned how to form guide questions from the boldface headings in your text. Use those questions to check your comprehension while reading. When you finish a boldface-headed section, take a moment to recall your guide questions and answer them mentally or on paper. Your ability to answer your questions will indicate your level of comprehension.

2. *Ask yourself thought-provoking questions.* To be certain that your comprehension is complete and that you are not recalling only superficial factual information, ask yourself questions that require you to think about content. Try to focus on the higher-level thinking skills: application, analysis, synthesis, and evaluation. Here are a few examples:

   Can I apply this information to a real-life situation?

   How does this reading assignment fit with the topics of this week's class lectures?

   How does this material fit with what I already know about the topic?

   Can I identify a principle that this material illustrates?

3. *Use internal dialogue.* Internal dialogue—mentally talking to yourself—is another excellent way to check your reading and learning. Rephrase, in your own words, the message the author is communicating. If you cannot express the ideas in your own words, your understanding is probably incomplete. The following examples of internal dialogue illustrate how the technique is used.

   You are reading an essay that argues convincingly that capital punishment does not stop crime. As you finish reading each stage of the argument, you rephrase it in your own words.

   While reading a section in a math textbook, you mentally outline the steps to follow in solving a sample problem.

   As you finish each boldface section in an anthropology chapter, you summarize the key points in your own words.

This chapter has shown you several active reading techniques, but each takes time and initially may slow you down. Considering all the competing pressures you face, you may be wondering whether you can afford the time to experiment with these techniques. However, each of these techniques will save you time in the long run. You will learn more while you are reading and will have to spend less time after reading to learn the material.

EXERCISE 1–15

Choose a section from one of your own textbooks. Read it, and check your comprehension by using both guide questions and thought-provoking questions. List your questions on a sheet of paper. List the positive and negative comprehension signals you noted as you read.

EXERCISE 1–16

Select another section from one of your textbooks and experiment with the technique of internal dialogue to check your comprehension. On a sheet of paper, describe the technique you used and evaluate its effectiveness.

SUMMARY

Learning style refers to each person's unique way of learning. The Learning Style Questionnaire assesses five aspects of learning style. Active reading plays a critical role in college success. Concentration is among the skills you need to be an active reader. You can improve your concentration by

- eliminating distractions.
- learning to focus your attention.
- assessing your concentration.

Thinking about what you read involves six stages:

- knowledge
- comprehension
- application
- analysis
- synthesis
- evaluation

Previewing helps you become familiar with the chapter's content and organization before reading it. It enables you to

- make predictions.
- anticipate content, development, and organization.

When you create guide questions, you establish a focus and purpose for your reading.

Finally, comprehension checking helps you maintain and evaluate your comprehension.

Psychology

PREREADING QUESTION

Think of a person to whom you are attracted. Why are you attracted to him or her?

Factors Affecting Interpersonal Attraction

Josh R. Gerow

1   Now let's look at some empirical evidence related to attraction. What determines whom you will be attracted to? What factors tend to provide the rewards, or the positive reward/cost ratios, that serve as the basis for strong relationships? Here we'll describe four common principles related to interpersonal attraction.

Reciprocity

2   Our first principle is perhaps the most obvious one. Not surprisingly, we tend to value and like people who like and value us (Backman & Secord, 1959; Curtis & Miller, 1986). Remember that we've already noted, in our discussion of operant conditioning, that the attention of others often can be a powerful reinforcer. This is particularly true if the attention is positive, supportive, and affectionate. Research indicates that the value of someone else caring for us is particularly powerful when that someone initially seemed to have neutral or even negative attitudes toward us (Aronson & Linder, 1965). That is, we are most attracted to people who like us now, but who didn't originally. The logic here is related to attribution. If someone we meet for the first time expresses nothing but positive feelings and attitudes toward us, we are likely to attribute their reaction internally to the way the person is—rather shallow and the sort who just likes everybody. But if someone at first were to express neutral, or even slightly negative, feelings toward us and then were to become more and more positive, we might have a different, more positive view of their ability to judge others.

Proximity leads to liking, which is why teenagers who go to the same school are likely to form friendships.

Proximity

3   Our second principle suggests that physical closeness, or proximity, tends to produce attraction. Sociologists, as well as your own personal experience, will tell you

that people tend to establish friendships (and romances) with others with whom they have grown up, worked, or gone to school. Similarly, social-psychological studies consistently have found that residents of apartments or dormitories tend to become friends with those other residents living closest to them (Festinger et al., 1950). Being around others gives us the opportunity to discover just who can provide those interpersonal rewards we seek in friendship.

4

mere exposure phenomenon
the tendency to increase our liking of people and things the more we see of them

There may be another social-psychological phenomenon at work here called the **mere exposure phenomenon.** Research, pioneered by Robert Zajonc (1968), has shown with a variety of stimuli that liking tends to increase with repeated exposure to stimuli. Examples of this phenomenon are abundant in everyday life. Have you ever bought a CD that you have not heard previously, assuming that you will like it because you have liked all the other CDs this performer made? The first time you listen to your new CD, however, your reaction may be lukewarm at best, and you may be disappointed in your purchase. Not wanting to feel that you've wasted your money, you play the CD a few more times over the next several days. What often happens is that soon you realize that you like this CD after all. The mere exposure effect has occurred, and this commonly happens in our formation of attitudes about other people as well. Apparently, familiarity is apt to breed attraction, not contempt. I also have to add that although there seems to be ample evidence that the mere exposure phenomenon is real, there remains considerable disagreement about *why* familiarity and repeated interactions breed attraction (e.g., Birnbaum & Mellers, 1979; Kunst-Wilson & Zajonc, 1980).

Physical Attractiveness

5
Our physical appearance is one personal characteristic that we cannot easily hide. It is always on display in social situations, and it communicates something about us. People are aware of the role of appearance in nonverbal, interpersonal communication and may spend hours each week doing whatever can be done to improve the way they look.

6
The power of physical attractiveness in the context of dating has been demonstrated experimentally in a classic study directed by Elaine Walster (Walster et al., 1966). University of Minnesota freshmen completed a number of psychological tests as part of an orientation program. The students were then randomly matched for dates to an orientation dance, during which they took a break and evaluated their assigned partners. This study allowed researchers the possibility of uncovering intricate, complex, and subtle facts about interpersonal attraction, such as which personality traits might tend to mesh in such a way as to produce attraction. As it turned out, none of these complex factors, so carefully controlled for, was important. The effect of physical attractiveness was so powerful that it wiped out all other effects. For both men and women, the more physically attractive their date, the more they liked the person and the more they wanted to go out again with that individual.

7
Numerous studies of physical attractiveness followed this one. Some of these studies simply gave subjects a chance to pick a date from a group of several potential partners (usually using descriptions and pictures). Not surprisingly, subjects almost invariably selected the most attractive person available to be their date (Reis et al., 1980).

8   You may have noticed, however, that in real life we seldom have the opportunity to request a date without at least the possibility of being turned down. When experimental studies began to build in the possibility of rejection, an interesting effect emerged: Subjects stopped picking the most attractive candidate and started selecting partners whose level of physical attractiveness was more similar to their own. This behavior has been called the **matching phenomenon,** and it is an effect that has been verified by naturalistic observation studies (Walster & Walster, 1969).

matching phenomenon
the tendency to select partners whose level of physical attractiveness matches our own

Similarity

9   There is a large body of research on the relationship between similarity and attraction, but the findings are consistent, and we can summarize them briefly. Much of this research has been done by Donn Byrne and his colleagues (e.g., Byrne, 1971). It indicates that there is a strong positive relationship between attraction and the proportion of attitudes held in common. Simply put, the more similar another person is to you, the more you will tend to like that person (Buss, 1985; Davis, 1985; Rubin, 1973). Sensibly, we also tend to be repelled, or put off, by persons we believe to be dissimilar to us (Rosenbaum, 1986).

10   Perhaps you know a happily married couple for whom this sweeping conclusion does not seem to fit. At least some of their behaviors seem to be quite dissimilar, almost opposite. Perhaps the wife appears to be the one who makes most of the decisions while the husband simply seems to follow orders. It may very well be the case, however, that this apparent lack of similarity in behavior exists only on the surface. There may be an important similarity that makes for a successful marriage here: Both have the same idea of what a marriage should be like—wives decide and husbands obey. In such a case, the observed differences in behavior are reflecting a powerful similarity in the view of the roles of married couples.

—Gerow, *Psychology: An Introduction,* pp. 654–56

VOCABULARY REVIEW

1. For each of the words listed below, use context; prefixes, roots, and suffixes (see Chapter 3); and/or a dictionary to write a brief definition or synonym of the word as it is used in the reading.

   a. empirical (para. 1) _____

   b. reciprocity (para. 2) _____

   c. proximity (para. 3) _____

   d. phenomenon (para. 4) _____

   e. invariably (para. 7) _____

   f. dissimilar (para. 9) _____

2. Underline new specialized terms introduced in the reading.

COMPREHENSION QUESTIONS

1. Write a list of guide questions useful in reading and reviewing this reading.
2. Check your level of comprehension. What positive or negative signals did you sense?
3. What are the four principles discussed in this reading?
4. Explain the mere exposure phenomenon.
5. Explain the matching phenomenon.

THINKING CRITICALLY

1. Think of someone to whom you are attracted. Which of the principles of attraction can account for your attraction?
2. Can you think of other factors not discussed in this reading that may account for interpersonal attraction?
3. Describe an instance in which you experienced the mere exposure phenomenon.
4. Have you observed or experienced the matching phenomenon? If so, describe the situation in which it occurred.

LEARNING/STUDY STRATEGY

For each of the four principles of attraction, the author describes one or more experiments that are related to the principle. To review this research, complete the following study chart.

Principle	Author(s)	Summary of Findings
1. Reciprocity		
2. Proximity		
3. Physical attractiveness		
4. Similarity		

Multimedia Activities

1. **Index of Learning Styles Questionnaire**
   http://www2.ncsu.edu/unity/lockers/users/f/felder/public/ILSdir/ilsweb.html
   Try another learning style assessment at this site from North Carolina State University. Compare your results with those from the assessment in this book. How do online tests differ from those on paper? Which do you prefer? Is this a result of your learning style?

2. **Improving Your Concentration**
   http://www.ksu.edu/counseling/concentr.html
   Kansas State University offers some interesting ideas to keep your mind from wandering, being distracted, and much more. Try some of these techniques, and keep track of what works for you. In what other areas of your life could these ideas be useful? Discuss with your friends the potential benefits of techniques such as meditation, yoga, and acupuncture.

Take a Road Trip to
New Orleans!

If your instructor has asked you to use the Reading Road Trip CD-ROM or Website, be sure to visit the Active Reading module for multimedia tutorials, exercises, and tests.

CHAPTER 2

FUNDAMENTAL COMPREHENSION SKILLS

LEARNING OBJECTIVES
- ✦ To identify what is important in a chapter
- ✦ To learn how to vary your reading rate
- ✦ To learn how to read selectively

Many beginning college students are overwhelmed by the amount of required reading. Comments such as "I can't keep up!" and "I'll never get all this read by Friday!" are common.

Other students complain that although they spend large amounts of time reading and studying, they do not earn top grades. The problem may be that they have not comprehended ideas fully. They may not have distinguished main ideas from supporting details and have not grasped the relationships among ideas.

This chapter presents techniques that enable you to read better and more efficiently. There are no easy tricks to becoming a faster reader; textbook reading must always be relatively slow and deliberate. However, if you can learn to locate what is important and then find essential supporting details, your reading will be smoother and faster. You will find, too, that you will learn more as you read, which will enable you to accomplish more as you study and review. The key to success when you are faced with large amounts of reading, then, is selectivity: sorting out what is important and focusing your attention on it.

LOCATING MAIN IDEAS AND SUPPORTING DETAILS

Not all sentences within a paragraph are equally important. In fact, there are three levels of importance:

> Most important: the main idea
>
> Less important: primary supporting details
>
> Least important: secondary supporting details

As you read a paragraph, you should be sorting ideas according to their relative importance and paying more attention to some than to others. Here, you will learn how to identify these levels of importance as well as how ideas fit and work together in a paragraph.

Finding the Main Idea

A **paragraph** can be defined as a group of related ideas. The sentences are related to one another and all are about the same person, place, thing, or idea. The common subject or idea is called the **topic**—what the focus of the entire paragraph is about. As you read the following paragraph, you will see that its topic is elections.

> Americans elect more people to office than almost any other society. Each even year, when most elections occur, more than 500,000 public officials are elected to school boards, city councils, county offices, state legislatures, state executive positions, the House of Representatives and the Senate, and of course, every fourth year, the presidency. By contrast with other countries, our elections are drawn-out affairs. Campaigns for even the most local office can be protracted over two or three months and cost a considerable amount of money. Presidential campaigns, including the primary season, last for at least ten months, with some candidates beginning to seek support many months and, as noted earlier, even years before the election.
>
> —Baradat, *Understanding American Democracy*, p. 163

Each sentence of this paragraph discusses or describes elections. To identify the topic of a paragraph, then, ask yourself: *"What or who is the paragraph about?"*

The **main idea** of a paragraph is what the author wants you to know about the topic. It is the broadest, most important idea that the writer develops throughout the paragraph. The entire paragraph explains, develops, and supports this main idea. A question that will guide you in finding the main idea is, *"What key point is the author making about the topic?"* In the above paragraph, the writer's main idea is that elections in America are more numerous and more drawn out than in other countries.

Topic Sentence

Often, but not always, one sentence expresses the main idea. This sentence is called the **topic sentence.**

To find the topic sentence, search for the one general sentence that explains what the writer wants you to know about the topic. A topic sentence is a broad, general statement; the remaining sentences of the paragraph provide details about or explain the topic sentence.

In the following paragraph, the topic is the effects of high temperatures. Read the paragraph to find out what the writer wants you to know about this topic. Look for one sentence that states this.

Environmental psychologists have also been concerned with the effects that extremely high temperatures have on social interactions, particularly on aggression. There is a common perception that riots and other more common displays of violent behaviors are more frequent during the long, hot days of summer. This observation is largely supported by research evidence (Anderson, 1989; Anderson & Anderson, 1984; Rotton & Frey, 1985). C. A. Anderson (1987, 1989) reported on a series of studies showing that violent crimes are more prevalent in hotter quarters of the year and in hotter years, although nonviolent crimes were less affected. Anderson also concluded that differences in crime rates between cities are better predicted by temperature than by social, demographic (age, race, education), and economic variables. Baron and Ransberger (1978) point out that riots are most likely to occur when the outside temperature is only moderately high, between about 75° and 90° F. But when temperatures get much above 90° F, energy (even for aggression) becomes rapidly depleted, and rioting is less likely to occur.

—Gerow, *Psychology: An Introduction*, p. 553

The paragraph opens with a statement and then proceeds to explain it by citing research. The first sentence of the paragraph functions as a topic sentence, stating the paragraph's main point: High temperatures are associated with aggressive behavior.

The topic sentence can be located anywhere in the paragraph. However, there are several positions where it is most likely to be found.

Topic Sentence First   Most often, the topic sentence is placed first in the paragraph. In this type of paragraph, the author first states his or her main point and then explains it.

There is some evidence that colors affect you physiologically. For example, when subjects are exposed to red light, respiratory movements increase; exposure to blue decreases respiratory movements. Similarly, eye blinks increase in frequency when eyes are exposed to red light and decrease when exposed to blue. This seems consistent with intuitive feelings about blue being more soothing and red being more arousing. After changing a school's walls from orange and white to blue, the blood pressure of the students decreased while their academic performance improved.

—DeVito, *Human Communication*, p. 182

Here, the writer first states that there is evidence of the physiological effects of colors. The rest of the paragraph presents that evidence.

Topic Sentence Last   The second most likely place for a topic sentence to appear is last in the paragraph. When using this arrangement, a writer leads up to the main point and then directly states it at the end.

Is there a relationship between aspects of one's personality and that person's state of physical health? Can psychological evaluations of an individual be used to predict physical as well as psychological disorders? Is there such a thing as a disease-prone personality? *Our response is very tentative, and the data are not all supportive, but for the moment we can say yes, there does seem to be a positive correlation between some personality variables and physical health.*

—Gerow, *Psychology: An Introduction,* p. 700

In this paragraph, the author ponders the relationship between personality and health and concludes with the paragraph's main point: that they are related.

Topic Sentence in the Middle   If it is placed neither first nor last, then the topic sentence appears somewhere in the middle of the paragraph. In this arrangement, the sentences before the topic sentence lead up to or introduce the main idea. Those that follow the main idea explain or describe it.

There are 1,500 species of bacteria and approximately 8,500 species of birds. The carrot family alone has about 3,500 species, and there are 15,000 known species of wild orchids. *Clearly, the task of separating various living things into their proper groups is not an easy task.* Within the insect family, the problem becomes even more complex. For example, there are about 300,000 species of beetles. In fact, certain species are disappearing from the earth before we can even identify and classify them.

—Wallace, *Biology: The World of Life,* p. 283

In this paragraph, the author first gives several examples of living things for which there are numerous species. Then he states his main point: Separating living things into species is not an easy task. The remainder of the paragraph offers an additional example and provides further information.

Topic Sentence First and Last   Occasionally, the main idea is stated at the beginning of a paragraph and again at the end, or elsewhere in the paragraph. Writers may use this organization to emphasize an important idea or to explain an idea that needs clarification. At other times, the first and last sentences together express the paragraph's main idea.

Many elderly people have trouble getting the care and treatment they need for their ailments. Most hospitals, designed to handle injuries and acute illness that are common to the young, do not have the facilities or personnel to treat the chronic degenerative diseases of the elderly. Many doctors are also ill-prepared to deal with such problems. As Fred Cottrell points out, "There is a widespread feeling among the aged that most doctors are not interested in them and are reluctant to treat people who are as little likely to contribute to the future as the aged are reputed to." *Even with the help of Medicare, the elderly in the United States often have a difficult time getting the health care that they need.*

—Coleman and Cressey, *Social Problems,* p. 277

The first and last sentences together explain that many elderly people in the United States have difficulty obtaining needed health care.

EXERCISE 2–1   *Underline the topic sentence(s) of each of the following paragraphs.*

Paragraph 1

People of nearly every culture have given names to patterns in the sky. The pattern that the Greeks named Orion, the hunter, was seen as a supreme warrior called *Shen* by the ancient Chinese. Hindus in ancient India also saw a warrior, called *Skanda*, who rode a peacock as the general of a great celestial army. The three stars of Orion's belt were seen as three fisherman in a canoe by Aborigines of northern Australia. As seen from southern California, these three stars climb almost straight up into the sky as they rise in the east, which may explain why the Chemehuevi Indians of the California desert saw them as a line of three sure-footed mountain sheep. These are but a few of the many names, each accompanied by a rich folklore, given to the pattern of stars that we call Orion.

—Bennett et al., *The Cosmic Perspective,* p. 28

Paragraph 2

Language consists of a large number of *symbols.* The symbols that constitute language are commonly referred to as words—labels that we have assigned to concepts, or our mental representations. When we use the word *chair* as a symbol, we don't use it to label just one specific instance of a chair. We use the word as a symbol to represent our concept of chairs. As symbols, words need not stand for real things in the real world. We have words to describe objects or events that cannot be perceived, such as *ghost* or, for that matter, *mind.* With language we can communicate about owls and pussycats in teacups and a four-dimensional, time-warped hyperspace. Words stand for cognitions, or concepts, and we have a great number of them.

—Gerow, *Psychology: An Introduction,* p. 250

Paragraph 3

Body mass is made up of protoplasm, extracellular fluid, bone, and adipose tissue (body fat). One way to determine the amount of adipose tissue is to measure the whole-body density. After the on-land mass of the body is determined, the underwater body mass is obtained by submerging the person in water. Since water helps support the body by giving it buoyancy, the apparent body mass is less in water. A higher percentage of body fat will make a person more buoyant, causing the underwater mass to be even lower. This occurs because fat has a lower density than the rest of the body.

—Timberlake, *Chemistry: An Introduction to General, Organic, and Biological Chemistry,* p. 30

Paragraph 4

Early biologists who studied reflexes, kineses, taxes, and fixed action patterns assumed that these responses are inherited, unlearned, and common to all members of a species. They clearly depend on internal and external factors, but until recently, instinct and learning were considered distinct aspects of behavior. However, in some very clever experiments, Jack Hailman of the University of Wisconsin showed that certain stereotyped behavior patterns require subtle forms of experience for their development. In other words, at least some of the behavior normally called instinct is partly learned.

—Mix et al., *Biology, The Network of Life,* p. 532

Paragraph 5

On election day in 1972, at 5:30 P.M. Pacific Standard Time, NBC television news declared that Richard Nixon had been reelected president. This announcement came several hours before the polls were closed in the western part of the United States. In 1988, polls in a dozen western states were still open when CBS and ABC announced that George Bush had been elected president. These developments point to the continuing controversy over the impact of election night coverage on voter turnout.

—Keefe et al., *American Democracy,* p. 186

Finding an Implied Main Idea

Although most paragraphs do have a topic sentence, some do not. Such paragraphs contain only details or specifics that, taken together, point to the main idea. The main idea, then, is implied but not directly stated. In such paragraphs, you must infer, or reason out, the main idea. This is a process of adding up the details and deciding what they mean together or what main idea they all support or explain. Use the following steps to grasp implied main ideas:

- Identify the topic by asking yourself, "What is the one thing the author is discussing throughout the paragraph?"
- Decide what the writer wants you to know about the topic. Look at each detail and decide what larger idea each explains.
- Express this idea in your own words.

Here is a sample paragraph; use the preceding steps to identify the main idea.

> As recently as 20 years ago, textbooks on child psychology seldom devoted more than a few paragraphs to the behaviors of the neonate—the newborn through the first 2 weeks of life. It seemed as if the neonate did not do much worth writing about. Today, most child psychology texts devote substantially more space to discussing the abilities of newborns. It is unlikely that over the past 20 years neonates have gotten smarter or more able. Rather, psychologists have. They have devised new and clever ways of measuring the abilities and capacities of neonates.
>
> —Gerow, *Psychology: An Introduction,* p. 319

The topic of this paragraph is the neonate. The author's main point is that coverage of neonates in psychology texts has increased as psychologists have learned more about them.

EXERCISE 2–2

Read the following section from an ecology textbook and underline the topic sentence in each paragraph. Monitor your comprehension and list positive or negative comprehension signals (see Chapter 1, p. 25) you received while reading. Compare your list with those of other students in the class.

PROTECTING THE OZONE LAYER

News that the ozone layer was damaged caught public attention, and the international response to limit ozone depletion can be seen as a success story. Curtailing emissions of CFCs [chlorofluorocarbons, molecules that contain both chlorine and fluorine atoms] and other chemicals that release chlorine or its chemical neighbor, bromine, took considerable retooling in industry, but substantial progress in this direction has been made.

Before any political mandates were laid down, industry had realized the good publicity that could be gained from "ozone-friendly" products. The general public started to purchase spray cans that used non-CFC propellants, and by the late 1980s most of these products were labeled as CFC-free. This was a case of consumer demand providing industry with an incentive to change.

In 1987, the Montreal Protocol was established, an agreement that established goals to reduce the emissions of ozone-depleting chemicals. The agreement has been progressively strengthened at subsequent meetings, both in the number of signatories, which has risen from 24 to 92 nations, and in the schedule of emissions reduction. The 1992 phase of this agreement led to signatory nations phasing out CFC-11 and CFC-12, the worst offenders among the chemicals, by 1996. Whether a global ban on CFCs can be realized will depend on policies adopted by developing nations with burgeoning populations and huge potential demands for refrigeration and air conditioning. At present these countries, such as China and India, still use CFCs, and the potential exists for a significant increase in CFC production as a larger proportion of their populations can afford refrigerators. The onus will fall on the developed nations to encourage use of more modern technology so that the work of the Montreal Protocol is not undone.

Although adherence to the Montreal Protocol has greatly reduced CFC emissions, the chemicals used in place of CFCs are not as benign as once thought. As CFCs were phased out they were replaced by "ozone-friendly" HCFCs. But, as noted above, HCFCs still degrade the ozone layer. HCFCs will be phased out by 2003. HCFCs are gradually being replaced by hydrofluorocarbons (HFCs), which are believed to be truly ozone friendly. However, the chemical structure of HFCs, like CFCs and HCFCs, trap heat and will be potent greenhouse gases.

Other chlorine- and bromine-based chemicals are also under scrutiny in the United States. Methyl chloride, a solvent, was phased out in 1996, and methyl bromide, an agricultural pesticide, will be phased out in 2010 in MDCs [more developed countries] and the amount used in LDCs [less developed countries] will be frozen at 1995–1998 levels by 2002. Within the United States, methyl bromide will no longer be used after 2001.

Controlling nitrous oxides from automobile exhaust emissions has been addressed by the Clean Air Act of 1990; however, agricultural emissions of N_2O are likely to increase as agriculture becomes increasingly reliant on fertilizer inputs. Agricultural N_2O outputs are not large enough to cause or maintain a depleted ozone layer, but they will slow its recovery.

–Bush, *Ecology of a Changing Planet*,
pp. 357–58

Positive signals: _____

_____

_____

Negative signals: _____

_____

_____

EXERCISE 2–3

Select a two- to three-page excerpt from one of your textbooks and underline the topic sentence of each paragraph.

Recognizing Primary and Secondary Details

Supporting details are those facts, reasons, examples, or statistics that prove or explain the main idea of a paragraph. Though all the details in a paragraph support the main idea, not all details are equally important. As you read, try to identify and pay attention to the most important, primary details. These primary details directly explain the main idea. Secondary, less important details may provide additional information, offer an example, or further explain one of the primary details. You might visualize the structure of a paragraph as follows:

> MAIN IDEA
>> Primary detail
>>> Secondary detail
>>> Secondary detail
>> Primary detail
>>> Secondary detail
>> Primary detail

Read the following paragraph. The topic is boxed, the main idea is double-underlined, and primary details are single-underlined.

Our data on the kinds of people who are more likely to read magazines are better than our data on the number who do. Surveys show, not surprisingly, that the amount of magazine reading is highly correlated with education. The more educated people are, the more time they are likely to spend reading magazines. We also know that women tend to read magazines more than men do. This is shown by various kinds of data, including the fact that magazines that appeal primarily to women outsell magazines that appeal primarily to men. It may seem strange or out of date to you for anyone in the 1980s to be talking about men's magazines or women's magazines. However, there is little evidence that the sexual revolution is erasing the clear distinctions between men's and women's tastes in magazines. Men are more likely than women to read magazines that cover news on business and finance, mechanics and science, sports, outdoor life, and those that include photographs of women in various states of undress. Men also have a higher probability of reading the general newsmagazines. Women, on the other hand, are more likely to read magazines with useful household information (recipes, home decor, child care, and gardening) or fashion and beauty information.

—Becker, *Discovering Mass Communication,* p. 159

This paragraph begins with a topic sentence. The primary details present what is known about magazine readership patterns, and the secondary details further explain and offer examples of these patterns.

To determine the importance of a particular detail, decide whether it directly explains the main idea or explains or provides further information about one of the primary details.

EXERCISE 2–4

Read the following excerpt from a psychology textbook. For each paragraph, draw a box around the topic sentence and underline the primary details. What types of details did the author provide? When you have finished, evaluate your comprehension by using internal dialogue (see Chapter 1, p. 26) to summarize the key points of the excerpt in your own words.

PSYCHOLOGY AND SPORT

Sport psychology is another new and exciting area of applied psychology. Although it has had a long history in Europe, sport psychology has become an organized focus of attention in this country only within the last 15 to 20 years. **Sport psychology** is "the application of psychological principles to sport and physical activity at all levels of skill development" (Browne & Mahoney, 1984, p. 605). There are many potential applications of psychology to sports and athletes. We'll review just two: analyzing the psychological characteristics of athletes and maximizing athletic performance.

The Psychological Characteristics of Athletes

Psychology's history is filled with research on the measurement of individual differences. Wouldn't it be useful to be able to predict who might become a world-class athlete on the basis of psychological testing? There are physiological differences between athletes and nonathletes—amount of muscle, muscle type, height, weight, lung capacity, and so on. Are there any differences between athletes and nonathletes on personality measures?

Generally, research in this area has been less than satisfactory and results often confirm the obvious. Differences tend to be small, but athletes usually score higher than nonathletes on tests of assertion, dominance, aggression, and need for achievement; they score lower on anxiety level, depression, and fatigue (Browne & Mahoney, 1984; Cox, 1990; Morgan, 1980). This is particularly true when the athletes are at a high skill level. Athletes in some sports, such as hockey and football, are more tolerant of pain than are athletes in other sports, such as golf and bowling (e.g., Ryan & Kovacic, 1966). Tolerance of pain, however, may be more of an outcome (result of their activity) for some athletes than a determinant of success.

This last point raises a problem that has plagued research on the personality of the athlete: Just how shall we define *athlete?* Given the differences among hockey players, golfers, long-distance runners, pocket billiards players, cowboys, bowlers, rock climbers, gymnasts, and so on, it is surprising that research can find *any* significant differences between athletes and nonathletes. In fact, when general trends are sought, they are often not found (e.g., Fisher, 1977).

Maximizing Athletic Performance

Of practical importance to coaches and athletes is the performance of the athlete in competition, and what can be done to maximize that performance.

One area of interest focuses on manipulating the arousal level of the athlete. The athlete in competition surely needs to be aroused and motivated to perform— "psyched up" to his or her best. Psychologists also know that too much arousal can interfere with athletic performance—that optimum levels of arousal can vary as a function of the task at hand. For example, making a long putt in golf requires a low level of arousal, blocking a shot in volleyball requires a slightly higher level, making a tackle in football a higher level, and a bench press in weight lifting requires a very high level of arousal (e.g., Cox, 1990, p. 98). . . . Psychologists can help athletes be sensitive to appropriate levels of arousal while maintaining concentration on the task at hand. This often involves training athletes to be sensitive to such indicators as their own blood pressure, respiration and heart rates, muscle tension and the like (Harris, 1973; Landers, 1982). . . . In a similar vein, psychologists now claim that the so-called home field advantage (Varca, 1980) often may be exaggerated, particularly in important games (Baumeister, 1985; Baumeister & Steinhilber, 1984). The argument is that frenzied, yelling, screaming hometown fans may raise arousal levels of the home team beyond the point of maximum efficiency. The negative effect of fans' reactions is more potent when teams are on offense than when they are playing defense, and it is clearly more potent in end-of-season playoff and championship games.

One sports psychologist, Michael Mahoney, commenting on Olympic athletes, has said, "At this level of competition, the difference between two athletes is 20 percent physical and 80 percent mental" (quoted in Kiester, 1984a, pp. 20–21). To the extent that this observation is accurate, psychologists have tried to help athletes to do their best—to give what is called their peak performance. Mental practice, or "imagery," combined, of course, with physical practice, has proven beneficial (e.g., Smith, 1987). In addition to manipulating acceptable levels of arousal, mental practice is useful in the following:

1. Mentally rehearsing a particular behavioral pattern. (Think about—mentally picture—that golf swing and the flight of the ball before you step up to the tee.)

2. Reducing negative thoughts that may interfere with performance. (Forget about an earlier error and focus on positive experiences, perhaps past victories.)

3. Rehearsing one's role in a team sport. (Mentally practice what you are supposed to do and when you are supposed to do it in various game situations.)

4. Setting realistic goals. (Don't get tense worrying about a competitor in this race, simply try to better your last performance; e.g., Creekmore, 1984; Fenker &

Lambiotte, 1987; Kiester, 1984a, 1984b; Ogilvie & Howe, 1984; Scott & Pelliccioni, 1982; Smith, 1987; Suinn, 1980.)

Obviously, using mental imagery is not a simple matter, nor is it the only way in which athletes can improve their performances. It's just one technique with which sports psychologists can help.

—Gerow, *Psychology: An Introduction,* pp. 554–57

ADJUSTING YOUR RATE TO MEET COMPREHENSION DEMANDS

Do you read the newspaper in the same way and at the same speed at which you read a biology textbook? Do you read an essay for your English class in the same way and at the same speed at which you read a mystery novel? Surprisingly, many people do.

If you are an efficient reader, however, you read the newspaper more quickly and in a different way than you read a biology textbook. Usually, the newspaper is easier to read, and you have a different purpose for reading it. Efficient readers adapt their speed and comprehension levels to suit the material.

To adapt your rate, you need to decide how you will read a given item. How you will read depends on why you are reading and how much you need to remember. A number of variables work together. To read efficiently, you must create a balance among these factors each time you read.

Rate and comprehension are the two main factors that you must keep in balance; as your reading rate increases, your comprehension may decrease. Your goal is to achieve a balance that suits the nature of the material and your purpose for reading it. The following steps will help you learn to vary your reading rate.

1. *Assess the text's difficulty.* Factors such as difficulty of the language, length, and organization all affect text difficulty. Usually, longer or poorly organized material is more difficult to read than shorter or well-organized material. Numerous typographical aids (italics, headings, etc.) can make material easier to read. As you preview an assignment, notice these features and estimate how difficult the material will be to read. There is no rule to use in adjusting your speed to compensate for differing degrees of difficulty. Instead, use your judgment to adjust your reading rate and style to the material.

2. *Assess your familiarity with and interest in the subject.* Your knowledge of and interest in a subject influence how fast you can read. Material you are interested in or that you know something about will be easier for you to read, and you can increase your speed.

3. *Define your purpose.* The reason you are reading an assignment should influence how you read it. Different situations demand different levels of comprehension and recall. For example, you can read an article in *Time* magazine assigned as a supplementary reading in sociology faster than you

TABLE 2–1   LEVELS OF COMPREHENSION

Desired Level of Comprehension	Type of Material	Purpose in Reading	Range of Reading Rates
Complete, 100%	Poetry, legal documents, argumentative writing	Analysis, criticism, evaluation	Under 200 wpm
High, 80–100%	Textbooks, manuals, research documents	High comprehension recall for exams, writing research reports, following directions	200–300 wpm
Moderate, 60–80%	Novels, paperbacks, newspapers, magazines	Entertainment enjoyment, general information	300–500 wpm
Selective, below 60%	Reference materials, catalogues, magazines	Overview of material, location of specific facts, review of previously read material	600–800 wpm

can read your sociology text because the magazine assignment does not require as high a level of recall and analysis.

4. *Decide what, if any, follow-up activity is required.* Will you have to pass a multiple-choice exam on the content? Will you be participating in a class discussion? Will you summarize the information in a short paper? The activities that follow your reading determine, in part, the level of comprehension that is required. Passing an exam requires a very high level of reading comprehension, whereas preparing for a class discussion requires a more moderate level of comprehension or retention.

Table 2–1 above shows the level of comprehension required for various types of material and gives approximate reading rates appropriate for each level.

EXERCISE 2–5

For each of the following situations, define your purpose and indicate the level of comprehension that seems appropriate.

1. Reading the end-of-chapter discussion questions in a business marketing text as part of your chapter preview.

   Purpose: _____

   Comprehension level: _____

2. Reading a critical essay that analyzes a Shakespearean sonnet you are studying in a literature class.

   Purpose: _____

   Comprehension level: _____

3. Reading an encyclopedia entry on poverty to narrow down a term paper assignment to a manageable topic.

   Purpose: _____

   Comprehension level: _____

4. Reading a newspaper article on a recent incident in the Middle East for your political science class.

   Purpose: _____

   Comprehension level: _____

5. Reading an excerpt from a historical novel set in the Civil War period for your American history class.

   Purpose: _____

   Comprehension level: _____

Measure Your Reading Rate

To verify that you are adjusting your reading rate to suit the material and your purpose for reading, measure your reading rate in a variety of situations and make comparisons. The following is an easy method of estimating your reading rate on whatever material you are reading.

1. *After you have chosen a passage in a book or article, count the total number of words in any three lines.* Divide that total by 3. Round to the nearest whole number. This will give you the average number of words per line.

2. *Count the number of lines in the article or passage* (or on one page if it is longer than one page). Multiply the number of words per line by the total number of lines. This will give you a fairly accurate estimate of the total number of words.

3. *As you read, time yourself.* Record the hour, minute, and second of your starting time (for example, 4:20:00). Start reading when the second hand of the clock reaches 12. Record your finishing time. Subtract your starting time from your finishing time.

4. *Divide the total reading time into the total number of words.* To do this, round the number of seconds to the nearest quarter of a minute and then divide. For example, if your total reading time was 3 minutes and 12 seconds, round it off to 3¼ or 3.25, minutes and then divide. Your answer will be your words-per-minute (wpm) score.

   Example:

   Total number of words on 3 lines: 23

   Divide by 3 and round: $23 \div 3 = 7\frac{2}{3} = 8$

   Total number of lines in article: 120

Multiply number of words per line by number of lines:

$8 \times 120 = 960$ (total words)

Subtract starting time from finishing time: 1:13:28

$-\underline{1:05:00}$

8:28

Round to nearest quarter minute: 8.25 minutes

Divide time into total number of words:

$960 \div 8.25 = 116 +$ a fraction (your wpm score)

EXERCISE 2–6

Measure how effectively you adjust your reading rate by reading each of the following materials for the purpose stated. Fill in your reading rate in the space provided, and then compare your results with those given in Table 2–1.

1. Material: A legal document (insurance policy, financial aid statement, credit card agreement)

   Purpose: Complete understanding

   Rate: _____

2. Material: A three-page assignment in one of your textbooks

   Purpose: High comprehension; recall for an exam

   Rate: _____

3. Material: An article in a favorite magazine

   Purpose: Moderate comprehension; entertainment

   Rate: _____

Reading Selectively to Improve Your Reading Efficiency

As part of learning how to adjust your reading rate, you should accept the idea that there is nothing sacred about the printed word. Many students erroneously believe that anything that appears in print must be true, valuable, and worth reading. Actually, the importance and value of printed information are affected by whether you need to learn it and whether you can use it in a practical way. Depending on the kind of material and your purpose for reading it, many times you may need to read only some parts and may skip over others. You might read selectively when:

1. *You are searching for specific information.* If you are looking up the date of a historical event in your history text, you skip over everything in the chapter except the exact passage that contains the information. This technique of skipping everything except the specific information for which you are looking is called *scanning.*

2. *A high level of comprehension is not needed.* If you are not trying to remember a major portion of the facts and details, then you might concentrate on reading only main ideas. This method of reading only main ideas is called *skimming*.

3. *You are familiar with what you are reading.* In a college chemistry course, for example, you might find that the first few chapters of your text are basic if you have already studied high school chemistry. You could afford to skip basic definitions and the explanations and examples of principles that you already know. Do not, however, decide to skip an entire chapter or even large sections within it; there just may be some new information included. You may find that more exact and detailed definitions are given or that a new approach is taken toward a particular topic.

4. *The material does not match your purpose in reading.* Suppose that, in making an assignment in your physics text, your instructor told you to concentrate only on theories, laws, and principles presented in the chapter. As you begin reading the chapter, you find that the first topic discussed is Newton's law of motion, but the chapter also contains a biographical sketch of Newton giving detailed information about his life. Because your purpose in reading the chapter is to focus on theories, laws, and principles, it would be appropriate to skip over much of the biographical information.

5. *The writer's style allows you to skip information (portions).* Some writers include many examples of a particular concept or principle. If, after reading two or three examples, you are sure that you understand the idea being explained, quickly glance at the remaining examples. Unless they present a new aspect or different point of view, skip over them. Other writers provide detailed background information before leading into a discussion of the intended topic. If a chapter starts out by summarizing information that was covered in a chapter you just read last week, it is not necessary to read this information again carefully unless you feel you need to review.

EXERCISE 2–7 | *The following items suggest different reading situations and describe the material to be read. For each item, decide whether you should (a) read the material completely, (b) read parts and skip other parts, or (c) skip most of the material.*

1. Your computer science instructor has just returned a test on a chapter on programming in BASIC. She indicates that the class's overall performance on this test was poor and suggests that the chapter be reviewed. You received a grade of 77 on the test. How should you reread this chapter?
2. You have just attended English class, where your instructor discussed Shakespeare's *Richard III*. During his discussion, he made numerous references to Machiavelli's *The Prince*. You have never read this second work but think it's important to know something about it. How would you read it?

3. You are doing research for a sociology term paper on world trends in gender inequality. You are looking for information and statistics on recent income and employment trends. You have located several books from the 1960s on the topic of gender inequality in the United States. How would you read these books?

4. Your American history instructor has assigned each student to read a historical novel for the purpose of getting a realistic picture of what life was like and how people lived during a certain period. As you are reading, you come to a detailed two-page description of decorative glass making in Sandwich, Massachusetts. How should you read these two pages?

5. Your zoology professor has assigned a number of brief outside readings along with the chapters in your regular textbook. He has put them on reserve in the college library for the use of all his classes. This is the only place where they can be used. He did not say whether you would be tested on these readings. How would you read them?

SUMMARY

The skills you have learned in this chapter enable you to improve your comprehension, adjust your reading rate, and read selectively.

While you read paragraphs, focus on identifying three types of information:

- the main idea
- primary supporting details
- secondary supporting details

The topic sentence can take several positions:

- first
- last
- in the middle
- first and last

In some paragraphs, the main idea may be implied rather than directly stated. Primary details directly support the main idea, whereas secondary details provide additional information or further explanation of primary details.

Your reading rate should vary to suit the material and your purpose for reading it. Measuring your reading rate can help you assess whether you are reading at the proper rate for good comprehension. You should read selectively when you need only main ideas, a specific fact, or the answer to a question; when you are very familiar with the material; when the material does not match with your purpose; and when the style or type of material is conducive to skipping information.

ART APPRECIATION

PREREADING QUESTIONS

1.   Do you know what issue-oriented art is?
2.   What do you think its purpose is?

Issue-Oriented Art

Duane Preble and Sarah Preble

1   Many artists in the last twenty years have sought to link their art directly to important or controversial questions. Issue-oriented artists believe that if they limit their art to aesthetic matters, then their work will be only a distraction from pressing problems. Furthermore, they recognize that what we see has a powerful influence on how we think, and they do not want to miss an opportunity to influence both.

2   Mierle Laderman Ukeles, spurred by New York's ongoing garbage crisis and her own experiences as a mother, began to consider the importance to society of "maintenance work," the repetitive tasks such as garbage collection that are necessary for social functioning. Since 1978, Ukeles has been an unsalaried artist-in-residence for New York City Department of Sanitation, where she makes pieces that are based on the apparent everydayness of Conceptual Art. In 1979 and 1980 she joined the daily rounds of sanitation workers and their supervisors; then for eleven months she completed an eight-hour-a-day performance piece in which she shook the hands of the more than 8,500 workers taking care of New York's mountains of garbage. With each handshake she said, "Thank you for keeping New York City alive."

Mierle Laderman Ukeles. THE SOCIAL MIRROR. *New York, 1983.*

20-cubic yard garbage collection truck fitted with hand-tempered glass mirror with additional strips of mirrored acrylic.

Photo: D. James Dee. Courtesy Ronald Feldman Fine Arts, New York.

3   For a parade, Ukeles covered the sides of a garbage truck with mirrors, creating THE SOCIAL MIRROR. The piece enabled people to see themselves as the starting point of the process, the source of the garbage. In the 1990 piece LANDFILL CROSS SECTION, she installed layers of a landfill, including its methane gas vents, beside a stairway so that viewers could see what happened to some of the waste that they generated. The result was not only educational, but a surprisingly interesting visual composition.

Mierle Laderman Ukeles. LANDFILL CROSS SECTION. *1990. with New York City Department of Sanitation,* Garbage Out Front: A New Era of Public Design, *Municipal Art.*
Layers of clays, soils, geosynthetic materials, methane venting system.
Photo: D. James Dee. Courtesy: Ronald Feldman Fine Arts, New York.

4   Photographer Richard Misrach is similarly motivated by concern for the environment. His photograph SUBMERGED LAMPPOST, SALTON SEA captures the silent yet ironic beauty of a small town in California that was flooded by a misguided irrigation system. In other works he has documented in chilling detail the bloated carcasses of animals killed on military proving grounds in Nevada. His brand of nature photography is in opposition to the common calendars that include soothing views of pristine landscapes. He wants us to know that such scenes are fast disappearing.

5   Barbara Kruger was trained as a magazine designer, and this profession shows in her piece UNTITLED (I SHOP THEREFORE I AM). She invented the slogan, which sounds as though it came from advertising. The position of the hand, too, looks like it came from an ad for aspirin or sleeping medication. Our products define us, don't they? We are what we shop for, and often we buy a product because of what it will say about us and not for the thing itself. These are some of the messages present in this simple yet fascinating work. Perhaps its ultimate irony is that the artist had it silkscreened onto a shopping bag.

Barbara Kruger. UNTITLED (I SHOP THEREFORE I AM). *1987.*
Photographic silkscreen/vinyl, 111" x 113".
Photo: Collection of the Broad Art Foundation, Santa Monica. Courtesy: Mary Boone Gallery, New York.

Richard Misrach. SUBMERGED LAMPPOST, SALTON SEA. *1985.*
Photograph (chromogenic color print).
Photo: Copyright Richard Misrach 1985. Courtesy Fraenkel Gallery.

6   Artists who create works about racism and class bias have often attempted to show how common practices of museum display may unwittingly contribute to such problems. In 1992, the Maryland Historical Society invited African-American artist Fred Wilson to rearrange the exhibits on one floor to create an installation called MINING THE MUSEUM. He spent a year preparing for the show, rummaging through the Society's basement and documentary records; the results were surprising. He found no portraits, for example, of noted African-American Marylanders Benjamin Banneker (who laid out the boundaries of the District of Columbia), Frederick Douglass (noted abolitionist and journalist), or Harriet Tubman (founder of the Underground Railroad). He found instead busts of Henry Clay, Andrew Jackson, and Napoleon Bonaparte, none of whom ever lived in Maryland. He exhibited those three busts next to three empty pedestals to symbolize the missing African Americans. He set out a dis-

Fred Wilson. MINING THE MUSEUM. *1992.*
Detail of installation. Cigar Store Indians facing photographs of Native American Marylanders.
Photo: Jeff Goldman.
Maryland Historical Society.

play of Colonial Maryland silverware and tea utensils, but included a pair of slave shackles. This lesser-known form of metalwork was perhaps equally vital to the functioning of nineteenth-century Maryland. He dusted off the Society's collection of wooden cigarstore Indians and stood them, backs to viewers, facing photographs of real Native Americans who lived in Maryland. In an accompanying exhibition brochure he wrote that a museum should be a place that can make you think. When MINING THE MUSEUM was on display, attendance records soared.

7   Brazilian artist Cildo Meireles communicates his concerns about environmental destruction through the impact of large-scale installations such as OLVIDO (OBLIVION). A conical form

Cildo Meireles. OLVIDO (OBLIVION). *1987–89.*
Native American tent, banknotes, bones, candles, soundtrack. 157½" x 315".
Courtesy of the artist and Galerie Lelong, New York.

shingled with paper money stands on a deep layer of bones—symbols of death. Candles, important to Catholic religious practice, form an encircling wall. The leaflike money on the central cone is currency from the nations of North, Central, and South America, which previously had indigenous populations; it represents the greed and exploitation that have doomed generations of Native Americans. The installation includes a soft sound track that evokes sounds of chanting priests or perhaps distant traffic—but is actually the sound of chain saws rapidly destroying rain forests. Meireles comes from a family long known for its advocacy of Native rights, and this installation denounces the destruction of indigenous cultures and the environment in which they once thrived.

8   William Kentridge's animated films trace the emergence of a new South Africa as it comes to grips with its history of apartheid. HISTORY OF THE MAIN COMPLAINT tells a story of a real estate speculator who is rendered semi-conscious in an auto acci-dent. As he slowly comes to himself in the hospital, his gradually clarifying memory tells him in flashbacks that others died in the crash, and also that he was the cause of it. The protagonist's story is an allegory of South Africa itself as it slowly awakens from the grim reality of racism. The artist made this film laboriously, in the fashion of an old cartoon, drawing hundreds of the story's moments in charcoal on paper and then photographing them in sequence.

Preble and Preble, *Artforms,* pp. 485–88

VOCABULARY PREVIEW

1. For each of the words listed below, use context; prefixes, roots, and suf-fixes (see Chapter 3); and/or a dictionary to write a brief definition or syn-onym of the word as it is used in the reading.

a. aesthetic (para. 1) _____

b. motivated (para. 4) _____

c. misguided (para. 4) _____

d. opposition (para. 4) _____

e. slogan (para. 5) _____

f. unwittingly (para. 6) _____

g. indigenous (para. 7) _____

2. Underline new specialized terms introduced in the reading.

COMPREHENSION QUESTIONS

1. Underline the topic sentence of each paragraph. If the main idea is implied, write a sentence stating the author's main idea.
2. Explain what issue-oriented art is.

3. How have museums been biased in common display practices?
4. How does issue-oriented art use everyday or common objects to make a point?

THINKING CRITICALLY

1. What other issues do you think could be accurately portrayed using art?
2. Does the author present a biased or an objective view of issue-oriented art?
3. What evidence does the author offer that issue-oriented art can affect people's opinions and thoughts? Is it sufficient?
4. Why do you think the use of everyday objects is important in issue-oriented art?
5. What additional information would you like to have about museum exhibits to evaluate whether or not they are biased?
6. Do you think issue-oriented art is effective? Why or why not?

LEARNING/STUDY STRATEGY

Assume this reading was assigned as a topic for a class discussion by your art appreciation instructor. Reread and annotate the reading in preparation for the class discussion.

Multimedia Activities

1. **What is a Topic Sentence?**
   http://www.cerritos.edu/reading/topic1.html
   Review how to locate the topic sentence of a paragraph with these tips and exercises from Cerritos College. Pay attention to the way you speak. Do you use topic sentences? Try putting more of them into your conversations and see if you are expressing yourself more clearly.

2. **Effective Reading Tutorial**
   http://www.jcu.edu.au/studying/services/studyskills/effreading/index.html
   Try this online module for improving your reading rate and comprehension from James Cook University in Australia.

Take a Road Trip to
Maine and St. Louis!

If your instructor has asked you to use the Reading Road Trip CD-ROM or Website, be sure to visit the Main Idea and Supporting Details modules for multimedia tutorials, exercises, and tests. You may also want to visit the Great Lakes to practice your inference skills.

CHAPTER 3

ESSENTIAL VOCABULARY SKILLS

LEARNING OBJECTIVES

✦ To learn techniques for vocabulary development
✦ To develop skill in using context clues
✦ To use word parts to expand your vocabulary
✦ To handle technical and specialized vocabulary

words are used to convey ideas

Your vocabulary can be one of your strongest academic assets or one of your worst liabilities. Language is the primary vehicle of thought, expression, and communication. Vocabulary is the basic unit of language. If your vocabulary is limited, your potential for self-expression, effective communication, and adequate comprehension of oral or printed materials also is limited. Conversely, a strong vocabulary can have both immediate (academic) and long-term (career) effects.

TECHNIQUES FOR VOCABULARY DEVELOPMENT

read professional journals to determine the kinds of terms

Here are some basic techniques for vocabulary development that can produce immediate results.

Be Selective

An unabridged (most nearly complete) dictionary lists approximately 300,000 words. Be realistic: you'll never learn them all. Your first task, then, is to decide what to learn—that is, to be selective. Some words are more useful to you than others, depending on several factors—the most important being your college major and your career goals. If you are a business administration major and plan to get a job with a major corporation, your working vocabulary should be much different than if you are a biology major planning a career in genetic research.

Use What You Already Know

we have listening, reading, speak-ing, a writing vocabulary.

You may believe that you have one vocabulary and that it is either weak or strong. Actually, you have four different vocabulary levels: reading, writing, listening, and speaking. Although they share a common core of basic, functional words, these levels range widely in both size and content. For example, there are words that you recognize and understand as you read but that you never use in your own writing. Similarly, there are words that you understand when you listen to them but that you do not use when you speak. Probably your listening and reading vocabularies are larger than your speaking and writing vocabularies. In other words, you already know a large number of words, but many of them you do not use. Here are a few examples of words you may know but probably don't use:

✱ Use one to improve the other

conform	contour
congeal	contrite
congenial	cosmic
congenital	cosmopolitan
contort	cosmos

When strengthening your vocabulary, a good place to start is to experiment with words you already know but don't use regularly.

Use New Words You Have Learned

Incorporate the new words into your vocabulary

Make a point of using one new word each day, both in speaking and in writing.

Regardless of how much time you spend looking up and recording words, you probably will remember only those that you use fairly soon after you learn them. Forgetting occurs extremely rapidly after learning unless you take action to apply what you have learned.

Acquire the Necessary Tools

To develop a strong vocabulary, you must acquire the necessary tools. These include a dictionary and a thesaurus, as well as access to subject area dictionaries.

Buy a Dictionary   Students commonly ask, "Which dictionary should I buy?" There are several types of dictionaries, each with its own purpose. A pocket or paperback dictionary is an inexpensive, shortened version of a standard desk dictionary. It is small enough to carry with you and costs around $5. Although a pocket dictionary is convenient, its use is also limited. A desk dictionary is more extensive. A pocket edition lists about 50,000 to 60,000 words, whereas a standard desk edition lists up to 150,000 words. Also, the desk edition provides much more information about each word it lists. Desk dictionaries are usually hardbound and cost more than $20. Figure 3–1 is a comparison of entries from a pocket and a collegiate desk dictionary.

Figure 3–1   Comparison of Pocket and Collegiate Dictionaries

Pocket Dictionary	*Collegiate Dictionary*
di·lem′ma (di-lem′ə) *n.* a choice between alternatives equally undesirable.	di-lem-ma (dĭ-lĕm′ə) *n.* **1.** A situation that requires a choice between options that are or seem equally unfavorable or mutually exclusive. **2.** *Usage Problem.* A problem that seems to defy a satisfactory solution. **3.** *Logic.* An argument that presents an antagonist with a choice of two or more alternatives, each of which contradicts the original contention and is conclusive. [Late Latin, from Greek *dilemma,* ambiguous proposition : *di-,* two; see DI–′ + *lēmma,* proposition; see LEMMA] — **dil′em-mat′ic** (dĭl′ə-măt′ĭk) *adj.*
	USAGE NOTE: In its primary sense *dilemma* denotes a situation in which a choice must be made between alternative courses of action or argument. Although citational evidence attests to widespread use of the term meaning simply "problem" or "predicament" and involving no issue of choice, 74 percent of the Usage Panel rejected the sentence *Juvenile drug abuse is the great dilemma of the 1980's.* • It is sometimes claimed that because the *di-* in *dilemma* comes from a Greek prefix meaning "two," the word should be used only when exactly two choices are involved. But 64 percent of the Usage Panel accepts its use for choices among three or more options in the example *Ph.D. students who haven't completed their dissertations by the time their fellowships expire face a difficult dilemma; whether to take out loans to support themselves, to try to work part-time at both a job and their research, or to give up on the degree entirely.*

SOURCE: *The New American Webster Handy College Dictionary* (left) and *The American Heritage Dictionary of the English Language* (right)

Several standard dictionaries are available in both desk and paperback editions. These include *Random House Dictionary of the English Language, Webster's Collegiate Dictionary,* and *The American Heritage Dictionary of the English Language.* A third type of dictionary, the unabridged dictionary, is found in the reference section of the library. The unabridged edition provides the most nearly complete information on each word in the English language.

You should buy a pocket dictionary to carry with you regularly. Use it to check unfamiliar words or unusual spellings. Also, you should purchase a collegiate edition desk dictionary. It is not necessary to have the most up-to-date edition; a used dictionary is just as good and costs considerably less.

A desk dictionary provides complete and varied meanings of words as well as information on word origin and structure. It also contains useful reference information, such as tables of weights and measures, metric equivalents, lists of abbreviations, lists of signs and symbols, a punctuation guide, and information about the mechanics of English and of manuscript form. Biographical and geographical guides also may be included. Electronic dictionaries and dictionaries for phonetic spellers (those who spell the word the way it sounds) are also available.

Use a Thesaurus   A thesaurus is a dictionary of synonyms that groups together words with similar meanings. This type of dictionary is useful for locating a precise descriptive word to fit a particular situation. For example, suppose you are looking for a more precise term for the boldface expression in the following sentence in a term paper you are writing:

> Whether men and women react differently to similar situations is often **talked about** in popular magazine articles.

Figure 3–2 on page 58 shows a thesaurus entry for the phrase *talk about.*

Figure 3–2   Thesaurus Entry

> 12   discuss, debate, reason, deliberate, deliberate upon, exchange views *or* opinions, talk, talk over, hash over <nonformal>, talk of *or* about, rap <nonformal>, comment upon, reason about, discourse about, consider, treat, dissertate on, handle, deal with, take up, go into, examine, investigate, talk out, analyze, sift, study, canvass, review, pass under review, controvert, ventilate, air, thresh out, reason the point, consider pro and con; kick *or* knock around <nonformal>

SOURCE: *Roget's International Thesaurus*

Right away, you can identify a number of words that are more specific than the phrase *talked about*. The next step is to choose a word from the entry that most closely suggests the meaning you wish to convey. Words such as *debate* and *discuss* would be appropriate. The easiest way to do this is to substitute various choices in your sentence to see which works best; check the dictionary if you are not sure of a word's exact meaning. Many students misuse the thesaurus by choosing words that do not fit the context. Use a word only when you are familiar with all its shades of meaning. Remember, a misused word is often a more serious error than a wordy or an imprecise expression.

The most widely used thesaurus originally was compiled by Peter Mark Roget and is known today as *Roget's Thesaurus*; it is readily available in an inexpensive paperback edition.

| EXERCISE 3–1 | *Use a thesaurus to find a more specific or descriptive word to replace the underlined word in each of the following sentences. Revise the sentence, if necessary.* |

1. The jury made the <u>right</u> decision on the sexual discrimination case.
2. The videotape on the rights of victims shown in my criminal justice class was <u>dull</u>.
3. After completing three exams in one day, Joe seemed <u>tired</u>.
4. Dr. Rodriguez is a <u>good</u> teacher.
5. My friends thought the biology exam was <u>hard</u>.

Use Subject Area Dictionaries

Many academic fields have specialized dictionaries that list most of the important words used in that discipline. These dictionaries give specialized meanings for words and suggest how and when to use the words. For the field of nursing, for instance, there is *Taber's Cyclopedic Medical Dictionary*. Other subject area dictionaries include Henderson's *Dictionary of Biological Terms*, *The New Grove Dictionary of Music and Musicians*, and *A Dictionary of Economics and Business*.

Find out whether there are subject area dictionaries for the disciplines you are studying. Many such dictionaries are available only in hardback and are likely to be expensive; however, students often find them worth the initial investment. Most libraries have reference copies of many specialized dictionaries.

EXERCISE 3–2 | *For each of the courses you are taking, find out whether there is a subject area dictionary available. If so, record its title.*

Use a System for Learning Vocabulary

One of the most practical systems for expanding your vocabulary is the index card system. It works like this:

1. *Whenever you hear or read a new word that you want to learn, jot it down in the margin of your notes or mark it in the material you are reading.*

2. *Later, write each word on the front of an index card.* Then look up the meaning of each word, and write it on the back. You also might record a phonetic key for the word's pronunciation, if it is a difficult one, or a sample sentence in which the word is used. Sample index cards are shown in Figure 3–3 on the next page.

3. *Whenever you have a few spare minutes, go through your pack of index cards;* for each card, look at the word on the front and try to recall its meaning on the back. Then check the back of the card to see whether you were correct. If you were unable to recall the meaning or if you confused it with another word, retest yourself. Shuffle the cards after each use.

4. *After you have gone through your pack of cards several times, sort the cards into two piles, separating the words you know from those you have not learned.* Then, putting the known words aside, concentrate on the words still to be learned.

5. *Once you have mastered all the words, periodically review them to refresh your memory and to keep the words current in your mind.*

6. *Once you have learned the words, use them in your speech and/or writing and evaluate how effectively you have used them.* This step is perhaps the most important of all, because it moves you from the knowledge and comprehension levels of thinking to the application and evaluation levels (see Chapter 1).

This system is effective for several reasons. First, you can accomplish it in your spare time; you can even review your cards while you wait for a bus. Second, the system enables you to spend time learning what you do not know rather than wasting time studying what you already have learned. Finally, the system overcomes a major problem that exists in learning information that appears in list form. When the material is in a fixed order, you tend to learn it in that order and may be unable to recall the items when they appear in isolation or out of order. Shuffling the cards enables you to scramble the order of the words and avoid this problem.

Figure 3-3 Sample Index Cards

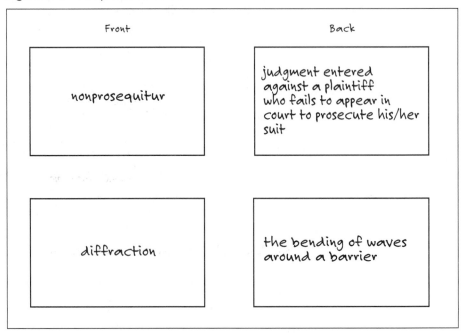

Front

Back

nonprosequitur

judgment entered
against a plaintiff
who fails to appear in
court to prosecute his/her
suit

diffraction

the bending of waves
around a barrier

EXERCISE 3-3

Academic Application

Over the next week, prepare a set of 15 to 20 index cards for new words used by your professor or introduced in your textbook. Include only words you feel you could use in your own speech or writing.

USING CONTEXT CLUES

Although a dictionary is invaluable, it is not practical to look up every new word you encounter. An alternative is to reason out the meaning of an unfamiliar word by using clues in the sentence or paragraph. Read the following paragraph, from which several words have been deleted. Fill them in after you have read the paragraph through once.

Karl Marx (1818–1883) was born _____ Germany. _____ father, a lawyer, and his _____ were both descended from long lines of rabbis. Marx _____ college and planned _____ practice law, but after becoming involved with a radical antireligious _____, he decided to devote his _____ to philosophy.

—Eshleman et al., *Sociology, An Introduction*, pp. 34–35

Certainly, you had no trouble filling in the missing words. You were able to do this because the paragraph contained enough information or clues about what was missing. Now imagine that instead of blanks, the paragraph contained several unfamiliar words. Often, you can "fill in" the meaning of the unknown words by using clues contained in the paragraph. Use these clues to determine the meanings of the boldface words in the following passage:

> The condition most feared among governments as a cause of war is power **asymmetry**—that is, an unfavorable tilt in the distribution of power. There is widespread conviction that whatever other **impetuses** to war may be present, a careful equilibration of power between **antagonists** will tend to prevent war, while a disequilibrium will invite aggression. . . .
>
> —Jones, *The Logic of International Relations*, p. 379

Although you may not have been able to define exactly words such as *asymmetry, impetuses,* and *antagonists,* you were probably able to make a reasonable guess about their meanings. You used the clues contained in the context (surrounding words and phrases) to arrive at the meaning.

Types of Context Clues

Now, let's look at various types of context clues. Each clue requires analysis of the word's context and the ideas that context contains.

Definition or Synonym   Frequently, a writer gives a brief definition or synonym for a word, usually in the same sentence as the word being defined. The definition may be the key idea of the sentence, as in the following examples.

> **Ethology** is the study of the behavior of animals in their natural settings.

At other times, the definition or synonym may be set apart from the key idea of the sentence through the use of commas, dashes, or parentheses.

> Experimental biology includes the study of learning, behavior, memory, perception, and **psychology** (biological bases of behavior).

> Most societies are **patriarchal**—males exert dominant power and authority.

You will find this type of clue used in most introductory college textbooks, especially in the first several chapters in which the "course language" is introduced.

Example Clues   Writers include examples to clarify or illustrate important concepts and ideas. If you are unfamiliar with a word or concept, often you can figure it out by studying the example.

> The use of **nonverbal communication,** such as a smile or gesture, usually reduces the risk of misinterpretation.

From the examples, *smile* and *gesture,* you know that nonverbal communication refers to "body language"—physical movements and facial expressions. Here are two other sentences that contain example clues.

Collecting **demographic data** on potential consumers, including age, marital status, residency, and income, is an essential part of market research.

Salary increases, promotions, privileges, and praise are forms of **extrinsic** rewards that motivate behavior.

You may have noticed that the examples in these sentences are signaled by certain words and phrases. *Such as* and *including* are used here. Other common signals are *for instance, to illustrate,* and *for example.*

Contrast Clues   Sometimes, you can determine the meaning of an unknown word from a word or phrase in the context that has an opposite meaning. Note, in the following sentence, how a word opposite in meaning from the boldface word provides a clue to its meaning.

Despite their seemingly **altruistic** actions, large corporations are self-interested institutions that exist to make profits.

Although you may not know the meaning of *altruistic,* you know it means the opposite of self-interested. The word *despite* suggests this. *Altruistic,* then, means "interested in the welfare of others." Here are two additional sentences containing contrast clues.

Studies of crowd behavior suggest that people in a crowd lose their personalities and act **impulsively,** rather than making reasoned decisions.

Polytheism, the worship of more than one god, is common throughout India; however, **monotheism** is the most familiar religion to Americans.

Each of these examples contains a word or phrase that indicates that an opposite or contrasting situation exists. Two such signals that were used in the examples are *rather than* and *however.* Other signal words that also show a contrasting idea include *but, despite, rather, while, yet,* and *nevertheless.*

Inference Clues   Many times, you can figure out the meaning of a word you do not know by using logical reasoning or by drawing on your own knowledge and experience. From the information given in the context, you can infer the meaning of a word you are not familiar with, as in the following sentence.

Confucius had a **pervasive** influence on all aspects of Chinese life, so much so that every county in China built a temple to him.

If every county in China built a temple to Confucius, you can imagine that his influence was widespread. You can infer, then, that *pervasive* means "spread throughout."

Similarly, in the following example, the general sense of the context provides clues to the meaning of the word.

In wind instruments such as the trumpet, sound is **emitted** directly by the vibrations of air columns in the instrument.

In this sentence, *emitted* means "sent out."

Sometimes your knowledge and experience can help you figure out an unknown word. Consider, for instance, the following sentence.

>   To **simulate** the weightless environment of outer space, astronauts are placed in a specially designed room.

Here, *simulate* means "to give the appearance of."

Limitations of Context Clues

Although context clues generally are useful, they do not always work. There will be words for which the context provides no clues. Also, you should recognize that context clues give you only a general sense of what the word means—not its exact or complete definition. If you've figured a word out from context clues and you feel it is worth learning, mark it and later check its complete meaning in a dictionary.

A final limitation of context is that it suggests the meaning of the word only as it is used in a particular context. Words have multiple meanings; the meaning you infer from a single context gives you only a limited understanding of the word.

EXERCISE 3–4

Use context clues to determine the meaning of each boldface word. Write a brief definition or synonym in the space provided.

1. People who practice **totemism,** the worship of plants, animals, or objects as gods, usually select for worship objects that are important to the community.

    Worshiping something

2. The tone of **percussion** instruments, such as drums and cymbals, depends in part on the geometry of the surface area.

    Hitting two objects making beat

3. A cult may recruit followers through **deception;** potential followers may not be told what the cult involves or what will be expected of them.

    lies

4. **Euthanasia,** sometimes called mercy killing, is a controversial issue among the families of terminally ill patients.

    Taking someones life to end suffering

5. Establishing a buying **motive,** such as hunger, safety, or prestige, is important in developing an advertising plan for a new product.

    _____

6. Our **paleolithic** ancestors relied on their own body power and the controlled use of fire to get things done. In later Stone Age societies, people used animals for muscle power.

    _____

7. Information, as well as rumors and gossip, is quickly spread through the office **grapevine**, although it is not recognized as an official channel of communication.

_____

8. New hourly employees in the firm are **accountable** to the training director, who, in turn, is accountable to the director of personnel.
   _responsible_____

9. In one culture, a man may be **ostracized** for having more than one wife, whereas in other cultures, a man with many wives is an admired and respected part of the group.
   _to kick out_____

10. **Homogeneous** groups, such as classes made up entirely of teenagers, social organizations of high-IQ people, and country clubs of wealthy families, have particular roles and functions in our society.
    _similar characteristics_____

EXERCISE 3–5

Working with a classmate, use context clues to determine the meaning of each word in boldface print in the following passage. Write a brief definition or synonym in the space provided.

ORGANIZATION OF RELIGION

Religious associations take the form of cult, sect, or church depending upon their degree of institutionalization and level of formality. **Cults** represent the most loosely structured and unconventional forms of organization. They consist of small numbers of persons who band together in order to express a new religious cause—a cause often at great **variance** from that of established religion. In Roman times Christians were members of a cult. Today **adherents** of the Reverend Moon's Unification Church—"Moonies"—can be considered [members of] a cult.

Most cults dissipate after a short period of time. They are held together only as long as their charismatic leaders are able to mobilize the loyalty and passion of followers. In order to remain viable, then, religious groups must move to another level of organization: They take the form of either sect or church.

A **sect** is a small religious association that generally appeals to poor, propertyless, or otherwise marginal members of society. As in the case of a cult, the sect frequently supports a cause that places its membership at odds with established religious organizations. Unlike cults, sects usually **emerge** out of established religious orders. Also unlike cults, sects perpetuate themselves over time by developing a loose structure usually consisting of a part-time minister from the congregation who leads a highly involved membership in a number of emotionally charged services. The recent "Born Again" movement in Protestantism is a case in point. On television weekly, the various "Born Again" groups gained enormous popularity in the early and mid-1980s but found themselves **tottering** after the highly publicized scandals of Jim and Tammy Bakker and Jimmy Swaggert in the latter part of the decade.

The most highly structured and conventional religious organization is known as the church. Unlike a sect, a church draws membership from the cultural and economic mainstream of a society. Thus the religious beliefs and rituals of a church generally reflect an acceptance of the **prevailing** social order. Also unlike a sect, a church typically **engages** a specialized and full-time minister (or rabbi) who leads the congregation and socializes new members in religious beliefs and rituals.

—Levin and Spates, *Starting Sociology,* pp. 251–52

1. _____
2. _____
3. _____
4. _____
5. _____
6. _____
7. _____
8. _____

WORD PARTS: THE MULTIPLIER EFFECT

Suppose you want to learn 50 new words. For each word you learn, your vocabulary increases by one word; if you learn all 50, then you've increased your vocabulary by 50 words. The vocabulary of the average young adult is 30,000 words. Adding 50 words is equal to a 0.17 percent increase—negligible at best. You may be thinking, "There must be a better way," and fortunately, there is. If you learn word parts—prefixes, roots, and suffixes (beginnings, middles, and endings of words)—instead of single words, your vocabulary will multiply geometrically rather than increase by one word at a time.

Learning word parts, then, produces a multiplier effect. A single prefix can unlock the meaning of 50 or more words. Think of the prefix *inter-*. Once you learn that it means "between," you can define many new words. Here are a few examples.

intercede	interscholastic
interconnect	intersperse
interracial	interstellar

interrelate	intertribal
interrupt	intervene

Similarly, knowledge of a single root unlocks numerous word meanings. For instance, knowing that the root *spec* means "to look or see" enables you to understand words such as

inspect	retrospect
inspector	retrospection
introspection	spectator
introspective	speculate
perspective	speculation

Learning word parts is a much more efficient means of building vocabulary than learning single words. The following sections list common prefixes, roots, and suffixes and provide practice in learning them. Before you begin to learn specific word parts, study the following guidelines.

1. In most cases, a word is built on at least one root.

2. Words can have more than one prefix, root, or suffix.
    a. Words can be made up of two or more roots (geo-logy).
    b. Some words have two prefixes (in-sub-ordination).
    c. Some words have two suffixes (beauti-ful-ly).

3. Words do not always have both a prefix and a suffix.
    a. Some words have neither a prefix nor a suffix (read).
    b. Others have a suffix but no prefix (read-ing).
    c. Others have a prefix but no suffix (pre-read).

4. Roots may change in spelling as they are combined with suffixes (arid, arable).

5. Sometimes, you may identify a group of letters as a prefix or root but find that it does not carry the meaning of the prefix or root. For example, in the word *internal*, the letters *i-n-t-e-r* should not be confused with the prefix *inter-*, which means "between." Similarly, the letters *m-i-s* in the word *missile* are part of the root and are not the prefix mis-, which means "wrong or bad."

Prefixes

Prefixes appear at the beginning of many English words and alter the meaning of the root to which they are connected. Table 3–1 groups 36 common prefixes according to meaning.

Learning word parts is particularly useful for science courses. Many scientific words are built from a common core of prefixes, roots, and suffixes. Chapter 17 offers several examples on page 487.

TABLE 3–1   COMMON PREFIXES

Prefix	Meaning	Example
Amount or Number		
bi-	two	bimonthly
deci-	ten	decimal
centi-	hundred	centigrade
equi-	equal	equidistant
micro-	small	microscope
milli-	thousand	milligram
mono-	one	monocle
multi-	many	multipurpose
poly-	many	polygon
semi-	half	semicircle
tri-	three	triangle
uni-	one	unicycle
Negative		
a-	not	asymmetrical
anti-	against	antiwar
contra-	against, opposite	contradict
dis-	apart, away, not	disagree
in-/il-/ir-/im-	not	illogical
mis-	wrongly	misunderstood
non-	not	nonfiction
un-	not	unpopular
pseudo-	false	pseudoscientific
Direction, Location, or Placement		
circum-	around	circumference
com-/col-/con-	with, together	compile
de-	away, from	depart
ex-/extra-	from, out of, former	ex-wife
hyper-	over, excessive	hyperactive
inter-	between	interpersonal
intro-/intra-	within, into, in	introduction
post-	after	posttest
pre-	before	premarital
re-	back, again	review
retro-	backward	retrospect
sub-	under, below	submarine
super-	above, extra	supercharge
tele-	far	telescope
trans-	across, over	transcontinental

| **EXERCISE 3–6** | *Using the list of common prefixes in Table 3–1 (p. 67), write the meaning of each of the following boldface words. If you are unfamiliar with the root, check its meaning in a dictionary.* |

1. a **multinational** corporation _____

2. **antisocial** behavior _____

3. **inefficient** study habits _____

4. **postglacial** period _____

5. **unspecialized** training _____

6. housing **subdivision** _____

7. **redefine** one's goals _____

8. a **semifinalist** _____

9. **retroactive** policies _____

10. a sudden **transformation** _____

| **EXERCISE 3–7** | *Select two classmates and, working as a team, record as many words as you can that begin with one of the following prefixes. Compare your findings with those of other classroom teams.* |

1. pre-
2. de-
3. mis-

Roots

Roots carry the basic or core meaning of a word. Hundreds of root words are used to build words in the English language. Table 3–2 (p. 69) lists 30 of the most common and most useful roots.

| **EXERCISE 3–8** | *Use the list of common roots in Table 3–2 to determine the meanings of the following boldface words. Write a brief definition or synonym of each, checking a dictionary if necessary.* |

1. **bioethical** issues _____

2. **terrestrial** life _____

3. to **desensitize** _____

4. to study **astronomy** _____

5. **synchronize** your watches _____

6. **visualize** the problem _____

7. a religious **missionary** _____

8. **biographical** data _____

9. a **geology** course _____

10. **pathological** behavior _____

TABLE 3–2   COMMON ROOTS

Root	Meaning	Example
aud/audit	hear	audible
aster/astro	star	astronaut
bio	life	biology
cap	take, seize	captive
chron(o)	time	chronology
corp	body	corpse
cred	believe	incredible
dict/dic	tell, say	predict
duc/duct	lead	introduce
fact/fac	make, do	factory
graph	write	telegraph
geo	earth	geophysics
log/logo/logy	study, thought	psychology
mit/miss	send	dismiss
mort/mor	die, death	immortal
path	feeling	sympathy
phono	sound, voice	telephone
photo	light	photosensitive
port	carry	transport
scop	see	microscope
scrib/script	write	inscription
sen/sent	feel	insensitive
spec/spic/spect	look, see	retrospect
tend/tent/tens	stretch or strain	tension
terr/terre	land, earth	territory
theo	god	theology
ven/vent	come	convention
vert/vers	turn	invert
vis/vid	see	invisible
voc	call	vocation

Suffixes

Suffixes are word endings that often change the part of speech of a word. For example, adding the suffix *-y* to the noun *cloud* produces the adjective *cloudy*. Accompanying the change in part of speech is a shift in meaning.

Often, several different words can be formed from a single root word with the addition of different suffixes. Some examples follow.

Root: class

root + suffix = class-ify, class-ification, class-ic

Root: right

root + suffix = right-ly, right-ful, right-ist, right-eous

If you know the meaning of the root word and the ways in which different suffixes affect the meaning of the root word, you will be able to understand a word's meaning when a suffix is added. A list of common suffixes and their meanings appears in Table 3–3.

EXERCISE 3–9

For each of the words listed, add a suffix so that the word will complete the sentence. Write the new word in the space provided.

1. *behavior*

   _____ therapy attempts to change habits and illnesses by altering people's responses to stimuli.

2. *atom*

   Uranium, when bombarded with neutrons, explodes and produces a heat reaction known as _____ energy.

3. *advertise*

   One important purpose of an _____ is to inform potential customers about the service or product and familiarize the public with the brand name.

4. *uniform*

   The _____ of a law requires that it must be applied to all relevant groups without bias.

5. *evolution*

   Darwin's theory of natural selection tied the survival of a species to its _____ fitness—its ability to survive and reproduce.

6. *compete*

   When food sources are not large enough to support all the organisms in a habitat, environmental _____ occurs.

7. *religion*

   During the Age of Reason in American history, _____ revivals swept the nation.

8. *perform*

Perhaps an administrator's most important duty is establishing conditions conducive to high employee motivation, which results in better job _____.

9. *effective*

A critical factor in evaluating a piece of literature or art is its _____—how strongly and clearly the artist's message has been conveyed to the audience.

10. *theory*

_____ have spent decades studying the theory of relativity.

TABLE 3–3 COMMON SUFFIXES	
Suffix	**Example**
State, Condition, or Quality	
-able	touchable
-ance	assistance
-ation	confrontation
-ence	reference
-ible	tangible
-ion	discussion
-ity	superiority
-ive	permissive
-ment	amazement
-ness	kindness
-ous	jealous
-ty	loyalty
-y	creamy
"One Who"	
-ee	tutee
-eer	engineer
-er	teacher
-ist	activist
-or	advisor
Pertaining to or Referring to	
-al	autumnal
-ship	friendship
-hood	brotherhood
-ward	homeward

Use your knowledge of context clues and word parts to determine the meaning of each boldface word. On a separate sheet of paper, write a brief definition of each word that fits its use in the sentence.

1. GLOBAL TECHNOLOGY

The advancement of technology is a **global** issue. The United States has been known as a world leader in the advancement of technology. To remain **competitive,** however, global research and development strategies must respond to changes in transportation, communication, information technology, and **merged** national markets. Intellectual capital is the critical resource in the global economy. The ability to **generate,** access, and rapidly use new knowledge and **convert** it (technology transfer) into marketable quality products and processes is the key to competitive advantage.

The **diffusion** of technological capabilities and expansion of the technically trained work force worldwide have strengthened the competitive position of industrialized countries and **enabled** many more to enter the marketplace. As a result, **dominance** by the United States in nearly all high-tech markets is being challenged.

In many countries, government-sponsored programs have reduced the costs and risks associated with technological development by **assuring** long-term financial commitment. Airbus Industries, for example, is a cross-national European consortium that has developed and produced airplanes through support of its partner companies in the form of repayable loans.

—Kinnear et al., *Principles of Marketing,* pp. 57–58

2. LINGUISTIC ANTHROPOLOGY

While all organisms have some way of communicating, and some animals, such as porpoises and chimpanzees, have highly developed means of communicating, humans have evolved a unique and extremely complex system. Without it, human culture as we know it would be impossible. The field of **linguistic anthropology** focuses on this aspect of human life. It is, in turn, divided into a number of **subfields.**

Descriptive linguistics deals with how languages are constructed and how the various parts (sound and grammar) are **interrelated** to form coherent systems of communication. Historical linguistics concerns the **evolution** of language—how languages grow and change. Sociolinguistics studies the relationship between language and social factors, such as class, ethnicity, age, and gender. Finally, a topic of interest to many anthropological linguists is language and culture, which examines the ways that language affects how we think and, *conversely,* how our beliefs and values might influence our linguistic patterns.

—Howard, *Contemporary Cultural Anthropology,* pp. 12–13

LEARNING SPECIALIZED AND SCIENTIFIC VOCABULARY

You probably have noticed that each sport and hobby has its own language—a specialized set of words with specific meanings. Baseball players and fans talk about no-hitters, home runs, errors, and runs batted in. Each academic discipline, too, has its own set of specialized words. These terms enable specialists to give accurate and concise descriptions of events, principles, concepts, problems, and occurrences.

One of the first tasks that you face in a new course is to learn its specialized language. This task is especially important in introductory courses where the subject is new and unfamiliar to you. In an introductory computer science course, for instance, you often start by learning how a computer functions. From that point, many new terms are introduced: *bit, byte, field, numeric characters, character positions, statements, coding, format,* and so forth.

In science courses, new terminology is especially important. Hundreds of new scientific terms are introduced in each course. For specific suggestions on learning scientific terminology, refer to Chapter 17, pages 486–88.

Specialized Terminology in Class Lectures

Often, the first few class lectures in a course are devoted to acquainting students with the nature and scope of the field and to introducing its specialized language. Many instructors devote considerable time to presenting the language of the course carefully and explicitly. Be sure to record each new term accurately for later review and study. Good lecturers give you clues to what terms and definitions are important to record. Some instructors make a habit of writing new words on the chalkboard; others may speak very slowly so that you can record definitions. Still other instructors may repeat a word and its definition several times or offer several variations of the word's meaning. As a part of your note-taking system, develop a consistent way of easily identifying new terms and definitions recorded in your notes. For instance, you might circle or draw a box around each new term or write "def." in the margin.

EXERCISE 3–11

Estimate the number of new terms that each of your instructors introduced during the first several weeks for each of your courses. Now check the accuracy of your estimates by reviewing the first two weeks of your class notes and the first several chapters of the textbook for each course you are taking. How many new terms and definitions were included for each course? Most students underestimate. Did you?

Specialized Terminology in Textbooks

The first few chapters in a textbook are generally introductory, too. They are written to familiarize you with the subject and acquaint you with its specialized language. In one economics textbook, 34 new terms were introduced in the first two chapters (40 pages). In the first two chapters (28 pages) of a chemistry book, 56 specialized words were introduced.

Textbook authors use various means to emphasize new terminology. In some texts, new vocabulary is printed in italics, boldface type, or colored print. Other texts indicate new terms in the margin of each page. Still the most common means of emphasis, however, is the "New Terminology" or

"Vocabulary" list that appears at the beginning or end of each chapter. Many texts also include a glossary of key terms at the back of the book.

EXERCISE 3–12 | *Review the first chapter from two of your texts and then answer the following questions.*

1. How many new terms are introduced in each?
2. If your texts contain glossaries, are all of these new terms listed?
3. Are most new words technical terms, or are they words in everyday use to which a specialized meaning is attached?
4. How does each textbook author call your attention to these new terms?

Learning Core Prefixes, Roots, and Suffixes

Terminology in a particular academic discipline often uses a core of common prefixes, roots, and suffixes. For example, in the field of human anatomy and physiology, the prefix *endo-* means "inner" and the root *derma* refers to "skin." Thus the word endoderm refers to the inner layer of cells in the skin. Numerous other words are formed by using the root *derma* in conjunction with a suffix.

As you are learning new terminology for each course, make a point of noticing recurring prefixes, roots, and suffixes. Compile a list of these word parts and their meanings, along with several examples of each one. A partial sample list for anthropology follows.

	MEANINGS	**EXAMPLES**
PREFIXES		
bi-	two	bipedalism
anti-	against	antibody
poly-	many	polygyny
ROOTS		
terra	earth, ground	territory
gene	unit of chromosomes	genotype
anthropo	human	anthropoid
SUFFIXES		
-us	one who	Australopithecus
-cene	era or epoch	Pleistocene
-cide	killing of	infanticide

EXERCISE 3–13 | *For one of your courses, identify five commonly used prefixes, roots, and suffixes. If you have difficulty, review the glossary of the text to discover commonly used word parts.*

Developing a Course Master File

For each course you are taking, set up a master file that includes new terminology to be learned and a list of essential prefixes, roots, and suffixes. Also include a list of frequently used signs, abbreviations, and symbols and their meanings.

In the sciences, numerous symbols are used in formulas. You'll save time and avoid frequent interruptions if you learn these symbols right away rather than having to refer to the text to translate each sign or symbol. Your course master file can be a big help in this effort.

An abbreviated version of a course master file for a course in American politics is shown in Figure 3–4.

Because each course is different, your course master file will change for each course you are taking. Check with the Learning Lab or Academic Skills Center at your college; it may offer lists of common prefixes and roots.

Figure 3–4 Sample Course Master File

New Terminology

Cabinet	Group of presidential advisors made up of secretaries who head government departments and the attorney general.
Deficit	An excess of government expenditures over federal revenues.
Bill	A proposed law that must be passed by Congress and signed by the President to become a law.

Prefixes, Roots, Suffixes

Prefix	Meaning	Example
anti-	against	antitrust
bi-	two	bicameral
sub-	under	subgovernments

Root	Meaning	Example
pol	political	policy
employ	to provide work	unemployment
pluri	many	pluralist

Suffix	Meaning	Example
-ism	a quality, doctrine, theory, or principle	capitalism
-ive	state, condition, or quality	progressive
-al	referring to	presidential

Abbreviations

CIA	Central Intelligence Agency
PAC	political action committee
FTC	Federal Trade Commission
CPI	Consumer Price Index
FEC	Federal Election Committee

EXERCISE 3–14

Begin preparing a master file for one of your courses. Using both your text and your lecture notes, begin with the first chapter and list new terms, prefixes, roots, and suffixes, as well as symbols and abbreviations.

SUMMARY

This chapter focused on basic techniques of vocabulary development. Some basic tools for vocabulary development are

- pocket and collegiate dictionaries
- a thesaurus
- subject area dictionaries
- the index card system

Often, you can determine the meaning of unfamiliar words by examining the context in which they appear. Four common types of context clues are

- definition or synonym
- example
- contrast
- inference

If you learn common word parts (prefixes, roots, and suffixes), you can unlock the meaning of thousands of words.

Each academic discipline has its own set of specialized and technical vocabulary. Aids to mastering specialized terminology include

- subject area dictionaries
- core prefixes, roots, and suffixes
- a course master file

Interpersonal Communication

PREREADING QUESTIONS

1. Do people always understand what you are saying?
2. Why does miscommunication occur?

What Words Can and Cannot Do

Richard L. Weaver, III

1   If we see a series of stones lying across a stream, we know they will help us get to the other side. But our experience with such stones tells us that some of the stones may be loose or covered with slime and could cause us to slip. Like these stones, words can help us to reach our goals, or they can cause us to stumble and fall. Let's look at some characteristics of language that affect our interpersonal communication.

2   When we talk to people, we often assume too quickly that we are being understood. If we tell people we are going to put on some music, we probably don't think about whether they are expecting to hear the kind of music we intend to play—we just turn it on. But think about the word *music* and how many different interpretations there are of it. (See Figure A on page 78.)

3   We depend on context and on nonverbal cues to give us the meaning of words. If we say we are going to put on some music, our friends may be able to predict from knowing our taste and from nonverbal cues (our mood) what we might play. But they have a good chance of being wrong. In our daily conversation, we use about 2,000 words. Of those 2,000, the 500 we use most often have more than 14,000 dictionary definitions. Think of the possibilities for confusion! The problem of figuring out what a person means by a certain word is compounded by the fact that even dictionary meanings change, and new words are constantly being added to the language.

4   **Denotative meanings.** *The* **denotative meaning** *of a word is its dictionary definition.* Dictionaries provide alternatives; we still must choose from those alternatives. The choice of what is "appropriate" or "inappropriate" is left to the user.

5   Some words have relatively stable meanings. If several people were to define a particular word special to their discipline, they would probably use about the same definition—an agreed-upon interpretation. To lawyers, the word *estoppel* has one precise, denotative meaning. Doctors would probably agree upon the definition of *myocardial infarction.* People in many disciplines depend on certain words having precise, unchanging meanings in order to carry on their work. There is little likelihood of confusion with denotative meanings because there is a direct relationship

Figure A One word may have many different interpretations.

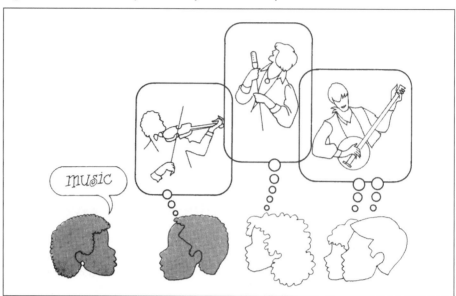

between the word and what it describes. Connotative meanings, on the other hand, depend a lot more than denotative meanings on our subjective thought processes. (See Figure B.)

6 **Connotative meanings.** *The connotative meaning of a word is the associations and overtones people bring to it.* Dictionary definitions would probably not help our friends predict the kind of music we would play or what we mean by "music." But their experience with us and with music will give them a clue as to what we mean. If "music" connotes the same thing to us and to our friends, there's less chance of misunderstanding.

7 When we hear a word, the thoughts and feelings we have about that word and about the person using it determine what that word ultimately means to us. This is the word's *connotative* meaning. Connotative meanings change with our experience. Just as we experience something different in every second of life that we

---

CONSIDER THIS

The belief that sitting down and talking will ensure mutual understanding and solve problems is based on the assumption that we can say what we mean, and that what we say will be understood as we mean it.

—Tannen, *That's Not What I Meant!* p. 124.

Figure B   Connotative meanings may depend a great deal on the perceiver's experience.

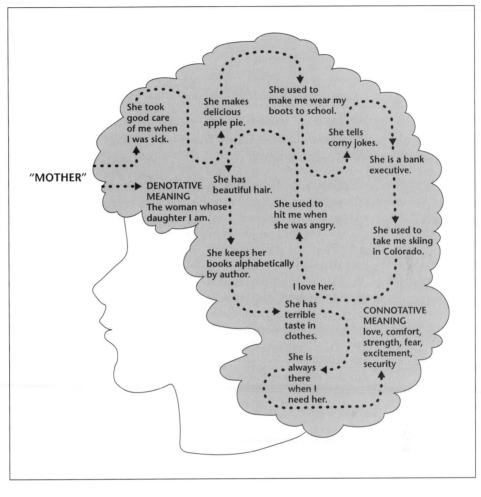

live, so does everyone else. And no two of these experiences are identical! It's no wonder there are infinitely many connotations for every word we use. Figure B illustrates the process through which words may accumulate their connotative meanings.

8   If a word creates pretty much the same reaction in a majority of people, the word is said to have a general connotation. Actually, the more general the connotation of a word, the more likely that meaning will become the dictionary meaning because most people will agree on what that word represents. The more general the connotation of a word, the less likely people are to misunderstand it.

9   Problems in interpersonal communication increase as we use words with many connotative meanings. Because these meanings are so tied to the particular feelings, thoughts, and ideas of other people, we have a bigger chance of being misunderstood when we use them. On the other hand, richly connotative words

give our language power. Note, for example, the differences between the following lists of words:

freedom	book
justice	piano
love	tree
liberty	teacher
music	fire

The words in the left column have many connotations; the words in the right column are more strictly denotative. "The teacher put the book on the piano" is an unambiguous statement. The sentence, "The love of freedom burns like a white flame in all of us" can be interpreted in numerous ways.

10   What does all this have to do with our use of words? First, we should recognize that words evoke sometimes unpredictable reactions in others. We should try to anticipate the reactions of others to our words as much as we can. For example, if we are talking to an art major, we may cause confusion or even produce a hostile response if we use the psychology-major jargon we have picked up. If we antici- pate this negative reaction, we'll leave the jargon in the psychology classroom.

11   Second, most words have both denotative and connotative meanings, and we should recognize that these meanings vary from person to person. People will react to words according to the meaning *they* give them. An effective communicator tries to recognize different reactions and to adapt to them. Remember as you communi- cate that meanings do *not* reside in the words themselves. *Meanings are in the minds of the people who use and hear the words. That is the essence of the trans- actional view of communication.*

—Weaver, *Understanding Interpersonal Communication,* pp. 230–33

VOCABULARY REVIEW

1. For each of the words listed below, use context; prefixes, roots, and suffixes; and/or a dictionary to write a brief definition or synonym of the word as it is used in the reading.

   a. nonverbal (para. 3) _____

   b. denotative (para. 4) _____

   c. connotative (para. 6) _____

   d. unambiguous (para. 9) _____

   e. jargon (para. 10) _____

   f. transactional (para. 11) _____

2. Underline new specialized terms introduced in the reading.

COMPREHENSION QUESTIONS

1. Explain the differences between denotative and connotative meanings.
2. Why do professions use words with agreed-upon denotative meanings?
3. According to this author, what are the causes of miscommunication?

THINKING CRITICALLY

1. Make a list of words with numerous connotations.
2. Give an example of a word whose connotative meaning changes with the speaker's experience.
3. International students often have difficulty understanding the connotations of English words. Why?
4. This reading focuses on miscommunication in speech. Do similar miscommunications occur in reading and writing? If so, do they stem from the same causes?
5. Do you think more or fewer misunderstandings occur in reading and writing than in speaking? Justify your answer.
6. Are there other causes of miscommunication not discussed in the reading? If so, what are they?

LEARNING/STUDY STRATEGY

Summarize the most important information in this reading.

Multimedia Activities

1. **Commonly Misused Words**

    http://www.cmu.edu/styleguide/trickywords.html#misused

    Be on the lookout for the easy-to-confuse words listed here by Carnegie Mellon University. Which words would you add to this list? Which words surprised you? Write a paragraph on the importance of proper usage. Why does it matter if people know what you mean?

2. **A Word A Day**

    http://www.wordsmith.org/awad/index.html

    Sign up to receive a word a day in your e-mail or read a newsletter about words at this interesting site for language lovers. Use the new words in your writing and speech.

Take a Road Trip to the
Library of Congress!

If your instructor has asked you to use the Reading Road Trip CD-ROM or Website, be sure to visit the Vocabulary Development module for multimedia tutorials, exercises, and tests.

CHAPTER 4

EVALUATING THE AUTHOR'S MESSAGE

LEARNING OBJECTIVES

✦ To make inferences and understand implied meanings
✦ To assess the author's credentials
✦ To distinguish between fact and opinion
✦ To identify the author's purpose
✦ To evaluate the data and evidence
✦ To analyze the author's tone
✦ To annotate as you read
✦ To synthesize your ideas

In college you will be reading many new kinds of material: research articles, essays, critiques, reports, and analyses. Your instructors expect you to be able to do much more than understand and remember the basic content. They often demand that you read critically—interpreting, evaluating, and reacting to assigned readings. To meet these expectations, you'll need to make solid inferences, recognize the author's tone, annotate as you read, and analyze and evaluate what you have read.

MAKE INFERENCES AS YOU READ

So far, we have been concerned primarily with the literal meanings of writing. You have been shown techniques to help you to understand what the author says and retain the literal, factual content. However, you often need to go beyond what authors *say* and to be concerned with what they *mean*. Look at the photograph shown in Figure 4–1 on page 84, which appeared in a psychology textbook. What do you think is happening here? Where is it happening? What are the feelings of the participants?

To answer these questions, you had to use any information you could get from the photo and make guesses based on it. The facial expressions, body

Figure 4–1

language, clothing, and other objects present in this photo implied or hinted at the emotions of those involved, the event that is occurring, and the locale of that event. This process of drawing conclusions, as you did, from these implied meanings is called "making an inference."

Inferences from the Given Facts

An inference is a reasoned guess about what you don't know made on the basis of what you do know. Inferences are common in our everyday lives. When you enter an expressway and see a long, slow-moving line of traffic, you might predict that there is an accident or roadwork ahead. When you see a puddle of water under the kitchen sink, you can infer that you have a plumbing problem. The inferences you make may not always be correct, even though you base them on the available information. The water under the sink might have been the result of a spill. The traffic you encountered on the expressway might be normal for that time of day, but you didn't know it because you aren't normally on the road then. An inference is only the best guess you can make in a situation, given the information you have.

EXERCISE 4-1

Study the photograph shown in Figure 4–1, and make inferences to answer the following questions.

1. What is happening in the photograph? _____

_____

_____

2. List the evidence shown in the photograph that supports your answer to Question 1. _____

_____

_____

3. This photograph was included in a sociology textbook chapter that discusses economic stratification (levels) in the United States. What does this photograph contribute to chapter content? _____

_____

_____

Inferences from Written Material

When you read the material associated with your college courses, you frequently need to make inferences. Writers do not always present their ideas directly. Instead, they often leave it to you to add up and think beyond the facts they present. You are expected to reason out, or infer, the meaning an author intended (but did not say) on the basis of what he or she did say. In a sense, the inferences you make act as bridges between what is said and what is not said but is meant.

There are several reasons why textbook authors and other writers require you to make inferences. Often, information is left out because it would make the message too long or would divert you from the central point. Sometimes an author assumes the readers know enough to fill in the omitted ideas. Other times, the writer believes that you will get more meaning or enjoyment from engaging in the thought process required to make an inference. Finally, some writers leave out pertinent information in order to make it easier to influence you to draw a desired conclusion, especially if you might have challenged the details had they been included. You can see, then, that making solid inferences is an important first step toward reading critically.

How to Make Inferences

Each inference you make depends on the situation, the facts provided, and your own knowledge and experience. Here are a few guidelines to help you see beyond the factual level and make solid inferences.

Know the Literal Meaning   Be sure you have a firm grasp of the literal meaning. You must understand the stated ideas and facts before you can move to higher levels of thinking, which include inference making. You should recognize the topic, main idea, key details, and organizational pattern of each paragraph you have read.

Notice Details   As you are reading, pay particular attention to details that are unusual or stand out. Often, such details will offer you clues to help you make inferences. Ask yourself

- What is unusual or striking about this piece of information?
- Why is it included here?

Read the following excerpt, which is taken from a business marketing textbook, and mark details that are unusual or striking.

MARKETING IN ACTION

Dressing Up the Basics in Idaho

In almost any grocery store across the United States, consumers can purchase ten pounds of Idaho-grown potatoes for less than $5.00. Despite this fact, Rolland Jones Potatoes, Incorporated, has been extremely successful selling a "baker's dozen" of Idaho potatoes for $18.95. The potatoes are wrapped in a decorative box that uses Easter grass.

The Baker's Dozen of Idaho potatoes is only one example of a growing phenomenon. Laura Hobbs, marketing specialist for the Idaho Department of Agriculture, reports that more than 200 Idaho farms produce specialty or value-added products. These goods typically consist of basic farm commodities that have been "dressed-up" with packaging. Consumers can choose from these products: microwave popcorn that comes on the cob and pops right off the cob, a bag of complete chili ingredients that makers claim won't cause embarrassing side-effects, and chocolate-covered "Couch Potato Chips."

Idaho farmers are supported by two groups, the Idaho Specialty Foods Association and Buy Idaho, whose goals are to help producers market and promote unique items. With the help of the groups, Idaho farmers are getting quite savvy. The marketers have discovered, for example, that packaging certain items together can increase their attractiveness. Hagerman's Rose Creek Winery found that sales of its wines soared when they were packaged in gift baskets with jars of Sun Valley brand mustard.

According to Hobbs, consumers attracted to the unique packaging provide a market for an endless variety of products, all of which are standard commodities transformed into new products through packaging. The value added through the unique packaging also provides opportunities to charge prices in ranges far above the prices of standard products—like $18.95 for 12 potatoes!

—adapted from Kinnear et al., *Principles of Marketing,* p. 301

Did you mark details such as the price of $18.95 for potatoes, corn that pops right off the cob, and chocolate-covered potato chips?

Add Up the Facts   Consider all of the facts taken together. To help you do this, ask yourself such questions as the following:

- What is the writer trying to suggest with this set of facts?
- What do all these facts and ideas seem to point toward or add up to?
- Why did the author include these facts and details?

Making an inference is somewhat like assembling a complicated jigsaw puzzle, in which you try to make all the pieces fit together to form a recognizable picture. Answering these questions will require you to add together all the individual pieces of information, which will enable you to arrive at an inference.

When you add up the facts in the article "Dressing Up the Basics in Idaho," you realize that the writer is suggesting that people are willing to pay much more than a product is worth if it is specially packaged.

Be Alert to Clues   Writers often provide you with numerous hints that can point you toward accurate inferences. An awareness of word choices, details included (and omitted), ideas emphasized, and direct commentary can help you determine a textbook author's attitude toward the topic at hand. In the foregoing excerpt, the authors offer clues that reveal their attitude toward increased prices for special packaging. Terms such as *dressed-up* and the exclamation point at the end of the last sentence suggest that the authors realize that the products mentioned are not worth their price.

In addition to these clues, writers of fiction also provide hints in their descriptions of characters and actions and through the conversations of their characters.

Consider the Author's Purpose   Also study the author's purpose for writing. If an author's purpose is to convince you to purchase a particular product, as in an advertisement, as you begin reading you already have a clear idea of the types of inferences the writer hopes you will make. For instance, here is a magazine ad for a stereo system.

If you're in the market for true surround sound, a prematched system is a good way to get it. The components in our system are built for each other by our audio engineers. You can be assured of high performance and sound quality.

Verify Your Inference   Once you have made an inference, check that it is accurate. Look back at the stated facts to be sure that you have sufficient evidence to support the inference. Also, be certain that you have not overlooked other equally plausible or more plausible inferences that could be drawn from the same set of facts.

EXERCISE 4–2   *Read each of the following statements and the sentences that follow. Place a check-mark in front of each sentence that is a reasonable inference that can be made from the statement.*

1. Political candidates must now include the Internet in their campaign plans.

   _____ a. Political candidates may host online chats to assess voter opinion.

   _____ b. Informal debates between candidates may be conducted online.

   _____ c. Internet campaigning will drastically increase overall campaign expenditures.

   _____ d. Television campaigning is likely to remain the same.

2. Half of the public education classrooms in the United States are now hooked up to the Internet.

   _____ a. Children are more computer literate than their parents.

   _____ b. Many students now have access to current world news and happenings.

   _____ c. Books are no longer considered the sole source of information on a subject.

   _____ d. Teachers have become better teachers now that they have Internet access.

3. The Internet can make doctors more efficient through the use of new software and databases that make patient diagnosis more accurate.

   _____ a. The cost of in-person medical care is likely to decrease.

   _____ b. Doctors may be able to identify patients with serious illness sooner.

   _____ c. Doctors are likely to pay less attention to their patients' descriptions of symptoms.

   _____ d. Information on the symptoms and treatment of rare illnesses is more readily available.

EXERCISE 4–3   *Read the following paragraph. A number of statements follow it; each statement is an inference. Label each inference as either*

PA—Probably accurate—there is substantial evidence in the paragraph to support the statement.

IE—Insufficient evidence—there is little or no evidence in the paragraph to support the statement.

While working for a wholesale firm, traveling to country stores by horse and buggy, Aaron Montgomery Ward conceived the idea of selling directly to country people by mail. He opened his business in 1872 with a one-page list of items that cost one dollar each. People could later order goods through a distributed catalog and the store would ship the merchandise cash on delivery (COD). The idea was slow to catch on because people were suspicious of a strange name. However, in 1875 Ward announced the startling policy of "satisfaction guaranteed or your money back." Contrasting with the former retailing principle of caveat emptor (Latin for "buyer beware"), this policy set off a boom in Ward's business.

—Frings, *Fashion: From Concepts to Consumer*, p. 11

_____ 1. Aaron Ward had experience in sales before he began his own business.

_____ 2. Country people were targeted because they do not have access to stores in cities.

_____ 3. Ward's mistake was to give every item on the list the same price.

_____ 4. Other stores in operation at the time did not offer money back guarantees.

_____ 5. Other mail order business quickly followed Ward's success.

EXERCISE 4–4   *Read the following passages, and then answer the questions. The answers are not directly stated in the passage; you will have to make inferences in order to answer them.*

Passage A "Is Laughter the Best Medicine?"

Lucy went to the hospital to visit Emma, a neighbor who had broken her hip. The first thing Lucy saw when the elevator door opened at the third floor was a clown, with an enormous orange nose, dancing down the hall, pushing a colorfully decorated cart. The clown stopped in front of Lucy, bowed, and then somersaulted to the nurses' station. A cluster of patients cheered. Most of them were in wheelchairs or on crutches. Upon asking for directions, Lucy learned that Emma was in the "humor room," where the film *Blazing Saddles* was about to start.

Since writer Norman Cousins's widely publicized recovery from a debilitating and usually incurable disease of the connective tissue, humor has gained new respectability in hospital wards around the country. Cousins, the long-time editor of the *Saturday Review,* with the cooperation of his physician, supplemented his regular medical therapy with a steady diet of Marx brothers movies and *Candid Camera* film clips. Although he never claimed that laughter alone effected his cure, Cousins is best remembered for his passionate support of the notion that, if negative emotions can cause distress, then humor and positive emotions can enhance the healing process (Cousins, 1979, 1989).

—Zimbardo and Gerrig, *Psychology and Life,* p. 501

1. What is the purpose of the story about Lucy and Emma?
2. What is a "humor room"?
3. What type of movie is *Blazing Saddles?*
4. Answer the question asked in the title.

Passage B "Oprah Winfrey—A Woman for All Seasons"

Oprah Winfrey—actress, talk-show host, and businesswoman—epitomizes the opportunities for America's women entrepreneurs. From welfare child to multimillionaire, Ms. Winfrey—resourceful, assertive, always self-assured, and yet unpretentious—has climbed the socioeconomic ladder by turning apparent failure into opportunities and then capitalizing on them.

With no playmates, Oprah entertained herself by "playacting" with objects such as corncob dolls, chickens, and cows. Her grandmother, a harsh disciplinarian, taught Oprah to read by age 2-½, and as a result of speaking at a rural church, her oratory talents began to emerge.

At age 6, Winfrey was sent to live with her mother and two half-brothers in a Milwaukee ghetto. While in Milwaukee, Winfrey, known as "the Little Speaker," was often invited to recite poetry at social gatherings, and her speaking skills continued to develop. At age 12, during a visit to her father in Nashville, she was paid $500 for a speech she gave to a church. It was then that she prophetically announced what she wanted to do for a living: "get paid to talk."

Her mother, working as a maid and drawing available welfare to make ends meet, left Oprah with little or no parental supervision and eventually sent her to live with her father in Nashville. There Oprah found the stability and discipline she so desperately needed. "My father saved my life," Winfrey reminisces. Her father—like her grandmother—a strict disciplinarian, obsessed with properly educating his daughter, forced her to memorize 20 new vocabulary words a week and turn in a weekly book report. His guidance and her hard work soon paid off, as she began to excel in school and other areas.

—Mosely et al., *Management: Leadership in Action*, p. 555

1. What is the author's attitude toward Winfrey?
2. What is the author's attitude toward strict discipline for children?
3. Is the author optimistic about business opportunities for women? How do you know?
4. What factors contributed to Winfrey's success?

ASSESS THE AUTHOR'S QUALIFICATIONS

Not everything that appears in print is accurate and competently reported. Also, there are varying levels of expertise within a field. Consequently, you must assess whether the material you are reading is written by an expert in the field who can knowledgeably and accurately discuss the topic. For example, a sociologist who has studied the criminal justice system is not necessarily an expert on problems of immigrant populations. A scientist who specializes in genetics cannot write authoritatively about the greenhouse effect. In some materials, the author's credentials are footnoted or summarized at the end of the work. In journal articles, the author's college or university affiliation is often included. Authors also may establish their expertise or experience in the field within the material itself.

EXERCISE 4–5

Read each statement and place a checkmark next to the individual who would seem to be the best authority on the subject.

1. One simple way to improve your diet is to put away the salt shaker.

    _____ a. Paula Weigel, registered dietician and nutritionist

    _____ b. John Mishler, life-long dieter

    _____ c. Maria Sanchez, columnist for *Food and Wine* magazine

2. The Dalai Lama is one of the great spiritual leaders of our time.

    _____ a. Richard Gere, film actor and follower of Buddhism

    _____ b. Alice Kohler, college student majoring in religion

    _____ c. Joseph Campbell, author and scholar of religion and mythology

3. Genetic engineering has enhanced both the quality and quantity of many crops, including soybeans, rice, and corn.

    _____ a. Craig Stinson, stockbroker

    _____ b. Andrew Burnette, television news reporter in the Midwest

    _____ c. Charlotte Corbeille, professor of agriculture at Iowa State University

EXERCISE 4–6

Working together with a classmate, discuss and identify who (title or job description) would be considered a qualified expert on each of the following topics.

1. the side effects of a prescription drug
2. building code laws for an apartment building
3. controlling test anxiety
4. immigration laws
5. influence of television violence on children

DISTINGUISH BETWEEN FACT AND OPINION

Facts are statements that can be tested as true or false—they are verifiable pieces of information. *Opinions* are statements that express feelings, attitudes, or beliefs that are neither true nor false. Here are a few examples of each.

Facts

Birth rates declined from 1960 to 1979.

The proportion of married women in the work force has steadily increased in the past 40 years.

Opinions

A drastic change is soon to occur in family structure.

Parenthood is the most rewarding human experience.

There is also what is known as expert opinion or testimony—the opinion of an authority. Ralph Nader represents expert opinion on consumer rights, for example. Here are a few examples of expert opinions.

Bill Gates, Chairman and Chief Software Architect Microsoft Corporation	"Right now, we're only scratching the surface of what computing technology can do."
David Satcher, former U.S. Surgeon General	"The prevalence of overweight and obesity has nearly doubled among children and adolescents since 1980. It is also increasing in both genders and among all population groups of adults."
Sir Edmund Hillary, one of the first two men to climb Mt. Everest	"Other mountains have more technically difficult routes than Everest, but none have that last 800 feet of extreme height."

Textbook authors, too, offer expert opinions, especially when they interpret events, summarize research, or evaluate trends. In the following paragraph, the author of a sociology textbook on marriage and the family interprets recent studies on sexuality.

> Recent studies of the history of sexuality in Western society have revealed that dramatic changes have taken place in beliefs and behavior. Among the most striking contrasts with our own times are the acceptance of bisexuality among men in ancient times and the disapproval of sexual pleasure in marriage for many centuries of the Christian era. The new studies also reveal that the sexual culture of any particular place and time is a complex mixture of expressive and repressive codes.
>
> —Skolnick, *The Intimate Environment,* p. 224

Some authors are careful to signal the reader when they are presenting an opinion. Watch for words and phrases such as:

apparently	this suggests	in my view	one explanation is
presumably	possibly	it is likely that	according to
in my opinion	it is believed	seemingly	

Here is an example:

> Among the many moons of Saturn is Titan, Saturn's only large moon and the second-largest in the solar system. Titan's hazy and cloudy atmosphere hides its surface, so we do not know whether Titan is geologically active. However, given

its relatively large size and icy composition, <u>it seems likely that</u> Titan has a rich geological history. Our understanding of Titan should improve dramatically when
NASA's *Cassini* spacecraft reaches Saturn in 2004.

—Bennett et al., *The Cosmic Perspective,* pp. 311–12

As you read a work, it is essential to distinguish between fact and opinion.
Factual statements from reliable sources can be accepted and used in drawing
conclusions, building arguments, and supporting ideas. Opinions, however, are
one person's point of view that you are free to accept or reject.

EXERCISE 4–7

*Read each of the following statements and identify whether it sounds like fact (F),
opinion (O), or expert opinion (EO).*

_____ 1. Most Americans feel strongly about the gun control issue.

_____ 2. Mosquitoes can transmit a disease known as encephalitis.

_____ 3. By 2005, more than 500 million people will use the Internet.

_____ 4. Marine biologists use the Internet in researching and identifying
plant and animal species.

_____ 5. Computer users often feel guilty and blame themselves when
their computer fails or performs an illegal operation.

_____ 6. Borders is the biggest music retailer on the Internet.

_____ 7. James Gleick, a well-known author who writes about technology,
notes that networked digital devices set the pace of change in
the computer field.

_____ 8. An increasing number of private citizens have their own
Web sites.

_____ 9. Personal Web sites give people a sense of power and importance.

_____ 10. Capron, an author of a textbook on computers, says Internet
traffic jams can be expected, creating slow response times in
sending and receiving messages.

EXERCISE 4–8

*Read each of the following statements. In each, underline the word or phrase that sug-
gests that the author is offering an informed opinion.*

1. According to recent studies, infants who use pacifiers may experience
delays in their speech development.

2. The candidate lost the election apparently because voters disapproved of
her negative campaigning tactics.

3. In my opinion, the Tour de France is the most demanding athletic event
in the world.

4. One explanation for the elementary school's declining enrollment is an aging population in the area.

5. It is likely that the drought will continue through the summer.

Each of the following paragraphs contains both fact and opinion. Read each paragraph and label each sentence as fact or opinion.

Paragraph 1

(1) Harriet Tubman was born a slave in Maryland in 1820 and escaped to Philadelphia in 1849. 2 Her own escape presumably required tremendous courage, but that was just the beginning. 3 Through her work on the Underground Railroad, Harriet Tubman led more than 300 slaves to freedom. 4 During the Civil War, Tubman continued her efforts toward the abolition of slavery by working as a nurse and a spy for the Union forces. 5 Today, Americans of all races consider Harriet Tubman one of the most heroic figures in our country's history.

Sentences: 1. _____ 2. _____ 3. _____ 4. _____ 5. _____

Paragraph 2

(1) Smokeless tobacco is used by approximately 5 million U.S. adults, most of whom are young males. 2 One explanation for the popularity of smokeless tobacco among young men is that they are emulating professional athletes who chew tobacco or use snuff. 3 In any major league baseball game, more than a few players with chewing tobacco bulging in their cheeks apparently believe the myth that smokeless tobacco is less harmful than cigarettes. 4 In reality, smokeless tobacco contains 10 times the amount of cancer-producing substances found in cigarettes and 100 times more than the Food and Drug Administration allows in foods and other substances used by the public. 5 Smokeless tobacco has been banned from minor-league baseball, a move that should be extended to all professional sports to help discourage the use of smokeless tobacco products.

Sentences: 1. _____ 2. _____ 3. _____ 4. _____ 5. _____

Paragraph 3

(1) Managed care plans have agreements with certain physicians, hospitals, and health care providers to give a range of services to plan members at a reduced cost. 2 There are three basic types of managed care plans: health maintenance organizations (HMOs), point-of-service plans (POS), and preferred provider organizations (PPO). 3 The PPO, in my opinion, is the best type of managed care plan because it merges the best features of traditional health insurance and HMOs. 4 As in traditional plans, participants in a PPO pay premiums, deductibles, and co-payments, but the co-pay under a PPO is lower (10 percent or less compared to the 20 percent co-pay under a traditional plan). 5 The best part of a PPO, though, is its flexibility: participants may choose their physicians and services from a list of preferred providers, or they may go outside the plan for care if they wish.

Sentences: 1. _____ 2. _____ 3. _____ 4. _____ 5. _____

IDENTIFY THE AUTHOR'S PURPOSE

Writers have many different reasons or purposes for writing. Read the following statements and try to decide why each was written:

1. Acute coronary syndromes are caused by a decrease or interruption of blood flow to the muscular tissue of the heart.

2. The new *Slumber-Rest* adjustable bed features a patented coil system and a triple thick mattress for night after night of deep, refreshing sleep. And with any *Slumber-Rest* bed purchased before January 1, you'll receive two luxurious down pillows.

3. A bad workman quarrels with his tools.

4. If your car engine is overheating, turn on the heater immediately. Pull over to the side of the road and open the hood as soon as possible.

5. Never open an e-mail attachment from an address you do not recognize. It could contain a virus.

Statement 1 was written to give information, 2 to persuade you to buy a bed, 3 to stimulate thought, 4 to explain how to handle an overheated car engine, and 5 to give advice.

In each of the examples, the writer's purpose was fairly clear, as it will be in most textbooks (to present information), newspaper articles (to communicate daily events), and reference books (to compile facts). However, in many other types of writing, authors have varied, sometimes less obvious, purposes. In these cases, an author's purpose must be inferred.

Often a writer's purpose is to express an opinion indirectly. Or the writer may want to encourage the reader to think about a particular issue or problem. Writers achieve their purposes by manipulating and controlling what they say and how they say it. The author's style and intended audience often reveal his or her purpose.

Writers have unique characteristics that distinguish their writing from that of others. One author may use many examples; another may use few. One author may use relatively short sentences; another may use long, complicated ones. The characteristics that make a writer unique are known as **style.** By changing style, writers can create different effects.

Writers may vary their styles to suit their intended audiences. A writer may write for a general-interest audience (anyone who is interested in the subject but is not considered an expert). Most newspapers and periodicals, such as *U. S. News & World Report* and *Newsweek,* appeal to a general-interest audience. On the other hand, a writer may have a particular interest group in mind. A writer may write for attorneys in the *ABA Journal* or for golf enthusiasts in *Golf Digest* or for antique collectors in the *World of Antiques.* A writer may also target his or her writing for an audience with particular political, moral, or religious attitudes. Articles in the *New Republic* often appeal to a particular political viewpoint, whereas the *Catholic Digest* appeals to a specific religious group.

Depending on the group of people for whom the author is writing, he or she will change the level of language, choice of words, and method of presentation. One step toward identifying an author's purpose, then, is to ask yourself the question, "Who is the intended audience?" Also ask yourself, "Why did the author write this?" In academic reading, you will most often find that the author's purpose is either to inform (present information) or to persuade. For example, an essay on state aid to private colleges may present information on current levels of funding, it may argue for an increased or decreased level of funding, or it may address both topics. Knowing the author's primary purpose will alert you to the type of critical questions you should ask.

EXERCISE 4–10 | *Based on the title of each of the following essays, predict whether the author's purpose is to inform or persuade.*

1. Changing habits: How shopping online is different
2. I got straight A's, but I wasn't happy.
3. Animals can't speak: We must speak for them!
4. Guns don't kill people; people kill people.
5. What the Bible says about the end of the world

EXERCISE 4–11 | *Read each of the following statements and decide for whom each was written. Write a sentence that describes the intended audience.*

1. Autumn is the best time of year to plant most trees, shrubs, and perennials. The warm days and cool nights of fall are ideal for root systems to develop, resulting in healthy, hardy plants.

   _____

2. Learning to play a musical instrument can have many rewards for your children. They will develop confidence as a result of successful individual study, and if they choose to play in a band or orchestra, their interpersonal skills and social awareness will be enhanced through their participation in a group. Most important, they will develop a satisfying lifelong leisure activity.

   _____

3. In the second season of the Women's United Soccer Association, the Carolina Courage defeated Mia Hamm and the Washington Freedom for the WUSA championship. Hamm continues to reign as the leading international scorer in women's soccer history.

   _____

4. For a refreshingly healthy way to quench your thirst, try Pauley's Parrot Juice. Pauley has cleverly combined the juice of pears and carrots to create natural, nutritious, and uniquely delicious Parrot Juice. And while

you're quenching your thirst, remember that one-third of all proceeds from Pauley's Parrot Juice goes to conservation efforts in the Amazon Rainforest.

5. When you are choosing a dog, it is important to identify a breed that matches your lifestyle. An apartment with a balcony may lend itself well to smaller breeds that do not require a great deal of outdoor exercise, whereas a house on acreage will provide a more physically demanding dog with the space it needs.

EVALUATE THE DATA AND EVIDENCE

Many writers who express their opinions, state viewpoints, or make generalizations provide data or evidence to support their ideas. Your task as a critical reader is to weigh and evaluate the quality of this evidence. You must examine the evidence and assess its adequacy. You should be concerned with two factors: the type of evidence being presented and the relevance of that evidence. Various types of evidence include

- personal experience or observation
- statistical data
- examples, descriptions of particular events, or illustrative situations
- analogies (comparisons with similar situations)
- historical documentation
- experimental evidence

Each type of evidence must be weighed in relation to the statement it supports. Acceptable evidence should directly, clearly, and indisputably support the case or issue in question.

EXERCISE 4–12

Study the photograph shown on page 98. Place a checkmark in front of those statements that seem reasonable based on the evidence shown in the photograph.

_____ 1. The men in the photo are over 40 years old.

_____ 2. The men in the photo are good friends.

_____ 3. The men in the photo dress in a similar way.

_____ 4. The men in the photo are being arrested.

_____ 5. The photo was taken in a suburban area.

_____ 6. Some of the men are sports fans or gang members.

EXERCISE 4–13 *For each of the following statements, discuss the type or types of evidence that you would need in order to support and evaluate the statement.*

1. Individuals must accept primary responsibility for the health and safety of their babies.
2. Apologizing is often seen as a sign of weakness, especially among men.
3. There has been a steady increase in illegal immigration over the past 50 years.
4. More college women than college men agree that abortions should be legal.
5. Car advertisements sell fantasy experiences, not means of transportation.

ANALYZE THE WRITER'S TONE

Suppose you are a customer service manager and a customer has complained about the assembly instructions for a computer workstation your company sells. You need to write a letter responding to the customer's complaints. You also need to send an e-mail message to the customer support department describing the problem. Would the two messages sound the same? Probably not. The letter to the customer would be friendly, polite, and accommodating, attempting to build goodwill and restore confidence in the company. The message to the customer support would be straightforward, direct, and factual. It would describe the problem and emphasize its seriousness. Each message, then, would have a different tone.

Tone refers to how a writer sounds to readers and how the writer feels about his or her topic. Recognizing an author's tone will help you interpret and evaluate his or her message. Tone also helps to suggest the author's purpose. Tone is revealed primarily thorough word choice and stylistic features such as sentence patterns and length. Tone, then, can reveal feelings. A writer can communicate surprise, disapproval, hate, disgust, admiration, gratitude, or amusement, for example.

Read the following statement, paying attention to the author's tone.

> "Although hazing is considered a time-honored tradition at many fraternities, any activity centered around the senseless humiliation of individuals and the reckless consumption of alcohol has no place on a college campus."

Here the author's disapproval is apparent. Through choice of words such as *humiliation* and *reckless*, as well as choice of detail, she makes the tone obvious. Here are a few examples of different tones. How does each make you feel?

- *Instructive*—"Before you begin any knitting project, always check your gauge. Using the yarn and needles called for in the instructions, knit a two-inch swatch and then compare it with the scale given in the pattern. By making adjustments before beginning the project, you can avoid problems later on."

- *Sympathetic*—"After the whales had beached themselves for a third time, the exhausted volunteers abandoned their rescue efforts and looked on grimly while the dying whales were euthanized."

- *Persuasive*—"Many frequent flyer programs allow you to donate points to charity. Your frequent flyer points may be used to help people with life-threatening medical conditions travel by plane to obtain the treatment they need, or to transport emergency relief personnel to the site of natural disasters, or simply to enable seriously ill children and their families to enjoy a trip to Disney World."

- *Humorous*—"A boy can run like a deer, swim like a fish, climb like a squirrel, balk like a mule, bellow like a bull, eat like a pig, or act like a jackass, according to climate conditions. A boy is a piece of skin stretched over an appetite. However, he eats only when he is awake. Boys imitate their Dads in spite of all efforts to teach them good manners." (former President Herbert Hoover; source: www.hooverassoc.org)

- *Nostalgic*—"The handwritten letter is a vanishing art. Although the convenience of e-mail can't be beat, when someone sits down with pen and paper to write a good, old-fashioned letter, it reminds us of a simpler, more thoughtful time."

Tone can also be used to help establish a relationship between writer and reader. Through tone a writer can establish a sense of a shared communication with the reader, drawing them together. Or a writer may establish a distance from the reader, keeping them apart. In the excerpts that follow, notice how in the first passage a formality, or distance, is evident, and in the second, how a familiarity and friendliness are created.

Passage 1

Meditation, which focuses awareness on a single stimulus, generally brings a subjective sense of well-being and relaxation, along with such physiological changes as decreased heart and respiratory rates and shifting EEG patterns of brain activity. There are three main types of meditation: concentrative, in which the meditator focuses on one chosen image or word; opening-up, in which the mediator's surroundings become part of the meditation; and mindfulness, in which the meditator focuses on whatever is most prominent at the moment.

—Kosslyn and Rosenberg, *Psychology: The Brain, the Person, the World,* p. 162

Passage 2

To begin evaluating a poem, first try to understand your own subjective response—don't pretend it doesn't exist. Admit, at least to yourself, whether the poem delights, moves, bores, or annoys you. Then try to determine what the poem seems designed to make you think and feel. Does it belong to some identifiable form or genre? (Is it, for instance, a love sonnet, narrative ballad, satire, or elegy?) How does its performance stack up against the expectations it creates? Considering those questions will give you some larger sense of perspective from which to evaluate the poem.

—Kennedy and Gioia, *Literature,* 2d edition, p. 789

To identify a writer's tone, pay particular attention to the words he or she uses, particularly their connotative meanings. Ask yourself: "How does the author feel about his or her subject and how is it revealed?" It is sometimes difficult to find the right word to describe a writer's tone. Table 4–1 list words that are often used to describe the tone of a piece of writing.

TABLE 4–1	WORDS FREQUENTLY USED TO DESCRIBE TONE			
abstract	condemning	formal	joyful	reverent
absurd	condescending	frustrated	loving	righteous
amused	cynical	gentle	malicious	sarcastic
angry	depressing	grim	melancholic	satiric
apathetic	detached	hateful	mocking	sensational
arrogant	disapproving	humorous	nostalgic	serious
assertive	distressed	impassioned	objective	solemn
awestruck	docile	incredulous	obsequious	sympathetic
bitter	earnest	indignant	optimistic	tragic
caustic	excited	indirect	outraged	uncomfortable
celebratory	fanciful	informative	pathetic	vindictive
cheerful	farcical	intimate	persuasive	worried
comic	flippant	ironic	pessimistic	
compassionate	forgiving	irreverent	playful	

EXERCISE 4–14

Read each of the following statements, paying particular attention to the tone. Then write a sentence that describes the tone. Prove your point by listing some of the words that reveal the author's feelings.

1. I could not believe my ears when the boy who bagged my groceries demanded a tip!
2. The spectacular house known as "Falling Waters" illustrates Frank Lloyd Wright's unparalleled genius as an architect.
3. It rained steadily all day, ruining our plans to go out on the boat.
4. The penalty for creating and launching a computer virus should include a personal apology to every single person whose computer was affected by the virus, and each apology should be typed—without errors!—on a manual typewriter.
5. When you are backpacking, you can reduce the risk of back injury by adjusting your pack so that most of its weight is on your hip belt rather than your shoulder straps.

EXERCISE 4–15

The following brief excerpt is taken from an article titled "Trash Troubles" that appeared in the periodical The World and I, *in November 1998. Using the guidelines you have learned in this chapter for evaluating the writer's message, answer the questions that follow.*

TRASH TROUBLES

Our accumulating piles of solid waste threaten to ruin our environment, pointing to the urgent need for not only better disposal methods but also strategies to lower the rate of waste generation.

As our ship surges forward, we notice a mound jutting up ahead, directly in our path. Like an iceberg, a much larger mass is hidden beneath the surface. If we keep running the vessel at current speed, we may have a major problem on our hands.

No, this not the Titanic. The ship we're on is our consumer-goods-dependent lifestyle that creates as much as a ton of solid waste per person each year. And the peak ahead is but the tip of a massive "wasteberg" that is 95 percent hidden from view: For every ton of trash we generate, there is an underlying loss of another 19 tons of industrial, agricultural, mining, and transportation wastes, building up into a mound that threatens to shatter our future.

The wasteberg entails a formidable economic and environmental challenge. For most local governments, solid waste management ranks behind only schools and highways as the major budget item. Improperly managed solid waste eats up dollars while polluting water supplies, threatening neighborhoods, and squandering natural resources.

So how is this odyssey progressing? Are we about to capsize on the wasteberg and drown, or can we successfully circumnavigate the threat? Better yet, can we shrink the wasteberg?

Circumnavigating the Wasteberg

The simplest way to steer around the wasteberg is to try to isolate wastes from their surrounding environment. This has been the major approach worldwide—solid waste management has usually meant solid waste disposal. Around the world, many nations have chosen incineration as the preferred way to dispose of solid waste. This is particularly the case where landfill sites are scarce. Japan, for example, has around 2,800 municipal incinerators that reduce solid wastes to ashes. In the United States, though, incineration has fallen strongly out of favor. Despite significant improvements in the technology, concerns that the incineration process may release toxic pollutants such as dioxins have brought this once-popular technology to near-obsolescence.

Shrinking the Wasteberg

For every pound of trash that goes into the waste basket, another 19 are released elsewhere in the environment—in forms ranging from industrial byproducts to fertilizer runoff to wasted energy. Thus if we reduce our generation of solid waste, the "leverage effect" is enormous: Each ton of trash kept out of the dump means that 19 tons of waste, along with related environmental impacts and the dollar cost of producing it, are avoided.

There are three major approaches to narrowing the waste stream: reducing, redesigning, and recycling. All require vigorous participation by both producers and consumers.

Reducing. Producers reduce waste through offering products that are less wasteful. Consumers reduce waste by using less of the product and using materials longer.

Redesigning. Producers offer alternative products that have a lower environmental impact than traditional ones, while continuing to meet given needs.

Recycling. Producers make reusable products, utilizing waste materials in manufacturing these goods. Consumers reuse the products and collect the materials to recycle out of the waste stream and back to the producers.

—Purcell, "Trash Troubles" in *The World and I*, p. 190

1. The author, Arthur H. Purcell, is the founder and director of the Resource Policy Institute, the author of *The Waste Watchers*, and a commentator for National Public Radio's "Marketplace." Evaluate his authority to discuss this topic.
2. Is the article primarily fact, opinion, or expert opinion? Support your answer with examples.
3. What is the author's purpose?
4. Evaluate the types and adequacy of the evidence the author provides.
5. Describe the author's tone.

EXERCISE 4–16 | *Working with another classmate, review the reading "Factors Affecting Interpersonal Attraction," which appears on page 28 in Chapter 1, and answer questions 2 through 5 from Exercise 4–15.*

ANNOTATE AS YOU READ

An important part of reading critically is to react to the author's ideas. You may agree, disagree, question, challenge, or seek further information, for example. To do so, begin by writing down your reactions while and after you read. Then, once you have finished, review your notes and evaluate the writer's ideas.

If you were reading the classified ads in a newspaper in search of an apartment to rent, you probably would mark certain ads. Then, when you phoned for more information, you might make notes about each apartment. These notes would be useful in deciding which apartments were worth visiting.

Similarly, in other types of reading, making notes—*annotating*—is a useful strategy. Annotating is a means of keeping track of your impressions, ideas, reactions, and questions as you read. Reviewing your annotations will help you form a final impression of the work. If a writing assignment accompanies the reading, your annotations will serve as an excellent source of ideas for a paper. This reading strategy is discussed in more detail in Chapter 11.

There are no fixed rules about how or what to annotate. In general, try to mark or note any ideas about the work that come to mind as you read or reread. Underline or highlight within the work and use the margins to write your notes. Your annotations might include

- questions
- opinions
- strong pieces of evidence
- key points
- ideas with which you disagree
- good or poor supporting data or examples
- inconsistencies
- key terms or definitions
- contrasting points of view
- key arguments
- words with strong connotations
- figures of speech (images that reveal the writer's feelings)

A sample annotation is shown in the following passage on the meaning of color. Read it carefully, noticing the types of markings and annotations that were made.

COLOR AND EMOTIONS

the issue or question

would like reference to these studies

The research in color preference led to a spin-off area of research, that of color and emotional response or moods. Researchers asked whether a reliable mood-color association exists and whether <u>color could influence one's emotional state</u>. Well-controlled research studies have shown that a definite color-mood tone association exists, although the color-mood association differed widely among people participating in the study. In fact, the studies showed all colors to be associated

*does not state
nature and
strength of
evidence*

with all moods in varying degrees of strength. Although certain colors are more strongly associated with a given mood or emotion, there was evidence to suggest a one-to-one relationship between a given color and a given emotion. What seemed to make the difference was how strongly a person associated a particular color with a particular mood or emotion.

*What evidence?
describe?*

Colors have been stereotyped by the public when it comes to emotions. In spite of physical evidence to the contrary, most people continue to equate red tones with excitement and activity and blue tones with passivity and tranquillity in color-mood association research. This is a learned behavior. From the time we are very young we learn to associate red with fire engines, stop lights, and danger signals that cause us to form an alert or danger association with red. Further, the red, orange, and yellow tones in fire further cause association between those colors and heat and kinetic energy. We have seen how cultural biases that are a part of our language further support the red equals excitement myth. These subconscious messages clearly affect the response to red. Blue tones, being associated with cool streams, the sky, and the ocean, continue to be equated with calm and tranquillity. This, too, is a learned response with which we are subtly surrounded from early childhood. In understanding color, it is important to differentiate between these culturally learned color associations and true biological responses.

*What are the
biological ones?*

How?

*Clothing design?
interior design?
building design?
—which one?*

*Could be expert
opinion, depending
on qualifications
of author*

Research on the emotional aspects of color has for the most part resulted in a gross oversimplification of a very involved process. Unfortunately, this oversimplification has been promoted heavily in the popular press. The design community too has jumped on the bandwagon, often making sweeping statements about color that are totally unsupported by anything but myth or personal belief. For example, one book refers to blue as "communicating cool, comfort, protective, calming, although may be slightly depressing if other colors are dark; associated with bad taste." There is of course no basis for these statements except as the personal opinion of the author, but too often these personal opinions become accepted as fact.

Summary

Colors do not contain any inherent emotional triggers. Rather, it is more likely that our changing moods and emotions caused by our own physiological and psychological makeup at the moment interact with color to create preferences and associations that we then link to the color-emotion response itself.

—Fehrman and Fehrman, *Color: The Secret Influence,* pp. 83–84

EXERCISE 4–17 | *Review and write annotations for "Trash Troubles," which appears on page 101.*

SYNTHESIZE YOUR IDEAS

After you have read (and perhaps reread) a piece of writing and made annotations, the final steps are to review your annotations and arrive at some conclusions and final impressions of the work. This is a creative as well as a logical process that involves looking for patterns and trends, noticing contrasts, thinking about the author's intentions, analyzing the effects of stylistic features, and determining the significance of the work. You might think of it as a process similar to evaluating a film after you have seen it or discussing a controversial television documentary. Your overall purpose is analysis: to arrive at an overall interpretation and evaluation of the work.

When analyzing a work, it may be helpful to write lists of words, issues, problems, and questions to discover patterns and evaluate the author's bias. Use the following questions to guide your analysis.

- What did the author intend to accomplish?
- How effectively did he or she accomplish this?
- What questions does the work raise and answer?
- What questions are ignored or left unanswered?
- What contributions to your course content and objectives does this work make?
- How does this work fit with your course textbook?
- How worthwhile is the material? What are its strengths and weaknesses?

EXERCISE 4–18   *Preview, read, and annotate the following essay titled "The Barbarity of Meat." Assume it is one of several articles your health and nutrition instructor assigned for a class discussion on vegetarianism. Pose several guide questions to focus your reading. Annotate as you read. Then analyze and evaluate the reading using the questions listed on p. 106.*

THE BARBARITY OF MEAT

The food industry downplays the connection between steak and cows

If, as some authors suggest, eating meat is indeed an important statement of human power, it might seem strange that we are apparently becoming progressively more uncomfortable with reminders of its animal origins. Consumer attitudes today are in a state of flux, not least for this reason. Whereas once it was sufficient simply to display whole animals and pieces of meat, the packing of the product is now a more delicate task. Most of us prefer not to think too directly about where our meat has come from, and unwelcome reminders can be distinctly off-putting. As one consumer put it, "I don't like it when you see . . . veins and things coming out of the meat . . . because it always reminds me of my own insides in a funny sort of a way. I suppose it's the idea of, like, blood flowing [that] makes you realize that this slab of meat was once a bit of functioning body, a bit like your own."

Meat marketing has responded accordingly, to assuage customers' sensitivity to the nature of the product. Nowadays, the consumer need never encounter animal flesh in its vulgar, undressed state. Instead it will come cooked and reshaped, in a sesame bun or an exotically flavored sauce, as a turkey roll or as chicken nuggets, in a crumb coating or a vacuum package, with not a hint of blood in sight. More and more butchers' windows sport fresh green vegetables, fragrant herbs, and perhaps a stir-fry mixture. A deliberate process of disguising the source of animal foods has gained momentum in the 20th century, reacting to our evident unease with the idea of eating dead animals: Said one butcher, "I deplore deliveries being carried into the front of my shop on the neck of a van driver—especially if they are not wrapped. . . . I can think of little more guaranteed to turn pedestrians off buying meat than the sight of pigs' heads flopping about as he struggles past them with the carcass."

The number of independent butchers' shops has declined considerably in recent years. Supermarkets have clearly derived particular competitive advantage from presenting meat in conspicuously hygienic conditions with all preparation completed out of sight. Often only the best cuts are displayed; bones, guts, and skin are nowhere to be seen. The hermetically sealed package is effectively dissociated from the animal to which its contents once belonged, a service that is clearly winning customers.

The names we give to the flesh of the main meat animals are another device whereby we reduce the unpleasant impact of having to acknowledge their identity. We do not eat cow, we eat beef; we do not eat pig, we eat pork; we do not eat deer, we eat venison. It is as if we cannot bear to utter the name of the beast whose death we have ordained.

To some, our willingness to consume meat as well as the many other assorted products of the animal industry, but apparent unwillingness to slaughter the beasts for ourselves or even to acknowledge our complicity in that process, is a matter for moral reproof. Said one critic, "I think the meat industry is very dishonest. The people are not allowed to be aware of what's going on. To them meat is wrapped up in cellophane in supermarkets; it's very divorced from the animal that it's coming from. . . . People don't go down on the factory farm to see what's really going on down there. I think if a lot of people did do that or [went] to the slaughterhouse to see how the meat is produced, then a lot of them would become vegetarians."

There is some evidence to support this belief. Many first-generation vegetarians and semivegetarians directly trace their abstinence to occasions when, for one reason or another, they were brought face to face with the connection between the meat on their plate and once-living animals. The particular incident related by any individual—be it the sight of carcasses being carried into a butcher's shop, or an encounter with vegetarian polemicism, or a visit to a slaughterhouse on daily business, or merely an unusually vivid flight of imagination—is of minor importance. What matters is that many people, when confronted with this ethical perplexity, seemingly prefer to forgo meat altogether rather than to condone the treatment of animals on their path from birth to plate. And equally important, perhaps, is how new this rebellion is, or rather how rapid its development has been in recent history.

—Fiddes, *Meat: A Natural Symbol,* pp. 100–01

1. Does the author establish his authority on the subject of vegetarianism?
2. Is the article primarily fact or opinion? Justify your answer.
3. What is the author's purpose? How effectively does he accomplish it?
4. Summarize the evidence the author offers in support of his main points.
5. Does the author anticipate and address objections to his argument? If so, what are the objections and how does he refute them?
6. What questions might be raised during a class discussion of this essay?

SUMMARY

Critical reading involves interpreting, evaluating, and reacting to ideas.

An inference is a reasoned guess about what you do not know on the basis of what you do know. To make inferences as you read,

- know the literal meaning
- notice details
- add up the facts
- be alert for clues
- verify your inference

To assess an author's ideas, ask the following questions.

- Is the author a qualified expert?
- What are the facts and what are the opinions?
- What is the author's purpose?
- Is the author biased?
- How strong are the data and evidence?

Tone refers to how a writer sounds to his or her readers and how the writer feels about his or her topic. To recognize an author's tone, pay particular attention to the author's word choice and stylistic features.

To react to an author's ideas, annotate during and after reading, and synthesize your ideas using the following questions.

- What did the author intend to accomplish?
- How effectively did he or she accomplish this?
- What questions does the work raise and answer?
- What questions are ignored or left unanswered?
- What contributions to your course content and objectives does this work make?
- How does this work fit with your course textbook?
- How worthwhile is the material? What are its strengths and weaknesses?

Sociology/Contemporary Issues

PREREADING QUESTIONS

1. Can you predict two arguments the author might use to support his view that drugs should not be legalized?
2. What kinds of questions might the author reasonably pose regarding drug legalization?
3. Do you believe drugs should be legalized?

Why Drug Legalization Should Be Opposed

Representative Charles B. Rangel

Charles Rangel, a U.S. Congressman from the state of New York, has served 14 terms of office. Rangel, who holds a law degree, has worked to further affirmative action and to limit international drug trafficking.

1   In my view, the very idea of legalizing drugs in this country is counterproductive. Many well-meaning drug legalization advocates disagree with me, but their arguments are not convincing. The questions that I asked them twenty years ago remain unanswered. Would all drugs be legalized? If not, why? Would consumers be allowed to purchase an unlimited supply? Are we prepared to pay the medical costs for illnesses that are spawned by excessive drug use? Who would be allowed to sell drugs? Would an illegal market still exist? Would surgeons, bus drivers, teachers, military personnel, engineers, and airline pilots be allowed to use drugs?

2   Drug legalization threatens to undermine our society. The argument about the economic costs associated with the drug war is a selfish argument that coincides with the short-sighted planning that we have been using with other social policies. With any legalization of drugs, related problems would not go away; they would only intensify. If we legalize, we will be paying much more than the $30 billion per year we now spend on direct health care costs associated with illegal drug use.

3   Drug legalization is not as simple as opening a chain of friendly neighborhood "drug" stores. While I agree that some drugs might be beneficial for medicinal purposes, this value should not be exploited to suggest that drugs should be legalized. Great Britain's experience with prescription heroin should provide a warning. Until 1968, British doctors were freely allowed to prescribe drugs to addicts for medicinal purposes. Due to the lack of rigorous controls, some serious problems became associated with this policy. Doctors supplied drugs to non-addicts, and addicts supplied legally obtained drugs to the general population resulting in an increased rate of addiction. There is plenty of evidence to show that drug legalization has not worked in other countries that have tried it. The United States cannot afford such

experiments when the data shows that drug legalization policies are failing in other countries.

4   In minority communities, legalization of drugs would be a nightmare. It would be a clear signal that America has no interest in removing the root causes of drug abuse: a sense of hopelessness that stems from poverty, unemployment, inadequate training, and blight. Legalization of drugs would officially sanction the total annihilation of communities already at risk. Instead of advocating drug legalization, we should focus our efforts on rebuilding schools, strengthening our teachers, improving housing, and providing job skills to young people.

5   The issue should not be whether or not drugs should be legalized. Rather, we need to focus on changing the way the war on drugs is being fought. The real problems are our emphasis on incarceration, including mandatory minimum sentences, the unfair application of drug laws, the disparity in sentencing between crack cocaine and powder cocaine, and the failure to concentrate on the root causes of drug abuse. These shortcomings in our drug policy should not become a license for legalization. Many critics of the drug war have the knowledge and skills to improve our national drug control policy. Instead of supporting the Drug Czar, they use their resources to blast all efforts to eradicate drugs in this country. It is a shame that many educated and prominent people suggest that the only dangerous thing about drugs is that they are illegal.

6   If we are truly honest, we must confess that we have never fought the war on drugs as we have fought other adversaries. The promotion of drug legalization further complicates the issue. We must continue our efforts to stop the flow of illegal drugs into our country. Most importantly, we need to remove the root causes of drug abuse and increase our focus in the areas of prevention and treatment through education. Rather than holding up the white flag and allowing drugs to take over our country, we must continue to focus on drug demand as well as supply if we are to remain a free and productive society.

—Rangel, *Criminal Justice Ethics,* Vol. 17, No. 2 (Summer/Fall 1998), p. 2

VOCABULARY REVIEW

1. For each of the words listed below, use context; prefixes, roots, and suffixes; and/or a dictionary to write a brief definition or synonym of the word as it is used in the reading.

   a. advocates (para. 1) _____

   b. spawned (para. 1) _____

   c. undermine (para. 2) _____

   d. exploited (para. 3) _____

   e. blight (para. 4) _____

   f. sanction (para. 4) _____

   g. annihilation (para. 4) _____

h. incarceration (para. 5) _____

i. disparity (para. 5) _____

j. eradicate (para. 5) _____

2. Underline new specialized terms introduced in the reading.

COMPREHENSION QUESTIONS

1. Identify three reasons why the author is opposed to legalizing drugs.
2. What effect does the author believe drug legalization would have?
3. What cue words in the first paragraph suggest the author may have a bias?
4. Does the author propose an alternative solution for the drug problem? If so, what is that solution?
5. What does the author imply when he states that "[d]rug legalization is not as simple as opening a chain of friendly neighborhood 'drug' stores"?
6. According to the author, why did legalizing heroin in Great Britain by making it a prescription drug fail?

THINKING CRITICALLY

1. What is the author's purpose in writing this essay?
2. What do you believe is the strongest argument the author uses to support his position? Why is this a strong argument?
3. The author states that there is "plenty of evidence to show that drug legalization has not worked in other countries. . . ." Other than with information about Great Britain, does the author support this statement? How does this weaken or strengthen the author's argument?
4. The author believes that we will be paying much more money in health care costs if we legalize drugs. Do you agree or disagree? Why?
5. The author states that legalizing drugs "will undermine our society." Does he support this with generalizations or specific facts? Explain.
6. In general, do you think the author is essentially biased or essentially objective in presenting his arguments? On what do you base your assessment?

LEARNING/STUDY STRATEGY

Annotate the reading by highlighting why the author is opposed to legalizing drugs. Then record your ideas and reactions to these arguments.

Sociology/Contemporary Issues

PREREADING QUESTIONS

1. Has the current drug policy failed? Why do you think so?
2. Can you speculate about why the author believes it has failed?
3. Can you predict what the author will suggest the Office of Drug Policy do instead?

Let's Retire the Drug War

Jacob G. Hornberger

Hornberger is founder and president of the Future of Freedom Foundation. He holds a law degree and worked as a trial attorney. He has published numerous articles, delivered speeches nationwide, and written seven books on issues related to libertarianism.

1   Of all the domestic wars that the U.S. government has waged in the last several decades, the war on drugs has got to be the most immoral and destructive of them all. The drug war has constituted a frontal attack on individual liberty. It has provided an excuse for government officials to trample the Constitution, especially the provisions of the Fourth Amendment. It has caused death and destruction of innocent people, not only here in America but overseas as well. It has provided a means by which racism has been able to raise its ugly face in an innocent guise. And by everyone's standards, the war on drugs has failed to accomplish it's own purported goals despite at least 30 years of warfare.

2   What does it mean to be free? At the very least, freedom entails the right of every adult to sit in the privacy of his own home and do whatever he wants, as long as his conduct is peaceful and nonabusive. Drink beer. Smoke cigarettes. Snort cocaine. Watch dirty movies. Listen to music with obscene and violent lyrics. Read smutty books. Have sex. Eat fatty foods. Cuss. Even criticize government officials.

3   If a grown-up is subject to being punished by the state for engaging in any of this conduct, then no one in society is free. And it doesn't matter whether you yourself never engage in any of it. If the state has the power to punish anyone for doing it, then that's a society in which tyranny is reigning for everyone.

4   The drug war enables and encourages the police to peer into your windows, examine your trash, monitor your bank accounts, turn your children into stool pigeons and haul you into court and send you to jail for engaging in what public officials consider to be personal, immoral conduct within the privacy of your very own home. Is this the kind of country you want for yourself and your family?

5   Look what they've done to our Constitution, which our ancestors intended to be an impenetrable barrier against unreasonable searches and seizures. Whether you're in your car, at the airport, walking down the street, or even in your own

home, you're subject to be accosted and searched by the drug police and their drug dogs, especially if your skin happens to be dark.

6   What better way to wage bigoted wars against racial minorities than the drug war? Does anyone really believe that it's only a coincidence that federal and state penitentiaries are filled with blacks and Hispanics who have violated drug laws? That racial profiling takes place because cops have a good-hearted concern that Blacks and Hispanics are ingesting harmful substances?

7   "Ever since President Nixon declared war on drugs (and antiwar protesters), U.S. officials have invaded foreign countries; had drug-lords extradited to the United States; killed innocent people in drug raids; barged through doors all across America; executed countless search warrants, many of them based on perjured testimony; arrested, indicted, and incarcerated tens of thousands of nonviolent people; confiscated millions of dollars in private assets, much of it from innocent people; invaded the privacy of thousands of financial institutions; expanded the ranks of law-enforcement; and spent hundreds of millions of dollars.

8   What do they have to show for it after 30 years of warfare? Good intentions? Through it all, they've never answered two fundamentally important questions with respect to the issue of individual liberty. Why should the state have the power to punish adults for ingesting harmful substances? Doesn't the very essence of human liberty entail the unfettered right to engage in self-destructive behavior?

9   For more than three decades, the drug war has assaulted our liberty, invaded our privacy, trashed our Constitution, increased our taxes, and provided an innocent cover for government bigotry. It's time to put the war on drugs out to pasture.

—Hornberger, "Let's Retire the Drug War," *New York Beacon*
(December 27, 2000), p. 3

VOCABULARY REVIEW

1. For each of the words listed below, use context; prefixes, roots, and suffixes; and/or a dictionary to write a brief definition or synonym of the word as it is used in the reading.

   a. domestic (para. 1) _____

   b immoral (para. 1) _____

   c. frontal (para. 1) _____

   d. guise (para. 1) _____

   e. entails (para. 2) _____

   f. tyranny (para. 3) _____

   g. stool pigeons (para. 4) _____

   h. impenetrable (para. 5) _____

   i. ingesting (para. 8) _____

2. Underline new specialized terms introduced in the reading.

COMPREHENSION QUESTIONS

1. Identify three reasons why the author believes the war on drugs should end.
2. How does the author believe the war on drugs has violated the Constitution?
3. What tone does the author use in this selection?
4. What evidence does the author give to show that the war on drugs is racist?
5. What does the author imply when he says "What do they have to show for it after 30 years of warfare? Good intentions?"
6. How does the author justify the fact that he believes adults should be allowed to use drugs?

THINKING CRITICALLY

1. What is the author's purpose in writing this essay?
2. What do you believe is the strongest argument the author uses to support his position? Why?
3. What facts or statistics does the author offer to support his position? How does this affect his position?
4. Do you agree or disagree with the author's point of view with regard to drugs and privacy? Why?
5. What kinds of arguments might be offered in opposition to this author's point of view?
6. Do you feel that the author is convincing in this essay? Why or why not? If not, what kinds of things could the author add that would be convincing?

LEARNING/STUDY STRATEGY

Annotate the reading by listing the author's objections to the drug war. Then record your reactions to these ideas.

THINKING ABOUT THE PAIRED READINGS

INTEGRATING IDEAS

1. How do the authors' purposes differ in these two readings?
2. Compare the tone of the two readings.
3. Both authors express opinions. Which author better supports his opinions? Give an example of this.
4. What is a major difference in style between the two readings? How does the difference affect the reader in assessing which reading is more persuasive?

GENERATING NEW IDEAS

1. Using one quote from each source, write a one- to two-page paper stating whether you believe drugs should be legalized.
2. Make a list of the strengths and weaknesses of each selection.

Multimedia Activities

1. "Fact or Opinion" Quizzes

    http://cuip.uchicago.edu/www4teach/97/jlyman/default/quiz/factopquiz.html

    http://dhp.com/~laflemm/RfT/Tut2.htm

    Try these online quizzes. Pay attention to what you hear during the day and try to keep track of the facts and opinions. When do you hear more of one than the other?

2. **Differences Between Critical and Noncritical Thinking**

    http://library.usask.ca/ustudy/critical/critnoncrit.html

    Look over this helpful chart from the University of Saskatchewan Library and evaluate yourself. Compare the ways you behave while watching a movie, reading a textbook, viewing a Web site, and talking with friends.

Take a Road Trip to the
American Southwest!

If your instructor has asked you to use the Reading Road Trip CD-ROM or Website, be sure to visit the Critical Thinking module for multimedia tutorials, exercises, and tests.

CHAPTER 5

EVALUATING THE AUTHOR'S TECHNIQUES

LEARNING OBJECTIVES
+ To identify connotative language
+ To understand figurative language
+ To recognize bias
+ To discover missing information
+ To evaluate generalizations
+ To identify assumptions
+ To recognize manipulative language

Whether you are looking at famous paintings, watching an athlete breaking a world record, or tasting wonderful desserts, the same question comes to mind: How did they do it? You wonder *how* the artists accomplished such magnificent works, *how* the athlete trained, and *how* the desserts were made. You want to know what the artists, athlete, or chefs did to produce their end results. When reading an article or essay, you should ask a similar question: How did the writer achieve his or her results? In other words, ask what techniques (methods) the writer used to communicate the message. How did the writer make you feel sympathetic to her cause? How did the writer make you want to take a particular action? How did the writer change your opinion on an issue? Understanding a writer's techniques will help you think critically about the author's message and form reasonable judgments about the author and his or her message.

In this chapter we will examine the various techniques that writers use to express their ideas and manipulate their readers. We will study connotative and figurative language and examine how writers reveal bias, mislead through omission, and make generalizations and assumptions. We will also examine how writers use language to manipulate ideas using clichés, jargon, allusions, euphemisms, doublespeak, and hyperbole. Each topic will be addressed in the form of a question to guide your critical analysis.

DOES THE WRITER USE CONNOTATIVE LANGUAGE?

If you were wearing a jacket that looked like leather but was made out of man-made fibers, would you prefer it be called *fake* or *synthetic*? Would you rather be part of a *crowd* or *mob*? Would you rather be called *thin* or *skinny*?

Each of the above pairs of words has basically the same meaning. A *crowd* and a *mob* are both groups of people. Both *fake* and *synthetic* refer to something manmade. If the words have similar meanings, why did you choose *crowd* rather than *mob* and *synthetic* rather than *fake*? While the pairs of words have similar primary meanings, they carry different shades of meaning; each creates a different image or association in your mind. This section explores these shades of meaning, called connotative meanings.

All words have one or more standard meanings. These meanings are called **denotative meanings.** Think of them as those meanings listed in the dictionary. They tell us what the word names. Many words also have connotative meanings. **Connotative meanings** include the feelings and associations that may accompany a word. For example, the denotative meaning of *sister* is a female sibling. However, the word carries many connotations. For some, *sister* suggests a playmate with whom they shared their childhood. For others the term may suggest an older sibling who watched over them. Let us take another example, the word *dinner*. Its denotative meaning is "an evening meal," but its connotative meaning to many suggests a relaxed time to share food and conversation with family or friends.

Connotations can vary from individual to individual. The denotative meaning for the word *flag* is a piece of cloth used as a national emblem. To many, the American flag is a symbol of patriotism and love of one's country. To some people, though, it may mean an interesting decoration to place on their clothing. The word *dog* to dog lovers suggests a loyal and loving companion. To those who are allergic to dogs, however, the word *dog* connotes discomfort and avoidance—itchy eyes, a runny nose, and so forth.

Writers and speakers use connotative meanings to stir your emotions or to bring to mind positive or negative associations. Suppose a writer is describing how someone drinks. The writer could choose words such as *gulp, sip, slurp,* or *guzzle.* Each creates a different image of the person. Connotative meanings, then, are powerful tools of language. When you read, be alert for meanings suggested by the author's word choice. When writing or speaking, be sure to choose words with appropriate connotations.

EXERCISE 5–1	*For each of the following pairs of words, underline the word with the more positive connotation.*

1. dimple   dent

2. bold   sassy

3. cheap   frugal

4. displease   repel
5. tipsy   drunk
6. ache   agony
7. untidy   grubby
8. haughty   proud
9. deck hand   sailor
10. job   chore

EXERCISE 5–2

For each word listed, write a word that has a similar denotative meaning but a negative connotation. Then write a word that has a positive or neutral connotation.

WORD	NEGATIVE CONNOTATION	POSITIVE or NEUTRAL CONNOTATION
Example: costly	extravagant	expensive
1. leisurely	_____	_____
2. small	_____	_____
3. take	_____	_____
4. talk	_____	_____
5. satirize	_____	_____
6. farmer	_____	_____
7. choosy	_____	_____
8. delay	_____	_____
9. desire	_____	_____
10. famous	_____	_____

EXERCISE 5–3

Discuss the differences in connotative meaning of each of the following sets of words. Consult a dictionary, if necessary.

1. painful: hurtful—sore—excruciating
2. aware: familiar—alert—privy
3. room: chamber—study—cubicle
4. someone who travels: globe-trotter—tourist—pilgrim
5. understanding: mastery—insight—comprehension
6. harmony: agreement—conformity—order
7. education: literacy—schooling—breeding
8. proper: correct—appropriate—demure
9. seclusion: isolation—privacy—withdrawal
10. lovable: adorable—attractive—winning

DOES THE WRITER USE FIGURATIVE LANGUAGE?

Figurative language makes a comparison between two unlike things that share one common characteristic. If you say that your apartment looked as if it had been struck by a tornado, you are comparing two unlike things—your apartment and the effects of a tornado. Figurative language makes sense creatively or imaginatively, but not literally. You mean that the apartment is messy and disheveled. Figurative language is a powerful tool that allows writers to create images or paint pictures in the reader's mind. We all know the devastation caused by a tornado and have a visual picture of it. Figurative language also allows writers to suggest an idea without directly stating it. If you say the councilman bellowed like a bear, you are suggesting that the councilman was animal-like, loud, and forceful, but you have not said so directly. By planting the image of bear-like behavior, you have communicated your message to your reader.

There are three primary types of figurative language—similes, metaphors, and personification. A **simile** uses the words *like* or *as* to make the comparison:

> The computer hums like a beehive.

> After 5:00 P.M. our downtown is as quiet as a ghost town.

A **metaphor** states or implies the relationship between the two unlike items. Metaphors often use the word *is*.

> The computer lab is a beehive.

> After 5:00 P.M. our downtown is a ghost town.

Personification compares humans and nonhumans according to one characteristic, attributing human characteristics to ideas or objects. If you say "the wind screamed its angry message," you are giving the wind the humanlike characteristics of screaming, being angry, and communicating a message. Here are a couple more examples:

> The sun mocked us with its relentless stare.

> After two days of writer's block, her pen started dancing across the page.

Because figurative language is a powerful tool, be sure to analyze the author's motive for using it. Often, a writer uses figurative language as a way of describing rather than telling. A writer could say "The woman blushed" (telling) or "The woman's cheeks filled with the glow of a fire" (describing). Other times, however, figurative language is a means of suggesting ideas or creating impressions without directly stating them. When evaluating figurative language, ask the following questions:

- Why did the writer make the comparison?
- What is the basis of the comparison, that is, the shared characteristic?
- Is the comparison accurate?
- What images do you have in your mind? How do these images make you feel?

- Is the comparison positive or negative?
- Are several different interpretations possible?

EXERCISE 5–4 | *Explain the comparison in each of the following examples of figurative language.*

1. The view from the summit was like a painting.
2. Her memory was a blank tablet.
3. The library renovation project was an uncontrollable beast.
4. During the morning commute, the lanes of cars were snarled like a nest of snakes.
5. As the tide rolled in, the waves roared at her to escape quickly.

EXERCISE 5–5 | *Discuss how the writer of each of the following passages uses figurative language to create a specific impression.*

1.   As a vacation port of call, Southern California has got it all. It's like a giant geographic theme park. Want to lap up glistening waves and bury your feet in the sand? The beach beckons. How about thick forests with fir- and pine-covered mountains? The majestic Angeles National Forest is a quick drive from Los Angeles. I prefer to use Dante's "Inferno" as my Baedeker [a guidebook for travelers]. Every summer, whenever I get the itch for a little rest and relaxation, I venture deep into the inner circle of hell—otherwise known as Palm Springs.
    —Weingarten, "Palm Springs in August: The Ducks Use Sunblock,"
    New York Times (August 9, 2002)

2.   Thick as a truck at its base, the Brazil-nut tree rises 10 stories to an opulent crown, lord of the Amazon jungle. It takes the tree a century to grow to maturity; it takes a man with a chain saw an hour to cut it down. "It's a beautiful thing," nods Acelino Cardoso da Silva, a 57-year-old farmer. "But I have six hungry people at home. If the lumberman turns up, I'll sell."
    —Margolis, "A Plot of Their Own," *Newsweek* (January 21, 2002)

3.   If parenting is like an endurance race, senior year should be the section where parents triumphantly glide toward the finish line with a smiling graduate-to-be alongside. Instead, it's often more like heartbreak hill at the 20-mile mark of the Boston marathon, the bump that leaves parents exhausted and wondering what they were thinking 17 years ago.
    —Dunnewind, "Launching Kids to Independence," *Seattle Times* (August 17, 2002)

EXERCISE 5–6 | *Convert each of the following statements to an expression of figurative language.*

Example: I am nervous. I feel as if I have a thousand butterflies fluttering in my stomach.

1. He was hungry. _____

2. The clouds were beautiful. _____

3. Everyone argued. _____

4. The test was hard. _____

5. My friend laughed. _____

IS THE AUTHOR FAIR OR BIASED?

Think of a television commercial you have seen recently, perhaps for a particular model of car. The ad tells you the car's advantages—why you want to buy it—but does it tell you its disadvantages? Does it describe ways in which the model compares unfavorably with competitors? Certainly not. Do you feel the ad writer is being unfair? Now let us say you know nothing about e-book readers and want to learn about them. You find an article titled, "What you need to know about e-book readers." If the author of this article told you all the advantages of e-book readers, but none of its disadvantages, would you consider the article unfair? We expect advertisers to present a one-sided view of their products. We expect other forms of writing, however, to be honest and forthright. If a writer is explaining instant messaging, he or she should explain it fully, revealing both strengths and weaknesses. To do otherwise is to present a biased point of view. You can think of bias as a writer's prejudice. If an author is biased, then, he or she is partial to one point of view or one side of a controversial issue. The author's language and selection of facts provide clues about his or her bias.

In the following excerpt from a biology text, the author's choice of words (see underlining) and sarcastic comment in parentheses reveal his attitude toward seal hunters.

> Greenpeace is an organization dedicated to the preservation of the sea and its great mammals, notably whales, dolphins, and seals. Its ethic is <u>nonviolent</u> but its <u>aggressiveness</u> in protecting our oceans and the life in them is becoming legendary.
>
> Greenpeace volunteers routinely place their lives in <u>danger</u> in many ways, such as by riding along the backs of whales in inflatable zodiacs, keeping themselves between the animal and the harpoons of ships giving <u>chase</u>. They have pulled alongside Dutch ships to stop the <u>dumping</u> of <u>dangerous toxins</u> into the sea. They have placed their zodiacs directly in the paths of ships <u>disrupting delicate</u> breeding grounds of the sea with soundings and have forced some to turn away or even abandon their efforts. They have confronted hostile sealers on northern ice floes to try to stop them from <u>bludgeoning</u> the baby seals in the birthing grounds, skinning them on the spot, and leaving the mother sniffing at the <u>glistening red corpse</u> of her baby as its skin is <u>stacked</u> aboard the ship on the way to warm the <u>backs of very fashionable people</u> who gather where the bartender knows their favorite drink. (The mother seal would be <u>proud</u> to know that her dead baby had nearly

impressed some bartender.) They have petitioned the International Whaling Commission to establish rules and enact bans.

—Wallace, *Biology: The World of Life*, p. 754

To detect bias, ask the following questions:

- Is the author acting as a reporter—presenting facts—or as salesperson—providing only favorable information?
- Does the author feel strongly about or favor one side of the issue?
- Does the author use connotative or figurative language to create a positive or negative image?
- Does the author seem emotional about the issue?
- Are there other views toward the subject that the writer does not recognize or discuss?

EXERCISE 5–7

Read each of the following statements, and place a checkmark in front of each that reveals bias.

_____ 1. Cities should be designed for the pedestrian, not the automobile.

_____ 2. There are more channels than ever before on cable television.

_____ 3. The current system of voter registration is a sham.

_____ 4. Professional sports have become elitist.

_____ 5. Space exploration costs millions of dollars each year.

EXERCISE 5–8

Describe the author's bias in each of the following statements.

1. The greatest immediate danger to the future of our firearm rights is the media hype typified in a *Washington Times* headline, "Gun Control Drops Off the Screen." Don't for one second buy into it. The goal of the anti-gun-rights crowd this election year is power—total control of the national legislature, and they will try to get it by lulling gun owners into thinking the threat has passed. They want gun owners to stay home election day.

—LaPierre, "Standing Guard," *American Rifleman* (August 2002)

2. I have expressed in the past that police officers should refrain from enforcing immigration laws so that police departments can maintain good relations with Hispanics. If Latinos fear that police will report them or their family members to the immigration service, they might fear coming forward to help solve crimes.

—Salinas, "Will All Hispanic Men Be Suspect?"
Seattle Post-Intelligencer (July 30, 2002)

3. This should end the argument [against video violence], but, unfortunately, we in the video industry know it won't. Movements seeking to blame the media for society's problems are not just popular within religiously conservative groups, but are

also the unspoken fears of everyday parents whose worst nightmare is a Columbine-type massacre in their own backyards. Where children are concerned—especially one's own—reason and the First Amendment can quickly fly out the window.

—Villa, "Winning in the Courts but Losing in the Court of Public Opinion,"
Video Store (January 20–26, 2002)

4.   Those clamoring to shut down the farmers, however, should look hard at the prospect of a prairie full of subdivisions and suburban pollution: car exhaust, lawn and garden fertilizers, wood stoves, sewage. Certainly, the smoke from field burning is an annoyance, particularly to the hard-hit Sandpoint area, and to some it's a health hazard. But the benefits the sturdy farmers produce 50 weeks of the year shouldn't be dismissed casually.

—Oliveria, "Burning Will Go; That's Not All Good," *Spokesman Review* (July 24, 2002)

5.   Money doesn't grow on trees, but some trees might as well be pure gold. The world's voracious (and growing) appetite for wood, paper, and other forest products is driving a stampede to mow down forests. Much of this logging is illegal.

—Haugen, "Logging Illogic," *World Watch* (September/October 2002)

WHAT ISN'T THE AUTHOR TELLING ME?

Writers mislead by omission. Writers may omit essential details, ignore contradictory evidence, or selectively include only details that favor their position. They may also make incomplete comparisons, use the passive voice, or use unspecified nouns and pronouns.

Suppose, in describing home schooling, an author states "Many children find home schooling rewarding." But what is the author not telling us? If the author does not tell us that some children find home schooling lonely and feel isolated from their peers, the author is not presenting a fair description of home schooling. The writer has deliberately omitted essential details that a reader needs to understand home schooling.

Suppose the same writer describes a research study that concludes that home schooled children excel academically. The writer, to be fair, should also report that other studies have demonstrated that home schooled children do not differ in academic achievement from traditionally educated students. In this case the writer has ignored contradictory evidence, reporting only evidence that he or she wants the reader to know.

In describing a home school environment, suppose the writer reports that "the home environment is ideal" and goes on to describe features such as comfortable home surroundings, flexible scheduling, and supportive parental mentoring. To be fair, the writer should also point out what the home environment lacks. A home environment may lack a library of instructional software, collaborative learning activities with classmates, or the services of learning support specialists. The writer, then, selectively reported details, telling us what was positive and omitting negative details.

Suppose the writer concludes his or her article on home schooling by saying, "Home schooling is the better route to follow to produce a well-educated child." What the writer has not told us is what route home schooling is better than. Is it better than a private school? Is it better than a public school? Is it better than hiring a private tutor? The writer has made an incomplete comparison.

One way writers avoid revealing information is to use a particular sentence structure that does not identify who performed a specified action. In the sentence *The cup broke* you do not know who broke the cup. In the sentence *The bill was paid* you do not know who paid the bill. This sentence pattern is called the passive voice. Here are a few more examples of the passive voice. In each, notice what information is missing.

> The tax reform bill was defeated.

> The accounting procedures were found to be questionable.

> The oil spill was contained.

Another way writers avoid revealing information is to use nouns and pronouns that do not refer to a specific person or thing. The sentence *They said it would rain by noon* does not reveal who predicted rain. The sentence *It always happens to me* does not indicate what always happens to the writer. Here are a few more examples.

> They say the enemy is preparing to attack.

> Anyone can get rich with this plan; many people have already.

> Politicians don't care about people.

To be sure you are getting full and complete information, ask the following questions:

- What important information is omitted? (What have you not told me?)
- What contradictory evidence is not reported?
- Has the author selectively reported details to further his or her cause?
- Does the author explain incomplete comparisons?
- What else do I need to know?

To answer these questions, it may be necessary to do additional reading or research, either on the Internet or in your college library. Try to locate another article on the same topic and notice what additional information is included.

EXERCISE 5–9 | *For each of the following statements, indicate what information is missing.*

1. Our neighborhood was ruined by the water treatment plant.
2. They raised test scores in that state.
3. People were hurt by welfare reform.
4. Some animal testing has been banned in other countries.

5. Athletes are overpaid.
6. They say the Columbia River has too many dams.
7. Anyone can get on the Internet.
8. They filed charges.
9. Orchestras in many cities have gone out of business.
10. The check was probably forged.

DOES THE AUTHOR MAKE AND SUPPORT GENERALIZATIONS?

Suppose you are reading an article that states that "Musicians are temperamental people." Do you think that every musician who ever wrote or performed a song or played a musical instrument is temperamental? Can you think of exceptions? This statement is an example of a generalization. A **generalization** is a reasoned statement about an entire group (musicians) based on known information about part of the group (musicians the writer has met or observed). A generalization requires a leap from what is known to a conclusion about what is unknown. Generalizations may be expressed using words such as *all, always, none,* or *never.* Some statements may imply but not directly state that the writer is referring to the entire group or class. The statement "Musicians are temperamental people" suggests but does not directly state that all musicians are temperamental. Here are a few more generalizations:

Rich people are snobs.

Chinese food is never filling.

Pets are always troublesome.

The key to evaluating generalizations is to evaluate the type, quality, and amount of evidence given to support them. Here are a few more generalizations. What type of evidence would you need to convince you that each is or is not true?

College students are undecided about future career goals.

Fast food lacks nutritional value.

Foreign cars outperform similar American models.

For the generalization about college students, you might need to see research studies about college students' career goals, for example. And, then, even if studies did conclude that many college students are undecided, it would not be fair to conclude that every single student is undecided. If no evidence is given, then the generalization is not trustworthy and should be questioned.

You can also evaluate a generalization by seeing whether the author provides specifics about the generalization. For the statement "Pets are always troublesome," ask what kind of pets the author is referring to—a pet potbellied pig, an iguana, or a cat? Then ask what is meant by troublesome—does it mean the animal is time consuming, requires special care, or behaves poorly?

Another way to evaluate a generalization is to try to think of exceptions. For the generalization *Medical doctors are aloof and inaccessible*, can you think of a doctor you have met or heard about who was caring and available to his or her patients? If so, the generalization is not accurate in all cases.

EXERCISE 5–10

Read each of the following statements and place a checkmark before each generalization.

_____ 1. The Internet is changing America.

_____ 2. Influenza causes severe epidemics every two years.

_____ 3. Most drug cases start with busts of small, local dealers and move to a search of their suppliers.

_____ 4. Attending college is essential for economic success and advancement.

_____ 5. Colds are caused by viruses, not bacteria, not cold weather, and not improper diet.

EXERCISE 5-11

Read each of the following paragraphs and underline each generalization.

1. Child care workers are undereducated in relation to the importance of their jobs. A whole generation of children is being left day after day in the hands of women with little more than high-school-level education. These children will suffer in the future for our inattention to the child care employment pool.

2. Americans have had enough of libraries providing Internet pornography to children. They want filtering on all computers or computers out of libraries. When will librarians listen to their customers (who also pay their salaries)?

3. For the past few years, drivers have been getting worse. Especially guilty of poor driving are the oldest and youngest drivers. There should be stricter tests and more classes for new drivers and yearly eye exams and road tests for drivers once they hit age 60. This is the only way to ensure the safety of our roads.

EXERCISE 5–12

For each of the following generalizations, indicate what questions you would ask and what types of information you would need to evaluate the generalization.

1. Vegetarians are pacifists and they do not own guns.
2. Most crimes are committed by high school dropouts.
3. It always rains in Seattle.
4. Private school students get a better education than public school students.
5. Scientists don't believe in any kind of higher power.

EXERCISE 5–13 *Review "Psychology and Sport," which appears on page 41 in Chapter 2. Working with a classmate, locate and underline generalizations the author makes. Discuss whether the author provides adequate evidence to support each generalization.*

WHAT ASSUMPTIONS IS THE AUTHOR MAKING?

Suppose a friend asked you, "Have you stopped cheating on your girlfriend?" This person, perhaps not a friend after all, is making an assumption. He or she is assuming that you already have been cheating. An **assumption** is an idea or principle the writer accepts as true and makes no effort to prove or substantiate. Usually, it is a beginning or premise on which he or she bases the remainder of the statement. Assumptions often use words such as *since, if,* or *when.* Here are a few more examples.

- You're going to make that mistake again, are you? (The assumption is that you have already made the mistake at least once.)
- When you're mature, you'll realize you made a mistake. (The assumption is that you are not mature now.)
- You are as arrogant as your sister. (The assumption is that your sister is arrogant.)
- My dog is angry. (The assumption is that dogs have and can express emotions.)

Each of the above statements makes no attempt to prove or support the hidden assumption; it is assumed to be true.

Writers often make assumptions and make no effort to prove or support them. For example, an author may assume that television encourages violent behavior in children and proceed to argue for restrictions on TV viewing. Or a writer may assume that abortion is morally wrong and suggest legal restrictions on how and when abortions are performed. If a writer's assumption is wrong or unsubstantiated, then the statements that follow from the assumption should be questioned. If television does not encourage violent behavior, for example, then the suggestion to restrict viewing should not be accepted unless other reasons are offered.

EXERCISE 5–14 *Read each of the following statements and then place a checkmark before those choices that are assumptions made by the writer of the statement.*

1. Cosmetics should not be tested on animals, since they may cause pain, injury, or even death.

   _____ a. Animals have the right to avoid pain and suffering.

   _____ b. Cosmetics should be tested on people.

   _____ c. Animals should be anesthetized before research is conducted.

2. Teacher's aides lack advanced college degrees: therefore, they are unable to teach children effectively.

_____ a. Teachers aides should obtain advanced degrees.

_____ b. Advanced college degrees are needed in order to teach effectively.

_____ c. Teachers who hold advanced degrees are not necessarily effective teachers.

3. Border states in the U.S. must take action to curb illegal immigration; otherwise, state funds will be quickly exhausted.

_____ a. The writer opposes using state funds to help illegal immigrants.

_____ b. Illegal immigrants must enter the U.S. legally to receive state aid.

_____ c. State funding guidelines should be revised.

EXERCISE 5-15   *For each statement listed below, identify at least one assumption.*

1. Grocery stores should reduce the number of weekly sale items and lower overall prices.
2. Eliminating essay exams from psychology courses would diminish students' writing abilities.
3. More public transit should be added to our cities to reduce traffic and pollution.
4. Endangered species should be bred in captivity to ensure their survival.
5. Artists do not need grants from the government because they sell their works for such high prices.
6. Hunters serve their communities by keeping down the deer population.
7. Lobbyists hinder the work of our elected officials; these groups should be banned from Washington, DC.
8. Doing away with unions would increase productivity in our country.
9. Learning a foreign language is a waste of time; Americans can get by anywhere.
10. Violence in sports affects everyone. Such brutality corrupts play, a form of free expression.

EXERCISE 5- 16   *Identify the assumption(s) in each of the following passages.*

1.   Most kids, of course, listen barely if at all to what adults say. Instead they watch what adults do. And, for better or worse, there may be no lesson we impart to them

so efficiently as how we adults react to events that upset us, from a fender-bender to a threatening new era of conflict.

—Editorial, "Raising the Sept. 11 Generation," *Chicago Tribune* (September 9, 2002)

2.   Speaking from developments in my own family, there are way too many young students out there whose focus centers on partying, dress competition, music, souped-up cars and sex. Goal-setting and accomplishment in their studies as they prepare themselves for what is a highly competitive world do not figure too prominently in their day-to-day lives.

—Editorial, "School's First Week Provides a Few Bright Exceptions," *Toronto Star* (September 6, 2002)

3.   Most products—from cigarette lighters to medicine bottles—have to be designed to protect against foreseeable misuse. But there is no regulator to help the plaintiffs: guns and tobacco are the only products that the Consumer Product Safety Commission does not oversee. And even though lawsuits have often helped push up safety standards elsewhere, there are plenty of conservative judges who do not think it is the courts' job to create gun laws.

—Editorial, "From the hip; Gun control," *The Economist* (US) (November 23, 2002)

4.   In the meantime, a disturbing message is being sent to the guys and girls in the little leagues. Practice hard, work out, eat nutritiously—and sneak illegal steroids because, after all, winning and setting records are everything. And besides, if you make it big, you'll have enough money to care for your broken body.

—Editorial, "Steroids Should Be Tagged Out," *San Jose Mercury News* (June 4, 2002)

5.   Britain on Wednesday marked the 150th anniversary of its public toilets. This reminds us of the barbaric lack of such facilities in the United States. Along with an increasingly chaotic and unfair health system, sparse public transportation and a paucity of neighborhood parks, the absence of public loos here evokes America's depressing distance from the perfect place that pathological patriots assert that it is.

—Editorial, "Sign of Civilization," *Providence Journal* (August 16, 2002)

DOES THE AUTHOR USE MANIPULATIVE LANGUAGE?

Writers can shape their readers' thinking and response to their message by the language they choose to express it. Writers use a variety of language manipulation techniques to achieve a particular effect, to communicate their message in a particular way, and to appeal to specific groups of people. These techniques include clichés, jargon, allusions, euphemisms, doublespeak, and hyperbole.

Clichés

A **cliché** is a tired, overused expression. Here are a few examples:

Curiosity killed the cat.

Bigger is better.

Absence makes the heart grow fonder.

He is as blind as a bat.

These everyday expressions have been overused; they are so commonly used that they no longer carry a specific meaning. They have become pat expressions, used by writers without much thought or creativity. Because the expressions are so common, many readers tend to accept them at face value rather than to evaluate their meaning and appropriateness. When you recognize a cliché, ask yourself the following questions:

- Why did the writer use the cliché?
- Why did the writer not use a fresh expression instead?

Numerous clichés used throughout a piece of writing may suggest that the writer has not thought in depth about the topic or has not made the effort to express his or her ideas in an interesting and unique way.

- *Is the writer trying to gloss over or skip over details by using a cliché?* Clichés often oversimplify a situation that is complex. In trying to decide which courses to register for, a student may say, "Don't put off till tomorrow what you can do today." Actually the student *could* register today, but it may be better to wait until he or she has had time to think, do research, and talk to others about course selection.

- *Is the writer trying to avoid directly stating an unpopular or unpleasant idea?* Suppose you are reading an article on controlling world terrorism. After describing recent acts of terrorism, the writer concludes the article with the cliché, "What will be, will be." What dies this cliché really say? The expression is a common one and is commonly accepted. However, in this context, the cliché suggests (but does not directly state) that nothing can be done about terrorism, a unpopular viewpoint that would receive criticism if directly expressed.

- *Is the cliché fitting and appropriate?* Suppose in writing an article on college financial aid, the writer admonishes students not to spend their financial aid loan before they receive it, by saying, "Don't count your chickens before they are hatched." The writer's audience would be better served if the writer, instead, had offered more detail, explaining that loan checks are often delayed, and that spending money before it is received may cause serious financial problems.

- *What does the use of clichés reveal about the author?* Use of clichés may signal that a writer is not fully aware of his or her audience or interested in accommodating them. A writer who packs an article full of clichés is not aware that his or her readers prefer fresh, descriptive information, rather than standard clichés.

EXERCISE 5–17 *For each of the following clichés, explain its meaning and then think of a situation in which it would be untrue or inappropriate.*

Example:

Cliché: Don't change horses in midstream.

Meaning: You should not try to change something once you have begun.

Situation: If you realize you have made a poor decision and there is a way to correct it, you should correct it. For example, if you realize you are registered for the wrong level math course, try to drop the course or change to the appropriate level course.

1. Better late than never.
2. Opportunity doesn't knock twice.
3. Good fences make good neighbors.
4. Money makes the world go round.
5. If you don't have anything nice to say, don't say anything at all.

EXERCISE 5–18 *Replace each of the following clichés with more specific information that fits the context.*

Example: The university president did not want to "toot his own horn," but he enumerated all his accomplishments of the past year.

Replacement: The university president didn't want to brag . . .

1. My older sister turned 40 this year. She is over the hill.
2. The mayor and the governor are like two peas in a pod.
3. Not sure of his itinerary, the salesman decided to play it by ear.
4. The students made sure to read the fine print on their new lease.
5. Our new senator rubs me the wrong way.

Jargon

Jargon refers to words, phrases, and specialized terms used by a particular academic field or special interest group that is not readily understood by the general public. Librarians speak jargon when communicating with each other, for example:

> We are considering several different solutions for the aggregation question that will allow our patrons more targeted periodical database searching.

Doctors use specialized language when communicating treatments to other medical professionals, for example:

> During the technique for nursemaid's elbow reduction, put your thumb in the antecubital fossa, then apply longitudinal traction.

Computer users who communicate through e-mail and instant messaging use words and symbols that carry specialized meaning to other users, for example:

> GTG . . . TTYL = got to go . . . talk to you later

Jargon, when read by people who are not a member of the group that uses it, tends to confuse, isolate, or exclude those readers. A writer may use jargon to appear more knowledgeable or even superior to his or her readers. Unknowing, noncritical readers may accept ideas simply because they are defended by jargon, assuming that the writer must be knowledgeable in order to use complex, unfamiliar terminology.

If a writer uses jargon you do not understand, you may not be the writer's intended audience. This may be the case in reading a medical journal such as the *Journal of the American Medical Association*, which is intended for medical doctors who understand the jargon being used. If you are the intended audience, the writer may be purposely trying to manipulate you. Writers may purposely use jargon to assume a position of authority. As another example, a writer of a general interest article on organ transplants may use obtuse medical terminology to present facts that, if presented in layman's terms, may be unpleasant or objectionable.

EXERCISE 5–19

Underline the jargon in each of the following statements and discuss how appropriate the language is for you. Can you use context to figure out new terms? Would you continue reading the rest of the article? Is the jargon confusing or manipulative?

1. Place-based education, which draws from local culture, history, and geography to create a meaningful curriculum, can occur in any type of setting, but it holds particular promise for rural home schooling. Place-based educators use local particulars to teach universal concepts, engage students in community life, and involve people and resources unique to the home community.
   —Jaycox, "Rural Home Schooling and Place-Based Education," *ERIC Digest* (December 1, 2001)

2. Extinction is actually a normal process in the course of evolution. Throughout geological time, many more species have become extinct than exist today. These species slowly disappeared because of climatic changes and the inability to adapt to such conditions as competition and predation.
   —"Endangered Species," *Funk & Wagnalls New World Encyclopedia*

3. Russian air-launched weapons manufacturer Bazalt has begun to develop a family of low-cost precision-guided munitions in the wake of its air force's combat

experience in Chechnya, and from watching the U.S. shift to precision-guided air-launched ordnance in its recent combat operations. Work is underway on the development of a glide-bomb wing-kit and terminal-guidance seekers intended to provide the Russian air force with a low-cost short-range standoff attack weapon based around its existing iron bomb inventory. The system is called the FAB-500MPK.

—Barrie, "Russia's Bazalt Working On Standoff Bomb Kit,"
Aviation Week & Space Technology (August 5, 2002)

Allusions

Allusions are references to well-known religious, literary, artistic, or historical works or sources. A writer may refer to a biblical verse, a character in a famous poem or novel, a line in a well-known song, or a historical figure such as Napoleon or George Washington. An allusion makes a connection or points to similarities between the writer's subject and the reference. Writers usually assume that educated readers will recognize and understand their allusions. Here are a few examples of allusions.

- A writer describes a person as having the patience of Job. In the Bible, Job is a righteous man whose faith was tested by God.
- An article on parental relationships with children refers to the Oedipus complex. Oedipus was a figure in Greek mythology who unknowingly killed his father and married his mother. He blinded himself when he discovered what he had done. The Oedipus complex is controversial but refers to a child's tendency to seek sexual fulfillment from a parent of the opposite sex.

If you encounter an allusion you do not understand, check it on the Internet using a search engine such as Google (www.google.com) by typing in the key words of the allusion. The following reference sources may also be helpful:

Merriam-Webster's Dictionary of Allusions

Dictionary of Historical Allusions and Eponyms

The Facts on File Encyclopedia of Word and Phrase Origins

Writers may include numerous literary or scholarly allusions to give their writing the appearance of scholarship. Do not be overly impressed by a writer's use of allusions, particularly obscure ones. A writer may use allusions to divert readers' attention from the lack of substantive detail or support. When evaluating a writer's use of allusions, ask the following questions:

- What does the allusion mean?
- Why did the writer include the allusion?
- What does the allusion contribute to the overall meaning of the work?

EXERCISE 5–20 *For each of the following statements, explain the meaning of the allusion.*

1. The mayor looked around the hurricane-ravaged city and pondered the Herculean task that lay ahead in rebuilding the lives and homes destroyed.
2. Emily's mother hoped her new regimen of yoga and raw foods would be her fountain of youth.
3. "Whoa, Twilight Zone," the two new friends said to each other when they realized how many coincidences linked them.
4. Her grandparents finally came out of the Dark Ages and bought an answering machine and cordless phone.
5. The campaign manager sought to discover and exploit the opponent's Achilles' heel.
6. Many small business people find themselves in a Catch-22 when they realize they must compete in a world of e-commerce but cannot afford to create an e-commerce Web site.
7. When she realized her best friend had joined in with others to betray her, she muttered, "Et tu, Brute?"
8. With a grin like the Cheshire Cat, the defendant sat waiting for the jury's verdict.
9. He awoke from a Kafkaesque dream feeling anxious and lonely, frightened of what his day would bring.
10. The little boy likened himself to George Washington as he confessed to breaking the neighbor's window with his baseball.

Euphemisms

What do these sentences have in common?

He suffered combat fatigue.

The company is downsizing.

Capital punishment is controversial.

Each uses an expression called a euphemism. A **euphemism** is a word or phrase that is used in place of a word that is unpleasant, embarrassing, or otherwise objectionable. The expression *combat fatigue* is a pleasant way to refer to the psychological problems of veterans caused by their experiences in war, *downsizing* replaces the word *firing*, and *capital punishment* is a substitute for *death penalty*.

The word *euphemism* comes from the Greek roots *eu-*, meaning "sounding good," and *-pheme*, meaning "speech." Euphemisms have a long history going back to ancient languages and cultures. Ancient people thought of names as an extension of things themselves. To know and say the name of a person or object gave power over the person or thing. Thus calling something by its name was avoided, even forbidden. God, Satan, deceased relatives, and hunted animals would often be referred to indirectly. For example, in one culture God was called The Kindly One; the bear was called The Grandfather. Today, many euphemisms are widely used in both spoken and written language. Here are a few more examples:

> The foreign spy was put out of circulation. (the spy was killed)

> He was hit by friendly fire. (accidentally shot by a member of his own country)

> My brother works as a sanitation engineer. (janitor or garbage collector)

Euphemisms tend to minimize or downplay something's importance or seriousness. They are often used in politics and advertising. They can be used to camouflage actions or events that may be unacceptable to readers or listeners if bluntly explained. For example, the word *casualties* of a war may be used instead of the phrase *dead soldiers* to lessen the impact of the attack. To say that a politician's statement was *at variance with the truth* has less impact and is less forceful than to say that the politician lied.

A writer may use a euphemism to alter your perception of a situation by lessening its harshness, ugliness, severity, or seriousness. When a writer uses a euphemism, substitute the everyday meaning of the euphemism and notice whether the writer's message changes.

EXERCISE 5–21

For each of the underlined euphemisms, write a substitution that does not minimize or avoid the basic meaning of the term.

Example: The theater had only one <u>ladies' room</u>.

<u>The theater had only one women's bathroom.</u>

1. The councilman has entered a <u>substance abuse</u> program.
2. <u>Body counts</u> started out high, but then were revised to lower numbers.
3. Reporters are not required to reveal their <u>confidential sources</u>.
4. The high school teacher found her senior English students to be <u>unmotivated</u>.
5. A new <u>correctional facility</u> will be built near Deer Run housing development.
6. You may experience <u>precipitation</u> over the holiday weekend.
7. My midwife says I might feel <u>under the weather</u> during the first trimester of my pregnancy.
8. Richard's parents were surprised to see just how <u>cozy</u> his apartment was.
9. Several countries considered a <u>preemptive strike</u> against the uncooperative nation.
10. Everyone wondered how Aurora would make ends meet now that she was <u>between jobs</u>.

Doublespeak

Doublespeak is deliberately unclear or evasive language. Often, it exaggerates or overstates information that could be expressed simply. William Lutz, an expert on doublespeak, defines it as "language that pretends to communicate but does not," in his book *Beyond Nineteen Eighty-Four*. Here is an example: "the letter from the air force colonel in charge of safety said that rocket boosters weighing more than 300,000 pounds 'have an explosive force upon surface impact that is sufficient to exceed the accepted overpressure threshold of physiological damage for the exposed personnel.'" What does the colonel's statement mean in simple words? If a 300,000 pound rocket falls on a person, it will kill him or her. The language the colonel used is an example of doublespeak.

Here is a humorous example of the use of doublespeak, attributed to Everett Dirksen, former U.S. senator:

> I am reminded of the man who filled in an application for an insurance policy. One of the questions he had to answer was, "How old was your father when he died and of what did he die?" Well, his father had been hanged, but he did not want to put that on his application. He puzzled it out for a while. He finally wrote, "My father was 65 when he died. He came to this end while participating in a public function when the platform gave way."
>
> —Grazian, "How Much Do Words Really Matter?"
> *Public Relations Quarterly* (Summer 1998) p. 37

Here are a few more examples, along with their everyday meanings:

detainees—hostages

downsizing the company—firing employees

vertically deployed antipersonnel devices—bombs

Doublespeak uses euphemisms, but it tangles language in other ways as well that are intended to confuse or overwhelm the listener or reader. Doublespeak also may use technical language (jargon) that is likely to be unfamiliar to the audience. Doublespeak also may use inflated language—words that tend to make something seem more important or complex than it really is. Doublespeak also may use long, polysyllabic words. It may scramble the order of words in a sentence to create confusion or avoid giving complete information. For example, writers may use the passive voice to avoid saying who performed an action. In the sentence "The bombs were released, injuring many civilians," we do not know who released the bombs.

When reading doublespeak, be suspicious of the writer's motives. Ask yourself:

- Why is the writer being purposefully evasive or unclear?
- What is he or she trying to hide?

EXERCISE 5–22   *Untangle each of the following examples of doublespeak and write a translation in simple English.*

Example: Most hospitals are reluctant to publicize negative patient care outcomes.

Hospitals are reluctant to publicize patient deaths.

1. Jessamyn's advisor suggested she try a course in human kinetics figuring that the outcomes from this class would cause an upward development in the calculation of her GPA.
2. The positive economic adjustments at our most-liked eating establishment were meant to counter the recent negative contributions to profit.
3. My female sibling went on a caloric reduction program two seasons prior to her nuptials.
4. More than several students have forgone cowhide back-mounted equipment for those of the vegetarian variety.
5. The drug enterprise leader was apprehended following his deployment of an intrusion detection device.
6. Large amounts of previously owned parts were strewn about the public waste reception center.
7. How much time do our education users spend on task or attending to their learning facilitators?
8. My personal manual database indicates I must procure a social expression product for my chronologically gifted neighbor.
9. In the event of a nonroutine operation, follow the relocation drill.
10. Preliminary reports show a negative gain in test scores in the state's public schools.

Hyperbole

Hyperbole is a deliberate, excessive, and obvious exaggeration. If you say, "I could eat a ton of those chocolate chips cookies!" you are obviously exaggerating. Hyperbole is used for special effect, and it is a way of creating emphasis. It also may be a way of suggesting meaning without directly stating it. If, for instance, a writer, in describing a person's appearance, states that *he could pass for a clown in the circus*, the writer is suggesting, but not directly stating, that the person is comical, gaudy, overstated, and out of place. Here are a few more examples:

> An exasperated commuter exclaimed, "You can't get anywhere in this city during rush hour!"

> The European immigrant bricklayers built our city.

To evaluate the use of hyperbole, ask the following questions:

- What was the hyperbole?
- What is suggested but not directly stated?

EXERCISE 5–23 | *Explain what each of the following examples of hyperbole suggests but does not directly state.*

1. No one understands Stephen Hawking's books.
2. The Internet holds the answers to all your questions.

3. I have a mountain of homework papers to correct.
4. The major car companies control the transportation habits of all Americans.
5. Snow never stops falling here; winter will never end.

SUMMARY

Writers use a variety of techniques to express their ideas and to manipulate their readers. Understanding the writer's techniques will help you think critically about his or her message and form reasonable judgments about the author and the message. Critical readers should be alert for:

- Connotative language that suggests the feelings and associations that may accompany a word.
- Figurative language that makes comparisons between two unlike things. Three types of figurative language are simile, metaphor, and personification.
- Bias. Writers may present a one-sided viewpoint on a topic or issue.
- Missing information. Writers should always ask: "What is the author not telling me?"
- Generalizations. A generalization is a reasoned statement about an entire group based on known information about part of the group. Generalizations may be reasonable or unfounded, depending on the evidence on which they are based.
- Assumptions. An assumption is an idea or principle the writer accepts to be true and makes no effort to prove or substantiate. Assumptions may be accurate or inaccurate.
- Manipulative language. Writers use a variety of techniques to achieve a particular effect, to communicate their message in a particular way, or to appeal to specific groups of people. These techniques include clichés, jargon, allusions, euphemisms, doublespeak, and hyperbole.

INTEGRATING
IDEAS

◆

PAIRED
READINGS

Political Science

PREREADING QUESTIONS

1. Why is the rebuilding of the World Trade Center site controversial?
2. What kind of memorial is appropriate for the World Trade Center site?

Look at What They've Done

Anna Quindlen

1   The site is as tidy and anonymous now as a hospital room after the patient has left, or died. The slabs of pale concrete look like the beginning of something, not its end, as though at any moment workers, whistling, carrying lunch, will begin to raise the girders and frame the walls as workers have done in New York City for as long as anyone can remember.

2   It does not look like a mass grave. It does not look like a crime scene. It does not look like a historical site. It is all of those.

3   It looks like a development opportunity. And that it should not be.

4   Now that the wreckage of the World Trade Center has been cleared away, those left behind face a lesser, different sort of danger, but a danger nonetheless. And that is that what really happened here, the carnage and the suffering and the blind hatred and the sheer destruction will be muted by an impulse so strong that it may well count as a national disease. It has many names: moving ahead, getting past it, closure, healing.

5   But healing is for wounds. Grief is for deaths.

6   New York City is built on commerce, the capital of capitalism. So it was inevitable that some of the first public conversations about the site of the most dev-astating injury in the nation's history would concern real-estate development. "A fantastic opportunity," one architect called it. How pernicious is America's chronic amnesia that less than a year since those buildings dropped, taking thousands with them in pain and terror, what it all comes down to is square footage?

7   One of the earliest proposals for the site was for the world's tallest building and a memorial dominated by statues of two women representing the muses History and Memory, one holding a tablet, the other a torch. It is impossible to believe that anyone who thinks this event should be commemorated with a sky-scraper and classical statuary has any idea what happened to that place, or this country.

8   This has always been a nation willing to sell out its past for putative progress. A new country, a young country, it sees itself as a tabula rasa, which is why archival photographs of its greatest city show charming and even inspired buildings where now stand great hulking misanthropic glass cubes.

9   More cubes rise every day. There is the need for office space. The Twin Towers provided an acre of it on every floor.

10   But let them rise elsewhere. There is a great emptiness now, 16 acres of breathtaking ground-level flatness at the center of predictable vertical thrust. And that emptiness speaks powerfully, not just of the end of two buildings but of thousands of deaths and a sense of indomitability whose loss is measured in eyes cast up on the city streets whenever a plane flies low.

11   It was a moment like no other in the country's history. It should be commemorated like no other. It should reflect what viewers see in "In Memoriam," the unflinching HBO documentary about the events of September 11. The music to the film is the heartbreaking "Adagio for Strings" by Samuel Barber, but the real soundtrack is the disembodied voices of people repeating these words: oh my God.

12   Sometimes blasphemy becomes a prayer.

13   Twenty-one years ago, anonymous entry 1,026 won the design competition for a memorial to the most corrosive conflict in American history, the Vietnam War. An undergraduate at Yale, a 21-year-old Chinese-American woman named Maya Lin, had created in her mind's eye two walls of black polished granite in the shape of a broad V, inscribed with the names of the more than 50,000 Americans who had died.

14   The design immediately came under virulent attack, from veterans groups and from conservative politicians. They wanted columns, flagpoles, a tablet, a torch, something redolent of that American sense that everything, eventually, can be transmuted into triumph.

15   They could not see that Lin's design was something different, something almost mystical, the visual evocation of all the things the war really represented, sorrow and pain and memory.

16   It is now the most visited memorial in Washington.

17   Perhaps another, smaller moment in history also suggests what the Trade Center site demands. It is the moment on Air Force One, when Jacqueline Kennedy wiped her husband's blood from her face. "I should have left it there," she said later. "Let them see what they've done."

18   The tragic cavern in lower Manhattan is not a design or a development problem but a test of the spiritual and emotional depth of an entire nation. The demands of democracy should not be confused with those of capitalism. To honor a tragedy of this magnitude requires a response of comparable magnitude. Maybe Maya Lin could suggest how best that could be done. But maybe, looking at the flattened plain where once so many worked and where so many died, the answer is to honor the emptiness by leaving it as a mute memorial. Are we a people so pinched of heart that we would trade memory for real estate? If so, the terrorists really have won.

—Quindlen, "Look at What They've Done," *Newsweek* (June 3, 2002), p. 68

VOCABULARY REVIEW

1. For each of the words listed below, use context; prefixes, roots, and suffixes; and/or a dictionary to write a brief definition or synonym of the word as it is used in the reading.

    a. anonymous (para. 1) _____

    b. carnage (para. 4) _____

c. closure (para. 4) _____

d. pernicious (para. 6) _____

e. putative (para. 8) _____

f. archival (para. 8) _____

g. disembodied (para. 11) _____

h. corrosive (para. 13) _____

i. virulent (para. 14) _____

2. Underline new specialized terminology introduced in the reading.

COMPREHENSION QUESTIONS

1. What is the author's main point in the essay?
2. What did some of the first public discussions about the World Trade Center site propose it be used for?
3. What does the Vietnam Memorial represent?
4. Why did Jacqueline Kennedy later say she should have left her husband's blood on her face?
5. Why does the author refer to the assassination of President Kennedy?
6. What reasons does the author offer in support of her suggested plan for the site?

THINKING CRITICALLY

1. In paragraph 18, the author says that this site should not be about capitalism. In what way is capitalism part of the site no matter how the site is memorialized?
2. What information is not included in this essay that would help the reader decide how the site should be memorialized?
3. Identify the generalization the author makes in paragraph 8.
4. Explain the allusion to the muses in paragraph 7.
5. Identify and explain the figurative expression used in paragraph 10.
6. Underline words and phrases in paragraph 18 that have strong connotative meaning.

LEARNING/STUDY STRATEGY

Outline the argument the author uses.

INTEGRATING
IDEAS

◆

PAIRED
READINGS

Political Science

PREREADING QUESTIONS

1. What should a Ground Zero memorial convey?
2. What criteria should be used to choose a memorial?

Architect Is Off the Mark on Ground Zero Mound

Editorial, March 11, 2002,
Engineering News-Record

1   Saying that buildings would be inappropriate for the 16-acre site of the World Trade Center in New York City, architect Tadao Ando, the winner of the 2002 Gold Medal of the American Institute of Architects, has instead graciously offered a diametrically opposed scheme: a 200-meter-diameter mound of earth, covered in grass and rising 30 m. The mound, symbolizing a partial globe protruding from the earth, would "remind people of the courage after Sept. 11 and of the responsibility America has for the rest of the world," said Ando while explaining his scheme recently in Washington, D.C., where he accepted the Gold Medal.

2   "What I saw Sept. 11 was not only a question of architecture, it was a question of a violent attack on an architectural symbol of American power—the World Trade Center," he said. The attack was a kind of knock on the door of America because the attackers wanted to make their presence felt to a power that had ignored them, he implied.

3   Ando made it clear he thought the attack "very unfortunate." But at the same time, he said it gave a lot of people a greater awareness that there is something on the other side of the world. "The act of terror is something we cannot forgive," he said, "but it gives us all a lesson" of how we might live better together. "Whatever you build [at Ground Zero] will be the center of the world. You should try to make something that will reflect all of the world," Ando said.

4   Ando may be an architectural genius, but he doesn't have a clue as to what is appropriate at the WTC site. He joins a long line of other people presenting crackpot ideas. It behooves all Americans to be aware of a world outside their own circumstances. But as far as a message from Ground Zero, a globe symbolizing this awareness is wholly inappropriate. Americans, however arrogant at times, need not make amends to the terrorists for their egregious deeds. It is not a place for Americans to reach out, as if apologizing for being the victim. And rather than symbolizing Planet Earth, the dirt pile seems more like the burial mound for victims that it is.

5   There will be plenty more discussions about the form of a permanent memorial at Ground Zero. Whatever is built should be just that—a memorial to the victims of a heinous and inexcusable act and a reminder of that act. Ando says he endeavors to use architecture to foster community, to bring people together, to touch their hearts and to enrich lifestyles. America, despite its faults, has been endeavoring to do that for hundreds of years. It has been and remains the land of opportunity for all people.

—"Architect Is Off the Mark on Ground Zero Mound,"
ENR: Engineering News-Record (March 11, 2002), p. 48

VOCABULARY REVIEW

1. For each of the words listed below, use context; prefixes, roots, and suffixes; and/or a dictionary to write a brief definition or synonym of the word as it is used in the reading.

   a. diametrically (para. 1) _____

   b. protruding (para. 1) _____

   c. behooves (para. 4) _____

   d. arrogant (para. 4) _____

   e. egregious (para. 4) _____

   f. heinous (para. 5) _____

   g. endeavors (para. 5) _____

2. Underline new specialized terminology introduced in the reading.

COMPREHENSION QUESTIONS

1. Why does Ando propose a mound for a memorial?
2. What does Ando feel the attack demonstrated?
3. Why does the author believe Ando's proposal is wrong?
4. What credentials does Ando have?

THINKING CRITICALLY

1. Underline examples of connotative language used in this essay.
2. Do you agree with the author's statement that Ground Zero is not a place for America to reach out to the world? Why or why not?
3. What kind of bias does Ando hold?
4. Explain the figurative expression used in paragraph 2—"a kind of knock on the door."

5. Underline the generalization in paragraph 5.

LEARNING/STUDY STRATEGY

1. Write a summary of this essay.
2. Draw a sketch of how Ando's design would appear based on the description in the selection.

THINKING ABOUT THE PAIRED READINGS

INTEGRATING IDEAS

1. In what ways are the two readings similar?
2. In what ways are they different?
3. In what ways do the authors' purposes differ?

GENERATING NEW IDEAS

Create a list of your own suggestions for ways to memorialize Ground Zero.

Multimedia Activities

1. **Similes, Metaphors, and Personification**
   http://www.learn.co.uk/default.asp?WCI=Unit&WCU=1746
   Explore this interactive site by following the list of links on the left. Try writing some poetry of your own using these techniques.

2. **Writing Techniques in Advertising**
   http://www.stanford.edu/group/step/vosovic/american_literature/debate%201/propaganda.html
   Try this assignment from a class at Stanford University. Be sure to scroll all the way down to the assignment page.

Take a Road Trip to the
American Southwest!

If your instructor has asked you to use the Reading Road Trip CD-ROM or Web site, be sure to visit the Critical Thinking module for multimedia tutorials, exercises, and tests.

CHAPTER 6

READING AND EVALUATING ARGUMENTS

LEARNING OBJECTIVES

✦ To recognize the elements of an argument
✦ To recognize types of arguments
✦ To evaluate arguments
✦ To recognize errors in logical reasoning

An argument between people can be an angry exchange of ideas and feelings. Family members might argue over household chores or use of the family car. Workers may argue over policies and procedures on the job. To be effective, however, an argument should be logical and should present well-thought-out ideas. It may involve emotion, but a sound argument is never simply a sudden, unplanned release of emotions and feelings.

An argument, then, always presents logical reasons and evidence to support a viewpoint. In a government course, you might read arguments for or against free speech; in a literature class, you may read a piece of literary criticism that argues for or against the value of a particular poem, debates its significance, or rejects a particular interpretation.

Here is a brief argument. As you read, notice that the argument offers reasons to support the viewpoint that baseball players' use of steroids is harmful.

IGNORING THE RISKS HARMS
PLAYERS' HEALTH AND THEIR REPUTATIONS

Olympic athletes who take steroids risk being banned from competition, internationally disgraced and forced to hand back tainted medals. NFL or NBA players face suspension and loss of salary for four or five games, maybe more. But a baseball player who uses steroids can take home one of the game's most cherished honors—and brag about it. That's because baseball management and the players union, both of which should be concerned with protecting ballplayers' health, can't work together to confront a problem that risks turning the national pastime into a muscle-bound freak show.

The ostrichlike attitude—and the rampant drug use that has resulted—set up baseball for its latest scandal. Retired slugger Ken Caminiti told *Sports Illustrated* he used steroids in 1996 when he hit 40 home runs, drove in 130 runs, batted .326 for the San Diego Padres—and won the National League's coveted Most Valuable Player Award.

While Caminiti has since backed away from his assertions that half of all major league players are on steroids, the magazine's report confirmed baseball's worst-kept secret: Use of steroids and other high-risk potions like human-growth hormones, amphetamines and ephedrine is widespread and growing. Not only are chemically pumped muscles popping out of uniforms, some players can't make their batting helmets fit because the drugs have caused their heads to swell and change shape.

Doping rumors have tainted baseball's image for two decades. Suspicions abound as to whether the recent crop of muscled home-run hitters runs on talent or on black-market chemicals.

Doctors suspect steroid use is a major factor in the increase of career-shortening muscle tears and tendon ruptures among major leaguers. The drug, which is illegal unless prescribed by a physician, elevates a user's testosterone, increasing muscle mass. But even a well-trained body can't always cope with the strains created by chemically enhanced strength.

Among former users—football players, weightlifters and others—steroids are blamed for heart and liver damage, endocrine-system imbalance, elevated cholesterol levels, strokes, aggressive behavior and genital dysfunction.

Yet neither baseball's owners nor the players union has ever cared enough about the drug issue—or the players' long-term health—to take it seriously. Management says it wants a drug-testing program in a new contract now being negotiated. The union until now has thrown up vague arguments about privacy rights and fears that owners will use test results unfairly against players.

Both sides, fixated on money issues, treat drug testing as a low priority. To the owners, it's a bargaining chip that can be dropped in exchange for economic concessions. To the players union, it distracts from efforts to maximize already huge salaries.

Their willingness to do nothing ignores the reality that doping is cheating.

Players using steroids to smash records corrupt baseball's traditions. By refusing to call them on it, baseball squanders high salaries on injury-prone players. And it unfairly taints the accomplishments of players who succeed on natural talent.

Fair ball, indeed.

—"Today's Debate," *USA Today* (June 4, 2002), p. 12A

PARTS OF AN ARGUMENT

An argument has three essential parts. First, an argument must address an **issue**—a problem or controversy about which people disagree. Abortion, gun control, animal rights, capital punishment, and drug legalization are all examples of issues. Second, an argument must take a position on an issue. This position is called a **claim.** An argument may claim that capital punishment should be outlawed or that medical use of marijuana should be legalized. Finally, an argument offers **support** for the claim. Support consists of reasons and evidence that the claim is reasonable and should be accepted. An argument may also include a fourth part—a **refutation.** A refutation considers opposing viewpoints and may attempt to disprove or discredit them.

In the argument above, the issue is baseball players' use of steroids. Notice that the title and first paragraph of the argument clearly identify the issue. The author's claim is that baseball players' use of steroids is unhealthy and unfair and that owners and players need to take the issue seriously. The author builds his or her argument by offering reasons why steroid use is unhealthy and unfair. In this argument, the author does not refute objections to his or her claim. An opposing viewpoint to the author's argument may be that steroid use creates enhanced performance, which makes the game more fun and competitive for fans. To refute this argument, the author would need to provide evidence that fans dislike extraordinary feats of performance and would prefer to see the game go back to the way it used to be played before players used drugs.

Types of Claims

The claim is the position or stand the writer takes on the issue. You might think of it as his or her viewpoint. Here are a few sample claims on the issue of animal rights.

> Animals should have none of the rights that humans do.

> Animals have limited rights: freedom from pain and suffering.

> Animals should be afforded the same rights as humans.

There are three common types of claims. A **claim of fact** is a statement that can be proven or verified by observation or research, as in the following example.

> Within ten years, destruction of rain forests will cause hundreds of plant and animal species to become extinct.

A **claim of value** states that one thing or idea is better or more desirable than another. Issues of right versus wrong or acceptable versus unacceptable lead to claims of value. The argument about baseball players' use of steroids is a claim of value. The author argues that steroid use is not acceptable because it is harmful to both the players and the game of baseball.

Here is another example. The following claim of value asserts that mandatory community service is appropriate.

> Requiring community service in high school will produce more community-aware graduates.

A **claim of policy** suggests what should or ought to be done to solve a problem. The following claim of policy suggests action to be taken to combat school violence.

To reduce school violence, more gun and metal detectors should be installed in public schools.

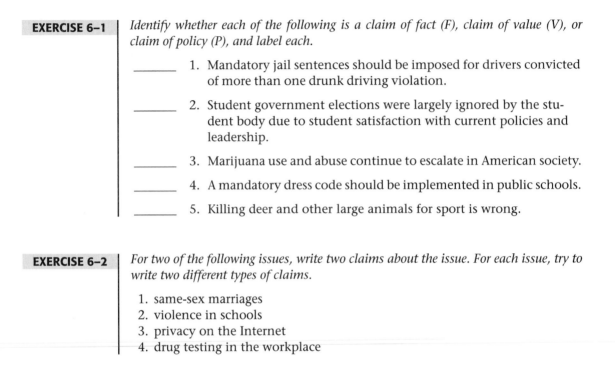

EXERCISE 6–1   *Identify whether each of the following is a claim of fact (F), claim of value (V), or claim of policy (P), and label each.*

_____   1. Mandatory jail sentences should be imposed for drivers convicted of more than one drunk driving violation.

_____   2. Student government elections were largely ignored by the student body due to student satisfaction with current policies and leadership.

_____   3. Marijuana use and abuse continue to escalate in American society.

_____   4. A mandatory dress code should be implemented in public schools.

_____   5. Killing deer and other large animals for sport is wrong.

EXERCISE 6–2   *For two of the following issues, write two claims about the issue. For each issue, try to write two different types of claims.*

1. same-sex marriages
2. violence in schools
3. privacy on the Internet
4. drug testing in the workplace

Types of Support

Three common types of support are reasons, evidence, and emotional appeals. A **reason** is a general statement that supports a claim. It explains why the writer's viewpoint is reasonable and should be accepted. In "Ignoring the Risks Harms Players' Health and Their Reputations," the author's two primary reasons why steroids should not be used: they are unhealthy and they are unfair.

Evidence consists of facts, statistics, experiences, comparisons, and examples that demonstrate why the claim is valid. The author of "Ignoring the Risks Harms Players' Health and Their Reputations " offers medical facts that demonstrate that steroids are unhealthy. He or she also offers an example of a player, Caminiti, who used steroids. The example illustrates a situation in which a player received a coveted award while using steroids.

Emotional appeals are ideas that are targeted toward needs or values that readers are likely to care about. Needs include physiological needs (food, drink, shelter) and psychological needs (sense of belonging, sense of accomplishment, sense of self-worth, sense of competency). An argument favoring gun control, for example, may appeal to a reader's need for safety, while an argument favoring restrictions on sharing personal or financial information may appeal to a reader's need for privacy and financial security.

In "Ignoring the Risks Harms Players' Health and Their Reputations," the author appeals to a reader's sense of fairness—players should not be allowed to succeed by using drugs rather than natural talent. The writer also appeals to the reader's sense of nostalgia by mentioning baseball traditions that are being corrupted.

EXERCISE 6–3 | *Identify the type(s) of evidence used to support each of the following brief arguments.*

1. Many students have part-time jobs that require them to work late afternoons and evenings during the week. These students are unable to use the library during the week. Therefore, library hours should be extended to weekends.
2. Because parents have the right to determine their children's sexual attitudes, sex education should take place in the home, not at school.
3. No one should be forced to inhale unpleasant or harmful substances. That's why the ban on cigarette smoking in public places was put into effect in our state. Why shouldn't there be a law to prevent people from wearing strong colognes or perfumes, especially in restaurants since the sense of smell is important to taste?

INDUCTIVE AND DEDUCTIVE ARGUMENTS

Two types of arguments—inductive and deductive—are common. An **inductive argument** reaches a general conclusion from observed specifics. For example, by observing the performance of a large number of athletes, you could conclude that athletes possess physical stamina. A **deductive argument**, on the other hand, begins with a general statement, known as a major premise, and moves toward a more specific statement, known as the minor premise. For example, from the major premise that "Athletes possess physical stamina," you can reason that because Anthony is an athlete (the minor premise), he must possess physical stamina.

Both types of arguments begin with statements that are assumed to be correct. Basically, both follow a general pattern of "If that is so, then this is so . . ." At times, an argument may be more complex, involving several steps—"If that is so, and this happens, then this should be done." You can visualize each type of argument as shown in Figure 6–1 on the next page.

EXERCISE 6–4 | *For each of the following inductive arguments, supply the missing pieces.*

1. Evidence: Prof. Hong wears jeans and flannel shirts to class.

   Evidence: Prof. Hutchinson wears khaki pants and running shoes when he lectures.

   Evidence: _____

   Conclusion: Professors on this campus dress casually for class.

Figure 6–1 Inductive and Deductive Arguments

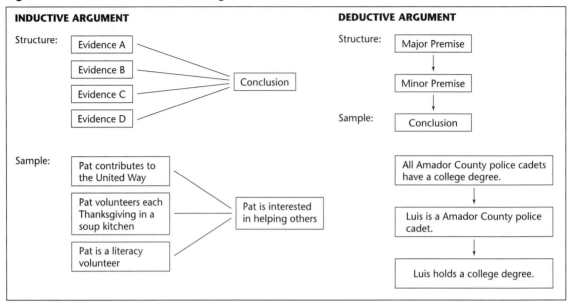

2. Evidence: Many people walk down the street talking on their cellular phones.

   Evidence: Most families own at least two cellular phones.

   Evidence: In restaurants and in shopping malls people can be observed using their cellular phones.

   Conclusion: _____

EXERCISE 6–5

For each of the following deductive arguments, supply the conclusion.

1. Major Premise: All students with yearly averages above 3.5 are offered a summer internship.

   Minor Premise: Jacqueline has a yearly average of 3.7.

   Conclusion: _____

2. Major Premise: Most elementary school children's absences from school are due to illness.

   Minor Premise: Quinne, a fifth grade student, was absent yesterday.

   Conclusion: _____

STRATEGIES FOR READING AN ARGUMENT

Arguments need to be read slowly and carefully. Count on reading an argument more than once. The first time you read it, try to get an overview of its three essential elements: issue, claim, and support. Then reread it more carefully to closely follow the author's line of reasoning and to identify and evaluate the evidence provided.

Think Before You Read

1. *What does the title suggest?* Before you read, preview the essay (see p. 16) and ask yourself what the title suggests about the issue and claim or support. The title of the *USA Today* argument on baseball players' use of steroids, for example, suggests the author's position on the issue.

EXERCISE 6–6   *For each of the following titles, predict the issue and claim the essay addresses.*

1. "A Former Smoker Cheers New Legislation"
2. "Overflowing, Overcrowded Jails: New Solutions"
3. "The Right to Die My Way"
4. "The Effects of Unchecked Immigration"
5. "Indecent Proposal: Internet Censorship"

2. *Who is the author, and what are his or her qualifications?* Check to see if you recognize the author, and if so, evaluate whether he or she is qualified to write about the issue. For example, an article written by professional golfer Tiger Woods would be an authoritative source on the issue of ethics in professional golf. If the same argument were written by a state senator or a medical doctor, it would have less credibility. The specific qualifications of the author have a bearing on the worth of the evidence provided.

3. *What is the date of publication?* Checking the date will prompt you to consider whether new, even possibly contradictory, evidence has recently developed.

4. *What do I already know about the issue?* Try brainstorming using a two-column list. Label one column "pro" and the other "con," and list as many ideas as you can in each. By thinking about the issue on your own, you are less likely to be swayed by the writer's appeals and more likely to think and evaluate the reasons and evidence objectively.

EXERCISE 6–7   *Preview but do not read the following argument. (For previewing guidelines, see p. 16.) Complete the activities that follow. Read the argument after you have finished the next section, "Read Actively."*

POOR ACCOUNTABILITY MARS NATIONAL GUARD'S REPUTATION

Our view: States resist tighter federal oversight; military readiness falters. For 365 years, the National Guard and its forebears have protected Americans in peacetime and in war, not only from enemies foreign and domestic, but also from natural disasters. At this moment, Guardsmen are risking their lives to keep the peace in

Bosnia and to keep watch over Iraq while thousands more play a vital role in projecting U.S. forces into landlocked Afghanistan.

But that popular image of the Guard masks deep and festering problems exposed this week by USA TODAY reporters Dave Moniz and Jim Drinkard. In state after state, the Guard is mismanaged and politicized to a point where its military reliability is questionable. It is in dire need of stronger federal oversight, which states, Congress and the Guard itself are loath to accept.

Among abuses documented by USA TODAY and often unpunished under deficient state-by-state Guard disciplinary codes:

- Rosters are padded with "phantom" soldiers. Within individual National Guard units, as many as 20% of soldiers reported on the rolls are no longer with the service, meaning that if Guard units were called up, they might not be fit for duty.

- Serious misconduct by top officials. Guard generals have committed serious offenses at twice the rate of regular Army and Air Force generals during the past five years. In recent years, serious allegations have been confirmed against nine states' top officers as well as the general who oversees the Guard. These range from drunkenness and sexual misconduct to filing false paperwork and misusing government planes.

- Ineffective discipline and oversight. Of nine states where the Guard's top officer was investigated, only one changed the selection process and one added new sexual-harassment regulations.

Worse, those findings may present only an outline of the troubles. The military would open Guard investigative files only in cases USA TODAY already knew about.

At the heart of the problem is the fact that the National Guard is made up of independent state fiefdoms without common rules of conduct and only weak oversight from the Pentagon. Governors and state congressional delegations fiercely protect the state Guards' independence and the $13 billion in federal appropriations that go with it.

When military investigators from outside the Guard determine that allegations of misconduct have merit, officers can only recommend action. State Guard officials and their political superiors are free to ignore their suggestions. And they do.

In one Illinois case, four military investigations left a colonel accused of serious misconduct including inappropriate sexual relationships largely unscathed. Only when the FBI stepped in and taped him offering a Jeep Cherokee to a witness was he sent to jail. Now the officer faces civil suits claiming he raped female Guard members.

The solution is simple to identify, though politically tricky to implement. The National Guard must be held to the same standards and the same judicial system as the rest of the military. Crimes from rape to the faked paperwork that inflates Guard numbers are taken far more seriously in the rest of the military, where the Uniform Code of Military Justice is rigorously enforced.

Unfortunately, neither the National Guard nor the governors who serve as its fierce protectors will back such changes. A time of national emergency could prick the conscience of Congress. Indeed, Congress has already asked for an investigation of the facts exposed by USA TODAY. But the threat of withholding federal dollars, which fund 95% of the Guard, could also persuade states.

True, the Guard has "non-military" duties such as responding to natural disasters and riots and is constitutionally required in most cases to report to state governors, not the president. More accountability need change none of that.

With U.S. troops risking their lives in the caves of Afghanistan and the military girding itself for the next stages of the war on terror, America needs all of her troops in fighting form. New accountability for the National Guard will ensure its readiness.

—USA Today (December 21, 2001), p. 13A

1. What does the title suggest about the issue, claim, or evidence?
2. What do you already know about the issue? Brainstorm a two-column "Pro-Con" list.

Read Actively

When reading arguments, it is especially important to read actively. For general suggestions on active reading, see Chapter 1. Use the following specific strategies for reading arguments:

1. *Read once for an initial impression.* Do not focus on specifics; instead, try to get a general feel for the argument.

2. *Read the argument several more times.* First identify the specific claim the writer is making and start to identify the reasons and evidence that support it. Read the argument again to examine whether the writer acknowledges or refutes opposing viewpoints.

3. *Annotate as you read.* Record your thoughts; note ideas you agree with, those you disagree with, questions that come to mind, additional reasons or evidence overlooked by the author, and the counterarguments not addressed by the author.

4. *Highlight key terms.* Often, an argument depends on how certain terms are defined. In an argument on the destruction of forests, for example, what does "destruction" mean? Does it mean building homes within a forest, or does it refer to clearing the land for timber or to create a housing subdivision? Highlight both the key terms and the definitions the author provides.

5. *Diagram or map to analyze structure.* Because many arguments are complex, you may find it helpful to diagram or map them. By mapping the argument you may discover unsubstantiated ideas, reasons for which evidence is not provided, or an imbalance between reasons and emotional appeals. Use the format shown in Figure 6–2 on the next page to help you analyze an argument's structure. Figure 6–3 on page 155 shows you how the argument presented in "Poor Accountability Mars National Guard's Reputation" on pages 151–53 is mapped.

Figure 6–2   The Structure of an Argument

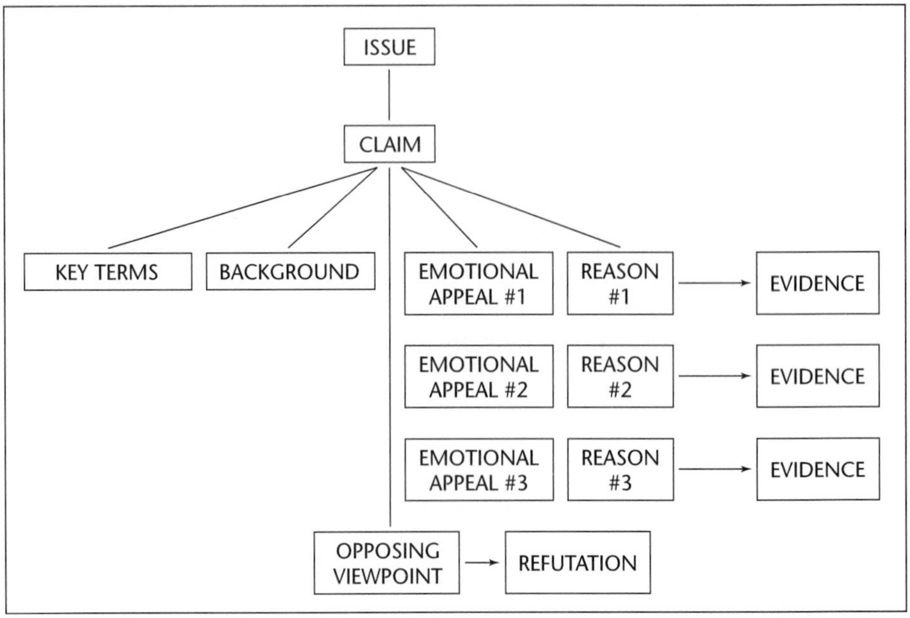

STRATEGIES FOR EVALUATING ARGUMENTS

Once you have understood the article by identifying what is asserted and how it is asserted, the next step is to evaluate the soundness, correctness, and worth of the argument. Specifically, you must evaluate evidence (both type and relevancy), definitions of terms, cause-effect relationships, value systems, and counterarguments, as well as recognize emotional appeals.

Types of Evidence

The validity of an inductive argument rests, in part, on the soundness and correctness of the evidence provided to draw the conclusion. The validity of a deductive argument, on the other hand, rests on the accuracy and correctness of the premises on which the argument is based. Evaluating each type of argument involves assessing the accuracy and correctness of statements on which the argument is based. Often, writers provide evidence to substantiate their observations or premises. As a critical reader, your task is to assess whether the evidence is sufficient to support the claim. Here are some suggestions for evaluating each type of evidence.

Personal Experience   Writers often substantiate their ideas through experience and observation. Although a writer's personal account of a situation may provide an interesting perspective on an issue, personal experience should not be

Figure 6–3   A Map of an Argument

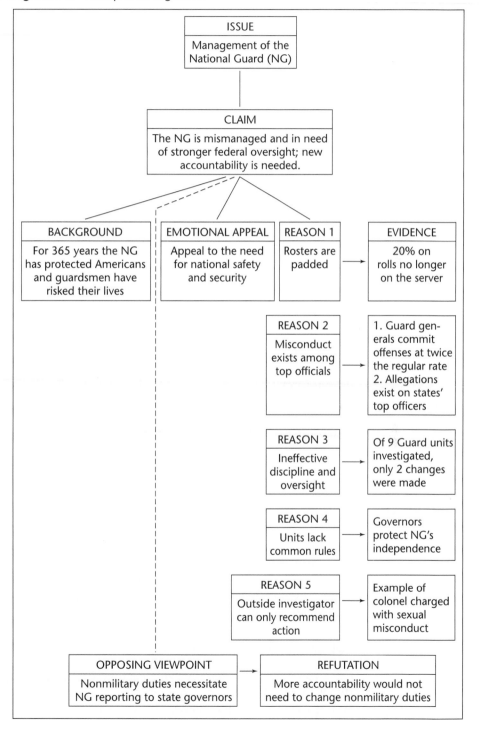

accepted as proof. The observer may be biased or may have exaggerated or incorrectly perceived a situation.

Examples   Examples are descriptions of particular situations that are used to illustrate or explain a principle, concept, or idea. To explain what aggressive behavior is, your psychology instructor may offer several examples: fighting, punching, and kicking. Examples should not be used by themselves to prove the concept or idea they illustrate, as is done in the following sample.

> The American judicial system treats those who are called for jury duty unfairly. It is clear from my sister's experience that the system has little regard for the needs of those called as jurors. My sister was required to report for jury duty the week she was on vacation. She spent the entire week in a crowded, stuffy room waiting to be called to sit on a jury and never was called.

The writer's sister's experience may be atypical, or not representative, of what most jurors experience.

Statistics   Many people are impressed by statistics—the reporting of figures, percentages, averages, and so forth—and assume they are irrefutable proof. Actually, statistics can be misused, misinterpreted, or used selectively to give other than the most objective, accurate picture of a situation. Suppose you read that magazine X has increased its readership by 50 percent while magazine Y made only a 10 percent increase. From this statistic, some readers might assume that magazine X has a wider readership than Y. However, if provided with complete information, you can see that this is not true. The missing, but crucial, statistic is the total readership of each magazine before the increase. If magazine X distributed 20,000 copies, and increased its circulation by 50 percent, its readership would total 30,000. However, if magazine Y's circulation was already 50,000, a 10 percent increase (bringing the new total to 55,000) would still give it the larger readership despite the fact that it made the smaller increase. Approach statistical evidence with a critical, questioning attitude.

Comparisons and Analogies   Comparisons or analogies (extended comparisons) serve as illustrations and are often used in argument. Their reliability depends on how closely the comparison corresponds or how similar it is to the situation to which it is being compared. For example, Martin Luther King Jr., in his famous letter from the Birmingham jail, compared nonviolent protesters to a robbed man. To evaluate this comparison, you would need to consider how the two are similar and how they are different.

Relevancy and Sufficiency of Evidence

Once you have identified the evidence used to support an argument, the next step is to decide whether there is enough of the right kind of evidence to lead you to accept the writer's claim. This is always a matter of judgment; there are no easy rules to follow. You must determine whether the evidence provided directly supports the claim and whether sufficient evidence has been provided.

Suppose you are reading an article in your campus newspaper that states Freshman Composition should not be required of all students at your college. As evidence, the writer includes the following.

> Composition does not prepare us for the job market. Besides, the reading assignments have no relevancy to modern times.

This reason provides neither adequate nor sufficient evidence. The writer does nothing to substantiate his statements of irrelevancy of the course to the job market or modern times. For the argument to be regarded seriously, the writer would need to provide facts, statistics, expert opinion, or other forms of documentation.

EXERCISE 6–8

Reread the argument "Poor Accountability Mars National Guard's Reputation" on page 151, paying particular attention to the type(s) of evidence used. Then answer the questions that follow.

1. What type(s) of evidence is/are used?
2. Is the evidence convincing?
3. Is there sufficient evidence?
4. What other types of evidence could have been used to strengthen the argument?

Definition of Terms

A clear and effective argument carefully defines key terms and uses them consistently. For example, an essay arguing for or against animal rights should state what is meant by the term, describe or define those rights, and use that definition through the entire argument.

The following two paragraphs are taken from two different argumentative essays on pornography. Notice how in the first paragraph the author carefully defines what he means by pornography before proceeding with his argument, whereas in the second the term is not clearly defined.

Paragraph 1—Careful Definition

There is unquestionably more pornography available today than 15 years ago. However, is it legitimate to assume that more is worse? Pornography is speech, words, and pictures about sexuality. No one would consider an increase in the level of speech about religion or politics to be a completely negative development. What makes speech about sexuality different?

—Lynn, "Pornography's Many Forms: Not All Bad," *Los Angeles Times*

Paragraph 2—Vague Definition

If we are not talking about writing laws, defining pornography doesn't pose as serious a problem. We do have different tastes. Maybe some of mine come from my middle-class background (my mother wouldn't think so!). I don't like bodies presented without heads, particularly female bodies. The motive may sometimes be the protection of the individual, but the impression is decapitation, and I also happen to be someone who is attracted to people's faces. This is a matter of taste.

—Rule, "Pornography Is a Social Disease," *The Body Politic*

Cause-Effect Relationships

Arguments are often built around the assumption of a cause-effect relationship. For example, an argument supporting gun control legislation may claim that ready availability of guns contributes to an increased number of shootings. This argument implies that availability of guns causes increased use. If the writer provides no evidence that this cause-effect relationship exists, you should question the accuracy of the statement.

Implied or Stated Value System

An argument often implies or rests on a value system (a structure of what the writer feels is right, wrong, worthwhile, and important). However, everyone possesses a personal value system, and although our culture promotes many major points of agreement (murder is wrong, human life is worthwhile, and so forth), it also allows points of departure. One person may think telling lies is always wrong; another person may say it depends on the circumstances. Some people have a value system based on religious beliefs; others may not share those beliefs.

In evaluating an argument, look for value judgments and then decide whether the judgments are consistent with and acceptable to your personal value system. Here are a few examples of value judgment statements.

Abortion is wrong.

Financial aid for college should be available to everyone regardless of income.

Capital punishment violates human rights.

Recognizing and Refuting Opposing Viewpoints

Many arguments recognize opposing viewpoints. For example, the author of "Poor Accountability Mars National Guard's Reputation" recognizes that state governors and state congressional delegations want to keep the National Guard under their control to preserve the Guard's independence and receive the federal appropriations to operate it. The author also states the Guard has nonmilitary responsibilities that require it to report to state governors instead of federal officials.

Many arguments also attempt to refute opposing viewpoints (explain why they are wrong, flawed, or unacceptable). Basically, the author finds weaknesses in the opponent's argument. One way to do this is to question the accuracy, relevancy, or sufficiency of the opponent's evidence. Another way is to disagree with the opponent's reasons. The author of the argument on the National Guard refutes the argument that the Guard must remain under state control because it has nonmilitary duties by stating that more accountability would not need to change that relationship.

When reading arguments that address opposing viewpoints, ask yourself the following questions.

- Does the author address opposing viewpoints clearly and fairly?
- Does the author refute the opposing viewpoint with logic and relevant evidence?

Unfair Emotional Appeals

Emotional appeals attempt to involve or excite readers by appealing to their emotions, thereby controlling the reader's attitude toward the subject. Several types of emotional appeals are described below.

1. *Emotionally charged or biased language.* By using words that create an emotional response, writers establish positive or negative feelings. For example, an advertisement for a new line of fragrances promises to "indulge," "refresh," "nourish," and "pamper" the user. An ad for an automobile uses phrases such as "limousine comfort," "European styling," and "animal sleekness" to interest and excite readers.

2. *False authority.* False authority involves using the opinion or action of a well-known or famous person. We have all seen athletes endorsing underwear or movie stars selling shampoo. This type of appeal works on the notion that people admire celebrities and strive to be like them, respect their opinion, and are willing to accept their viewpoint.

3. *Association.* An emotional appeal also is made by associating a product, idea, or position with others that are already accepted or highly regarded. Patriotism is valued, so to call a product All-American in an advertisement is an appeal to the emotions. A car being named a Cougar to remind you of a fast, sleek animal, a cigarette ad picturing a scenic waterfall, or a speaker standing in front of an American flag are other examples.

4. *Appeal to "common folk."* Some people distrust those who are well educated, wealthy, highly artistic, or in other ways distinctly different from the average person. An emotional appeal to this group is made by selling a product or idea by indicating that it is originated from, held by, or bought by ordinary citizens. A commercial may advertise a product by showing its use in an average household. A politician may describe her background and education to suggest that she is like everyone else; a salesperson may dress in styles similar to his clients.

5. *Ad hominem.* An argument that attacks the holder of an opposing viewpoint, rather than his or her viewpoint, is known as ad hominem, or an attack on the man. For example, the statement, "How could a woman who does not even hold a college degree criticize a judicial decision?" attacks the woman's level of education, not her viewpoint.

6. *"Join the crowd" appeal.* The appeal to do, believe, or buy what everyone else is doing, believing, or buying is known as crowd appeal or the bandwagon effect. Commercials that proclaim their product as the "#1 best-selling car in America" are appealing to this motive. Essays that cite opinion polls on a controversial issue in support of a position—"68% of Americans favor capital punishment"—are also using this appeal.

ERRORS IN LOGICAL REASONING

Errors in reasoning, often called logical fallacies, are common in arguments. These errors invalidate the argument or render it flawed. Several common errors in logic are described next.

Circular Reasoning

Also known as begging the question, this error involves using part of the conclusion as evidence to support it. Here are two examples.

> Cruel medical experimentation on defenseless animals is inhumane.

> Female police officers should not be sent to crime scenes because apprehending criminals is a man's job.

In circular reasoning, because no evidence is given to support the claim, there is no reason to accept the conclusion.

Hasty Generalization

This fallacy means that the conclusion has been derived from insufficient evidence. Here is one example: you taste three tangerines and each is sour, so you conclude that all tangerines are sour. Here is another: by observing one performance of a musical group, you conclude the group is unfit to perform.

Non Sequitur ("It Does Not Follow")

The false establishment of cause-effect is known as a non sequitur. To say, for example, that "Because my doctor is young, I'm sure she'll be a good doctor" is a non sequitur because youth does not cause good medical practice. Here is another example: "Arturio Alvarez is the best choice for state senator because he is an ordinary citizen." Being an ordinary citizen will not necessarily make someone an effective state senator.

False Cause

The false cause fallacy is the incorrect assumption that two events that follow each other in time are causally related. Suppose you opened an umbrella and then tripped on an uneven sidewalk. If you said you tripped because you opened the umbrella, you would be assuming false cause.

Either-Or Fallacy

This fallacy assumes that an issue is only two sided, or that there are only two choices or alternatives for a particular situation. In other words, there is no middle ground. Consider the issue of censorship of violence on television. An either-or fallacy is to assume that violence on TV must be either allowed or banned. This fallacy does not recognize other alternatives such as limiting access through viewing hours, restricting certain types of violence, and so forth.

EXERCISE 6–9   *Identify the logical fallacy in each of the following statements.*

1. All African-American students in my biology class earned A grades, so African-Americans must excel in life sciences.
2. If you are not for nuclear arms control, then you're against protecting our future.
3. My sister cannot do mathematical computations or balance her check-book because she has math anxiety.
4. A well-known mayor, noting a decline in the crime rate in the four largest cities in his state, quickly announced that his new "get-tough on crimi-nals" publicity campaign was successful and took credit for the decline.
5. I always order a fruit pastry for dessert because I am allergic to chocolate.

EXERCISE 6–10   *Read the following pair of arguments that appeared in* USA Today, *and answer the questions that follow.*

Argument 1

REGULATING CLONING: RESEARCHERS HIDE LAB, THWARTING REGULATORS. TIME FOR A BAN?

Within the next week, a Canadian company will use the DNA of a dead infant to clone the world's first human being at an undisclosed U.S. location, says the company's scientific director. Fortunately, independent scientists are skeptical that Brigitte Boisselier's team at CLONAID will succeed. Even the cloning of less-complex mammals is successful in fewer than one in 25 tries. But the fact that Boisselier and other scientists say they are proceeding with human-cloning experiments is a disturbing sign of how quickly science is outpacing ethics and law.

News of human-cloning experiments has touched off a scramble among law-makers anxious to prevent the gruesome deaths of deformed newborns, and harm to surrogate mothers. They have good cause to worry.

To date, the few animal clones that didn't die before or shortly after birth mostly suffered birth defects ranging from incomplete immune systems to unexplained explosions in weight. Scientists who have conducted animal cloning testified before a congressional subcommittee last week that attempts to clone humans could result in hundreds of failures before a healthy child is born.

First there would be miscarriages and pregnancy problems that could put surrogate mothers' lives at risk. If babies were born, most would die within days. Any survivors would be time bombs, because even the most knowledgeable scientists don't know what would happen years from now.

Until those facts change, cloning an entire individual would be a reckless disregard of human life. The difficulty comes in calibrating a ban on human cloning that won't outlaw or discourage promising lines of research involving the cloning of human cells.

If successful, for example, human-tissue cloning could rebuild new organs to replace diseased ones or provide perfectly matched cell implants to arrest such degenerative diseases as arthritis and Alzheimer's.

Responsibility for striking a balance falls to the U.S. Food and Drug Administration. It says CLONAID's plan requires approval and that it is investigating. But the FDA's authority is legally untested, and the company just thumbs its nose at the agency, flaunting the secrecy of its U.S. location. Clearly, the deterrence to cloning is not high enough.

The FDA could address this by taking a more aggressive and public stance. On rare occasions, it has filed criminal charges against those who willfully violated regulations, and that seems a sensible step in this case. So does enlisting Canada's help.

But the FDA is not geared to police work or fast action. It reviews experimentation slowly and cautiously.

A longer-term solution is to ban by law any implantation of a cloned fetus into a surrogate mother, an approach the House Energy and Commerce Committee is considering. That limited approach poses the least risk of undermining useful research, though it still might be vulnerable to mischief from abortion opponents seeking legal leverage to assert a form of fetal rights.

As science advances and the debate over cloning matures, the ban could and should be revisited periodically.

While Americans are deeply divided over many moral issues surrounding reproduction, one thing is clear: Cloning humans before there's reason to believe the practice is safe is unnecessary and just plain wrong.

—Regulating Cloning: Researchers Hide Lab, Thwarting Regulators.
Time for a Ban? *USA Today* (April 5, 2001), p. 10A

Argument 2

REGULATING CLONING: HUMAN CLONING REPRESENTS OPPORTUNITY; NO COMPARISON WITH CATTLE. THINK OF PARENTS' WISHES

How could a baby, not even born yet, have created so much fear around the world and in this country in the past four years?

Since the day the announcement of his potential birth was made, all of the possible unfavorable outcomes have been predicted, ignoring the wishes and the commitment of the parents who desire a baby through this method. There are infertile couples, homosexual couples and parents who have lost a child, and they all know that the baby will be the belated twin of one of them or of a dead child–nothing less, nothing more. They are calling us by the thousands, and we will do it, whether it is done in the USA or elsewhere.

For the past four years, cloning-success rates have greatly increased (as could be expected of a new technology), reaching such levels as 15%–20% for cattle. That example compares well with human in-vitro-fertilization success rates of 30%–40%. The reported defects have been different depending on the species studied. For instance, the problems of large offspring observed in cattle cloning have also been observed in calves resulting from in-vitro fertilization. These defects have never been observed in humans born through the same method, which means that these defects are specific to cattle, not to cloning.

Those who are familiar with human-assisted reproductive technologies know that our knowledge of human reproduction is far more advanced than that of other mammals. We could work 10 years on cattle and learn nothing relevant to humans.

CLONAID scientists are well trained and have been perfecting egg enucleation and heteronuclear transfer, which makes us very confident about the outcome.

The cycle of acceptation for new technologies and theories starts with high disgust, followed by mild critics and ending with those saying, "I always knew it was a good thing." Centuries ago, people were burned at the stake for holding unpopular views; today we do not risk our lives but our reputation. Isn't this worth it?

The more I read the letters of the parents, the stronger I am in conducting this research, and I will fight as much as it is humanely possible so that the freedom of scientific inquiry and the freedom to make a personal reproduction choice are fully respected.

I believe that one day we will reach eternal life through this technique, so I am also fighting for the right of the future reborns, or should we say the resurrected.

—Boisselier, Regulating Cloning: Human Cloning Represents Opportunity;
No Comparison with Cattle. Think of Parents' Wishes,
USA Today (April 5, 2001), p. 10A

For each argument:

1. Identify the claim.
2. Outline the primary reasons used to support the claim.
3. What types of evidence are used?
4. Evaluate the adequacy and sufficiency of the evidence.
5. What emotional appeals are used?
6. Does the author recognize or refute counterarguments?

Compare the arguments:

1. Compare the types of evidence used.
2. Which argument did you find more convincing? Why?
3. What further information would be useful in assessing the issue?

SUMMARY

An argument presents logical reasons and evidence in support of a particular viewpoint.

An argument has three essential parts:

- the issue—a problem or controversy about which people disagree
- the claim—the position the writer takes on the issue
- support—the reasons and evidence that suggest the claim is reasonable and should be accepted

Some arguments include a refutation that considers opposing viewpoints and may attempt to disprove or discredit them.

There are three types of claims:

- A claim of fact is a statement than can be verified through observation or research.
- A claim of value states that one thing or idea is better or more desirable than another.
- A claim of policy suggests what should or ought to be done to solve a problem.

There are three common types of support: reasons, evidence, and emotional appeals.

Two types of arguments are inductive and deductive:

- Inductive arguments reach a general conclusion from observed specifics.
- Deductive arguments begin with a general statement (major premise), move toward a more specific statement (minor premise), then reach a conclusion.

The chapter presents strategies for reading and evaluating arguments.

Six types of emotional appeals are emotionally charged language, false authority, association, appeal to "common folk," ad hominem, and "join the crowd" appeal.

Errors in logical reasoning include circular reasoning, hasty generalization, non sequitur, false cause, and either-or fallacy.

INTEGRATING
IDEAS

◆

PAIRED
READINGS

Environmental Studies

PREREADING QUESTIONS

1. What is the ANWR?
2. How might the ANWR be harmed by oil drilling?

Arctic Oil: Black Gold or Fool's Gold?

Paula Abend

1   As George W. Bush's administration prepares to govern, one wildlife issue is sure to spark intense debate: opening up the coastal plain of the Arctic National Wildlife Refuge (ANWR) to oil drilling and development.

2   First set aside by President Eisenhower 40 years ago, this unbroken landscape of arctic and subarctic habitat is home to such a wealth of wildlife that it has been dubbed "America's Serengeti." Polar and grizzly bear, caribou, musk ox, Dall sheep, wolf, arctic fox, and more than 100 species of migratory birds use the land. Twenty-one species of marine mammals live in the waters off the refuge.

3   But in 1980, when the Alaska National Interest Lands Conservation Act passed and formally established the refuge, oil interests and environmentalists were already battling over the land. Unable to resolve the debate, Congress exempted the 1.5-million-acre coastal plain from the wilderness protection afforded the rest of the original refuge.

4   Yet the U.S. Fish and Wildlife Service calls the coastal plain the "biological heart" of the refuge, a critical area of wildlife activity. The migratory, 130,000-member Porcupine caribou herd depends on the coastal plain to calve and raise its young. It is also an important onshore denning area for polar bears.

5   Oil-drilling proponents claim that disruptions to wildlife would be minimal. But a group of 250 scientists recently joined forces to warn that the risks to wildlife are substantial. Studies of caribou living near Alaska's Prudhoe Bay oil fields show decreased birth rates, altered migration patterns, and poorer overall condition. Polar-bear mothers have been known to abandon dens when disturbed, an event that may prove fatal to cubs. Huge water reservoirs that will be dug along rivers will permanently scar habitat vital to musk ox and other wildlife. And the roads, pipelines, power plants, airports, living quarters, and other supporting infrastructure would industrialize a priceless wilderness. Despite claims of better technology, there are currently between 500 and 1,000 oil spills a year in Prudhoe Bay.

6   The oil industry already has access to about 95 percent of Alaska's North Slope. Is access to ANWR's coastal plain really needed? No one knows for sure how much oil is at stake, but the most often used estimate equals a 200-day supply for the

United States—an amount, say environmentalists, that could easily be saved by increasing the gas mileage of cars. And according to the Tellus Institute, a nonprofit research and consulting firm, a national energy efficiency program would create about 10 times the number of jobs that could be expected from oil development in the ANWR.

7   With the executive branch firmly behind oil drilling, it will be up to Congress to protect the ANWR's coastal plain, so let your representative and senators know how you feel.

—Abend, "Arctic Oil: Black Gold of Fool's Gold?"
Animals (winter 2001), p. 4

VOCABULARY REVIEW

1. For each of the words listed below, use context; prefixes, roots, and suffixes; and/or a dictionary to write a brief definition or synonym of the word as it is used in the reading.

   a. administration (para. 1) _____

   b. conservation (para. 3) _____

   c. resolve (para. 3) _____

   d. exempted (para. 3) _____

   e. migratory (para. 4) _____

   f. calve (para. 4) _____

   g. denning (para. 4) _____

   h. infrastructure (para. 5) _____

2. Underline new specialized terms introduced in the reading.

COMPREHENSION QUESTIONS

1. What is the author's claim?
2. How did some of the animals respond to development near the Prudhoe Bay oil fields?
3. Why did Congress exempt the coastal plain from protection?
4. Name two likely risks to wildlife if drilling commences.
5. According to the author, how can the United States increase oil supplies and create jobs without opening the ANWR to development?
6. What does the author urge her readers to do?

THINKING CRITICALLY

1. What is the author's purpose in writing this article?
2. What issue is at the core of her argument?

3. How relevant are the details she provides? Is there important information that she has not included?
4. How effective is her use of statistics?
5. What assumptions does she make?

LEARNING/STUDY STRATEGY

Using the model shown in Figure 6–2, diagram the structure of the argument.

Environmental Studies

PREREADING QUESTIONS

1. How could drilling in the ANWR benefit the United States?
2. What is the climate of the coastal plain? What plants and animals live there?

ANWR Oil: An Alternative to War Over Oil

Walter J. Hickel

1   The Senate Democrats have stubbornly refused to allow any oil exploration along the rim of the Arctic National Wildlife Refuge (ANWR) in Alaska. Despite this latest vote, however, the issue is not going to go away. Given our continuing precarious dependence on overseas oil suppliers ranging from Saddam Hussein to the Saudis to Venezuela's Castro-clone Hugo Chavez, sensible Americans will continue to press Congress in the months and years ahead to unlock America's great Arctic energy storehouse.

2   I'm an Alaskan who believes the coastal plain of ANWR should be opened for intelligent exploration of its energy potential. ANWR is owned by all Americans. The very small portion of the refuge with oil potential can be explored and drilled without damaging the environment. At a time when America is dependent for vital energy supplies on overseas oil-producing countries, some of which are allied with terrorist groups, it makes no sense for us to ignore a region within our own borders that could supply up to a third of a trillion dollars worth of domestic energy— enough to replace completely all imports from Saudi Arabia or Iraq for a generation. There are already 171 million acres of land in Alaska fenced off for conservation and wilderness preservation. That's an area larger than the state of Texas.

3   ANWR's coastal plain, the only part of the refuge where oil is suspected to exist, is a flat and featureless wasteland that experiences some of the harshest weather conditions in the world. Temperatures drop to nearly −700°F. There are no forests or trees. At all.

4   For ten months a year, the plain is covered with snow and ice and is devoid of most living things. Then, for a few weeks, a carpet of lichen and tundra emerges from beneath the snow. During that brief period, the migratory Porcupine caribou herd (named for the Porcupine River), one of Alaska's 20 caribou herds, may graze and calve on the plain. The animals seek breezes from the Beaufort Sea to help them cope with the blizzard of mosquitoes that hatch with the spring.

5   In 2001, the Porcupine herd didn't calve on the coastal plain. It gave birth to its young many miles to the east, across the Canadian border. It calved in Canada the previous year as well. There is nothing magical about the area.

6   It's unlikely that exploration and drilling on the coastal plain will harm the caribou. Most biologists expect the animals will react to the presence of human activity the same way the Central Arctic herd adjusted to oil development at Prudhoe Bay (the region to the immediate west of ANWR's coastal plain). That herd has not only survived, but flourished. In 1977, as the Prudhoe region started delivering oil to America's southern 48 states, the Central Arctic caribou herd numbered 6,000; it has since grown to 27,128.

7   It is important to note that in the Arctic, oil drilling is restricted to the wintertime. And from early fall to early May, the Porcupine herd is not on the coastal plain at all. It roams south to the Porcupine Mountains and east into Canada.

8   ANWR covers an enormous area nearly as much as New Hampshire, Vermont, Massachusetts, and Connecticut combined. The most beautiful sections of ANWR—8 million acres—are federally mandated wilderness areas where the only tolerated human activity is hiking, backpacking, camping, and rafting. No motorized vehicles are permitted, and no development of any kind is allowed. This wilderness heart of ANWR includes the mountains of the Brooks Range. Journalists often use images of these mountains when describing the coastal plain region and its rich energy supplies, but the Brooks Range will not be touched by development.

9   When it set up ANWR, Congress recognized that the 1.5 million acre coastal plain possesses unique potential for large oil and gas reserves. It was stipulated that these resources could be developed at any time if Congress so voted. As a result, scientists have studied this area for more than 20 years, and their work has produced estimates of recoverable oil ranging up to 16 billion barrels. Most of these scientists recommend that exploration be allowed.

10   To compare how much petroleum may lie beneath ANWR, consider that the entire rest of the U.S. contains 21 billion barrels of recoverable oil. The monetary value of ANWR's pumpable oil is projected by the U.S. Energy Information Agency to be between $125 billion and $350 billion. This doesn't even count the region's vast natural gas potential.

11   How much would an oil reservoir that size, just a few miles from the already-built-and-paid-for trans-Alaska pipeline, mean to America and our energy future? The government estimates the coastal plain could produce 600,000 to 1,900,000 barrels of oil per day. This new source of Alaskan oil could more than supplant all of our annual oil imports from Saudi Arabia or Iraq and ensure that the trans-Alaska oil pipeline would continue to deliver domestically produced energy to American consumers for decades to come.

12   I have visited many oil-producing regions throughout the world. The production techniques are often primitive and risky, both for the workers and the environment. The technology used in Alaska's Arctic to find and develop oil is the best in the world. When and if development takes place on the ANWR coastal plain, there will be little traceable disturbance. Seismic tests to locate the oil, and the actual drilling after that, will take place in the winter, using ice roads that will melt later. Small gravel drilling pads, only six acres in size, will be used to tap vast fields and will be removed when drilling is complete. Alaska's "North Slope" oil workers take pride in challenging visitors to find any trace of winter work activities after the snow melts.

13   If oil is discovered in ANWR, the size of the surface area disturbed will be dramatically less than when Prudhoe Bay was developed 30 years ago. Experts estimate that less than 2,000 acres will be touched—out of the 1.5 million acres on the coastal plain, and the 19 million acres in ANWR as a whole.

14   The opposition to opening ANWR "isn't really economic, humanitarian, or even environmental. It is spiritual," wrote a *New York Daily News* columnist. "If all the oil in the refuge could be neatly sucked up with a single straw, the naturalists would still oppose it because [to them] human activity in a pristine wilderness is, in itself, an act of desecration."

15   That is an extreme philosophical position. America's access to energy is a serious national security issue. Overdependence on foreign oil exposes us to energy blackmail and compromises our ability to protect our citizens and assist our friends in times of crisis. Our goal as Americans must be to produce as much energy as we can for ourselves. This need not undermine efforts to conserve energy nor undercut the push to discover alternate energy sources. We must extend the energy sources that are practical today, even as we pursue possible alternatives for the future.

16   Rather than shutting down the Alaska pipeline and our other Arctic oil infrastructure we should be linking them to the vast untapped resources that await us on ANWR's coastal plain. That will not only make America safer and stronger economically; it will provide the rest of the world with an environmentally responsible model of how to produce energy the right way.

17   It makes no sense to ignore a region within our own borders that could supply up to a third of a trillion dollars worth of domestic energy—enough to replace completely all annual imports from Saudi Arabia. Oil development would touch less than 2,000 acres in ANWR. Meanwhile, 171 million acres of land in Alaska are already fenced off for conservation and wilderness preservation

—Hickel, "ANWR Oil: An Alternative to War Over Oil,"
The American Enterprise (June 2002)

VOCABULARY REVIEW

1. For each of the words listed below, use context; prefixes, roots, and suffixes; and/or a dictionary to write a brief definition or synonym of the word as it is used in the reading.

   a. precarious (para. 1) _____

   b. Castro-clone (para. 1) _____

   c. devoid (para. 4) _____

   d. lichen (para. 4) _____

   e. tundra (para. 4) _____

   f. mandated (para. 8) _____

   g. stipulated (para. 9) _____

   h. supplant (para. 11) _____

    i. pristine (para. 14) _____

    j. desecration (para. 14) _____

2. Underline new specialized terms introduced in the reading.

COMPREHENSION QUESTIONS

1. What claims does the author make?
2. What are the reasons in support of the claim?
3. How have the animals of Prudhoe Bay adapted to development by humans?
4. What technology will be used to minimize the environmental impact?
5. What benefits will drilling have for the United States? For the world?
6. How much land is set aside for conservation in Alaska? How much of that is in the ANWR? How big is the coastal plain? How much land would be needed for oil drilling?

THINKING CRITICALLY

1. What personal details does the author provide? Why does he do this? How effective is this technique?
2. In what way does the author use emotional appeal?
3. Does the author refute any opposing viewpoints? If so, which one(s)?
4. How does the author use repetition in the article? How does this contribute to the argument?
5. How appropriate is the article's title? What other titles might be used?

LEARNING/STUDY STRATEGY

Using the model shown in Figure 6–2, diagram the structure of the argument.

THINKING ABOUT THE PAIRED READINGS

INTEGRATING IDEAS

1. How do the arguments differ in their purposes?
2. Each article describes the wildlife differently. Explain these differences.
3. Which reading did you find more convincing? Why?
4. What further information would you like in order to take a position on this issue?

GENERATING NEW IDEAS

1. Write a paper on the Arctic drilling issue using one or both of the readings to support your viewpoint.
2. Write a letter to your congressional representative or senator urging him or her to either support or reject opening up the coastal plain to oil drilling.

Multimedia Activities

1. **Identifying the Argument of the Essay**
   http://commhum.mccneb.edu/argument/summary.htm
   Try this online tutorial in critical reasoning from Metropolitan Community College in Nebraska. Make notes about the new concepts you learn.

2. **Logic in Argumentative Writing**
   http://owl.english.purdue.edu/handouts/general/gl_argpers.html
   Review the common terms and concepts used in reasoning, and try the online exercises at this site from Purdue University. Use some of these ideas to analyze the conversations you have with your friends or discussions you hear on TV or the radio. Apply them to editorials in the newspaper or political speeches.

Take a Road Trip to the
American Southwest!

If your instructor has asked you to use the Reading Road Trip CD-ROM or Website, be sure to visit the Critical Thinking module for multimedia tutorials, exercises, and tests.

CHAPTER 7

PATTERNS OF ACADEMIC THOUGHT

LEARNING OBJECTIVES

✦ To recognize common academic thought patterns
✦ To use thought patterns to focus your reading

This term, you probably are taking courses in several different disciplines. You may study psychology, anatomy and physiology, mathematics, and English composition all in one semester. During one day, you may read a poem, solve math problems, and study early developments in psychology. These diverse tasks seem difficult to master because you treat each course differently from every other. Consequently, you are forced to shift gears for each course, developing new approaches and strategies.

What few students realize is that a biologist and a psychologist, for example, think about and approach their subject matter in similar ways. Both carefully define terms, examine causes and effects, study similarities and differences, describe sequences of events, classify information, solve problems, and enumerate characteristics. The subject matter and language they use differ, but their approaches to the material are basically the same. Regardless of their field of expertise, researchers, textbook authors, and your professors use standard approaches, or patterns of thought, to organize and express their ideas. The more familiar you become with these patterns, the easier your reading assignments will be.

PATTERNS: A FOCUS FOR READING

Let's begin by trying a few learning experiments.

Experiment 1. Supply the missing numbers in the following numeric sequence.

1, 5, 7, 8, 12, 14, 15, _____, _____, _____

Experiment 2. Study each of the following drawings briefly, and then continue reading.

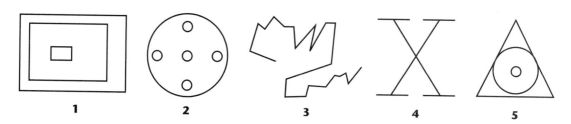

Next, close the book and quickly sketch each of the drawings you studied.

Now let's analyze your performance. In the first experiment, the last three digits are 19, 21, and 22. If you were correct, you realized the numbers increased successively by 4, by 2, and by 1, and then the pattern repeated. Now supply the next three numbers. Did you get 26, 28, and 29? It is an easy task now that you know the pattern. Reconstructing the entire sequence from memory also is a simple task now that you know the pattern.

For the second experiment, you probably sketched some or all of drawings 1, 2, 4, and 5 correctly. But did you get drawing 3 correct? Probably not. Why? Drawing 3 is irregular and has no pattern.

From these experiments, you can see that patterns make certain tasks easier to complete and that they facilitate your memory and recall. Patterns exist for ideas as well; we will refer to them as **thought patterns.**

Familiarity with these basic thought patterns will enable you to approach all of your courses more effectively. You will find textbook chapters easier to read if you can identify the thought pattern(s) by which they are organized. The same patterns also are used by your professors as they lecture. Lectures will be easier to follow and your notes will be better organized if you can identify these patterns.

Commonly used academic thought patterns include

definition

classification

order or sequence

cause and effect

comparison and contrast

listing/enumeration

These patterns can work for you in several ways.

1. *Patterns provide a focus for reading by enabling you to anticipate the author's thought development.* For example, from a heading or topic sentence alone, you often can predict the thought pattern that the section or paragraph will follow. When you encounter "Types of Government Spending," you might expect to read about how government spending is divided or classi-

fied. Or suppose you read the following topic sentence: "Vaporization, or evaporation as it is also called, is the change from a liquid to a gas." Here, you would anticipate vaporization to be further defined in the paragraph. If your professor announced, "Today we'll consider the impact of stress upon health," then you could expect the speaker to use a cause-and-effect pattern of development.

2. *Patterns help you remember and recall what you read.* Information that is grouped, chunked, or organized is easier to store than single, unrelated bits of information. Also, the manner in which information is stored in memory influences the ease with which it is retrieved. Thought patterns provide a vehicle for organizing information, and they function as retrieval clues for subsequent recall.

3. *Patterns are useful in your own writing;* they help you organize and express your ideas in a more coherent, comprehensible form. As you write essay exam answers, class assignments, or term papers, thought patterns will provide a base or structure around which you can effectively develop ideas.

The following section describes each thought pattern listed above. In subsequent chapters, you will see how these patterns are used in specific academic disciplines.

ACADEMIC THOUGHT PATTERNS

Definition

Each academic discipline has its own specialized vocabulary (see Chapter 3). One of the primary purposes of introductory textbooks is to introduce students to this new language. Consequently, definition is a commonly used pattern throughout most introductory-level texts.

Suppose you were asked to define the word *comedian* for someone unfamiliar with the term. First, you would probably say that a comedian is a person who entertains. Then you might distinguish a comedian from other types of entertainers by saying that a comedian is an entertainer who tells jokes and makes others laugh. Finally, you might mention, by way of example, the names of several well-known comedians who have appeared on television. Although you may have presented it informally, your definition would have followed the standard, classic pattern. The first part of your definition tells what general class or group the term belongs to (entertainers). The second part tells what distinguishes the term from other items in the same class or category. The third part includes further explanation, characteristics, examples, or applications.

Here are two additional examples.

Term	General Class	Distinguishing Characteristics
Stress	Physiological reaction	A response to a perceived threat
Mutant	Organism	Carries a gene that has undergone a change

See how the term *genetics* is defined in the following paragraph, and notice how the term and the general class are presented in the first sentence. The remainder of the paragraph presents the distinguishing characteristics.

> Genetics is the scientific study of heredity, the transmission of characteristics from parents to offspring. Genetics explains why offspring resemble their parents and also why they are not identical to them. Genetics is a subject that has considerable economic, medical, and social significance and is partly the basis for the modern theory of evolution. Because of its importance, genetics has been a topic of central interest in the study of life for centuries. Modern concepts in genetics are fundamentally different, however, from earlier ones.
>
> —Mix et al., *Biology: The Network of Life,* p. 262

Writers often provide clues that signal the thought pattern being used. These signals may occur within single sentences or as transitions or connections between sentences. (Transitional words that occur in phrases are italicized here to help you spot them.) Examples of transitional words or phrases used for the definition pattern are shown below.

TRANSITIONAL WORDS
genetics *is* . . .
bureaucracy *means* . . .
patronage *refers to* . . .
aggression *can be defined as* . . .
deficit is *another term* that . . .
balance of power *also means* . . .

EXERCISE 7–1   *Read the following paragraphs and answer the questions that follow.*

A. The French satirist and social reformer Voltaire (1694–1778) once defined the family as a "group of people who cannot stand the sight of each other but are forced to live under the same roof." The American poet Robert Frost (1875–1963) in his narrative poem *Death of the Hired Man* has one character observe, "Home is the place where, when you have to go there, They have to take you in." Whether home and family prove burdensome depends upon one's maturity level, emotional stability, and willingness to work on the difficulties which arise from close relationships. Most would agree, however, that there are few households which glide serenely along on a perpetually even keel.

—Janaro and Altshuler, *The Art of Being Human,* p. 334–35

1. What is the definition of family as used in this paragraph?
2. How is home defined?
3. What transitional word(s) is/are used with family?
4. What transitional word(s) is/are used with home?
5. What general class do both home and family belong to according to this paragraph?

B. The **integumentary** system is the external covering of the body, or the skin. It waterproofs the body and cushions and protects the deeper tissues from injury. It also excretes salts and urea in perspiration and helps regulate body temperature. Temperature, pressure, and pain receptors located in the skin alert us to what is happening at the body surface.

—Mareib, *Essentials of Human Anatomy and Physiology,* p. 3

1. What is the definition of the integumentary system?
2. What transitional word is used in this paragraph?
3. List three things the integumentary system does.
4. How does the skin alert us to what is happening at the body surface?
5. What does the integumentary system excrete?

C. Given that Congress designated the 1990s as "the decade of the brain," it is not surprising that one of the emerging specialties in psychology is concerned with brain functioning. **Neuropsychologists** are trained to diagnose disorders of the brain. Using various tests, they try to identify specific brain areas that may be malfunctioning. They often conduct research to identify early symptoms that predict the development of disorders such as Huntington's disease. They also devise rehabilitation programs to help patients regain as much of their abilities as possible after suffering brain damage, strokes, or traumatic brain injury.

—Davis and Palladino, *Psychology,* p. 40

1. What general class do neuropsychologists belong to?
2. What is a distinguishing characteristic of neuropsychologists?
3. How do neuropsychologists identify specific brain areas that may be malfunctioning?
4. What kind of research do neuropsychologists often perform?
5. Why do neuropsychologists devise rehabilitation programs?

EXERCISE 7–2 | *Read the following passage about polarization and answer the questions that follow.*

Another way in which language can obscure differences is in its preponderance of extreme terms and its relative lack of middle terms, a system that often leads to polarization. **Polarization** is the tendency to look at the world in terms of opposites and to describe it in extremes—good or bad, positive or negative, healthy or sick, intelligent or stupid. It's often referred to as the fallacy of "either-or" or "black or white." Most people exist somewhere between the extremes. Yet there's a strong tendency to view only the extremes and to categorize people, objects, and events in terms of these polar opposites.

Problems are created when opposites are used in inappropriate situations. For example, "The politician is either for us or against us." The politician may be for us in some things and against us in other things, or may be neutral.

In correcting this tendency to polarize, be aware of implying (and believing) that two extreme classes include all possible classes—that an individual must be one or the other, with no alternatives ("Are you prochoice or prolife?"). Most people, most events, most qualities exist between polar extremes. When others imply that there are only two sides or alternatives, look for the middle ground.

—DeVito, *Human Communication*, p. 124

1. What is the purpose of the passage?
2. Highlight the topic sentence of each paragraph. If there is no stated main idea, write a sentence expressing the main idea.
3. Highlight all transitional words.
4. What is the definition of polarization?
5. Why is polarization often a problem?
6. What are some examples of polarized opposites?
7. What do polarized opposites exclude?
8. What is the solution to the problem of polarization?

EXERCISE 7–3

Using the definition pattern described above, work with a classmate to write a two-part definition for each of the following terms.

1. robot
2. age discrimination
3. fiction
4. adolescence
5. phobia

Classification

If you were asked to describe types of computers, you might mention desktop, laptop, and notebook computers. By dividing a broad topic into its major categories, you are using a pattern known as **classification.**

This pattern is widely used in many academic subjects. For example, a psychology text might explain human needs by classifying them into two categories: primary and secondary. In a chemistry textbook, various compounds may be grouped and discussed according to common characteristics, such as the presence of hydrogen or oxygen. The classification pattern divides a topic into parts on the basis of common or shared characteristics.

Here are a few examples of topics and the classifications or categories into which each might be divided.

movies: comedy, horror, mystery

motives: achievement, power, affiliation, competency

plant: leaves, stem, roots

Note how the following paragraph classifies the various types of cancers.

The name of the cancer is derived from the type of tissue in which it develops. Carcinoma (carc = cancer; omo = tumor) refers to a malignant tumor consisting of epithelial cells. A tumor that develops from a gland is called an adenosarcoma (adeno = gland). Sarcoma is a general term for any cancer arising from connective tissue. Osteogenic sarcomas (osteo = bone; genic = origin), the most frequent type of childhood cancer, destroy normal bone tissue and eventually spread to other areas of the body. Myelomas (myelos = marrow) are malignant tumors, occurring in middle-aged and older people, that interfere with the blood-cell-producing function of bone marrow and cause anemia. Chondrosarcomas (chondro = cartilage) are cancerous growths of cartilage.

—Tortora, *Introduction to the Human Body,* p. 56

Examples of transitional words and phrases that indicate the classification pattern follow.

TRANSITIONAL WORDS
there are *several kinds* of chemical bonding . . .
there are *numerous types of* . . .
reproduction can be *classified as* . . .
the human skeleton is *composed of* . . .
muscles *comprise* . . .
one type of communication . . .
another type of communication . . .
finally, there is . . .

EXERCISE 7–4   *Read the following paragraphs and answer the questions that follow.*

A. The reptiles made one of the most spectacular adaptive radiations in all of Earth history. One group, the pterosaurs, took to the air. These "dragons of the sky" possessed huge membranous wings that allowed them rudimentary flight. Another group of reptiles, exemplified by the fossil *Archaeopteryx,* led to more successful flyers: the birds. Whereas some reptiles took to the skies, others returned to the sea, including fish-eating plesiosaurs and ichthyosaurs. These reptiles became proficient swimmers, but retained their reptilian teeth and breathed by means of lungs.

—Tarbuck and Lutgens, *Earth Science*, p. 309

1. List the classifications of reptiles included in this paragraph.
2. Highlight the transitional words in this paragraph that signal the classification pattern.
3. Which classification does Archaeopteryx belong to?
4. Which classification of reptiles could swim proficiently?
5. What is another name for pterosaurs?

B. From the hundreds of billions of galaxies, several basic types have been identified: spiral, elliptical, and irregular. The Milky Way and the Great Galaxy in Andromeda are examples of fairly large **spiral galaxies.** Typically, spiral galaxies are disk-shaped with a somewhat greater concentration of stars near their centers, but there are numerous variations. Viewed broadside, arms are often seen extending from the central nucleus and sweeping gracefully away. One type of spiral galaxy, however, has the stars arranged in the shape of a bar, which rotates as a rigid system. This requires that the outer stars move faster than the inner ones, a fact not easy for astronomers to reconcile with the laws of motion. Attached to each end of these bars are curved spiral arms. These have become known as **barred spiral galaxies.** The most abundant group, making up 60 percent of the total is the **elliptical galaxies.** These are generally smaller than spiral galaxies. Some are so much smaller, in fact, that the term dwarf has been applied. Because these dwarf galaxies are not visible at great distances, a survey of the sky reveals more of the conspicuous large spiral galaxies. As their name implies, elliptical galaxies have an ellipsoidal shape that ranges to nearly spherical, and they lack spiral arms. Only 10 percent of the known galaxies lack symmetry and are classified as **irregular galaxies.** The best-known irregular galaxies, the Large and Small Magellanic Clouds in the Southern Hemisphere, are easily visible with the unaided eye.

—Tarbuck and Lutgens, *Earth Science*, pp. 620–21

1. What are the three primary classifications of galaxies?
2. What determines how a galaxy is classified?
3. Highlight the transitional words that signal the classification pattern.
4. How can the types of spiral galaxies be classified?
5. What is another name for elliptical galaxies?

EXERCISE 7–5   *Read the following passages and answer the questions that follow.*

Passage A

TYPES OF BONES

The bones of the body may be classified into four principal types on the basis of shape: long, short, flat, and irregular. **Long bones** have greater length than width and consist of a shaft and extremities (ends). They are slightly curved for strength. Long bones consist mostly of compact bone (dense bone with few spaces) but also contain considerable amounts of spongy bone (bone with large spaces). The details of compact and spongy bone are discussed shortly. Long bones include bones of the thighs, legs, toes, arms, forearms, and fingers.

Short bones are somewhat cube-shaped and nearly equal in length and width. They are spongy except at the surface where there is a thin layer of compact bone. Short bones include the wrist and ankle bones.

Flat bones are generally thin and composed of two more or less parallel plates of compact bone enclosing a layer of spongy bone. Flat bones afford considerable pro-tection and provide extensive areas for muscle attachment. Flat bones include the cranial bones, the sternum (breastbone), ribs, and the scapulas (shoulder blades).

Irregular bones have complex shapes and cannot be grouped into any of the three categories just described. They also vary in the amount of spongy and com-pact bone present. Such bones include the vertebrae (backbones) and certain facial bones.

—Tortora, *Introduction to the Human Body,* p. 100

1. What is the purpose of this passage?
2. Highlight the topic sentence of each paragraph. If there is no stated main idea, write a sentence expressing the main idea.
3. Highlight transitional words that signal the classification pattern.

4. What are the four principal types of bones?
5. What is the basis of classification (how are they divided)?
6. How can long bones be classified?
7. Why are irregular bones a separate classification?

Passage B

Fossils are of many types. The remains of relatively recent organisms may not have been altered at all. Such objects as teeth, bones, and shells are common examples. Far less common are entire animals, flesh included, that have been preserved because of rather unusual circumstances. Remains of prehistoric elephants called mammoths that were frozen in the Arctic tundra of Siberia and Alaska are examples, as are the mummified remains of sloths preserved in a dry cave in Nevada.

Given enough time, the remains of an organism are likely to be modified. Often fossils become *petrified* (literally, "turned into stone"), meaning that the small internal cavities and pores of the original structure are filled with precipitated mineral matter. In other instances *replacement* may occur. Here the cell walls and other solid material are removed and replaced with mineral matter. Sometimes the microscopic details of the replaced structure are faithfully retained.

Molds and casts constitute another common class of fossils. When a shell or other structure is buried in sediment and then dissolved by underground water, a *mold* is created. The mold faithfully reflects only the shape and surface marking of the organism; it does not reveal any information concerning its internal structure. If these hollow spaces are subsequently filled with mineral matter, *casts* are created.

A type of fossilization called *carbonization* is particularly effective in preserving leaves and delicate animal forms. It occurs when fine sediment encases the remains of an organism. As time passes, pressure squeezes out the liquid and gaseous components and leaves behind a thin residue of carbon. Black shales deposited as organic-rich mud in oxygen-poor environments often contain abundant carbonized remains. If the film of carbon is lost from a fossil preserved in fine-grained sediment, a replica of the surface, called an *impression*, may still show considerable detail.

—Tarbuck and Lutgens, *Earth Science*, pp. 278–79

1. What is the purpose of the passage?
2. Highlight the topic sentence of each paragraph. If there is no stated main idea, write a sentence expressing the main idea.
3. Highlight all transitional words.
4. What are the four main classifications of fossils?
5. What are the two types of modified fossils?
6. How are molds and casts distinguished?
7. Which type of fossilization is most effective for leaves?

| **EXERCISE 7–6** | *Divide each of the topics listed below into several groups or categories.* |

1. foods _____

2. cars _____

3. arts _____

4. laws _____

5. pollutants _____

Order or Sequence

If you were asked to summarize what you did today, you probably would mention key events in the order in which they occurred. In describing how to write a particular computer program, you would detail the process step by step. If asked to list what you feel are your accomplishments so far this week, you might present them in order of importance, listing your most important accomplishment first. In each case, you are presenting information in a particular sequence or order. Each of these examples illustrates a form of the thought pattern known as **order,** or **sequence.** Let us look at several types of order.

Chronology   **Chronological order** refers to the sequence in which events occur in time. This pattern is essential in the academic disciplines concerned with the interpretation of events in the past. History, government, and anthropology are prime examples. In various forms of literature, chronological order is evident; the narrative form, used in novels, short stories, and narrative essays, relies on chronological order.

The following paragraph uses chronology to describe how full-scale intervention in Vietnam began.

> The pretext for full-scale intervention in Vietnam came in late July 1964. On July 30, South Vietnamese PT (patrol torpedo) boats attacked bases in the Gulf of Tonkin inside North Vietnamese waters. Simultaneously, the *Maddox,* an American destroyer, steamed into the area to disrupt North Vietnamese communication facilities. On August 2, possibly seeing the two separate missions as a combined maneuver against them, the North Vietnamese sent out several PT boats to attack the destroyer. The *Maddox* fired, sinking one of the attackers, then radioed the news to Washington. Johnson ordered another ship into the bay. On August 3 both destroyers reported another attack, although somewhat later, the commander of the *Maddox* radioed that he was not sure. Nonetheless, the president ordered American planes to retaliate by bombing inside North Vietnam.
>
> —Wilson et al., *The Pursuit of Liberty: A History of the American People,* p. 493

Examples of transitional words and phrases that indicate chronological order include the following.

TRANSITIONAL WORDS
in ancient times . . .
at the start of the battle . . .
on September 12 . . .
the *first* primate species . . .
later efforts . . .

Other clue words are

> then, before, during, by the time, while,
> afterward, as, after, thereafter, meanwhile,
> at that point

Process   In disciplines that focus on procedures, steps, or stages by which actions are accomplished, writers often employ the **process** pattern. These subjects include mathematics, natural and life sciences, computer science, and engineering. The pattern is similar to chronology, in that the steps or stages follow each other in time. Transitional words often used in conjunction with this pattern are similar to those used for chronological order.

Note how this pattern is used in a paragraph explaining what occurs in the brain during sleep.

> Let us track your brain waves through the night. As you prepare to go to bed, an EEG records that your brain waves are moving along at a rate of about 14 cycles per second (cps). Once you are comfortably in bed, you begin to relax and your brain waves slow down to a rate of about 8 to 12 cps. When you fall asleep, you enter your *sleep cycle,* each of whose stages shows a distinct EEG pattern. In Stage 1 sleep, the EEG shows brain waves of about 3 to 7 cps. During Stage 2, the EEG is characterized by *sleep spindles,* minute bursts of electrical activity of 12 to 16 cps. In the next two stages (3 and 4) of sleep, you enter into a very deep state of relaxed sleep. Your brain waves slow to about 1 to 2 cps, and your breathing and heart rate decrease. In a final stage, the electrical activity of your brain increases; your EEG looks very similar to those recorded during stages 1 and 2. It is during this stage that you will experience REM sleep, and you will begin to dream.
>
> —Zimbardo and Gerrig, *Psychology and Life,* p. 115

Order of Importance   This pattern of ideas sometimes expresses order of priority or preference. Ideas are arranged in one of two ways: from most to least important, or from least to most important. In the following paragraph, the causes of the downward trend in the standard of living are arranged in order of importance.

> The United States' downward trend in standard of living has many different causes, of which only a few major ones can be identified here. Most important is probably deindustrialization, the massive loss of manufacturing jobs as many U.S. corporations move their production to poor, labor-cheap countries. But deindustrialization hurts mostly low-skilled manufacturing workers. Most of the well-educated, high-skilled employees in service industries are left unscathed. Deindustrialization alone is therefore not enough to explain the economic decline. Another major factor is the great increase in consumption and decrease in savings. Like their government, people spend more than they earn and become deeply in debt. Those who do practice thrift still have an average rate of savings significantly lower than in countries with fast-growing economies. The habits of high consumption and low saving may

have resulted from the great affluence after the Second World War up until the early 1970s (Harrison, 1992).

—Thio, *Sociology,* p. 255

Order of importance is used in almost every field of study. Commonly used clues that suggest this pattern are

TRANSITIONAL WORDS
is *less* essential than . . .
more revealing is . . .
of *primary* interest is . . .

Other clue words are

first, next, last, most important, primarily, secondarily

Spatial Order Information organized according to its physical location, or position or order in space, exhibits a pattern known as **spatial order.** Spatial order is used in academic disciplines in which physical descriptions are important. These include numerous technical fields, engineering, and the biological sciences.

You can see how the following description of a particular type of blood circulation relies on spatial relationships.

> Pulmonary circulation conducts blood between the heart and the lungs. Oxygen-poor, CO_2-laden blood returns through two large veins (venae cavae) from tissues within the body, enters the right atrium, and is then moved into the right ventricle of the heart. From there, it is pumped into the pulmonary artery, which divides into two branches, each leading to one of the lungs. In the lung, the arteries undergo extensive branching, giving rise to vast networks of capillaries where gas exchange takes place, with blood becoming oxygenated while CO_2 is discharged. Oxygen-rich blood then returns to the heart via the pulmonary veins.
>
> —Mix et al., *Biology: The Network of Life,* pp. 663–64

Diagramming is of the utmost importance in working with this pattern; often, a diagram accompanies text material. For example, a diagram makes the functions of the various parts of the human brain easier to understand. Lecturers often refer to a visual aid or chalkboard drawing when providing spatial descriptions. Examples of transitional words and phrases that indicate spatial order follow.

TRANSITIONAL WORDS
the *left side* of the brain . . .
the *lower* portion . . .
the *outer* covering . . .
beneath the surface . . .

Other transitional words are

next to, beside, to the left, in the center, externally

EXERCISE 7–7 | *Read the following paragraphs and answer the questions that follow.*

A. The following paragraph uses the spatial pattern.

> **Skeletal muscle tissue** is named for its location—attached to bones. Skeletal muscle tissue is also *voluntary* because it can be made to contract by conscious control. A single skeletal muscle fiber (cell) is cylindrical and appears *striated* (striped) under a microscope; when organized in a tissue, the fibers are parallel to each other. Each muscle fiber has a plasma membrane, the **sarcolemma,** surrounding the cytoplasm, or **sarcoplasm.** Skeletal muscle fibers are multinucleate (more than one nucleus), and the nuclei are near the sarcolemma.
>
> —Tortora, *Introduction to the Human Body,* p. 77

1. Briefly describe skeletal muscle tissue.
2. Highlight the transitional words used to indicate the spatial pattern.
3. How are skeletal muscle fibers or cells arranged in a tissue?
4. Where can the sarcolemma (or plasma membrane) be found in muscle fibers?
5. Where are the nuclei in skeletal muscle fibers located?

B. The following paragraph uses the chronology pattern.

> Only two presidents have been impeached. The House impeached Andrew Johnson, Lincoln's successor, in 1868 on charges stemming from his disagreement with radical Republicans. He narrowly escaped conviction. Richard Nixon came as close to impeachment as anyone since. On July 31, 1974, the House Judiciary Committee voted to recommend his impeachment to the full House as a result of the **Watergate** scandal. Nixon escaped a certain vote for impeachment by resigning. In 1998, the House voted two articles of impeachment against President Clinton on party-line votes. The public clearly opposed the idea, however, and the Senate voted to acquit the president on both counts in 1999.
>
> —Edwards, *Government in America*, p. 416

1. How many events are described in this paragraph?
2. Highlight the transitional words that are used to indicate the chronology pattern.
3. Which event occurred most recently?
4. When was Andrew Johnson impeached?
5. Whose impeachment episode occurred in 1974?

C. The following paragraph uses the process pattern.

> BMI [body mass index] is an index of the relationship of height and weight. It is one of the most accurate indicators of a person's health risk due to excessive weight, rather than "fatness" per se. Although many people recoil in fright when they see they have to convert pounds to kilograms and inches to meters to calculate BMI, it really is not as difficult as it may seem. To get your kilogram weight, just divide your weight in pounds (without shoes or clothing) by 2.2. To convert your height to meters squared, divide your height in inches (without shoes) by 39.4, then square this result. Sounds pretty easy and it actually is. Once you have these

basic values, calculating your BMI involves dividing your weight in kilograms by your height in meters squared.

$$BMI = \frac{\text{Weight (in lbs)} \div 2.2 \text{ (to determine weight in kg)}}{(\text{Height [in inches]} \div 39.4)^2 \text{ (to determine height in meters squared)}}$$

Healthy weights have been defined as those associated with BMIs of 19 to 25, the range of the lowest statistical health risk. A BMI greater than 25 indicates over-weight and potentially significant health risks. The desirable range for females is between 21 and 23; for males, it is between 22 and 24. A body mass index of over 30 is considered obese. Many experts believe this number is too high, particularly for younger adults.

—Donatelle, *Access to Health*, p. 264

1. What process is being described in this paragraph?
2. Highlight the transitional words that are used to signal the process pattern.
3. What is the first step in the process?
4. Is a BMI of 23 considered healthy?
5. How do you convert height to meters squared?

D. *The following paragraph uses the spatial order pattern.*

The nucleus is bound by a double membrane barrier called the **nuclear membrane** or **nuclear envelope.** Between the two membranes is a fluid-filled "moat," or space. At various points, the two layers of the nuclear membrane approach each other and fuse, and nuclear pores penetrate through the fused regions. Like other cellular membranes, the nuclear membrane is selectively permeable, but passage of substances through it is much freer than elsewhere because of its relatively large pores. The nuclear membrane encloses a jellylike fluid called **nucleoplasm** in which the nucleoli and chromatin are suspended.

—*Mareib,* Essentials of Human Anatomy and Physiology, *p. 55*

1. What is being described in this paragraph?
2. Highlight the transitional words that are used to signal the spatial order pattern.
3. What is between the two outer membranes of a nucleus?
4. What is inside the nucleoplasm?
5. If you read this description in a textbook, what would you expect to accompany it?

E. *The following paragraph uses the order of importance pattern.*

Media resources are being reassembled in a new pattern, with three main parts. The first is the traditional mass media that will continue to be for a long time the most important element in the pattern in terms of their reach and influence. The second consists of the advanced electronic mass media, operating primarily within the new information utility, and competing increasingly with older media services. Finally, there are newer forms of personal electronic media, formed by clusters of like-minded people to fulfill their own professional or individual information needs. Internet chat rooms and personalized Web pages are fast-expanding examples of this development. Each of these parts of the evolving mass-communications pattern deserves separate scrutiny.

–Dizard, *Old Media, New Media,* p. 179

1. What does this paragraph describe?
2. Highlight the transitional words that are used to signal the pattern.
3. Why is traditional mass media the most important type of resource?
4. Which type of media resource competes the most with the traditional mass media?
5. What are some examples of personal electronic media?

EXERCISE 7–8   *Read the following passages and answer the questions that follow.*

Passage A

The shape of a state may affect its ability to consolidate its territory and control circulation across its borders. A circle would be the most efficient shape on an isotropic plain because a circular state would have the shortest possible border in relation to its territory, and that shape would allow all places to be reached from the center with the least travel. States with shapes closest to this model are sometimes called *compact states.* Bulgaria, Poland, and Zimbabwe are examples. *Prorupted states* are nearly compact, but they have at least one narrow extension of territory. Namibia and Thailand are examples. If these extensions reach out to navigable waterways, the extensions are called *corridors. Elongated states* are long and thin, such as Chile or Norway, and *fragmented states* consist of several isolated bits of territory. *Archipelago states,* made up of several strings of islands, such as Japan or the Philippines, are fragmented states. Still other states, called *perforated states*, are interrupted by the territory of another state enclosed entirely within them. South Africa, for example, is perforated by Lesotho, and Italy is perforated by the Vatican and by San Marino.

The shape of a state's territory may influence the government's ability to organize that territory, but this is not always true. A topographic barrier such as a mountain chain may effectively divide even a compact state. Bolivia and Switzerland, for example, are compact in shape, but mountain chains disrupt their interiors. For some of their regions, trade across international borders is easier than trade with other regions of their own country. The people throughout an archipelago state, by contrast, may be successfully linked by shipping.

Before drawing any conclusions about political control from the shape of a state alone, one must consider the distribution of topographic features, the state's population and resources, and whether any centrifugal forces such as economic or cultural ties straddle the state's borders.

—Bergman and Renwick, *Introduction to Geography,* pp. 442–43

1. What is the purpose of the passage?
2. Highlight the topic sentence of each paragraph. If there is no stated main idea, write a sentence expressing the main idea.
3. Highlight all transitional words.
4. What kind of study aid would help you understand this passage?

5. What is a state that is nearly circular in shape called?
6. What is a corridor?
7. What is a perforated state?

Passage B

The first American daily newspaper was printed in Philadelphia in 1783, but such papers did not proliferate until the technological advances of the mid-nineteenth century. The ratification of the First Amendment in 1791, guaranteeing freedom of speech, gave even the earliest American newspapers freedom to print whatever they saw fit. This has given the media a unique ability to display the government's dirty linen, a propensity that continues to distinguish the American press today.

Rapid printing and cheap paper made possible the "penny press," which could be bought for a penny and read at home. In 1841, Horace Greeley's *New York Tribune* was founded, and in 1851, the *New York Times* started up. By the 1840s, the telegraph permitted a primitive "wire service," which relayed news stories from city to city faster than ever before. The Associated Press, founded in 1849, depended heavily on this new technology.

At the turn of the century, newspaper magnates Joseph Pulitzer and William Randolph Hearst ushered in the era of "yellow journalism." This sensational style of reporting focused on violence, corruption, wars, and gossip, often with a less than scrupulous regard for the truth. On a visit to the United States at that time, young Winston Churchill said that "the essence of American journalism is vulgarity divested of truth." In the midst of the Spanish-American conflict over Cuba, Hearst once boasted of his power over public opinion by telling a news artist "You furnish the pictures and I'll furnish the war."

Newspapers consolidated into **chains** during the early part of the twentieth century. Today's massive media conglomerates (Gannet, Knight-Ridder, and Newhouse are the largest) control newspapers with 78 percent of the nation's daily circulation. Thus, three of four Americans now read a newspaper owned not by a fearless local editor but by a corporation headquartered elsewhere. Often these chains control television and radio stations as well.

—Edwards, *Government in America*, pp. 223–24

1. What is the purpose of the passage?
2. Highlight the topic sentence of each paragraph. If there is no stated main idea, write a sentence expressing the main idea.
3. Highlight all transitional words.
4. How did the American print media begin?
5. When was the *New York Times* founded?
6. What era began at the turn of the century?
7. How are most newspapers owned today?

Passage C

DEATH FROM INFECTIOUS DISEASES

The single leading communicable cause of death in the world today is the human immunodeficiency virus (HIV), which causes AIDS. It was responsible for 2.7 million deaths in 1999, almost 5 percent of all deaths. Acquired immune-deficiency syndrome (AIDS) is a viral disease that destroys the body's ability to fight infections. It is believed that the AIDS virus emerged in Africa in the 1950s; by 2000 about 35 million people worldwide had contracted the AIDS virus, and 15,000 new infections were occurring each day. India was probably the country with the greatest number of infected people (about 3.5 million), but two-thirds of all people infected were in sub-Saharan Africa. In several African countries, AIDS-related illnesses were the leading cause of adult death. AIDS has shortened life expectancy 17 to 20 years in Botswana, Zimbabwe, and Zambia. AIDS causes massive human suffering, and it also has a pernicious economic impact.

The second leading communicable cause of death is diarrheal diseases, responsible for about 4 percent of all deaths. The most important of these is cholera. New strains of cholera appear regularly, and they are spread through contaminated water and poor sanitation. Cholera periodically surges out of Asia.

Tuberculosis is the third leading communicable cause of death, causing about 3 percent of the total. Approximately one-third of the human population carries TB bacilli in their bodies, but in the vast majority of cases the disease is latent and cannot be transmitted. New strains of drug-resistant tuberculosis, however, are multiplying, and the war against this disease continues.

—Bergman and Renwick, *Introduction to Geography*, pp. 182–83

1. What is the purpose of the passage?
2. Highlight the topic sentence of each paragraph. If there is no stated main idea, write a sentence expressing the main idea.
3. Highlight all transitional words.
4. What is AIDS?
5. What is the most important type of diarrheal disease?
6. What is the leading cause of adult death in several African countries?
7. What percent of deaths is caused by tuberculosis?
8. What standard is used to place these diseases in order of importance?

Passage D

Even before you take your first bite of pizza, your body has already begun a series of complex digestive responses. Your mouth prepares for the food by increasing production of **saliva.** Saliva contains mostly water, which aids in chewing and swallowing, but it also contains important enzymes that begin the process of food breakdown, including amylase, which begins to break down carbohydrates. Enzymes are protein compounds that facilitate chemical reactions but are not altered in the process. From the mouth, the food passes down the **esophagus,** a 9- to 10-inch tube that connects the mouth and stomach. A series of contractions and relaxations by the muscles lining the esophagus gently move food to the next digestive organ, the **stomach.** Here food mixes with enzymes and stomach acids. Hydrochloric acid begins to work in combination with pepsin, an enzyme, to break down proteins. In most people, the stomach secretes enough mucus to protect the stomach lining from these harsh digestive juices.

Further digestive activity takes place in the **small intestine,** a 20-foot coiled tube containing three sections: the *duodenum,* the *jejunum,* and the *ileum.* Each section secretes digestive enzymes that, when combined with enzymes from the liver and the pancreas, further contribute to the breakdown of proteins, fats and carbohydrates. Once broken down, these nutrients are absorbed in the bloodstream to supply body cells with energy. The liver is the major organ that determines whether nutrients are stored, sent to cells or organs, or excreted. Solid wastes consisting of fiber, water, and salts are dumped into the large intestine, where most of the water and salts are reabsorbed into the system and the fiber is passed out the anus. The entire digestive process takes approximately 24 hours.

—Donatelle, *Access to Health*, pp. 223–24

1. What is the purpose of the passage?
2. Highlight the topic sentence of each paragraph. If there is no stated main idea, write a sentence expressing the main idea.
3. Highlight all transitional words.
4. What pattern is used to describe digestion?
5. How does food travel from the mouth to the stomach?
6. What role does the liver play?
7. What happens in the stomach?

EXERCISE 7–9   *Read each of the following opening sentences from a textbook reading assignment, and anticipate whether the material will be developed using chronology, process, order of importance, or spatial order. Then underline the portion(s) of the sentence that suggest(s) the pattern you choose.*

1. Several statistical procedures are used to track the changes in the divorce rate.

   _____

2. The immune system's ability to defend against an almost infinite variety of antigens depends on a process called clonal selection.[1]

   _____

3. We have no idea how many individuals comprised the human species in our earliest days, and we don't know much more about our numbers in recent times.[2]

   _____

4. There are sources of information about corporations that might help an investor evaluate them. One of the most useful is the *Value Line Investment Survey*.

   _____

5. Human development begins at conception, when the father's sperm cell unites with the mother's ovum.[3]

   _____

6. In the human digestive system, the breakdown of food particles begins in the mouth, where chewing breaks food apart and increases the surface area on which enzymes can act.[4]

---

7. The two atrioventricular (AV) valves, one located at each atrial-ventricular junction, prevent backflow into the atria when the ventricles are contracting.[5]

---

8. One of the most significant benefits of family therapy is the strengthening of the family unit.

---

9. The spinal cord is located within the spinal column; it looks like a section of rope or twine.

---

10. The transition from medieval to modern societies occurred from approximately 1400 to 1800.

Cause and Effect

The **cause-and-effect** pattern expresses a relationship between two or more actions, events, or occurrences that are connected in time. The relationship differs, however, from chronological order in that one event leads to another by *causing* it. Information that is organized in terms of the cause-and-effect pattern may

explain causes, sources, reasons, motives, and action

explain the effect, result, or consequence of a particular action

explain both causes and effects

Cause and effect is clearly illustrated by the following passage, which gives the sources of fashions or the reasons why fashions occur.

> Why do fashions occur in the first place? One reason is that some cultures, like ours, *value change:* what is new is good, what is newer is even better. Thus, in many modern societies clothing styles change yearly, while people in traditional societies may wear the same style for generations. A second reason is that many industries promote quick changes in fashion to increase sales. A third reason is that fashions usually trickle down from the top. A new style may occasionally originate from lower-status groups, as blue jeans did. But most fashions come from upper-class people who like to adopt some style or artifact as a badge of their status. But they cannot monopolize most status symbols for long. Their style is adopted by the

middle class, maybe copied or modified for use by lower-status groups, offering many people the prestige of possessing a high-status symbol.

—Thio, *Sociology*, p. 534

The cause-and-effect pattern is used extensively in many academic fields. All disciplines that ask the question "Why" employ the cause-and-effect thought pattern. It is widely used in the sciences, technologies, and social sciences.

Many statements expressing cause-and-effect relationships appear in direct order, with the cause stated first and the effect following: "When demand for a product increases, prices rise." However, reverse order is sometimes used, as in the following statement: "Prices rise when a product's demand increases."

| EXERCISE 7–10 | *Identify the cause and the effect in each of the following statements. Circle the cause and underline the effect.* |

1. Most nutritionists agree that long-term weight loss involves a combination of moderate dieting (say, eating 200 to 500 fewer calories a day than your body requires) and moderate exercise, both of which usually involve some behavior modification.[6]

2. When the body loses fluids, the kidneys stimulate the production of a hormone that activates the thirst drive.

3. Anorexia nervosa—a type of self-starvation—may be caused, in part, by our culture's emphasis on thinness.

4. The decrease in tensions between the former Soviet Union and the Western world has made it possible for the UN to become much more active than in the past.[7]

5. A computer program is easy or difficult to run, depending in part on the data entry system you choose.

The cause-and-effect pattern is not limited to an expression of a simple one-cause, one-effect relationship. There may be multiple causes, or multiple effects, or both multiple causes and multiple effects. For example, both slippery road conditions and your failure to buy snow tires (causes) may contribute to your car's sliding into the ditch (effect).

In other instances, a chain of causes or effects may occur. For instance, failing to set your alarm clock may force you to miss your 8:00 A.M. class, which in turn may cause you not to submit your term paper on time, which may result in a grade penalty. Transitional words or phrases that suggest the cause-and-effect pattern follow.

TRANSITIONAL WORDS

stress *causes* . . .
aggression *creates* . . .
depression *leads to* . . .
forethought *yields* . . .

mental retardation *stems from* . . .
life changes *produce* . . .
hostility *breeds* . . .
avoidance *results in* . . .

Other transitional words are

therefore, consequently, hence, for this reason, since

EXERCISE 7–11

Determine whether each of the following statements expresses single or multiple causes and single or multiple effects. Circle each cause; underline each effect.

1. Heavy drinking (three drinks or more per day) significantly increases the chance of having smaller babies with retarded physical growth, poor coordination, poor muscle tone, intellectual retardation, and other problems, collectively referred to as fetal alcohol syndrome (FAS).[8]

   _____

2. Psychogenic amnesia—a severe and often permanent memory loss—results in disorientation and the inability to draw on past experiences.

   _____

3. Social loafing, the tendency to work less when part of larger groups, may account for declining worker productivity and corporate profits in rapidly expanding businesses.

   _____

4. The world price of an internationally traded product may be influenced greatly, or only slightly, by the demand and supply coming from any one country.[9]

   _____

5. Insulin's main effect is to lower blood sugar levels, but it also influences protein and fat metabolism.[10]

   _____

EXERCISE 7–12

The following paragraphs are organized using the cause-and-effect pattern. Read them and answer the questions that follow.

Paragraph A

All objects continually radiate energy. Why, then, doesn't the temperature of all objects continually decrease? The answer is that all objects also continually absorb radiant energy. If an object is radiating more energy than it is absorbing, its temperature does decrease; but if an object is absorbing more energy than it is emitting, its temperature increases. An object that is warmer than its surroundings emits more energy than it receives, and therefore it cools; an object colder than its surroundings is a net gainer of energy, and its temperature therefore increases. An object whose temperature is constant, then, emits as much radiant energy as it receives. If it receives none, it will radiate away all its available energy, and its temperature will approach absolute zero.

—Hewitt, *Conceptual Physics,* p. 272

1. Explain why not all objects that radiate energy drop in temperature.
2. What happens to an object that radiates energy but does not absorb any?
3. Highlight the transitional words that signal the cause-and-effect pattern.
4. What causes an object's temperature to remain constant?
5. What is the effect of an object radiating away all of its available energy?

Paragraph B

It's the end of the term and you have dutifully typed the last of several papers. After hours of nonstop typing, you find that your hands are numb, and you feel an intense, burning pain that makes the thought of typing one more word almost unbearable. If you are like one of the thousands of students and workers who every year must quit a particular task due to pain, you may be suffering from a **repetitive stress injury (RSI)**. These are injuries to nerves, soft tissue or joints that result from the physical stress of repeated motions. One of the most common RSIs is **carpal tunnel syndrome,** a product of both the information age and the age of technology in general. Hours spent typing at the computer, flipping groceries through computerized scanners, or other jobs "made simpler" by technology can result in irritation to the median nerve in the wrist, causing numbness, tingling, and pain in the fingers and hands.

—Donatelle, *Access to Health,* p. 516

1. What is the cause of RSIs?
2. Highlight the transitional words that are used in this paragraph.
3. What kind of damage causes carpal tunnel syndrome?
4. What do students often do that can be a cause of RSIs?
5. What kinds of symptoms can result from RSI?

Paragraph C

CAUSES OF FITNESS-RELATED INJURIES

There are two types of injuries stemming from participation in fitness-related activities: overuse and traumatic. **Overuse injuries** occur because of cumulative, day-after-day stresses placed on tendons, bones, and ligaments during exercise. The forces that occur normally during physical activity are not enough to cause a ligament sprain or muscle strain, but when these forces are applied on a daily basis for weeks or months, they can result in an injury. Common sites of overuse injuries are the leg, knee, shoulder, and elbow joints. **Traumatic injuries,** which occur suddenly and violently, typically by accident, are the second major type of fitness-related injuries. Typical traumatic injuries are broken bones, torn ligaments and muscles, contusions, and lacerations. Most traumatic injuries are unavoidable—for example, spraining your ankle by landing on another person's foot after jumping up for a rebound in basketball. If your traumatic injury causes a noticeable loss of function and immediate pain or pain that does not go away after 30 minutes, you should have a physician examine it.

—Donatelle, *Access to Health,* p. 300

1. What is the cause of overuse injuries?
2. Highlight the transitional words that are used in this paragraph to signal the cause-and-effect pattern.
3. How do traumatic injuries often occur?
4. What kinds of injuries are typical traumatic injuries?
5. When should you have a traumatic injury examined?

EXERCISE 7–13   *Read the following passage about alcohol and answer the questions that follow.*

IMMEDIATE EFFECTS OF ALCOHOL

The most dramatic effects produced by ethanol occur within the central nervous system (CNS). The primary action of the drug is to reduce the frequency of nerve transmissions and impulses at synaptic junctions. This reduction of nerve transmissions results in a significant depression of CNS functions, with resulting decreases in respiratory rate, pulse rate, and blood pressure. As CNS depression deepens, vital functions become noticeably depressed. In extreme cases, coma and death can result.

Alcohol is a diuretic, causing increased urinary output. Although this effect might be expected to lead to automatic **dehydration** (loss of water), the body actually retains water, most of it in the muscles or in the cerebral tissues. This is because water is usually pulled out of the **cerebrospinal fluid** (fluid within the brain and spinal cord), leading to what is known as mitochondrial dehydration at the cell level within the nervous system. Mitochondria are miniature organs within the cells that are responsible for specific functions. They rely heavily upon fluid balance. When mitochondrial dehydration occurs from drinking, the mitochondria cannot carry out their normal functions, resulting in symptoms that include the "morning-after" headaches suffered by some drinkers.

Alcohol irritates the gastrointestinal system and may cause indigestion and heartburn if taken on an empty stomach. Long-term use of alcohol causes repeated irritation that has been linked to cancers of the esophagus and stomach. In addition, people who engage in brief drinking sprees during which they consume unusually high amounts of alcohol put themselves at risk for irregular heartbeat or even total loss of heart rhythm, which can cause disruption in blood flow and possible damage to the heart muscle.

—Donatelle, *Access to Health,* pp. 337–38

1. What is the purpose of the passage?
2. Highlight the topic sentence of each paragraph. If there is no stated main idea, write a sentence expressing the main idea.
3. Highlight all transitional words.

4. What does the reduction of nerve transmissions result in?
5. What is the result of the diuretic effect of alcohol?
6. Why does drinking alcohol sometimes result in indigestion and heartburn?
7. If alcohol causes irregular heartbeat or loss of heart rhythm, what can result?

Comparison and Contrast

The **comparison** thought pattern is used to emphasize or discuss similarities between or among ideas, theories, concepts, or events, whereas the **contrast** pattern emphasizes differences. When a speaker or writer is concerned with both similarities and differences, a combination pattern is used. The comparison-and-contrast pattern is widely used in the social sciences, where different groups, societies, cultures, or behaviors are studied. Literature courses may require comparisons among poets, among literary works, or among stylistic features. A business course may examine various management styles, compare organizational structures, or contrast retailing plans.

A contrast is shown in the following paragraph, which describes the purchasing processes of small and large businesses.

> Small businesses are likely to have less formal purchasing processes. A small retail grocer might, for example, purchase a computer system after visiting a few suppliers to compare prices and features, while a large grocery store chain might collect bids from a specified number of vendors and then evaluate those bids on pre-established criteria. Usually, fewer individuals are involved in the decision-making process for a small business. The owner of the small business, for example, may make all decisions, and a larger business may operate with a buying committee of several people.
>
> —Kinnear et al., *Principles of Marketing*, p. 218

Depending on whether a speaker or writer is concerned with similarities, differences, or both similarities and differences, the pattern might be organized in different ways. Suppose a professor of American literature is comparing two American poets, Whitman and Frost. Each of the following organizations is possible.

1. *Compare and then contrast the two.* That is, first discuss how Frost's poetry and Whitman's poetry are similar, and then discuss how they are different.

2. *Discuss by author.* For example, discuss the characteristics of Whitman's poetry; then discuss the characteristics of Frost's poetry; then summarize their similarities and differences.

3. *Discuss by characteristic.* For example, first discuss the two poets' use of metaphor; next discuss their use of rhyme, and then discuss their common themes.

Examples of transitional words and phrases that reflect these patterns follow.

TRANSITIONAL WORDS: CONTRAST

unlike Whitman, Frost . . .
less wordy than Whitman . . .
contrasted with Whitman, Frost . . .
Frost *differs from* . . .

Other contrast transitional words are

in contrast, however, on the other hand, as opposed to, whereas

TRANSITIONAL WORDS: COMPARISON

similarities between Frost and Whitman . . .
Frost is *as* powerful *as* . . .
like Frost, Whitman . . .
both Frost and Whitman . . .
Frost *resembles* Whitman in that . . .

Other comparison transitional words are

in a like manner, similarly, likewise, correspondingly, in the same way

EXERCISE 7–14 | *Read the following paragraphs and answer the questions that follow.*

A. When considering the relationship of Congress and the president, the basic differences of the two branches must be kept in mind. Members of Congress are elected from narrower constituencies than is the president. The people usually expect the president to address general concerns such as foreign policy and economic prosperity, while Congresspersons are asked to solve individual problems. There are structural differences as well. Congress is a body composed of hundreds of independent people, each with a different power base, and it is divided along partisan lines. Thus, it is difficult for Congress to act quickly or to project unity and clear policy statements.

—Baradat, *Understanding American Democracy*, p. 300

1. What two branches of the government are discussed?
2. Explain how these two branches are similar and/or different.
3. Highlight the transitional words that signal the comparison-and-contrast pattern.
4. Does this paragraph mainly use comparison, contrast, or both?
5. Why is it difficult for Congress to act quickly?

B. What are the main characteristics of this new postindustrial society? Unlike the industrial society from which we are emerging, its hallmark is not raw materials and manufacturing. Rather, its basic component is *information*. Teachers pass on knowledge to students, while lawyers, physicians, bankers, pilots, and interior decorators sell their specialized knowledge of law, the body, money, aerodynamics, and color schemes to clients. Unlike the factory workers in an industrial society, these workers don't *produce* anything. Rather, they transmit or use information to provide services that others are willing to pay for.

—Henslin, Social Problems, p. 154

1. What two things are being compared or contrasted?
2. Highlight the transitional words used to indicate the comparison-contrast pattern.
3. What is the postindustrial society based upon?
4. What did most workers in industrial society do at their jobs?
5. How is information connected to money in a postindustrial society?

C. You have already seen that homosexuality is more common among males than females, a finding that is supported by all researchers who have reported on this matter. Let's see what other differences they have found. One of the most significant is that lesbians are more likely to seek lasting relationships, place a premium on emotional commitment and mutual fidelity, and shun the bar scene (Wolf 1979; Lowenstein 1980; Peplau and Amaro 1982). Consequently, while most male homosexuals have "cruised" (sought impersonal sex with strangers), fewer than 20 percent of lesbians have done so. As a result, lesbians tend to have fewer sexual partners than do male homosexuals. Psychologist Alan Bell and sociologist Martin Weinberg (1978) interviewed about 1500 homosexuals. They found that almost half the white and one third the African-American homosexual males had at least 500 different sexual partners. About 28 percent of the white sample had more than 1000 different partners. Although their sample is large, it is not representative of homosexuals, because their research focused heavily on bars and steam baths. Bell's and Weinberg's findings do, however, support other studies indicating promiscuity among male homosexuals.

—Henslin, Social Problems, p. 74

1. What are two differences between lesbians and gay males?
2. Highlight the transitional words that are used to indicate the comparison-contrast pattern?
3. Why is the research cited in this paragraph not representative of all homosexuals?
4. What does it mean to "cruise"?
5. What percent of white homosexual males had more than 1000 partners?

EXERCISE 7–15 | *Read the following passage about behavior and answer the questions that follow.*

MODELS OF ABNORMAL BEHAVIOR

In their efforts to identify and explain abnormal behaviors, psychologists often adopt models, or general views of what causes those behaviors. Models help by pointing out which symptoms are most important, directing attention to their likely causes and suggesting possible treatments.

The Medical Model

Near the end of the eighteenth century, physicians began to document their patients' symptoms and to note which ones occurred together. The occurrence of groups of symptoms, called *syndromes,* helped physicians identify underlying diseases and develop treatments. Approaching abnormal behaviors just as one would approach medical illnesses is known as the **medical model.**

Psychiatrist Thomas Szasz (1993) argues for limiting the medical model to conditions resulting from actual brain dysfunctions. In his opinion, this model has been expanded to cover behaviors that are perhaps annoying or inappropriate but do not constitute diseases of the brain. For example, the list of proposed or recognized diseases includes shoplifting, pathological gambling, and nicotine dependence. According to Szasz, applying the medical model to such behaviors does not advance our understanding of the causes of the problems and allows people to avoid taking responsibility for their problems by attributing them to a disease process.

Accumulating evidence shows that a number of psychological disorders are related to elevated or reduced levels of certain neurotransmitters or structural abnormalities in the brain. What's more, evidence is increasing that heredity plays a significant role in the development of some psychological disorders.

The Psychological Models

In contrast to the medical model, various *psychological models* emphasize the importance of mental functioning, social experiences and learning histories in trying to explain the causes of abnormal behaviors. Sigmund Freud's **psychodynamic model** focuses on unconscious conflicts involving the id, ego and superego or fixations at an early stage of psychosexual development. For example, anxiety is seen as a warning that the ego is about to be overwhelmed by conflict. The **behavioral model,** by contrast, focuses on environmental factors that mold human and animal behaviors. Behavioral theorists such as John B. Watson and B. F. Skinner propose that we learn both normal and abnormal behaviors through the principles of classical conditioning, operant conditioning, and modeling. In contrast to the behavioral model, the **cognitive model** focuses on understanding the content and processes of human thought. Cognitive psychologists claim that to understand human behavior, we must look beyond actual events to understand how people interpret those events.

—Davis and Palladino, *Psychology,* pp. 535–36

1. What is the purpose of the passage?
2. Highlight the topic sentence of each paragraph. If there is no stated main idea, write a sentence expressing the main idea.
3. Highlight all transitional words.
4. What is the medical model of approaching abnormal behavior?
5. How do psychological models contrast with the medical model?
6. Which psychological model relies on understanding the content and processes of human thought?
7. Why does Szasz argue for limiting the use of the medical model?

EXERCISE 7–16 *Read each of the following opening sentences from a textbook reading assignment and predict whether a comparison, contrast, or combination pattern will be used.*

1. In Rembrandt's *Self-Portrait* and Frank Auerbach's *Head of Michael Podro,* the artists' responsiveness to both the reality of their subjects and the physical nature of paint and painting is clearly visible.[11]

   _____

2. The Enlightenment celebrated the power of reason; however, an opposite reaction, Romanticism, soon followed.[12]

   _____

3. The small group develops in much the same way that a conversation develops.[13]

   _____

4. Think of the hardware in a computer system as the kitchen in a short-order restaurant: It's equipped to produce whatever output a customer (user) requests, but it sits idle until an order (command) is placed.[14]

   _____

5. One important conceptual issue that arises frequently in economics is the distinction between stock and flow variables.[15]

   _____

EXERCISE 7–17

Write five sentences that express either a comparison or a contrast relationship. Exchange your sentences with a classmate, asking him or her to identify the pattern used.

Listing/Enumeration

If asked to evaluate a film you saw, you might describe the characters, plot, and technical effects. These details about the film could be arranged in any order; each detail provides further information about the film, but they have no specific relationship to one another. This arrangement of ideas is known as **listing** or **enumeration**—giving bits of information on a topic by stating them one after the other. Often, there is no particular method of arrangement for those details.

The following list of managers' difficulties in problem solving could have been presented in any order without altering the meaning of the paragraph.

> Although accurate identification of a problem is essential before the problem can be solved, this stage of decision making creates many difficulties for managers. Sometimes managers' preconceptions of the problem prevent them from seeing

the situation as it actually is. They produce an answer before the proper question has ever been asked. In other cases, managers overlook truly significant issues by focusing on unimportant matters. Also, managers may mistakenly analyze problems in terms of symptoms rather than underlying causes.

—Pride et al., *Business,* p. 189

This pattern is widely used in college textbooks in most academic disciplines. In its loosest form, the pattern may be simply a list of items: factors that influence light emission, characteristics of a particular poet, a description of an atom, a list of characteristics that define poverty.

Somewhat tighter is the use of listing to explain, support, or provide evidence. Support may be in the form of facts, statistics, or examples. For instance, the statement "The incidence of white collar crime has dramatically increased over the past 10 years" would be followed by facts and statistics documenting the increase. The transitional words or phrases used for this pattern include the following.

TRANSITIONAL WORDS
one aspect of relativity . . .
a second feature of relativity . . .
also, relativity . . .
there are *several* characteristics of . . .
(1) . . . , *(2)* . . . , *and (3)* . . .
(a) . . . , *(b)* . . . , *and (c)* . . .

Other transitional words are

in addition, first, second, third, finally, another

EXERCISE 7–18 | *Read the following paragraphs and answer the questions that follow.*

A. By far the most important committees in Congress are the standing committees. Currently 16 standing committees in the Senate and 22 in the House receive the bills that are introduced in Congress. The standing committees are assigned subject-matter jurisdiction by the rules of their respective house, and their titles reflect their general area of expertise. Hence, we have the Senate Finance Committee, the House Agriculture Committee, the Senate Budget Committee, the House Judiciary Committee, and so on. The authority of the standing committees includes the power to study legislation, to subpoena witnesses or information, to remand bills to subcommittees, to vote bills dead, to table bills (putting them aside, thus allowing them to die quietly at the end of the congressional term), to amend bills, to write bills (amending a bill or writing an entirely new version of a bill is called **marking-up**), or to report the bill to the floor.

—Baradat, *Understanding American Democracy,* p. 202

1. What is the topic of the paragraph?
2. What types of information does this paragraph list?

3. Highlight the transitional words used in this paragraph to indicate the listing pattern.
4. What is the purpose of standing committees in general?
5. List two powers of standing committees.

B. Minorities come into existence, then, when, due to expanded political boundaries or migration, people with different customs, languages, values or physical characteristics come under control of the same state organization. There, some groups who share physical and cultural traits discriminate against those with different traits. The losers in this power struggle are forced into minority group status; the winners enjoy the higher status and greater privileges that their dominance brings. Wagley and Harris noted that all minorities share these five characteristics: (1) They are treated unequally by the dominant group. (2) Their physical or cultural traits are held in low esteem by the dominant group. (3) They tend to feel strong group solidarity because of their physical or cultural traits—and the disabilities these traits bring. (4) Their membership in a minority group is not voluntary but comes through birth. (5) They tend to marry within their group. Sharing cultural or physical traits, having similar experiences of discrimination, and marrying within their own group create a shared identity—sometimes even a sense of common destiny. These shared experiences, however, do not mean that all minority groups have the same goals.

—Henslin, *Social Problems,* p. 252

1. How do minorities come into existence?
2. Highlight the transitional words used to indicate the listing pattern.
3. How does minority status impact marriage?
4. At what stage of life does a person enter an already existing minority group?
5. How is a shared identity or destiny created among minorities?

C. Voters make two basic decisions at election time. The first is whether to vote. Americans' right to vote is well established, but in order to do so citizens must go through the registration process. America's unique registration system is one major reason why turnout in American elections is much lower than in most other democracies. The 1996 election was another in a long string of low-turnout elections. Second, those who choose to vote must decide for whom to cast their ballots. Over a generation of research on voting behavior has helped political scientists understand the dominant role played by three factors in voters' choices: party identification, candidate evaluations, and policy positions.

—Edwards, *Government in America,* p. 330

1. What two categories are listed or enumerated in this paragraph?
2. What transitional words are used to indicate the listing or enumeration pattern?
3. What is a major reason why voter turnout is low in America?
4. List the factors involved in voters' choices.
5. What is the first decision a voter must make in an election?

EXERCISE 7–19   *Read the following passage about economics and answer the questions that follow.*

FOUR ECONOMIC PROBLEMS FACING THE UNITED STATES

Capitalism provides the setting for understanding problems of social inequality in the United States. Within this broad context of wealth and poverty are more specific issues that affect the future direction of the U.S. economy. Let's look at four of the problems that spell future trouble.

The first is a decline in people's **real income** (income in constant dollars, that is, adjusted for inflation). For 25 years, from the end of World War II until 1970, the real income of U.S. workers rose steadily. For the past 30 years, however, real income has declined. The situation is deceptive, for workers have more dollars in their paychecks than they used to, but those dollars don't go as far. In spite of fat raises, *each five-year period since 1970 has brought a decline in purchasing power.* Workers don't just *feel* poorer—they *are*.

The second major problem is taxes. Someone coined the term *Tax Freedom Day* to refer to the day when the average American has earned enough to pay his or her annual taxes. Politicians keep promising tax cuts, but because they never deliver on their promise Tax Freedom Day has been pushed forward relentlessly. It now falls on May 6 (Keating 1998). On average, each of us must work for the government for more than four months before we have a cent for our own needs!

The third major problem is that the U.S. savings rate has dropped to a low not seen even during the Great Depression of the 1930s. Americans save less than people in all other industrialized nations—just one-sixth of what the Japanese save. The significance of our drop in savings is that we have less money to invest in new plants and equipment, which may undermine our ability to compete in international trade or to increase our living standard.

Fourth, we import foreign goods at such a frenzied pace that the United States has become the largest debtor nation in the world. Each year, the amount that we spend on products we buy from other nations amounts to almost $200 billion more than the amount we get from selling to them. These mountains of debt cannot keep piling up indefinitely. Just as individuals must repay what they borrow or else get into financial trouble, so it is with nations. To finance **national debt** (the total amount the U.S. government owes), we must pay $250 billion a year in interest (*Statistical Abstract* 1998: Table 538). This is money that we cannot use to build schools and colleges, hire teachers, rebuild our cities, pay for medical services for the poor, operate Head Start programs, or pay for any other services to help improve our quality of life.

—Henslin, *Social Problems,* pp. 216–18

1. What is the purpose of the passage?
2. Highlight the topic sentence of each paragraph. If there is no stated main idea, write a sentence expressing the main idea.
3. Highlight all transitional words.
4. What is real income?
5. Why are taxes a problem for the U.S. economy?
6. How much do Americans save in comparison to the Japanese?
7. How does importing goods negatively affect the U.S. economy?

EXERCISE 7–20 | *Identify and circle the topics listed below that might be developed by using the listing pattern.*

1. The Impact of Budget on Crime Prevention
2. The Aims of Legal Punishment
3. America: A Drugged Society?
4. Varieties of Theft
5. Homicide and Assault: The Current Picture

Mixed Patterns

Thought patterns are often combined. In describing a process, a writer may also give reasons why each step must be followed in the prescribed order. A lecturer may define a concept by comparing it to something similar or familiar. Suppose an essay in your political science textbook opens by stating, "The distinction between 'power' and 'power potential' is an important one in considering the balance of power." You might expect a definition pattern (where the two terms are defined), but you also might anticipate that the essay would discuss the difference between the two terms (contrast pattern).

In the passage below, the author uses both definition and listing to explain child abuse.

CHILD ABUSE

Children raised in families in which domestic violence and/or sexual abuse occur are at great risk for damage to personal health and well-being. The effects of such violent acts are powerful and can be very long-lasting. **Child abuse** refers to the systematic harm of a child by a caregiver, generally a parent. The abuse may be sexual, psychological, physical, or any combination of these. Although exact figures are lacking, many experts believe that over 2 million cases of child abuse occur every year in the United States, involving severe injury, permanent disability, or death. Child abusers exist in all gender, social, ethnic, religious, and racial groups.

Certain personal characteristics tend to be common among child abusers: having been abused as a child, having a poor self-image, feelings of isolation, extreme frustration with life, higher stress or anxiety levels than normal, a tendency to abuse drugs and/or alcohol, and unrealistic expectations of the child. It is also estimated that from one half to three quarters of men who batter their female partners also batter children. In fact, spouse abuse is the single most identifiable risk factor for predicting child abuse. Finally, children with handicaps or other "differences" are more likely to be abused.

—Donatelle, *Access to Health,* p. 107

EXERCISE 7–21 | *The following paragraph describes the beginnings of Earth's atmosphere. Read the paragraph and answer the questions that follow.*

Earth's very earliest atmosphere probably was swept into space by the *solar wind,* a vast stream of particles emitted by the Sun. As Earth slowly cooled, a more enduring atmosphere formed. The molten surface solidified into a crust, and gases that had been dissolved in the molten rock were gradually released, a process called **outgassing.** Outgassing continues today from hundreds of active volcanoes worldwide. Thus, geologists hypothesize that Earth's original atmosphere was made up of gases similar to those released in volcanic emissions today: water vapor, carbon dioxide, nitrogen, and several trace gases.

—Tarbuck and Lutgens, *Earth Science,* p. 298

1. Which patterns are used in this paragraph?
2. Highlight the transitional words used to indicate the patterns.
3. What happened to the first atmosphere the Earth had?
4. How does outgassing occur?
5. What was the original atmosphere probably composed of?

EXERCISE 7–22 *The following passage uses mixed patterns. Read the passage and answer the questions that follow.*

WEATHERING

All materials are susceptible to weathering. Consider, for example, the synthetic rock we call concrete, which closely resembles the sedimentary rock called conglomerate. A newly poured concrete sidewalk has a smooth, fresh look. However, not many years later, the same sidewalk will appear chipped, cracked, and rough, with pebbles exposed at the surface. If a tree is nearby, its roots may grow under the concrete, heaving and buckling it. The same natural processes that eventually break apart a concrete sidewalk also act to disintegrate natural rocks, regardless of their type or strength.

Why does rock weather? Simply, weathering is the response of Earth materials to a changing environment. For instance, after millions of years of uplift and erosion, the rocks overlying a large body of intrusive igneous rock may be removed. This exposes the rock to a whole new environment at the surface. The mass of crystalline rock, which formed deep below ground where temperatures and pressures are much greater than at the surface, is now subjected to very different and comparatively hostile surface conditions. In response, this rock mass will gradually change until it is once again in equilibrium, or balance, with its new environment. Such transformation of rock is what we call *weathering.*

There are two kinds of weathering—mechanical and chemical. Mechanical weathering is the physical breaking up of rocks into smaller pieces. Chemical weathering actually alters a rock's chemistry, changing it into different substances. Although we will consider these two processes separately, keep in mind that they usually work simultaneously in nature.

—Tarbuck and Lutgens, *Earth Science,* p. 61

1. What is the purpose of the passage?
2. Highlight the topic sentence of each paragraph. If there is no stated main idea, write a sentence expressing the main idea.
3. Highlight all transitional words.

4. Which patterns are utilized in this passage?
5. Why do rocks weather?
6. What is the difference between mechanical and chemical weathering?
7. What kind of rock is concrete similar to?

EXERCISE 7–23

For each of the following topic sentences, anticipate what thought pattern(s) the paragraph is likely to exhibit. Record your prediction in the space provided. Underline the word(s) that suggest the pattern(s) you chose.

1. Another form of learning that does not fit neatly into the mold of classical or operant conditioning is learning through insight.

   _____

2. GNP (gross national product) is an economic measure that considers the total value of goods and services that a country produces during a given year.

   _____

3. Diseases of the heart and blood vessels—cardiovascular diseases—are the leading cause of death in the United States today.[16]

   _____

4. Impulse conduction in neurons has been compared to electrical impulses in, say, a copper wire, but the analogy is not a good one.[17]

   _____

5. The body's first line of defense against infection consists of several kinds of nonspecific resistance, so named because they do not distinguish one invader from another.[18]

   _____

6. Research suggests that obsessive-compulsive disorder has a biological basis.[19]

   _____

7. Nervous systems consist of two major types of cells: neurons (nerve cells), which are specialized for carrying signals from one location in the body to another, and supporting cells, which protect, insulate, and reinforce neurons.[20]

   _____

8. Both Neoclassicism and Romanticism had their beginnings in rebellion.[21]

   _____

9. Some astute observers have noted that when we find ourselves in an energy crunch, as when Iraq invaded Kuwait and threatened the Saudi oil fields in 1990, the first response of our national leaders is to act to insure our continued access to Middle East oil.[22]

   _____

10. Before the twentieth century, most of the population of Latin America resembled the populations of antiquity, with high birthrates offset by high death rates.[23]

EXERCISE 7–24 *Choose a one- or two-page section of one of your textbooks and determine the pattern of each major paragraph. Then identify the overall pattern of the section as a whole.*

EXERCISE 7–25 *Turn to the table of contents of this text. Predict the thought pattern(s) that any five of the readings will follow. Ask a classmate to confirm or disagree with the patterns you identified.*

Other Useful Patterns of Organization

The patterns presented in the previous section are the most common. Table 7–1 on the next page presents a brief review of those patterns and their corresponding transitional words. However, writers do not limit themselves to these six patterns. Especially in academic writing, you may find one or more of the patterns listed in Table 7–2 (p. 209), as well. Here is a brief overview of each of these additional patterns.

Statement and Clarification   Many writers make a statement of fact and then proceed to clarify or explain that statement. For instance, a writer may open a paragraph by stating that "The best education for you may not be the best education for someone else." The remainder of the paragraph would then discuss that statement and make its meaning clear by explaining how educational needs are individual and based on one's talents, skills, and goals. Transitional words associated with this pattern are listed in Table 7–2.

In the following paragraph about sex ratios, the writer uses statement and clarification.

> Sex ratios in the poor countries do not show a consistent pattern. In some poor countries men outnumber women, but in others, in tropical Africa, for example, women outnumber men. In fact, variations in sex ratios can be explained only by a combination of national economic and cultural factors. In the countries of North America and Europe and in Japan, women may suffer many kinds of discrimination, but they are not generally discriminated against when it comes to access to medical care.

—Bergman and Renwick, *Introduction to Geography,* p. 185

Notice that the writer begins with the statement about sex ratios in poor countries and then goes on to clarify this fact. The author uses the transitional words "in fact."

Summary   A summary is a condensed statement that provides the key points of a larger idea or piece of writing. The summaries at the end of each chapter of this text provide a quick review of the chapter's contents. Often writers summarize what they have already said or what someone else has said. For example, in a psychology textbook you will find many summaries of research. Instead of asking you to read an entire research study, the textbook author will summarize the study's findings. Other times a writer may repeat in condensed form what he or she has already said as a means of emphasis or clarification. Transitional words associated with this pattern are listed in Table 7–2.

In the following paragraph about the magazine industry, the author uses the summary method of organization.

TABLE 7–1	A REVIEW OF PATTERNS AND TRANSITIONAL WORDS	
Pattern	**Characteristics**	**Transitional Words**
Definition	Explains the meaning of a word or phrase	is, refers to, can be defined as, means, consists of, involves, is a term that, is called, is characterized by, occurs when, are those that, entails, corresponds to, is literally
Classification	Divides a topic into parts based on shared characteristics	classified as, comprises, is composed of, several varieties of, different stages of, different groups that, includes, one, first, second, another, finally, last
Order or Sequence	Describes events, processes, procedures, spatial relationships, and order of importance	first, second, later, before, next, as soon as, after, then, finally, meanwhile, following, last, during, in, on, when, until
Cause-Effect	Describes how one or more things cause or are related to another	*Causes:* because, because of, for, since, stems from, one cause is, one reason is, leads to, causes, creates, yields, produces, due to, breeds, for this reason *Effects:* consequently, results in, one result is, therefore, thus, as a result, hence
Comparison-Contrast	Discusses similarities and/or differences among ideas, theories, concepts, objects, or persons	*Similarities:* both, also, similarly, like, likewise, too, as well as, resembles, correspondingly, in the same way, to compare, in comparison, share *Differences:* unlike, differs from, in contrast, on the other hand, instead, despite, nevertheless, however, in spite of, whereas, as opposed to
Listing/Enumeration	Organizes lists of information, characteristics	the following, several, for example, for instance, one, another, also, too, in other words, first, second

Pattern	Characteristics	Transitional Words
Statement and Clarification	Indicates that information explaining an idea or concept will follow the topic sentence	in fact, in other words, clearly, evidently, obviously
Summary	Indicates that a condensed review of an idea or piece of writing will be given	in summary, in conclusion, in brief, to summarize, to sum up, in short, on the whole
Generalization and Example	Provides examples that clarify a broad, general statement	for example, for instance, that is, to illustrate, thus
Addition	Indicates that additional information will follow the topic sentence	furthermore, additionally, also, besides, further, in addition, moreover, again

TABLE 7–2   A REVIEW OF ADDITIONAL PATTERNS AND TRANSITIONAL WORDS

In summary, the magazine industry is adapting to the new world of electronic multimedia information and entertainment, with formats that will be quite different from the familiar ones. Computer-generated publishing has become the norm in the magazine business, expanding beyond its uses in producing newsletters and other specialized publications. Most general circulation magazines already rely heavily on desktop computers, interacting with other electronic equipment to produce high-quality, graphics-filled products.

—Dizard, *Old, Media, New Media,* p. 169

Notice that the writer summarizes many facts about how the magazine industry uses electronic multimedia information and that the transitional words "in summary" are used.

Generalization and Example   Examples are one of the best ways to explain something that is unfamiliar or unknown. Examples are specific instances or situations that illustrate a concept or idea. Often writers may present a general statement, or generalization, and then explain it by giving examples to make its meaning clear. In a social problems textbook, you might find the following generalization: Computer theft by employees is on the increase. The section might then go on to offer examples from specific companies in which employees insert fictitious information into the company's computer program and steal company funds. Transitional words associated with this pattern are listed in Table 7–2.

In the following paragraph about dreams, the writer uses generalization and example.

Different cultures place varying emphases on dreams and support different beliefs concerning dreams. For example, many people in the United States view dreams as irrelevant fantasy with no connection to everyday life. By contrast, people in other cultures view dreams as key sources of information about the future, the spiritual world, and the dreamer. Such cultural views can influence the probability of dream recall. In many modern Western cultures, people rarely remember their dreams upon awakening. The Parintintin of South America, however, typically remember several dreams every night (Kraeke, 1993) and the Senoi of Malaysia discuss their dreams with family members in the morning (Hennager, 1993).

—Davis and Palladino, *Psychology,* p. 210

Notice that the writer begins with the generalization that different cultures place different emphases on dreams and then goes on to give examples of the way specific cultures treat dreams. Note the use of the transitional words "for example."

Addition   Writers often introduce an idea or make a statement and then supply additional information about that idea or statement. For instance, an education textbook might introduce the concept of homeschooling and then provide in-depth information about its benefits. This pattern is often used to expand, elaborate on, or discuss an idea in greater detail. Transitional words associated with this pattern are listed in Table 7–2.

In the following paragraph about pathogens, the writer uses addition.

Some pathogens [disease-causing organisms] evolve and mutate naturally. Also, patients who fail to complete the full portion of their antibiotic prescriptions allow drug-resistant pathogens to multiply. The use of antibiotics in animal feed and sprayed on fruits and vegetables during food processing increases opportunities for resistant organisms to evolve and thrive. Furthermore, there is evidence that the disruption of Earth's natural habitats can trigger the evolution of new pathogens.

—Bergman and Renwick, *Introduction to Geography,* p. 182

Notice that the writer states that some pathogens mutate naturally and then goes on to add that they also mutate as a result of human activities. Note the use of the transitional words "also" and "furthermore."

EXERCISE 7–26   *For each of the following statements, identify the pattern that is evident and write its name in the space provided. Choose from among the following patterns: statement and clarification, summary, generalization and example, and addition.*

1. _____ In short, physical anthropologists are still waiting to locate the remains that will connect present day humans with early hominids.

2. _____ Humans have been using pictures to communicate and make sense of their environment since they first evolved. Cave paintings and the creation of constellation figures are just a few examples.

3. _____ Anthrax is a strain of bacteria that is spread through inhalation. Anthrax can also be contracted cutaneously, through contact with the skin.

4. _____ Pedophiles (criminals who molest children) generally cannot be rehabilitated. In fact, many types of therapy have been tried without success.

5. _____ Internet bulletin boards and listservs make it possible for people to casually meet other people that they would not otherwise come into contact with. For instance, a popular listserv made up of tea enthusiasts comprises members from all over the globe.

6. _____ Frogs are able to breathe underwater by absorbing oxygen from the water through their skin. Besides breathing underwater, frogs are also able to breathe while in air, but their skin must be wet in order to absorb oxygen from the air.

7. _____ The Moro reflex in human infants is best summed up as a holdover from life in the trees. When the infant perceives the feeling of falling, it spreads its arms and hands in an attempt to prevent a fall from the branches.

8. _____ What is considered as instinct in animals is often the manifestation of a highly developed sense. As a case in point, salmon are able to return to their spawning stream using a highly developed sense of smell.

9. _____ Crustaceans have exoskeletons instead of internal skeletons. To illustrate this, think of how a lobster has a shell on the outside that can be removed and that once inside the shell, there is only meat.

10. _____ Circulation numbers are crucial in increasing ad revenues for magazines. In fact, many magazines give free or very low cost subscriptions in order to boost their circulation numbers and support increases in ad revenues.

EXERCISE 7–27 *Read each of the following paragraphs and identify the predominant organizational pattern used. Write the name of the pattern in the space provided. Choose from among the following patterns: statement and clarification, summary, generalization and example, and addition.*

1. **Managing Emotional Responses**

Have you have gotten all worked up about something you thought was happening only to find that your perceptions were totally wrong or that a communication problem had caused a misrepresentation of events? If you're like most of us, you probably have. We often get upset not by realities but by our faulty perceptions. For example, suppose you found out that everyone except you is invited to a party. You might easily begin to wonder why you were excluded. Does someone dislike you? Have you offended someone? Such thoughts are typical. However, the reality of the situation may have absolutely nothing to do with your being liked or disliked. Perhaps you were sent an invitation and it didn't get to you.

—Donatelle, *Access to Health,* p. 81

Pattern: _____

2. A serious problem with some drugs is **addiction,** or **drug dependence.** That is, people come to depend on the regular consumption of a drug in order to make it through the day. When people think of **drug addiction,** they are likely to think of addicts huddled in slum doorways, the dregs of society who seldom venture into daylight—unless it is to rob someone. They don't associate addiction with "good," middle-class neighborhoods and "solid citizens." But let's look at drug addiction a little more closely. Although most people may think of heroin as the prime example of an addictive drug, I suggest that nicotine is the better case to consider. I remember a next-door neighbor who stood in his backyard, a lit cigarette in his hand, and told me about the operation in which one of his lungs was removed. I say "I remember," because soon after our conversation he died from his addiction.

—Henslin, *Social Problems,* p. 93

Pattern: _____

3. **The Challenges of Cable TV**

The more immediate challenge to the Big Three television networks, however, came from cable television. The networks were at a structural disadvantage in their attempts to match cable's appeal. They had only one channel with which to reach the home audiences that advertisers wanted. Moreover, network program costs rose as advertising revenues fell. This was especially true of the more popular programs networks had to offer in order to keep what was left of their competitive prime-time edge.

—Dizard, *Old Media, New Media,* p. 87

Pattern: _____

4. Internet-based electronic commerce continues to develop at a rapid rate despite the economic slowdown in 2000. In fact, it's estimated that e-commerce will account for over 8.6 percent of worldwide sales of goods and services within just a few years. Recent surveys by *The Standard* and *InternetWeek*, widely read industry magazines, indicate that there are several thousand Internet-based companies, also referred to as **do**t **coms,** that make up only 10 percent to 15 percent of Internet economy revenue and jobs. But the Internet economy has evolved to include the millions of traditional, so-called brick-and-mortar, companies, and a large majority of these better-managed companies utilizing the Internet are operating profitable e-business operations. Clearly, Fortune 1000 and Global 2000 companies, especially in industries, such as chemicals, energy, financial services, manufacturing, retail and utilities, are pushing ahead aggressively with entire portfolios of e-business projects. And according to another survey by *Interactive Week* magazine, budgets for Internet

products and services will continue to rise, in some large companies by as much as 20 percent.

—Beekman, *Computer Confluence: IT Edition,* p. 47

Pattern: _____

5. In summary, the publishing industry is undergoing major changes, brought on by demographic shifts, financial upheavals, and the pressure of new technologies. Instability and reassessment are common to all parts of the industry—newspapers, magazines, and books—but the situation in each sector is distinct enough to warrant examining them separately.

—Dizard, *Old Media, New Media,* p. 157

Pattern: _____

6. For each American who commits suicide, about ten attempt it. Although many more women than men attempt suicide, more men than women succeed at it. This is likely because the women's attempts are more a 'cry for help,' while the men are more serious about accomplishing the act. In addition, men tend to choose methods that allow less intervention, such as guns, while women are more likely to use pills. Also guns provide less time to change one's mind or to allow someone to intervene.

—Henslin, *Social Problems,* p. 336

Pattern: _____

7. Be careful not to evaluate negatively the cultural differences you perceive. Be careful that you don't fall into the trap of ethnocentric thinking, evaluating your culture positively and other cultures negatively. For example, many Americans of Northern European descent evaluate negatively the tendency of many Hispanics and Southern Europeans to use the street for a gathering place, for playing Dominoes, and for just sitting on a cool evening. Whether you like or dislike using the street in this way, recognize that neither attitude is logically correct or incorrect. This street behavior is simply adequate or inadequate for *members of the culture.*

—DeVito, *Human Communication,* p. 103

Pattern: _____

8. In short, the view that a drug is good or bad depends not on objective conditions but on subjective concerns. It is a matter of how people define matters. People's definitions, in turn, influence how they use and abuse drugs, whether or not a drug will be legal or illegal, and what social policies they want to adopt. This is the central sociological aspect of drug use and abuse, one that we shall stress over and over in this chapter.

—Henslin, *Social Problems,* p. 91

Pattern: _____

9. Human migration has by no means come to an end. Large-scale migrations still make daily news. The United Nations' Universal Declaration of Human Rights

affirms anyone's right to leave his or her homeland to seek a better life elsewhere, but it cannot guarantee that there will be anyplace willing to take anyone. As in the past, the major push and pull factors behind contemporary migration are economic and political. Also, people are trying to move from the poor countries to the rich countries and from the politically repressed countries to more democratic countries. In addition, millions of people are fleeing civil and international warfare. Pressures for migration are growing, and in coming years they may constitute the world's greatest political and economic problem.

—Bergman and RenwicK, *Introduction to Geography,* p. 197

Pattern: _____

10. "I'll lose my job if they find out what I sent you." Most companies keep copies of all e-mail that is sent and received, and most do spot checks of the contents. When the above statement was discovered among an employee's outgoing messages, a company security officer wondered whether she had uncovered corporate espionage. Was the message sender giving away—or perhaps selling—company secrets? In this case it was easy to find out: The security officer simply extracted the attachment that had been sent with the message. It turned out to be pornographic material—and the employee did indeed lose his job over this incident.

—Capron and Johnson, *Computers: Tools for an Information Age,* p. 328

Pattern: _____

APPLYING ACADEMIC THOUGHT PATTERNS

Now that you are familiar with the basic thought patterns, you are ready to use these valuable structures to organize your learning and shape your thinking. Patterns give ideas shape or form, thereby making them more readily comprehensible. Look for these patterns as you read, listen for them in lectures, and use them in completing assignments and writing papers.

Subsequent chapters in this text will demonstrate the use of patterns in specific learning situations and in specific academic disciplines. Although it is not within the scope of this text, you also will discover that academic thought patterns are useful in organizing and answering essay questions and writing term papers.

SUMMARY

Recognition of an author's or speaker's thought pattern aids comprehension and recall and also allows you to anticipate idea development. Six thought patterns are common.

- *Definition.* An object or idea is explained by describing the general class or group to which it belongs and then specifying how it differs from others in the same group (distinguishing characteristics).

- *Classification.* Classification divides a topic into parts or categories on the basis of common or shared characteristics.
- *Order or sequence.* There are four forms of the order or sequence pattern. Chronology refers to the arrangement of events in time; process focuses on the order in which procedures or steps are accomplished; order of importance expresses priority or preference; and spatial order refers to physical location, position, or order.
- *Cause and effect.* Causal relationships between two or more events or actions are shown with this pattern. Causes may be implied or directly stated, and often multiple causes and/or multiple effects are evident.
- *Comparison and contrast.* This pattern emphasizes similarities and/or differences among ideas, concepts, people, or events.
- *Listing/enumeration.* This pattern is a means of presenting pertinent information about or in support of a topic, either step by step or with no inherent order.

Other commonly used thought patterns are

- *Statement and clarification.* This pattern indicates that information explaining an idea or concept will follow the topic sentence.
- *Summary.* This pattern indicates that a condensed review of an idea will be given.
- *Generalization and example.* This pattern provides one or more examples of a broad, general statement.
- *Addition.* this pattern indicates that additional information will follow the topic sentence.

INTEGRATING
IDEAS

◆

PAIRED
READINGS

Biology

PREREADING QUESTIONS

1. What thought pattern(s) do you anticipate this reading will use?
2. What do you already know about right-brain and left-brain dominance?

The Human Brain

Robert A. Wallace

1   Now we come to the rather interesting notion of the human brain talking about itself. Perhaps it is because of this strange twist that we encounter so many endless accolades about this great organ. Let's begin with some basic descriptions.

2   The human brain is divided into three parts: the hindbrain, the midbrain, and the forebrain. The **hindbrain** consists of the medulla, the cerebellum, and the pons. The hindbrain is sometimes called the "old brain" because it evolved first. These structures still dominate the brain of some animals, as we have seen. The **midbrain,** logically enough, is the area between the forebrain and hindbrain and connects the two. The **forebrain,** or "new brain," consists of the two cerebral hemispheres and certain internal structures.

THE HINDBRAIN

The Medulla

3   As a rough generality, the more subconscious, or mechanical, processes are directed by the more posterior parts of the brain. For example, the hindmost part, the **medulla,** is specialized as a control center for such basic functions as breathing, digestion, and heartbeat. In addition, it is an important center of control for certain charming activities such as swallowing, vomiting, and sneezing. As we have already seen, it connects the spinal cord and the more anterior parts of the brain.

The Cerebellum and Pons

4   Above the medulla and more toward the back of the head is the **cerebellum,** which is concerned with balance, equilibrium, and coordination. Do you suppose there might be differences between athletes and nonathletes in this part of the brain? (Apparently there are, but the differences are slight.) Do you think this "lower" center of the brain is subject to modification through learning? (Can you improve your coordination through practice?) The **pons,** which is the portion of the brainstem just above the medulla, acts as a bridge connecting certain parts of the brain. For instance, it connects the cerebellum and the cerebral cortex, accenting the relationship between the cerebellar part of the hindbrain and the more "conscious" centers of the forebrain.

Figure A   The human brain in surface view (1) and in sagittal section (2). Note that there is so much regularity in the convolutions that some have been named.

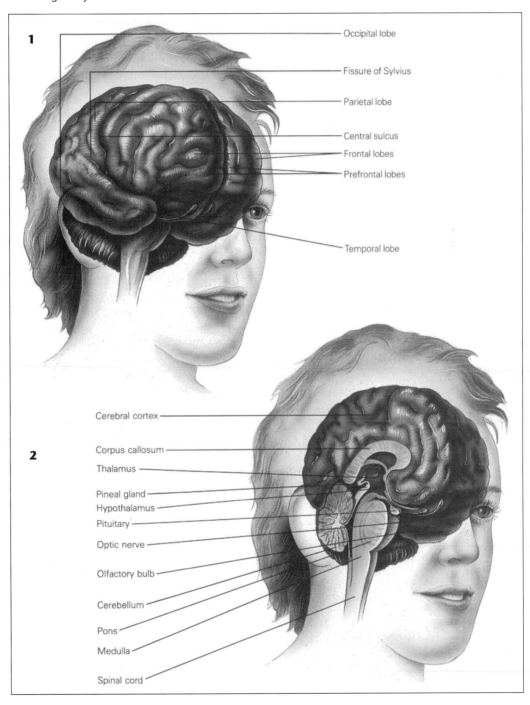

THE MIDBRAIN

5   The **midbrain** connects the hindbrain and forebrain by numerous tracts. In addition, certain parts of the midbrain receive sensory input from the eyes and ears. In vertebrates, sound is processed here before being sent to the forebrain. The midbrain has a more complex role in fishes and amphibians than in reptiles, birds, and mammals because in the latter group, many of its functions are taken over by the forebrain.

THE FOREBRAIN

The Thalamus and Reticular System

6   The thalamus and hypothalamus are located at the base of the forebrain. The **thalamus** is rather unpoetically called the "great relay station" of the brain. It consists of densely packed clusters of nervous cells that presumably connect the various parts of the brain—between the forebrain and the hindbrain, between different parts of the forebrain, and between parts of the sensory system and the cerebral cortex.

7   The thalamus contains a peculiar neural structure called the **reticular system,** an area of interconnected neurons that are almost feltlike in appearance. The reticular system runs through the medulla, pons, and thalamus and extends upward to the cerebral cortex. The role of the reticular system is still a bit mysterious, but several interesting facts are known about it. For example, it bugs your brain. Every afferent and efferent pathway to and from the brain sends side branches to the reticular system as it passes through the thalamus. So all the brain's incoming and outgoing communications are "trapped." Also, these reticular neurons are rather unspecific. That is, the same neuron may respond to stimuli from, say, the hand, foot, ear, or eye. It has been suggested that the reticular system serves to activate the appropriate parts of the brain upon receiving a stimulus. In other words, the reticular system activates the part of the brain that is needed for the particular task at hand. If there is no incoming stimulus—no need for conscious activity—the system sends fewer signals, quieting the brain. You may have noticed it is much easier to fall asleep lying on a soft bed in a quiet, darkened room than on a pool table in a disco. With the quietness, the reticular system receives fewer messages and the brain is lulled rather than aroused. On those nights when you have the "big eye" and just can't sleep, the cause may be continued (possibly spontaneous) firing of reticular neurons.

8   The reticular system may also regulate which impulses are allowed to register in your brain. When you are engrossed in a television program, you may not notice that someone has entered the room. But when you are engaged in even more absorbing activities, it might take a general stimulus on the order of an earthquake to distract you. Such filtering and selective depression of stimuli apparently takes place in the reticular system.

The Hypothalamus

9   The **hypothalamus** is a small body, densely packed with cells. It helps regulate the internal environment as well as some aspects of behavior. For example, the hypothalamus helps to control heart rate, blood pressure, and body temperature. It also plays a part in the regulation of the pituitary gland, as we learned earlier. And it con-

trols such basic drives as hunger, thirst, and sex. So now you know what to blame for all your problems. Experimental electrical stimulation of various centers in the hypothalamus can cause a cat to act hungry, angry, cold, hot, benign, or horny.

The Cerebrum

10   For many people the word *brain* conjures up an image of two large, deeply convoluted gray lobes. What they have in mind, of course, is the outside layer of the two cerebral hemispheres, the dominant physical aspect of the human brain. The **cerebrum** is present in all vertebrates, but it assumes particular importance in humans. In some animals, it is essentially an elaborate refinement that implements behavior that could be performed to some degree without it. It has a far greater importance in other animals.

HEMISPHERES AND LOBES

11   The human cerebrum consists of two hemispheres, the left and the right, each of these being divided into four lobes. At the back is the **occipital lobe,** which receives and analyzes visual information.

12   The **temporal lobe** is at the side of the brain. It roughly resembles the thumb on a boxing glove, and it is bounded anteriorly by the fissure of Sylvius. The temporal lobe shares in the processing of visual information, but its main function is auditory reception.

13   The **frontal lobe** is right where you would expect to find it—at the front of the cerebrum, just behind the forehead. This is the part that people hit with the heel of the palm when they suddenly remember what they forgot. One part of the frontal lobe is the center for the regulation of precise voluntary movement. Another part functions importantly in the use of language, and damage here results in speech impairment.

14   The area at the very front of the frontal lobe is called the **prefron area,** if you follow that. Whereas it was once believed that this area was the seat of intellect, it is now apparent that its principal function is sorting out information and ordering stimuli. In other words, it places information and stimuli into their proper context. The gentle touch of a mate or the sight of a hand protruding from the bathtub drain might both serve as stimuli, but they would be sorted differently by the prefrontal area. Up until a few years ago, parts of the frontal lobe were surgically removed in efforts to bring the behavior of certain aberrant individuals more into line with what psychologists had decided was the norm. The operation was called a frontal lobotomy, and it resulted in passive and unimaginative individuals. Fortunately, the practice has been largely discontinued, largely because chemical treatments now meet the same objectives.

15   The **parietal lobe** lies directly behind the frontal lobe and is separated from it by the central sulcus. This lobe receives stimuli from the skin receptors, and it helps to process information regarding bodily position. Even if you can't see your feet right now, you have some idea of where they are thanks to neurons in the parietal lobe. Damage to the parietal lobe may produce numbness and may cause a person to perceive his or her own body as wildly distorted and to be unable to perceive spatial relationships in the environment.

TWO BRAINS, TWO MINDS?

16   The best way to begin a banal conversation a few years ago was, "What sign are you?" Today, though, sophisticates may lead with, "Are you right-brained or left-brained?" Some of the findings of one of the most fascinating branches of neural research have indeed filtered into the public consciousness.

17   The question is based on information that has been accumulating since the middle of the last century when A. L. Wigam, a British physician, performed autopsies on men who had led somewhat normal lives with only half a brain. That is, one hemisphere had been destroyed by accident or other trauma. The question then arose, since we only need half a brain, then why do we have two? At first it was assumed that this was another case where nature had built in redundancy, or backup, in a critical system.

18   Brain research has revealed a fascinating fact: the hemispheres are not duplicates at all, but structures with quite different specializations. To oversimplify, the left hemisphere is the center of logical, stepwise reasoning, of mathematics and language. It processes information in a fragmentary, sequential manner, sorting out the parts of questions and dealing with each quite rationally. (*Star Trek's* Spock was definitely left-brained.) The right brain, on the other hand, is the center of awareness for music and art. Imagination swells from this lobe and it sees things in their entirety (holistically), often solving problems through insight, as it compares relationships.

19   The flexibility of the two hemispheres has been shown when one is damaged and the other takes over its role. Such flexibility, by the way, may be greater in left-handers than in right-handers. It seems that the brain centers of south-paws are generally more diffuse, less localized, with functions more equally dispersed between the two hemispheres. Brain damage to left-handers may produce different symptoms than right-handers with similar injuries.

20   The two halves of the brain are connected by a great, broad tract of nerve fibers, about 4 inches wide, called the **corpus callosum.** Information from each half can be communicated to the other half via the corpus callosum. Thus, special abilities of the two parts of the brain can be integrated and allow us to solve problems, perform tasks, and appreciate life's offerings by a grand union of complex and differing abilities.

21   Or maybe not. Evidence indicates that usually one hemisphere is dominant and inordinately influences how we approach life. Furthermore, some researchers argue that the hemispheres compete with each other for our attention. Such arguments, at this point, quickly extend beyond science and enter the realm of philosophy.

—Wallace, *Biology: The World of Life,* pp. 604–14

VOCABULARY REVIEW

1. For each of the words listed below, use context; prefixes, roots, and suffixes; and/or a dictionary to write a brief definition or synonym of the word as it is used in the reading.

a. afferent (para. 7) _____

b. efferent (para. 7) _____

c. banal (para. 16) _____

d. redundancy (para. 17) _____

e. specializations (para. 18) _____

f. fragmentary (para. 18) _____

g. realm (para. 21) _____

2. Underline new specialized terms introduced in the reading.

COMPREHENSION QUESTIONS

1. Which area of the brain is responsible for each of the following functions?

   a. balance and coordination _____

   b. regulation of heart rate _____

   c. vision _____

   d. hearing _____

   e. sorting out information _____

2. Describe the specializations of the right brain and of the left brain.
3. Explain what happens when one brain hemisphere is damaged.
4. Why do left-handed people have more flexibility between hemispheres than right-handed people?
5. Identify the overall thought pattern(s) used in this reading.
6. Underline transitional words that signal the overall pattern(s).

THINKING CRITICALLY

1. If the author of the reading were present, what questions would you like to ask him about right-brain or left-brain dominance or brain functioning?
2. Why does the author defer the argument in paragraph 21 to a philosopher?
3. Are you right- or left-brained? That is, which hemisphere dominates your thinking and behavior?

LEARNING/STUDY STRATEGY

Draw a sketch of the brain. Label its parts.

Psychology

PREREADING QUESTIONS

1. Do men and women think differently? How?
2. How are male and female brains different?

Are There "His" and "Hers" Brains?

Carole Wade and Carol Tavris

1   A second stubborn issue concerns the existence of sex differences in the brain. Historically, findings on male-female brain differences have often flip-flopped in a most suspicious manner, a result of the biases of the observers rather than the biology of the brain (Shields, 1975). For example, in the 1960s, scientists speculated that women were more "right-brained" and men were more "left-brained," which supposedly explained why men were "rational" and women "intuitive." Then, when the virtues of the right hemisphere were discovered, such as creativity and ability in art and music, some researchers decided that *men* were more right-brained. But it is now clear that the abilities popularly associated with the two sexes do not fall neatly into the two hemispheres of the brain. The left side is more verbal (presumably a "female" trait), but it is also more mathematical (presumably a "male" trait). The right side is more intuitive ("female"), but it is also more spatially talented ("male").

2   To evaluate the issue of sex differences in the brain intelligently, we need to ask two questions: Do male and female brains differ physically? And if so, what, if anything, do these differences have to do with behavior?

3   Let's consider the first question. Many anatomical and biochemical sex differences have been found in animal brains, especially in areas related to reproduction, such as they hypothalamus (McEwen, 1983). Human sex differences, however, have been more elusive. Of course, we would expect to find male-female brain differences that are related to the regulation of sex hormones and other aspects of reproduction. But many researchers want to know whether there are differences that affect how men and women think or behave—and here, the picture is murkier.

4   For example, in 1982, two anthropologists autopsied 14 human brains and reported an average sex difference in the size and shape of the *splenium,* a small section at the end of the corpus callosum, the bundle of fibers dividing the cerebral hemispheres (de Lacoste-Utamsing & Holloway, 1982). The researchers concluded that women's brains are less lateralized for certain tasks than men's are—that men rely more heavily on one or the other side of the brain, whereas women tend to use both sides. This conclusion quickly made its way into newspapers, magazines, and even textbooks as a verified sex difference.

5   Today, however, the picture has changed. In a review of the available studies, neuroscientist William Byne (1993) found that only the 1982 study reported the splenium to be larger in women. Two very early studies (in 1906 and 1909) found that it was larger in men, and 21 later studies found no sex differences between the two sexes, differences that paled in comparison with the huge individual variations *within* each sex (Bishop & Wahlsten, 1997). Most people are unaware of these findings because studies that find no differences rarely make headlines.

6   Researchers are now looking for other sex differences in the brain, such as in the density of neurons in specific areas. One team, examining nine brains from autopsied bodies, found that the women had an average of 11 percent more cells in areas of the cortex associated with the processing of auditory information; all of the women had more of these cells than did any of the men (Witelson, Glazer, & Kigar, 1994).

7   Other researchers are searching for sex differences in the brain areas that are active when people work on a particular task. In one study (Shaywitz et al., 1995), 19 men and 19 women were asked to say whether pairs of nonsense words rhymed, a task that required them to process and compare sounds. MRI scans showed that in both sexes an area at the front of the left hemisphere was activated. But in 11 of the women and none of the men, the corresponding area in the right hemisphere was also active. These findings are further evidence for a sex difference in lateralization, at least for this one type of language function. Such a difference could help explain why left-hemisphere damage is less likely to cause language problems in women than in men after a stroke (Inglis & Lawson, 1981; McGlone, 1978).

8   Over the next few years, research may reveal additional anatomical and information processing differences in the brains of males and females. But even if such differences exist, we must then ask our second question: *What do the differences mean for the behavior of men and women in real life?*

9   Some popular writers have been quick to assume that brain differences explain, among other things, women's allegedly superior intuition, women's love of talking about feelings and men's love of talking about sports, women's greater verbal ability, men's edge in math ability, and why men won't ask for directions when they are lost. But there are at least three problems with these conclusions:

10   1 *These supposed gender differences in behavior are stereotypes;* the overlap between the sexes is greater than the difference between them. Although some differences may be statistically significant, most are small in practical terms.

11   2 *A biological difference does not necessarily have behavioral implications.* In the rhyme-judgment study, for example, men and women performed equally well, despite the differences in their MRIs—so what do those brain differences actually mean in practical terms? When it comes to explaining how brain differences are related to more general abilities, speculations are as plentiful as ants at a picnic, but at present they remain just that—speculations (Blum, 1997; Hoptman & Davidson, 1994). To know whether sex differences in the brain translate into significant behavioral differences, we would need to know much more about how brain organization and chemistry affect human abilities and traits.

12   3 *Sex differences in the brain could be the result rather than the cause of behavioral differences.* Remember that experiences in life are constantly sculpting the

circuitry of the brain, affecting the way brains are organized and how they function—and males and females often have different experiences.

13   Thus, the answer to our second question, whether physical differences are linked to behavior, is "No one really knows." It is important to keep an open mind about new findings on sex differences in the brain, but because the practical significance of these findings (if any) is not clear, it is also important to be cautious and aware of how such results might be exaggerated and misused.

—Wade and Tavris, *Psychology*, pp. 130–32

VOCABULARY REVIEW

1. For each of the words listed below, use context; prefixes, roots, and suffixes; and/or a dictionary to write a brief definition or synonym of the word as it is used in the reading.

   a. existence (para. 1) _____

   b. biases (para. 1) _____

   c. intuitive (para. 1) _____

   d. hemispheres (para. 1) _____

   e. spatially (para. 1) _____

   f. elusive (para. 3) _____

   g. hypothalamus (para. 3) _____

   h. splenium (para. 4) _____

   i. lateralized (para. 4) _____

   j. speculations (para. 11) _____

2. Underline new specialized terms introduced in the reading.

COMPREHENSION QUESTIONS

1. What did researchers decide about the brain once the right hemisphere abilities were discovered?
2. What questions need to be asked to evaluate if sex is responsible for brain differences?
3. How do male and female brains differ in physical makeup?
4. Why are the differences between male and female brains not as significant as they might seem?
5. What do scientists need to know to determine if sex differences in the brain are related to general abilities?
6. Explain how sex differences in the brain might actually be the result and not the cause of behavioral differences.

7. Why is it important to keep an open mind about sex differences in the brain?

8. What is the overall thought pattern used throughout the reading?

THINKING CRITICALLY

1. How might the findings about sex differences in the brain be misused?

2. Why do you think the author characterizes some traits as "male" and some as "female"? Is this an accurate characterization? Can you name some other traits that are considered typically male or typically female?

3. Why do you think it is important to understand how male and female brains are different? What possible uses could there be for this information?

4. Why do scientists study which areas of the brain are used for different tasks?

5. Are you convinced by this selection that there are significant differences in male and female brains? Why or why not?

6. Describe other types of physical differences between men and women that impact behavior.

LEARNING/STUDY STRATEGY

Write a summary of this selection.

THINKING ABOUT THE PAIRED READINGS

INTEGRATING IDEAS

1. What is the purpose of each reading?

2. In what ways are these readings similar, and how are they different?

3. Which reading was easier to read? Explain your reasons.

4. Assume you are preparing for an essay exam. How would you study each reading? How would your strategies differ?

GENERATING NEW IDEAS

1. Identify one famous historical figure and write a one-page paper describing whether and how that person is left- or right-brained or how you could argue both ways.

2. Based on the reading "Are There 'His' and 'Hers' Brains?" summarize a short story you could write describing a world in which sex differences in the brain are fully understood and accounted for.

Multimedia Activities

1. **Rhetorical Patterns for Organizing Documents**
   http://www.ecf.utoronto.ca/~writing/handbook-rhetoric.html
   The University of Toronto presents this site, which reviews the ways information is organized.
   Choose some objects and activities you experience in your daily life. Write about them according
   to the appropriate guidelines presented here.

2. **Logic Patterns**
   http://www.learner.org/teacherslab/math/patterns/logic.html#activities
   Try these online logic pattern activities from The Teacher's Lab, the Annenberg/CPB Math
   and Science Project. Observe patterns in your daily life. When do you find yourself sorting and
   classifying?

Take a Road Trip to
Ellis Island and the Statue of Liberty!

If your instructor has asked you to use the Reading Road Trip CD-ROM or Website, be sure to visit the
Patterns of Organization module for multimedia tutorials, exercises, and tests.

CHAPTER 8

LEARNING FROM TEXTBOOKS

LEARNING OBJECTIVES

✦ To become familiar with standard textbook format
✦ To use textbook features to facilitate learning
✦ To devise systematic approaches for textbook study
✦ To learn systematic retention and recall techniques

In many college courses, the textbook is your primary source of information. Each term you will spend hours reading, reviewing, and studying textbooks. Class lectures are often coordinated with reading assignments in the course text, written assignments require you to apply or evaluate ideas and concepts presented in the textbook, and term papers explore topics introduced in the text.

This chapter presents strategies for using textbooks as efficiently as possible. It describes the standard format, identifies features that aid learning, discusses systematic approaches to textbook study, and presents recall and retention strategies.

TEXTBOOK FORMAT

When you first examine a textbook, it may seem like an overwhelming collection of facts and ideas. However, textbooks are highly organized, well-structured sources of information. They follow specific patterns of organization and are uniform and predictable in format and style. Once you become familiar with these structures, you will come to regard textbooks as easy-to-use resources and valuable guides to learning.

Preface

A textbook usually begins with an opening statement called a preface, in which the author describes the text. The preface often specifies

- structure or organization of the book
- major points of emphasis

- distinctive features
- author's reasons for writing the text
- intended audience
- special learning features
- author's qualifications
- references or authorities consulted when writing

Reading the preface gives you a firsthand impression of the author and his or her attitudes toward the text. Think of it as a chance to get a glimpse of the author as a person.

Some authors include, instead of or in addition to a preface, an introduction titled "To the Student." Written specifically for you, it contains information similar to that in a preface. The author may also include an introduction directed "To the Instructor." Although it may often be quite technical, discussing teaching methodologies and theoretical issues, it may contain some material of interest to students as well. Figure 8–1 shows an excerpt from the preface of a computer science text. Marginal annotation and underlining have been added to call your attention to its contents.

EXERCISE 8–1 | *Read or reread the preface in Academic Reading and in one of your other textbooks. Using the list above as a guide, list on your own paper the types of information each preface provides.*

Table of Contents

The table of contents is one of the first things a professor looks at to evaluate a book. It is also one of the first things you should look at after you have purchased a textbook. The table of contents is an outline of the textbook's main topics and subtopics. It shows the organization of the text and indicates the interrelations among the topics. You can easily identify predominant thought patterns used throughout the text.

Besides using the table of contents to preview a text's overall content and organization, be sure to refer to it before reading particular chapters. Although chapters are organized as separate units, they are related. To understand a given chapter, note what topics immediately precede and follow it.

Recent textbooks may include a brief table of contents listing only unit and chapter titles, followed by a complete table of contents that lists subheadings and various learning aids contained within each chapter. The brief table of contents is most useful for assessing the overall content and structure of the entire text, whereas the complete one is more helpful when you are studying individual chapters.

Figure 8–2 on page 231 shows a brief table of contents excerpted from a sociology textbook. You can see that the text approaches the study of sociology by examining first the sociological perspective, followed by the basic concepts of the social framework. It then considers how people are differentiated and

Figure 8–1   Excerpt from a Preface

What Is Computer Confluence?

book is part of a multimedia package

Computer Confluence is more than a textbook; it's the confluence of three information sources: an illustrated textbook, a multimedia CD-ROM, and a timely World Wide Web site on the Internet. This integrated learning package takes advantage of the unique strengths of three media types:

advantages of textbooks

- *Computer Confluence,* the text. In spite of the talk about a paperless future, a book's user interface still has many advantages: You can read it under a tree or on the subway, you can bend the corners and scribble in the margins, you can study the words and pictures for hours without suffering from eyestrain or backache. A well-written text can serve as a learning tool, a reference work, a study guide, and even a source of motivation and inspiration. A textbook is no substitute for a good teacher, but a good textbook can almost always make a good teacher better. This book, which started out as *Computer Currents* in 1994, has served as an information-age guidebook for thousands of students through its first two editions.

CD-ROM uses

- *Computer Confluence,* the CD-ROM. A CD-ROM may not be as warm and friendly as a good book, but it can deliver video, audio, animation, and other dynamic media that can't be printed on paper. A well-designed CD-ROM can encourage exploration through interactivity. The *Computer Confluence* CD-ROM supplements and reinforces the material in the book with state-of-the-art 3-D animation, audio, and video. It also includes a software sampler for hands-on experimentation and interactive study materials that provide student feedback.

Web site uses

- *Computer Confluence,* the Web site (http://www.computerconfluence.com). The information in computer books and CD-ROMs has a short shelf life. The Internet makes it possible to publish up-to-the-minute news and information regularly and link that information to other sources around the world. The Internet can also serve as a communication conduit for on-line discussion and research. An extensive collection of timely, media-rich Web pages keeps the information in *Computer Confluence* current. The pages include late-breaking news, multimedia tidbits, and links to the most important computer and information technology sites, all organized by chapter and topic. The Web site also includes discussion areas where students, instructors, and authors can meet on-line. Students can also visit the Web site to take practice quizzes and submit answers to on-line exercises.

Computer Confluence presents computers and information technology on three levels:

levels of thinking on which the book focuses

- Explanations: *Computer Confluence* clearly explains what a computer is and what it can (and can't) do; it explains the basics of information technology clearly and concisely.

- Applications: *Computer Confluence* clearly illustrates how computers and networks can be used as practical tools to accomplish a wide variety of tasks and solve a wide variety of problems.

- Implications: *Computer Confluence* puts computers in a human context, illustrating how information technology affects our lives, our world, and our future.

Who Is Computer Confluence For?

intended audience

Computer Confluence: Exploring Tomorrow's Technology is designed especially for the introductory computer class for both nonmajors and majors. *Computer Confluence* is also appropriate for introductory computer science classes, discipline-specific computer courses offered through other departments, high school courses, and adult education courses. *Computer Confluence* can also serve as a self-study guide for anyone who's motivated to understand the changing technological landscape. . . .

How Is Computer Confluence Organized?

The book consists of 16 chapters organized into five broad sections:

overall organization: 5 key topics

1. *Approaching Computers: Hardware and Software Fundamentals*

2. *Using Computers: Essential Applications*

3. *Exploring with Computers: Networks and Gateways*

4. *Mastering Computers: Issues, Algorithms, and Intelligence*

5. *Living with Computers: Information Age Implications*

(continued)

content review
of each part

> Part 1 provides the basics: a brief historical perspective, a nontechnical discussion of computer and Internet basics, and an overview of hardware and software options. These chapters quickly introduce key concepts that recur throughout the book, putting the student on solid ground for understanding future chapters. Part 2 covers the most important and widely used computer applications, including word processing, spreadsheets, graphics, multimedia tools, and databases. These applications, like those in Parts 3 and 4, are presented in terms of concepts and trends rather than keystrokes. Part 3 explores the world of networks, from simple interoffice LANs to the massive global infrastructure that's evolving from the Internet. Part 4 begins with a discussion of information technology risks and related ethical issues; it then explores the process and the problems of creating software, including the curious field of computer science known as artificial intelligence. Part 5 explores the far-reaching impact of computers on our work, our schools, our homes, our society, and our future.

focus of
the text

> Throughout the five parts, the book's focus gradually flows from the concrete to the controversial and from the present to the future. Individual chapters have a similarly expanding focus. After a brief introduction, each chapter flows from concrete concepts that provide grounding for beginners toward abstract, future-oriented questions and ideas.

instructional
aids

> Each chapter includes instructional aids to help students master the material quickly. Key terms are highlighted in boldface type for quick reference; secondary terms are italicized. Terms are defined in context, in a glossary at the end of the text, and in the CD-ROM's hypertext glossary. Each chapter begins with a list of objectives and ends with a chapter summary; a list of key terms; collections of review questions, discussion questions, and projects; and an annotated list of sources and resources for students who want more information or intellectual stimulation.

Source: Beekman, *Computer Confluence,* pp. xix–xxi

treated unequally, the institutions that society creates, and, finally, the causes and results of social change. The thought pattern used to organize the textbook's contents is *classification.*

Figure 8–3 on page 232 is an excerpt from the detailed table of contents that appears in the same textbook. The chapter discusses how socialization occurs. The predominant thought pattern is evident: *order* and *sequence.* Both process and chronological sequence patterns are evident in individual chapter sections, as marked on the figure.

EXERCISE 8–2

Turn to the table of contents of one of your textbooks. Choose a unit or part that you have not read but that will be assigned soon. Predict and list the thought pattern(s) of as many sections of the chapters as possible. Then, when you read the chapter, confirm or reject each of your predictions.

Appendix

The appendix of a textbook contains supplementary information that does not fit within the framework of the chapters. Often, the appendix offers valuable aids. For example, one physics text contains five appendixes:

Appendix A. Systems of Measurement

Appendix B. More About Motion

Figure 8–2   Brief Table of Contents

Source: Thompson and Hickey, *Society in Focus,* p. vii

    Appendix C. Graphing

    Appendix D. More About Vectors

    Appendix E. Exponential Growth and Doubling Time[1]

The textbook includes these appendixes for the reader's convenience, and the text refers to each one frequently.

Figure 8–3   Detailed Table of Contents

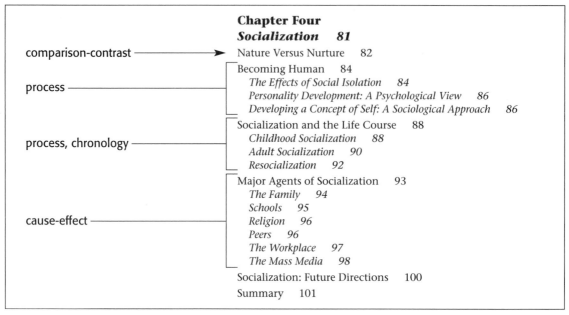

Source: Thompson and Hickey, *Society in Focus,* p. ix–x

Glossary

A glossary is an alphabetical listing of new vocabulary words that are used in the text. The meaning of each word is also included. Located in the back of the text, the glossary serves as a mini-dictionary. To make it even more convenient to use, take some paper clips and attach one to the first page of the glossary in each of your texts. The paper clips will enable you to turn directly to the glossary without hunting and fumbling.

The glossary is easier to use than a regular dictionary. As you know, many words have several meanings, and regular dictionaries list all of the most common meanings. To find the meaning of a word in a dictionary, you have to sort through all the meanings until you find one that suits the way the word is used in the text. A glossary, on the other hand, lists only one meaning—the meaning intended by the author of your text.

The glossary can serve as a useful study aid, particularly at the end of a course when you have completed the text. The glossary is actually a list of words that you should have learned. The easiest way to check whether you have learned these new terms is to go through each column of the glossary, covering up the meanings with an index card or folded sheet of paper. Read each word and try to write a definition for it or just make up the definition mentally. Then uncover the meaning and see whether you were correct. Keep track of the terms you miss, and study them later.

Index

At the end of most texts, you will find an alphabetical subject index that lists topics covered in the text, along with page references. Although its primary function is to enable you to locate information on a specific topic, it can also be used as a study aid for final exams. If you have covered most or all of the chapters in the text, then you should be familiar with each topic indexed. For example, suppose the index of an economics textbook includes the following.

> Saving, 487
>> desired, equilibrium national income and, 497–499
>> domestic, economic development and, 751
>> marginal propensity to save and, 490–491
>> national, 518–519
>> private, 511
>> public, 511–512
>> short- and long-run effects of, 728–729

To review for an exam, you can look at each index entry and test your recall. In the economics textbook example you would ask yourself, "What is the equilibrium national income? How does it relate to desired saving? What is the difference between national and public saving? What are the effects of saving?" and so forth.

Some texts also include a name index that enables you to locate references to individuals mentioned in the text.

The checklist in Figure 8–4 on page 234 is provided to help you quickly assess a textbook's content and organization.

EXERCISE 8–3 | *Use the checklist in Figure 8–4 to analyze the content and organization of one of your textbooks. Check each item that describes your textbook.*

Academic Application

TEXTBOOK LEARNING FEATURES

Most college textbooks are written by professors who are experienced teachers. They understand how students learn, and they know which topics and concepts usually cause students difficulty. Their purpose in writing is not only to present information but also to help students learn actively. Consequently, most textbooks contain numerous learning aids: chapter previews, marginal

Figure 8–4   Textbook Checklist

Preface

- States the purpose of the text
- Indicates intended audience
- Explains book organization
- Includes author's credentials
- Describes distinctive features
- Discusses major points of emphasis
- Describes learning aids

Table of Contents

- Includes brief table of contents
- Groups chapters into parts or sections
- Indicates thought pattern(s) throughout the text

Appendix

- Offers useful tables and charts
- Includes supplementary documents
- Describes background or reference material

Glossary

- Includes definitions of special terms
- Provides pronunciation guide, as well as word meanings

Index

- Includes subject index
- Offers separate name index

notes, special-interest boxes or inserts, review questions, lists of key terms, summaries, and references. A textbook is a guide to learning—a source that directs your attention, shows you what is important, and enables you to read actively. Learning will be easier if you use the textbook's learning aids to best advantage.

Chapter Preview

Research indicates that if readers have some knowledge of the content and organization of material *before* they begin to read it, their comprehension and recall increase. Consequently, numerous textbooks begin each chapter with some kind of preview. There are several common forms.

Chapter Objectives   Some texts list the objectives of each chapter beneath the chapter title, as is done in this book. The objectives help to focus your attention on important ideas and concepts. They usually are listed in the order in which the topics appear in the chapter, presenting an abbreviated outline of the main topics.

Chapter Outline   Other texts provide a brief outline of each chapter's contents. Formed from the headings and subheadings used throughout the chapter, the outline reflects both the content and the organization of the chapter. A sample outline from a psychology text is shown in Figure 8–5. As you study a chapter outline, pay attention to the sequence and progression of topics and look for thought patterns.

Figure 8–5 Chapter Outline

CHAPTER THIRTEEN
Development over the Life Span

From Conception to the First Year
  Prenatal Development
  The Infant's World

Cognitive Development
  The Ability to Think
  The Ability to Speak

Gender Development

Moral Development
  Moral Judgments: Reasoning About Morality
  Moral Emotions: Acquiring Empathy, Guilt, and Shame
  Moral Action: Learning to Behave Morally

Adolescence
  The Physiology of Adolescence
  The Psychology of Adolescence

Adulthood
  The Biological Clock
  The Social Clock

Are Adults Prisoners of Childhood?

Think About It: Puzzles of Psychology
  How Long Should We Prolong Life?

Taking Psychology with You
  Bringing Up Baby

Source: Wade and Tavris, *Psychology,* p. 491

Chapter Overview Some textbook authors provide a preview section in which they state what the chapter is about, explain why certain topics are important, focus the reader's attention on key issues, or indicate how the chapter is related to other chapters in the book. Overviews may be labeled "Chapter Preview," "Overview," a less obvious title such as "Memo," or, as in the sample shown in Figure 8–6 on page 236 (taken from a biology text), with no title at all, but presented on the opening page of the chapter following the objectives.

Each type of preview can be used to activate and monitor your learning before you begin, while you are reading, and after you finish the chapter.

Figure 8–6   Chapter Overview

All the known field mice in the universe must live on whatever this planet can provide for them. They run little risk of depleting their planet's resources, however, because their needs are few—a warm hole, a little food, and a little social acceptance. It's a good thing for them that their requirements are so few, because they have only the resources that their planet can provide. Should they deplete or foul those resources, they would be in a bit of a fix, because *that's all there is.* The point is not too subtle, is it? We share the planet with the field mice. And our resources, too, are limited. But their gentle touch on the great, delicate globe is far from our sledgehammer impact.

In this chapter, we will review the state of some of the resources and energy necessary to life and try to see just how our impact is influenced by something very ephemeral and hard to pin down—our values. We will approach the question of whether our behavior and values could or should be based on our access to the Earth's resources and energy. And how have we treated our heritage?

We will consider the Earth's resources to be in one of two categories, renewable and nonrenewable. **Renewable resources** are those that do not exist in set amounts—they can be reused or replenished at least as fast as we use them. If we cut a pine tree, we can grow another one (assuming that the topsoil didn't wash away because we cut the first one). **Nonrenewable resources** are those that exist in set amounts on the planet and cannot be replenished. Once used, they are gone, or they are changed so much that they are difficult to recover in their original form. The two gallons of gasoline your auto consumed on your date last night is an example.

Source: Wallace, *Biology: The World of Life,* p. 535

Before Reading
- Use the chapter preview to activate your prior knowledge on the subject. Recall what you already know about the subject by trying to anticipate the chapter's main points.
- Use chapter previews to predict the predominant thought patterns.
- Use previews to anticipate which portions or sections of the chapter will be the most difficult or challenging.

While Reading
- Use the preview as a guide to what is important to learn.
- Mark or underline key information mentioned in the preview.

After Reading
- Use the preview to monitor your comprehension.
- Test your ability to recall key information.
- Immediately review any material you were unable to recall.

EXERCISE 8–4 | *Refer to the chapter outline in Figure 8–5 to answer the following questions.*

1. What predominant thought pattern(s) do you predict the chapter will use? Why?

   _____

2. Which section do you feel will be the most difficult to read and learn? Justify your choice.

   _____

3. What guide questions could you ask to guide your reading?

_____

EXERCISE 8–5

Refer to the chapter overview in Figure 8–6 to answer the following questions.

1. What do you know about the connections between resources, energy, and human life? Activate your prior knowledge by listing several issues or problems associated with this topic.

_____

2. What predominant thought pattern(s) do you predict the chapter will use?

_____

3. Besides listing the topics that will be covered in this chapter, what does the author do to focus attention on the key issues?

_____

Marginal Notations

Textbooks used to have wide, empty margins that were useful to students for jotting notes. Recently, some textbook authors have taken advantage of this available space to offer comments on the text; pose questions based on the text; provide illustrations, examples, and drawings; or identify key vocabulary. Figure 8–7, excerpted from an economics text, illustrates one type of marginal notation.

In the excerpt, brief definitions of key terms are given in the margin next to the sentences in which the terms are first introduced.

Figure 8–7   Marginal Notations

Inflation and Deflation

Inflation
The situation in which the average of all prices of goods and services in an economy is rising.

Deflation
The situation in which the average of all prices of goods and services in an economy is falling.

During World War II, you could buy bread for 8 to 10 cents a loaf and have milk delivered fresh to your door for about 25 cents a half gallon. The average price of a new car was less than $700, and the average house cost less than $3,000. Today bread, milk, cars, and houses all cost more—a lot more. Prices are more than 10 times what they were in 1940. Clearly, this country has experienced quite a bit of *inflation* since then. We define **inflation** as an upward movement in the average level of prices. The opposite of inflation is **deflation,** defined as a downward movement in the average level of prices. Notice that these definitions depend on the *average* level of prices. This means that even during a period of inflation, some prices can be falling if other prices are rising at a faster rate. The prices of electronic equipment have dropped dramatically since the 1960s, even though there has been general inflation.

Source: Miller, *Economics Today,* p. 153

Refer to marginal notes once you have read the text to which they correspond. Use them to review and monitor your comprehension, as well. If the marginal notes are in the form of questions, then you should go through the chapter, section by section, answering each question. Test your ability to define each term in your own words.

EXERCISE 8–6 *Read the excerpt and marginal notations in Figure 8–7. Monitor your comprehension by writing your own definitions of* inflation *and* deflation *without reference to the figure. Compare your definitions with those given in the notations.*

Special-Interest Inserts

Many textbooks contain, within or at the end of the chapter, brief articles, essays, or commentaries that provide a practical perspective or an application of the topic under discussion. Typically, these inserts are set apart from the text by using boxes or shaded or colored print. Usually, too, the insert titles suggest their function. They might be called "Focus," "Counterpoint," or "Today's Problems." In a chapter on drug abuse, a sociology textbook might include a vivid narrative of the life of a drug addict. An economics text might describe specific situations in which key concepts are applied. Figure 8–8 shows an insert from an introductory business textbook. Each chapter contains one or more "Web Connections." The one shown in Figure 8–8 appeared in a chapter on entrepreneurship and small businesses and extends chapter content by providing a description of the SBA's (Small Business Association) Web site, useful to

Figure 8–8   Special Interest Insert

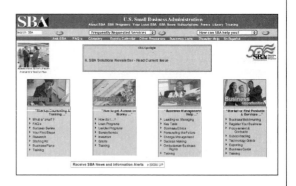

Source: www.sba.gov

anyone operating a small business. When reading and studying chapters that offer article inserts, try the following approach.

- Read the insert *after* you have read the text material on the page.
- Determine the purpose of the insert, and mark in the margin the concept or principle to which the insert refers.
- When reviewing for exams, especially essay exams, quickly review the chapter inserts, especially if your instructor has emphasized them.

EXERCISE 8–7 | *Read the insert shown below, which is taken from a business textbook chapter on human resources—the hiring, development, and maintenance of a workforce. Then answer the following questions using your own paper.*

1. What aspect of human resources does this boxed insert investigate?
2. Summarize the information presented in this box.
3. How useful do you feel this information would be in studying the chapter?
4. What did you learn about the recruitment process from this box?

IT'S A WIRED WORLD
Companies Put Web to Work as Recruiter

At DVCi Technologies' office in New York, employees never know who's looking over their shoulders. Their moves are broadcast live to the world via a Webcam as part of the company's effort to attract new hires by giving them a glimpse behind the scenes.

The video show is the latest example of how companies are using Web sites as an increasingly creative recruiting tool. It's no longer enough to post jobs on the Internet. Employers today are attracting candidates with such tactics as downloaded video and audio feeds, online employment tests, and real-time chats with recruiters.

"We had to differentiate ourselves," says Haim Ariav at DVCi Technologies <www.dvci-muffin-head.com>, a provider of Internet solutions. His movements—a wave, pen chewing, typing—are broadcast online at www.recruitcam.com. "It's been phenomenal. We've hired a lot of people through it, and we're still getting e-mail."

How others are using Web sites:

- *Giving visitors a behind-the-scenes look.* The U.S. Army's Web site <www.army.mil> includes a virtual tour of barracks. Visitors can click and drag their computer mouse to see sweeping views of bedrooms, laundry rooms, and courtyard. Visitors can also chat with online cyber-recruiters or download a video of an Abrams M1A2 tank.

- *Letting job candidates "meet" current employees.* Visitors to Chicago-based Andersen Consulting's Web site <www.arthuranderson.com> can view pictures of employees and read messages. Entries range from "I love water skiing" to "my job gives me satisfaction and balance." At San Jose, California-based Cisco Systems <www.cisco.com>, visitors can join in an online program called "Make Friends at Cisco." Job candidates can ask to get in touch with current workers to grill them about what it's like to work there.

- *Staying in touch with potential hires.* At Sprint's site <www.sprint.com>, job seekers can send e-mail about their ideal job. The company will send automatic e-mail if future job postings match the criteria. "There are a lot of ways to establish long-term relationships with this tool," says Sonja Ambur, national staffing director in Kansas City, Missouri. "Every company is looking at ways to maximize the Internet as a recruiting tool."

Some job seekers say the tactics work. Marta Sant, 28, took a job with DCVi Technologies after viewing the company through its Webcam. "I looked at the pictures and thought it was fun," says Sant, senior art directior. "I e-mail my friends and family, and they can see me."

Source: Ebert and Griffin, *Business Essentials,* p. 226

Review Questions

Some textbook chapters conclude with a set of review questions. Read through these questions *before* you read the chapter. They serve as a list of what is important in the chapter. Usually, the questions are listed in the order in which they appear in the chapter, forming an outline of important topics. As you read and locate answers to the questions in the text, be sure to underline or mark them. Read the review questions again *after* you finish the chapter and use them to test your recall.

Be aware that review questions are a useful—but by no means sufficient—review. These questions often test only factual recall of specific information. They seldom require you to pull together ideas and compare them, assess causes, or react to the information presented.

Lists of Key Terms

Lists of key terms are often found at the end of each chapter. Usually, only specialized terms that are introduced for the first time in that chapter are included. Glancing through the list before reading the chapter will familiarize you with these terms and make reading go more smoothly.

Chapter Summaries

The end-of-chapter summary is useful both before and after you read a chapter. Before reading, the summary familiarizes you with the chapter's basic organization and content. After reading the chapter, it provides an excellent review and helps you to tie together, or consolidate, the major points.

Suggested Readings or References

Many authors provide a list of suggested readings at the end of each chapter or section. This list refers you to additional sources that provide more information on topics discussed in the chapter. References given in this list provide a useful starting point when you are researching a topic discussed in the chapter.

The evaluation list shown in Figure 8–9 will enable you to quickly assess the learning aids that a chapter provides.

Texts Without Learning Features

Instructors are always careful to select textbooks that help their students learn. However, not all textbooks have all the features described in this section. For instance, one of your texts may not include a list of key terms, and another may lack marginal notations. When a text lacks a feature that you find particularly helpful, construct the feature yourself. Prepare your own list of key terms; write your own marginal notations. If your text lacks special-interest boxes that discuss how the material can be applied, take a few moments to think of your

Figure 8–9   Evaluation List

- Chapter preview
    Are thought patterns evident?
    How could the preview be used for review?

- Marginal notes
    How can the notes be used for study and review?

- Special-interest inserts
    How are inserts related to chapter content?
    How much emphasis should be given to the inserts?

- Review questions
    Do the questions provide an outline of chapter content? (Compare them with chapter headings.)
    What types of thinking do the questions require? Are they primarily factual, or do they require critical thinking?

- Key terms
    How many words are already familiar?
    How difficult do you predict the chapter will be?

- Chapter summary
    Does the summary list the main topics the chapter will cover?
    Is a thought pattern evident?

- Suggested readings
    What types of sources are listed?
    To which topics do they refer?

own applications. You will find that writing your own features will be at least as helpful as using those supplied by the textbook author.

EXERCISE 8–8

Academic
Application

Use the evaluation list shown in Figure 8–9 to analyze how the author of one of your current textbooks guides your learning. Write a brief critique of the textbook, including both strengths and weaknesses.

SYSTEMATIC APPROACHES TO TEXTBOOK READING

Throughout this text, you have learned numerous strategies and techniques to improve your textbook reading skills, and you may ask how you can combine them most effectively. Several systems have been developed that integrate these techniques into a step-by-step procedure for learning as you read. In this book, we focus on one particularly useful system.

The SQ3R Reading/Study System

Developed in the 1940s, the SQ3R system has been used successfully for many years and has proved effective in increasing retention of information. It is especially useful for textbooks and other highly factual, well-organized materials. Basically, SQ3R is a way of learning as you read. Its name is taken from the first letter of each step. First we will summarize the steps, and then we will apply the system to a sample selection.

Survey   Become familiar with the overall content and organization of the material. You already have learned this technique and know it as previewing.

Question   Formulate questions about the material that you expect to be able to answer as you read. As you read each successive heading, turn it into a question. This step is similar to establishing guide questions, a topic discussed in Chapter 1.

Read   As you read each section, actively search for the answers to your guide questions. When you find the answers, underline or mark the portions of the text that concisely state the information.

Recite   Probably the most important part of the system, "recite" means that after each section or after each major heading, you should stop, look away from the page, and try to remember the answer to your question. If you are unable to remember, look back at the page and reread the material. Then test yourself again by looking away from the page and "reciting" the answer to your question. This step is a form of comprehension and retention assessment that enables you to catch and correct weak or incomplete comprehension or recall. Here, you are operating primarily at the knowledge and understanding levels of thinking.

Review   Immediately after you have finished reading, go back through the material again, reading titles, introductions, summaries, headings, and graphic material. As you read each heading, recall your question and test yourself to see whether you still can remember the answer. If you cannot, reread that section. Once you are satisfied that you have understood and recalled key information, move toward the higher-level thinking skills. Consider applications, analyze, synthesize, and evaluate the material. Ask questions. Some students like to add a fourth "R" step—for "React."

Now, to get a clear picture of how the steps in the SQ3R method work together to produce an efficient approach to reading/study, let's apply the method to a textbook reading. Suppose you have been assigned the article on the next page on nonverbal communication for a communication class. Follow each of the SQ3R steps in reading this section.

Survey   Preview the article, noting introductions, headings, first sentences, and typographical clues. Refer to Chapter 1, page 16, for more information on previewing. From this prereading, you should have a good idea of what information this article will convey and should know the general conclusions the authors draw about the subject.

Question   Now, using the headings as a starting point, develop several questions to which you expect to find answers in the article. Think of these as guide questions (see Chapter 1, page 22). You might ask such questions as:

What are the major types of nonverbal cues?

What are spatial cues?

What messages are communicated at each of the four distances?

Read   Now read the selection through. Keep your questions in mind. Stop at the end of each major section and proceed to the next step.

Recite   After each section, stop reading and check to see whether you can recall the answer to the corresponding question.

Review   When you have finished reading the entire article, take a few minutes to reread the headings, recall your questions, and write answers to your questions to see how well you can remember the answers.

TYPES OF NONVERBAL CUES

You now have a definition of nonverbal communication, you know how much nonverbal communication counts, you understand the characteristics most nonverbal cues share, and you know the functions and forms, so it is time to examine the types of nonverbal cues. In this section, spatial cues, visual cues, vocal cues, touch, time, and silence will be discussed.

Spatial Cues
Spatial cues are the distances we choose to stand or sit from others. Each of us carries with us something called informal space. We might think of this as a bubble; we occupy the center of the bubble. This bubble expands or contracts depending on varying conditions and circumstances such as these:

- Age and sex of those involved.
- Cultural and ethnic background of the participants.
- Topic or subject matter.
- Setting for the interaction.
- Physical characteristics of the participants (size or shape).
- Attitudinal and emotional orientation of partners.
- Characteristics of the interpersonal relationship (like friendship).
- Personality characteristics of those involved.

In his book *The Silent Language,* Edward T. Hall, a cultural anthropologist, identifies the distances that people assume when they talk with others. He calls these distances intimate, personal, social, and public. In many cases, the adjustments that occur in these distances result from some of the factors listed above.

Intimate distance. At an **intimate distance** (0 to 18 inches), you often use a soft or barely audible whisper to share intimate or confidential information. Physical contact becomes easy at this distance. This is the distance we use for physical comforting, lovemaking, and physical fighting, among other things.

Personal distance. Hall identified the range of 18 inches to 4 feet as **personal distance.** When you disclose yourself to someone, you are likely to do it within this distance. The topics you discuss at this range may be somewhat confidential and usually are personal and mutually involving. At personal distance you are still able to touch another if you want to. This is likely to be the distance between people conversing at a party, between classmates in a casual conversation, or within many work relationships. This distance assumes a well-established acquaintanceship. It is probably the most comfortable distance for free exchange of feedback.

Social distance. When you are talking at a normal level with another person, sharing concerns that are not of a personal nature, you usually use the **social distance** (4 to 12 feet). Many of your on-the-job conversations take place at this distance. Seating arrangements in living rooms may be based on "conversation groups" of chairs placed at a distance of 4 to 7 feet from each other. Hall calls 4 to 7 feet the close phase of social distance; from 7 to 12 feet is the far phase of social distance.

The greater the distance, the more formal the business or social discourse conducted is likely to be. Often, the desks of important people are broad enough to hold visitors at a distance of 7 to 12 feet. Eye contact at this distance becomes more important to the flow of communication; without visual contact one party is likely to feel shut out and the conversation may come to a halt.

Public distance. **Public distance** (12 feet and farther) is well outside the range for close involvement with another person. It is impractical for interpersonal communication. You are limited to what you can see and hear at that distance; topics for conversation are relatively impersonal and formal; and most of the communication that occurs is in the public-speaking style, with subjects planned in advance and limited opportunities for feedback.

—Weaver, *Understanding Interpersonal Communications,* pp. 215–18

How SQ3R Improves Your Reading Efficiency

The SQ3R system improves your reading efficiency in three ways. It increases your comprehension, it enhances your recall, and it saves you valuable time by encouraging you to learn as you read.

Your comprehension is most directly improved by the Survey and Question steps. By surveying or prereading, you acquire an overview of the material that serves as an outline to follow as you read. In the Question step, you are focusing your attention and identifying what is important to look for as you read.

Your recall of the material is improved through the Recite and Review steps. By testing yourself while reading and immediately after you finish, you build a systematic review pattern that provides the repetition needed to promote learning and recall.

Finally, because you are learning as you are reading, you will save time later when you are ready to study the material for an exam. Since you already have learned the material through recitation and review, you will find that you need much less time to prepare for an exam. Instead of learning the material for the first time, you can spend the time reviewing. You also will have time to consider applications, to pull the material together, to analyze it, and to evaluate its usefulness.

Adapting the SQ3R System

To make the best use of SQ3R, you must adapt the procedure to fit the material you are studying. You also must adjust the system to suit how you learn and to fit the kind of learning that is expected.

Adapting SQ3R to Suit the Material   Your texts and other required readings vary greatly from course to course. To accommodate this variation, use the SQ3R system as a base or model. Then add, vary, or rearrange the steps to fit the material.

For example, when working with a mathematics text, you might add a Study the Sample Problems step in which you analyze the problem-solving process. When reading an essay, short story, or poem for a literature class, add a React step in which you analyze various features of the writing, including the writer's style, tone, purpose, and point of view (see Chapter 15). For textbooks with a great deal of factual information to learn, you might add Underline, Take Notes, or Outline steps.

Adapting SQ3R to Suit Your Learning Style   Throughout your school experience, you probably have found that some learning techniques work better for you than others. Just as everyone's personality is unique, so is everyone's learning style. Refer to the Learning Style Questionnaire discussed in Chapter 1, page 3.

Try to use knowledge of your learning style to develop your own reading/study system. Experiment with various study methods and adapt the SQ3R system accordingly. For instance, if writing outlines helps you recall information, then replace the Recite step with an Outline step, and make the Review step a Review of Outline step. Or if you have discovered that you learn well by listening, replace the Recite and Review steps with Tape Record and Listen steps, in which you dictate and record information to be learned and review by listening to the tape.

There are numerous possibilities for developing your own reading/study system. The best approach is to test variations until you find the most effective system.

EXERCISE 8–9   *Get together with other students taking the same course (or courses within the same discipline or department). Discuss and prepare a list of modifications to the SQ3R system that would be appropriate for your course's content and learning requirements.*

EXERCISE 8–10   *Use the SQ3R system to read one of the readings included in this text. Write your questions on a separate sheet, and underline your answers in the reading selection.*

EXERCISE 8–11   *Apply the SQ3R system to a chapter in one of your other textbooks. List your questions on a separate sheet, and underline the answers in your textbook. Evaluate the effectiveness of your approach and decide on any modifications needed.*

RETENTION AND RECALL STRATEGIES

Although the SQ3R system is an effective means of improving both comprehension and recall, it cannot ensure complete retention by itself. Periodic review, pattern recognition, association, visualization, mnemonic devices, and the use of writing also are helpful in learning and retaining the text material.

Periodic Review

Immediate review is effective and increases your ability to recall information, but it is not sufficient for remembering material for long periods of time. To remember facts and ideas permanently, you will need to review them periodically, going back and refreshing your recall on a regular basis. For example, suppose you are reading a chapter on criminal behavior in your sociology text, and a midterm exam is scheduled in four weeks. If you read the chapter, reviewed it immediately afterward, and then did nothing with it until the exam a month later, you would not remember enough to score well. To achieve a good grade, you need to review the chapter periodically. You might review the chapter once several days after reading it, again a week later, and once again a week before the exam. Then, when the time comes to study the chapter for the exam, you will find that you are still basically familiar with the chapter's content and you will not need to spend valuable study time becoming reacquainted with the material. Instead, studying will be a matter of learning specifics and organizing particular information into a format that will be easily remembered during the exam. You also will have time to consider how to apply what you have learned—a higher-level thinking skill.

Pattern Recognition

When you read about academic thought patterns in Chapter 7, you learned that it is easier to remember information that has a pattern or structure than it is to remember material that is randomly arranged. Now that you are familiar with the six basic academic thought patterns, you can learn to use these patterns to help you organize ideas.

In some chapters, the patterns will be clearly evident. In others, as well as in articles and essays, a pattern may not be as obvious. You may find it necessary to outline the material or rearrange it into a more meaningful pattern. Chapter 11 describes techniques for organizing information.

Association of Ideas

Association is a useful way to remember new facts and ideas. It involves connecting information that is new and unfamiliar to facts and ideas you already know. For instance, if you are reading a management text for a business class and are trying to remember a list of the characteristics of successful entrepreneurs, you might try to associate each characteristic with a person you know who exhibits that trait.

Using association involves stretching your memory to see what the new information has in common with what you already know. When you find a connection between the known and the unknown, you can retrieve from your memory the new information along with the old.

Visualization

Visualizing, or creating a mental picture of what you have read, often aids recall. The effectiveness of this technique definitely depends on the type of material you are reading. When you are reading descriptive writing in which the writer intends to create a mental picture, visualization is an easy task. When you are reading about events, people, processes, or procedures, visualization is again relatively simple. However, visualization of abstract ideas, theories, philosophies, and concepts may not be possible. Instead, you may need to create in your mind, or on paper, a visual picture of the *relationship* between ideas. For example, suppose you are reading about the invasion of privacy and learn that there are arguments for and against the storage of personal data on each citizen in large computer banks. You might create a visual image of two lists: advantages and disadvantages.

Mnemonic Devices

Memory tricks and devices, often called mnemonics, are useful in helping you recall lists of factual information. You might use a rhyme, such as "Thirty days hath September, April, June, and November. . . ." Another device involves making up a word or phrase in which each letter represents an item you are trying to remember. If you remember the name Roy G. Biv, for example, you will be able to recall the colors in the light spectrum: *r*ed, *o*range, *y*ellow, *g*reen, *b*lue, *i*ndigo, *v*iolet.

Use of Writing to Enhance Learning

Your senses of sight, hearing, and touch all can be used to help you remember what you read. Most of the time, you use just one sense—sight—as you read. However, if you are able to use more than one sense, you will find that recall is easier. Activities such as underlining, highlighting, note taking, and outlining involve your sense of touch and enable you to reinforce your learning. These activities also force you to organize and consolidate information. Chapter 11 discusses each of these techniques in detail.

EXERCISE 8–12

Five study/learning situations follow. Decide which of the aids to retention described in this section—periodic review, pattern recognition, association, visualization, mnemonic devices, and the use of writing—might be useful in each situation, and list the aids after each item. Explain why each would be helpful.

1. In a sociology course, you are assigned to read about and remember the causes of child abuse.

   _____

2. You are learning to simplify radicals in a mathematics class.

   _____

3. You are studying mitosis, the multistage process of cell division, in a biology class.

   _____

4. In economics, you are studying the law of demand. The law states, "The price of a product and the amount purchased are inversely related: if the price rises, the quantity demanded falls; if the price falls, the quantity demanded increases."

   _____

5. You are studying the similarities and differences between plant and animal cells for a biology class.

   _____

SUMMARY

Textbooks contain numerous features to enable you to read, study, and learn as efficiently as possible.

- The preface and table of contents provide keys to the overall organization.
- The appendix, glossary, and index organize and supplement the content.

Numerous learning aids are featured within a textbook chapter:

- chapter previews
- marginal notes
- special-interest inserts
- review questions
- lists of key terms
- references

You can read your textbook most effectively if you use a systematic approach that integrates prereading and postreading. The SQ3R system is a five-step process:

- survey
- question
- read
- recite
- review

Additional strategies to ensure retention and recall are

- periodic review
- pattern recognition
- association
- visualization
- use of mnemonic devices
- use of writing

**INTEGRATING
IDEAS**

◆

**PAIRED
READINGS**

Biology

PREREADING QUESTIONS

1. How would you define thinking?
2. Do you believe animals can think?

Do Animals Think?

Michael C. Mix, Paul Farber, and Keith I. King

1   Scientists have investigated the human organism from a mechanistic viewpoint for over a century. Their underlying assumption has been that humans could be viewed as elegant chemical machines that follow predictable natural laws. This approach has had stunning success. We know a great deal about the human body, we can design drugs to alleviate various ailments, and we can counter numerous conditions that cause suffering or death. Although science can tell us a great deal about our physical condition by treating the human body as a machine, no one doubts that humans, unlike machines, are conscious creatures. <u>Our own consciousness is evident. What about animals?</u>

2   To those of us who have pets, such as dogs or cats, it is difficult to think of them as machines without self-awareness—as entities more akin to our washing machines, personal computers, and blow-dryers than to our family members and friends (see Figure A). Can it be that our clever dog, Cassie, that "comforts" us when we are down, leaps with "joy" when we return from work, and has "outsmarted" the neighbor's dog that used to "steal" her food, is simply a genetically programmed automaton? Or that ZiZi, our neighbor's cat, that would seemingly "favor" starvation to dry cat food and that, if not a connoisseur of lasagna, is known to "prefer"—very definitely—smoked salmon to canned tuna, is, in her behavior, just reflecting an idiosyncratic program rather than expressing a conscious preference?

3   Until shortly after World War I, it seemed obvious to scientists that animals had feelings and that they could think. Charles Darwin believed that female birds showed aesthetic preferences in their choice of mates and that sexual selection was strongly influenced by it.

4   Many writings done in the late nineteenth century on the animal mind, however, were uncritical and highly anthropomorphic. Human desires, fears, and attitudes were attributed to animals, and numerous stories were accepted <u>without any careful attempts at verification.</u> It is not surprising, then, that when we read this literature today, much of it seems comical.

5   Psychologists in the 1920s reacted strongly to this uncritical literature and took the position that it was <u>not possible to verify</u> whether or not animals could think. They concluded that the question of animals' thinking was not a meaningful topic for science because it <u>could not be tested experimentally.</u> Instead, psychologists

Figure A   (1) Can this animal think? (2) Do pet tricks reflect thinking ability?

focused on the observable behavior of animals. They argued that in establishing a scientific psychology, it was irrelevant whether animals thought. They intended to establish scientific laws about how animals learn and behave that could be verified by other scientists. To psychologists like James Watson or B. F. Skinner, the private mind of the animal, if it existed, was closed to human investigation.

Ethologists who studied animal behavior, for the most part, were equally dismissive about probing the inner world of animals. A few workers were interested in how the world might "look" to animals, which have different sense organs than humans, but the primary thrust of ethology was in documenting repeatable patterns of behavior and in comparing these patterns with the object of establishing evolutionary connections.

Modern animal behavior draws on knowledge derived from psychology, ethology, and an ever-growing body of research in the fields of genetics, ecology, neurophysiology, and neuroanatomy. Until recently, all of these areas of research had been far removed from discussions of animal thought or animal awareness.

A well-known investigator of animal behavior, Donald Griffin of Rockefeller University, argues that neglecting animal awareness and thinking is not only an overreaction to the naive acceptance of undocumented animal stories but also a blind spot that retards advances in the scientific understanding of animal behavior. Griffin believes that mental experiences in animals could have an adaptive value— the better an animal understands its environment, the better it can adjust its behavior to survive and reproduce in it. He is also interested in animal communication, which he feels can sometimes be used to convey information about objects or

9. T: cites behaviors that involve an accurate evaluation in complex environment
MI: They have to makes choices like when to hunt and where

10 T: Psycologists were outspoken in their regetion of consiousness
MI: Some tests may be possible and evidance can be gathered.

11. T: It's too early to tell what researchers will conclude about animal awareness
MI: further reasearce must be neccessary for formulating a scientific conlusion

events that are distant in time or space. This form of information may suggest awareness.

[9] In support of his ideas, Griffin cites various behaviors that seem to involve accurate evaluation in complex environments. For example, he refers to a classic study on the prey selection of wagtails, a type of bird found in southern England. These birds feed on fly eggs and on a number of small insects. Each day they must make several choices on where to hunt, when to move on to hunt in another area, and whether to join a flock or hunt alone. Scientists who study these wagtails have shown that they hunt with great proficiency. Although proficiency is not necessarily an indicator of awareness, Griffin argues that in cases where accurate evaluation of a changing and complex environment occurs, it is reasonable to consider that the animal is consciously thinking about what it is doing. Cooperative hunting by lions and the cultural transmission of behavior such as the potato washing done by Japanese macaques . . . are other examples of behaviors that suggest to Griffin and others that animals are aware and can think.

[10] At present, Griffin and analysts who agree with him are in the minority in the scientific community. How can the question of animal thinking be resolved? One way is to attempt to design experiments that might give an indication one way or the other. Psychologists in the early twentieth century were very outspoken in their rejection of animal consciousness, claiming that testing for it was impossible. Griffin has proposed that some tests may be possible and that evidence can be gathered to support his position. He argues that once we have a better understanding of the electrical signals that are correlated with conscious thinking in humans, we could search for equivalents in animals. If none were found, that would suggest that his hypothesis of animal awareness is false. The strongest supporting evidence of Griffith's hypothesis involves cases in which animal communication is active and specialized, information is exchanged, and the receiving animal responds interactively. To Griffin, such cases are compelling examples of conscious and intentional acts.

[11] It is too early to tell what researchers of animal behavior will conclude about animal awareness. Further research on interesting phenomena, such as animal communication, will ultimately provide the results necessary for formulating a scientific conclusion. Until then, we are confident that people will continue to discuss the world with their dogs and cats.

—Mix et al., *Biology: The Network of Life*, pp. 551–52

VOCABULARY REVIEW

1. For each of the words listed below, use context; prefixes, roots, and suffixes; and/or a dictionary to write a brief definition or synonym of the word as it is used in the reading.

   a. entities (para. 2) _____

   b. connoisseur (para. 2) _____

   c. anthropomorphic (para. 4) _____

d. ethologists (para. 6) _____

e. dismissive (para. 6) _____

2. Underline new specialized terms introduced in the reading.

COMPREHENSION QUESTIONS

1. Why did psychologists in the 1920s declare that the question of animal thinking was not meaningful?
2. How do ethologists approach the study of animal behavior?
3. What evidence does Donald Griffin offer in support of animals' ability to think?
4. Explain what Griffin means by "adaptive value" (para. 8).
5. What types of additional evidence are needed to change the opinion of the scientific community?
6. What learning features does this excerpt include?

THINKING CRITICALLY

1. What does the last sentence of the reading suggest about humans?
2. Does the reading contain any clues about the author's answer to the question of whether animals can think?
3. Evaluate the evidence offered by Griffin. Do you feel it is sufficient and convincing?

LEARNING/STUDY STRATEGIES

1. Write a brief set of notes for the reading. (Refer to pages 363–65 for suggestions on note taking.)
2. What thought pattern(s) is (are) evident in the reading?
3. What retention or recall strategies would be helpful in learning this material?
4. Did you use SQ3R when reading the material? If so, how did you find it helpful?

INTEGRATING
IDEAS

◆

PAIRED
READINGS

Biology

PREREADING QUESTIONS

1. Do you think parrots are capable of communicating through the use of words?
2. What thought patterns do you anticipate this reading will use?

The Subject Is Alex
Kenn Kaufman

1   At first sight Alex appears out of place, somebody's pet brought in for the day and plopped down in a corner of the modern research laboratory at the University of Arizona. But the impression is wrong. Alex is the research. An African Grey, *Psittacus Erithacus,* he lacks the gaudy greens and yellows of many species. Despite his silky sheen and crimson tail feathers, he seems duller than the average parrot. Perched on the back of a metal folding chair with newspapers unceremoniously spread underneath, he shifts his feet nervously and turns an owlish eye toward anyone who approaches.

2   "Alex, how many?" A researcher holds up a purple metal key and a larger green plastic key. The parrot stares, turning his head slowly: The question hangs for fifteen silent seconds. Why expect an answer? Doesn't "to parrot" mean "to mimic mindlessly"? But then the parrot says, "Two."

3   The same two keys are held up with a different question. "Which is *bigger*?" Again the parrot stares, pauses, then says, "Green key." Next is a wooden Popsicle stick. "What matter?" Again the long pause, again a correct answer: "Wood."

4   Getting the stick as a reward, Alex splinters it in his massive beak. It's strange to watch this bird perform—especially strange for anyone with a background in traditional science. For years the assumption had been that "talking" birds are nothing but mimics, attaching no meaning to their "words." But this parrot seems to crush that assumption as easily as he crushes Popsicle sticks. Alex is impressive—and so is the scientist who trained him.

5   Irene Pepperberg was well on her way to earning a Ph.D. in chemical physics from Harvard when, in 1973, her professional interest began to shift toward animals. The *Nova* programs on public service television provided the spark: It was the first time, she says, that TV had shown wild animals as they really were and had suggested scientific studies of them were worthwhile. Especially compelling were programs on animal communication: voices of birds and attempts to teach sign language to chimpanzees. "Suddenly," Pepperberg says, "mathematical modeling of the reaction pathways of molecules seemed a lot less exciting than trying to understand communication in animals."

6   "Most people felt that the brain structure of birds wouldn't allow for much intelligence," she says, "or that the striatal area in birds couldn't handle information

as well as the cortex in mammals. But a different brain type didn't have to be fundamentally inferior. Birds had done well in experiments with problem-solving based on numbers. Otto Koehler had ravens, jackdaws and Grey parrots that could match numbers of spots up to eight. Pastore's canaries could pick out the third item from a series. Logler had an African Grey parrot trained on numbers up to eight.

7   "In all these tests the birds 'responded' by picking a certain item. There was no vocal response. In the 1940's and 1950's a psychologist named Mowrer tried to teach parrots to use words for objects, and that effort failed. But I thought it should be possible to teach a bird to use at least a few vocal labels. The vocal behavior of birds is such a rich subject. Some individual marsh wrens, for example, will use hundreds of different songs, and a lot is known about how some birds learn their songs in different context—suggesting that they attach some meaning to the sounds. So why not see if those meanings could be attached to specific objects?"

8   Her Ph.D. work complete, Pepperberg wound up in Indiana on the academic periphery of Purdue University. Her husband had a job there; she did not. But Purdue agreed to let her use lab space if she would raise the funds for her research. She designed her own study and, in June 1977, bought Alex, a thirteen-month-old Grey parrot chosen at random in a Chicago pet store.

9   "The Grey parrot was the logical species," she says, "It had done so well with numbers in Logler's tests. Besides, if you think about wild parrots, they live in social groups. Most are in tropical forests, where the foliage is dense, and they might need complex vocal signals to stay in touch."

10   Pepperberg's logic sounds simple in retrospect. At the outset, however, launching her study was far from easy. She wrote grant proposals, but no one was interested in funding an offbeat "talking bird" experiment. So she scraped up used equipment, enlisted volunteer help, and endured the mild putdowns of other scientists.

11   Within a few months it appeared Alex was catching on; within a couple of years it was beyond doubt. In a paper entitled "Functional Vocalizations by an African Grey Parrot" published in 1981, Pepperberg reported Alex could identify more than thirty objects by name, shape, and color; he had averaged 80 percent accuracy over some two hundred tests. This was a breakthrough, the first solid evidence that a bird could attach meanings to sounds, labels to objects. But the experiments went on from there.

12   "OKAY, ALEX, BACK to the chair." It's a rule of the lab: On the counter top, the floor, or someone's shoulder, Alex can clown around or request whatever he wants, but when he sits on the back of the metal chair, he has to work. "Alex, what's this?" "Rrrock!" says Alex. Irene Pepperberg hands him the rock, which he turns over in his bill a couple of times before dropping it on the floor.

13   Next question: "What color?" Alex eyes the blue toy truck and reaches for it. Pepperberg pulls it away. "No. Tell me what color?" Alex pauses and then says, "Want a nut." Pepperberg speaks sharply and turns away: "No! Bad parrot! Pay attention. What color?" Finally he gets it out ("Blhoo"), and gets to play with the truck.

14   Then he has a request of his own: "Want pah-ah." "Better!" says Pepperberg, "Say it better." Alex tries again. "Want pah-ssdah." "Okay, that's pretty good," says Pepperberg, and hands him a piece of raw pasta. He crunches it hard, sending a

shower of fragments to join the accumulation of crushed shredded-wheat squares, Popsicle sticks, and grapes on the newspaper below.

15   Then Pepperberg holds up three spools of different sizes and color. "Which is smaller?" Show Alex a paper triangle and ask, "What shape?" and he'll say, "Three-corner." Show him five Popsicle sticks dyed red and ask, "What color?" and he'll say, "Rose." Then ask, "How many?" and he'll say, "Five." He is clearly responding to the question itself, as well as to the objects. He understands "different" and "same" and can answer questions about relationships: Show him a blue-dyed cork and blue key and ask, "What's the same?" he will answer, "Color." Show him two identical squares of rawhide and ask, "What's different?" and he will say, "None." Substitute a pentagon for one square, and he will answer, "Shape."

16   To do these things Alex must understand the questions, analyze several qualities, compare them, and search his vocabulary; he is processing information on several levels. None of this is simple memorization. On questions of size or color or shape, "different" or "same," Alex scores slightly *better* with new objects than with familiar ones; novelty seems to focus his attention.

17   It's an incredible performance for a bird. But Alex did not reach this level by accident. Every detail of his training and testing has been carefully considered.

18   For example, Alex regularly nuzzles and scratches with Pepperberg and all the student assistants. This is essential. The parrot is highly social and needs this interplay. If it felt no bond with researchers, it would never cooperate. On the other hand major problems could result if the bird felt a strong "pair bond" with one person—parrots can be violently jealous about their "mates." Thus, assistants were brought in to interact with Alex from the beginning.

19   Alex does not seem to know the meaning of "bad parrot" or "good parrot" or "pay attention," but tones of approval and disapproval are enough to influence him. Another factor to reinforce learning: appropriate rewards. Past experiments with birds had rewarded "correct behavior" with food. But when Alex names an object correctly he is rewarded with the object itself; he may examine it, scratch himself with it, or chew it for several minutes before he loses interest and drops it.

20   The language training rests on a technique developed by German biologist Dietmar Todt, who found the Grey parrot learned phrases most quickly from two trainers: One formed a bond with the parrot; the other acted as both "rival" and model. For the parrot to gain the attention of its "mate," it learned to mimic simple phrases used repeatedly by the model/rival. In Pepperberg's study no one person took the role of Alex's mate. Trainers took turns "training" each other to name objects while Alex watched and listened; eventually he joined in.

21   The initial aim was to teach Alex to use words for objects, something no bird had been proven to do before. Next the focus moved to categories of color and shape, to numbers, to concepts such as similarity and difference. At every stage Alex was subjected to rigorous tests. The results had to be above question—beyond any suggestion the bird was receiving cues from the researchers. Tests were administered by students who had not taken part in the training. Pepperberg kept score of Alex's answers but sat with her back turned, unable to see the objects being presented. Each response had to be clear enough to be understood. Alex would get no hints, no leniency.

22 But as the tests became more complex, Alex continued to score around 80 percent accuracy in his answers, far above what would have been possible by chance alone. Carefully documenting the parrot's progress, Pepperberg published one scientific paper after another.

23 Researchers trying to open two-way communication with animals are caught in the crossfire of a controversy that has been running for decades. On one side are the strict behaviorists, who suggest that animals have no real thought processes, no consciousness, no awareness of their own actions. At the other extreme are those who maintain that animals may indeed be thinking and that science should inquire what they are thinking about. Joining this far-reaching debate are psychologists, linguists, and philosophers who ask: What is awareness? What is language? Do things like "belief" and "desire" really exist, even in humans?

24 The arguments continue, but the study of animal minds—now dignified with the name "cognitive ethology"—is gaining stature as a legitimate field. Researchers have managed to open limited dialogues with various mammals: chimpanzees, gorillas, orangutans, dolphins, sea lions. And joining this cast of "smart" mammals on stage is one Grey parrot. "We haven't gone as far as the chimpanzee or marine mammal studies," says Pepperberg. "But up to this point Alex has performed as well as the chimps or dolphins." No other researcher has taken bird communication to this level.

25 For Pepperberg the Grey parrot was a calculated choice as a promising study species. But parrots also represent the endangered wildlife of the tropics. "There are more than three hundred parrot species," she says, "mostly in the tropics, and nearly one-fourth of those could be considered endangered in the wild. These are intelligent, adaptable birds, and they could probably survive alongside 21st Century humanity given a chance. But the cage-bird trade doesn't give them a chance." She favors legislation now being considered that would ban the import of wild birds. "Wild-caught parrots make inferior pets, and a shocking number of wild parrots die in transport. If someone really has the time to devote to a pet parrot, the only responsible approach is to buy one that has been raised by a reputable breeder.

26 "If my research could affect public awareness," she concludes, "I'd like people to realize that a parrot is not just a bundle of bright feathers. A parrot is a creature with mental capabilities beyond what we would have guessed—a creature that deserves respect. As civilized beings, we can't go on blithely destroying the habitat and populations of wild parrots."

—Kaufman, "The Subject Is Alex," Audubon Magazine
(September–October 1991)

VOCABULARY REVIEW

1. For each of the words listed below, use context; prefixes, roots, and suffixes; and/or a dictionary to write a brief definition or synonym of the word as it is used in the reading.

a. mimic (para. 2) _____

b. compelling (para. 5) _____

c. periphery (para. 8) _____

d. retrospect (para. 10) _____

e. reinforce (para.19) _____

f. rival (para. 20) _____

g. leniency (para. 21) _____

h. calculated (para. 25) _____

i. blithely (para. 26) _____

2. Underline new specialized terms introduced in the reading.

COMPREHENSION QUESTIONS

1. How did Pepperberg become interested in studying communication with parrots?
2. Why did Pepperberg choose to study parrots instead of other animals?
3. What kinds of thinking does Alex demonstrate when answering questions asked by Pepperberg?
4. Describe the methods Pepperberg uses to teach Alex.
5. Explain the controversy among scientists about two-way communication with animals.

THINKING CRITICALLY

1. What is Pepperberg's attitude toward the capture and sale of wild parrots?
2. Do you think that Pepperberg's work with Alex establishes that parrots can think? If not, what further information or experiments are needed to answer the question: "Do Animals Think?"
3. What does Pepperberg think about keeping parrots as pets?
4. What kinds of information is Alex able to learn?

LEARNING/STUDY STRATEGIES

1. What thought pattern is used throughout this reading?
2. Write a set of notes that would be useful if you were writing a research paper that argues that animals can think.

THINKING ABOUT THE PAIRED READINGS

INTEGRATING IDEAS

1. Compare the position each reading takes on whether animals can think.
2. Compare the organization of the two readings.
3. Compare the purpose of each of the readings. What is each intended to accomplish?

GENERATING NEW IDEAS

1. Design an experiment that would evaluate whether an animal could think. Explain what you would have the animal do and how you would determine whether thought occurred.
2. If you were to write a research paper on animal intelligence, what further information would you need? Explain what sources you would consult and what information you would need.

Multimedia Activities

1. **Academic Success: Reading Textbooks**
    http://www.dartmouth.edu/~acskills/success/reading.html
    Dartmouth College offers several online handouts designed to help students read textbooks more effectively and efficiently. Two featured documents are "Six Reading Myths" and "Harvard Report on Reading." Read them over and discuss with your classmates how these documents apply to your current experiences. Offer each other suggestions for improving your reading skills.

2. **Mnemonics: Memory Techniques**
    http://www.bucks.edu/~specpop/mnemonics.htm
    Some easy-to-use memory techniques are presented in chart form on this site from Bucks County Community College. Try out each of these techniques over the next few days. Keep track of which ones work best for you.

Take a Road Trip to
Mount Rushmore!

If your instructor has asked you to use the Reading Road Trip CD-ROM or Website, be sure to visit the Memorization and Concentration module for multimedia tutorials, exercises, and tests.

CHAPTER 9

READING GRAPHICS

LEARNING OBJECTIVES

- ✦ To develop reading strategies for graphics
- ✦ To learn to read different types of graphics

Many college textbooks include graphics such as maps, diagrams, charts, tables, or graphs. Some students find graphics intimidating, mainly because they have not learned how to approach them. All graphic devices serve the same primary functions. First, graphics summarize and condense written information, making it easier to comprehend and retain. In this respect, graphics actually save you time by eliminating lengthy written explanations. To illustrate, first study the table in Figure 9–1 on the next page. Then read the paragraph that begins to present the factual information contained in the table.

Which would you rather read, the table or the paragraph? The paragraph is dull, routine reading, whereas the table presents the same information concisely and in a more interesting format. The table also makes it easier to understand the relationship between individual bits of information. A glance at the table tells you that 19.1 percent of adolescent boys engaged in three problem behaviors, compared to 2.6 percent of girls. (Locating this information would be much more difficult if it were presented only in paragraph form.) By providing a visual picture of the information, graphics also make relationships, trends, and patterns easier to grasp.

It is tempting to skip over the graphic aids included in textbooks. Stopping to study a graph or chart takes time and may seem to interrupt your flow of reading. Because graphics do not present information in words (there are no statements to underline or remember), you may think they are unimportant. Actually, graphics often are more important than the paragraphs that surround them. They are included to call your attention to, emphasize, and concisely describe a relationship.

Figure 9–1   Sample Graphic

Co-occurrence of Three Serious Problem Behaviors Among Adolescent Girls and Boys

NUMBER OF SERIOUS PROBLEM BEHAVIORS	FEMALES	MALES
None	57.4%	21.9%
One		
Sex	15.5	26.6
Substance use	7.9	2.8
Total	23.4	29.4
Two		
Sex/substance use	14.0	27.0
Substance use/assault	2.6	2.5
Total	16.6	29.5
Three		
Sex/substance use/assault	2.6	19.1

Paragraph:

57.4 percent of females exhibited no serious problem behaviors, 23.4 percent engaged in one (sex or substance use), 16.6 percent reported serious engagement in two problem behaviors, and 2.6 percent had been involved in all three. The males in the sample were more generally involved than females in problem behaviors, but 21.9 percent had not engaged seriously in any of the three problem behaviors. About 29 percent of the males had engaged seriously in one problem behavior (primarily sex), nearly 30 percent had engaged in two (primarily sex combined with substance use), and 19.1 percent had engaged in all three.

Source: Conger and Galambos, *Adolescence and Youth,* pp. 296–97

HOW TO READ GRAPHICS

Here are some general suggestions that will help you get the most out of graphic elements in the material you read.

1. *Read the title or caption.* The title tells you what situation or relationship is being described.

2. *Determine how the graphic is organized.* If you are working with a table, note the column headings. For a graph, note what is marked on the vertical and horizontal axes.

3. *Note any symbols and abbreviations used.*

4. *Determine the scale or unit of measurement.* Note how the variables are measured. For example, does a graph show expenditures in dollars, thousands of dollars, or millions of dollars?

5. *Identify the trend(s), pattern(s), or relationship(s) the graphic is intended to show.* The following sections will discuss this step in greater detail.

6. *Read any footnotes.* Footnotes, printed at the bottom of a graph or chart, indicate how the data were collected, explain what certain numbers or headings mean, or describe the statistical procedures used.

7. *Check the source.* The source of data is usually cited at the bottom of the graph or chart. Unless the information was collected by the author, you are likely to find listed a research journal or publication from which the data were taken. Identifying the source is helpful in assessing the reliability of the data.

TYPES OF GRAPHICS

All graphics describe some type of relationship. Not coincidentally, these relationships correspond to the thought patterns we examined in Chapter 7.

Tables: Comparison and Classification of Information

Sociologists, psychologists, scientists, economists, and business analysts frequently use tables to organize and present statistical evidence. A table is an organized display of factual information, usually numbers or statistics. Its purpose is to classify information so that comparisons can be made between or among data.

Take a few minutes now to study Figure 9–2 on page 264, using the suggestions listed above. Then use the following steps to analyze the table.

1. *Determine how the data are classified, or divided.* This table classifies sources of sound according to level of intensity. Note that the relative sound intensity and the effects of prolonged exposure are also included.

2. *Make comparisons and look for trends.* This step involves surveying the rows and columns, noting how each entry compares with the others. Be sure to compare columns and rows, noting both similarities and differences and focusing on trends. In Figure 9–2, you might compare the relative intensities of several common sounds to which you are exposed.

3. *Draw conclusions.* Decide what the data show. You can conclude from Figure 9–2 that prolonged exposure to some sounds is dangerous. Often you will find clues, and sometimes direct statements, in the paragraphs that correspond to the table. The portion of the text that refers you to the table often makes a general statement about what the table is intended to highlight.

Figure 9–2 Interpreting a Table

The Intensity of Some Common Sounds

Sound Source Exposure	Decibels (dbA)	Relative Sound Intensity	Effect on Hearing (Prolonged Exposure)
	0*	1	Audibility threshold
Breathing	10	10	
Whisper, rustling leaves	20	100	Very quiet
Quiet rural nighttime	30	1000	
Library, soft music	40	10,000	
Normal conversation	50	100,000	Quiet
Average office	60	1,000,000	
Vacuum cleaner	70	10,000,000	Annoying
Garbage disposal	80	100,000,000	Possible hearing damage
City traffic, diesel truck	90	1,000,000,000	Hearing damage (8 hours or more exposure)
Garbage truck, chain saw	100	10,000,000,000	Serious hearing damage (8 hours or more exposure)
Live rock band; portable stereo held close to ear	110	100,000,000,000	
Siren (close range); jet takeoff (200 yds)	120	1,000,000,000,000	Hearing pain threshold
Crack of gunfire	130	10,000,000,000,000	
Aircraft carrier deck	140	100,000,000,000,000	Eardrum ruptures
Jet takeoff (close range)	150	1,000,000,000,000,000	

*The threshold of hearing is 0 decibels because the scale is logarithmic, and the logarithm of 1 is 0.

Source: Byer and Shainberg, *Living Well: Health in Your Hands,* p. 788

Once you have drawn your conclusions, stop, think, and react. For example, you might consider what the data in Figure 9–2 suggest about your daily activities.

EXERCISE 9–1

Study the table shown in Figure 9–3, and answer the accompanying questions.

1. What is the subject of the table? _____

2. Describe how the data are organized. _____

3. Overall, which age group spends the most total time getting news? Which age group spends the least? _____

4. Which age group has the largest percent of people who did not get any news yesterday? _____

5. Which news source is used most often by all groups combined? _____

6. What overall trends does this table suggest? _____

Figure 9–3 Interpreting a Table

SPENDING TIME WITH THE NEWS

The PEW Research Center asked a representative sample of the population how much time they spent during an average day getting the news from TV, newspapers, and radio. The table below shows the results, broken down by age.

<table>
<tr><th></th><th colspan="5">Spending Time With the News
(Avg. Minutes Yesterday*)</th></tr>
<tr><th></th><th>Total</th><th>Paper</th><th>TV</th><th>Radio</th><th>No News
Yesterday</th></tr>
<tr><td>All</td><td>66</td><td>18</td><td>31</td><td>17</td><td>14%</td></tr>
<tr><td>18–24</td><td>48</td><td>9</td><td>26</td><td>13</td><td>25%</td></tr>
<tr><td>25–29</td><td>50</td><td>11</td><td>23</td><td>16</td><td>17%</td></tr>
<tr><td>30–34</td><td>54</td><td>11</td><td>24</td><td>19</td><td>15%</td></tr>
<tr><td>35–49</td><td>63</td><td>16</td><td>28</td><td>19</td><td>14%</td></tr>
<tr><td>50–64</td><td>71</td><td>21</td><td>34</td><td>16</td><td>14%</td></tr>
<tr><td>65+</td><td>96</td><td>33</td><td>44</td><td>19</td><td>6%</td></tr>
</table>

*All averages are estimated.
SOURCE: Reprinted by permission of the PEW Research Center for the People & Press from their Web site: http://www.people-press.org/medsec3.htm.

Source: Edwards, Watterburg, and Lineberry, *Government in America,* p. 226

Graphs: Relationships Among Variables

Graphs depict the relationship between two or more variables such as price and demand or expenditures over time. Put simply, they are pictures of relationships between two or more sets of information. As you read and study in various academic disciplines, you will encounter many variations of a few basic types of graphs.

Linear Graphs   In linear graphs, information is plotted along a vertical and a horizontal axis, with one or more variables plotted on each. The resulting graph makes it easy to see the relationship between the variables. A sample linear graph is shown in Figure 9–4 on page 266. The line graph compares the amount of beef and poultry consumed in the United States between 1973 and 1999.

In addition to the comparison, the graph also allows you to see total consumption of red meat and poultry together through these years. The graph enables you to determine the general trend or pattern among the variables. Generally, this graph shows a slight, steady decrease in beef consumption along with a slight, steady increase in poultry consumption, while total consumption of the products combined is more stable.

Figure 9–4 A Sample Linear Graph

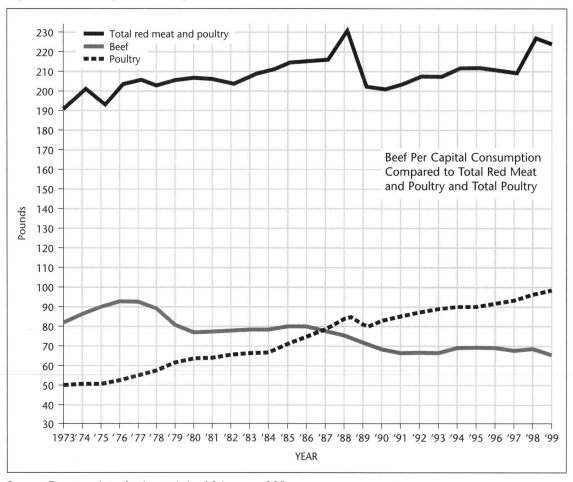

Source: Damron, *Introduction to Animal Science,* p. 325

A graph can show one of three general relationships: positive, inverse, or independent. Each of these is shown in Figure 9–5.

1. *Positive relationships.* When both variables increase or decrease simultaneously, the relationship is positive and is shown on a graph by an upwardly sloping line. In Figure 9–5, Graph A shows the relation between how long a student studied and his or her exam grade. As the study time increases, so does the exam grade.

2. *Inverse relationships.* Inverse relationships occur when one variable increases while the other decreases, as shown in Graph B. Here, as the exam grade increases, the amount of time spent watching TV decreases. The inverse relationship is shown by the line or curve that slopes downward and to the right of the point of origin.

Figure 9–5   Relationships Shown by Graphs

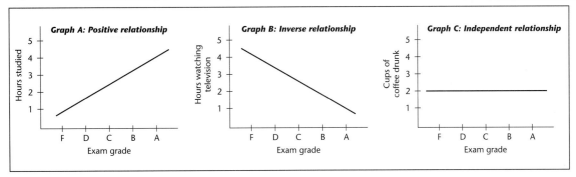

3. *Independent relationships.* When the variables have no effect on or relation-ship to one another, the graph looks like Graph C. There, you can see that the amount of coffee drunk while studying has no effect on exam grades.

From these three relationships, you can see that linear graphs may suggest a cause-and-effect relationship between the variables. However, do not assume that simply because two variables both change, one is acting on the other. Two events may occur at the same time but have no relation to one another. For example, your grades may improve during a semester in which you modify your diet, but the change in diet did not cause your grades to improve. Once you have determined the trend and the nature of the relationship that a linear graph describes, be sure to jot these down in the margin next to the graph. These notes will save you time as you review the chapter.

EXERCISE 9–2   *What type of relationship (positive, inverse, or independent) would each of the follow-ing linear graphs show?*

1. In a graph that plots the way effective use of study time is related to semester grade point average, what type of relationship would you expect?

   _____

   _____

2. In a graph that plots the way time spent reading is related to time spent playing tennis, what relationship would you predict?

   _____

   _____

3. What type of relationship would be shown by a graph that plots the way time checking a dictionary for unknown words is related to reading speed?

   _____

   _____

| **EXERCISE 9–3** | *Study the graph shown in Figure 9–6, and answer the following questions.* |

1. What is the purpose of this graph?

   _____

2. What type of relationship (positive, inverse, or independent) does this graph show between the types of revenue and years?

   _____

3. What trend does this graph reveal about individual income taxes?

   _____

4. Which source of income has experienced the largest increase?

   _____

5. Which two sources have changed least?

   _____

6. What overall trend does this graph reveal about federal revenues?

   _____

Figure 9–6   Interpreting a Linear Graph

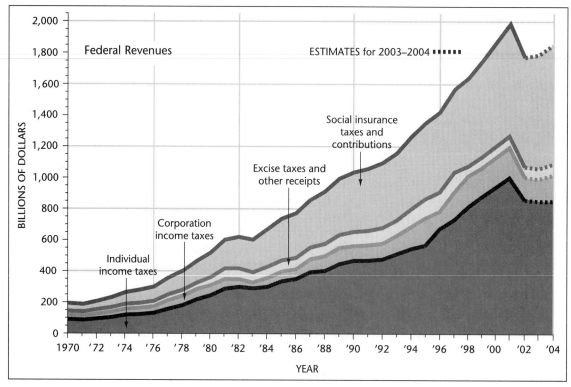

Source: Edwards et al., *Government in America,* p. 523

Figure 9–7 Sample Circle Graph

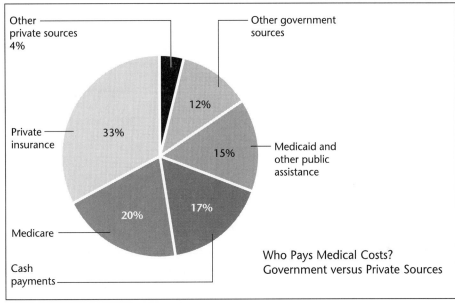

Source: Edwards et al., *Government in America,* p. 622

Circle Graphs A circle graph, also called a pie chart, is used to show the relationships of parts to the whole or to show how given parts of a unit have been divided or classified. Figure 9–7 is a circle graph that shows the sources of payment of medical costs. In this graph, payments are divided into six categories. Notice that private insurance covers only one-third of health care costs and that government sources (Medicare and Medicaid combined with other government sources) pay for nearly half.

Circle graphs often are used to emphasize proportions or to show the relative size or importance of various parts. You can see from this graph that private insurance is the greatest source of medical payments, and that other private sources make up the smallest identified source.

EXERCISE 9–4

Study the circle graphs shown in Figure 9–8 on page 270, and answer the accompanying questions.

1. What are these circle graphs intended to show?

   _____

2. Where does the largest portion of the federal dollar come from?

   _____

3. Where does the largest portion go?

   _____

4. What percent of the federal government dollar comes from corporation income taxes?

_____

5. What percent is spent on interest?

_____

Bar Graphs   A bar graph is often used to make comparisons between quantities or amounts. The horizontal scale often measures time and the vertical scale quantity. A sample bar graph is shown in Figure 9–9. It depicts trends in aging from 1950 to 2050.

EXERCISE 9–5   _Study the bar graph shown in Figure 9–9, and answer the questions below._

1. What is the purpose of the graph? _____

_____

2. In what year will the population over age 65 be the greatest in size? _____

3. Which age group is projected to increase
the most in size from 1990 to 2050? _____

4. What overall trends does this bar graph suggest? _____

_____

Figure 9–8   Comparing Circle Graphs

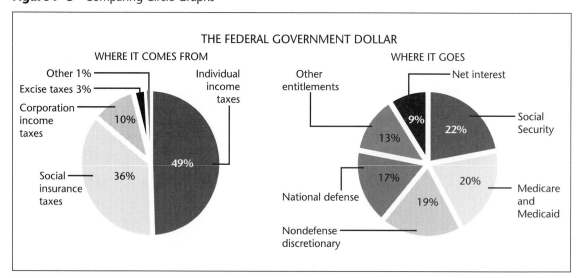

Source: U.S. Government Printing Office, _Budget of the U.S. Government, Fiscal Year 2000._

Figure 9–9   Sample Bar Graph

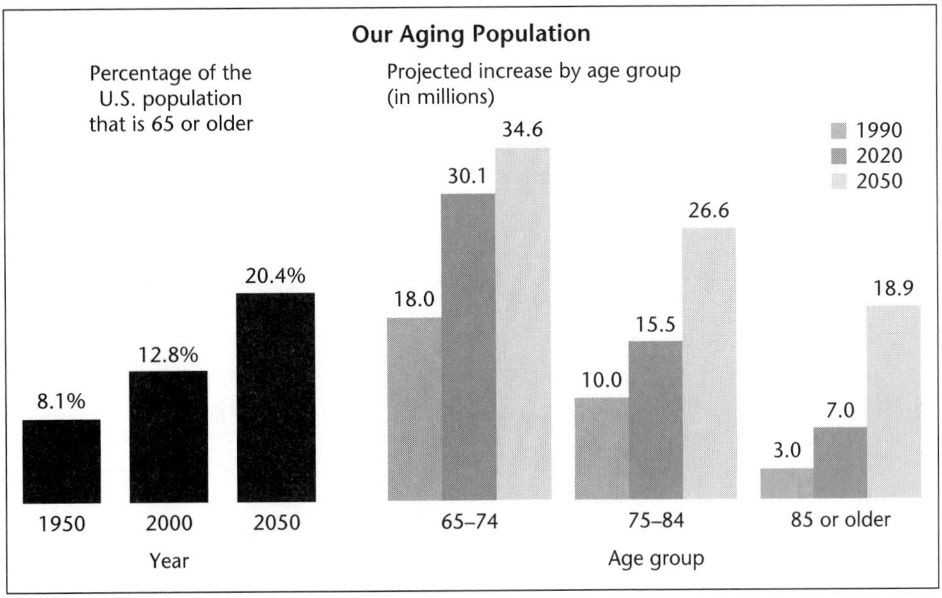

Our Aging Population

Percentage of the
U.S. population
that is 65 or older

8.1% — 1950
12.8% — 2000
20.4% — 2050
Year

Projected increase by age group
(in millions)

1990
2020
2050

65–74: 18.0, 30.1, 34.6
75–84: 10.0, 15.5, 26.6
85 or older: 3.0, 7.0, 18.9
Age group

Source: Donatelle, *Health: The Basics,* p. 354

Diagrams: Explanations of Processes

Diagrams are often included in technical and scientific as well as business and economic texts to explain processes. Diagrams are intended to help you see relationships between parts and understand sequences. Figure 9–10 on page 272, which is taken from a geography textbook, shows how the food chain works. It shows how plant-eating animals, called herbivores, begin the food chain by eating plants, how carnivores (meat-eating animals) consume herbivores, and how animal bodily wastes return nutrients to the soil. These nutrients may be used for new plant growth, thus creating a cyclical relationship.

Reading diagrams differs from reading other types of graphics in that diagrams often correspond to fairly large segments of text. This means you have to switch back and forth frequently between the text and the diagram to determine what part of the process each paragraph is discussing.

Because diagrams of processes and the corresponding text are often difficult, complicated, or highly technical, plan to read these sections more than once. Use the first reading to grasp the overall process. In subsequent readings, focus on the details of the process, examining each step and understanding how the process unfolds.

One of the best ways to study a diagram is to redraw it without referring to the original, including as much detail as possible. Redrawing is a true test of whether you understand the process you have diagrammed. Alternatively, you can test your understanding and recall of the process illustrated in a diagram by explaining it step by step in writing, using your own words.

Figure 9–10 Sample Diagram

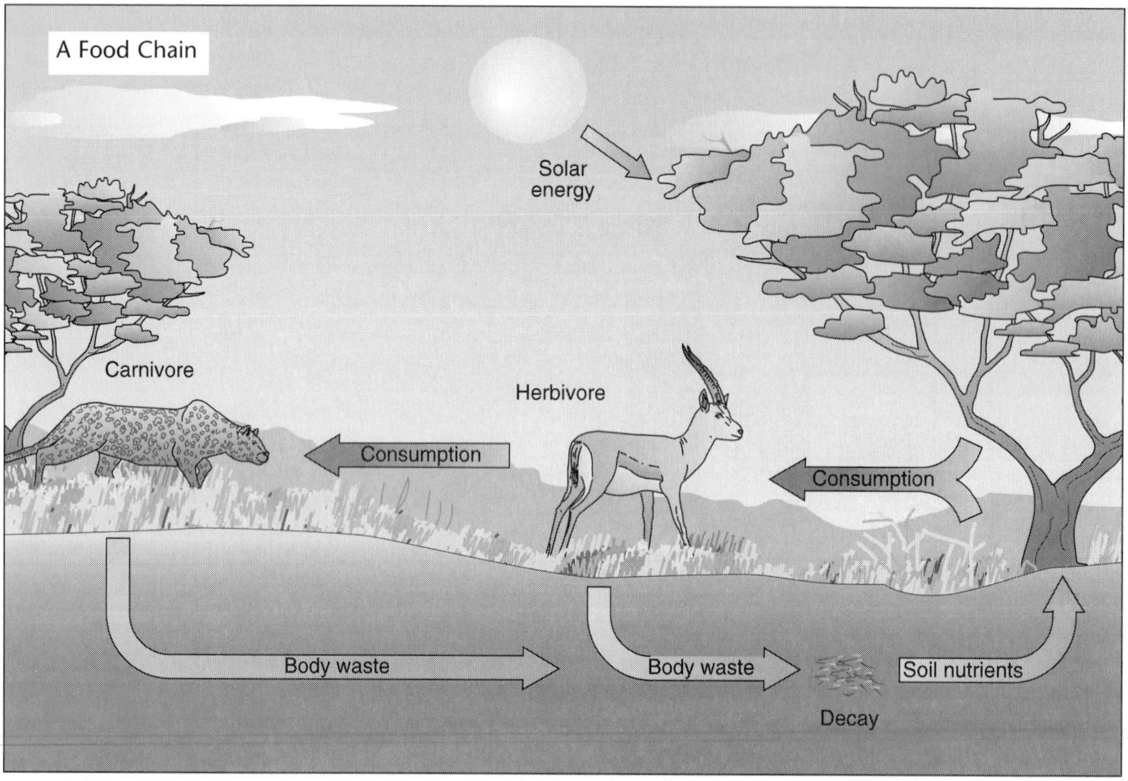

Source: McKnight, *Physical Geography: A Landscape Appreciation,* 4th ed.

EXERCISE 9–6

Study the diagram in Figure 9–11, which shows how the AIDS virus spreads in the bloodstream. Then answer the following questions.

1. What type of cell does the AIDS virus attack?

____

2. Why doesn't the host cell reject the AIDS virus?

____

____

____

3. Explain how the AIDS virus spreads beyond the first cell it attacks.

____

____

____

Figure 9–11 Sample Diagram

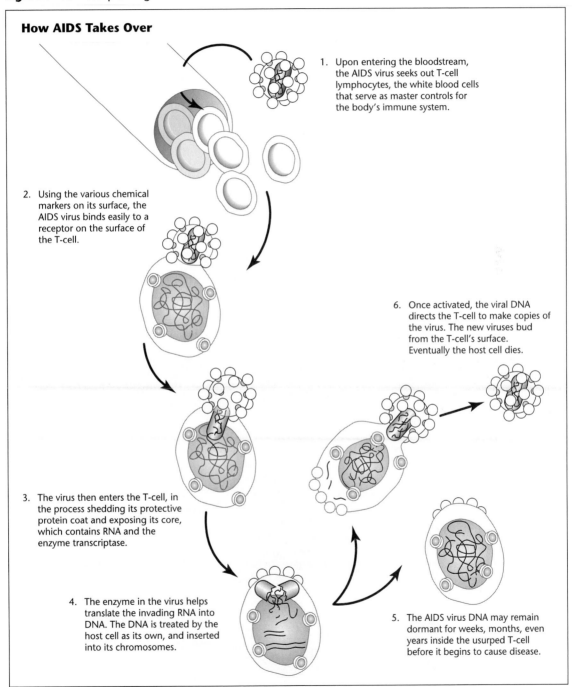

How AIDS Takes Over

1. Upon entering the bloodstream, the AIDS virus seeks out T-cell lymphocytes, the white blood cells that serve as master controls for the body's immune system.

2. Using the various chemical markers on its surface, the AIDS virus binds easily to a receptor on the surface of the T-cell.

3. The virus then enters the T-cell, in the process shedding its protective protein coat and exposing its core, which contains RNA and the enzyme transcriptase.

4. The enzyme in the virus helps translate the invading RNA into DNA. The DNA is treated by the host cell as its own, and inserted into its chromosomes.

5. The AIDS virus DNA may remain dormant for weeks, months, even years inside the usurped T-cell before it begins to cause disease.

6. Once activated, the viral DNA directs the T-cell to make copies of the virus. The new viruses bud from the T-cell's surface. Eventually the host cell dies.

Source: Wallace, *Biology: The World of Life,* p. 567

Photographs: A Visual Impression

Photographs are often considered an art form, but they serve some of the same purposes as other graphics: they are used in textbooks in place of verbal descriptions to present information. Photographs are also used to spark your interest and, often, to draw out an emotional response or impression. Study the photograph shown in Figure 9–12.

This photograph appears on a page of a biology textbook chapter titled "Resources, Energy and Human Life." The photograph of Dian Fossey, a scientist who studied gorilla behavior, reveals the trusting relationship she established with gorillas. Use the following steps to understand photographs.

1. Read the caption to discover the subject and context of the photograph.

2. If the photo is referred to in the text, read the text before studying the photograph. What details are emphasized? What conclusions are drawn?

3. Study the photograph. What is your first overall impression? What details did you notice first? Answering these questions will lead you to discover the purpose of the photograph.

Figure 9–12   Sample Photograph

Much of what we know in science is due to simple observation. Dian Fossey told us a great deal about mountain gorillas by being able to move among them. The arrogant, tough, and dedicated Fossey was instrumental in protecting these shy beasts from poachers (who sell gorilla hands to wealthy Europeans to be used for ashtrays) until she was killed by an assailant in her mountain cabin.

Source: Wallace, *Biology: The World of Life,* p. 38 (text); Peter Weit, Corbis/Sygma (photo)

EXERCISE 9–7 | *Study the photograph shown in Figure 9–13. Then answer the questions below.*

1. What emotional reaction does this photograph elicit?

   _____

   _____

2. Why would it be included in a sociology textbook chapter titled "Third World Problems"?

   _____

   _____

Maps: Physical Relationships

Maps describe relationships and provide information about location and direction. They are commonly found in geography and history texts, and they also appear in ecology, biology, and anthropology texts. Most of us think of maps as describing distances and locations, but maps are also used to describe placement of geographical and ecological features such as areas of pollution, areas of population density, or political data (voting districts).

Figure 9–13   Interpreting a Photograph

Source: Charles Caratini, Corbis/Sygma

When reading maps, use the following steps.

1. Read the caption. This identifies the subject of the map.

2. Use the legend or key to identify the symbols or codes used.

3. Note distance scales.

4. Study the map, looking for trends or key points. Often, the text that accompanies the map states the key points that the map illustrates.

5. Try to visualize, or create a mental picture of, the map.

6. As a learning and study aid, write, in your own words, a statement of what the map shows.

Now refer to the map shown in Figure 9–14, which is taken from a biology textbook.

This map shows the number of different species of trees located in North America. The caption notes trends and explains that diversity is affected by changes in longitude and latitude.

Figure 9–14 Sample Map

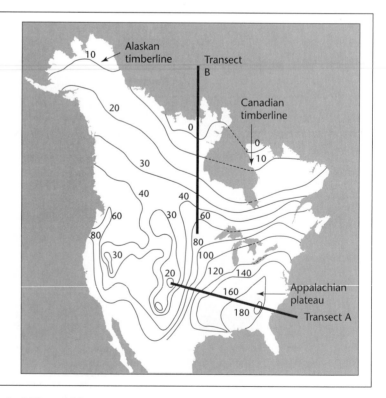

Tree Species in North America

Tree species diversity in North America decreases from east to west and from south to north. Along transect A, the change in species diversity is primarily associated with increasing longitude, whereas along transect B, species diversity decreases with increasing latitude. The lines delineate areas, each labeled with the number of species that grow there.

Source: Mix et al., *Biology: The Network of Life,* p. 128

Figure 9–15   Sample Map

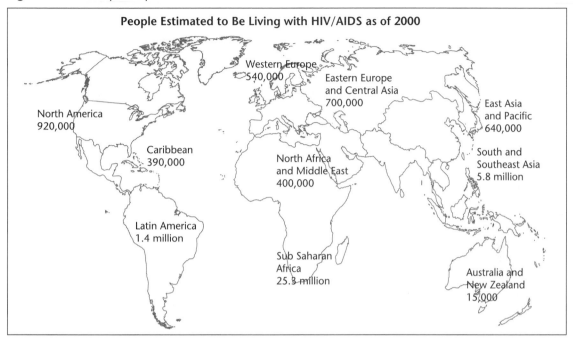

People Estimated to Be Living with HIV/AIDS as of 2000

Western Europe
540,000

Eastern Europe
and Central Asia
700,000

North America
920,000

East Asia
and Pacific
640,000

Caribbean
390,000

North Africa
and Middle East
400,000

South and
Southeast Asia
5.8 million

Latin America
1.4 million

Sub Saharan
Africa
25.3 million

Australia and
New Zealand
15,000

Source: Powers and Dodd, *Total Fitness and Wellness,* p. 320

EXERCISE 9–8

Study the map shown in Figure 9–15, and answer the following questions.

1. What is the purpose of the map? _____

   _____

2. What area has the lowest incidence of HIV/AIDS infection? _____

   _____

3. In what area is the largest number of people infected with HIV/AIDS?

   _____

4. How does the number of HIV/AIDS-infected people in North America
   compare with that of the other areas represented in this map?

   _____

EXERCISE 9–9

*Use the following statistics to construct a graphic that organizes some or all of the
information on population growth. Exchange your creation with a classmate, and
offer each other ideas for improvement.*

1. In 1970, the world population was 3,632 million.
2. In 1990, the world population was 5,320 million.

3. In 2000, the world population was 6,080 million.
4. In 1970, the population of Africa was 344 million.
5. In 1990, the population of Africa was 660 million.
6. In 2000, the population of Africa was 805 million.
7. In 1970, the population of Asia was 2,045 million.
8. In 1990, the population of Asia was 3,111 million.
9. In 2000, the population of Asia was 3,688 million.
10. In 1970, the population of Europe was 462 million.
11. In 1990, the population of Europe was 499 million.
12. In 2000, the population of Europe was 729 million.

EXERCISE 9–10

Select two different graphic devices used in a textbook chapter you have read recently, and answer the following questions about each.

1. What is the subject of the graphic?
2. What is its purpose?
3. If it presents data, how is it organized? If it is a diagram or photo, how does it achieve its purpose?
4. What is its source, and how recent is it?

SUMMARY

Graphics summarize and condense information and emphasize or clarify relationships. It is important to remember to do the following things when reading graphics.

- Read the caption.
- Determine the organization of the graphic.
- Note symbols, abbreviations, and/or scales.
- Identify trends or patterns.
- Study footnotes.
- Check the source of information.

Several types of graphics are described.

- Tables are used to compare and classify data or information.
- Graphs depict relationships among variables.
- Diagrams present visual representations of processes or sequences.
- Photographs provide visual impressions and often provoke an emotional response.
- Maps are used to describe physical relationships.

INTEGRATING IDEAS

◆

PAIRED READINGS

American Government

PREREADING QUESTIONS

1. What kinds of voting patterns would you expect to see in the U.S.?
2. How would you categorize U.S. voters?

Voting Patterns
James M. Henslin

1   Year after year, Americans show consistent voting patterns. From Table A, you can see that the percentage of people who vote increases with age. The exception is those ages 21 to 24. This table also shows how significant race-ethnicity is. Non-Hispanic whites are more likely to vote than are African Americans, white Latinos are the least likely to vote. The significance of race-ethnicity is so great that Latinos are less than half as likely to vote as are non-Hispanic whites. A crucial aspect of the socialization of newcomers to the United States is to learn the U.S. political system.

2   Table A also shows that voting increases with education. College graduates are more than twice as likely to vote as those who don't complete high school. Employment and income are also significant. People who make less than $35,000 a year are twice as likely to vote as those who make less than $5,000. Finally, note that women are slightly more likely than men to vote.

3   **Social Integration**   How can we explain the voting patterns shown in Table A? Look at the extremes. Whites who are older, more educated, affluent, and employed are the most likely to vote. Those least likely to vote are Latinos who are poor, younger, less educated, and unemployed. From these extremes, we can draw this principle: *The more that people feel they have a stake in the political system, the more likely they are to vote.* They have more to protect, and they feel that voting can make a difference. In effect, people who have been more rewarded by the political and economic system feel more socially integrated. They vote because they perceive that elections directly affect their own lives and the type of society in which they and their children live.

4   **Alienation and Apathy**   In contrast, those who gain less from the system—in terms of education, income, and jobs—are more likely to feel alienated from politics. Looking at themselves as outsiders, many feel hostile to the government. Some feel betrayed, believing that politicians have sold out to special-interest groups. They are convinced that all politicians are liars. Minorities who feel the U.S. political system is a "white" system are less likely to vote.

5   From Table A, we see that many highly educated people with good incomes also stay away from the polls. Many people do not vote because of voter apathy, or indifference. Their view is that "next year will just bring more of the same, regardless

TABLE A   WHO VOTES IN U.S. ELECTIONS?

	1980	1984	1988	1992	1996	2000
Overall						
Americans Who Vote	59%	60%	57%	61%	54%	55%
Age						
18–20	36	37	33	39	31	28
21–24	38	44	46	33	24	24
25–34	55	58	48	53	43	44
35–44	64	64	61	64	55	55
45–64	69	70	68	70	64	64
65 and up	65	68	69	70	67	68
Sex						
Male	59	59	56	60	53	53
Female	59	61	58	62	56	56
Race/Ethnicity[a]						
Whites	61	61	59	64	56	56
African Americans	51	56	52	54	51	54
Latinos	30	33	29	29	27	28
Education						
Grade school only	43	43	37	35	28	27
High school dropout	46	44	41	41	34	34
High school graduate	59	59	55	58	49	49
College dropout	67	68	65	69	61	60
College graduate	80	79	78	81	73	72
Marital Status						
Married	NA	NA	NA	NA	NA	50
Divorced	NA	NA	NA	NA	NA	38
Labor Force						
Employed	62	62	58	64	55	56
Unemployed	41	44	39	46	37	35
Income[c]						
Under $5,000	38	39	35	NA	NA	21[b]
$5,000 to $9,999	46	49	41	NA	NA	24
$10,000 to $14,999	54	55	48	NA	NA	30
$15,000 to $24,999	59	63	56	NA	NA	35
$25,000 to $34,999	67	74	64	NA	NA	40
$35,000 to $49,999	74	74	70	NA	NA	44
$50,000 to $74,999	NA	NA	NA	NA	NA	50
$75,000 and over	NA	NA	NA	NA	NA	57

[a]Only these racial-ethnic groups are listed in all sources.

[b]Because the breakdown of voting by income for the year 2000 is not contained in the 2001 source, data for 1998 from U.S. Census Bureau, *Current Population Report,* P20–523, 2000: Tables 1, 5, 7, 8, 9 is used.

[c]For years preceding 1998, the category $35,000 to $49,999 is actually $35,000 and over, except for 1998, which is an average of $35,000 to $49,900 and over $50,000.

Sources: Statistical Abstract 1991:Table 450; 1997:Table 462; *Statistical Abstract* 2001:Table 401.

TABLE B   HOW THE TWO-PARTY PRESIDENTIAL VOTE IS SPLIT

	1988	1992	1996	2000
Women				
Democrat	50%	61%	65%	56%
Republican	50%	39%	35%	44%
Men				
Democrat	44%	55%	50%	44%
Republican	56%	45%	50%	56%
African Americans				
Democrat	92%	94%	99%	97%
Republican	8%	6%	1%	3%
Whites				
Democrat	41%	53%	54%	45%
Republican	59%	47%	46%	55%
Latinos				
Democrat	NA	NA	NA	61%
Republican	NA	NA	NA	39%
Asian Americans				
Democrat	NA	NA	NA	62%
Republican	NA	NA	NA	38%

Source: *Statistical Abstract* 1999:Table 464; Galup Poll 2000, *Los Angeles Times Exit Poll,* November 7, 2001.

of who is president." A common attitude of those who are apathetic is "What difference will one vote make when there are millions of voters?" Many see little difference between the two major political parties.

6   Alienation and apathy are so common that *half* of the eligible voters do not vote for president, and *two-thirds* of the nation's eligible voters don't bother to vote for candidates for Congress (*Statistical Abstract* 2000:Table 480).

7   **The Gender Gap in Voting**   Historically, men and women have voted the same way. Now, as Table B illustrates, when they go to the ballot box, they are somewhat more likely to vote for different presidential candidates. Where men are split between Democrats and Republicans, women are more likely to vote for Democratic candidates. In addition to this gender gap, this table also illustrates the much larger racial-ethnic gap in politics. Note how few African Americans vote for a Republican presidential candidate.

8   As we saw in Table A, voting patterns reflect life experiences, especially economic circumstances. On average, women earn less than men and African Americans earn less than whites. As a result, at this point in history women and African Americans tend to look more favorably on government programs that redistribute income.

—Henslin, *Sociology: A Down-to-Earth Approach,* pp. 450–52

VOCABULARY REVIEW

1. For each of the words listed below, use context; prefixes, roots, and suffixes; and/or a dictionary to write a brief definition or synonym of the word as it is used in the reading.

a. consistent (para. 1) _____

b. significance (para. 1) _____

c. socialization (para. 1) _____

d. affluent (para. 3) _____

e. integrated (para. 3) _____

f. alienated (para. 4) _____

g. apathetic (para. 5) _____

h. redistribute (para. 8) _____

2. Underline new specialized terms introduced in the reading.

COMPREHENSION QUESTIONS

1. What is the main point of the selection?
2. What is the lowest education level at which voting always exceeds 50%?
3. What principle is illustrated about voting patterns in this selection?
4. What is voter apathy?
5. What political party are minorities more likely to vote for?
6. Why do women and African-Americans tend to vote Democrat?
7. What year had the greatest overall voter turnout?
8. In what year or years did most men vote Republican?

THINKING CRITICALLY

1. In Table A, what trend is evident about voter turnout among whites and among African-Americans from 1980 to 2000?
2. Refer to Table A. For the year 2000, within which category is there the largest variation of voter turnout? Within which category is there the least variation?
3. Can you think of possible explanations for the fact that married people vote more often than divorced people?
4. Women voted Democratic in higher numbers than ever before in 1996. What explanation can you offer for this?
5. What do you think can be done to improve voter turnout?

LEARNING/STUDY STRATEGIES

1. Predict an essay question that might be based on this reading.
2. Construct a chart that summarizes voting patterns.

American Government

PREREADING QUESTIONS

1. In what countries might you expect to find low voter turnout?
2. What do you think causes a person to become politically active?

Political Participation

James N. Danziger

1 Once categories of political action are established, a basic research question is: How many people participate in each category, both within and across various national political contexts? In studying participation, Milbrath and Goel (1972) argue that only a small proportion of the population can be termed "gladiators"— those people who are active in the most demanding forms of political action, such as protest and extensive partisan political work. They concluded that only about 5 percent of the adults in the United States were gladiators and more than half of the adults were either "observers" or "apathetics." More recent empirical research reports that about one in five adults in the United States engages in no political activity and another one-fifth do little more than vote.

2 Some empirical data compare levels of participation across many countries. The most reliable of these comparative data measure voting in national elections. Table A on page 284 provides these data for selected countries. The most striking observation about these figures is the huge variation in voting level, ranging from a reported 98 percent in Vietnam to only 28 percent in Haiti. Notice the very high voter turnout in countries such as Cuba and North Korea (which reports voting participation at about 99 percent). In such countries, voting is primarily a symbolic act that is supposed to express support for the existing political leadership, not an action in which citizens select their leaders. Unlike Vietnam and Cuba, nearly every country in Table A does now offer the voters a choice among candidates. However, there is considerable variation in the extent to which the choice is genuine and the votes really do determine the top leadership. There are some countries (e.g., Kenya, Singapore, Zimbabwe) where one group is virtually assured of victory and other countries (e.g., Algeria, Myanmar) where the top leadership or the military has repudiated the elections if they do not approve of the electoral results. These variations regarding the act of voting alert us to a general problem in cross-national analyses of micropolitical data—the same action or belief might have a quite different meaning and significance in different settings.

3 The most consistent finding in virtually all recent comparative research on participation in democracies is clear: Most people do not regularly engage in high levels of political activity. Apart from voting, which *is* a political act completed by many/most citizens (Table A), high levels of persistent political activity tend to be uncommon in most political systems. For example, Dalton (1996) finds that

TABLE A   VOTING PARTICIPATION IN SELECTED COUNTRIES: PERCENTAGE OF ADULTS VOTING IN NATIONAL ELECTION

Country	Percentage	Election Year	Country	Percentage	Election Year
Vietnam	98%	1998	Czech Republic	74%	1998
Cuba	97	1997	Bangladesh	73	1996
Singapore	96	1996	Netherlands	73	1998
Australia	92	1998	United Kingdom	71	1997
Mongolia	92	1993	Costa Rica	70	1998
Cambodia	90	1997	Russia	69	1996
Indonesia	87	1999	Poland	68	1995
Denmark	85	1998	Kenya	66	1993
Uruguay	85	1994	Portugal	66	1996
South Africa	85	1999	South Korea	64	1996
Italy	83	1996	Canada	62	1997
Greece	82	1993	India	62	1998
Turkey	85	1995	Algeria	60	1999
Slovak Republic	84	1998	Japan	60	1996
Iran	81	2000	Colombia	59	1998
France	80	1995	Ukraine	59	1999
Palestine (territory)	80	1996	Hungary	56	1998
Sweden	80	1998	United States	49	1996
Israel	79	1996	Ireland	48	1997
Mexico	78	1994	Guatemala	39	1996
Norway	78	1997	Pakistan	37	1997
Spain	77	1996	Nigeria	31	1993
Taiwan	76	1996	Haiti	28	1995
Sri Lanka	75	1994			

Sources: *Facts on File* (various, biweekly); *Electoral Studies Journal* (various, quarterly).

fewer than one in ten citizens engages in active, partisan activities in the four Western democracies in his study.

4   A second broad finding is that some citizens are willing to engage occasionally in more activist modes of political participation. While very few citizens participate in violent protests against people or property, Table B indicates that a significant number of people perform certain less-conventional political acts, including some actions that require considerable effort or risk. In the majority of countries listed in the table, 30 percent or more of the citi-

"I'M HAVING SECOND THOUGHTS ABOUT THE ELECTION... I'M NOT SURE I VOTED AGAINST THE RIGHT PERSON."

zens have engaged in at least one "challenging act" (e.g., a lawful demonstration, boycott, or building occupation).

5   A third broad observation is based on these empirical participation studies. There is substantial variation, from country to country, in the proportion of citizens who undertake various forms of conventional and unconventional political action. In the data in Table B, the difference in rates of activity (from highest to lowest) between countries is often a ratio of 3:1 or higher (except for voting). For example, nearly four out of five Canadians have signed a petition whereas fewer than one in ten Nigerians has done so. And more than one in three Italians and Russians have participated in a lawful demonstration, compared to about one in twenty Turks or Hungarians. In some countries, there can be an explosion of protest behavior and political violence against the regime during periods of unsatisfactory political or economic conditions. Such political behavior can manifest itself in strikes, violent demonstrations, insurrections, and revolutionary action.

TABLE B   LEVEL OF LESS-CONVENTIONAL POLITICAL ACTIONS IN SELECTED COUNTRIES

| | Mode of Political Action | | | |
Country	Sign Petition	Boycott	Lawful Demonstration	Occupy Building
Belarus	27%	5%	18%	1%
Brazil	50	10	19	2
Bulgaria	22	4	15	2
Canada	77	23	22	3
Chile	23	4	30	4
Denmark	51	11	27	2
France	54	12	33	8
Great Britain	75	14	14	10
Hungary	18	2	4	0.1
India	25	17	17	1
Italy	48	11	36	8
Mexico	35	7	22	5
Nigeria	7	13	20	2
Japan	62	4	13	0.4
Poland	14	6	12	4
Russia	30	5	33	1
South Africa	34	15	15	2
South Korea	42	11	20	11
Sweden	72	17	23	0.2
Turkey	14	6	6	2
United States	72	18	16	2

Note: About one thousand respondents in each country indicated whether they had engaged in the action.

Source: *World Values Survey, 1990–1991* 1994.

6   In democratic countries, about which we have the most systematic empirical data, the evidence generally supports the conclusion that most individuals employ the conventional modes of voting and contacting public (elected or appointed) officials as the key means of achieving political objectives. But data like those in Table B, which reveal a notable level of unconventional participatory modes involving protest or political violence, have increased recognition among analysts that individuals' choices of political action might not conform to the democratic model. It is also clear that many individuals continue to rely on nongovernmental channels to achieve objectives that could be pursued by contacting public officials.

—Danziger, *Understanding the Political World*, pp. 51–54

VOCABULARY REVIEW

1. For each of the words listed below, use context; prefixes, roots, and suffixes; and/or a dictionary to write a brief definition or synonym of the word as it is used in the reading.

   a. contexts (para. 1) _____

   b. apathetics (para. 1) _____

   c. symbolic (para. 2) _____

   d. repudiated (para. 2) _____

   e. partisan (para. 3) _____

   f. regime (para. 5) _____

   g. empirical (para. 6) _____

2. Underline new specialized terms introduced in the reading.

COMPREHENSION QUESTIONS

1. What three key findings about political participation does this textbook excerpt present?
2. Why are voting levels high in Cuba and North Korea?
3. According to Table A, what was the voter turnout in Norway?
4. Does Canadian voter turnout exceed U.S. voter turnout? If so, by how much?
5. What methods of political participation are most used in democratic countries?
6. According to Table B, in which country are citizens least likely to occupy a building, boycott, or participate in a lawful demonstration?

THINKING CRITICALLY

1. According to Table B, which form of political participation is most widely accepted? Which is least widely accepted?
2. Based on Table A and the text of the selection, analyze Australia's voter turnout.
3. What does the cartoon in this selection imply about American voters?
4. What type of graph would best reflect the data in Table B?

LEARNING/STUDY STRATEGIES

1. Predict an essay question that might be based on this reading selection.
2. Sketch a graph based on the information in Table A.

THINKING ABOUT THE PAIRED READINGS

INTEGRATING IDEAS

1. The two readings contain a total of four graphs. Which graph was the most useful? Why?
2. Identify the thought patterns used to organize each reading.
3. What information would you use from each reading to make a speech to a group of high school students about their responsibility to participate in the political process?
4. Write a letter to the editor of your local newspaper. Your purpose is to urge members of your community to become more involved in the political process. Use information or statistics from one or both readings to support your ideas.

GENERATING NEW IDEAS

1. Write a list of suggestions that could be used in a brochure designed to encourage college students to increase their political participation.
2. Assuming that apathy may be a major reason that eligible voters in the U.S. do not vote, write an essay about the steps you would take to increase voting if you held a political office.
3. Discuss whether or not you would participate in a demonstration on the White House lawn. Choose a specific issue, and explain why you think it is or is not important enough to participate in a protest.

Multimedia Activities

1. **Charts and Graphs**

   http://www.kcmetro.cc.mo.us/longview/ctac/GRAPHS.HTM

   The Critical Thinking Across the Curriculum Project from Longview Community College invites you to analyze the way statistical information is represented visually. Look through some newspapers and magazines with a friend to locate charts and graphs. Analyze their reliability based on the information presented on this site. What is your perception of the media's use of statistics?

2. **American Factfinder**

   http://www.factfinder.census.gov/servlet/BasicFactsServlet

   Try using the "Basic Facts" tools on the U.S. Census Web site to find either tables or maps illustrating the information of your choice. Explore other areas of the site also. How do you prefer the statistics to be displayed?

Take a Road Trip!

If your instructor has asked you to use the Reading Road Trip CD-ROM or Website, be sure to use the CD throughout the course for multimedia tutorials, exercises, and tests.

CHAPTER 10

READING ONLINE

LEARNING OBJECTIVES

- ✦ To locate electronic sources more effectively
- ✦ To evaluate Internet sources
- ✦ To read electronic text
- ✦ To develop new reading and thinking strategies for reading electronic sources

Increasingly, college students are finding the Internet to be a valuable and useful resource. The Internet is a worldwide network of computers through which you can access a wide variety of information and services. Through the Internet, you can access the **World Wide Web** (WWW), a system of Internet servers that allows exchange of information of specially formatted documents. It connects a vast array of resources (documents, graphics, and audio and video files) and allows users to move between and among them easily and rapidly. Many instructors use the Internet and have begun requiring their students to do so. In this chapter, you will learn to read and study electronic sources differently than you do print sources.

Although in most courses, your textbook is still your primary source of information, more and more instructors expect their students to use the Internet to supplement their textbook or obtain additional, more current information by visiting Web sites on the Internet. (Textbooks, no matter how up to date they may be, often do not contain information learned within the past year.)

Other instructors expect their students to consult Internet sources in researching a topic for a research paper. Many students, too, are finding valuable information on personal or special interests on the Internet.

For example, Maria Valquez, a student majoring in liberal arts, over the course of a week conducted the following activities using electronic sources.

- Visited an online writing center, http://www.purdue.edu, for help with an English paper.
- Searched for Web sites on the topic of tattooing for a sociology research paper.
- Sent and received e-mail from friends.
- Checked the weather in her hometown in anticipation of a weekend trip.

- Visited a Latino student Web site for ideas for organizing a Latino student group on her campus.
- Ordered a music CD from Amazon.com, an online book and music store.

Electronic sources are becoming increasingly important in many students' academic and personal lives. Therefore, it is important to know how Web sites are structured, how to locate useful sources, how to evaluate the sources you locate, how to understand differences from print sources, and how to navigate through them in an efficient way.

Although this chapter focuses on using electronic sources, you should realize that the Internet is not always the best source of information. Sometimes it is easier and quicker to find a piece of information in a book or other traditional sources.

LOCATING ELECTRONIC SOURCES ON THE WEB

Begin by gaining access to the Internet. In addition to a computer, you will need a modem and a browser, such as Microsoft Explorer or Netscape Navigator. You will also need an Internet service provider (ISP) to connect your computer to the Internet. Your college's computer center, your telephone or cable company, or a commercial service provider such as America Online can connect you. You will need a name you use online, called a username, and a password. If you need help getting started, check with the staff in your college's computer lab.

Identifying Keywords

To search for information on a topic, you need to come up with a group of specific words that describe your topic; these are known as **keywords.** It is often necessary to narrow your topic in order to identify specific keywords. For example, if you searched the topic home-schooling, you would find thousands of sources. However, if you narrowed your topic to home-schooling of primary grade children in California, you would identify far fewer sources.

There are three basic groups of search tools you can use to locate information: subject directories, search engines, and meta-search engines.

Using Subject Directories

Subject directories classify Web resources by categories and subcategories. Some offer reviews or evaluations of sites. Use a subject directory when you want to browse the Web using general topics or when you are conducting a broad search. A subject directory would be helpful if you were looking for sites about parenting issues or wanted to find a list of organizations for animal welfare. Two useful subject directories are INFOMINE http://infomine.ucr.edu and Yahoo! http://www.yahoo.com.

Using a Search Engine

A **search engine** is a computer program that helps you locate information on a topic. Search engines search for keywords and provide connections to documents that contain the keywords you instruct it to search for. Depending on your topic, some search engines are more useful than others. In addition, each search engine may require a different way of entering the keywords. For example, some may require you to place quotation marks around a phrase ("capital punishment"). Other times, you may need to use plus signs (+) between keywords ("home schooling" + "primary grades" + "California"). The quotation marks around "home schooling" will create a search for those words used as a phrase, rather than as single terms. Be sure to use the "help" feature when you use a new search engine to discover the best way to enter keywords.

Using Meta-Search Engines

You can search a number of search engines at the same time and combine all the results in a single listing using a **meta-search engine.** Use these types of engines when you are searching for a very specific or obscure topic or one for which you are having trouble finding information. Table 10–1 describes several popular search and meta-search engines.

TABLE 10–1   USEFUL SEARCH AND META-SEARCH ENGINES

Name	URL	Description
Google	http://www.google.com	An extensive and very popular tool. Has basic and advanced (menu-based) searching. Many extra features such as translation, domain/file type searches, and filtering. Online help provided.
AltaVista	http://www.altavista.com	A powerful search engine with basic and advanced (menu-based) searching. Also offers searches for audio, video, and images. Provides news, subject guide, filtering, translation, and Internet portal features. Online help provided.
Yahoo!	http://www.yahoo.com	Biggest subject directory on Web. Pages are organized in a searchable directory. A few advanced features available. Internet portal and site recommendations.
Infomine	http://infomine.ucr.edu/	Academic and research sites compiled, organized, and annotated by college and university librarians. Basic and advanced searching (tips provided). Users can submit sites for inclusion.
Ixquick	www.ixquick.com	A meta-search engine covering at least nine other search tools. Features music, picture, and news searches. Search results are rated.
ProFusion	www.profusion.com	This meta-search tool searches major engines or subject-specific databases and resources. Basic and advanced searching. Results are ranked.

EXERCISE 10–1 *Use one of the search tools listed above to locate three sources on one of the following topics. Then use a different tool or different search engine to search the same topic again. Compare your results. Which engine was easier to use? Which produced more sources?*

1. The Baseball Hall of Fame
2. Telecommuting
3. Oil drilling in Alaska
4. Parenting issues

EVALUATING INTERNET SOURCES

Although the Internet contains a great deal of valuable information and resources, it also contains rumor, gossip, hoaxes, and misinformation. In other words, not all Internet sources are trustworthy. You must evaluate a source before accepting it. Here are some guidelines to follow when evaluating Internet sources.

Discover the Purpose of Web Sites

There are thousands of Web sites, and they vary widely in purpose. Table 10–2 summarizes five primary types of Web sites.

EXERCISE 10–2 *Determine the purpose of each of the following Web sites using the information in Table 10–2. Some sites may have more than one purpose. Be sure to investigate the whole site carefully and explain your choices.*

1. College Finder: http://www.college-finder.info/
2. Israel—A Country Study: http://lcweb2.loc.gov/frd/cs/iltoc.html
3. Hedgehog-o-Rama: http://neuro-www2.mgh.harvard.edu/hedgehog/ hedgehogmain.html
4. Public Citizen: http://www.citizen.org/
5. Affordable Low Cost Health Care: http://www.whole-health.biz/

Evaluate the Content of a Web Site

When evaluating the content of a Web site, evaluate its appropriateness, its source, its level of technical detail, its presentation, its completeness, and its links.

Evaluate Appropriateness   To be worthwhile a Web site should contain the information you need. It should answer one or more of your search questions. If the site touches upon answers to your questions but does not address them in detail, check the links on the site to see if they lead you to more detailed information. If they do not, search for another, more useful site.

TABLE 10–2   TYPES OF WEB SITES

Type	Purpose and Description	Domain	Sample Sites
Informational	To present facts, information, and research data. May contain reports, statistical data, results of research studies, and reference materials.	.edu or .gov	http://www.haskins.yale.edu/ http://www.census.gov/
News	To provide current information on local, national, and international news. Often supplements print newspapers, periodicals, and television news programs.	.com or .org	http://news.yahoo.com/ http://www.theheart.org/ index.cfm
Advocacy	To promote a particular cause or point of view. Usually concerned with a controversial issue; often sponsored by nonprofit groups	.com or .org	http://www.goveg.com/ http://www.bradycampaign.org/
Personal	To provide information about an individual and his/her interests and accomplishments. May list publications or include the individual's resume.	Varies. May contain .com, .org, .biz, .edu, .info. May contain a tilde (~)	http://www.jessamyn.com/ http://www.srmi.biz/ resumeJohn.html http://www.maryrussell.info/
Commercial	To promote goods or services. May provide news and information related to products.	.com, .biz, .info	http://www.nmgroup.biz/ http://www.alhemer.com/ http://www.vintageradio.info/

Evaluate the Source   Another important step in evaluating a Web site is to determine its source. Ask yourself "Who is the sponsor?" and "Why was this site put up on the Web?" The sponsor of a Web site is the person or organization who paid for it to be created and placed on the Web. The sponsor often suggests the purpose of a Web site. For example, a Web site sponsored by Nike is designed to promote its products, while a site sponsored by a university library is designed to help students use its resources more effectively.

If you are uncertain of who sponsors a Web site, check its URL, its copyright, and the links it offers. The ending of the URL often suggests the type of sponsorship, as you will see below. The copyright indicates the owner of the site. Links may also reveal the sponsor. Some links may lead to commercial advertising; others may lead to sites sponsored by nonprofit groups, for example.

Another way to check the ownership of a Web site is to try to locate the site's home page. You can do this by using only the first part of its URL—up to the first slash (/) mark. For example, suppose you found information on Medicare on the Internet at the URL http://www.pha.org.au/friends_of_ medicare/frame_friends_of_medicare.html. This page deals with Medicare, but it begins by talking about Australia. If you wanted to track its source, you could go back in the URL to http://www.pha.org.au and discover that the sponsoring organization is the Public Health Association of Australia.

Evaluate the Level of Technical Detail   A Web site should contain the level of detail that is suited to your purpose. Some sites may provide information that is too sketchy for your search purposes; others assume a level of background knowledge or technical sophistication that you lack. For example, if you are writing a short, introductory-level paper on global warming, information on the University of New Hampshire's NASA Earth Observing System site (http://www.eos-ids.sr.unh.edu/) may be too technical and contain more information than you need, unless you have some previous knowledge in that field.

Evaluate the Presentation   Information on a Web site should be presented clearly; it should be well written. If you find a site that is not clear and well written, you should be suspicious of it. If the author did not take time to present ideas clearly and correctly, he or she may not have taken time to collect accurate information, either.

Evaluate Completeness   Determine whether the site provides complete information on its topic. Does it address all aspects of the topic that you feel it should? For example, if a Web site on Important Twentieth Century American Poets does not mention Robert Frost, then the site is incomplete. If you discover that a site is incomplete, search for sites that present a more thorough treatment of the topic.

Evaluate the Links   Many reputable sites supply links to related sites. Make sure that the links work and are current. Also check to see if the sites to which you are sent are reliable sources of information. If the links do not work or the sources appear unreliable, you should question the reliability of the site itself. Also determine whether the links provided are comprehensive or present only a representative sample. Either is acceptable, but the site should make clear the nature of the links it is providing.

EXERCISE 10–3   *Evaluate the content of two of the following sites. Explain why you would either trust or distrust the site for reliable content.*

1. http://www.lassetersgold.info/
2. http://www.earlham.edu/~peters/knotlink.htm
3. http://www.age-of-the-sage.org/psychology/

Evaluate the Accuracy of a Web Site

When using information on a Web site for an academic paper, it is important to be sure that you have found accurate information. One way to determine the accuracy of a Web site is to compare it with print sources (periodicals and books) on the same topic. If you find a wide discrepancy between the Web site and the printed sources, do not trust the Web site. Another way to determine the accuracy of a site's information is to compare it with other Web sites that address the same topic. If discrepancies exist, further research is needed to determine which site is more accurate.

The site itself will also provide clues about the accuracy of its information. Ask yourself the following questions:

- Are the author's name and credentials provided? A well-known writer with established credentials is likely to author only reliable, accurate information. If no author is given, you should question whether the information is accurate.
- Is contact information for the author included on the site? Often, sites provide an e-mail address where the author may be contacted.
- Is the information complete or in summary form? If it is a summary, use the site to find the original source. Original information has less chance of error and is usually preferred in academic papers.
- If opinions are offered, are they presented clearly as opinions? Authors who disguise their opinions as facts are not trustworthy. (See fact and opinion, Chapter 4, p. 91.)
- Does the writer make unsubstantiated assumptions or base his or her ideas on misconceptions? If so, the information presented may not be accurate.
- Does the site provide a list of works cited? As with any form of research, sources used to put information up on a Web site must be documented. If sources are not credited, you should question the accuracy of the Web site.

It may be helpful to determine whether the information is available in print form. If it is, try to obtain the print version. Errors may occur when the article or essay is put up on the Web. Web sites move, change, and delete information, so it may be difficult for a reader of an academic paper to locate the Web site that you used in writing it. Also, page numbers are easier to cite in print sources than in electronic ones.

EXERCISE 10–4   *Evaluate the accuracy of two of the following Web sites.*

1. http://www.idausa.org/facts/pg.html
2. http://member.triped.com/~fedinfo/tax-page.html
3. http://home.fuse.net/ufo/maysville.html

Evaluate the Timeliness of a Web Site

Although the Web is well known for providing up-to-the-minute information, not all Web sites are current. Evaluate the timeliness by checking

- The date on which the Web site was mounted (put on the Web).
- The date when the document you are using was added.
- The date when the site was last revised.
- The date when the links were last checked.

This information is usually provided at the end of the site's home page or at the end of the document you are using.

EXERCISE 10–5 | *Evaluate the timeliness of two of the following Web sites, using the directions given above.*

    1. http://www.amguard.net/
    2. http://www.krysstal.com/democracy.html
    3. http://www.idausa.org/facts/pg.html

EXERCISE 10–6 | *Evaluate each of the sites you examined for Exercise 10–2. Assign a rating of 1–5 (1 = low reliability; 5 = high reliability). Be prepared to discuss your ratings.*

EXERCISE 10–7 | *Visit a Web site and become familiar with its organization and content. Evaluate it using the suggested criteria. Then write a brief paragraph explaining why the Web site is or is not a reliable source.*

READING ELECTRONIC TEXT

Reading electronic text (also called hypertext) is very different from reading traditional printed text such as textbooks or magazines or newspaper articles. The term electronic text, as used in this chapter, refers to information presented on a Web site. It does not refer to articles and essays that can be downloaded from Searchbank or from an e-journal, for example. Because Web sites are unique, they require a different mind-set and different reading strategies. If electronic text is new or unfamiliar to you, you need to change the way you read and the way you think when approaching Web sites. If you attempt to read Web sites the same way you read traditional text, you may lose focus or perspective, miss important information, or become generally disoriented. Text on Web sites is different in the following ways from traditional print text.

- *Reading Web sites involves paying attention to sound, graphics, and movement, as well as words.* Your senses, then, may pull you in several different directions simultaneously. Banner advertisements, flashing graphics, and colorful drawings or photos may distract you. Some Web sites are available in two formats—graphical and text-only. This is most common for academic sites. If you are distracted by the sound and graphics, check to see if a text-only version of the site is available.

- *Text on Web sites comes in brief, independent screenfuls, sometimes called nodes.* These screenfuls tend to be brief, condensed pieces of information. Unlike traditional text, they are not set within a context, and background information is often not supplied. They do not depend on other pages for meaning either. In traditional print text, paragraphs and pages are dependent— you often must have read and understood a previous one in order to comprehend the one that follows it. Electronic pages are often intended to stand alone.
- *Text on Web sites may not follow the traditional main idea–supporting details organization of traditional paragraphs.* Instead, the screen may appear as a group of topic sentences without detail.
- *Web sites are multidirectional and unique; traditional text progresses in a single direction.* When reading traditional text, a reader usually follows a single direction, working through the text from beginning to end as the author has written it. Web site text is multidirectional; each electronic reader creates his or her own unique text, by following or ignoring different paths. Two readers of the same Web site may read entirely different material, or the same material in a different order. For example, one user of the National Library of Medicine site shown in Figure 10–1 on the next page might begin by reading "New & noteworthy"; another user might start by looking for information using MEDLINEplus; a third might begin by clicking on the NIH link.
- *Web site text requires readers to make decisions.* Because screens have menus and links, electronic readers must always make choices. They can focus on one aspect of the topic and ignore all others, for example, by following a path of links. Readers of print text, however, have far fewer choices to make.
- *Web sites allow readers the flexibility to choose the order in which to receive the information.* Partly due to learning style, people prefer to acquire information in different sequences. Some may prefer to begin with details and then come to understand underlying rules or principles. Others may prefer to begin in the opposite way. Electronic sources allow readers to approach the text in any manner compatible with their learning style. A pragmatic learner may prefer to move through a site systematically, either clicking or ignoring links as they appear on the screen from top to bottom, for example.
- *Web sites use new symbol systems.* Electronic texts introduce new and sometimes unfamiliar symbols. A flashing or blinking light may suggest a new feature on the site, or an underlined word or a word in a different color may suggest a link.

EXERCISE 10–8 | *Locate a Web site on a topic related to one of the end-of-chapter readings in this text. Write a list of characteristics that distinguish it from the print readings.*

Figure 10–1 Web Sites are Multidirectional

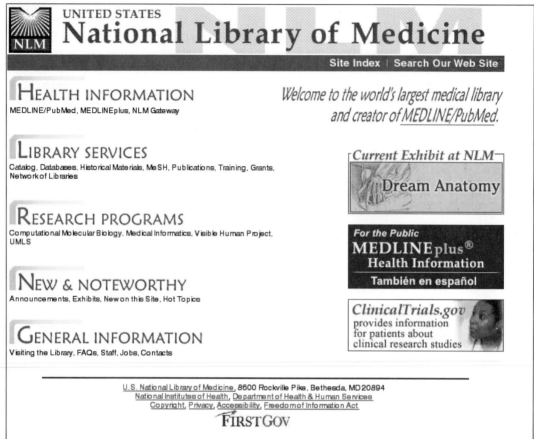

Source: The National Library of Medicine (http://www.nlm.nih.gov/)

Changing Your Reading Strategies for Reading Electronic Text

Reading electronic text is relatively new to the current generation of college students. (This will no doubt change with the upcoming generations who, as children, will learn to read both print and electronic text.) Most current college students and teachers first learned to read using print text. We have read print text for many more years than electronic text; consequently, our brains have developed numerous strategies or "work orders" for reading traditional texts. Our work orders, however, are less fully developed for electronic text. Electronic texts have a wider variety of formats and more variables to cope with than traditional texts. A textbook page is usually made up of headings, paragraphs, and an occasional photo or graphic. Web sites have vibrant color, animation, sound, and music as well as words.

Reading is not only different, but it also tends to be slower on the computer screen than on print sources. Your eyes can see the layout of two full pages in a book. From the two pages, you can see headings, division of ideas, and subtopics. By glancing at a print page, you get an initial assessment of what it contains. You can tell, for example, if a page is heavily statistical (your eye will see numbers, dates, symbols) or is anecdotal (your eye will see capitalized proper names, quotation marks, and numerous indented paragraphs for dialogue, for example). Because you have a sense of what the page contains and how it is organized, you can read somewhat faster. Because a screen holds fewer words, you get far less feedback before you begin to read.

DEVELOPING NEW WAYS OF THINKING AND READING

Reading of electronic sources demands a different type of thinking than print sources. A print source is linear—it goes in a straight line from idea to idea. Electronic sources, due to the presence of links, tend to be multidirectional and let you follow numerous paths (see illustration).

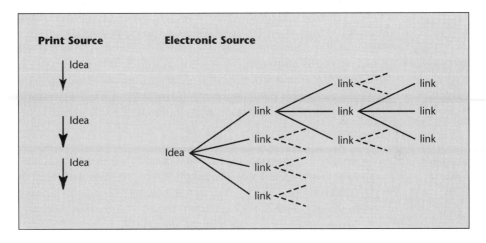

Reading electronic text also requires new strategies. The first steps to reading electronic text easily and effectively are to understand how it is different (see preceding section) and realize that you must change and adapt how you read. Some specific suggestions follow.

Focus on Your Purpose

Focus clearly on your purpose for visiting the site. What information do you need? Because you must create your own path through the site, unless you fix in mind what you are looking for, you may wander aimlessly, wasting valuable time, or even become lost, following numerous links that lead you farther and farther away from the site at which you began.

Get Used to the Site's Design and Layout

Each Web site has unique features and arranges information differently.

1. *When you reach a new site, spend a few minutes getting used to it and discovering how it is organized.* Scroll through it quickly to determine how it is organized and what information is available. Ask yourself the following questions.
   - What information is available?
   - How is it arranged on the screen?

2. *Expect the first screen to grab your attention and make a main point.* (Web site authors know that many people [up to 90 percent] who read a Web page do not scroll down to see the next page.)

3. *Get used to the colors, flashing images, and sounds before you attempt to obtain information from the site.* Your eye may have a tendency to focus on color or movement, rather than on print. Because Web sites are highly visual, they require visual as well as verbal thinking. The author intends for you to respond to photos, graphics, and animation.

4. *Consider both the focus and limitations of your learning style.* Are you a spatial learner? If so, you may have a tendency to focus too heavily on the graphic elements on the screen. If, on the other hand, you are a verbal learner, you may ignore important visual elements or signals. If you focus *only* on the words and ignore color and graphics on a particular screen, you will probably miss information or may not move through the site in the most efficient way. Review your learning style (p. 6), and consider both your strengths and limitations as they apply to electronic text.

EXERCISE 10-9

In groups of two or three students, consider at least two aspects of learning style. For each, discuss the tendencies, limitations, and implications these particular learning styles may have for reading electronic text. For example, consider how a visual learner would approach a Web site with numerous links and buttons. Then consider how a creative learner's approach might differ.

EXERCISE 10-10

Locate two Web sites that you think are interesting and appealing. Then answer the following questions.

1. How does each use color?
2. How does each use graphics?
3. Do the sites use sound or motion? If so, how?

Pay Attention to How Information Is Organized

Because you can navigate through a Web site in many different ways, it is important to have the right expectations and to make several decisions before you begin.

Figure 10–2   A Web Page with Links

In the newest Embodied Conversational Agent project, <u>Rea</u>, we are working with <u>Matthew Stone</u> to integrate a natural language generation engine (SPUD) and are now generating hand gestures and sentences as one single process, in real time. This work addresses the challenges of specifying an underlying representation of discourse that is capable of driving generation of several modalities. We have also integrated into Rea the ability to engage in social chit-chat as a way of reducing interpersonal distance and increasing trust between the user and the system.

We have also integrated the foundations of the Embodied Conversational Agent work into the design of a 3D graphical online world (<u>BodyChat</u>), an interactive kiosk (<u>MACK</u>), and an animator's tool, <u>BEAT</u>, which allows animators to input typed text that they wish to be spoken by an animated human figure, and to obtain as output appropriate and synchronized nonverbal behaviors and synthesized speech in a form that can be sent to a number of different animation systems.

In studies of these systems at the Gesture and Narrative Language Group, we have shown that these autonomously-generated conversational signals are more important to user satisfaction and efficiency than some simple facial displays of emotion (Cassell & Thorisson 1998), and than the ability to directly manipulate the interface (Cassell & Vihjalmsson, 1998). A recent experiment demonstrated that Rea's social chit-chat significantly increases the trust that people have in the system, particularly for *extroverted users*.

For publications about the Embodied Conversational Agents, see <u>publications</u>. Press clippings about this work may be seen <u>here</u>. By the way, Rea has now made her debut on the world stage as a permanent exhibit at the Deutsche Telekom Future Labs.

Source: http://web.media.mit/edu/~justine/research.html

Some Web sites are much better organized than others. Some have clear headings and labels that make it easy to discover how to proceed; others do not and will require more thought before beginning. For example, if you are reading an article with 10–15 underlined words (links), there is no prescribed order to follow and these links are not categorized in any way. Figure 10–2 shows an excerpt from a Web site discussing the Embodied Conversational Agent research of an associate professor at MIT. Notice that it has numerous links built into paragraphs that lead the reader to supplemental material.

Use the following suggestions to grasp a site's organization.

1. *Use the site map, if provided, to discover what information is available and how it is organized.* A sample site map, from a Web site sponsored by the National Association of Independent Fee Appraisers, is shown in Figure 10–3 on the next page. This site presents information about the Association and its activities. Notice that the links are categorized by subject: Education, News, Membership Information, and so forth.

Figure 10–3 A Web Site Map

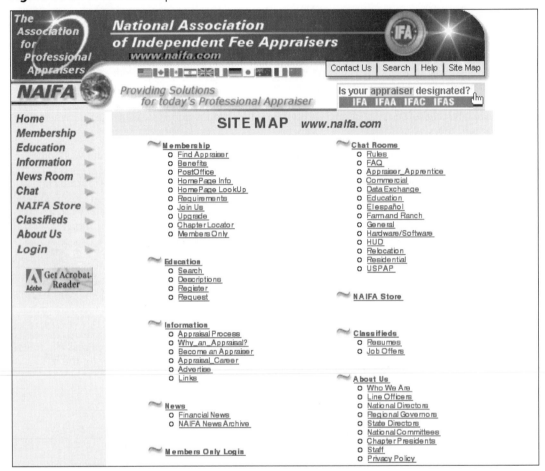

Source: The National Association of Independent Fee Appraisers (http://www.naifa.com/sitemap.html)

2. *Consider the order in which you want to take in information.* Choose an order in which to explore links; avoid randomly clicking on link buttons. Doing so is somewhat like randomly choosing pages to read out of a reference book. Do you need definitions first? Do you want historical background first? Your decision will be partly influenced by your learning style.

3. *Consider writing brief notes to yourself as you explore a complicated Web site.* Alternatively, you could print the home page and jot notes on it.

4. *Expect shorter, less detailed sentences and paragraphs.* Much online communication tends to be briefer and more concise than in traditional sources. As a result, you may have to mentally fill in transitions and make inferences about relationships among ideas. For example, you may have to infer similarities and differences or recognize cause and effect connections.

EXERCISE 10–11 *Visit two Web sites on the same topic. Write a few sentences comparing and contrasting the sites' organization and design.*

Use Links to Find the Information You Need

Links are unique to electronic text. Here's how to use them.

1. *Plan on exploring links to find complete and detailed information.* Links—both remote links (those that take you to another site) and related links within a site—are intended to provide more detailed information on topics introduced on the home page.

2. *As you follow links, be sure to bookmark your original site and other useful sites you come across so you can find them again.* **Bookmarking** is a feature on your Internet browser that allows you to record Web site addresses and access them later by simply clicking on the site name. Different search engines use different terms for this function. Netscape uses the term *Bookmarks;* Microsoft Explorer calls it *Favorites.* In addition, Netscape has a *GO* feature that allows a user to retrace the steps of the current search.

3. *If you use a site or a link that provides many pages of continuous paragraphs, print the material and read it offline to save time.*

4. *If you find you are lacking background on a topic, use links to help fill in the gap or search for a different Web site on the same topic that is less technical.*

5. *If you get lost, use the history feature found in most Internet browsers.* It allows you to backtrack or retrace the links your followed in a search. In Netscape, for example, clicking on "Back," takes you back one link at a time; "History" keeps track of all searches over a given period of time and allows you to go directly to a chosen site, rather than backtracking step by step.

EXERCISE 10–12 *For one of the Web sites you visited earlier in the chapter or a new site of your choice, follow at least three links and then answer the following questions.*

1. What type of information did each contain?
2. Was each source reliable? How do you know?
3. Which was the easiest to read and follow? Why?

SUMMARY

Reading electronic sources requires unique reading and thinking skills.

Locating sources on the World Wide Web (WWW) involves identifying keywords and using a search engine.

To evaluate a Web site, consider the following:

- purpose of the site
- content
- accuracy
- timeliness

Web sites differ from print text in the following ways:

- Web sites involve graphics, sound, color, and animation.
- Language on Web sites tends to be brief.
- Screens are often independent of one another.
- Web sites are multidirectional, require decision making, and allow flexibility.

Electronic text should be read differently than print text. Be sure to

- identify the purpose of the site.
- familiarize yourself with the site's design and layout.
- pay attention to how the information is organized.
- use links to find additional information.

Archaeology

PREREADING QUESTIONS

1. How do archaeologists know there might be an important artifact buried under the earth?
2. What can artifacts reveal about the past?

Slices of the Past

Alan Hall

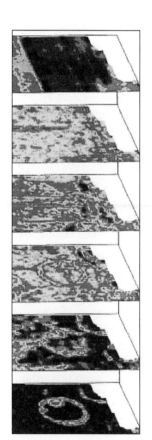

Series of Radar Images probe beneath an alfalfa field (top) in Japan to reveal the long-buried circular moat of an ancient burial mound (bottom).

1   When archaeologists suspect than an important find lies buried beneath the earth, they reach for their shovels, hoping to hit some clue of a buried city or important burial site; sometimes they even call in backhoes and trenching machines. But now, a University of Denver anthropology professor has come up with a ground-breaking alternative that may turn traditional archaeology upside down.

2   Lawrence B. Conyers and his colleague, Dean Goodman, have adapted a technology known as "ground penetrating radar" to pioneer a new era of "non-invasive" archaeology. By pumping radar pulses into the ground and creating images of the radar reflections on a computer, they can obtain detailed pictures of a potentially important site before the first shovel of dirt is lifted. Then, the researchers can decide whether to dig—and where to dig— while doing the least damage to important artifacts.

3   "Archaeologists tend to be very low-tech people," Conyers says. "They have a tendency to be more comfortable digging in the dirt than working with computers. But this radar can help to locate sites and objects that you can't see on the surface. It can help us save sites that could be destroyed with traditional excavation techniques."

4   Ground-penetrating radar has been used for decades for everything from locating buried family treasures hidden from the Nazis to finding the engines of the ValuJet crashed in the Everglades. Conyers has used the technology, and the software written by Goodman, to: map a Mayan village buried under 15 feet of volcanic ash in Ceren, El Salvador; create images of a Mayan ceremonial center buried in a sugar cane field in

Field Work. Conyers and his team have set up their radar base station at a site near Bluff, Utah, believed to conceal an ancient ceremonial room, or kiva, of the ancient Anasazi people.

Coatzalmaguapa, Guatemala; locate 1,700-year-old kiln sites and a large village buried in wind-blown sand between two ceremonial pyramids in Peru; and disclose details of ancient burial sites in Japan.

5   Closer to his home base in Denver, Conyers has employed the new technique to reveal the history of the ancient Anasazi people of the American West. Because of their sacred nature, the issue of whether to disturb these sites is crucial to their descendants. Near Bluff, Utah, Conyers and his colleagues pinpointed a subterranean kiva, used in ceremonial rites by the Anasazi people. "Even though the people that constructed this kiva have been dead for more than 900 years, these sites are still very sacred," says Conyers. "So radar was a method that we could use to first image what was there and then adjust our excavation procedures to dig only in certain spots to test our scientific ideas."

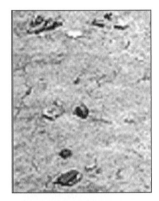

Fragments of Pottery
litter the ground at a site near Bluff, Utah, where Conyers and his colleagues located a village of Anasazi "pit houses". The broken ceramics were dated about A.D. 1100.

6   Nearby, Conyers and his colleagues also found a field littered with shards of pottery that dated to 1100 A.D. By searching the area with radar, they located a village of Anasazi "pit houses." Archaeologists usually use this type of evidence to locate sites, but of course have no idea where they are under the ground, says Conyers. "The typical way of finding the buried houses of this sort is to randomly dig test pits or drill auger holes—or, even worse, use backhoe trenchers that really destroy the site.

7   Mapping these sites using traditional excavation methods would have cost millions of dollars and taken many years. Conyers, using ground-penetrating radar and 3-D imaging software developed by Goodman, can map a site for a fraction of the cost in as little as three weeks. Many buried sites would not have been discovered without the ground-penetrating radar technology and would be potentially at risk from construction and erosion.

8   The next step for Conyers is the creation of moving 3-D images that will allow people to take video "tours" of archaeological sites that have not been unearthed. Maybe those people who Conyers refers to as "dirt archaeologists" will soon retire their shovels.

Related Reading

"Ground-penetrating Radar: An Introduction for Archaeologists," by Lawrence B. Conyers and Dean Goodman, Altamira Press, Walnut Creek, California, 1997.
                    —Hall, "Slices of the Past," *Scientific American—Exhibit: Radar Archaeology*
                    (June 22, 1998) (http://www.sciam.com)

[By clicking on the "burial mound" link, the following site was located.]

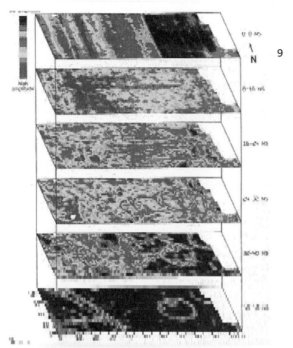

BURIAL MOUND

9   RADAR SURVEY, conducted by Dean Goodman, in Japan revealed a circular burial mound with a burial inside it, which shows up clearly in the bottom slice. The straight line at the left is probably an old fence line when the area was used for horse corrals about 500–600 years ago (Edo Period). The burial moat is much older, probably at least 1100 years old (Kofun Period). The surface is an alfalfa field. "As is usual in these surveys, there were no surface indicators of what was below the ground," says Conyers.

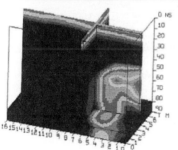

10   IMAGE is a 3-dimensional cutaway of a burial chamber that was found by Dean Goodman on a mound on the Island of Kyushu in Japan. It contained the remains of a warrior with a variety of artifacts, including bronze swords. This is a 3-D cutaway image of this chamber. It reveals a main chamber and a vertical shaft that leads to an offering below the burial.

Images: Lawrence B. Conyers and Dean Goodman, from "Ground-penetrating Radar: An Introduction for Archaeologists," Altamira Press, Walnut Creek, California, 1997.

Back to <u>Slices of the Past</u>

—"Burial Mound," *Scientific American—Exhibit: Radar Archaeology*
(June 22, 1998) (http://www.sciam.com)

VOCABULARY REVIEW

1. For each of the words listed below, use context; prefixes, roots, and suffixes; and/or a dictionary to write a brief definition or synonym of the word as it is used in the reading.

   a. alternative (para. 1) _____

   b. potentially (para. 2) _____

   c. artifacts (para. 2) _____

   d. excavation (para. 3) _____

   e. disclose (para. 4) _____

   f. subterranean (para. 5) _____

   g. shards (para. 6) _____

2. Underline new specialized terms introduced in the reading.

COMPREHENSION QUESTIONS

1. Why is the radar procedure referred to as noninvasive?
2. Name two important advantages of using the ground-penetrating radar.
3. What is the usual way of finding buried artifacts?
4. Why do archaeologists not like to use backhoe trenchers?
5. Why was it important to use radar to examine the subterranean kivas used by the Anasazi people?
6. How long does it take to map a site using this new radar technique, compared with traditional excavation?
7. What did the radar survey conducted by Dean Goodman reveal?

THINKING CRITICALLY

1. What would you do if you wanted to know more about Lawrence B. Conyers?
2. What does Conyers mean by the term *dirt archaeologists*?
3. For what other nonarchaeological situation can you imagine using ground-penetrating radar?
4. Do you think archaeologists should be permitted to dig up sacred sites? Explain.
5. How did this Web site differ from a textbook?
6. How useful did you find the link to "burial mound"?

LEARNING/STUDY STRATEGY

Design a study sheet explaining the different types of remote sensing.

Archaeology

PREREADING QUESTIONS

1. Why is the study of archaeology important?
2. What is remote sensing?

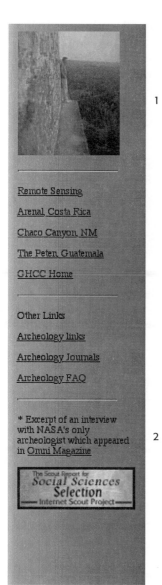

Remote Sensing

Arenal, Costa Rica

Chaco Canyon, NM

The Peten, Guatemala

GHCC Home

Other Links

Archeology links

Archeology Journals

Archeology FAQ

* Excerpt of an interview with NASA's only archeologist which appeared in Omni Magazine

The Scout Report for Social Sciences Selection — Internet Scout Project

Archaeology

Tom Sever

1 Much of human history can be traced through the impacts of human actions upon the environment. The use of remote sensing technology offers the archaeologist the opportunity to detect these impacts which are often invisible to the naked eye. This information can be used to address issues in human settlement, environmental interaction, and climate change. Archaeologists want to know how ancient people successfully adapted to their environment and what factors may have led to their collapse or disappearance. Did they overextend the capacity of their landscape, causing destructive environmental effects which led to their demise? Can this information be applied to modern day societies so that the mistakes of the past are not repeated?

2 Remote sensing can be used as a methodological procedure for detecting, inventorying, and prioritizing surface and shallow-depth archaeological information in a rapid, accurate, and quantified manner. Man is a tropical creature who has invaded every environment on earth successfully; now we are ready to explore, and eventually colonize, the delicate environments of Space. Understanding how ancient man successfully managed Earth is important for the success of current and future societies.

3   "The stereotype has archaeologists just digging up spearheads and pottery and anthropologists just writing down the words of primitive tribes. But we're examining how people adapted to their environment throughout time, how they experienced environmental shift, why cultures come and go. Soils associated with artifacts are as important as the artifacts themselves—probably more relevant to us than the actual objects. Now more than ever, archaeological research is interdisciplinary: botany, forestry, soil science, hydrology—all of which contribute to a more complete understanding of the earth, climatic shifts, and how people adapt to large regions. This understanding is critical to future decision making affecting the planet.

4   In Costa Rica, the culture survived repeated volcanic explosions that repeatedly destroyed the environment, explosions equal to the force of a nuclear blast. Other cultures, like the advanced Maya societies, did not survive or recover from similar eruptions. Did it have to do with the size and violence of the eruption, the way they farmed their land over time, or territorial and political struggle?"

> We have not inherited the earth from our fathers,
> we are borrowing it from our children
>
> Amish Farmer

—Sever, "Archaeology," Global Hydrology and Climate Center, NASA/Marshall Space Flight Center Web site (http://www.msfc.nasa.gov)

[By clicking on the "Remote Sensing" link, the following site was located.]

ARCHAEOLOGICAL REMOTE SENSING

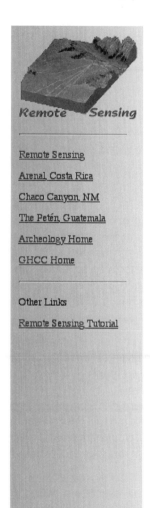

Remote Sensing

Remote Sensing

Arenal, Costa Rica

Chaco Canyon, NM

The Petén, Guatemala

Archeology Home

GHCC Home

Other Links

Remote Sensing Tutorial

5   Now more than ever, archaeological research is interdisciplinary: botany, forestry, soil science, hydrology—all of which contribute to a more complete understanding of the earth, climatic shifts, and how people adapt to large regions.

6   As a species, we've been literally blind to the universe around us. If the known <u>electromagnetic spectrum</u> were scaled up to stretch around the Earth's circumference, the human eye would see a portion equal to the diameter of a pencil. Our ability to build detectors that see for us where we can't see, and computers that bring the invisible information back to our eyesight, will ultimately contribute to our survival on Earth and in space.

7   The spectrum of sunlight reflected by the Earth's surface contains information about the composition of the surface, and it may reveal traces of past human activities, such as agriculture. Since sand, cultivated soil, vegetation, and all kinds of rocks each have distinctive temperatures and emit heat at different rates, sensors can "see" things beyond ordinary vision or cameras. Differences in soil texture are revealed by fractional temperature variations. So it is possible to identify loose soil that had been prehistoric agricultural fields, or was covering buried remains. The Maya causeway was detected through emissions of infrared radiation at a different wavelength from surrounding vegetation. More advanced versions of such multi-spectral scanner (Visible & IR) can detect irrigation ditches filled with sediment because they hold more moisture and thus have a temperature different from other soil. The ground above a buried stone wall, for instance, may be a touch hotter than the surrounding terrain because the stone absorbs more heat. Radar can penetrate darkness, cloud cover, thick jungle canopies, and even the ground.

8   Remote sensing can be a discovery technique, since the computer can be programmed to look for distinctive "signatures" of energy emitted by a known site or feature in areas where surveys have not been conducted. Such "signatures" serve as recognition features or fingerprints. Such characteristics as elevation, distance from water, distance between sites or cities, corridors, and transportation routes can help to predict the location of potential archaeological sites.

9   ## Computational Techniques Used to Analyze Data

1.   sun-angle correction
2.   density slicing

3. band ratioing
4. edge enhancement
5. synthetic color assignment
6. filtering
7. multichannel analysis

Remote Sensing Instruments

10   Aerial Photography:
Many features which are difficult or impossible to see standing on the ground become very clear when seen from the air. But, black and white photography only records about twenty-two perceptible shades of gray in the visible spectrum. Also, optical sources have certain liabilities; they must operate in daylight, during clear weather, on days with minimal atmospheric haze.

11   Color Infrared Film (CIR):
Detects longer wavelengths somewhat beyond the red end of the light spectrum. CIR film was initially employed during World War II to differentiate objects that had been artificially camouflaged. Infrared photography has the same problems that conventional photography has; you need light and clear skies. Even so, CIR is sensitive to very slight differences in vegetation. Because buried archaeological features can affect how plants grow above them, such features become visible in color infrared photography.

12   Thermal Infrared Multispectral Scanner (TIMS):
A six channel scanner that measures the thermal radiation given off by the ground, with accuracy to 0.1 degree centigrade. The pixel (picture element) is the square area being sensed, and the size of the pixel is directly proportional to sensor height. For example, pixels from Landsat satellites are about 100 feet (30 m) on a side, and thus have limited archaeological applications. However, pixels in TIMS data measure only a few feet on a side and as such can be used for archaeological research. TIMS data were used to detect ancient Anasazi roads in Chaco Canyon, NM.

13   Airborne Oceanographic Lidar (ADI):
A laser device that makes "profiles" of the earth's surface. The laser beam pulses to the ground 400 times per second, striking the surface every three and a half inches, and bounces back to its source. In most cases, the beam bounces off the top of the vegetation cover and off the ground surface; the difference between the two gives information on forest height, or even the height of grass in pastures. As the lidar passes over an eroded footpath that still affects the topography, the pathway's indentation is recorded by the laser beam. The lidar data can be processed to reveal tree height as well as elevation, slope, aspect, and slope length of ground features. Lidar can also be used to penetrate water to measure the morphology of coastal water, detect oil forms, fluorescent dye traces, water clarity, and organic pigments including chlorophyll. In this case, part of the pulse is reflected off the water

surface, while the rest travels to the water bottom and is reflected. The time elapsed between the received impulses allows for a determination of water depth and subsurface topography.

14   Synthetic Aperture Radar (SAR):
SAR beams energy waves to the ground and records the energy reflected. Radar is sensitive to linear and geometric features on the ground, particularly when different radar wavelengths and different combinations of the horizontal and vertical data are employed. Different wavelengths are sensitive to vegetation or to ground surface phenomena. In dry, porous soils, radar can penetrate the surface. In 1982, radar from the space shuttle penetrated the sand of the Sudanese desert and revealed ancient watercourses. Using airborne radar in Costa Rica, prehistoric footpaths have been found.

15   Microwave Radar:
Beaming radar pulses into the ground and measuring the echo is a good way of finding buried artifacts in arid regions (water absorbs microwaves). Man-made objects tend to reflect the microwaves, giving one a "picture" of what is underground without disturbing the site.

Selected Papers

"**Remote Sensing Methods,**" In *Advances in Science and Technology for Historic Preservation,* edited by Ray Williamson, Plenum Press. (In Press).

"**Remote Sensing,**" In *American Journal of Archaeology,* 99:83–84, 1995.

"**Applications of Ecological Concepts and Remote Sensing Technologies in Archaeological Site Reconnaissance,**" with F. Miller and D. Lee. (In *Applications of Space-Age Technology in Anthropology,* edited by Clifford Behrens and Thomas Sever. NASA, Stennis Space Center, MS, 1991.)

"**Remote Sensing,**" Chapter 14 of *Benchmarks In Time and Culture: Introductory Essays in the Methodology of Syro-Palestinian Archaeology.* Scholars Press. March, 1988.

"**Cultural and Ecological Applications of Remote Sensing.**" Final Report of a Conference Sponsored by the National Science Foundation. With Daniel Gross and Paul Shankman. University of Boulder Colorado, Boulder. April, 1988.

"**Conference on Remote Sensing: Potential for the Future.**" NASA, Stennis Space Center, Science and Technology Laboratory, SSC, MS., January, 1985.

—Global Hydrology and Climate Center, NASA/Marshall Space
Flight Center Web site (http://www.msfc.nasa.gov)

VOCABULARY REVIEW

1. For each of the words listed below, use context; prefixes, roots, and suffixes; and/or a dictionary to write a brief definition or synonym of the word as it is used in the reading.

   a. impacts (para. 1) _____

   b. demise (para. 1) _____

   c. methodological (para. 2) _____

   d. prioritizing (para. 2) _____

   e. quantified (para. 2) _____

   f. emit (para. 7) _____

   g. infrared (para. 7) _____

   h. perceptible (para. 10) _____

   i. optical (para. 10) _____

   j. camouflaged (para. 11) _____

   k. eroded (para. 13) _____

   l. morphology (para. 13) _____

   m. porous (para. 14) _____

2. Underline new specialized terms introduced in the reading.

COMPREHENSION QUESTIONS

1. Why do archaeologists need remote sensing?
2. What is the value of research that allows archaeologists to uncover previously invisible information?
3. Describe one archaeological discovery that was made using remote sensing.
4. What characteristics can predict the potential of an archaeological site?
5. Why might the ground above a buried stone wall be a little warmer than the ground surrounding it?
6. Name and briefly describe one remote sensing instrument.

THINKING CRITICALLY

1. If you did not understand the term *remote sensing,* what would you do?
2. What is the purpose of the quotation given in paragraphs 3–4?
3. Which of the remote sensing instruments might be useful in environmental preservation and conservation of wetland and coastal areas?
4. Name two advantages of reading material electronically (as opposed to a print source) that this electronic reading provided?

5. If you wanted additional information on synthetic aperture radar, how would you go about finding it?
6. Evaluate this Web site using the criteria suggested in the chapter.

LEARNING/STUDY STRATEGIES

1. Locate at least three additional electronic articles on ground-penetrating radar.
2. Evaluate each source you identify.

THINKING ABOUT THE PAIRED READINGS

INTEGRATING IDEAS

1. Which of the two readings do you think offers the most information?
2. Compare the author's purpose in both readings.
3. How do the readings differ?
4. Which of the two readings offers a more scientifically based definition of radar as used in the study of archaeology? Explain your answer.
5. If you came across these two readings online, which one would you find more "user friendly" and why?

GENERATING NEW IDEAS

1. Visit one or both of the Web sites from which these readings were taken. Search for updated information on research tools in archaeology. Write a brief summary of your findings.
2. Write a cause-and-effect essay explaining how technology has affected and changed the field of archaeology.

Multimedia Activities

1. **Worst of the Web/Best of the Web**

   http://www.worstoftheweb.com/

   http://www.webbyawards.com/main/webby_awards/winner_list.html

   Explore some links from these sites and try to determine why they were given their respective "awards." Do you have sites that you return to over and over? What about them appeals to you? What types of sites do you avoid? Why?

2. **Web Page Evaluation Sheet**

   http://www.duke.edu/~de1/evaluate.html

   Print this page and use it to evaluate Web sites you use.

Take a Road Trip!

If your instructor has asked you to use the Reading Road Trip CD-ROM or Website, be sure to use the CD throughout the course for multimedia tutorials, exercises, and tests.

CHAPTER 11

USING WRITING TO LEARN

LEARNING OBJECTIVES

- ✦ To use writing to monitor your comprehension
- ✦ To use highlighting to improve textbook reading
- ✦ To use note taking to organize, synthesize, and retain ideas
- ✦ To use mapping to show relationships
- ✦ To use summaries to condense information
- ✦ To use writing as a discovery process

Most students think of writing in college as something they do for others—writing essay exams and term papers, for example. Writing is a vehicle of expression, of course, but it is also a very effective way to learn. You can use it, for example, to organize your ideas, pull information together, discover what you think about an issue, or make a difficult reading assignment understandable.

Research studies indicate that you learn information more easily if you elaborate upon it. *Elaboration,* which means "building upon," is a process of expanding your thinking. It involves the multilevel thinking skills discussed in Chapter 1: building connections, developing associations, seeing relationships, and considering applications. Elaboration makes information meaningful and, therefore, easier to recall. Writing is one way to help you elaborate. It forces you to think about the material, to make connections, and to consider applications. This chapter discusses ways to use writing to strengthen comprehension and offers numerous writing strategies that facilitate learning. Not all strategies work equally well for everyone. Experiment to discover which work well for you.

WRITING TO ASSESS AND STRENGTHEN COMPREHENSION

Writing is an excellent means of assessing your comprehension. Let us suppose you are reading a difficult assignment in your political science text. You realize you are not understanding much of it, so you need to try a new approach. One effective technique is to test yourself as you read. After each paragraph, write the main point of the paragraph in your own words. Your writing could take any number of different forms: a summary sentence, an outline, or a list. If you cannot do this, then you know you have not fully understood the paragraph and you need to reread it.

Try the same kind of self-test when you finish a section. Finally, when you have completed the assignment, write a review of key points. Any time you cannot state or recall key points, you need to do more work.

Not only is writing a good way to test whether you are understanding what you read, but it also will improve your comprehension of difficult or complicated material. When you are reading a complex argument for a logic course, you can improve your understanding by writing a list of the argument's main points. Writing each point forces you to think about each one, so connections and relationships become more apparent. Writing also forces you to spend enough time with the material to understand it fully.

Similarly, when you are solving math problems, writing will increase your understanding of the process. Listing the steps used to solve the problem makes the process "real" and more manageable. Writing makes problem solving practical rather than theoretical. There are many other situations in which writing strengthens comprehension. You can use writing to summarize case studies, explain how a process works, or describe similarities and differences among readings.

EXERCISE 11–1

Suppose you have been assigned three chapters to read in your psychology textbook. The next exam in psychology will emphasize these three chapters. Because of time limitations, your instructor will not discuss the chapters in class. Form groups of three or four students, and discuss the following issues.

1. How you would learn the chapters' content
2. What writing strategies you would use
3. How you would know when you were adequately prepared for the exam

HIGHLIGHTING AND ANNOTATING TEXTBOOKS

Highlighting and annotating are excellent means of improving your comprehension and recall of textbook assignments. Highlighting forces you to decide what is important and to sort the key information from less important material. Sorting ideas this way improves both comprehension and recall. To decide what to highlight, you must think about and evaluate the relative importance of each idea. Highlighting has the following added benefits.

- Highlighting keeps you physically active as you read.
- The physical activity focuses your attention and improves your concentration.
- Highlighting helps you discover how ideas are related.
- Highlighting is a good test of whether you understand what you are reading. If you have difficulty deciding what to highlight, it indicates that you are not comprehending the material.

How to Highlight

To highlight textbook material most effectively, apply these guidelines.

1. *Analyze the assignment.* Preview the assignment, and define what type of learning is required. This will help you determine how much and what type of information you need to highlight.

2. *Assess your familiarity with the subject.* Depending on your background knowledge, you may need to highlight only a little or a great deal. Do not waste time highlighting what you already know. In chemistry, for example, if you already have learned the definition of a mole, then do not highlight it.

3. *Read first, then highlight.* Finish a paragraph or self-contained section before you highlight. As you read, look for signals to academic thought patterns. Each idea may seem important as you first encounter it, but you must see how it fits in with the others before you can judge its relative importance.

4. *Use the boldface headings.* Headings are labels that indicate the overall topic of a section. These headings serve as indicators of what is important to highlight. For example, under the heading "Objectives of Economic Growth," you should be certain to highlight each objective.

5. *Highlight main ideas and only key supporting details.* Try to keep academic thought patterns in mind.

6. *Avoid highlighting complete sentences.* Highlight only enough so that your highlighting makes sense when you reread it. In the following selection, note that only key words and phrases are highlighted. Now read only the highlighted words. Can you grasp the key idea of each paragraph?

BIOMES

By using imagination, we can divide the earth's land into several kinds of regions called biomes, areas of the earth that support specific assemblages of plants. As would be expected, certain kinds of animals occupy each type of biome, since different species of animals are dependent on different sorts of plant communities for food, shelter, building materials, and hiding places. . . .

Tropical rain forests are found mainly in the Amazon and Congo Basins and in Southeast Asia. The temperature in this biome doesn't vary much throughout the year. Instead, the seasons are marked by variation in the amount of rainfall throughout the year. In some areas, there may be pronounced rainy seasons. These forests support many species of plants. Trees grow throughout the year and reach tremendous heights, with their branches forming a massive canopy overhead. The forest floor, which can be quite open and easy to travel over, may be dark and steamy. Forests literally swarm with insects and birds. Animals may breed throughout the year as a result of the continual availability of food. Competition is generally considered to be very keen in such areas because of the abundance of species.

—Wallace, *Biology: The World of Life,* pp. 708, 710

7. *Move quickly through the document as you highlight.* If you have understood a paragraph or section, then your highlighting should be fast and efficient.

8. *Develop a consistent system of highlighting.* Decide, for example, how you will mark main ideas, how you will distinguish main ideas from details, and how you will highlight new terminology. Some students use a system of symbols such as brackets, asterisks, and circles to distinguish various types of information; others use different colors of highlighters to make distinctions. The specific coding system you devise is unimportant; what is important is that you devise some consistent approach to highlighting. At first, you will need to experiment, testing various systems. However, once you have settled on an effective system, use it regularly.

9. *Use the 15–25 percent rule of thumb.* Although the amount you will highlight will vary from course to course, try to highlight no more than 15 to 25 percent of any given page. If you exceed this figure, it often means that you are not sorting ideas as efficiently as possible. Other times, it may mean that you should choose a different strategy for reviewing the material. Remember, the more you highlight, the smaller your time-saving dividends will be as you review. The first paragraph of the following excerpt provides an example of effective highlighting.

> ### Biomes (cont'd)
>
> Temperate deciduous forests once covered most of the eastern United States and all of Central Europe. The dominant trees in these forests are hardwoods. The areas characterized by such plants are subject to harsh winters, times when the trees shed their leaves, and warm summers that mark periods of rapid growth and rejuvenation. Before the new leaves begin to shade the forest floor in the spring, a variety of herbaceous (nonwoody) flowering plants may appear. These wildflowers are usually perennials, plants that live and produce flowers year after year. In the early spring, they don't have time to manufacture the food needed to grow and bloom suddenly. Instead, they draw on food produced and stored in underground parts during the previous year. Rainfall may average 75 to 130 centimeters or more each year in these forests and is rather evenly distributed throughout the year.
>
> People who live in temperate deciduous biomes often consider the seasonal changes as both moving and fascinating. They describe a certain joy that swells within them each spring and a secret pensiveness that overcomes them in the fall as the days darken and the forests become more silent. (Perhaps we are exceeding technical descriptions here, but these are my favorite places.)
>
> **Taiga** (pronounced "tie-gah") is quite unmistakable; there is nothing else like it. It is confined almost exclusively to the Northern Hemisphere and is identified by the great coniferous forests of pine, spruce, fir, and hemlock that extend across North America, Europe, and Asia. Some of these trees are the largest living things on earth.
>
> Taiga is marked by long, cold, wet winters and short summer growing seasons. The forest is interrupted here and there by extensive bogs, or muskegs, which are the remains of large ponds. The forest floor is usually covered by a carpet of needles. In the dim light at ground level, there may be mosses, ferns, and a few flowering

plants. One may move silently on the muffling needles through the Canadian taiga observing a host of mammals, including porcupines, moose, bear, rodents, hares, and wolverines.

Tundra is the northernmost land biome. It is covered throughout most of the year by ice and snow. This biome is most prevalent in the far north (arctic tundra), but it may also appear at high elevations in other parts of the world (alpine tundra). For example, in the United States, it may be seen in the high Rocky Mountains. Tundra appears in places where summer usually lasts two to four months, just long enough to thaw a few feet of the soil above the permafrost, or permanently frozen soil. Thaw brings soggy ground, and ponds and bogs appear in the depressions. The plant life consists mostly of lichens, herbs, mosses, and low-lying shrubs and grasses, as well as a few kinds of trees, such as dwarf willows and birches. Such plants obviously must be hardy, but their hardiness disguises their fragility. Once disturbed, these areas take very long periods to restore themselves.

—Wallace, *Biology: The World of Life,* pp. 712–13

EXERCISE 11–2 | *Finish highlighting the preceding passage.*

Evaluating Your Highlighting

As with any learning strategy, you must ask the question "Is it working?" Your final answer, of course, will come when you take your first major examination. If you were able to review the material within a reasonable time and you earn an acceptable grade, you will know your system was effective.

There are two common mistakes you can make when you are highlighting.

Highlighting too much. Using the tired, worn-out "rather safe than sorry" rule, you may tend to highlight almost every idea on the page. Highlighting nearly everything is about as effective as highlighting nothing because no sorting occurs: key ideas are not distinguished from other, less important, ones. Highlighting too much can become a way of escaping or postponing the real issue: deciding what to learn.

Highlighting too little. If you find you are highlighting less than 10 percent per page, this often is a signal that you are having difficulty understanding the material. If you cannot explain the content of a given section in your own words, then you have not understood it. If, however, you understand what you read but are highlighting very little, then you may need to redefine your purpose for reading.

Evaluate your own highlighting by

- Selecting a sample page, highlighting it, and rereading only your highlighting. Then ask yourself the following questions: "Does my highlighting convey the key ideas of the passage?" "Can I follow the author's train of thought and his or her progression of ideas by reading only my highlighting?" "Is the highlighting appropriate for my purposes?"

- Compare your highlighting with that of another student. Although there will be individual differences, both sets of highlighting should emphasize the same key ideas.

EXERCISE 11–3 | *Evaluate your highlighting in Exercise 11–2 by using one of the preceding suggestions.*

Marginal Annotation

In many situations, highlighting alone is not a sufficient means of identifying what to learn. It does not separate the main ideas from the examples, and each of these from new terminology. Nor does it give you any opportunity to comment on or react to the material. Therefore, it is often necessary to make marginal annotations as well as to highlight.

Annotating is an active reading process. It forces you to monitor your comprehension as well as react to ideas. Table 11–1 suggests various types of annotation used in marking a political science textbook chapter.

Annotation as a means of analysis and evaluation is discussed on page 103 in Chapter 4. Review this section now for additional suggestions on how to annotate effectively.

EXERCISE 11–4 | *Add annotations to the excerpt that you highlighted in Exercise 11–2 and compare them with those of another student.*

EXERCISE 11–5 | *Select a two- to three-page excerpt from one of your textbooks. Read, highlight, and annotate the selection. Do you feel the combination of processes is more effective than highlighting alone? Why or why not?*

EXERCISE 11–6 | *Working with another student in the class, choose one of the end-of-chapter readings in this text. Assume it is a reading assignment for one of your courses. Each of you should read, highlight, and annotate the selection. Then discuss similarities and differences in your work and evaluate each other's annotations.*

EXERCISE 11–7 | *Choose a two- or three-page section from one of your textbooks and highlight it, using the guidelines suggested in this chapter. Then evaluate the effectiveness of your highlighting in preparation for an objective exam on the material.*

TABLE 11–1   MARGINAL ANNOTATION

Type of Annotation	Example
Circling unknown words	. . . redressing the apparent (asymmetry) of their relationship
Marking definitions	_def_ ⎰ To say that the balance of power favors one party over another is to introduce a disequilibrium.
Marking examples	ex ⎰ . . . concessions may include negative sanctions, trade agreements . . .
Numbering lists of ideas, causes, reasons, or events	components of power include ① ② ③ self-image, population, natural resources, and geography ④
Placing asterisks next to important passages	* ⎰ Power comes from three primary sources . .
Putting question marks next to confusing passages	? → war prevention occurs through institutionalization of mediation . . .
Making notes to yourself	Check def in soc text · power is the ability of an actor on the international stage to . . .
Marking possible test items	⊤ There are several key features in the relationship . . .
Drawing arrows to show relationships	. . . natural resources . . . , . . . control of industrial manufacture capacity
Writing comments, noting disagreements and similarities	Can terrorism be prevented through similar balance? · war prevention through balance of power is . . .
Marking summary statements	sum ⎰ the greater the degree of conflict, the more intricate will be . . .

NOTE TAKING TO ORGANIZE IDEAS

Note taking is a writing strategy that can assist you in organizing information and pulling ideas together. It is also an effective way to pull together information from two or more sources—your textbook and class lectures, for example. Finally, note taking is a way to assess your comprehension and strengthen your recall. Use the following tips to take good notes.

1. *Read an entire section and then jot down notes.* Do not try to write notes while you are reading the material for the first time.

2. *As you read, be alert for academic thought patterns.* These patterns will help you organize your notes.

3. *Record all of the most important ideas in the briefest possible form.*

4. *Think of your notes as a list of the main ideas and supporting details of a selection.* Organize them to show how the ideas are related or to reflect the organization of the material.

5. *Use words and short phrases to summarize ideas.* Do not write in complete sentences.

6. *Write in your own words;* do not copy sentences or parts of sentences from the selection.

7. *Be highly selective.* Unless you are sure that a fact or idea is important to remember, do not include it. If you are not selective, you will find that your notes are nearly as long as the selection itself and you will save little time when you review the material.

8. *Use an outline system of indentation to separate main ideas and details.* As a general rule, the greater the importance of an idea, the closer it is placed to the left margin. Ideas of lesser importance are indented and appear closer to the center of the page. Your notes might follow a format such as this:

    TOPIC
        Main Idea
            Supporting detail
                fact
                fact
            Supporting detail
        Main Idea
            Supporting detail
            Supporting detail
                fact
                fact

As a further illustration of the techniques of note taking, study the notes shown in Figure 11–1. They are based on a portion of the excerpt on biomes that appears earlier in this chapter.

EXERCISE 11–8

Write a brief set of notes for the reading selection "Body Adornment: The Use of Cosmetics" at the end of this chapter. Working with a classmate, compare, discuss, and revise your notes.

Figure 11–1   Sample Notes

Biomes
- Regions of earth's land
- Each has own plants and animals

Tropical Rain Forests
- Amazon & Congo Basins and SouthEast Asia
- Seasons vary according to rainfall amount
- Trees grow throughout year
    - branches form canopy, forest floor dark, steamy
- Animals breed throughout year
    - keen competition

EXERCISE 11–9   *Select a three- to four-page section from one of your textbooks. Write a brief set of notes, including the key ideas.*

MAPPING TO SHOW RELATIONSHIPS

Mapping is a way of drawing a diagram to describe how a topic and its related ideas are connected. It organizes and consolidates information, often emphasizing a particular thought pattern. Mapping is a visual means of learning by writing.

This section discusses four types of maps: conceptual maps, process diagrams, part and function diagrams, and time lines. Each uses one of the thought patterns discussed in Chapter 7.

Conceptual Maps

A conceptual map is a form of outline that presents ideas spatially rather than in list form. It is a "picture" of how ideas are related. Use the following steps to construct a conceptual map.

1. Identify the topic and write it in the center of the page.

2. Identify ideas, aspects, parts, and definitions that are related to the topic. Draw each one on a line radiating from the topic.

3. As you discover details that further explain an idea already recorded, draw new lines branching from the idea that the details explain.

Figure 11–2 Sample Conceptual Map of Chapter 8

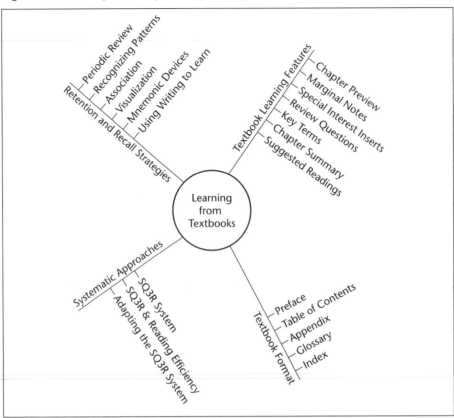

A map of Chapter 8 is shown in Figure 11–2. Take a moment now to refer to Chapter 8 before studying the map.

Process Diagrams

In the technologies and the natural sciences, as well as in many other courses, *processes* are an important part of the course content. A diagram that visually describes the steps, variables, or parts of a process will simplify learning. For example, the diagram in Figure 11–3 visually describes the steps in the search process for using library sources.

EXERCISE 11–10 | *Draw a conceptual map of Chapter 3 of this book.*

EXERCISE 11–11 | *Draw a conceptual map of the reading titled "Body Adornment: The Use of Cosmetics" at the end of this chapter.*

Figure 11–3 Sample Process Diagram

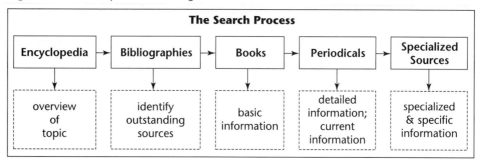

The following paragraph describes the sequential effects of taking the psychedelic drug LSD. Read the paragraph and then draw a process diagram that describes this response sequence. Compare your diagram with those of several other students.

Psychedelics are . . . a group of drugs that produce hallucinations and various other phenomena that very closely mimic certain mental disorders. These drugs include lysergic acid diethylamide (LSD), mescaline, peyote, psilocybin, and various commercial preparations such as Sernyl and Ditran.

Of these, LSD is probably the best known, although its use has apparently diminished since its heyday in the late 1960s. LSD is synthesized from lysergic acid produced by a fungus (ergot) that is parasitic on cereal grains such as rye. It usually produces responses in a particular sequence. The initial reactions may include weakness, dizziness and nausea. These symptoms are followed by a distortion of time and space. The senses may become intensified and strangely intertwined—that is, sounds can be "seen" and colors "heard." Finally, there may be changes in mood, a feeling of separation of the self from the framework of time and space, and changes in the perception of the self. The sensations experienced under the influence of psychedelics are unlike anything encountered within the normal range of experiences. The descriptions of users therefore can only be puzzling to nonusers. Some users experience bad trips or "bummers," which have been known to produce long-term effects. Bad trips can be terrifying experiences and can occur in experienced users for no apparent reason.

—Wallace, *Biology: The World of Life*, pp. 632–33

Part and Function Diagrams: Classification

In courses that deal with the use and description or classification of physical objects, labeled drawings are an important learning tool. In a human anatomy and physiology course, for example, the easiest way to learn the parts and functions of the brain is to draw it. To study, sketch the brain and test your recall of each part and its function. A sample part and function diagram of the brain appears at the end of Chapter 7 on page 217.

The following paragraph describes the outer layers of the earth. Read the paragraph, and then draw a diagram that will help you to visualize how the earth is structured.

OUTER LAYERS OF THE EARTH

The Earth's crust and the uppermost part of the mantle are known as the *lithosphere.* This is a fairly rigid zone that extends about 100 km below the Earth's surface. The crust extends some 60 km or so under continents, but only about 10 km below the ocean floor. The continental crust has a lower density than the oceanic crust. It is primarily a light granitic rock rich in the silicates of aluminum, iron, and magnesium. In a simplified view, the continental crust can be thought of as layered: On top of a layer of igneous rock (molten rock that has hardened, such as granite) lies a thin layer of sedimentary rocks (rocks formed by sediment and fragments that water deposited, such as limestone and sandstone); there is also a soil layer deposited during past ages in the parts of continents that have had no recent volcanic activity or mountain building.

Sandwiched between the lithosphere and the lower mantle is the partially molten material known as the *asthenosphere,* about 150 km thick. It consists primarily of iron and magnesium silicates that readily deform and flow under pressure.

—Berman and Evans, *Exploring the Cosmos,* p. 145

Time Lines

When you are studying a topic in which the sequence or order of events is a central focus, a time line is a helpful way to organize the information. Time lines are especially useful in history courses. To map a sequence of events, draw a single line and mark it off in year intervals, just as a ruler is marked off in inches. Then write each event next to the corresponding year. For example, the time line in Figure 11–4 displays major events during the presidency of Franklin D. Roosevelt. The time line shows the sequence of events and helps you to visualize them more clearly.

The following passage reviews the chronology of events in public school desegregation. Read the selection, and then draw a time line that will help you to visualize these historical events.

DESEGREGATING THE SCHOOLS

The nation's schools soon became the primary target of civil-rights advocates. The NAACP concentrated first on universities, successfully waging an intensive legal battle to win admission for qualified blacks to graduate and professional schools. Led by Thurgood Marshall, NAACP lawyers then took on the broader issue of segregation in the country's public schools. Challenging the 1896 Supreme Court decision *(Plessy v. Ferguson)* which upheld the constitutionality of separate but equal public facilities, Marshall argued that even substantially equal but separate schools

Figure 11–4   Sample Time Line

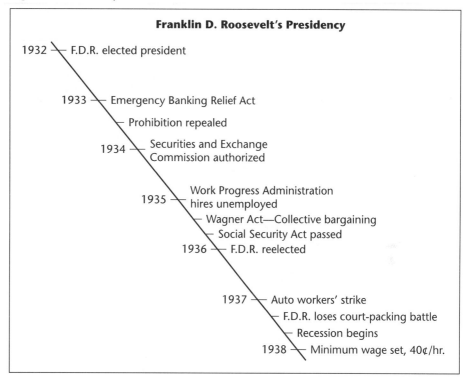

Franklin D. Roosevelt's Presidency

1932 — F.D.R. elected president

1933 — Emergency Banking Relief Act

— Prohibition repealed

1934 — Securities and Exchange
Commission authorized

1935 — Work Progress Administration
hires unemployed

— Wagner Act—Collective bargaining

— Social Security Act passed

1936 — F.D.R. reelected

1937 — Auto workers' strike

— F.D.R. loses court-packing battle

— Recession begins

1938 — Minimum wage set, 40¢/hr.

did profound psychological damage to black children and thus violated the Fourteenth Amendment.

A unanimous Supreme Court agreed in its 1954 decision in the case of *Brown v. Board of Education of Topeka.* Chief Justice Earl Warren, recently appointed by President Eisenhower, wrote the landmark opinion which flatly declared that "separate educational facilities are inherently unequal." To divide grade-school children "solely because of their race," Warren argued, "generates a feeling of inferiority as to their status in the community that may affect their hearts and minds in a way unlikely ever to be undone." Despite this sweeping language, Warren realized that it would be difficult to change historic patterns of segregation quickly. Accordingly, in 1955 the Court ruled that implementation should proceed "with all deliberate speed" and left the details to the lower federal courts.

The process of desegregating the schools proved to be agonizingly slow. Officials in the border states quickly complied with the Court's ruling, but states deeper in the South responded with a policy of massive resistance. Local White Citizen's Councils organized to fight for retention of racial separation; 101 congressmen and senators signed a Southern Manifesto in 1956 which denounced the *Brown* decision as "a clear abuse of judicial power." School boards, encouraged by this show of defiance, found a variety of ways to evade the Court's ruling. The most successful was the passage of pupil-placement laws . . . .

Southern leaders mistook Ike's silence for tacit support of segregation. In 1957, Governor Orville Faubus of Arkansas called out the national guard to prevent the integration of Little Rock's Central High School on grounds of a threat to public order . . . .

Despite the snail's pace of school desegregation, the *Brown* decision led to other advances. In 1957, the Eisenhower administration proposed the first general civil-rights legislation since Reconstruction. Strong southern resistance and compromise by both the administration and Senate Democratic leader Lyndon B. Johnson of Texas weakened the bill considerably. The final act, however, did create a permanent Commission for Civil Rights, one of Truman's original goals. It also provided for federal efforts aimed at "securing and protecting the right to vote." A second civil-rights act in 1960 slightly strengthened the voting-rights section.

—Divine et al., *America Past and Present,* pp. 890–91

SUMMARIZING TO CONDENSE IDEAS

Like note taking, summarizing is an excellent way to learn from your reading and to increase recall. A summary is a brief statement that reviews the key points of what you have read. It condenses an author's ideas or arguments into sentences written in your own words. A summary contains only the gist of the text, with limited explanation, background information, or supporting detail. Writing a summary is a step beyond recording the author's ideas; a summary must pull together the writer's ideas by condensing and grouping them. Writing a summary is a useful strategy when an overview of the material is needed, as in the following situations:

- Answering an essay question
- Reviewing a film or videotape
- Writing a term paper
- Recording results of a laboratory experiment or demonstration
- Summarizing the plot of a short story
- Quickly reviewing large amounts of information

Before writing a summary, be sure that you understand the material and that you have identified the writer's major points. Then use the following suggestions.

1. *As a first step, highlight or write brief notes for the material.*

2. *Write one sentence that states the writer's overall concern or most important idea.* To do this, ask yourself what one topic the material is about. Then ask what point the writer is trying to make about that topic. This sentence will be the topic sentence of your summary.

3. *Be sure to paraphrase, using your own words rather than those of the author.*

4. *Next, review the major supporting information that the author gives to explain the major idea.*

Figure 11–5   Sample Summary

> The earth is divided into regions called biomes. Each biome has its own species of plants and animals. Tropical rain forests have consistent temperatures but seasonal variation in rainfall. Trees grow throughout the year and animals breed year round. Both plants and animals are abundant in forests. Temperate deciduous forests have seasonal change in temperature; rainfall is evenly distributed. Tiaga, an area of coniferous pine forests, has long wet winters and short summers. Tundra refers to land covered by ice and snow most of the year. Plant life is limited to hardy lichens, herbs, mosses, low-lying shrubs, and dwarf trees.

5. *The amount of detail you include, if any, depends on your purpose for writing the summary.* For example, if you are writing a summary of a television documentary for a research paper, it might be more detailed than if you were writing it to jog your memory for a class discussion.

6. *Normally, present ideas in the summary in the same order in which they appear in the original material.*

7. *If the writer presents a clear opinion or expresses an attitude toward the subject matter, include it in your summary.*

8. *If the summary is for your own use only and is not to be submitted as an assignment, do not worry about sentence structure.* Some students prefer to write summaries using words and phrases rather than complete sentences.

A sample summary of the article on biomes that appears earlier in this chapter is shown in Figure 11–5.

EXERCISE 11–15

Write a summary of one of the end-of-chapter readings that you have already read. Working with a classmate, compare, discuss, and revise your summaries.

EXERCISE 11–16

Select a five- to six-page section from one of your textbooks. Write a brief summary of the section, using the guidelines suggested above.

BRAINSTORMING TO DISCOVER IDEAS

Brainstorming is a writing and thinking exercise that is particularly effective for generating ideas. It works like this: Suppose you are trying to think of a topic for a three-minute informative speech for your speech class. Begin by making a list of any topics that come into your mind. Write continuously. Do not be concerned about whether you are writing in complete sentences or whether the topics are practical or connected to one another. Write continuously for a set period—two or three minutes. When you have finished, reread what you have written. You will be surprised at the number of different topics you have discovered. Highlight those topics that are worth further exploration.

Brainstorming is also a way to get interested in a topic before beginning to read about it. Suppose you must read several lengthy research articles on the psychological effects of color. Before you start, brainstorm. List every possible effect of color and ways to measure its effects. Then read to confirm what you knew and to find out what you did not know.

EXERCISE 11–17   *Assume you will be reading several journal articles on drug testing in schools for a sociology class. Brainstorm for three minutes to discover what you already know about the issue.*

EXERCISE 11–18   *For each of the following statements, suggest one or more writing strategies that would enhance learning.*

1. Some math students are having difficulty because they confuse several similar types of problems and choose incorrect solutions.

   _____

2. A political science class does not have a standard textbook. Instead, the instructor assigns weekly library readings on which she bases class discussions and lectures.

   _____

3. An anthropology student is preparing for an essay exam. She plans to predict possible questions and answer them.

   _____

4. A student in a computer literacy course must learn procedures for merging files using word processing software.

   _____

5. For an English literature class, a student must write a paper comparing two poems by the same poet.

   _____

SUMMARY

Writing is a process that can strengthen your comprehension and facilitate learning. You can monitor your comprehension by self-testing using writing. Writing can strengthen your understanding of difficult or complex material by forcing you to analyze it step by step.

This chapter discusses five writing strategies.

- Highlighting and annotating are useful in textbook reading because they enable you to distinguish what is important to learn and remember.
- Note taking is a writing strategy for organizing information and pulling ideas together.
- Mapping—drawing a diagram that describes how a topic and its related ideas are connected—is an effective way to organize and consolidate information. The four types of maps are
  - conceptual maps
  - process diagrams
  - diagrams of part functions
  - time lines
- Summaries condense ideas and provide a review of key points.
- Brainstorming enables you to discover and clarify ideas, as well as to generate interest in your reading assignments.

INTEGRATING
IDEAS

◆

PAIRED
READINGS

Cultural Anthropology

PREREADING QUESTIONS

1. How could you define the term *cosmetics?*
2. Does the manner in which cosmetics are used vary from society to society?

Body Adornment:
The Use of Cosmetics

David Hicks and Margaret A. Gwynne

1   One way in which people adorn their bodies is by temporarily decorating their skin with cosmetics, the general term for preparations designed to improve the appearance of the body, or part of it, by directly but temporarily applying them to the skin. In Western society, cosmetics take the form of various mass-produced, petroleum-based, colored creams, oils, or powders. These are usually applied to the face, and are much more frequently used by females than by males. In other societies, the term *cosmetics* may refer to body as well as face paints, usually made by combining animal or vegetable oils with colored powders made from naturally occurring minerals.

2   The extent to which cosmetics are used in human societies, from the remote jungles of South America to

Cosmetics are universally used to beautify people, protect them from harm, express their social status, or identify them as members of particular groups. In Liberia, a Bassa girl being initiated into the Sande, an all-female secret society, is covered with a chalky white clay.

the high-fashion capitals of western Europe, suggests that the notion of adorning or enhancing the surface of the body, like the idea of covering it with clothing, comes close to being a human universal. There are differences of placement, emphasis, and extent among various traditions of cosmetic use, but the reasons for wearing cosmetics are similar.

3   In every society with a cosmetic tradition, including Western society, one reason bodies are decorated is to enhance them—to make them appear more perfectly in accord with society's ideals of beauty (although what is considered attractive varies widely from society to society). But in some societies, the use of cosmetics quite consciously provides other benefits as well. Cosmetics may protect people from harm, express their social status, or identify them as members of particular classes or families. Benefits of this kind are probably part of the reason behind Western cosmetic use also, although Western cosmetics users may not be aware of it.

4   If Westerners differ little from members of other societies in their primary motivations for applying cosmetics, they do differ from some in the relatively modest extent to which they decorate themselves. Cosmetic use in some societies is so extensive it would make the heavy-handed application of cosmetics to a female American screen star by a Hollywood makeup artist seem moderate.

5   A well-turned-out Nuba male from Kordofan Province in the Sudan of northern Africa is literally painted from head to foot. Among the Nuba, body painting begins in infancy, when a baby's scalp is decorated with either red or yellow paint, depending on its family membership (Faris 1972:30). Thereafter, body painting is used to suggest one's social and physical status as well as to beautify, and it becomes more and more complex with advancing age. A young Nuba boy, for example, wears simple, inconspicuous, red and greyish white decorations on his scalp, gradually earning the right to use increasingly elaborate, colorful, and extensive designs as he matures. Each change of age and status means a new kind of decoration for the boy, as with advancing years he earns the right to use more products in a wider range of colors and designs. (Westerners, too, sometimes use cosmetics as an age marker, as when an American girl is forbidden by her parents to wear lipstick until she has reached a certain age.)

6   The scalp, face, chest, back, arms, and legs of a young adult Nuba male may literally be covered with colorful designs (Faris 1972:18–19, 62), both purely decorative (straight and curved lines, dots, triangles, crosshatching) and representational (animals, airplanes, lightning, stars—even English words, which may or may not be intelligible to the Nuba). Often these designs are asymmetrically placed on the face or body and are strikingly modern looking. They may take up to an hour to apply and may be redone daily.

7   Decorating the body as well as the face with cosmetics is by no means limited to rural or small-scale societies. Some modern, urban girls and women in North Africa, the Middle East, and South Asia decorate their skin with henna, an orange-red dye made from leaves. Urban Moroccan women, for example, may be decorated on suitable occasions with fine lines and dots forming intricate designs. These are typically applied to the hands and feet, which then look as if they are clad in

lace gloves or stockings. Henna is applied at a "henna party," to which the girl or woman to be decorated invites her friends, a professional henna artist, and sometimes professional musicians or other entertainers. During the long and careful process of decorating, the guests eat, sing songs, tell jokes, and dance around the woman being decorated (Messina 1988).

8   Moroccan women who use henna say they apply it for a variety of reasons. A girl or woman may be decorated in preparation for a religious festival or her wedding, to cheer her up in late pregnancy, to soften her skin, to prevent spirits called *jinni* from causing illness or misfortune, or to calm her nerves. Whatever the reason, applying henna is cause for celebration; a henna party provides a "lively departure" from formal Islamic expectations of proper female behavior (Messina 1988:46). People from different regions admire different designs, and styles of decoration change constantly, but the designs themselves have no explicit meanings.

—Hicks and Gwynne, Cultural Anthropology, pp. 378–80

VOCABULARY REVIEW

1. For each of the words listed below, use context; prefixes, roots, and suffixes; and/or a dictionary to write a brief definition or synonym of the word as it is used in the reading.

    a. status (para. 3) _____

    b. inconspicuous (para. 5) _____

    c. elaborate (para. 5) _____

    d. representational (para. 6) _____

    e. asymmetrically (para. 6) _____

    f. explicit (para. 8) _____

2. Highlight new specialized terms introduced in the reading.

COMPREHENSION QUESTIONS

1. What main point about the use of cosmetics does this reading make?
2. How does the use of cosmetics differ between Western and other societies?
3. For what single purpose do all societies use cosmetics?
4. Explain how cosmetics are used by males in the Nuba society.
5. How do Moroccan women use henna?

THINKING CRITICALLY

1. What is the author's purpose for writing?
2. What generalizations do the authors make about the use of cosmetics? What types of evidence do the authors give to support their generalizations?

3. Discuss the use of cosmetics in Western society. For what purposes are they used? How does their use vary from subgroup to subgroup?

LEARNING/STUDY STRATEGIES

1. Draw a map that shows the key ideas of this reading.
2. Assume you have to write a short paper for a sociology class explaining why Western women use cosmetics. Review the reading, and make annotations that would help you develop ideas for your paper.

INTEGRATING
IDEAS

◆

PAIRED
READINGS

Cultural Anthropology

PREREADING QUESTIONS

1. In what ways do people decorate their bodies?
2. Do you think most people are comfortable with their bodies? Why?

The Decorated Body

France Borel

1   Human nakedness, according to social custom, is unacceptable, unbearable, and dangerous. From the moment of birth, society takes charge, managing, dressing, forming, and deforming the child—sometimes even with a certain degree of violence. Aside from the most elementary caretaking concerns—the very diversity of which shows how subjective the motivation is—an unfathomably deep and universal tendency pushes families, clans, and tribes to rapidly modify a person's physical appearance.

2   One's genuine physical makeup, one's given anatomy, is always felt to be unacceptable. Flesh, in its raw state, seems both intolerable and threatening. In its naked state, body and skin have no possible existence. The organism is acceptable only when it is transformed, covered with signs. The body only speaks if it is dressed in artifice.

3   For millennia, in the four quarters of the globe, mothers have molded the shape of their newborn babies' skulls to give them silhouettes conforming to prevalent criteria of beauty. In the nineteenth century, western children were tightly swaddled to keep their limbs straight. In the so-called primitive world, children were scarred or tattooed at a very early age in rituals which were repeated at all the most important steps of their lives. At a very young age, children were fitted with belts, necklaces, or bracelets; their lips, ears, or noses were pierced or stretched.

4   Some cultures have designed sophisticated appliances to alter physical structure and appearance. American Indian cradleboards crushed the skull to flatten it; the Mangbetus of Africa wrapped knotted rope made of bark around the child's head to elongate it into a sugarloaf shape, which was considered to be aesthetically pleasing. The feet of very young Chinese girls were bound and spliced, intentionally and irreversibly deforming them, because this was seen to guarantee the girls' eventual amorous and matrimonial success.[1]

5   Claude Levi-Strauss said about the Caduveo of Brazil: "In order to be a man, one had to be painted; whoever remained in a natural state was no different from the beasts."[2] In Polynesia, unless a girl was tattooed, she would not find a husband. An unornamented hand could not cook, nor dip into the communal food bowl. Pink lips were despicable and ugly. Anyone who refused the test of the tattoo was seen to be marginal and suspect.

6   Among the Tivs of Nigeria, women called attention to their legs by means of elaborate scarification and the use of pearl leg bands; the best decorated calves were known for miles around. Tribal incisions behind the ears of Chad men rendered the skin "as smooth and stretched as that of a drum." The women would laugh at any man lacking these incisions, and they would never accept him as a husband. Men would subject themselves willingly to this custom, hoping for scars deep enough to leave marks on their skulls after death.

7   At the beginning of the eighteenth century, Father Laurent de Lucques noted that any young girl of the Congo who was not able to bear the pain of scarification and who cried so loudly that the operation had to be stopped was considered "good for nothing."[3] That is why, before marriage, men would check to see if the pattern traced on the belly of their intended bride was beautiful and well-detailed.

8   The fact that such motivations and pretexts depend on aesthetic, erotic, hygienic, or even medical considerations has no influence on the result, which is always in the direction of transforming the appearance of the body. Such a transformation is wished for, whether or not it is effective.

9   The body is a supple, malleable, and transformable prime material, a kind of modelling clay, easily molded by social will and wish. Human skin is an ideal subject for inscription, a surface for all sorts of marks which make it possible to differentiate the human from the animal. The physical body offers itself willingly for tattooing or scarring so that, visibly and recognizably, it becomes a social entity.

10   The absolutely naked body is considered as brutish, reduced to the level of nature where no distinction is made between man and beast. The decorated body, on the other hand, dressed (if even only in a belt), tattooed, or mutilated, publicly exhibits humanity and membership in an established group. As Theophile Gautier said, "The ideal disturbs even the roughest nature, and the taste for ornamentation distinguishes the intelligent being from the beast more exactly than anything else. Indeed, dogs have never dreamed of putting on earrings."

11   So, it is by their categorical refusal of nakedness that human beings are distinguished from nature. The "mark makes unremarkable"—it creates an interval between what is biologically and brutally given in the animal realm and what is won in the cultural realm. The body is tamed continuously; social custom demands, at any price—including pain, constraint, or discomfort—that wildness be abandoned. Each civilization chooses—through a network of elective relationships which are difficult to determine—which areas of the body deserve transformation. These areas are as difficult to define and as shifting as those of eroticism or modesty. An individual alone eludes bodily modifications; they are the expression of a homogeneous collectivity which, at a chosen moment, comes to a tacit agreement to attack one or another part of the anatomy.

12   Whatever the choices, options, or differences may be, that which remains constant is the transformation of appearance. In spite of our contemporary western belief that the body is perfect as it is, we are constantly changing it: clothing it in musculature, suntan, or makeup; dying its head hair or pulling out its bodily hair. The seemingly most innocent gestures for taking care of the body very often hide a persistent and disguised tendency to make it adhere to the strictest of norms,

reclothing it in a veil of civilization. The total nudity offered at birth does not exist in any region of the world. Man puts his stamp on man. The body is not a product of nature, but of culture.

—Borel, "The Decorated Body," *Parabola,* Vol. 19, No. 3 (Fall 1994), p. 74

VOCABULARY REVIEW

1. For each of the words listed below, use context; prefixes, roots, and suffixes; and/or a dictionary to write a brief definition or synonym of the word as it is used in the reading.

   a. diversity (para. 1) _____

   b. subjective (para. 1) _____

   c. prevalent (para. 3) _____

   d. swaddled (para. 3) _____

   e. aesthetically (para. 4) _____

   f. spliced (para. 4) _____

   g. marginal (para. 5) _____

   h. scarification (para. 6) _____

   i. pretexts (para. 8) _____

   j. erotic (para. 8) _____

   k. inscription (para. 9) _____

   l. interval (para. 11) _____

   m. tacit (para. 11) _____

2. Highlight new specialized terms introduced in the reading.

COMPREHENSION QUESTIONS

1. What is the author's view of human nakedness?
2. How did the Mangbetus of Africa change the heads of children?
3. What was done to Chinese girls to alter their appearance? Why was this done?
4. Why did the men of the Congo check the stomachs of their brides before marrying them?
5. Describe how the Tiv women of Nigeria treated their legs.

THINKING CRITICALLY

1. What is the author's purpose in writing this article?
2. What can you conclude about human beauty from this reading?

3. In Polynesia, a girl without a tattoo would not be considered for marriage. Why do you think that was?
4. How do young men and women in the American culture decorate their bodies today?
5. The author states that humans decorate their bodies to designate their membership in an established group. In what other ways do humans signal group membership?

LEARNING/STUDY STRATEGY

Create a chart that lists the cultures referred to in this reading and describes the type of body decoration each used.

THINKING ABOUT THE PAIRED READINGS

INTEGRATING IDEAS

1. In what ways do the authors agree on the purposes for body decoration, and in what ways do they differ?
2. How do the two readings differ in content?
3. What do you think would be the best way to learn the information in these readings in light of what you have learned in this chapter?
4. If you were writing a ten-page research paper on the purposes and types of body decoration, what further information would you need?
5. What aspects of both readings apply to people in the U.S. today?
6. Of the two readings, which do you think was more difficult to read and remember? Why?

GENERATING NEW IDEAS

1. Take ten minutes to brainstorm ideas about body adornment in order to narrow a topic for a two-page paper.
2. Suppose you have a friend or relative who lives in a foreign country and is unfamiliar with western forms of body decoration. Your friend is planning to visit the U.S. soon. Write a letter to that person describing what unusual decorations he or she might expect to see.

Multimedia Activities

1. **PBS Timelines:**

   http://www.pbs.org/deepspace/timeline/index.html

   http://www.pbs.org/kera/usmexicanwar/timeline/index.html

   http://www.pbs.org/wgbh/amex/telephone/timeline/

   http://www.pbs.org/wnet/pharaohs/timeline1.html

   http://www.pbs.org/wgbh/amex/eleanor/timeline/index.html

   Many of the programs on PBS have accompanying Web sites with time lines. Visit the Internet pages above and evaluate their design and content. How well do they clarify the sequence of events and their importance? Write down your thoughts about the concept of time. Explain how you organize the passage of time in your own mind.

2. **Visual Organizers**

   http://www.bucks.edu/~specpop/visual-org.htm

   Explanations and examples of various ways to graphically represent information are presented here at this site created by Bucks County Community College. Create several of your own visual organizers centered around your life. Try topics such as your schedule, family history, future plans, friends, or ideas for a novel/movie/art project.

Take a Road Trip to
Florida (Spring Break)!

If your instructor has asked you to use the Reading Road Trip CD-ROM or Website, be sure to visit the Outlining, Summarizing, Mapping, and Paraphrasing module for multimedia tutorials, exercises, and tests.

CHAPTER 12

READING RESEARCH, REFERENCE, AND COLLATERAL ASSIGNMENTS

LEARNING OBJECTIVES

✦ To learn a systematic approach for reading research materials
✦ To develop alternative reading strategies
✦ To learn note taking
✦ To develop skills for reading collateral reading assignments
✦ To learn to evaluate sources
✦ To learn to synthesize and compare sources

Your political science professor assigns a 20-page research paper. Your psychology professor assigns a text and 30 related readings—research articles from *Science Digest*. Your marketing professor requires that you read and abstract two articles per week on topics related to her weekly lectures. You probably have discovered that your reading assignments are not limited to textbooks; many of your professors require that you locate sources, read research articles, and report your findings. Some professors distribute reading lists and direct you to read or write a specified number of abstracts. Others place materials to be read on reserve in the library. Still others assign a research paper on a related topic of your choice. You are expected to locate numerous sources, synthesize them, and come up with your own ideas on the topic.

Many students make the mistake of reading research and supplementary material in the same way they read their textbook assignments. Consequently, they become frustrated with the assignments, claiming, "I'll never finish the research for this paper" or "These reading assignments are impossible!" This chapter describes new approaches to reading, evaluating, and synthesizing research, reference, and collateral reading assignments that are distinct from textbook reading techniques.

READING RESEARCH MATERIALS

Reading research and reference materials is very different from reading textbooks. When reading textbooks, your goal is usually a high level of retention and recall. In reading research papers, however, complete retention is not always necessary. You may be searching for evidence to support an argument, reading widely to gain overall familiarity with a subject, or locating a particular statistic. Also, whereas textbooks have a consistent format and organization, research and reference sources differ widely in these characteristics. Consequently, you must adapt your reading strategy to suit the nature of the material. The following sections present a systematic approach to reading research and reference material when you must prepare a written report or research paper.

Define and Focus Your Topic

The first critical step in doing research for a written assignment is to define and focus your topic. It is a waste of time to begin a full search for information and to read numerous sources until you know exactly what you are looking for. Suppose you begin with a topic, such as "Hypnotism." This subject is much too broad. You could not possibly cover everything about hypnotism in one paper in any meaningful way. It may take two or three attempts at narrowing to arrive at a topic you can reasonably handle. For example, "Hypnotism" could be narrowed to "Uses of Hypnotism," then to "Modern Uses of Hypnotism," and finally to "Modern Medical Uses of Hypnotism."

To help narrow your topic, especially if it is one with which you are not familiar, some preliminary research or reading may be helpful. Here are some suggestions.

1. *Consult with your reference librarian to find out whether computerized searches are available.* Many libraries have access to data banks that identify all possible sources on a given topic. (Some libraries charge a fee for this service.)

2. *Read an encyclopedia entry to get an overview of the subject.*

3. *Check the* Reader's Guide to Periodical Literature *for listings on your topic.* Look through the list of articles for ideas on how to narrow your topic.

4. *Check the card catalogue or online computer system to see how your topic is subdivided.*

5. *Consult your instructor if you're not sure whether your topic is sufficiently narrow.*

Once you have narrowed your topic, try to establish a focus or direction for your research. Your paper should focus on, explore, and answer a question; it should take a position. For example, your paper on "Modern Medical Uses of Hypnotism" might discuss the ways hypnotism is useful in modern medicine, or it might take the position that hypnotism is of limited use in modern medical practice, or even that hypnotism is dangerous and that its use should be restricted.

EXERCISE 12–1 | *Assume that one of your professors has assigned a research paper on one of the following subjects. Choose one subject, and narrow it to a topic that is manageable in a ten-page paper.*

1. Environmental problems
2. Pornography
3. Test-tube babies
4. Professional sports

Devise a Search Strategy

In researching a topic, some students begin by gathering all the sources on the topic and then working through them randomly. This approach is time consuming and often repetitious. Instead, devise and follow a search strategy—an orderly way of sifting through available sources on your topic. A search strategy enables you to select the most suitable materials and to approach the topic in a logical fashion. A search strategy proceeds from general to specific. You begin by reading general materials that provide an overview of your topic. You then move gradually to more detailed sources that address a particular aspect of your topic. Of course, your search strategy depends on your topic, your familiarity with it, and the requirements of your assignments, but a common search strategy is shown in Table 12–1.

As you proceed through the search, you will find additional references. Each source will list its own references; eventually, the sources will converge. That is, you will come on the same sources several times and will begin to recognize authorities in the field. For example, as you research quality control in business and industry, you keep coming across the name of W. Edwards Deming, so you realize you need to know more about him and his ideas. If you have difficulty locating bibliographies or working through the search, reference librarians are ready to offer valuable, time-saving assistance.

TABLE 12–1 A SEARCH STRATEGY	
Source	**Purpose**
1. Encyclopedia	Obtain an overview; learn the language of the subject; discover subdivisions.
2. Bibliographies and Indexes (list of sources on a topic)	Locate a list of sources on the subject.
3. Books	Obtain basic information on the topic (or aspects of the topic).
4. Periodicals	Investigate particular aspects of the topic; obtain current or recent information.
5. Special sources (documents, directories, review of the literature, pamphlet files, media resources)	Zero in on specialized information.

Preview Sources

As you proceed through your search, it is useful to preview sources before delving into them. Previewing is an excellent research strategy; it enables you to select the most useful sources and to select sources of appropriate difficulty and complexity.

Let us assume you have located 15 books for a term paper on the psychological effects of terrorism on its victims. Your next step is to preview those sources to determine which are useful to your paper. If your paper requires current information, check the copyright date and eliminate any sources that are outdated. Next, glance through the table of contents to get an overall idea of the material covered by each source. Check the index to determine how extensively the source treats your specific topic. Select only those sources that provide a comprehensive treatment of your topic. Once you have identified these sources, randomly select a sample page in each and skim it to get a "feel" for the source. Pay particular attention to the level of difficulty. Is the source too basic, containing little more information than is in your course textbook? Or is the source too complicated? Does it assume extensive background knowledge of the subject, such as an extensive knowledge of psychoanalysis, for example? Previewing will enable you to select sources that contain sufficient information and that are of an appropriate degree of difficulty.

Define Your Purpose

Be sure to have a specific purpose for reading each reference source. Your purpose determines *how* you will read the material, as well as what type of note taking, if any, is necessary. To define your purpose, determine what level of comprehension and retention is expected. Is complete recall necessary, or is familiarity with key concepts sufficient? Your choice will hinge in part on the type of follow-up activity, if any, that will be involved. Will you be expected to write a summary or abstract, discuss the material in class, or use the information to write a term paper? (Refer to "Documentation and Note Taking" later in this chapter for suggestions.)

Comprehension is not an either/or situation. Rather, comprehension is a continuum; many levels of understanding are possible. In this respect, you might think of comprehension as similar to temperature: There is a wide range of conditions between freezing and boiling. And just as snowball fights go with freezing temperatures and cool drinks in the shade go with high temperatures, so are various levels of comprehension appropriate for various materials and types of assignments. An extremely high level of comprehension is necessary if you are reading a critical interpretation of a poem for an English literature paper. Each detail is important. However, a lower level of comprehension is appropriate for reading excerpts from a biography assigned for an American history course. Here, you would not be expected to recall each descriptive detail or bit of conversation.

The reading strategy you select is also shaped by the tasks that will follow your reading. If, for example, you are reading an encyclopedia article to get an

TABLE 12–2	LEVELS OF COMPREHENSION	
Level of Comprehension	Percentage of Recall	When Used
Complete	100%	Reading critical analysis; reading directions or procedures
High	90–100%	Reading a primary reference source
Moderate	70–90%	Reading for an overview of a subject
Low	50–70%	Reading to obtain background information; reading only for key ideas
Selective	50% or below	Looking up a statistic in an almanac; checking a date in a biographical dictionary

overview of a subject so that you can narrow a topic for a term paper, then complete comprehension is not needed. You require only an understanding of the major aspects or divisions of the subject in order to begin topic selection. Therefore, moderate to low comprehension is appropriate. Suppose, however, you are required to write a critical evaluation of a magazine article arguing against capital punishment. A high or complete level of comprehension is required, because you need to follow the argument carefully, search for points of inconsistency, and so forth.

Comprehension can, somewhat arbitrarily, be divided into five levels: complete, high, moderate, low, and selective, as described in Table 12–2. Study Table 12–2 before continuing to read.

EXERCISE 12–2

Working with a classmate, select a level of comprehension that seems appropriate for each of the following research situations.

1. Reading a biographical entry on Ella Fitzgerald in *The Encyclopedia of Jazz* for a term paper on the history of jazz.
2. Locating names of leaders of Third World countries in the *International Yearbook* and *Statesman's Who's Who*.
3. Reading the directions for using a computerized card catalogue.
4. Reading a source to verify that you have not missed any key information in sources you have already used.
5. Reading a newspaper review of a performance of *Cats* in preparation for a drama class discussion on audience responsiveness.

ALTERNATIVE READING STRATEGIES

Now that you have learned to gauge the level of comprehension appropriate for various reading assignments, the next step is to learn alternative reading strategies to meet these varied comprehension demands.

Most students are accustomed to reading everything completely. They read each word successively, from beginning to end. Few students realize there are other options available. Two alternative reading strategies are presented here: skimming and scanning.

When and How to Skim

Most textbook assignments must be read completely; complete or high comprehension is required. However, for some reading assignments that demand lower levels of comprehension, you can afford to read some parts and skip others. This strategy is known as **skimming.** Skimming is a technique in which you selectively read and skip in order to find only the most important ideas. Here are a few situations in which skimming is appropriate.

- *Reading a section of a textbook chapter that reviews the metric system.* If you have already learned and used the metric system, you can afford to skip over much of the material.
- *Reading a section of a reference book that you are using to complete a research paper.* If you have already collected most of your basic information, you might skim through additional references, looking only for new information not discussed in sources you have used before.
- *Sampling a two-page, 30-item supplementary reading list for a sociology class.* Your instructor has encouraged you to review as many of the items as possible. You anticipate that the final exam will include one essay question that is related to these readings. Clearly, you cannot read every entry, but you can skim a reasonable number.
- *Reviewing a textbook chapter you have already read.* To review the chapter for a class discussion, you could skim it.

In skimming, your goal is to identify those parts of any reading material that contain the main ideas. The type of material you are reading will, in part, determine how you should adapt your reading techniques. Authors use different patterns of organization and various formats, and skimming is a highly flexible technique that can be adapted to these varying structures and formats. To acquaint you with the process of skimming, here is the procedure. Generally, read the following items.

1. *The title.* The title announces the subject of the material and provides clues about the author's approach or attitude toward it.

2. *The subtitle or introductory byline.* Some material includes, underneath the title, a statement that further explains the title or is written to catch the reader's interest.

3. *The introductory paragraph.* The first paragraph often provides important background information and introduces the subject. It also may provide a brief overview of the treatment of the subject.

4. *The headings.* A heading announces the topic that will be discussed in the paragraphs that follow it. When read successively, the headings form an outline or a list of topics covered in the material.

5. *The first sentence of each paragraph.* Most paragraphs are built around a topic sentence that states the main idea of the paragraph. The most common position for the main idea is in the first sentence of the paragraph. If you read a first sentence that clearly is not the topic sentence, then you might jump to the end of the paragraph and read the last sentence. Your goal as you skim each paragraph should be to get an overview of its structure and content. The first sentence, if it functions as a topic sentence, usually states the main idea and provides clues about how the rest of the paragraph is organized.

6. *The remainder of the paragraph.* Quickly glance through the remainder of the paragraph. Let your eyes quickly sweep through the paragraph. Try to pick out words that answer questions such as "who," "what," "when," "where," or "how much" about the main idea of the paragraph. Also, note any words that indicate a continuation or a change in thought pattern as you glance through the paragraph. Try to pick up names, numbers, dates, places, and capitalized or italicized words and phrases. Note any numbered sequences too. This quick glance will add to your overall impression of the paragraph and will confirm that you have identified the main idea of the paragraph.

7. *The title or legend of any maps, graphs, charts, or diagrams.* The title or legend will state what is depicted and suggest what important event, idea, or relationship is emphasized.

8. *The last paragraph.* The last paragraph often provides a conclusion or summary for the article. It might concisely state the main points of the article, or it might suggest new ways to consider the topic.

Now that you are familiar with the procedure for skimming, you are probably wondering how fast to skim, how much to skip, and what level of comprehension to expect. Generally, your reading rate should be about three or four times as fast as you normally read. You should skip more than you read. Although the amount to skip varies according to the type of material, a safe estimate is that you should skip about 70 to 80 percent of the material. Because you are skipping large portions of the material, your comprehension will be limited.

To give you a better idea of what the technique of skimming is like, the following article has been highlighted to indicate the portions of the article that you might read when skimming. Of course, this is not the only effective way to skim this article. Depending on your purpose for reading it, you could identify different parts of the article as important. You also might select different key words and phrases while glancing through each paragraph.

AN OVERVIEW OF INTERNET SPEECH AND PRIVACY: THE ISSUE AT A GLANCE

The development of a new medium always creates new anxieties. Gutenberg's press prompted two centuries of debate over whether the spread of books would corrupt society. Privacy and free speech are already among the nations most difficult social issues; and it would be startling if the Internet did not raise new concerns about both of them.

Even the Internet itself is only the beginning. The electronic age is creating an entirely new medium, one that combines the interactive Internet with older media like TV, radio, print, mail, and the telephone. Few rules exist about what can be said or done over this new medium—and no one is really in charge of setting them. The Internet has no headquarters and doesn't exist as an official entity. Rather, it is the sum of millions of networked computers and telephone lines, all using an electronic Web language that, like English or Spanish, has dictionaries and grammars, but no controlling authority.

The questions of how to balance personal privacy and public safety have become all the more urgent since the Sept. 11 terrorist attacks. The "war on terrorism" evolves daily, even as the technology continues to evolve. The public's opinions about this medium are in flux—and their views on free speech and privacy were far from settled to begin with.

A Planet of Publishers

Press critic A. J. Liebling once said that "freedom of the press is guaranteed only to those who own one." Thanks to the Internet, millions of individuals now have the power that formerly only belonged to the owners of printing presses and broadcast licenses—the power to spread their views, whether profound or profane, to a worldwide audience. That has prompted a remarkable burst of creativity, but it has also provided hate groups and pornographers with a low-cost way of spreading their messages to anyone, including children, with a personal computer.

So far, the U.S. government has supported two approaches to dealing with offensive content: regulation and filtering. Two major attempts at regulation have been struck down by the courts, either in whole or in part. The first, the Communications Decency Act of 1996, would have made publishing "indecent" or "patently offensive" material on the Internet a federal offense. The U.S. Supreme Court, in *ACLU v. Reno*, came down firmly on the side of granting the highest free-speech protection to the Internet and struck down the indecency portions of the law. A second law, the Children's Online Protection Act, tried to ban material "harmful to minors." The Supreme Court sent the law back to a lower court for further review in May 2002, effectively blocking enforcement for the time being.

The other tactic, filtering, rests on the premise that technology can solve the problem technology created. Filters block out Web sites with offensive content, usually based on keywords or lists complied by the filter developer. Filter supporters say the technology is ideal because it empowers parents and blocks out speech without silencing the speaker. Critics say filters are a crude tool at best because they depend on keywords that could crop up on perfectly legitimate sites devoted to breast cancer, AIDS prevention, or the novel *Moby Dick.* A third federal law would have required all public libraries to use filters, but a federal court threw out the law in 2002, saying filters would block porn and protected speech alike.

Your Personal Fish Bowl

The Internet itself may seem anonymous, but it is far from private. E-mail can be easily intercepted by anyone with enough technical skill, and Web sites can track substantial information about users, either by voluntary registration or involuntarily through the use of "cookies"—files quietly stored on a visitor's computer that will identify them to the Web site on their next visit.

One way of making Internet communications more secure is encryption, the technique for coding messages so they can only be read by someone who has the encryption "key." Encryption programs have been available for years, and businesses contend that strong encryption is critical to keeping online commerce secure. But even before Sept. 11, law enforcement officials were concerned that criminals and terrorists will use the programs to send messages they can't break. Under heavy pressure from the technology industry, the Clinton administration had relaxed laws that treat advanced encryption technology as a munition and prevent its export overseas. In the wake of Sept. 11, the debate over encryption has been reopened, and Congress has already made it easier for authorities to use electronic surveillance.

But the ability of Web sites and hackers to collect information pales next to the newfound power technology gives to governments and marketers. "Data warehouses" are able to mix information from different sources to create a single, detailed profile of an individual, including vital statistics, how much they earn, what they buy, the state of their health, their interests, what they read, and more. And all of that information is for sale—to direct marketers, current and potential employers, or just anybody willing to pay for it. Already, as part of the war on terrorism, the federal government and financial services companies are discussing how to use their databases to flag suspicious activity.

Current privacy laws are rarely enforced and would offer spotty protection even if they were—for example, video store rental records are private under federal law, but medical records are not. The Supreme Court has upheld a federal law barring states from selling information they collect, such as voter registrations and motor vehicle records, to direct marketers. But there are few restrictions on what private companies may do with the information they collect.

The Learning Curve

Not surprisingly, the public is still learning about the Internet, and it shows in the volatile polling results. But the public's views on free speech have always been contradictory. Americans say they firmly believe in the right to express unpopular views, but often oppose specific examples, like flag-burning. More than one in four say the Internet is under-regulated, but nearly the same number say users, rather than government or private industry, should control the medium. Majorities say they would support bans on publishing child pornography (which is already illegal) or terrorist material on the Net.

Strong majorities of Americans say privacy is an essential right, outweighing the right of others to access information. Most say they are concerned about the privacy of their personal financial or medical information, but very few say their own privacy has been violated. Surveys since Sept. 11 show the public believes some tradeoffs of privacy and civil liberties may be justified in order to fight the war on terrorism.

Three Perspectives

Our Framing the Issue section offers three public approaches to the issues of free speech and privacy:

- Safeguard the Individual's Rights of Privacy and Free Speech. Private life is being turned inside out for all to see in this electronic age. That chills free speech and undermines democracy. Americans must have their rights protected through laws that ensure the right to keep personal information private, to send encrypted communications, and provide the highest level of free-speech protection to the Internet.

- Empower Consumers, not Regulators, to Protect Their Rights. Technology raises new challenges, but promises Americans unprecedented control over their privacy and in avoiding offensive material on the Internet. There is no need to regulate Internet content when individuals can do it themselves using "filter programs" that block out offensive material. Consumers, however, should have more say in how personal information is collected and used.

- Protect Communities by Curbing Overly Permissive Rights. The individual's rights of free speech and privacy are permitting those at the fringe of society to pollute the mainstream—by exploiting laws that permit them to promote violent pornography in cyberspace and send anonymous messages police can't decipher. The Internet is a public communications medium and public standards should apply. Public information should remain accessible in cyberspace.

—*Public Agenda Online,* June 2002

| **EXERCISE 12–3** | *After you have skimmed "An Overview of Internet Speech and Privacy: The Issue at a Glance," page 350, answer the following questions.* |

1. What is the purpose of the article?
2. What are the two ways in which the government has approached the problem of inappropriate content on the Internet?
3. Name at least one way privacy is compromised by the Internet.
4. How can the privacy of Internet users be safeguarded in the future?

| **EXERCISE 12–4** | *Skim "Giving Viruses a Cold Reception," and answer the following questions.* |

1. What is the main point of the article?
2. How are cold viruses transmitted?
3. What should you do to prevent colds?
4. List several symptoms that suggest that an infection may be more serious than a cold.
5. List several things to do to relieve cold symptoms.

GIVING VIRUSES A COLD RECEPTION

The immune system learns to recognize specific disease agents through exposure to them. Antigen exposure can occur through vaccination or by natural means. We acquire immunity to chickenpox, measles, mumps, tetanus, cholera, smallpox, and many other life-threatening diseases. So, one might wonder, if the immune system can do such amazing things, why can't it defend us from the common cold?

We are susceptible to at least 200 different cold-causing viruses. The most common type, rhinoviruses (literally "nose viruses"), cause about 30 to 50 percent of all colds in adults. As soon as the immune system learns to recognize and defend us from one, another comes along, and then another. This antigenic diversity creates quite a challenge for the immune system, so much so that most people succumb to one to six colds per year.

Nonspecific Resistance

Cold symptoms are not produced directly by the cold virus, but by the body's nonspecific immune response as it fights the virus. When viruses invade the cells lining the nasal passages, your body responds with inflammation and the production of extra mucus. This causes nasal congestion, a "stuffy nose." As mucous membranes in the nose accelerate their secretion of antibody-containing mucus, you get a runny nose. Congestion in the middle ear or sinuses can cause dizziness or a headache.

The "swollen glands" sometimes felt during a cold are actually swollen lymph nodes. The nodes swell as immune cells, including macrophages, T-cells, and B-cells, work overtime to fight pathogens. A sore throat can result from "postnasal drip" as the sinuses drain mucus into the throat. Throat tissue can also become dry and irritated from breathing through your mouth or coughing.

Like the nasal passages, the trachea and bronchial tubes become inflamed and produce extra secretions if invaded by the cold virus. A wheezing sound indicates airway congestion as mucus accumulates and restricts the flow of air. A "productive" cough assists the respiratory passages in getting rid of the mucus and the virus. A "nonproductive" or dry cough is usually caused by throat irritation. Your body may produce a fever to create an inhospitable climate for the virus. Most cold viruses prefer temperatures of 86 to 96° F (30 to 35.5° C). Since fever is a helpful part of your nonspecific resistance, medication should only be used if the fever exceeds 101.5° F (38.6° C) or is needed to treat accompanying aches and pains.

Cold Prevention

Despite its name, a cold is not caused by cold weather, wet feet, or getting cold, at least according to laboratory studies. Colds do occur more frequently in the winter than in the summer, but no one knows why. The incidence of colds usually rises sharply in the early fall and spring. Some believe that when children go back to school and are exposed to each other's viruses, they bring them home to their families.

Research indicates that most of the time cold viruses are transmitted from the hands of an infected person to the hands of a susceptible person. The virus can survive on the skin for only a few hours and must reach the nose in order to invade the body. On the face near the nose is no good, since the skin provides an effective barrier. The mucous membranes of the mouth are also an inhospitable environment; kissing seldom spreads colds.

If all goes well for the virus, eventually the hand delivers the virus to its new home, the person's respiratory system, by touching the mucous membranes of the nose or the eyes (the virus can travel down the tear duct to the upper nose). One study found that 40 to 90 percent of people with colds had rhinoviruses on their hands. The viruses were also found on about 15 percent of nearby objects, such as door knobs, telephones, and coffee cups.

It is not known what makes some people more susceptible to colds. Small children are the most susceptible, because their immune systems are still immature and haven't learned to recognize as many pathogens. People who are around children a lot also get colds more frequently. Smokers are more likely to catch colds than nonsmokers, partly because smoking inhibits the airway cilia that help move mucus. Some studies have shown that stress can decrease the effectiveness of the immune system, and many people believe that stress and fatigue increase their susceptibility to colds.

Given what we know about the transmission of colds, the single best way to prevent colds is frequent handwashing, especially when you're around people who have colds. Avoid sharing telephones, glasses, towels, and other objects with a person who has a cold. And try not to touch your nose or eyes.

Getting enough rest, eating well, exercising moderately, and managing stress certainly won't hurt and may help keep your resistance up. If you're a smoker, cold prevention is yet another good reason to quit.

What about vitamin C? Studies have failed to show that vitamin C prevents colds, although some research has found that it may lessen the severity of cold symptoms. Vitamin C also increases the intactness of cell membranes, so it may make them harder for viruses to penetrate.

Cold Self-Care

Since a cure for colds continues to elude medical researchers, the best we can do is to treat the symptoms. It's been said that with aggressive medical treatment a cold will disappear in seven days, while if left alone a cold will last a week. Nevertheless, symptom treatment can at least make us feel better until the cold has run its course.

The first step in cold self-care is to decide whether your symptoms are those of a cold or something more serious requiring medical attention. People who have heart disease, emphysema, diabetes, or another health condition should get professional advice before initiating self-care, especially before taking over-the-counter medication. Pregnant and lactating women should also check with their doctors before taking any medication.

Symptoms that indicate your infection may be more than a cold include:

1. Oral temperature over 103° F (39.5° C).
2. Sore throat with temperature above 101° F (38.5° C) for over 24 hours.

3. Temperature over 100° F (37.5° C) for three days.

4. Severe pain in ears, head, chest, or stomach.

5. Symptoms that persist more than a week.

6. Enlarged lymph nodes.

7. In a child, difficulty breathing or greater than normal irritability or lethargy.

Once you decide you have a cold, there are several things you can do to help yourself feel better. They include the following.

1. Chicken soup, broth, or other hot drinks. Your mother was right: hot fluids help relieve congestion by increasing the flow of nasal secretions. They also soothe irritated throats.

2. Gargle with salt water (¼ teaspoon salt in 8 oz. water) to soothe a sore throat.

3. Use a vaporizer or humidifier to increase humidity, especially if the air is very dry. Humid air is gentler on nose and throat.

4. Breathing steam gives your nose a temporary fever, creating an inhospitable environment for the virus. It also helps to thin the mucus causing a stuffy nose, and thus temporarily relieves congestion. The steam may also feel soothing to irritated throats and nasal passages.

5. While rest may not hasten your recovery, it may help you feel better. It's good to stay out of circulation for the first few days of a cold to keep others from getting it.

6. Many over-the-counter cold medications are available. If you decide you need something, avoid combination drugs that contain several active ingredients to treat several symptoms. If, instead, you buy single drugs for the symptoms you wish to treat, you will avoid taking unnecessary drugs and decrease unpleasant side effects.

Should You Exercise When You Have a Cold?

Many people wonder whether they should continue their exercise programs when they have a cold. Some hope that the exertion will create a fever and "burn out the cold," while others believe that the added stress of exercise will only exhaust an already overwhelmed immune system. At this point, there is nothing but anecdotal evidence for these two beliefs. As long as symptoms are mild, exercising doesn't appear to either prolong the cold or hasten recovery.

It is important to recognize, however, that colds can sometimes lead to more serious complications, such as secondary bacterial infection in the middle ear, sinuses, or respiratory system. Medical authorities generally advise rest during the initial days of infection, just to be sure that what you are catching (or that what is catching you) is really just a cold. People who insist on exercising should start slowly. If they begin to feel better after five or ten minutes, then the exercise is probably not harmful.

—Tortora, *Introduction to the Human Body: The Essentials of Anatomy and Physiology*, pp. 407–08

EXERCISE 12–5 *Working with another student, select and skim one of the end-of-chapter readings in this text. Then question each other on the main points of the reading by using the comprehension questions as guidelines.*

EXERCISE 12–6 *Look ahead to the chapter you will study next in one of your textbooks. Skim one or two sections of this chapter and write a brief summary including the main point and most important information. Then check the accuracy of your summary by reading those sections more closely.*

When and How to Scan

Have you ever become frustrated when trying to locate a statistic in an almanac or find a reference to a particular research study in a lengthy research review? Have you ever had to read an article completely in order to find a particular fact? These frustrations probably occurred because you were not scanning in the most effective, systematic manner. *Scanning* is a technique for quickly looking through reading material to locate a particular piece of information—a fact, a date, a name, a statistic.

Every time you use a dictionary to find a particular word, you are scanning. When you locate a call number in a card catalogue or find a book on a library shelf, you are scanning. In each case, you are looking for a particular piece of information, and your only purpose in looking through the material is to locate that information. In fact, when you scan you are not at all interested in anything else on the page, and you have no reason to notice or remember any other information.

Many people do not scan as efficiently as possible because they randomly search through the material, hoping to stumble on the information they are seeking. Scanning in this way is time consuming, is frustrating, and often forces the reader to "give up" and read the entire selection. The key to effective scanning is to approach the material in a systematic manner, as outlined in the following steps.

Know Your Purpose Fix in your mind what you are looking for. Scanning is effective only if you have a very specific purpose. Before you begin to scan, try to form very specific questions that you need to answer. For example, instead of scanning for information on the topic of abortions in New York state, it would be more effective to develop questions such as:

> How many abortions were performed in 2002?
>
> What rules and limitations restrict abortions?
>
> Where are the majority of abortions performed?

The more specific your purposes and questions are, the more effectively you will be able to scan.

Check the Organization   Before you begin to scan, check to see how the article or material is organized.

For graphics (maps, tables, graphs, charts, and diagrams), this step is especially important. The title of the item you are scanning and other labels, keys, and legends are important. They state what the graphics are intended to describe and tell you how they are presented.

For prose selections, assessing the organization is similar to previewing. Your purpose should be to notice the overall structure of the article so that you will be able to predict where in the article you can expect to find the information you are looking for. Headings are especially important because they clearly show how a selection is divided into subtopics.

Anticipate Clue Words   The next step is to anticipate clues that may help you locate the answer. For example, if you were trying to locate the population of New York City in an article on the populations of cities, you might expect the answer to appear in digits, such as 4,304,710, or in an estimate form using words such as "four million." If you were looking for the name of the researcher in a journal article, you would expect to find the name capitalized. In looking for the definition of a particular term, you might look for italics and you might scan for the word itself or for words or phrases such as "means," "can be defined as," or "refers to." As accurately as possible, then, try to fix the image of your clue words or phrases in your mind before you begin to scan.

Identify Probable Answer Locations   Using what you have learned from checking the organization of the material, try to identify places where you are likely to find the information you are looking for. You might be able to identify a column or section that could contain the needed information, you might be able to eliminate certain sections, or you might be able to predict that the information will probably appear in a certain portion of the article.

Use a Systematic Pattern   Once you know what you are looking for and can anticipate the location and form of your answer, you are ready to scan. Scanning should be organized and systematic. Do not randomly skip around, searching for clues. Instead, rhythmically sweep your eyes through the material. The pattern or approach you use will depend on the material. For material printed in narrow six- or seven-word columns (newspaper articles, for example), you might move your eyes straight down the middle, catching the phrases on each half of the line. For wider lines of print, a zigzag or Z pattern might be more effective. Using this pattern, you move your eyes back and forth, catching several lines in each movement. Each of these patterns is shown in Figure 12–1 on the next page. When you do come to the information you are looking for, it may almost seem as though the clue words "pop out" at you.

Confirm Your Answer   Once you think you have located the answer you have been looking for, read the sentence or two that contain the answer to confirm that it is the information you need. Often, you can be misled by headings and

Figure 12–1 Scanning Patterns

Narrow Columns

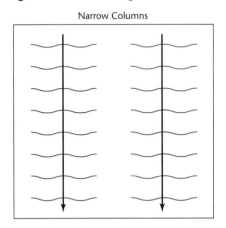

Wide Columns

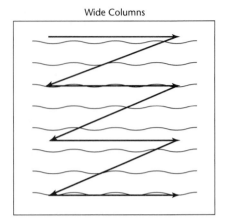

keywords that seem to indicate that you have found your answer when in fact you have located related information, opposite information, or information for another year, a different country, or a merely similar situation.

Now try out this procedure. Assume that you are writing a term paper on applications of genetic engineering and need to find out how it is regulated in agricultural production. You have located a reference book on animal science that contains the following section. Scan to find the answer to one of your research questions: What government agency determines the guidelines for genetically engineered foods coming from plants?

REGULATION OF GENETICALLY ENGINEERED PRODUCTS

Three federal agencies currently regulate genetically engineered products: the Environmental Protection Agency (EPA), the Food and Drug Administration (FDA), and the United States Department of Agriculture (USDA). In addition, most states monitor development and testing of genetically monitored products within their borders.

Animal and Plant Health Inspection Service (APHIS), a division of the United States Department of Agriculture, regulates genetically engineered products under several statutes. Genetically engineered crops are regulated under the Federal Plant Pest Act. This legislation enables APHIS to regulate interstate movement, importation into the United States, and field testing of altered crops.

The Food and Drug Administration has broad authority and primary responsibility for regulating the introduction of all new foods, including genetically engineered foods, under the Federal Food, Drug, and Cosmetic Act (FFDCA). Two different sets of provisions in the FFDCA pertain to genetically engineered foods. The first are the "adulteration" provisions, which give the FDA authority to remove unsafe foods from the market. The other pertinent section of the act requires premarket approval of food additives. In 1992, the FDA released guidelines for genetically engineered foods coming from plant sources. These guidelines can be found in the Federal Register, and vol. 57, pages 22984 and 22986–88. Because the FDA has authority over drug approval, it also has authority over drugs produced through biotechnological means. In this case, the fact that a drug is produced through biotechnology is not the issue. The FDA already had authority over drugs.

The Environmental Protection Agency oversees genetically engineered microbial pesticides and certain crops that are genetically engineered to produce their own pesticides under the Federal Insecticide, Fungicide, and Rodenticide Act (FIFRA). The FFDCA authorized the FDA to set tolerances and establish exemptions for pesticide residues on and in food crops. Nonpesticidal, nonfood microbial products are regulated under the Toxic Substances Control Act (TSCA). The regulation under which the TSCA Biotechnology Program functions is titled "Microbial Products of Biotechnology; Final Regulation Under the Toxic Substances Control Act," which can be found in the Federal Register, vol. 62, No. 70, pages 17909–58. This rule was developed under TSCA because intergeneric microorganisms are considered new chemicals under the act.

Animal vaccines are regulated under the Virus, Serum, and Toxin Act; and engineered poultry and livestock fall under various meat inspection statutes. Transgenic animals other than poultry and livestock are not regulated for environmental risks.

—Damron, *Introduction to Animal Science*, pp. 202–03

Scanning Lists and Tables

In scanning information in list form, the most important step is to become familiar with how the writer has arranged the information. Check the overall organization, and then see whether it is divided in any particular way. For instance, a TV program schedule is organized by day of the week, but it is also arranged by time. In scanning a table of metric equivalents, you would see that it is arranged alphabetically but that it is subdivided into measures of volume, length, and so on. Column titles, headings, and any other clues are important to show the organization of the material.

Many reference books that are arranged alphabetically have guide words at the top of each page to indicate the words or entries that are included on that page. For instance, in the upper-right or upper-left corner of a page of a dictionary, you might find the two words *cinder-circle*. These guide words indicate that the first entry on the page is *cinder* and that the last entry on the page is *circle*. Guide words are valuable shortcuts to help you quickly locate the appropriate page to scan. For lengthy alphabetical material that does not include guide words, you should check the first entry and the last entry on a page to determine whether that page contains the item you are looking for.

In scanning columnar material, often you will be able to scan for a specific word, phrase, name, date, or place name, and it may not be necessary to guess at the form of your answer. For example, in scanning an almanac to find the length of Lake Ontario, you are looking for one very specific statistic. Similarly, you can check *Taber's Cyclopedic Medical Dictionary* just for a description of brittle diabetes.

When scanning material that is arranged alphabetically, focus on the first letter of each line until you reach the letter that begins the word you are

360 CHAPTER 12

Figure 12–2 Environmental Resource Handbook

4409 Illinois Audubon Society
425 B N Gilbert Street
PO Box 2418
Danville, IL 61834
217-446-5085
Fax: 217-446-6375
http://www.illinoisaudubon.org

A membership organization dedicated to the preservation of Illinois Wildlife and the habitats which support them. Has sanctuaries and native education and land acquisition programs, and publishes quarterly magazines and newsletters.

Publication Date: 1916 28 Pages Quarterly
ISSN: 1061-9801
Marilyn F. Campbell, Executive Director

4410 Illinois Environmental Council – IEC Bulletin
197 West Cook
Suite 15
Springfield, IL 62704-2527
217-544-5954
Fax: 217-544-5958
E-mail: iec@ilenviro.org
http://www.ilenviro.org

The IEC is a coalition of over 70 environmental, conservation and health groups.

Bi-Monthly

4411 In Brief
223 South King
4th Floor
Honolulu, HI 96813
808-599-2436
Fax: 808-521-6841
E-mail: eajushi@earthjustice.org
http://www.earthjustice.org

Newsletter of Earthjustice, a non-profit public interest law firm dedicated to protecting the magnificent places, natural resources and wildlife of this earth and to defending the right of all people to a healthy environment. We bring about far-reaching change by enforcing and strengthening environmental laws on behalf of hundreds of organizations and communities.

Quarterly
David Henkin, Staff Attorney

4412 Iowa Cooperative Fish & Wildlife Research Unit, Annual Report
Iowa State University Science Hall
II
Ames, IA 50011
515-294-3056
Fax: 515-294-5468

Publication Date: 1932 Annual

4413 Iowa Native Plant Society Newsletter
Botany Department
Iowa State University
Ames, IA 50011-1020
515-294-9499
Fax: 515-294-1337
E-mail: dlewis@iastate.edu

An organization of amateur and professional botanists and native plant enthusiasts who are interested in the scientific, educational and cultural aspects, as well as the preservation and conservation of the native plants of Iowa. The Society was organized in 1995 to create a forum where plant enthusiasts, gardeners and professional botanists could exchange ideas and coordinate activities such as field trips, workshops, and restoration of natural areas.

Publication Date: 1995   12 pages 3/4 times X year
Tom Rosburg, President
Deb Lewis, Contact Person

4414 Journal of Economic Entomology
Journal of Entomology
9301 Annapolis Road
Lanham, MD 20706-3115
301-731-4535
Fax: 301-731-4538
E-mail: esa@entsoc.org
http://www.entsoc.org

Contributions report on the economic significance of insects and are divided into categories by subject matter: apiculture and social insects; arthropods in relation to plant disease; biological and microbial disease; ecology and behavior; ecotoxicology; extension; field and forage crops; forest entomology; horticultural entomology; household and structural entomology; insecticide resistance and resistance management; medical entomology; plant resistance; sampling and biostatistics.

6 Times a Year

4415 Land and Water Magazine
Land and Water
PO Box 1197
918 B 1st Avenue South
Fort Dodge, IA 50501-1197
515-576-3191
Fax: 515-576-2606
E-mail: landandwater@dodgenet.com
http://www.landandwater.com

Edited for contractors, engineers, architects, government officials and those working in the field of natural resource management and restoration from idea stage through project completion and maintenance.

44 pages
Amy Dencklau, Publisher
Teresa Doyle, Editor

4416 Leaves Newsletter
Michigan Forest Association
1558 Barrington
Ann Arbor, MI 48103-5603
734-665-8279
Fax: 734-913-9167
E-mail: mfa@i-star.com
http://www.mfa.nu

An organization composed mainly of private owners of small woodlands. Our purpose is to promote good forest management and stewardship of all forest lands.

Monthly
McClain B. Smith Jr., Executive Director

4417 MACC Newsletter
Alba Press
10 Juniper Road
Belmont, MA 02478
617-489-3930
Fax: 617-489-3935
E-mail: staff@maccweb.org
http://www.maccweb.org

Published six times a year, each issue features carefully chosen technical and interpretive articles, updates on government actions and policies.

Source: *Environmental Resource Handbook*, p. 372

looking for. Then focus on the first two letters until you reach the two-letter combination you seek. Successively widen your focus until you are looking for whole words.

EXERCISE 12–7

Scan Figure 12–2 from the Environmental Resource Handbook *to locate the answers to the following questions.*

1. Who sponsors *Leaves Newsletter*?
2. How often is *Journal of Economic Entomology* published?
3. What is the Web address for *In Brief*?
4. When was the Iowa Native Plant Society organized?
5. How many groups are in the IEC (Illinois Environmental Council)?

EXERCISE 12–8

Scan Figure 12–3 (p. 362) from A to Zoo: Subject Access to Children's Picture Books *to locate the answers to the following questions.*

1. How many books feature the holiday Sukkot?
2. Who wrote the book, *Hooray! It's Passover!*?
3. Which book was written by Valerie Tripp?
4. How many books on this page were written by Eve Bunting?
5. For which holiday is the least number of books listed?

Scanning Prose Materials

Prose materials are more difficult to scan than columnar material. Their organization is less apparent, and the information is not so concisely or obviously stated. And unless the headings are numerous and concise, you may have to scan large amounts of material with fewer locational clues. To scan prose materials, you must rely heavily on identifying clue words and predicting the form of your answer.

It is useful to think of scanning prose materials as a floating process in which your eyes drift quickly through a passage searching for clue words and phrases. Your eyes should move across sentences and entire paragraphs, noticing only clue words that indicate you may be close to locating the answer. As you become skilled at scanning prose material, your clue words will "pop out" at you as though they were in boldface print.

EXERCISE 12–9

Scan the article titled "Giving Viruses a Cold Reception" on pp. 353–55 and answer the following questions.

1. How many cold-related viruses are humans susceptible to?

   _____

2. What is the difference between a "productive" and a "nonproductive" cough?

   _____

Figure 12–3   A to Zoo: Subject Access to Children's Picture Books

Holidays – Mother's Day

Anderson, Laurie Halse. *No time for Mother's Day*
Balian, Lorna. *Mother's Mother's Day*
Bunting, Eve (Anne Evelyn). *The Mother's Day mice*
Howe, James. *The case of the missing mother*
Kroll, Steven. *Happy Mother's Day*
Livingston, Myra Cohn. *Poems for mothers*
Morgan, Allen. *Matthew and the midnight money van*
Sharmat, Marjorie Weinman. *Hooray for Mother's Day!*
Tripp, Valerie. *Happy, happy Mother's Day*
Wynot, Jillian. *The Mother's Day sandwich*

Holidays – New Year's

Andersen, H. C. (Hans Christian). *The little match girl*, ill.
    by Rachel Isadora
    The little match girl, ill. by Blair Lent
    The little match girl, ill. by Jerry Pinkney
Chiomruom, Sothea. *Dara's Cambodian New Year*
Grifalconi, Ann. *The bravest flute*
Holabird, Katharine. *Angelina ice skates*
Janice. *Little Bear's New Year's party*
Kudler, David. *The Seven Gods of Luck*
Modell, Frank. *Goodbye old year, hello new year*
Ziefert, Harriet. *First Night*

Holidays – Passover

Adler, David A. *A picture book of Jewish holidays*
    A picture book of Passover
Auerbach, Julie Jaslow. *Everything's changing – It's pesach!*
Behrens, June. *Passover*
Feder, Harriet K. *Not yet, Elijah!*
Fishman, Cathy Goldberg. *On Passover*
Hawxhurst, Joan C. *Bubbe and Gram, my two grand-mothers*
Hirsh, Marilyn. *I love Passover*
    One little goal
Kimmelman, Leslie. *Hooray! it's Passover!*
Manushkin, Fran. *The matzah that Papa brought home*
    Miriam's cup
Newman, Lesléa. *Matzo ball moon*
Portnoy, Mindy Avra. *Matzah ball*
Rosen, Anne. *A family Passover*
Rothenberg, Joan. *Matzah ball soup*
Rouss, Sylvia A. *Sammy Spider's first Passover*
Schotter, Roni. *Passover magic*
Schwartz, Lynne Sharon. *The four questions*
Silverman, Erica. *Gittel's hands*
Simon, Norma. *The story of Passover*
Swartz, Leslie. *A first Passover*
Wikler, Madeline, *My first seder*
Wohl, Lauren L. *Matzoh mouse*
Zalben, Jane Breskin. *Happy Passover, Rosie*
Zusman, Evelyn. *The Passover parrot*

Holidays – Purim

Cohen, Barbara. *Here come the Purim players!*, ill. by
    Beverly Brodsky McDermott
    Here come the Purim players!, ill. by Shoshana Mekibel
Gerstein, Mordicai. *Queen Esther the morning star*
Nerlove, Miriam. *Purim*
Schotter, Roni. *Purim play*

Suhl, Yuri. *The Purim goat*
Topek, Susan Remick. *A costume for Noah*
Wikler, Madeline. *The Purim parade*

Holidays – Ramadan

Ghazi, Suhaib Hamid. *Ramadan*

Holidays – Rosh Hashanah

Fishman, Cathy Goldberg. *On Rosh Hashanah and
    Yom Kippur*
Gellman, Ellie. *It's Rosh Hashanah!*
Goldin, Barbara Diamond. *World's birthday*
Kahn, Katherine Janus. *The shofar calls to us*
Kimmelman, Leslie. *Sound the shofar!*

Holidays – St. Patrick's Day

Bunting, Eve (Anne Evelyn). *St. Patrick's Day in the
    morning*
Calhoun, Mary. *The hungry leprechaun*
Dillon, Jana. *Lucky O'Leprechaun*
Janice. *Little Bear marches in the St. Patrick's Day parade*
Kroll, Steven. *Mary McLean and the St. Patrick's Day
    parade*
O'Donnell, Elizabeth Lee. *Patrick's day*
Schertle, Alice. *Jeremy Bean's St. Patrick's Day*
Zimelman, Nathan. *To sing a song as big as Ireland*

Holidays – Sukkot

Groner, Judyth Saypol. *All about Sukkot*
Lepon, Shoshana. *Hillel builds a house*
Polacco, Patricia. *Tikvah means hope*
Zalben, Jane Breskin. *Leo and Blossom's Sukkah*

Holidays – Thanksgiving

Alcott, Louisa May. *An old-fashioned Thanksgiving*
Anderson, Laurie Halse. *Turkey pox*
Balian, Lorna. *Sometimes it's turkey*
Behrens, June. *The feast of Thanksgiving*
Berenstain, Stan. *The Berenstain bears and the prize
    pumpkin*
Borden, Louise. *Thanksgiving is . . .*
Brown, Marc Tolon. *Arthur's Thanksgiving*
Bunting, Eve (Anne Evelyn). *How many days to
    America?*
    A turkey for Thanksgiving
Carlson, Nancy L. *A visit to grandma's*
Child, Lydia Maria. *Over the river and through the wood*
Cowley, Joy. *Gracias, the Thanksgiving turkey*
Dalgliesh, Alice. *The Thanksgiving story*
De Paola, Tomie (Thomas Anthony). *My first
    Thanksgiving*
Devlin, Wende. *Cranberry Thanksgiving*
Dragonwagon, Crescent. *Alligator arrived with apples*
George, Jean Craighead. *The first Thanksgiving*
Gibbons, Gail. *Thanksgiving Day*
Hopkins, Lee Bennett. *Merrily comes our harvest in*
Ipcar, Dahlov. *Hard scrabble harvest*
Jackson, Alison. *I know an old lady who swallowed a pie*
Janice. *Little Bear's Thanksgiving*
Koller, Jackie French. *Nickommoh!*
Kraus, Robert. *How Spider saved Turkey*

Source: *A to Zoo: Subject Access to Children's Picture Books*, 6th ed., p. 382

3. Why are small children most susceptible to colds?

   _____

4. What effects might vitamin C have on cold viruses?

   _____

5. How does breathing steam relieve cold symptoms?

   _____

DOCUMENTATION AND NOTE TAKING

As you read reference sources for a research paper, documentation and note taking are important. You must record carefully the sources you use and take clear and concise notes to use when writing your paper.

Documentation Format and Systems

Documentation—recording the sources you use—is necessary for preparing the footnotes and bibliography of any paper you write. As you use sources, you will need to keep a record of the complete title, author, publisher, place, date, and pages referred to. Before you begin, select the format you will use for the paper's bibliography, and use this format to record sources as you use them. Several documentation styles are available; often a particular style is preferred in a specific academic discipline. The two most common styles are those of the MLA and the APA, which are explained in the following manuals. Instructors usually require one style or the other.

> Gibaldi, Joseph. *MLA Handbook for Writers of Research Papers,* 6th ed. New York: MLA, 2003.

> American Psychological Association. *Publication Manual of the American Psychological Association,* 4th ed. Washington, DC: APA, 1994.

Documentation rules are complex and may seem picky and annoying, especially if you have to learn different styles for different courses, but there is good reason for them. If your source is fully documented, your reader can follow up, explore further, or research a topic in more depth. Documentation also may be useful to you. As you complete your paper, for example, you may need to return to a source to get an important date you missed or to check a name spelled two different ways in your notes.

Many researchers list their sources on 3 x 5 inch index cards, which make it possible to alphabetize rapidly when preparing the bibliography. For each source, record the library call number in addition to bibliographic information. (This will save you time should you need to locate the source again.) A sample source card is shown in Figure 12–4 (p. 364).

Figure 12–4 Sample Source and Note-Taking Cards

Source Card

```
                                                    • T J
                                                       211
                                                    • C69
                                                       1995


        Critchlow, Arthur J.

        Introduction to Robotics

        New York : Macmillan, 1995,

        pp. 39-51
```

Note Card

```
    Critchlow, P. 42                    Payback on
                                        investment
    formula for      =    capital cost of system
    payback               yearly    _  operations
                          savings      cost

              (P  =   c   )
                     s-o

    Capital includes robot, auxiliary, safety
    equipment, installation, and training
    Operations include overhead and maintenance,
    wages and salaries of operators
```

Note-Taking Cards

For taking notes, 5 x 8 inch or 4 x 6 inch index cards are best. Use a separate card for each subtopic or aspect of your topic. In the upper-left corner, record the author's last name and the pages you used. In the upper-right corner, record the subtopic. Be sure to write on only one side of the card. A sample note-taking card is also shown in Figure 12–4. Here are a few suggestions for taking good research notes.

Record the information in your own words instead of copying the author's words. By recording the author's wording, you run the risk of using it in your paper, perhaps without realizing that you have done so. Whenever you use an author's words or ideas instead of your own, you are required to use quotation marks and/or give proper credit by indicating the author and source from which the material was taken. Failure to give credit is known as **plagiarism**. Plagiarism is a form of theft and therefore a serious error; many institutions penalize students who either knowingly or unknowingly plagiarize.

Try to summarize and condense information. You will find that it is impossible to record all the information that appears in your sources. If you have already made a note once, do not spend time writing it again. (You might, however, want to note the fact that there is common agreement in a number of sources about the information.) Occasionally, you may need to check back through your notes to see what you already have recorded.

Record useful quotes. If you find a statement that strongly supports your thesis, you may want to include it as a quotation in your paper. Copy it down exactly and place it in quotation marks in your notes, along with its page reference. Photocopy important articles so you can refer to them while you work.

READING COLLATERAL ASSIGNMENTS

In addition to the course textbook, many professors assign collateral readings. These assignments are drawn from a variety of sources: other textbooks, paperbacks, newspapers, periodicals, scholarly journals, and reference books. Often, your professor will place the required book or periodical on reserve in the library. This means the book is held at the reserve desk, where its use is restricted to a specified period of time. Collateral assignments may present

- new topics not covered in your text
- updated information
- alternative points of view
- applications or related issues
- realistic examples, case studies, or personal experiences

Reading collateral assignments requires different skills and strategies than reading textbooks. Unless the assignment is from another textbook, you may find that the material is not as well or as tightly organized as it would be in a textbook. It may also be less concise and factual.

Analyzing the Assignment

First, determine the purpose of the assignment: how is it related to the course content? Listen carefully as your professor announces the assignment; he or she often provides important clues. Next, determine what type and level of recall are necessary. If the purpose of an assignment is to present new and important topics not covered in your text, then a high level of recall is required. If, on the other hand, an assignment's purpose is to expose you to alternative points of view on a controversial issue, then key ideas are needed but highly factual recall is not.

Choosing Reading and Study Strategies

Depending on the purpose of the assignment and the necessary level and type of recall, your reading choices range from a careful, thorough reading to skimming to obtain an overview of the key ideas presented. Before you begin, you need to select a strategy to enable you to retain and recall the information. Table 12–3 lists examples of supplementary assignments and their purposes and suggests possible reading and retention strategies for each. The table shows how strategies vary widely to suit the material and the purpose for which it was assigned.

TABLE 12-3   STRATEGIES FOR COLLATERAL READINGS

Assignment	Purpose	Reading Strategies	Retention Strategies
Historical novel for American history course	To acquaint you with living conditions of the period being studied	Read rapidly, noting trends, patterns, characteristics; skip highly detailed descriptive portions.	Write a brief synopsis of the basic plot; make notes (including some examples) of lifestyles, living conditions (social, religious, political, as well as economic).
Essay on exchange in Moroccan bazaars (street markets) for economics course	To describe system of barter	Read for main points, noting process, procedures, and principles.	Underline key points.
Article titled "What Teens Know about Birth Control" assigned in a maternal care nursing course	To reveal attitudes toward, and lack of information about, birth control	Read to locate topics of information, misinformation, and lack of information; skip details and examples.	Prepare a three-column list: information, misinformation, and lack of information.

Working on Nonprint Collateral Assignments

Occasionally, a professor may ask you to view videotapes, films, lectures, or television documentaries. Approach these assignments as you would approach a reading assignment. It is particularly important to determine your purpose and to take adequate notes at the time because it is usually difficult, or impossible, to review the material later. Making notes on nonprint materials is, in some ways, similar to taking notes on class lectures. In the case of films, dramatic recreations, or performances, your notes should reflect your impressions as well as a brief review of the content.

EXERCISE 12–10 | *Summarize how you would approach each of the following collateral assignments. What would be your purpose? What reading and study strategies would you use?*

1. Reading a *Time* magazine article about a recent incident of terrorism for a discussion in your political science class.
2. Reading two articles that present opposing opinions and evidence about the rate of the spread of AIDS throughout the United States.
3. Reading a recent journal article on asbestos control to obtain current information for a term paper on the topic.
4. Reading a case study of an autistic child for a child psychology course.
5. Reading IBM's end-of-the-year statement for stockholders for a business class studying public relations strategies.

EVALUATING SOURCES

Through your research and supplementary reading, you will encounter a variety of sources ranging from newspaper editorials to professional journal research reports. Not all sources are equal in accuracy, scholarship, or completeness. In fact, some sources may be inaccurate, and some may be purposely misleading. Other sources that were once respected are now outdated and have been discredited by more recent research. Part of your task as a researcher is to evaluate available sources and select those that seem the most reliable and appropriate. Use the following suggestions in evaluating sources. Also refer to Chapter 10 for suggestions on evaluating Internet sources.

1. *Assess the authority of the author.* In standard reference books such as encyclopedias and biographical dictionaries, you can assume the publisher has chosen competent authors. However, when using individual source materials, it is important to find out whether the author is qualified to write on the subject. Does he or she have a degree or experience in the field? What is the author's present position or university affiliation? This information may appear in the preface or on the title page of a book. In journal articles, a brief paragraph at the end of the article or on a separate page in the

journal may summarize the author's credentials. If the author's credentials are not provided, then it may be necessary to consult reference sources to establish or verify the author's qualifications. Sources such as *Who's Who, Directory of American Scholars,* and numerous biographical dictionaries are available in the library reference section. By appraising the sources the author cites (footnotes and bibliography), you also can judge the competence of the author.

2. *Check the copyright date.* The date the source was published or revised is indicated on the back of the title page. Especially in rapidly changing fields such as computer science, the timeliness of your sources is important. Using outdated sources can make a research paper incomplete or incorrect. Consult at least several current sources, if possible, to discover recent findings and new interpretations. Suppose that in doing research on regulations for day care centers, you have located several articles. One was written in 1993, another in 1996, another in 2002. The 1993 and 1996 articles may be outdated because regulations change frequently.

3. *Evaluate the fulfillment of the work's purpose.* Does the work accomplish what it promises? Purposes are often stated or implied in the title, subtitle, preface, and introduction. Does the author recognize appropriate limitations, or does he or she claim the source is a complete study of a topic?

4. *Assess the intended audience.* For whom is the work intended? Some sources are written for children, others for young adults, and others for a general-interest audience. The work should suit the audience in format, style, complexity of ideas, and amount of detail. Some sources may be too technical and detailed for your purposes. For example, if a book on control of water pollution is written for engineers, then it may be too complicated.

5. *Verify one source against another.* If you find information that seems questionable, unbelievable, or disputable, verify it by locating the same information in several other reputable sources. Ask your reference librarian for assistance, if necessary. If you do verify the information in other sources, then you can be reasonably confident that the information is acceptable. You cannot, however, assume that it is correct—only that it is one standard or acceptable approach or interpretation. For instance, in researching global warming, you might encounter several theories of its cause and many projections of its long-range effects. Eventually, you will recognize the more standard theories and the more widely accepted projections.

6. *Look for a consensus of opinion.* As you read differing approaches to or interpretations of a topic, sometimes it is difficult to decide what source(s) to accept. When you encounter differing opinions or approaches, the first thing to do is locate additional sources; in other words, do more reading. Eventually, you will discover the consensus.

7. *Evaluate statistics carefully.* Many students regard statistical figures as correct and indisputable and assume that no interpretation or evaluation of statis-

tics is required. Actually, statistics must be carefully evaluated, along with the conclusions the authors draw from them. Suppose you read a statement that "at present, a recent survey indicated that 52 percent of single-parent household heads lack a high school diploma, compared to 22 percent in 1965." To evaluate this statistic, you might ask questions such as, "What year is the 'present'? How were these data obtained? How many single-parent households were surveyed? How were they surveyed? What was the survey response rate? How is a high school diploma defined? Does it include high school equivalency diplomas? How were the 1965 data obtained?" You can see that the answers to these questions can influence how the statistics should be interpreted. In general, ask questions about

- sample size (the size of the group studied)
- sample composition (who was included)
- method of obtaining the data
- definition of terms

Approach statistics as critically, then, as you would any other type of information.

8. *Consider whether the article is fact or opinion.* Question the author's purpose, the use of generalizations, any basic assumptions, and the type of evidence presented. For a review of these criteria, refer to the section in Chapter 4 titled "Distinguish Between Fact and Opinion."

EXERCISE 12–11

What questions would you ask when evaluating each of the following sources?

1. An article in *Newsweek* reporting a dramatic increase in domestic violence in the United States.

   _____

2. An article written by the president of Chrysler Corporation describing effective and ineffective business management strategies.

   _____

3. An essay in a right-to-life pamphlet reporting a high incidence of injury and maternal death resulting from abortion. Other articles, using other sources, report a much lower incidence.

   _____

4. An article, published in an advertising trade journal, titled "Teenage Drinking: Does Advertising Make a Difference?"

   _____

5. An article in *TV Guide* titled "Should TV Stop Projecting Election Winners?"

   _____

SYNTHESIZING AND COMPARING SOURCES

The first step in comparing several works or different sections within the same work is to read, annotate, and analyze each text. Once you have studied each carefully, you are ready to discover the similarities and differences among them. Compare the works on the basis of such factors as

- overall theme or position
- types and quality of supporting evidence
- degree of bias shown in each work
- authority of each author
- author's purpose
- points of agreement and disagreement
- how each work approached the subject
- effectiveness of each work in persuading or educating you
- types of arguments used
- style
- intended audience

Make notes as you study each work, both in the margins of the works themselves and on separate pieces of paper. Then study your annotations and notes, looking for similarities and differences. Try to put into your own words what you discover. When you write about the two works, rather than just thinking about them, it forces you to clarify your ideas.

Ask questions such as these.

- On what do the sources agree?
- On what do the sources disagree?
- How do they differ?
- Are the viewpoints toward the subject similar or different?
- Does each source provide supporting evidence for major points?

To initiate a discussion on the issue of computer privacy, a business professor distributed two excerpts from articles on the topic. In preparation for the discussion, the instructor asked the class to read both accounts and be prepared to discuss them in class. One student read and annotated each selection as shown below.

Account 1

The advent of e-commerce is, however inadvertently, endangering privacy. Companies have long boasted about the efficiency, convenience and personalized service that distinguish commerce online. But that promise hinges on the merchants' intimate knowledge of their customers' tastes and behavior. For starters, *types of information collected* they know who their customers are, where they live and their credit card numbers. And the more someone buys, the more the seller finds out about him: likes bourbon and trash novels; sends someone not his wife flowers every Wednesday.

Any Web site operator can reconstruct a visitor's every move on his site: what pages he viewed, what information he entered and the Internet service he uses.

does not tell us what to do about the problem

> Privacy advocates warn that most online companies won't fight subpoenas seeking access to those logs. Security guru Richard Smith, founder of Phar Lap Software, likens Web sites to VCRs "constantly recording when you come in, who you talked to and maybe what you talked about."
> —Sandberg, "Losing Your Good Name Online," *Newsweek,* September 20, 1999, p. 57

Account 2

exchange of personal information

marketing databases

organization

businesses and agencies that collect information

> We live in an information age, and data is one of the currencies of our time. Businesses and government agencies spend billions of dollars every year to collect and exchange information about you and me. More than 15,000 specialized marketing databases contain 2 billion consumer names, along with a surprising amount of personal information. The typical American consumer is on 25 marketing lists. Many of these lists are organized by characteristics like age, income, religion, political affiliation, and even sexual preference—and they're bought and sold every day.
>
> Marketing databases are only the tip of the iceberg. Credit and banking information, tax records, health data, insurance records, political contributions, voter registration, credit card purchases, warranty registrations, magazine and newsletter subscriptions, phone calls, passport registration, airline reservations, automobile registrations, arrests, Internet explorations—they're all recorded in computers, and we have little or no control over what happens to most of these records once they're collected.
> —Beekman, *Computer Confluence: Exploring Tomorrow's Technology,* p. 204

Then the student made notes and wrote the following paragraph.

Paragraph

Sandberg discusses the types of information that can be collected from e-commerce and focuses on personal data collected by online merchants and from Web sites. Beekman states that information that is collected becomes part of a database and explains that other businesses and agencies collect information, as well. Both emphasize that privacy may be endangered.

EXERCISE 12–12

Assume you are taking a business retailing course. Your instructor has asked you to read each of the following brief descriptions of Jeff Bezos, the founder of Amazon.com, an online bookstore. Using information from both articles, write a paragraph summarizing Bezos' personality and leadership style.

Statement 1

MEDIA PROFILES: JEFF BEZOS

Amazon.com's Jeff Bezos is often portrayed in press coverage as charismatic, ambitious and a shrewd businessman. He has also been characterized as a fun-loving guy with a great sense of humor. He has been heralded as an Internet success story, even in the wake of the dot-com bust. In interviews he is known to be light-hearted, laughing and joking with reporters. Bezos, 37, is also well known for participating in high-profile charitable work. Recently he played in a tennis tournament with Bill Gates, Andre Agassi and Pete Sampras to benefit breast care and cancer research, despite the fact that he reportedly didn't own a pair of tennis shoes a week before the tournament. Bezos combined his sense of humor with his charitable intentions again when he starred in a goofy Taco Bell commercial for "the hot new handheld," the Taco Bell chicken quesadilla. Bezos' proceeds went to the Special Olympics foundation, with a deal for Taco Bell to match this donation. On Sept. 11, Bezos had Amazon.com change gears, canceling the planned promotion of a major partnership with Target Stores. Amazon.com's homepage became a donation site for the Red Cross. At 5:15 p.m. (PDT) on Sept. 11, Amazon.com launched the donation box, raising more than $100,000 in the first four hours. Much has been made of his fall from the heights of being named Time's "Man of the Year" in 1999, yet he is still widely viewed as one of the few leaders left in the e-commerce arena. Although Bezos ranked fourth overall in the CEO MediaShare, he topped the list in Brand Power this year, signaling his strengthening ties to the company he built.

—"Media Profiles: Jeff Bezos," *Adweek Magazine's Technology Marketing* (December 2001), p. 22

Statement 2

IN E-BIZ, MOST ARE BEZOS WANNABES

Is he a humble technology visionary or the P. T. Barnum of e-business? Amazon.com founder and CEO Jeff Bezos is probably some of both. He pioneered personalization in business-to-consumer e-commerce as well as the growth-at-all-costs business strategy. Both have been widely copied. But the individual is not so easy to clone. Bezos is one of those rare individuals who has a grasp of technology, business, finance (some would debate that) and human nature and, above all, has the willingness to act on his vision and the ability to sell it.

New ideas come easily to him. Amazon's personalization technology is great but tends to put customers in a box of past purchases. What about the random walk through a bookstore that we all sometimes take to challenge ourselves with new subjects and ideas? He's thinking of that, too. Although not yet implemented, in his recent PC Expo keynote in New York he discussed a "serendipity knob" that, when pressed, would give you a list of books that would be different from—perhaps the opposite of—what would otherwise be predicted from your earlier book buys. One imagines a person who bought a biography of Vince Lombardi and an NFL pictorial volume being presented with tomes chronicling Italian baroque art and contemporary feminism. Why not?

So the serendipity knob is not far off, from a man who says we're still in "the Kitty Hawk era of personalization." However, Bezos does caution that although these things are not that difficult to accomplish on a small scale, when you want to do them for millions of customers—any of whom might be logging on at the same time—the task becomes much harder.

The other side of the Bezos coin is his ability to sell his vision to the investment community. This skill was tested recently when a bond analyst wrote an emperor's-new-clothes report on the company's bonds that sent its stock down 19 percent in one day. Bezos and company responded with vehemence, but an objective analysis still places the bonds in the junk category. The real question is whether Amazon will run out of cash before it is profitable, and, here, Bezos says not to worry.

Bezos may be replaced by a bean counter at some point, but it's hard to imagine any other entrepreneur who has accomplished so much, so fast in a completely new field. In five short years at the helm of Amazon, Bezos has earned his place in the pantheon of business greats.

—Gibson, "In E-biz, Most Are Bezos Wannabes," *e-Week* (July 10, 2000), p. 62

SUMMARY

This chapter discusses reading strategies for nontextbook materials and presents a systematic approach for reading research sources. The steps include

- defining and focusing your topic
- devising a search strategy
- previewing sources
- defining your purpose for reading

Two alternative reading strategies will help you get the most from research materials.

- Skimming is a rapid reading technique that enables you to quickly obtain main ideas only.
- Scanning is a process of searching for a specific piece of information.

As you read reference sources, a note card system can help you with documentation and note taking. Collateral reading assignments require that you analyze the assignment and select the appropriate reading and study strategies. Finally, evaluating sources is an important step in reading research. To compare and synthesize several works, focus on similarities and differences among them.

INTEGRATING
IDEAS

◆

PAIRED
READINGS

English

PREREADING QUESTIONS

1. What is Internet plagiarism?
2. How can teachers stop this type of cheating?

Lessons in the School of Cut and Paste

Katie Hafner

1   To a student at Spring Lake Park High School outside Minneapolis, it seemed like a formatting problem: the margins on the research paper he was trying to print out for an English class this spring were not aligning correctly. But when he complained to Jane Prestebak, a librarian whose duties include running the school's computer labs, she immediately suspected the actual cause. Ms. Prestebak took the first five words of text and put them in a search engine. Up came the Web site from which the student had taken the paper, in its entirety, margin formatting and all. When she confronted the student, he was taken aback to be caught so swiftly, by a 43-year-old school librarian of all people. "Maybe a teacher who wasn't as computer literate as I am wouldn't have known to be suspicious," Ms. Prestebak said. She alerted the student's teacher, who decided to turn the incident into a lesson in scholarly ethics. "The student needed a wake-up call," Ms. Prestebak recalled. "His teacher allowed him to rewrite it and hand it in again a week later. It gave us a chance to reteach him."

2   At a time when Internet literacy seems in inverse proportion to age, a new generation of students is faced with an old temptation made easier than ever: taking the work of others and passing it off as one's own. In this era of cut and paste, hundreds of sites offer essays and research papers on topics as abstruse and challenging as Shakespeare's "Troilus and Cressida" and Sartre's "Being and Nothingness," some at no charge. And e-mail has made it simpler for students to borrow from one another's work.

3   Indeed, a scandal last month at the University of Virginia, where 122 students are being investigated for possible plagiarism of term papers for an introductory physics course, not only revealed how precarious the notion of an honor system can be, but also painted in sharpest relief how easy cheating has become. Donald McCabe, a management professor at Rutgers University in Newark who conducts periodic surveys on cheating at college campuses, recently surveyed 4,500 high school students at 25 schools around the country. When it comes to plagiarizing from the Web, he found, high schools seem to present a far larger problem.

4   More than half of the high school students surveyed admitted either downloading a paper from a Web site or copying a few sentences from a Web site

without citation. On the college level, Dr. McCabe said, just 10 to 20 percent of those surveyed acknowledged such practices. Often, teachers are suspicious from the start. "If a student hasn't done a lick of work or produced anything during the stages of a research paper, then suddenly this beautifully typed-up paper materializes, that's a sign," said Cathy Aubrecht, an English teacher at Hononegah High School in Rockton, Ill. At other times, the problem presents itself in a more subtle fashion. "I have kids every year who have a hard time understanding that ideas can be plagiarized as well," she said. "If you get a good idea from someplace, or a concept is related to you via a book or Internet site, it needs to be recognized. But they assume that everything is public domain."

5   Dr. McCabe said he was deeply concerned about the cavalier attitude toward plagiarism among students coming up through high school and beginning to enter college. "Many students say, 'We're way ahead of our teachers when it comes to the Internet,'" Dr. McCabe said. "And they say, 'Everybody's doing it.'" In high school, moreover, the consequences are not so grave as they are in college. High school students caught cheating are usually given a stern lecture or, at worst, a failing grade. On rare occasions, seniors will not be allowed to graduate. College students caught plagiarizing, especially at institutions with strict honor codes, are often suspended and may even be expelled, Dr. McCabe said.

6   Dr. McCabe said he believed there was less cheating in college than in high school not only because of the consequences but also because students take college more seriously. At the same time, Dr. McCabe said there was a "steady erosion" of students' sense of right and wrong when it came to plagiarism. When he reads the comments accompanying his surveys, he said, he is struck by how readily students place the blame for their cheating on societal problems and pressures. "The college students say, 'When Clinton can do this,' or 'When Milken can do that,' who can blame them for what they do? It's very, very pervasive." This is a line of justification Dr. McCabe said he increasingly saw among high school students as well. "High school students tend to blame the competitiveness of the college admissions process," he said.

7   At the same time, the Web has made it much easier to catch plagiarists. A growing number of educators routinely use Web-based services for detecting unoriginal work. Turnitin.com, a popular service, offers a simple method that allows both teachers and students to submit papers to electronic scrutiny. The service compares the paper against millions of Web sites, a database of previous submissions and papers offered by the so-called term-paper mills. Turnitin.com then sends a report with the results to the teacher. High schools using this service pay around $1,000 a year for an unlimited number of submissions. Colleges pay roughly $2,000. Dr. John M. Barrie, a founder of Turnitin.com, estimated that of all the work submitted to the site, nearly one-third is copied in whole or in part from another source. "When it comes to cheating, at the top of the list is plagiarism, and at the top of that list are students cutting and pasting, mostly from the Internet," Dr. Barrie said. He said about 1,000 institutions subscribe to the service. Roughly 60 percent are high schools and the rest are colleges. A handful of middle schools subscribe to the service, and Dr. Barrie said he has also had inquiries from some elementary schools. Such services are surprisingly effective, especially as a deterrent.

8   Dr. Steven Hardinger, a chemistry lecturer at the University of California at Los Angeles, said he had students submit their own papers to Turnitin.com, with the results sent to him. "The use of Turnitin.com as a deterrent is perhaps much more valuable than as a way to ferret out plagiarism," Dr. Hardinger said. "We really hate to see plagiarists and hate to punish them, but we want them to know we're watching."

9   Dr. Jamie McKenzie, editor of From Now On—The Educational Technology Journal, an online publication at www.fno.org, said he saw a more disquieting problem associated with youthful plagiarists—what he calls "mental softness." "Students are caught up in a cut-and-paste mentality that relates to an old belief that longer is better," Dr. McKenzie said. "They're confusing the size of their pile, of what they've accumulated, with wisdom. Instead of finding the right stuff, they're just finding lots of stuff. They don't think of it as cheating. They are simply collecting information and don't understand the whole concept of intellectual property."

10   Even when caught, many high school students are relatively blasé about their transgression. Dr. Peter G. Mehas, superintendent of schools in Fresno County, Calif., blames parents, at least partly. He said he was chagrined to see a shift in parents' attitudes over his 30 years as an educator. "Some of the teachers who have stood up and said, 'This is cheating,' are accused of being too harsh and too strict," Dr. Mehas said. "I have some parents complain, saying, 'Why give the kid an F just because he plagiarized four or five points?'" Each spring, he receives about 200 calls from parents, "asking why someone's little darling isn't graduating," Dr. Mehas said. "In the cases where the child has been caught plagiarizing," he added, "what I hear is, 'Well, it's really not cheating, he just didn't cite all the sources.'" But Dr. Mehas stands firm on his decision to deny graduation to plagiarists. He said that many school districts remain silent about the problem because it reflects poorly on them. "It's our responsibility to say there are consequences when you sign your name to something you have not produced," he said.

11   When confronted with the notion of serious consequences, high school students do appear to pay attention. Nancy Breedlove, the writing center coordinator at Hononegah High School, told a group of students about a sports writer for the local newspaper, the Rockford Register Star, who was recently fired after he admitted using quotations from an article in the Star Tribune of Minneapolis without attributing them. "We wanted to let them know that not just in the academic world, but in the professional world, it could hurt them," Ms. Breedlove said. The story had an impact. "You could have heard a pin drop in the room." Ms. Breedlove said she was willing to do whatever it took to reinforce her point. "I just hope that somehow the kids do get the message," she said, "because this new temptation has been put out there, and it begins with www."

—Hafner, "Lessons in the School of Cut and Paste,"
New York Times (June 28, 2000), p. G1

VOCABULARY REVIEW

1. For each of the words or phrases listed below, use context; prefixes, roots, and suffixes; and/or a dictionary to write a brief definition or synonym of the word as it is used in the reading.

a. aligning (para. 1) _____

b. inverse proportion (para. 2) _____

c. abstruse (para. 2) _____

d. precarious (para. 3) _____

e. relief (para. 3) _____

f. cavalier (para. 5) _____

g. scrutiny (para.7) _____

h. deterrent (para. 7) _____

i. ferret out (para. 8) _____

j. disquieting (para. 9) _____

k. blasé (para. 10) _____

l. chagrined (para. 10) _____

2. Underline new specialized terms introduced in the reading.

COMPREHENSION QUESTIONS

1. What factors contribute to the prevalence of Internet plagiarism?
2. What penalties for plagiarism does the author discuss?
3. Why should students be penalized for Internet plagiarism?

THINKING CRITICALLY

1. Imagine that your college is considering subscribing to a service such as Turnitin.com. Using information from the reading, write a paragraph expressing your thoughts on the matter.
2. What are some larger issues in society and education that you think might contribute to the fact that many students cheat in high school and college?
3. How does this reading affect your knowledge of and attitude toward using the Internet for research?
4. If you had to explain to a child in fifth grade how to use information from a web site in a paper, what would you say?
5. Do you think there is more cheating in high school or college? What may contribute to the difference?

LEARNING/STUDY STRATEGIES

1. Draw a conceptual map of this reading.
2. Write a summary of this reading.

INTEGRATING
IDEAS

◆

PAIRED
READINGS

Music

PREREADING QUESTIONS

1. Who are the people discussed in this article?
2. What consequences for plagiarism does this story reveal?

Bolton Loses Court Fight with Isleys

Frank Saxe

1   Although his legal options have been exhausted and he will be forced to pay nearly $1 million out of his own pocket, Michael Bolton is hardly conceding defeat in his effort to call his 1991 top five pop hit "Love Is A Wonderful Thing" his own. For the past nine years, Bolton, cowriter Andrew Goldmark, and Sony Music Publishing locked horns with the Isley Brothers, who say the Bolton/Goldmark composition plagiarized their little-known 1966 song of the same name.

2   Bolton's court fight with the Isley Brothers ended Jan. 22 when the U.S. Supreme Court refused to hear Bolton's appeal of a May 2000 decision by the 9th U.S. Circuit Court of Appeals in San Francisco. The appeals court upheld a 1994 lower-court ruling that ordered the artist, Goldmark, and Sony Publishing to turn over $52 million in profits from the sales of Bolton's version of the song to the Isley Brothers (BillboardBulletin, May 11, 2000). After deciding the songs shared a number of the same elements, a trial jury ruled that the pair plagiarized the Isley Brothers song of the same name. The jury found that there were five instances where Bolton and Goldmark lifted from the original Isley Brothers song.

3   "I didn't expect [the Supreme Court] to hear this case, although I would have been overwhelmed at the possibility of seeing some justice in this case," Bolton told Billboard in an exclusive interview. "[Andy and I] were so 100% involved in the independent creation of this song. To have it torn from you forever and then to be fined for it is an atrocity that is psychologically a very tough pill to swallow."

4   Bolton maintains that he never heard the Isley Brothers' song. The Isley Brothers, through a representative, declined to comment on the Supreme Court's decision. Bolton's attorneys, including Harvard University law professor Alan Dershowitz, had asked the top court to reject the earlier decision. They argued that a national standard should be created to help guide artists and the courts in terms of what qualifies as copyright infringement. The Recording Industry Assn. of America (RIAA) agreed and filed a brief with the Supreme Court supporting Bolton in his appeal. The RIAA declined to comment.

5   Under the appeals court's ruling, the Isleys are to be paid $42 million from Sony Music, $932,924 from Bolton, $220,785 from Goldmark, and the balance from Bolton and Goldmark's music publishing company. The original jury found that 66% of the song's profits resulted from copyright-infringing elements and that 28% of the profits of the album "Time, Love & Tenderness" were derived from the track, which won Bolton and Goldmark a Grammy.

6   The legal process, which wound through three courts, from California to the Supreme Court, was a "maddening" process, says Bolton. "In this case, you have a song that never charted on The Billboard Hot 100; it never charted on the R&B charts, where the Isley Brothers had tremendous amounts of airplay; it never received a citing on the BMI or ASCAP [airplay tracking sheets]; there was not one receipt for the supposedly commercially released single—there was none of the usual evidence that shows up where the plaintiff's burden is to prove a reasonable amount of access." He also points out that there are more than 150 songs copyrighted with titles close to "Love Is A Wonderful Thing."

7   Although Bolton has covered many R&B classics and has based his career on a soulful sound, he says he has never owned a single Isley Brothers record. "I was not an Isley Brothers fan," he says. "Nothing to take away from Ronald Isley's singing, but I was a Marvin Gaye, Otis Redding, Ray Charles, and Smokey Robinson fan."

8   In a surprising twist, in January 2000 Bolton was among the parties bidding for a portion of Ronald Isley's assets after Isley filed for bankruptcy, including Isley's share of the Isley Brothers' catalog. The Pullman Group was the eventual winner (Billboard, Jan. 22, 2000). Bolton believes that by allowing the lower court's decision to stand, the Supreme Court ruling will subject other artists to similar suits. But music industry attorneys contacted by Billboard disagree, saying the Supreme Court's reluctance to review the case is neither significant nor precedent-setting. Steve England, an attorney with the Washington, D.C., firm Arnold & Palmer, notes that the Supreme Court reviews just 3% of the cases it is presented. "A case like this, which presents a number of factual questions, is not a very attractive case for the Supreme Court to take," says England.

9   "It's hardly a surprise that the court didn't take it, since there's not a lot of novel issues in the case," agrees William Coats, an attorney with the firm Howrey Simon, Arnold & White.

10   Englund also believes that this case will not lower the amount of evidence that will be required to prove access. "Just as this case is bound up in its facts, so is the next one," he says. Yet he agrees with Bolton that the evidence presented to the jury was "thin" and "circumstantial," adding, "That is a troubling aspect of the case."

11   Bolton is in the studio recording his first album under a new contract with Jive Records. When he returns to the road, fans can expect to still hear him sing "Love Is A Wonderful Thing," he says. "It will always be mine, in my heart and in Andy's. It will always be my song."

—Saxe, "Bolton Loses Court Fight with Isleys," *Billboard,*
Vol. 113, No. 5 (February 3, 2001), p. 8

VOCABULARY REVIEW

1. For each of the words or phrases listed below, use context; prefixes, roots, and suffixes; and/or a dictionary to write a brief definition or synonym of the word as it is used in the reading.

   a. conceding (para. 1) _____

   b. locked horns (para. 1) _____

   c. upheld (para. 2) _____

   d. atrocity (para. 3) _____

   e. copyright infringement (para. 4) _____

   f. derived (para. 5) _____

   g. plaintiff (para. 6) _____

2. Underline new specialized terms introduced in the reading.

COMPREHENSION QUESTIONS

1. What did the courts find that Bolton did wrong?
2. What is the penalty? How was this figured?
3. What evidence does Bolton say was missing from the case?
4. Why did the U.S. Supreme Court decline to hear Bolton's case?

THINKING CRITICALLY

1. Evaluate the case as presented in the article. Do you think the decision was fair? Why or why not?
2. Discuss the penalty. Is it too severe? Why or why not?
3. How could the music industry prevent copyright infringement?
4. Do you think plagiarism can be unintentional? Explain your answer.
5. Where would you look for more information on this case?

LEARNING/STUDY STRATEGIES

1. Create a time line of the events discussed in this reading.
2. Write a short speech defending Michael Bolton based on the information in the article.

THINKING ABOUT THE PAIRED READINGS

INTEGRATING IDEAS

1. How are the readings similar?
2. How do the articles differ?
3. If you were to use these two articles to teach high school students about plagiarism, how would you relate the second one to the first?

GENERATING NEW IDEAS

1. Find and evaluate your school's policy on plagiarism. Pay attention to how detailed the rules and punishments are and how clearly they are explained. What changes would you make?
2. Usually when we think of plagiarism, we think of the written word in print. These articles reveal other places plagiarism occurs—Internet and music. Brainstorm ideas for a paper that covers other types of cheating, plagiarism, or copyright infringement.

Multimedia Activities

1. **Plagiarism**

   http://www.indiana.edu/~wts/wts/plagiarism.html

   This site from Indiana University offers a clear treatment of plagiarism, explaining why it is wrong and how to avoid it, using numerous examples. Look at some articles in scholarly journals. Keep track of how many times the authors give credit to another. Does the amount surprise you? Why or why not?

2. **Guide to Library Research**

   http://www.lib.duke.edu/libguide/home.htm

   A comprehensive online tutorial from Duke University covering "Seven Steps of the Research Process." Familiarize yourself with the contents of this tutorial, and bookmark it for future reference. Ask your librarian for a quick overview of your library's resources.

Take a Road Trip to
Seattle!

If your instructor has asked you to use the Reading Road Trip CD-ROM or Website, be sure to visit the Note Taking and Textbook Highlighting module for multimedia tutorials, exercises, and tests.

CHAPTER 13

READING IN THE SOCIAL SCIENCES

LEARNING OBJECTIVES

✦ To learn why social sciences are "sciences"
✦ To discover specialized reading techniques for the social sciences
✦ To learn what common thought patterns to anticipate
✦ To adapt your study techniques for social science courses

The social sciences are concerned with the study of people, their development, and how they function together and interact. These disciplines deal with the political, economic, social, cultural, and behavioral aspects of human beings. The social sciences include psychology, anthropology, sociology, political science, and economics. History, which is sometimes considered one of the humanities, and geography, which is sometimes treated as a physical science, are included among the social sciences for the purposes of this book. During your college career, you probably will take at least two or three social science courses; many students take more.

As you select these courses, it is helpful to understand the basic focus and approach of each discipline. Each one of the social sciences focuses on selected aspects of human behavior, social relationships, or social systems and the laws or principles that govern them. Table 13–1 on the next page provides an overview of each discipline and shows how they differ by giving examples of the questions each discipline would ask about a particular topic—in this case, an accident on an oil tanker in the Gulf of Mexico resulting in a major oil spill.

WHY STUDY THE SOCIAL SCIENCES?

On many campuses, courses in the social sciences are among the most popular. Because social science courses focus on how people develop, behave, and interact, students find they learn a great deal about themselves and those around them. They also learn answers to many questions they have always

TABLE 13–1   THE SOCIAL SCIENCE DISCIPLINES TOPIC: OIL SPILL

Discipline	Overview	Questions
Anthropology	Examines concepts, customs, and rules in different societies and cultures	Does each country involved view the spill the same way? What rules and customs must be followed?
Economics	Studies how goods, services, and wealth are produced, consumed, and distributed within societies	How will environmental damage affect the economy of each country?
Geography	Focuses on the surface of the earth, its divisions, climate, inhabitants, and resources	What environmental damage has occurred? How will the spill affect the ecology of each area involved?
History	Provides a chronological record of past events; tells story of people's usable past	What other oil spills have occurred? How is this spill similar to and different from others?
Political science	Studies political power, governments, processes	How will each country be compensated for environmental damage? Who will decide the amount of compensation?
Psychology	Focuses on human mental processes and behavior	How will the pilot and crew of the tanker cope with the accident and its effects?
Sociology	Deals with human relationships, social systems, and societies	What leadership patterns emerged on the tanker after the accident? How were the cleanup efforts organized? What groups were most active?

wondered about: Why do some people commit violent crimes? Why and how do people fall in love? What can we learn from events of the past? Why is religion important in our lives, and how did it evolve? What factors determine how many jobs are available in a given city?

Social science courses are required courses for many college degrees because social science links to many other fields. If you plan to become a nurse, interacting with patients is important. If you plan to work in business, your success often depends on understanding people and the economy in which you are working. If you plan to work as a commercial Web site designer, you have to understand what motivates people to purchase goods and services. You can see, then, that social science courses are valuable in the workplace because all jobs require you to interact with people to some degree.

THE SOCIAL SCIENCES: A SCIENTIFIC APPROACH

Although each social science focuses on a different aspect of human life, they have much in common. Each is interested in general laws, principles, and generalizations that describe how events, facts, and observations are related. The author of your social science textbook and your course instructor are both social scientists, and their approach to problems and the way they organize ideas are similar and predictable. Once you are familiar with this approach, you'll find social science courses much easier to handle.

All social sciences use the scientific method. This is a systematic way of drawing conclusions about events and observations. Social scientists insist on evidence and proof and are careful to avoid subjectivity, judgments, and bias. The scientific method is a means of discovering the rules and principles that govern human behavior.

Five steps are commonly included in the scientific approach. You might think of them as a logical process that scientists follow in investigating problems.

1. *Problem or Research Question.* A researcher poses a problem or research question.

2. *Observations.* Researchers record what they can observe about a given problem or behavior. They emphasize facts and measurable, observable behaviors.

3. *Formulation of Hypothesis.* On the basis of observations, researchers form a preliminary hypothesis. A hypothesis is a statement about a relationship or occurrence that can be tested or evaluated.

4. *Research Design.* Researchers design a plan to gather the data necessary to test the hypothesis. This plan may include survey research, the use of secondary data, or an experiment with control and experimental groups.

5. *Data Analysis.* Data from the experiment are analyzed, and the hypothesis is supported or rejected. These findings often are published or shared with other researchers.

An overview of the method and an example of its use are shown on the next page in Table 13–2. In this case, the problem is "What are the effects of portraying violence on television?"

The scientific method is the standard operating procedure for all social sciences. Consequently, textbooks in the social sciences share several characteristics.

1. *The emphasis is on facts.* Especially in introductory courses, an instructor's first task often is to acquaint you with what has already been discovered—known principles, rules, and facts—so that you can use this information to approach new problems and situations. Consequently, you must comprehend and retain large amounts of factual information. Refer to "Locating Main Ideas and Supporting Details" in Chapter 2 and "Retention and Recall Strategies" in Chapter 8 for specific suggestions.

2. *Many new terms are introduced.* Each social science has developed an extensive terminology to make its broad topics as objective and as quantifiable as possible.

TABLE 13–2	THE SCIENTIFIC METHOD
Step	**Example**
Problem or question	Does the portrayal of violence on television produce aggressive behavior in viewers?
Observations	A great deal of violence is shown on television. Crime rates are increasing.
Hypothesis	Children who watch highly violent TV programs exhibit more aggressive behavior than children who watch nonviolent programs.
Research design	Two groups established; TV watching habits of each group controlled. Aggression measured by hidden observers during play periods following viewing. An aggression score is assigned for each group.
Data analysis	Viewers of violent programs received aggression scores three times higher than viewers of nonviolent programs. The research result supports the hypothesis that viewing violence produces aggressive behavior.

3. *Graphics are important.* Refer to Chapter 9, "Reading Graphics," for specific suggestions on reading and interpreting charts, tables, and graphs.

4. *Research references are stressed.* Many texts present research studies as supporting evidence. In introductory courses, the outcome of the research and what it proves or suggests usually are most important.

5. *Theories and their creators are emphasized.* Often, the social scientists who have developed important theories are discussed at length.

Now that you are familiar with the scientific method, you will understand how social scientists approach their subject matter and how you will be expected to think and analyze information in social science courses. You will have a competitive advantage over other students who mistakenly regard social science courses as subjective or unscientific.

SPECIALIZED READING TECHNIQUES

Especially in introductory-level social science courses, you will need to learn a large volume of information. Use the following suggestions to read social science materials and retain as much information as possible.

Identify Key Terms

The key to mastering any new discipline is to learn its language: specialized and technical terms unique to the discipline. The social sciences use precise terminology to describe observations as well as processes. Terminology in the social sciences includes everyday words with specialized meanings as well as new words not used elsewhere. Instructors recognize the importance of learning terminology; consequently, often they include items on their exams to test your knowledge of key terms. Refer to Chapter 3 for specific suggestions for learning specialized terminology.

In social science courses, it is particularly important to learn

- Terms that describe general behavior and organizational patterns
  Examples: denial, power, aggression, primary/secondary groups, free trade
- Names of stages and processes
  Examples: Piaget's stages of cognitive development, Maslow's hierarchy of needs
- Laws, principles, theories, and models
  Examples: figure-ground principles, income/expenditures model, models of attention, Keynesian theory
- Names of important researchers and theorists
  Examples: Marx, Freud, Skinner, Durkheim, Leakey

Understand Theories

An important part of most social science courses is the study of theories that explain various behaviors. A theory is a set of propositions that explains a certain phenomenon or occurrence. You might, for example, develop a theory to explain why your roommate cannot fall asleep without music or why your history professor always opens class with the same comment. A theory is a reasoned explanation of an observable occurrence. Theories are often tested using the scientific method. In sociology, you may study exchange theory, which explains social behavior as a series of exchanges or trade-offs involving rewards (benefits) and costs. In economics, you may study the natural rate hypothesis that states that workers do not immediately react to changes in wages.

When studying theories, read to find the following information:

- What is the theory?
- Who proposed the theory?
- When was it proposed? (Is it recent or historical?)
- What behavior or occurrence does it explain?
- What evidence or rationale is offered that the theory is correct?
- What use or application does the theory have?

Read the following excerpt from a sociology text. Note how the text has been marked to indicate the answers to each of the questions listed above.

CONFLICT THEORY

behavior —— ⎯⎯ Conflict theory also had its origins in early sociology, especially in the work of
origin — Marx. Among its more recent proponents are such people as Mills, Coser, and
recent proponents — Dahrendorf. They share the view that society is best understood and analyzed in
statement of theory   terms of conflict and power.

rationale

Karl Marx began with a very simple assumption: the structure of society is determined by economic organization, particularly the ownership of property. Religious dogmas, cultural values, personal beliefs, institutional arrangements, class structures—all are basically reflections of the economic organization of a society. Inherent in any economic system that supports inequality are forces that generate revolutionary class conflict, according to Marx. The exploited classes eventually recognize their submissive and inferior status and revolt against the dominant class of property owners and employers. The story of history, then, is the story of class struggle between the owners and workers, the dominators and the dominated, the powerful and the powerless.

applications

Contemporary conflict theorists assume that conflict is a permanent feature of social life and that as a result societies are in a state of constant change. Unlike Marx, however, these theorists rarely assume that conflict is always based on class or that it always reflects economic organization and ownership. Conflicts are assumed to involve a broad range of groups or interests: young against old, male against female, or one racial group against another, as well as workers against employers. These conflicts result because things like power, wealth, and prestige are not available to everyone—they are limited commodities, and the demand exceeds the supply. Conflict theory also assumes that those who have or control desirable goods and services will defend and protect their own interests at the expense of others.

—Eshleman et al., *Sociology: An Introduction,* p. 46

In some texts, you may find several theories presented to explain a single phenomenon. Often, these theories are not compatible, and they may even be contradictory. In this case, first make certain that you understand each theory; then examine how they differ and consider the evidence offered in support of each.

EXERCISE 13-1

Write a summary of the conflict theory described above. Refer to page 330 for suggestions on writing summaries. Compare your summary with those of several classmates.

EXERCISE 13-2

Read this excerpt from a psychology textbook, and answer the questions that follow.

KOHLBERG'S THEORY OF MORAL DEVELOPMENT

How children learn to reason about and make judgments about what is right and wrong is an aspect of cognitive development that has received considerable attention (Darley & Schultz, 1990; Vitz, 1990). Piaget included the study of moral development in his theory, arguing that morality is related to cognitive awareness, and that children are unable to make moral judgments until they are at least 3 or 4 years old (Piaget, 1932/1948).

Lawrence Kohlberg (1963, 1969, 1981, 1985) has offered a theory that focuses on moral development. Like Piaget's approach, Kohlberg's is a theory of stages, of moving from one stage to another in an orderly fashion. Kohlberg's database comes from the responses made by young boys who were asked questions about stories that involve a moral dilemma. A commonly cited example concerns whether a man should steal a drug in order to save his wife's life after the pharmacist who invented the drug refuses to sell it to him. Should the man steal the drug; why or why not?

On the basis of responses to such dilemmas, Kohlberg proposed three levels of moral development, with two stages (or "orientations") at each level. The result is the six stages of moral development. . . . For example, a child who says that the man should not steal the drug because "he'll get caught and be put in jail" is at the first, *preconventional*, level of reasoning because the prime interest of the child is simply with the punishment that comes from breaking a rule. A child who says that the man should steal the drug because "it will make his wife happy, and probably most people would do it anyway" is reflecting a type of reasoning at the second, *conventional*, level because the judgment is based on an accepted social convention, and social approval matters as much as or more than anything else. The argument that "no, he shouldn't steal the drug for a basically selfish reason, which in the long run would just promote more stealing in the society in general" is an example of moral reasoning at the third, *postconventional*, level because it reflects complex, internalized standards. Notice that what matters most is not the choice the child makes, but the reasoning behind the choice.

—Gerow, *Psychology: An Introduction,* p. 290

1. Who proposed the theory?
2. What is it intended to explain?
3. Explain the three levels in your own words.
4. How did Kohlberg arrive at the theory?
5. What practical uses can you see for the theory?
6. Underline terminology in the passage that is important to learn.
7. Construct a story about a moral dilemma, and indicate responses at each of the three levels.

Read Research Reports

Because the social sciences rely heavily on observation, research, and experimentation based on the scientific method, textbooks often include brief descriptions of, or references to, research studies. When such references are made to other works, the source of the reference is indicated in parentheses as shown in the excerpt below. Footnotes or endnotes sometimes are used to provide more detailed information.

When reading reports about research, keep these guidelines in mind:

- Determine who conducted the research.
- Identify its purpose.
- Find out how the research was done.

- Understand the results of the research.
- Find out what theory the results support or what conclusion was drawn.
- Discover the implications and applications of the research. Ask "Why is it important?"

The following excerpt from a sociology textbook describes research on masculine and feminine behavior. See how the marked passage reflects the guidelines given above.

Purpose

Although biologically men are men and women are women, roles—that is, definitions of masculine and feminine behavior—differ widely from one culture to another. The discovery of cross-cultural variation in gender was one of the earliest kinds of evidence against the idea that each sex has a "natural" temperament and set of interests. In American culture, for example, it is considered "feminine" to be artistic and emotional, but in other cultures men are supposed to be more emotionally expressive and artistic than women. Margaret Mead's (1935) classic study of sex and temperament in three cultures was the earliest <u>study of the variability of gender patterning.</u> In one of the New Guinea tribes, the Arapesh, both men and women were found to be cooperative, unaggressive, and gentle. In contrast, the Mundugumor prescribed what would be a masculine temperament in our culture for both sexes—ruthlessness, aggressiveness, and severity. Neither the Arapesh nor the Mundugumor emphasized a contrast between the sexes. In a third New Guinea tribe, the Tchambuli, however, there was such a contrast, but it was the reverse of sex-role temperament in our culture. Tchambuli women tended to be aggressive, domineering, and managerial, whereas the men tended to be dependent, artistic, and sensitive. In short, the study concludes that sex differences are arbitrary and do not reflect any underlying predisposition.

Results

Conclusion

—Skolnick, *The Intimate Environment: Exploring Marriage and the Family,* pp. 193–94

EXERCISE 13–3

Read the following excerpt from a psychology textbook, and answer the questions that follow.

Researchers have looked at the relationship between adolescent drug use and psychological health (Shedler & Block, 1990). Participants in this investigation were 18-year-olds who had been under study since they were 3 years old. Based on their level of drug use, they were divided into one of three groups: (1) *abstainers* (N = 29), who had never tried any drug; (2) *experimenters* (N = 36), who had used marijuana "once or twice, or a few times" and who tried no more than one other drug; and (3) *frequent users* (N = 20), who used marijuana frequently and tried at least one other drug. There were no socioeconomic or IQ differences among the groups.

The researchers found that *frequent users* were generally maladjusted, alienated, deficient in impulse control, and "manifestly" distressed. The *abstainers* were overly anxious, "emotionally constricted," and lacking in social skills. These same results were apparent when the researchers examined records from when the same subjects were 7 and 11 years old. Generally, the *experimenters* were better adjusted and psychologically "healthier" than either of the other two groups. The authors of this study are concerned that their data may be misinterpreted—that their data might be taken to indicate "that drug use might somehow improve an adolescent's psychological health." Clearly, this interpretation would be in error. You recognize these as correlational data from which no conclusion regarding cause and effect is justified.

While drug use among adolescents is a matter of great concern, there is evidence that we need not get hysterical about infrequent drug use among teenagers.

—Gerow, *Psychology: An Introduction,* pp. 305–06

1. Who conducted the research?
2. What was its purpose?
3. What methods were used?
4. What were the results?
5. What did the results demonstrate?
6. What is the practical value of the research?
7. Why did the author feel compelled to caution against misinterpretation?

Read to Make Comparisons and Connections

In the social sciences, the ability to see relationships among different ideas and concepts is a necessary skill. Often neither your instructor nor your textbook will make explicit, direct comparisons, yet you will be expected to compare or contrast ideas and concepts. Suppose you are reading about three forms of imperfect economic competition: monopoly, oligopoly, and monopolistic competition. You would, of course, be expected to understand each form. However, you must also know how they are similar, how they are different, and in what economic situation each is found.

When making comparisons, keep the following question in mind: "What does what I am reading have to do with other topics in the chapter?" Then spend a few minutes thinking about how the topics and ideas in the chapter are connected to one another. Begin by reviewing the chapter using the steps you used to preview it (see Chapter 1). Then study your text's detailed table of contents and review the lecture notes that correspond to the chapter. For example, one student connected the forms of imperfect competition to other market variables she had learned in economics: number of sellers, ease of entry, product type, price influence, and price level. Then she drew the chart shown in Table 13–3 on the next page to compare the three forms according to the market variables that she identified.

In addition to charts, you can organize comparisons by making outlines or lists or by drawing maps that summarize similarities and differences (refer to Chapter 11).

TABLE 13–3   SAMPLE COMPARISON CHART

	Forms of Imperfect Competition		
	Monopoly	Oligopoly	Monopolistic Competition
Number of sellers	One	Several	Many
Entry	Difficult	Less difficult	Easy
Product	Unique	Homogeneous or differentiated	Differentiated
Price influence	Price makers	Price makers	Limited price makers
Price level	Higher price, lower quantity than competition	Somewhat higher price and lower quantity than competition	Slightly higher price than competition and frequently higher production costs

EXERCISE 13–4

Read the following excerpt from a sociology textbook chapter titled "Religious Groups and Systems," and make comparisons between Hinduism and Buddhism by listing, charting, or mapping. Compare your work with the work of other students, discussing its relative effectiveness.

HINDUISM

The great majority of Hindus in the world live in India and Pakistan. In India, approximately 85 percent of the population is Hindu. Hinduism has evolved over about 4000 years and comprises an enormous variety of beliefs and practices. It hardly corresponds to most Western conceptions of religion because organization is minimal, and there is no religious hierarchy.

Hinduism is so closely intertwined with other aspects of the society that it is difficult to describe it clearly, especially in regard to castes . . . . Hindus sometimes refer to the ideal way of life as fulfilling the duties of one's class and station, which means obeying the rules of the four great castes of India: the Brahmins, or priests; the Kshatriyas, warriors and rulers; the Vaisyas, merchants and farmers; and the Sudras, peasants and laborers. A fifth class, the Untouchables, includes those whose occupations require them to handle "unclean objects."

These classes encompass males only. The position of women is ambiguous. In some respects, they are treated as symbols of the divine, yet in other ways, they are considered inferior beings. Traditionally, women have been expected to serve their husbands and to have no independent interests, but this is rapidly changing.

Although caste is a powerful influence in Hindu religious behavior, a person's village community and family are important as well. Every village has gods and goddesses who ward off epidemics and drought. Hindu belief holds that the universe is populated by a multitude of gods (polytheism) who behave much as humans do, and worship of these gods takes many forms. Some are thought to require sacrifices, others are worshipped at shrines or temples, and shrines devoted to several gods associated with a family deity are often erected in private homes.

To Hindus, the word *dharma* means the cosmos, or the social order. Hindus practice rituals that uphold the great cosmic order. They believe that to be righteous, a person must strive to behave in accordance with the way things are. In a sense, the Hindu sees life as a ritual. The world is regarded as a great dance determined by one's karma, or personal destiny, and the final goal of the believer is liberation from this cosmic dance. Hindus also believe in *transmigration of souls*: After an individual dies, that individual's soul is born again in another form, as either a higher or lower being, depending on whether the person was righteous or evil in the previous life. If an individual becomes righteous enough, the soul will be liberated and will cease to be reborn into an earthly form and will exist only as spirit.

A fundamental principle of Hinduism is that our perceptions of the external world are limitations. When we think about one thing, we are cut off from the infinite number of things we are not thinking about but could be. If we think of nothing, we become in tune with the universe and freed of these limitations. One means of doing this is through meditation.

The actual belief systems of India are extremely confusing to Westerners, because so many different tribal religions have been assimilated into Hinduism, but the basic nature of polytheism in general and of Hinduism in particular permits new gods to be admitted.

BUDDHISM

It is impossible to precisely determine the number of Buddhists because many people accept Buddhist beliefs and engage in Buddhist rites while practicing other religions such as Shintoism, Confucianism, Taoism, or Hinduism.

Buddhism is thought to have originated as a reaction against the Brahminic tradition of Hinduism in the fifth century B.C. At this time, a prince named Siddhartha Gautama was born in northern India to a prosperous ruling family. As he grew older, he was distressed by the suffering he witnessed among the people. At the age of 29, he left his wife and family to go on a religious quest. One day, sitting under a giant fig tree, he passed through several stages of awareness and became the Buddha, the enlightened one. He decided to share his experience with others and became a wandering teacher, preaching his doctrine of the "Four Noble Truths": (1) this life is suffering and pain; (2) the source of suffering is desire and craving; (3) suffering can cease; and (4) the practice of an "eightfold path" can end suffering. The eightfold path consisted of right views, right intentions, right speech, right conduct, right livelihood, right effort, right mindfulness, and right concentration. It combined ethical and disciplinary practices, training in concentration and meditation, and the development of enlightened wisdom. This doctrine was Buddha's message until the age of 80, when he passed into final nirvana, a state of transcendence forever free from the cycle of suffering and rebirth.

After Buddha's death, legends of his great deeds and supernatural powers emerged. Stories were told of his heroism in past lives, and speculations arose about his true nature. Some groups viewed him as a historical figure, whereas others placed him in a succession of several Buddhas of the past and a Buddha yet to come. Differing views eventually led to a diversity of Buddhist sects in different countries. Some remained householders who set up Buddha images and established many holy sites that became centers of pilgrimage. Others became monks, living in monastic communities and depending on the laity for food and material support. Many monks became beggars, and in several Southeast Asian countries, they still go on daily alms rounds. They spend their days in rituals, devotions, meditation, study, and preaching. Flowers, incense, and praise are offered to the image of the Buddha. These acts are thought to ensure that the monks will be reborn in one of the heavens or in a better place in life, from which they may be able to attain the goal of enlightenment.

In every society where Buddhism is widespread, people combine Buddhist thought with a native religion, supporting the monks and paying for rituals in the temples. These societies are also organized around other religions, however.

Today, the integration of Buddhism into many cultures has resulted in different interpretations of the way to Buddhahood. Yet we can supposedly reach Nirvana by seeing with complete detachment, by seeing things as they really are without being attached to any theoretical concept or doctrine.

—Eshleman et al., *Sociology: An Introduction*, pp. 356–58

Read to Make Practical Applications

In many courses, instructors want students to apply what they learn to everyday, practical situations. Consequently, instructors expect and encourage students to use their reasoning skills to go beyond what is stated in the text and consider practical applications of textbook information. For example, your psychology instructor may ask this question on a midterm exam.

> Five-year-old Sammy tells his grandmother that three dinosaurs are hiding in his closet. Knowing this is not true, his grandmother spanks Sammy. Grandmother should be
>
> a. encouraged to be consistent, spanking Sammy whenever he talks about dinosaurs.
> b. reminded that children of this age often confuse fantasy and reality.
> c. thanked for acting as a good role model for Sammy.
> d. told that her authoritarian response will improve his ability to relate to adults.

Or, in your American government class, the following question might appear on an essay exam.

> Project the key political issues that will be involved in the next presidential election.

To be prepared for questions such as these, consider the practical applications of what you read. Try to relate each idea to a real-life situation, and, if possible, connect the material to your own experience.

Focus on Large Ideas

Because many social science courses present a great deal of factual information, it is easy to become convinced that the facts are all you need to learn. Actually, factual information is only a starting point, a base from which to approach the real content of a course. Most social science instructors expect you to go beyond facts to analysis—to consider the meaning of facts and details. Many students fail to understand the overriding concepts of their courses because they are too concerned with memorizing information. They fail to ask, "Why do I need to know this? Why is this important? What principle or trend does this illustrate?" Table 13–4 gives examples of details from a course in American history and the more important trends, concepts, or principles they represent.

Be certain you stay focused on major ideas; after you preview a chapter, write a list of key topics and concepts you expect to read about. After you have read about each one, check it off on your list. Before you continue, mentally review what you have learned. After completing an assignment, return again to your list to reestablish what is important and recheck your recall. Restate each idea in your own words; if you can do so, you can be confident that you understand the ideas, rather than just recall the author's words.

TABLE 13–4   IDENTIFYING KEY CONCEPTS

Topics	Facts	Importance
The slavery controversy	On May 22, 1856, Representative Brooks from South Carolina approached Senator Sumner of Massachusetts (who had recently given a speech condemning the South for trying to extend slavery) on the floor of the Senate and beat him with a cane until he was near death.	The antagonism between the North and South had become bitter and violent by 1856.
Annexation of territories to the U.S.	Texas was annexed in 1845. In 1845 and 1846 a great controversy arose over the Oregon territory. The Democrats wanted to make all of the Oregon territory (stretching north above today's border into British Columbia) part of the U.S. The British also claimed this land. A war over the territory was barely avoided.	In the late 1840s a belief called *Manifest Destiny* was wide-spread. People felt it was the fate of the U.S. to spread from the Atlantic Ocean to the Pacific Ocean and eventually take over the entire continent.
Industry	Henry Ford perfected the Model T for manufacture in 1914, and by 1924 more than 40,000 workers were working in the first mass-production assembly line factory.	This began the trend toward mass production, which led the second Industrial Revolution.

THOUGHT PATTERNS IN THE SOCIAL SCIENCES

Four thought patterns that predominate in the social sciences are comparison and contrast, cause and effect, listing, and definition. Table 13–5 describes the uses of each pattern and includes several examples from a specific discipline.

TABLE 13–5	THOUGHT PATTERNS IN THE SOCIAL SCIENCES	
Pattern	**Uses**	**Topical Examples**
Comparison and contrast	To evaluate two sides of an issue; to compare and contrast theories, groups, behaviors, events	*Anthropology* Limbic and nonlimbic communication Theories of aggression Anatomical comparison: archaic and modern Relative versus chrono-metric dating methods
Cause and effect	To study behavior and motivation; to examine connections between events, actions, behaviors	*Economics* Price determination Factors affecting indi-vidual's demand curve Aggregate effects of taxes Factors influencing consumption and saving
Listing	To present facts, illustrations, or examples; to list research findings	*Sociology* Types of adult socialization Three sociological research methods Myths about old age Agencies of socialization
Definition	To label and describe behaviors, social systems, laws, cycles, etc.	*Political Science* Coercive power Utilitarian power Capitalism Conservatism

EXERCISE 13–5   *Figure 13–1 is a chapter outline from a sociology textbook. Read the headings and subheadings and identify the thought pattern of each shaded section. For some headings, more than one pattern may be identified. Refer to Chapter 7 for a review of thought patterns.*

EXERCISE 13–6   *Form groups of three students, and have each student bring a social science textbook to class. Each group should select one text and, using the table of contents, work together to agree on a list of patterns likely to appear in the first five chapters.*

Figure 13–1   Chapter Outline

Socialization	
Nature Versus Nurture	Religion
Becoming Human	Peers
The Effects of Social Isolation	The Workplace
Personality Development: A Psychological View	The Mass Media
Developing a Concept of Self:	**Socialization: Future Directions**
A Sociological Approach	*Box 4.1 Sociological Focus:*
Socialization and the Life Course	*Nature Versus Nurture:*
Childhood Socialization	*The Case of Willie Bosket Jr.*
Adult Socialization	*Box 4.2 Applied Sociology:*
Resocialization	*Resocialization in a Marine Corps Boot Camp*
Major Agents of Socialization	
The Family	
Schools	

Source: Thompson and Hickey, *Society in Focus: An Introduction to Sociology,* p. 81

ADAPTING YOUR STUDY TECHNIQUES

Use the following suggestions in adapting your study methods to the social science field.

1. *Schedule several 2- to 3-hour blocks of time per week for reading, review, and study.* Avoid last-minute cramming. Study that is distributed over several periods is more effective than one marathon session.

2. *Recognize that understanding is not the same as learning and recall.* Do not assume that because you have read an assignment, you have learned it. To ensure learning, use writing to organize the information. Refer to Chapter 11 for specific strategies.

3. *Use the SQ3R system, or your own adaptation of it, to learn the material.* Review this system in Chapter 8. Writing is useful in the recitation step because it allows for greater retention of information through multiple sensory stimulation.

4. *Review frequently.* Review each assignment immediately after you have read it and again the next day. Add periodic reviews to your regular study sessions.

5. *Make connections between topics and chapters.* Each topic is an essential part of the discipline, as is every chapter. Information gained in one chapter should be used and applied in subsequent chapters.

6. *Use the study guide.* Many social science textbooks have a study guide that may be purchased separately. These guides contain useful reviews, sample test questions, and additional practice materials.

7. *Keep a log of total hours studied per week.* The log will help maintain your motivation and enable you to see how the grades you are earning are related to the amount of time you spend studying.

Test-Taking Tips
Preparing for Exams in the Social Sciences

Many exams you will take in social science courses will be objective: multiple choice, true-false, matching, or fill-in-the-blank. Your task in these types of questions is to recognize correct answers. To prepare for objective exams, use the following suggestions:

1. *Attend review classes if your instructor conducts them.*

2. *Prepare study sheets.* Organize and summarize important information from your notes and your text on topics you expect the exam to cover.

3. *Use index cards to record factual information that you must learn* (names, dates, definitions, theories, research findings). Record the name, date, name of theory, and so forth on the front of the card, and record what the person is noted for, the event, or the theory itself on the back. Test yourself by reading the front of the card and trying to recall what is on the back. Shuffle the pack of cards so that you do not learn the material in a fixed order.

4. *Review previous exams and quizzes.* Look for patterns of errors, and identify kinds of questions you missed (knowledge or critical thinking), as well as topics that you need to review.

SUMMARY

This chapter describes reading strategies for the social sciences. All social sciences use the scientific method, which is a systematic way of drawing conclusions about events or observations.

The specialized reading techniques necessary for the social sciences are

- identifying key terminology
- understanding theories
- reading reports of research
- making comparisons
- making applications
- focusing on large ideas

Four thought patterns predominate in the social sciences:

- comparison and contrast
- cause and effect
- listing
- definition

Sociology

PREREADING QUESTIONS

1. What is a crowd?
2. How is one crowd different from another?

Crowd Behavior

J. Ross Eshleman, Barbara J. Cashion, and Laurence A. Basirico

CHARACTERISTICS OF CROWDS

A **spatially proximate collective** exists when people are geographically close and physically visible to one another. The most common type of spatially proximate collective is the **crowd,** a temporary group of people in face-to-face contact who share a common interest or focus of attention. This common interest may be unexpected and unusual, but it is not necessarily so. Although people in a crowd interact a good deal, the crowd as a whole is organized poorly if at all. According to Turner (1985), crowds have four features that make them a unique area for study: anonymity, suggestibility, contagion, and emotional arousability.

Most types of collective behavior involve *anonymity.* People who do not know those around them may behave in ways that they would consider unacceptable if they were alone or with their family or neighbors. During a riot, the anonymity of crowd members makes it easier for people to loot and steal. In a lynch mob, brutal acts can be committed without feelings of shame or responsibility. Whatever the type of crowd, the anonymity of the individuals involved shifts the responsibility to the crowd as a whole.

Handwritten annotations:

T: A spatially proximate collective exists when people are close & visible to one another

1. MI a crowd is a temporary group of people that share an intrest.

2. T: Most types of collective behavior involve anonymity

MI: crowd members makes it easier for people to loot and steal

MI: People may behave in ways they would consider unacceptable with family and neighbors

Crowds exist when many people are in face-to-face contact and share a common interest. Some crowds, such as at a sporting event or outdoor concert, may behave collectively by shouting, clapping, jumping, or waving when the performers engage in a particular activity: a home run or touchdown, a hit song, an emotionally charged speech, and so forth.

Because crowds are relatively unstructured and often unpredictable, crowd members are often highly *suggestible.* People who are seeking direction in an uncertain situation are highly responsive to the suggestions of others and become very willing to do what a leader or group of individuals suggests, especially given the crowd's anonymity.

The characteristic of *contagion* is closely linked to anonymity and suggestibility. Turner (1985) defines this aspect of crowd behavior as "interactional amplification." As people interact, the crowd's response to the common event or situation increases in intensity. If they are clapping or screaming, their behavior is likely to move others to clap or scream, and contagion increases when people are packed close together. An alert evangelist, comedian, or rock singer will try to get the audience to move close to one another to increase the likelihood of contagion and to encourage the listeners to get caught up in the mood, spirit, and activity of the crowd.

A fourth characteristic is *emotional arousal.* Anonymity, suggestibility, and contagion tend to arouse emotions. Inhibitions are forgotten, and people become emotionally charged to act. In some cases, their emotional involvement encourages them to act in uncharacteristic ways. During the Beatles concerts in the early 1960s, for example, teenage girls who were presumably quite conventional most of the time tried to rush on stage and had to be carried away by police. The combination of the four characteristics of crowds makes their behavior extremely volatile and frightening.

Although these four aspects of crowd behavior may be seen in almost any crowd, their intensity varies. Some crowds permit greater anonymity than others, and some have higher levels of suggestibility and contagion, yet one or more of these characteristics may not appear at all. The presence or absence of certain crowd features can be used to organize crowds into different categories.

TYPES OF CROWDS

All crowds are spatially proximate and temporary, and every crowd shares a common focus. However, some crowds are very low in emotional arousal and are highly unstructured, whereas others are quite emotional, aggressive, and even dangerous to one's safety.

The literature on collective behavior, following the lead of Herbert Blumer (1939), tends to label the nonemotional, unstructured crowd as a **casual crowd.** People who stop to look at an animated holiday display or who gather to watch a street musician would be of this type. Another type of crowd, sometimes called a **conventional crowd,** is more highly structured and occurs, for example, when spectators gather at a baseball game, attend a concert, or ride on an airplane. Although the participants are generally unknown to one another (anonymous), they have a specific goal or common purpose and are expected to follow established norms and procedures. At symphony concerts, for example, people applaud at the end of the music (an established procedure). When the music is being played, however, they do not run up and down the aisles or call out to a friend at the opposite side of the concert hall (not an established procedure).

The . . . crowds that attract the most public attention are called **acting crowds,** the behavior of which is centered around and typifies aroused impulses. The two most dramatic forms of acting crowds are mobs and riots.

Mobs are groups that are emotionally aroused and ready to engage in violent behavior. They are generally short-lived and highly unstable. Their violent actions often stem from strong dissatisfaction with existing government policies or social circumstances; extreme discontentment with prevailing conditions is used to justify immediate and direct action. Disdainful of regular institutional channels and legal approaches, mobs take matters into their own hands.

Most mobs are predisposed to violence before their actions are triggered by a specific event. When feelings of frustration and hostility are widespread, leaders can easily recruit and command members. With aggressive leadership, an angry, frustrated mob in an atmosphere of hostility can be readily motivated to riot, commit lynchings, throw firebombs, hang people in effigy, or engage in destructive orgies.

Mob violence has erupted in many different circumstances. During the French Revolution of the 1780s and 1790s, angry mobs stormed through Paris, breaking into the Bastille prison for arms and calling for the execution of Louis XVI. In nineteenth-century England, enraged workers burned the factories in which they worked. Lynchings of blacks in the United States for real or imagined offenses continued into the twentieth century, often with little or no opposition from the formal agencies of control—police, courts, and public officials. Although lynch mobs are uncommon today, occasional instances of mob behavior take place over civil rights issues such as busing or housing, during political conventions and rallies, and among student or labor groups angry about perceived injustices. In 1987, for example, mob violence erupted in all-white Forsyth County, Georgia, when a white mob disrupted a march by whites and blacks protesting discriminatory antiblack housing policy.

Riots are collective actions involving mass violence and mob actions. The targets of their hostility and violence are less specific than those of mobs, and the groups involved are more diffuse. Most riots result from an intense hatred of a particular group with no specific person or property in mind. Destruction, burning, or looting may be indiscriminate, and unfocused anger can lead to violent acts against any object or person who happens to be in the wrong area at the wrong time. Like mobs, rioters take actions into their own hands when they feel that institutional reaction to their concerns about war, poverty, racial injustices, or other problems is inadequate.

—Eshleman et al., *Sociology: An Introduction*, pp. 487–90

VOCABULARY REVIEW

1. For each of the words listed below, use context; prefixes, roots, and suffixes; and/or a dictionary to write a brief definition or synonym of the word as it is used in the reading.

   a. anonymity (para. 1, 2) _____

   b. suggestible (para. 1, 3) _____

    c. contagion (para. 1, 4) _____

    d. arousal (para. 1, 5) _____

    e. evangelist (para. 4) _____

    f. uncharacteristic (para. 5) _____

    g. volatile (para. 5) _____

    h. typifies (para. 9) _____

    i. disdainful (para. 10) _____

    j. channels (para. 10) _____

    k. predisposed (para. 11) _____

    l. effigy (para. 11) _____

    m. orgies (para. 11) _____

    n. diffuse (para. 13) _____

    o. indiscriminate (para. 13) _____

2. Underline new specialized terms introduced in the reading.

COMPREHENSION QUESTIONS

1. Identify and explain the four features of a crowd.
2. Name two characteristics that all crowds have in common.
3. Describe the difference between a "casual" crowd and a "conventional" crowd.
4. What are two forms of acting crowds?
5. Describe a mob and give an example of one.
6. How do mobs and riots differ from one another?

THINKING CRITICALLY

1. Explain how school pep rallies make use of the four features of a crowd to engage the spectators.
2. How can we use our knowledge of crowds to prevent crowd violence?
3. Give a specific example of a persuasive leader inciting a crowd to violence.
4. Explain why the right of people to assemble is often the first right restricted by leaders who gain governmental control forcibly.

LEARNING/STUDY STRATEGIES

1. Review the section on "Characteristics of Crowds" by completing the following study chart on features of crowds and how they support unacceptable behaviors by individuals within the crowd.

FEATURE	SUPPORTS UNACCEPTABLE BEHAVIOR BY:
1.	
2.	
3.	
4.	

2. What is the overall thought pattern used in this reading?

ONLINE RESEARCH: CROWD BEHAVIOR*

Sociology, like the other social sciences, has many practical applications. For example, examine these sites on the World Wide Web (WWW) that describe two different types of crowd management. Then answer the questions that follow.

1. Go to http://crowdsafe.com/taskrpt/chpt1.html to access "Crowd Management," part of a report on managing crowd behavior at public events such as concerts. In the second section, "Crowd Behavior," sociologist Dr. Irving Goldaber is quoted as saying that various "sociological signals" received by people attending an event can influence their behavior. What specific examples does the report give of these signals?
2. Go to http://www.animationartist.com/2002/07_jul/features/digitalcrowds.htm. Read over the first page of the article, "Digital Crowds." Discuss how crowd behavior and management is important to filmmakers and video game creators.

*If either of these sites is unavailable, use a search engine to locate a new Web site on the same topic.

The SOCIAL SCIENCES on the Internet

The Internet has numerous resources available for research in the social sciences, including directories and Web guides to help you find material relevant to your studies, journals and databases, references works, and government resources. Here is a list of useful academic Web sites to get you started.

Directories/Web Guides

The Virtual Library: Social Sciences
http://vlib.org/SocialSciences.html

Yahoo! Social Science
http://dir.yahoo.com/Social_Science/

Open Directory Project: Social Sciences
http://dmoz.org/Science/Social_Sciences/

Journals/Indexes/Databases

Social Sciences Electronic Journals
http://www.clas.ufl.edu/users/gthursby/socsci/ejournal.htm

ERIC
http://www.eric.ed.gov/

References

The Internet Public Library: Social Sciences Resources
http://www.ipl.org/ref/RR/static/soc00.00.00.html

Galileo Internet Resources from the University System of Georgia
http://www.usg.edu/galileo/internet/social/socialsc.html

Government Resources

National Center for Education Statistics
http://nces.ed.gov/

USGS National Mapping Information
http://mapping.usgs.gov/

Multimedia Activities

Practice your reading and research skills on the Web.

1. **University of Pennsylvania Museum of Archaeology and Anthropology**
   http://www.upenn.edu/museum/Collections/ourgalleries.html
   Write down some questions about different cultures that you would expect to be answered at this Web site. Include questions that stem from the thought patterns of the social sciences. Then view one of the galleries featured on the Web site and find the answers to your questions. Review the information and write a short essay or teach a friend about what you learned.

2. **American Psychological Society: Psychological Research on the Net**
   http://psych.hanover.edu/Research/exponnet.html
   Take part in some online experiments and contribute to important research. A special September 11 section consists of studies that ask questions about your thoughts, feelings, and actions since the terrorist attacks.

CHAPTER 14

READING IN BUSINESS

LEARNING OBJECTIVES

- ✦ To understand the focus of business courses
- ✦ To develop specialized reading techniques for business
- ✦ To discover thought patterns commonly used in business
- ✦ To adapt study techniques for business courses

Business is a diverse field that includes business management, information systems, accounting, finance, statistics, retailing, organizational behavior, and corporate strategy. In general, business is concerned with the production and sale of economic goods or services that satisfy people's needs and yield a profit. Because business is a broad field, course work for a degree in business often includes requirements in such related fields as computer science, economics, and communications.

BUSINESS: A FOCUS ON ORGANIZATION AND MANAGEMENT

Suppose you decided to start a new business that would produce and sell six varieties of gourmet desserts throughout the country. Now suppose you hired 200 employees and that all you told your workers was that their job was to make and sell these desserts. Your business would probably be a dismal failure; none of your employees would know what to do or how to do it. Your business lacked two essential ingredients: organization and management. These ingredients also are a key to your success in getting the most from your business courses.

Organization is a system or structure, and management is a process by which all parts of the system—employees, technology, job responsibilities, and resources—are combined and coordinated. In business courses, you study how businesses are set up and how they are made to operate effectively. These two key aspects, however, encompass numerous other areas: product development, communication, marketing, labor relations, retailing, advertising, financing, banking, accounting, computer systems, legal aspects, and international trade.

Business courses are practical, then. They deal with aspects of creating or operating a business. Business courses are interrelated. Business economics courses use concepts from accounting; marketing courses use concepts from management courses, and so on. Math is also an important part of some business courses. For advice on reading mathematics, see Chapter 16.

Why Study Business?

All of us are in contact with businesses on a daily basis. When you stop for gas, buy a sandwich, or pick up the telephone, you are involved in a business transaction. The world of business surrounds us. Business courses have a number of advantages, as follows:

- Business courses can make you a savvy, better-informed consumer. You discover how to make better-informed buying decisions and how to spend your money wisely.
- Business courses will help you make career decisions. You will discover a wide range of employment opportunities.
- Business courses will help you become a successful employee. Getting a job is only the first step to a successful career; you must be proficient at it. By learning how businesses operate, you will be able to contribute effectively to your company.
- Business courses will help you start your own business. If you plan to start your own business, business courses will give you the knowledge and skills to make your business a success.

Current Hot Topics in Business

Whenever you take a course, you should always try to discover the trends, issues, and themes that are emphasized. Identifying these "hot topics" will help you predict essay exam questions, choose worthwhile topics for papers and assignments, and make valuable contributions to class discussions.

In business courses, there are at least five current topics:

- **Globalization of Business.** Growing numbers of U.S. companies are doing business with firms in other countries. U.S. businesses compete in foreign markets, and the number of international trade agreements continues to grow. Consequently, it is important to recognize business as an international venture and understand the role of the U.S. in the world market.
- **Role of Technology.** As technology continues to develop and change, so must businesses change and adapt to keep pace. The Internet, telecommunications, computers, and robotics all have an impact on business. For example, growing numbers of businesses have Web sites; increasing numbers of employees are telecommuting (working at home), and small robots are used increasingly in manufacturing. Awareness of technology will keep you on the cutting edge of business growth and change.

- **Importance of Diversity.** Today's workforce consists of individuals from a variety of cultural and ethnic groups. A wider range of interests, social customs, and value systems is represented. Diversity can be a strong advantage for a company by offering a variety of resources and perspectives.

- **Growth and Role of Small Businesses.** Increasingly, small businesses are a major source of employment. A report to the president on the state of small businesses estimates that nearly 71 percent of future employment is likely to come from small businesses. Besides providing employment, small businesses provide competition and are responsible for change and innovation. Many people mistakenly think of businesses as only large corporations. By recognizing the role and importance of small businesses, you will approach business courses with a broadened perspective.

- **Importance of Ethical Decisions and Social Responsibility.** There is an increasing emphasis in business on making ethical decisions and demonstrating social responsibility. Business ethics is the application of moral standards to business situations. Ethical issues include fairness and honesty, conflict of interest (between personal and business interests), and communication. Using misleading advertising, falsifying information, taking bribes, and endangering a consumer's health are examples of ethical problems that companies strive to avoid.

SPECIALIZED READING TECHNIQUES

Business courses often require you to read and work with models, case studies and specialized graphics. The following sections describe these features and offer strategies for reading each one.

Reading Models

Because business courses focus on organization and management, many texts include models to describe these structures and processes. A model is an overall plan or representation that describes how something is designed, how it functions, or why it occurs.

Models contain general features or characteristics that pertain to many situations. For example, you could construct a model that describes the enrollment/advisement/registration process at your college. It would describe the procedures most students follow from the time they apply for college admission to the time they first attend classes.

Models also may function as explanations of complex processes. For example, you may study models of decision making, information processing, or leadership. These models contain all the pertinent variables, factors, and characteristics that control how something works or explain why it occurs. Diagrams often accompany text descriptions of the model.

The following excerpt shows a model and accompanying introductory explanation taken from a business text. It describes how a company develops short-term financial plans. The remainder of the chapter from which this introduction was taken provides detailed information about the process. The excerpt has been annotated to indicate the types of information to look for as you read models.

SHORT-TERM (OPERATING) FINANCIAL PLANS

purpose/function

time frame

key parts

reference to diagram

Short-term (operating) financial plans specify short-term financial actions and the anticipated impact of those actions. These plans most often cover a 1- to 2-year period. Key inputs include the sales forecast and various forms of operating and financial data. Key outputs include a number of operating budgets, the cash budget, and pro forma [document prepared in advance] financial statements. The entire short-term financial planning process is outlined in the flow diagram of Figure A (p. 409).

summary of model

Short-term financial planning begins with the sales forecast. From it production plans are developed that take into account lead (preparation) times and include estimates of the required types and quantities of raw materials. Using the production plans, the firm can estimate direct labor requirements, factory overhead outlays, and operating expenses. Once these estimates have been made, the firm's pro forma income statement and cash budget can be prepared. With the basic inputs—pro forma income statement, cash budget, fixed asset outlay plan, long-term financing plan, and current period balance sheet—the pro forma balance sheet can finally be developed. Throughout the remainder of this chapter, we will concentrate on the key outputs of the short-term financial planning process: the cash budget, the pro forma income statement, and the pro forma balance sheet.

—Gitman, *Principles of Managerial Finance,* pp. 581–82

When reading and studying models, be sure to:

1. *Find out what the model represents and why it is considered a model.* In the example above, the model explains the short-term financial planning process and factors that affect it. You should also know who developed the model and when it was developed. A model often is named after the person who proposed it.

2. *Determine how the model was derived.* Was it developed through study and research (theory), or by observing and working with the actual process (practice)? (In the previous excerpt, the text author does not include information on the development of the model under discussion.)

3. *Analyze the model closely.* Identify each stage or step, and understand the relationship between the parts or steps. If a diagram such as the one shown in the preceding excerpt is not included, try to draw one.

4. *Summarize the model in your own words, including its key features.* This will test your understanding and strengthen your recall.

Figure A   The Short-Term (Operating) Financial Planning Process

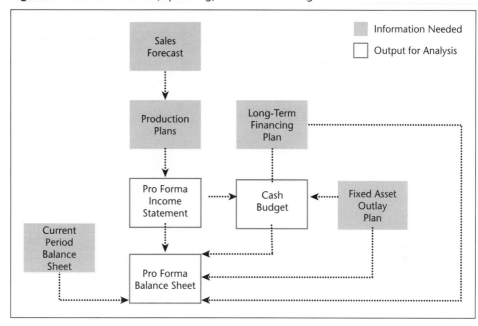

5. *Examine the model critically.* Does it account for all aspects or variations of the process? What are its limitations?

6. *Determine the usefulness or application of the model.* How and when can you use it? To what practical situations will it apply? The author may suggest applications or this task may be left to the reader.

7. *If more than one model is presented for a given process, focus on their similarities and differences.*

EXERCISE 14–1

The following excerpt presents a model of group collaboration—the process whereby members of a group work together toward a common goal. Study the model and answer the accompanying questions.

CHARACTERISTICS OF GROUP COLLABORATION

Group collaboration has several characteristics. One characteristic is *when* the collaboration takes place and another is *where* it takes place. This section examines these characteristics to provide a basis for understanding workgroup information systems.

Time and Place of Collaboration

Two of the basic characteristics of group collaboration are *time* and *place*—the "when" and "where" of collaboration. The figure on page 410 titled "Time and place

Figure A   Time and Place of Group Collaboration

Same time • Different place   Different time • Different place

PLACE

Different

Same

Same time • Same place   Different time • Same place

Same   Different

TIME

of group collaboration," shows these characteristics in two dimensions. If two or more people collaborate, they may do so at the same time or at different times. To work together at the same time, they could be in a room together or talk by telephone. To collaborate at different times, they could leave voice messages, send faxes, use overnight delivery, or send regular mail.

People may also work together at the same place or at different places. They may be in the same room or building, making it possible for them to have direct contact. Alternatively, they may be at widely separated locations, in which case they cannot have direct contact without extensive travel.

The figure shows four possible combinations of these characteristics. People working at the same time and place can collaborate directly. A face-to-face meeting is an example of this type of collaboration. People working at the same time but in different places often use the telephone for collaboration. Conference calls also are common in this situation. When people work at different times but at the same place, they collaborate by leaving messages, either on the telephone or by paper notes. Putting written messages in mailboxes in staff mail rooms is a common way of communicating in this situation. The most complex situation is when people working at different times and places need to collaborate. Voice messages, faxes, overnight deliveries, and regular mail are used in this situation.

Form of Communication

Another way of characterizing group collaboration is by the *form* that the communication between people takes—the "what" of collaboration. The figure on page 411 titled "Forms of communication in group collaboration," summarizes some of

Figure B   Forms of Communication in Group Collaboration

Audio communication

Live   Recorded

Visual communication

Live   Recorded

Still   Moving

Document (data) communication

Text   Numbers   Table   Diagram   Graph

the forms taken. Perhaps the most often used form of communication in business is *audio communication;* people talk to each other, either in person or on the telephone. Audio communication is not only what is said, but also how it is said. Tone, inflection, and other characteristics of speech often express information. In addition to live, verbal communication, recorded sound is used in group collaboration. Voice mail, taped sound, and other recorded sound are part of audio communication.

A second form of communication in group collaboration is *visual communication,* specifically sights of people or other real things. When groups meet in person, the members of the group can see each other. Their facial expressions and body language give visual clues that provide information about what they are saying and thinking. Recorded sights also are used in some collaborative situations. Still pictures or moving images on video tape may be shown to groups for discussion.

A final form of communication used in group collaboration is *document* (or *data*) *communication.* Documents may contain text, numbers, table, diagrams, graphs, and other written representations of information. Examples are a report sent to members of a team, a table of data examined by committee members, a diagram of a design examined by several people, and a graph of data discussed by a group.

—Nickerson, *Business and Information Systems,* pp. 263–65

1. What is the model intended to show?
2. Summarize the process described in the model.
3. Evaluate the model. Does the model account for all possibilities? What are its limitations?
4. Of what practical use is the model? When might you use it?

Reading Case Studies

Case studies often are included in business texts. Case studies are reports of single incidents or evaluations of a particular individual, firm, or transaction. They describe how a particular business is organized or how it manages a particular problem or process. They may be intended to introduce a concept, illustrate a principle, describe a situation, or provoke discussion and evaluation. Case studies also give you insights into and experience with actual problems or situations you may face on the job. In some texts, case studies are referred to as "business profiles" or simply as "cases." Other texts include a short case study, known as a "vignette," that provides a brief insight into a particular problem or issue.

The brief case study that follows appears in a marketing text. As you read it, try to discover why it was included in a chapter titled "Managing the Business Enterprise." The excerpt has been annotated to indicate the kinds of information presented.

This case study describes how a small company, Maine Roasters, has faced competition from Starbucks. The case was included to provide an example of how a small business operates and copes with competition.

When reading a case study, keep the following questions in mind.

1. What is the subject of the case study?

2. What key points does it make about the subject of the chapter?

3. What is the case study intended to demonstrate? For example, does it illustrate practical problems? Discuss limitations? Point out advantages or disadvantages? Demonstrate a process? Describe a management strategy? Demonstrate a particular philosophy or approach?

GROUNDS FOR THE DEFENSE

Maine Roasters
versus
Starbucks

In some ways it's like David and Goliath—a small upstart New England coffee retailer called Maine Roasters going toe-to-toe with Starbucks www.starbucks.com, the fastest-growing and, arguably, the highest-profile food and beverage company in the United States. To understand the competitive dynamics of this situation, let's

background about Starbucks first find out how Starbucks became the big kid on the block. It was started in Seattle in 1971 by three coffee aficionados. Their primary business at the time was buying premium coffee beans, roasting them, and then selling the coffee by the pound. The business performed modestly well and soon grew to nine stores, all in the Seattle area. When they thought their business growth had stalled in 1987, the three partners sold Starbucks to a former employee named Howard Schultz. Schultz promptly reoriented, trading in bulk coffee sales for retail coffee sales through the firm's coffee bars.

Starbucks' status today Today Starbucks is not only the country's largest coffee importer and roaster of specialty beans but also the largest specialty coffee bean retailer in the United States. There are more than 2,100 Starbucks locations in the United States. The firm has revenues of over $1.7 billion a year, annual profits of almost $102 million, and a workforce of more than 37,000 employees.

Starbucks in competition with Maine Roasters Given the enormous marketing and financial muscle that a company like Starbucks brings to the table, imagine how Rand Smith, the owner of Maine Roasters www.maineroasters.qpg.com, a small coffee shop in Portland, Maine, reacted when he heard that the coffee Goliah was coming to town. "It's Maine versus the national giant," said Smith, who decided to load whatever slingshot he could find.

Maine Roasters' strategy Smith's strategy was grounded in the passion and loyalty that exist among Maine residents for the sanctity of their home state. He has mounted a finely tuned plan for portraying Starbucks as a big bully from the "outside" and his own upstart operation as the homespun underdog. To promote this image, every morning he dispatches a team of his employees to stand outside the Starbucks restaurant closest to his own store to pass out chocolate drops and to encourage Starbucks customers to "Support a Maine-owned-and-operated company." So far, his efforts are paying off. The locaL paper, for example, has editorialized against corporate heavyweights, community groups have picketed Starbucks, and there has even been a spate of vandalism against Starbucks, usually involving broken store windows. Smith does not condone such tactics, but he no doubt privately sees each stone being thrown through a Starbucks window as a metaphor for the stone with which David felled Goliath in an earlier time.

local support So far, Maine Roasters is holding its own in its hometown of Portland, Maine. Rand Smith's strategy of pitching his small company as a David to Starbucks' Goliath has attracted considerable local sympathy. But Smith faces some other problems, too. For one thing, even as he pitches his business as a local, down-home operation, his original business plan called for more than 30 stores spread throughout New England. (As of yet, only a handful have been opened.) Smith openly acknowledges the inherent contradiction in his portrayal of Starbucks and his own vision. He also sees the day when he might very well be interested in selling his company—and thinks Starbucks might be the most logical buyer. In an

Starbucks' effect on business plan especially ironic twist, he actually credits Starbucks with boosting sales at his coffee shops by educating consumers about specialty coffees and, thus, broadening the local market.

Starbucks' effect on sales

—Ebert and Griffen, *Business Essentials,* pp. 114–15, 134–35

Read the following brief case study taken from a business textbook chapter titled "An Overview of Marketing," and answer the questions that follow.

CAMPBELL SOUP SERVES UP VARIETY

Over 120 years ago, the Campbell Soup Company introduced canned condensed soup and gave the world its first convenience food. Since then, those well-known red and white labels and the sigh "Mmmm, mmmm, good" have become symbols of American culture. However, today's increasingly health-conscious consumers often spurn canned soup in favor of those made with fresh ingredients. Although sales of the popular brand total $1.1 billion, earning the line 48.9 percent of the canned soup market, Campbell faces declining domestic sales. Turning to global markets, the company's executives hope that by the year 2000, more than half of the firm's profits will come from sales outside the United States.

Experts caution that strong cultural and regional tastes and preferences make food more difficult to translate to foreign markets than soda or laundry detergent. The editor of *Food and Drink Daily* recently stressed the importance of recognizing the unique characteristics of individual global market segments. Just because Americans love to ladle out clam chowder and tomato soup by the bowl full doesn't mean those same flavors appeal to customers around the world. Marketers at Campbell know that demographics, lifestyle, and geography influence customer choices, with diet especially sensitive to local fancies. To avoid potential pitfalls that differences often create, Campbell conducts extensive research in specific consumer segments before generating and marketing brands.

All over the globe, Campbell's research and taste tests are resulting in new, locally pleasing recipes. In Argentina, consumers don't take to the enduring American favorite, chicken noodle soup, but they do like split pea with ham. Emphasizing *Sopa de Campbell's* fresh ingredients, regional ads proclaim it "the real soup." Polish soup lovers, who eat an average of five bowls each week, can choose from eight varieties of Campbell's *zupa,* including *flaki*—tripe soup spiced with lots of pepper. To please Mexican palates, Campbell came up with hot and spicy Cream of Chile Poblano.

To become a major player in the global market, Campbell will face stiff competition. British consumers, for example, have known and preferred Heinz canned soup for many years. To attract more British shoppers, Campbell is creating new products developed specifically to meet English tastes. To expand its Japanese distribution from Tokyo and Osaka to include all of Japan, the soupmaker recently entered a joint venture with Nakano Vinegar Company of Japan.

Is the world ready for Campbell's soup? The company's CEO believes the answer is a resounding yes. His considerable international experience—as a former marketing executive with Colgate-Palmolive in South Africa and with Parke-Davis in Hong Kong—tells him that responding to consumer preferences leads to increased sales.

—Pride et al., *Business,* pp. 386–87

1. What is the purpose of the case study?
2. What is this case study intended to demonstrate about global marketing?

3. What does this study tell you about the problems of global marketing?
4. What motivated the Campbell Soup Company to explore global marketing?
5. What factors influence consumer choice of soups?

Graphics: Reading Organization Charts

Because the focus in the field of business is on organization and process, business texts frequently include graphs, charts, and tables to synthesize and/or summarize text material that describes those structures and processes. Chapter 9 offers general techniques for reading each of these graphic aids.

Particularly common in the field of business is the organization chart. Organization charts often are used to reflect structure or to define relationships; they may, for example, show levels of responsibility, roles, or functions. The chart shown in Figure 14–1 describes the organization of a corporation, emphasizing its financial structure.

Organization charts also may be used to describe group behaviors or define employee responsibilities. The impact of decisions or marketing strategies, and the classification of markets, also may be shown on an organization chart.

When reading organization charts, keep in mind the following tips.

1. *Read the text that accompanies the chart.* It should establish the context and provide details about the chart.

2. *Read the caption or title of the chart.* Note the key, abbreviations, or coding.

3. *Study the chart carefully.* Determine how the chart is organized. Charts often use a vertical or horizontal structure, moving from top to bottom or left to right in diminishing degrees of authority, importance, or responsibility. In Figure 14–1, the chart is organized vertically, with the positions of highest authority at the top.

4. *Decide how the items are related.* In Figure 14–1, each position on the same horizontal line is of equal importance.

5. *Determine what pattern, principle, or concept the chart describes.* Figure 14–1 on the next page describes the financial functions within a corporation.

EXERCISE 14–3   *Study the organization chart shown in Figure 14–2 on page 416, and answer the questions that follow.*

1. What is the chart intended to show?
2. Describe how the chart is organized and how the items are related.

EXERCISE 14–4   *Construct an organization chart that describes the structure of an organization (college, church, club, or business) with which you are familiar.*

Figure 14–1 Organization Chart

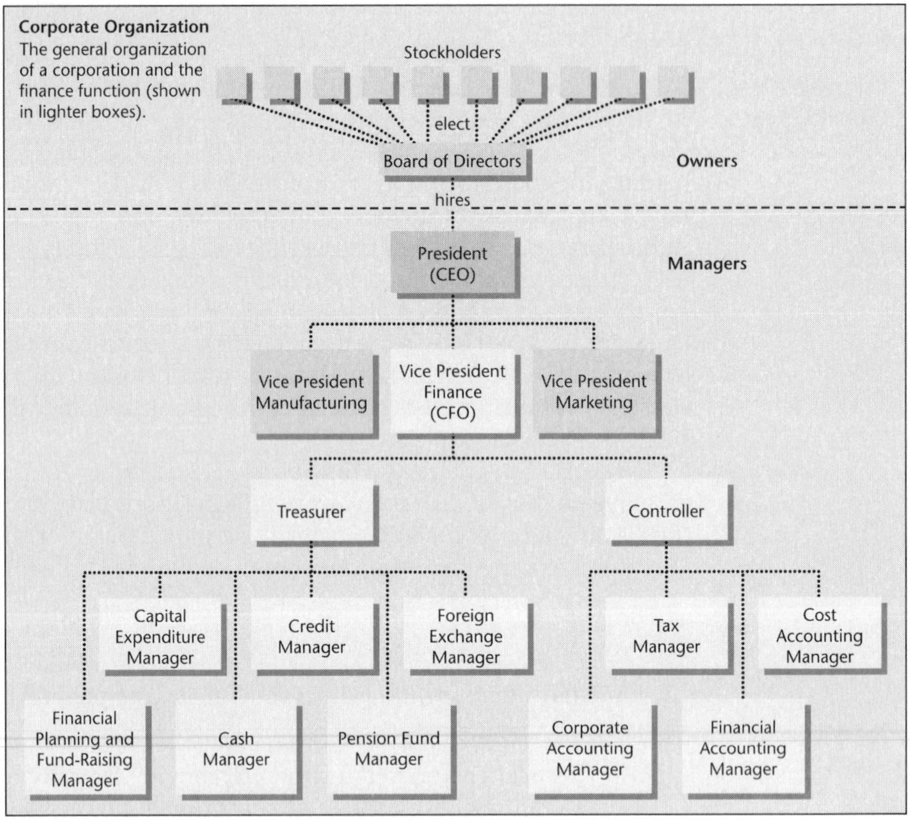

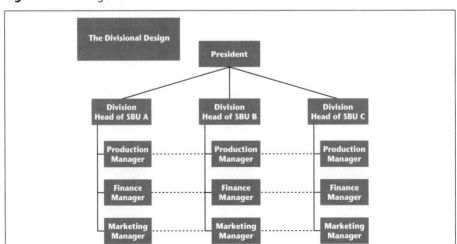

Source: Gitman, *Principles of Managerial Finance,* p. 8

Figure 14–2 Organization Chart

Source: Van Fleet, *Contemporary Management,* p. 251

Graphics: Reading Flowcharts

A flowchart is a specialized diagram that shows how a process or procedure works. Lines or arrows are used to show the direction (route or routes) through the procedure. Various shapes (boxes, circles, rectangles) enclose what is done at each stage or step. You could, for example, draw a flowchart to describe how to apply for and obtain a student loan or how to locate a malfunction in your car's electrical system.

A sample flowchart, taken from a business and information systems text, is shown in Figure 14–3; it describes the information flow related to sales.

Figure 14–3   Sample Flowchart

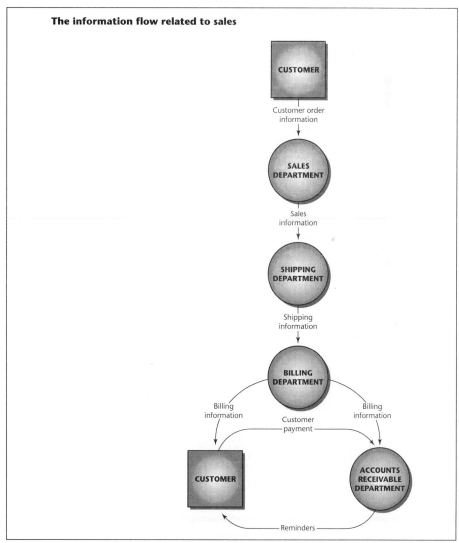

Source: Nickerson, *Business and Information Systems,* p. 40

To read flowcharts effectively, use the following suggestions:

1. Figure out what process the flowchart illustrates. Figure 14–3 shows the process by which information flows from a sale.

2. Next, follow the arrows, and read each step in the chart.

3. When you have finished, summarize the process in your own words. For example, you might write "When a customer places an order, the order information is transmitted to the sales department. The sales department sends sales information to the shipping department; the shipping department sends shipping information to the billing department who sends billing information to the customer and to the accounts receivable department. Customer payment is sent to the accounts receivable department, which also sends reminders to customers." Then try to draw the chart from memory without referring to the text. Compare your drawing with the chart, and note any discrepancies.

EXERCISE 14–5   *The flowchart shown in Figure 14–4, taken from a business text, describes a process for human resource planning. Study the chart and then, without referring to it, list the steps or sketch your own flowchart.*

Figure 14–4 Flowchart

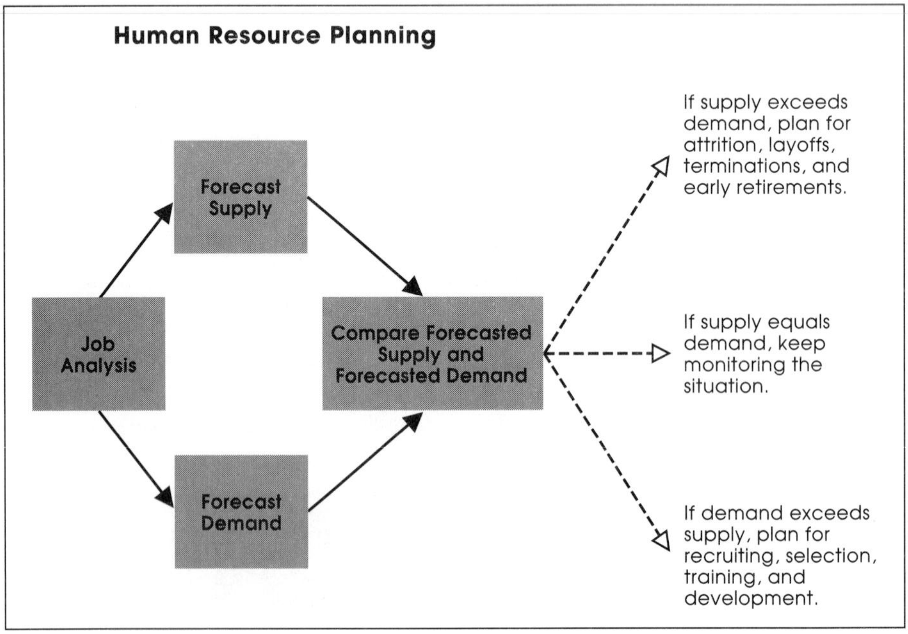

Source: Van Fleet, *Contemporary Management*, p. 270

THOUGHT PATTERNS IN BUSINESS

The three most common thought patterns you will find in business courses are classification, process, and enumeration, although others may be used as well. Refer to Chapter 7 for a complete discussion of these patterns.

Classification—subdividing a topic into its parts—is commonly encountered because it is an effective means of describing the components of management. Process—the study of how events occur—is used frequently because of the focus on *how* a business operates and is managed. Enumeration, or listing, is a commonly used pattern because much information in the business field is descriptive: listings of characteristics, factors, principles, and theories that affect a business's organization and management. A sample page from the table of contents of a business marketing text is shown in Figure 14–5. The figure is marked to indicate the patterns you should anticipate. As you can see, process, enumeration, and classification patterns appear, as well as definition and comparison-contrast.

Figure 14–5   Table of Contents

Source: Nickerson, *Business and Information Systems,* p. xvii

ADAPTING YOUR STUDY TECHNIQUES

Because the field of business is diverse and includes courses in a wide range of topics, it is especially important to adapt your study techniques to suit each course you are taking. Here are a few suggestions for handling your course load.

1. *Begin each class by analyzing course content.* Study course objectives, pay close attention to the course syllabus, and analyze your textbook's preface and individual chapter learning objectives for additional clues. Then select reading and study strategies for each course. Figure out what types of reading are required and what level of recall is demanded; then identify appropriate reading strategies to use. Refer to Chapter 2 for a discussion of adjusting your reading rate. Also select appropriate learning and review strategies and decide how writing could help you with each course. (Refer to Chapter 8 for a review of various strategies.)

2. *Take time to shift gears.* It is important to "shift gears" as you move from studying one course to studying another. Do this by taking a 10- to 15-minute break between study periods. As you begin working on the next course, spend a minute or two focusing your attention on it. You can do this easily by reviewing a previous assignment, your last set of lecture notes, or the last homework assignment you completed. Finally, preview your current assignment, define your goals, and set a time limit to complete the task. Monitor your comprehension as you work, by using the suggestions in Chapter 1.

3. *Use available text supplements.* Some business texts have accompanying study guides, problem sets, exercise books, or simulations. If they are recommended by your instructor, they will guide you in applying chapter content. These guides also will introduce you to the type of questions you may be asked on exams. Some of these materials are available on computer diskettes or CDs as well as in printed form.

4. *Use chapter aids.* Business textbook chapters typically contain numerous features that supplement and enhance basic chapter content. These include learning objectives, lists of keywords, chapter outlines, special-interest material, summaries, and review exercises. These features are intended to make the chapter easier to understand, study, and learn. Chapter 8 describes how to use each of these features effectively.

5. *Learn formulas and problem-solving strategies.* Some courses, such as accounting, investment, and finance, rely heavily on learning formulas and solving problems. For reading and study strategies useful in these courses, refer to Chapter 16, "Reading Mathematics."

Test-Taking Tips
Objective Exams

Exams in business are often objective. Refer to the test-taking tips in Chapter 13 for suggestions on preparing for objective exams. When taking exams, keep the following suggestions in mind.

1. *Be sure to arrive at the exam on time.* Sit in the front of the room; you will avoid distractions and be able to concentrate more easily.

2. *Preread the exam.* Look through the whole exam before beginning. Then plan your time: decide how much time to spend on each part.

3. *Read the directions carefully.*

4. *Leave nothing blank.* Guess if you are not sure of an answer; circle the question number so you can return to it later if you have time.

5. *Be sure to read all choices before answering a multiple-choice question;* often, the directions require you to select the "best" choice.

6. *If you are uncertain about a multiple-choice item, eliminate obviously wrong choices.* Then analyze those that remain. When two choices seem similar, analyze how they differ.

7. *Express similar or confusing choices in your own words.* Often, this process will help you discover the right answer.

SUMMARY

This chapter describes specialized reading strategies for business. This diverse field focuses on the organization and management of various types of businesses.

Specialized reading techniques involve

- interpreting models
- reading case studies
- understanding graphics (including organization charts and flowcharts) and supplemental readings

Three thought patterns predominate in business texts:

- classification
- process
- enumeration

Ideas for adapting study strategies to suit business courses are offered.

Marketing

PREREADING QUESTIONS

1.   What is a product life cycle?
2.   What factors influence how long a product's life cycle will last?

Marketing Throughout the Product Life Cycle

Michael R. Solomon and Elnora W. Stuart

1   The zipper is an example of a humble, low-tech product that has managed to live an exceptionally long life. Invented in the 1800s, the zipper was not used in men's clothing until the 1930s. These "hookless fasteners," as they were once called, were originally intended for use on high-buttoned shoes. It took time to be used in men's trousers because competitors argued that this "newfangled gadget" could result in serious injuries (ouch!). In 1936 the Prince of Wales adopted the zipper and was the first monarch to "sit on a throne bezippered."

product life cycle
Concept that explains how products go through four distinct stages from birth to death: introduction, growth, maturity, and decline.

2   In fact, many products have very long lives. The **product life cycle** is a useful way to explain how product features change over the life of a product. In chapter 9 we talked about how marketers go about introducing new products, but launching a product is only the beginning. Product marketing strategies must evolve and change as they continue through the product life cycle.

3   The concept of the product life cycle does not relate to a single brand but to the generic product. Thus, we talk about the life cycle of personal computers, not Compaq computers, of automobiles, not Mustangs. Some individual brands may have short life expectancies. Who remembers the Nash car, or Evening in Paris perfume? Others seem almost immortal: A Boston Consulting Group study found that 27 or 30 brands that were number one in 1930 are still number one today. These brands include Ivory soap, Campbell's soup, and Gold Medal flour.[5]

THE INTRODUCTION STAGE

introduction
The first stage of the product life cycle in which slow growth follows the introduction of a new product in the marketplace.

4   We can divide the life of a product into four separate stages. The first stage of the product life cycle, shown in Figure A, is **introduction** when customers get their first chance to purchase the good or service. During this early stage, a single company usually produces the product. If the product is accepted and profitable, competitors will follow with their own versions.

5   During the introduction stage, the goal is to get first-time buyers to try the product. Sales (hopefully) increase at a steady but slow pace. Also evident in Figure A, the company does not make a profit during this stage. Why? Two reasons:

Figure A   The Product Life Cycle

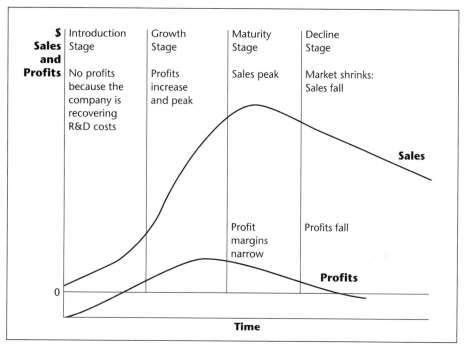

research and development (R&D) costs and heavy spending for advertising and other promotional costs.

6   During the introduction stage, pricing may be high to recover the research and development costs (demand permitting) or low to attract large numbers of consumers. For example, the Panasonic digital Palmcorder has a suggested retail price that's about double that of Panasonic's nondigital Palmcorders and is designed to appeal to consumers who are willing to pay dearly for the latest technological advances. The high cost helps Panasonic recover its R&D costs.

7   How long does the introduction stage last? As we saw in chapter 9's microwave oven example, it can be quite long. How long the introduction stage lasts depends on a number of factors, including marketplace acceptance and producer willingness to support the product during its start-up. In the case of the microwave, sales in countries such as Japan were much stronger, which supported the product through its long introduction stage.

8   Not all products make it past the introduction stage. For a new product to be successful, consumers must first know about it. Then they must believe that the product is something they need. Thus, marketing during this stage often focuses on informing consumers about the product, how to use it, and its benefits. Overall, 38 percent of all new products fail.[6]

9   One of the most noted examples of products that never got past the introduction stage is the Ford Edsel automobile. Introduced in 1957 and named after the

only son of Ford's founder, the Edsel was designed to compete with such cars as the Chrysler New Yorker. It boasted high horsepower, tail fins, three-tone paint jobs, wraparound windshields, a "horsecollar" grille, and a push-button gearshift. The problem was that consumers didn't like the Edsel (many considered it just plain ugly) and only 110,847 Edsels were made before Ford abandoned the car, making the word *Edsel* synonymous with failure.[7]

THE GROWTH STAGE

growth stage
The second stage in the product life cycle during which the product is accepted and sales rapidly increase.

10 The second stage in the product life cycle, the **growth stage,** sees a rapid increase in sales while profits increase and peak. Marketing's goal here is to encourage brand loyalty by convincing the market that this brand is superior to others in the categroy. In this stage marketing strategies may include the introduction of product variations to attract market segments and grow market share. When competitors appear, markets must use heavy advertising and other types of promotion. Price competition may develop, driving profits down. Some firms may seek to capture a particular segment of the market by positioning their product to appeal to a certain group.

THE MATURITY STAGE

maturity stage
The third and longest stage in the product life cycle in which sales peak and profit margins narrow.

11 The **maturity stage** of the product life cycle is usually the longest. Sales peak and then begin to level off and even decline while profit margins narrow. Competition grows intense when remaining competitors fight for a piece of a shrinking pie. Because most customers have already accepted the product, sales are often to replace a "worn-out" item or to take advantage of product improvements. For example, almost everyone owns a television so companies typically sell new TVs when consumers' sets die. During the maturity stage, firms will try to sell their product through all suitable retailers because product availability is crucial in a very competitive market. Consumers will not go far to find one brand when others are closer at hand.

12 To remain competitive and maintain market share during the maturity stage, firms may tinker with the marketing mix. Competitors may add new "bells and whistles" to their products' features, as when producers of potato chips and other snack foods modify their products. When consumers turned from high-fat snacks, chip makers gave them baked, "low-fat" products. In 1998 Frito-Lay introduced its WOW! Line of fat-free chips. And television manufacturers are hoping to invigorate sales with new flat-screen TVs.

13 Attracting new users of the product is another strategy used in the maturity stage. Market development, means introducing an existing product to a market that doesn't currently use it. Many U.S. firms are finding new markets in Eastern Europe for products whose domestic sales are lagging. For example, in the early 1990s, when IBM personal computers lost popularity in the United States, the company was able to capture a large percentage of the exploding Eastern European computer market.

THE DECLINE STAGE

decline stage
The final stage
in the product
life cycle in
which sales
decrease as
customer needs
change.

14 The **decline stage** of the product life cycle is characterized by a decrease in product category sales. Often this is because new technology has made the product obsolete, as when computers caused the decline of the typewriter. Although a single firm may still be profitable, the market as a whole begins to shrink, profits decline, and suppliers pull out. In this stage, there are usually many competitors with no one having a distinct advantage.

15 A firm's major product decision in the decline stage is whether or not to keep the product. Once the product is no longer profitable, it drains resources from the firm—resources that could help develop new products. If the decision is to drop the product, elimination may be handled in two ways: phase it out by cutting production in stages and letting existing stocks run out, or simply drop the product immediately. If the established market leader anticipates that there will be some residual demand for the product for a long time, it may make sense to keep the product on the market. The idea is to sell a limited quantity of the product with little or no support from sales, merchandising, advertising, and distribution and just let it "wither on the vine." Some classic products have been able to hang in there with little or no marketing support, such as the Pilot Stapler, which has been on the market for 70 years.

—Solomon and Stuart, *Marketing: Real People, Real Choices,* pp. 266–69

VOCABULARY REVIEW

1. For each of the words listed below, use context; prefixes, roots, and suffixes; and/or a dictionary to write a brief definition or synonym for the word as it is used in the reading.

   a. competitors (para. 1) _____

   b. generic (para. 3) _____

   c. expectancies (para. 3) _____

   d. profitable (para. 4) _____

   e. synonymous (para. 9) _____

   f. variations (para. 10) _____

   g. elimination (para. 15) _____

   h. residual (para. 15) _____

2. Underline new specialized terms introduced in the reading.

COMPREHENSION QUESTIONS

1. Why is a product life cycle considered only for generic products?
2. Name the four stages of a product life cycle.

3. Why doesn't the company make a profit during the introductory stage?
4. What two things need to happen for consumers to buy a product during the introductory stage?
5. What happens when price competition develops during the growth stage?
6. Why do most customers make purchases during the maturity stage?
7. If a product is phased out in the decline stage, what methods of elimination are used?
8. What is market development?

THINKING CRITICALLY

1. Give an example of a product you feel will be phased out and why.
2. If you wanted to increase the life cycle of a product, what steps could you take?
3. Give an example of a product not discussed in the selection that did not make it past the introductory stage. Why do you think this happened?
4. What kids of products would you expect to have long life cycles and why?
5. Name a product that is a favorite of yours that has had a long life cycle with little or no advertising support. Why do you think this product has lasted?

LEARNING/STUDY STRATEGY

Draw a chart that summarizes the factors that influence product life span. Use the following format.

Stage	Definition	Goal	Profits/Sales
1. Introduction			
2. Growth			
3. Maturity			
4. Decline			

ONLINE RESEARCH: PRODUCT LIFE CYCLE*

A large part of pushing a product through its life cycle is advertising. Visit these sites on the World Wide Web that provide more information on advertising, and answer the questions that follow.

*If either of these sites is unavailable, use a search engine to locate a new Web site on the same topic.

1. Read through the Advertising Timeline from the Web site of the American Advertising Museum (http://www.admuseum.org/museum/timeline/timeline.htm). What are the different techniques used in advertising? How do these techniques reflect the stages of a product's life cyle?

2. Advertising has become almost part of our daily existence. Read the scenarios at BadAds.org (http://www.badads.org/misc.shtml). Make a list of all the places you see advertising, and indicate whether you think these places are appropriate.

3. Read about product positioning at AdCracker.com (http://www.adcracker.com/position/). Make a list of memorable slogans. Have any of these influenced your buying habits?

BUSINESS on the Internet

The Internet has numerous resources available for research in the field of business, including directories and Web guides to help you find material relevant to your studies, journals and databases, references works, and government resources. Here is a list of useful Web sites to get you started.

Directories/Web Guides

Researching Companies Online
   http://home.sprintmail.com/~debflanagan/

Yahoo! Business and Economy
   http://dir.yahoo.com/business_and_economy/

Journals/Indexes/Databases

The Internet Public Library: Business and Economics Serials
   http://www.ipl.org/cgi-bin/reading/serials.out.pl?ty=long&id=bus00.00.00

Web-Ec List of Economics Journals
   http://netec.wustl.edu/WebEc/journals.html

Business News and Electronic Journals
   http://www.lib.washington.edu/subject/busecon/busnews/

References

Business Statistics
   http://www.lib.washington.edu/subject/BusinessStats/

Hoover's Online
   http://www.hoovers.com

Government Resources

U.S. Securities and Exchange Commission
   http://www.sec.gov/

Small Business Administration
   http://www.sba.gov/

Multimedia Activities

Practice your reading and research skills on the the Web.

1. **2000 State Occupational Employment and Wage Estimates**
   http://stats.bls.gov/oes/2000/oessrcst.htm
   The U.S. Bureau of Labor Statistics maintains a large site containing a great deal of information. Explore this section by picking a state and then an occupation category. View salary data for that occupation. Try comparing the data from different states. How can this information be useful?

2. **Researching Philanthropy—Top 100 U.S. Foundations by Total Giving**
   http://fdncenter.org/research/trends_analysis/top100giving.html
   Examine this chart compiled by the Foundation Center. Are you familiar with many of these organizations? What conclusions can you draw from this information? Find out more about a few of the foundations by following the links to their home pages. How much more information can you discover about their activities?

CHAPTER 15

READING IN THE HUMANITIES AND ARTS

LEARNING OBJECTIVES

✦ To learn specialized reading techniques for literature
✦ To develop an approach to studying visual arts
✦ To learn to read and use criticism
✦ To identify predominant thought patterns
✦ To adapt your learning skills for the humanities and arts

The humanities and the arts are areas of knowledge concerned with human thought and ideas and their creative expression in written or visual form. They deal with large, global questions such as, "What is worthwhile in life?" "What is moral?" "What is beautiful?" This chapter will consider two major branches of study: literature and the visual arts.

LITERATURE: A FOCUS ON IDEAS

Literature focuses on the search for reasons, values, and interpretation in all areas of human interest and experience. In literature classes, you will examine numerous literary works and will discuss and write about their value and meaning. Literature courses, then, concentrate on the analysis, subjective evaluation, and interpretation of ideas expressed through literary, philosophical, or artistic works. At first, literature courses may seem easier than other courses because most emphasize interpretation rather than factual recall. However, literature courses are demanding: they require critical reading, analysis, and evaluation.

Why Study Literature?

Literature describes human experience. It is a creative record of the thoughts, feelings, emotions, or experiences of other people. By reading literature, you can learn about yourself and understand both painful and joyful experiences without actually going though them yourself. For example, you can read a poem about the birth of a child and come to understand the range of feelings parents share, even though you may not be a parent. In other words, literature allows you to live vicariously, sharing the lives of others without physical participation.

READING AND ANALYZING LITERATURE

Literature includes poetry, drama, essays, short stories, and novels. Each is a literary form, or *genre,* through which a writer shares his or her view of the world and of humanity. The focus on reading any form of literature is interpretation. Your goal is to discover what the writer means. You are looking for a statement or message the writer is making about an issue, problem, attitude, or feeling. Use the following suggestions to guide your reading of literature.

- *Read slowly and carefully.* Literature uses language in unique ways that require interpretation and reaction. Consequently, you must read carefully and slowly, paying attention to numerous language features that provide clues to meaning. For example, observe word choice, syntax, and the order and arrangement of ideas.
- *Plan on reading the work several times.* Unlike some other types of material, a single reading is *not* sufficient to understand some literary works adequately. During the first reading, try to become familiar with the work and its literal meaning. On the second and subsequent readings, focus on the writer's message, on the significance of the work, and on literary concerns such as the use of language.
- *Ask questions to establish the literal meaning first; then work on interpretation.* In order to interpret and analyze a literary work, first try to understand it on a literal, or factual, level. An effective approach to reading literature is first to establish, "who did what, when, and where." Then ask why the writer wrote the piece and determine the message the writer is conveying.

Who?	Identify the subject or topic.
What is happening?	Describe the basic plot or sequence of events.
When/Where?	Establish the scene, setting, or context (for essays).
Why?	Why did the author write this?
Message?	What is the message the author is conveying and what is its significance?

This approach is shown in the following poem, "Mirror," written by Sylvia Plath.

Mirror
Sylvia Plath

I am silver and exact. I have no preconceptions.
Whatever I see I swallow immediately
Just as it is, unmisted by love or dislike.
I am not cruel, only truthful—
The eye of a little god, four-cornered.
Most of the time I meditate on the opposite wall.
It is pink, with speckles. I have looked at it so long
I think it is a part of my heart. But it flickers.
Faces and darkness separate us over and over.
Now I am a lake. A woman bends over me,
Searching my reaches for what she really is.
Then she turns to those liars, the candles or the moon.
I see her back, and reflect it faithfully.
She rewards me with tears and an agitation of hands.
I am important to her. She comes and goes.
Each morning it is her face that replaces the darkness.
In me she has drowned a young girl, and in me an old woman
Rises toward her day after day, like a terrible fish.

—*Crossing the Water* by Sylvia Plath

Questions	Responses
Who or What?	A mirror
What is happening?	Plath describes what the mirror reflects.
When/Where?	The mirror is hanging on a wall facing another wall.
Why?	Plath is using the mirror to comment on life and peoples' desire to know how they appear to others or to see their true selves.
Message?	The mirror is exact, accurate, and truthful. Life, in contrast, is affected, untruthful, and cruel.

- *Annotate as you read.* To understand the message, jot down your reactions, hunches, insights, feelings, and questions. Mark or underline words, sentences, or sections you feel are important statements, and words and phrases that provide clues to meaning. A sample annotation follows.

MIRROR
Sylvia Plath

consumes — I am silver and exact. I have no <u>preconceptions.</u> —— open—clear view
Whatever I see I(swallow)immediately

reality —— (Just as it is,)(unmisted by love or dislike.) —— unemotional,
untainted

I am <u>not cruel,</u> only <u>truthful</u> —— all
The eye of a little(god,)four-cornered. —— mirror is godlike—all knowing

reflecting
shows truth (Most of the time I meditate on the opposite wall.
whatever it is It is pink, with speckles. I have looked at it so long
I think it is a part of my heart. But it flickers.

deep, reflective —— Faces and darkness separate us over and over.)obstacles of life
Now I am a(lake.)A woman bends over me, searching for truth
<u>Searching my reaches for what she really is.</u> —— about herself

deceptive,
Then she turns to those <u>liars,</u> the(candles or the moon.) —— not faithful

not usually thought I see her back, and <u>reflect it faithfully.</u>
of as rewards She rewards me with(tears and an agitation of hands.)
I am important to her. She comes and goes. —— she comes and
Each morning it is her face that replaces the darkness. goes through reality

inescapable In me she has drowned a young girl, and in me an old woman) mirror
reality of aging Rises toward(her)day after day, like a terrible fish. holds
the past

- *Identify themes and patterns.* After you have read and annotated, the next
  step is to study your annotations, looking for themes and patterns. Try to
  discover how ideas work together to suggest themes. Themes are large or
  universal topics or subjects that are important to nearly everyone. A study
  of the Plath poem and annotations indicates that her theme is the realities
  of life. Possible themes in literature are

  - questions, issues, problems raised by the story: moral, political, philo-
    sophical, religious
  - abstract ideas: love, death, heroism, escapism, honor
  - conflicts: appearance versus reality, freedom versus restraint, poverty
    versus wealth, men against women, humans against society, humans
    versus nature
  - common literary topics: self-realization, inescapability of death, fall from
    innocence, search for the meaning of life

EXERCISE 15–1

*Refer to the multilevel thinking skills discussed in Chapter 1 and predict exam ques-
tions that might be asked about the Plath poem. Compare your questions with those of
another student.*

Understanding the Language of Literature

Literature is unique in its extensive use of descriptive, connotative, and figurative language to express images, attitudes, and feelings. In order to succeed in

your literature courses, you need to be able to use and understand the specialized vocabulary of literary works.

Descriptive Language   Writers often use words that create sensory impressions or responses. They are intended to help the reader re-create mentally what the author is describing. For example, in describing a stormy night, a poet may write, "Under the thunder-dark clouds, the storm mounts, flashes, and resounds." These terms give you a feeling about the storm and help you imagine its strength. Instead of saying two characters looked at each other, a novelist may write, "their eyes locked momentarily in a gaze, reflecting the strength of their opposing wills." Now, read the following paragraph. Note, in particular, the underlined words.

> Old men, old women, almost 20 million of them. They constitute 10 percent of the total population, and the percentage is steadily growing. Some of them, like <u>conspirators,</u> walk all <u>bent over, as if hiding some precious secret, filled with self-protection.</u> The body seems to gather itself around those vital parts, <u>folding shoulders,</u> arms, <u>pelvis like a fading rose.</u> Watch and you see how <u>fragile</u> old people come to think they are.
>
> —Curtin, "Aging in the Land of the Young,"
> *Nobody Ever Died of Old Age*

Connotative Language   The connotations of a word are the meanings it commonly suggests or implies beyond its primary, denotative meaning. Thus the word *dinner* denotes an evening meal but connotes a time of conversation, friendship, and interaction. The word *father* means "male parent" but often connotes a person who guides and directs. A connotative meaning may carry either a positive or a negative impression. For example, all of the following words mean an assembled group of people, but they have very different connotations.

crowd, congregation, mob, gang, audience, class

Read the following paragraph, which is taken from Martin Luther King Jr.'s "Letter from Birmingham Jail." He wrote it after being jailed for leading a civil rights demonstration.

> We have waited for more than 340 years for our constitutional and God-given rights. The nations of Asia and Africa are moving with <u>jetlike</u> speed toward gaining political independence, but we still <u>creep</u> at <u>horse-and-buggy pace</u> toward gaining a cup of coffee at a lunch counter. I guess it is easy for those who have never felt the <u>stinging darts of segregation</u> to say, "Wait." But when you have seen <u>vicious mobs lynch</u> your mothers and fathers at will and drown your sisters and brothers at whim; when you have seen <u>hate-filled</u> policemen <u>curse, kick,</u> and even kill your black brothers and sisters; when you see the vast majority of your 20 million Negro brothers <u>smothering</u> in an airtight <u>cage of poverty</u> in the midst of an affluent society; when you suddenly find your tongue twisted and your speech <u>stammering</u> as you seek to explain to your six-year-old daughter why she can't go to the public

amusement park that has just been advertised on television, and see tears <u>welling up</u> in her eyes when she is told that Funtown is closed to colored children, and see <u>ominous clouds of inferiority</u> beginning to form in her little mental sky, and see her beginning to distort her personality by developing an unconscious bitterness toward white people. . . then you will understand why we find it difficult to wait.

—King, "Letter from Birmingham Jail,"
Why We Can't Wait, p. 363

The underlined words reveal King's feeling toward segregation and discrimination. For example, notice that King uses the phrase "vicious mobs lynch" rather than "groups of people kill" and "hate-filled policemen curse, kick," instead of "policemen shout and strike." These choices of words are deliberate. King hopes to create an emotional response in his readers.

Figurative Language   Figurative language is a way of describing something that makes sense on an imaginative level but not on a literal or factual level. Many common expressions are figurative:

The exam was a piece of cake.

Sam eats like a horse.

He walks like a gazelle.

In each of these expressions, two unlike objects are compared on the basis of some quality they have in common. Take, for example, Hamlet's statement "I will speak daggers to her, but use none." Here the writer is comparing the features of daggers (sharp, pointed, dangerous, harmful) with something that can be used like daggers—words.

Figurative language is striking, often surprising, even shocking. This reaction is created by the unlikeness of the two objects being compared. To find the similarity and understand the figurative expression, focus on connotative meanings rather than literal meanings. For example, in reading the lines:

A sea

Harsher than granite

from an Ezra Pound poem, you must think not only of rock or stone but also of the characteristics of granite: hardness, toughness, impermeability. Then you can see that the lines mean that the sea is rough and resistant. Figurative words, which are also called figures of speech, are used to communicate and emphasize relationships that cannot be communicated through literal meaning. For example, the statement by Jonathan Swift, "She wears her clothes as if they were thrown on by a pitchfork," creates a stronger image and conveys a more meaningful description than saying "She dresses sloppily."

The three most common types of figurative expressions are similes, metaphors, and symbols. Similes make the comparison explicit by using the word *like* or *as*. Metaphors, on the other hand, directly equate the two objects. Here are several examples of each.

SIMILES

We lie back to back.
Curtains lift and fall,
like the chest of someone sleeping.

—Kenyon

Life, like a dome of many-colored glass,
stains the white radiance of Eternity.

—Shelley

METAPHORS

My Life has stood—a Loaded Gun—
In Corners—till a Day
The Owner passed—identified—
And carried Me away—

—Emily Dickinson

. . . his hair lengthened into sunbeams . . .

—Gustave Flaubert

For more on figurative language, refer to Chapter 5, page 118.

EXERCISE 15–2

Working with a group of classmates, make a list of figurative expressions you use in everyday speech.

EXERCISE 15–3

Explain the meaning of each of the following figures of speech. Several interpretations are possible.

Shall I compare thee to a summer's day?
Thou art more lovely and more temperate.

—Shakespeare

In plucking the fruit of memory,
one runs the risk of spoiling its bloom.

—Joseph Conrad

The scarlet of the maples can shake me like a cry
Of bugles going by.

—Carman

THE EAGLE

He clasps the crag with crooked hands;
Close to the sun in lonely lands,
Ringed with the azure world, he stands.

The wrinkled sea beneath him crawls;
He watches from his mountain walls,
And like a thunderbolt he falls.

—Tennyson

Symbols also make a comparison, but only one term of the comparison is stated. A symbol suggests more than its literal meaning. In fact, sometimes more than one meaning is suggested. In your everyday life, a flag is a symbol of patriotism; a four-leaf clover stands for good luck. A writer may describe a character dressed in white to symbolize her innocence and purity, but the words *innocence* and *purity* will not be mentioned. It is left to the reader to recognize the symbol and to make the comparison.

Symbols often are crucial to the writer's theme or essential meaning. For example, Hemingway's short story "A Clean, Well-Lighted Place" describes an aging man who visits a café. In this story, the café symbolizes an escape from loneliness, old age, and death. Hemingway's theme is the inevitability and inescapability of aging and death; the café closes, and the man's escape is short-lived. Melville's novel *Moby Dick* is the story of a white whale given the name Moby Dick. But the novel is about much more than an aquatic mammal; the whale takes on numerous meanings. The novel's characters imply he is the devil. Later, the whale seems to represent the forces of nature or the created universe.

Symbols, then, are usually objects—concrete items, not abstract feelings such as pity or hate. To recognize symbols, look for objects given a particular or unusual emphasis. The object may be mentioned often, or it may even be suggested in the title. The story or poem may open and/or close with reference to the object. Objects that suggest more than one meaning are possible symbols. Perhaps the best way to identify symbols is to look for objects that point to the author's theme.

EXERCISE 15–4 | *Reread Sylvia Plath's poem "Mirror" on page 431. Is the mirror a symbol? If so, what does it symbolize?*

EXERCISE 15–5 | *Read the following poem by Langston Hughes, and answer the questions that follow.*

THE NEGRO SPEAKS OF RIVERS
Langston Hughes

I've known rivers:
I've known rivers ancient as the world and older than the flow of
human blood in human veins.

My soul has grown deep like the rivers.

I bathed in the Euphrates when dawns were young.
I built my hut near the Congo and it lulled me to sleep.
I looked upon the Nile and raised the pyramids above it.
I heard the singing of the Mississippi when Abe Lincoln went down to
New Orleans, and I've seen its muddy bosom turn all golden in the
sunset.

I've known rivers:
Ancient, dusky rivers.

My soul has grown deep like the rivers.

—Hughes, *Selected Poems*

1. What does the river symbolize?
2. Explain any metaphors or similes the poem contains.

Reading and Analyzing Poetry

Poetry is a form of expression in which ideas are presented in a unique format. Poems are written in verse-lines and stanzas rather than paragraphs. Often, poetry requires more reading time and greater concentration than other types of material. In reading prose, you could skip a word in a paragraph and your comprehension of the whole paragraph would not suffer; poetry, however, is very compact and precise. Each word is important and carries special meaning. You have to pay attention to each word—its sound, its meaning, and its meaning when combined with other words. Here are a few guidelines to help you approach poetry effectively.

1. *Read the poem once straight through, without any defined purpose.* Be open-minded, experiencing the poem as it is written. If you meet an unknown word or confusing reference, keep reading.

2. *Use punctuation to guide your comprehension.* Although poetry is written in lines, do not expect each line to make sense by itself. Meaning often flows on from line to line, eventually forming a sentence. Use the punctuation to guide you, as you do in reading paragraphs. If there is no punctuation at the end of the line, consider it as a slight pause, with an emphasis on the last word.

3. *Read the poem a second time.* Identify and correct any difficulties, such as an unknown word.

4. *Notice the action. Who* is doing *what, when,* and *where?*

5. *Analyze the poem's intent.* Decide what it was written to accomplish. Does it describe a feeling or a person, express a memory, present an argument?

6. *Determine who is speaking.* Poems often refer to an unidentified "I" or "we." Try to describe the speaker's viewpoint or feelings.

7. *Establish the speaker's tone.* Is the author serious, challenging, saddened, frustrated? Read aloud; your intonation, your emphasis on certain words, and the rise and fall of your voice may provide clues. You may "hear" a poet's anger, despondency, or elation.

8. *Identify to whom the poem is addressed.* Is it written to a person, to the reader, to an object? Consider the possibility that the poet may be writing to work out a problem or as an emotional outlet.

9. *Reread difficult or confusing sections.* Read them aloud several times. Copying these sections word for word may be helpful. Look up unfamiliar words.

10. *Check unfamiliar references.* A poet may refer to people, objects, or events outside of the poem. These are known as *allusions*. Often, the allusion is important to the overall meaning of the poem. When you see Oedipus mentioned in a poem, you will need to find out who he was. Paperback books on mythology and literary figures are a good investment.

11. *Analyze the language of the poem.* Consider connotative meanings and study figures of speech.

12. *Look for the poet's meaning or the poem's theme.* Paraphrase the poem; express it in your own words and connect it to your own experience. Then put all the ideas together to discover its overall meaning. Ask yourself, "What is the poet trying to tell me?" "What is the message?"

Now read the poem "Dream Deferred," by Langston Hughes, applying the preceding guidelines.

DREAM DEFERRED
Langston Hughes

What happens to a dream deferred?

Does it dry up
like a raisin in the sun?
Or fester like a sore—
And then run?
Does it stink like rotten meat?
Or crust and sugar over—
like a syrupy sweet?
Maybe it just sags.
like a heavy load.

Or does it explode?

—Hughes, *The Panther and the Lash: Poems for Our Times*

One key to understanding the poem is the meaning of the word *deferred*. Here, it means put off or postponed. A dream deferred, then, refers to unfulfilled or postponed hopes. A poet questions what happens to a dream that is deferred and offers six alternatives. Note the connotative meanings of the first four choices: "dry up," "fester, "stink," "crust and sugar over." Each of these suggests some type of decay. The term sags suggests heaviness and inaction. The last alternative, "explode," is active: posing a threat and implying danger. The poet's purpose is to explore the negative consequences of unfulfilled hopes and to suggest that violent outcomes may result.

EXERCISE 15–6   *Read the following poem by Emily Dickinson, and use the guidelines for analyzing poetry to help you answer the questions below.*

BECAUSE I COULD NOT STOP FOR DEATH
Emily Dickinson

Because I could not stop for Death—
He kindly stopped for me—
The Carriage held but just Ourselves—
And Immortality.

We slowly drove—He knew no haste
And I had put away
My labor and my leisure too,
For His Civility—

We passed the School, where Children strove
At Recess—in the Ring—
We passed the Fields of Gazing Grain—
We passed the Setting Sun—

Or rather—He passed Us—
The Dews drew quivering and chill—
For only Gossamer,[1] my Gown—
My Tippet[2]—only Tulle—

We paused before a House that seemed
A Swelling of the Ground—
The Roof was Scarcely visible—
The Cornice[3]—in the Ground

Since then—'tis Centuries—and yet
Feels shorter than the Day
I first surmised the Horses' Heads
Were toward Eternity—

—*The Poems of Emily Dickinson*, ed. by Thomas H. Johnson

[1]A light, thin cloth
[2]Cape
[3]Section beneath roof

1. Summarize the literal action in the poem. Your summary should include answers to the questions given earlier in this chapter (who, what, where, when, and why).

2. Annotate the poem by marking words and phrases that describe death or the poet's attitude toward it.
3. What message is the author communicating about death?

Reading and Analyzing Short Stories and Novels

A short story is a brief work of prose narrative with an organized plot. It differs from the novel not only in length but also in magnitude: the size and proportion of the story, its scope, its impact, and its effects. A short story may discuss one event that shaped a person's life, whereas a novel describes the numerous actions that contribute to a character's development. However, both the short story and the novel share basic features.

Plot   The plot is the basic storyline—the sequence of events as they occur in the work. The plot, however, also consists of the actions through which the work's meaning is expressed. The plot often follows a predictable structure. Frequently, the plot begins by setting the scene, introducing the main characters, and providing background information needed to follow the story. Often, there is a complication or problem that arises. Suspense is built as the problem or conflict unfolds. Near the end of the story, events come to a climax: the point at which the outcome of the conflict will be decided. A conclusion quickly follows as the story ends.

Characterization   Characters are the actors in a narrative story. The characters reveal themselves by what they say—the dialog—and by their actions, appearance, thoughts, and feelings. The narrator, or person who tells the story, also may comment on or reveal information about the characters. Sometimes, the narrator is not the author, in which case you need to consider his or her characterization as well. As a critical reader, you need to analyze the characters' traits and motives, analyze their personalities, study their interaction, and examine character changes.

Setting   The setting is the time, place, and circumstances in which the action occurs. The setting provides a framework in which the actions occur and establishes an atmosphere in which the characters interact.

Point of View   The point of view is the way the story is presented or from whose perspective or outlook the story is told. Often, the author of a story is not the narrator. The story may be told from the perspective of a narrator who is not one of the characters or by one of the characters themselves. In analyzing the point of view, determine the narrator's role and function. Is the narrator accurate and knowledgeable (even all-knowing), or is his or her view limited or restricted? Sometimes the narrator is able to enter the minds of some or all of the characters, knowing their thoughts and understanding their actions and motivations. Other times, a narrator may be naive or innocent, unable to understand the actions or implications of the story.

Tone   The tone of a story suggests the author's attitude. Like tone of voice, tone in a story suggests feelings. Many ingredients contribute to tone, including the author's choice of details, characters, events, and situations. The tone of a story may be amusing, angry, or contemptuous. The author's feelings are not necessarily those of the characters or of the narrator. Instead, it is through the characters' actions and the narrator's description of them that we infer tone. The style in which a work is written often suggests the tone. Style means the way a writer writes, especially his or her use of language.

Theme   The theme of the story is the main point or message it conveys through all of the above elements. It is an insight into life revealed by the story. Themes are often large, universal ideas: life and death, human values, or human existence. To establish the theme, ask yourself, "What is the author trying to say about life by telling the story?" Try to explain it in a single sentence. If you are having difficulty stating the theme, try the following suggestions.

1. *Study the title.* Now that you have read the story, does it take on any new meanings?

2. *Analyze the main character.* Does he or she change? If so, how, and in reaction to what?

3. *Look for broad, general statements that a character or the narrator makes about life or the problems the characters face.*

4. *Look for symbols, figurative expressions, and meaningful names* (for example, Mrs. Goodheart), or objects that hint at bigger ideas.

Read "The Story of an Hour" by Kate Chopin, paying particular attention to each of the above features.

The Story of an Hour
Kate Chopin

Knowing that Mrs. Mallard was afflicted with heart trouble, great care was taken to break to her as gently as possible the news of her husband's death.

It was her sister Josephine who told her, in broken sentences; veiled hints that revealed in half concealing. Her husband's friend Richards was there, too, near her. It was he who had been in the newspaper office when intelligence of the railroad disaster was received, with Brently Mallard's name leading the list of "killed." He had only taken the time to assure himself of its truth by a second telegram, and had hastened to forestall any less careful, less tender friend in bearing the sad message.

She did not hear the story as many women have heard the same, with a paralyzed inability to accept its significance. She wept at once, with sudden, wild abandonment, in her sister's arms. When the storm of grief had spent itself she went away to her room alone. She would have no one follow her.

There stood, facing the open window, a comfortable, roomy armchair. Into this she sank, pressed down by a physical exhaustion that haunted her body and seemed to reach into her soul.

She could see in the open square before her house the tops of trees that were all aquiver with the new spring life. The delicious breath of rain was in the air. In the street below a peddler was crying his wares. The notes of a distant song which someone was singing reached her faintly, and countless sparrows were twittering in the eaves.

There were patches of blue sky showing here and there through the clouds that had met and piled one above the other in the west facing her window.

She sat with her head thrown back upon the cushion of the chair, quite motionless, except when a sob came up into her throat and shook her, as a child who has cried itself to sleep continues to sob in its dreams.

She was young, with a fair, calm face, whose lines bespoke repression and even a certain strength. But now there was a dull stare in her eyes, whose gaze was fixed away off yonder on one of those patches of blue sky. It was not a glance of reflection, but rather indicated a suspension of intelligent thought.

There was something coming to her and she was waiting for it, fearfully. What was it? She did not know; it was too subtle and elusive to name. But she felt it, creeping out of the sky, reaching toward her through the sounds, the scents, the color that filled the air.

Now her bosom rose and fell tumultuously. She was beginning to recognize this thing that was approaching to possess her, and she was striving to beat it back with her will—as powerless as her two white slender hands would have been.

When she abandoned herself a little whispered word escaped her slightly parted lips. She said it over and over under her breath: "free, free, free!" The vacant stare and the look of terror that had followed it went from her eyes. They stayed keen and bright. Her pulses beat fast, and the coursing blood warmed and relaxed every inch of her body.

She did not stop to ask if it were or were not a monstrous joy that held her. A clear and exalted perception enabled her to dismiss the suggestion as trivial.

She knew that she would weep again when she saw the kind, tender hands folded in death; the face that had never looked save with love upon her, fixed and gray and dead. But she saw beyond that bitter moment a long procession of years to come that would belong to her absolutely. And she opened and spread her arms out to them in welcome.

There would be no one to live for her during those coming years; she would live for herself. There would be no powerful will bending hers in that blind persistence with which men and women believe they have a right to impose a private will upon a fellow-creature. A kind intention or a cruel intention made the act seem no less a crime as she looked upon it in that brief moment of illumination.

And yet she had loved him—sometimes. Often she had not. What did it matter! What could love, the unresolved mystery, count for in face of this possession of self-assertion which she suddenly recognized as the strongest impulse of her being!

"Free! Body and soul free!" she kept whispering.

Josephine was kneeling before the closed door with her lips to the keyhole, imploring for admission. "Louise, open the door! I beg; open the door—you will make yourself ill. What are you doing, Louise? For heaven's sake open the door."

"Go away. I am not making myself ill." No; she was drinking in a very elixir of life through that open window.

Her fancy was running riot along those days ahead of her. Spring days, and summer days, and all sorts of days that would be her own. She breathed a quick prayer that life might be long. It was only yesterday she had thought with a shudder that life might be long.

She arose at length and opened the door to her sister's importunities. There was a feverish triumph in her eyes, and she carried herself unwittingly like a goddess of Victory. She clasped her sister's waist, and together they descended the stairs. Richards stood waiting for them at the bottom.

Someone was opening the front door with a latchkey. It was Brently Mallard who entered, a little travel-stained, composedly carrying his grip-sack and umbrella. He had been far from the scene of accident, and did not even know there had been one. He stood amazed at Josephine's piercing cry; at Richards' quick motion to screen him from the view of his wife.

But Richards was too late.

When the doctors came they said she had died of heart disease—of joy that kills.

—Chopin, *The Awakening: Selected Stories of Kate Chopin*

The plot of this short story involves a surprise ending: Mrs. Mallard learns that her husband, who she thought had been killed in a railroad disaster, is alive. She ponders his death and relishes the freedom it will bring. Upon discovering that her husband is not dead, Mrs. Mallard suffers a heart attack and dies. The key character is Mrs. Mallard; her thoughts and actions after learning of her husband's supposed death are the crux of the story. The setting is one hour in a time near the present in the Mallards' home. The story is told by a third-person narrator who is knowledgeable and understands the characters' actions and motives. In the story's last line, the narrator tells us that doctors assumed Mrs. Mallard died of "the joy that kills."

| EXERCISE 15–7 | *Answer the following questions about Chopin's "The Story of an Hour."* |

1. When did you first realize that Mrs. Mallard's reaction to her husband's death would be unusual? Underline words and phrases that led you to suspect her response would be unusual.
2. Explain the meaning of the phrase "the joy that kills."
3. What do Mrs. Mallard's response to the news of her husband's death and the surprise ending suggest about life and death and the nature of true happiness?

THE VISUAL ARTS: EXPRESSION WITHOUT WORDS

A work of art, such as a painting or a sculpture is the visual expression of an idea. The idea is expressed using a medium—a material such as canvas, clay, fiber, stone or paint. In a poem, the medium is words; in a sculpture, the medium may be marble. The medium is the vehicle through which the idea is expressed.

Why Study Art?

Many people study art because it is beautiful and they enjoy it. Art can arouse emotions and feelings, stimulate our imaginations, and help us think in new ways. It can enrich our lives. Besides providing enjoyment and enrichment, art also can be a form of communication. By studying the stained glass window in a cathedral, for example, you can learn how, during the Middle Ages, religion was taught to an illiterate population. Art may also have a spiritual (religious) value. Cave drawings may have been used by prehistoric humans to depict animals they valued for food or to magically exert control over them. Finally, art may have a functional value. Some works of art were useful in daily life. Intricately dyed or carved rawhide may have been used to transport personal goods, for instance. By studying works of art, we can learn about a society's religious beliefs and daily living habits.

How to Study Art

To study art, you have to think visually. Use the following suggestions to develop your visual thinking skills. As you read through this section, refer to a photograph taken by Dorothea Lange, *Migrant Mother, Nipomo, California, 1936* shown below.

Dorothea Lange, Migrant Mother, Nipomo, California, 1936.

Source: Copyright the Dorothea Lange Collection. The Oakland Museum, City of Oakland. Gift of Paul S. Taylor.

See as Well as Look   Looking means taking in what is before you in a physical, mechanical way. Your eyes focus on visual images. Seeing is a more active mental, as well as physical, process. It may require conscious effort. The distinction between looking and seeing is similar to that between hearing and listening. When you hear, you take in sound. When you listen, you understand meaning and grasp the speaker's message. When you see a work of art, you take away some meaning or understanding. What do you *see* in Lange's photograph?

Identify the Subject Matter   Decide who or what the work of art depicts or describes. For example, Michelangelo's "The Creation of Adam" describes, as its title suggests, the biblical creation of the first human. An Inuit stone carving may depict an animal valued by Inuit tribes, such as an eagle or bear. In Lange's photograph, the subject is a mother and her children.

Consider the Title   The title often offers clues that will help you construct an interpretation of the work. You should be aware that not all titles were given to the work by the original artist. The title of Lange's photograph is very revealing. We learn that the woman is a migrant worker and can infer that the children are her children. We also learn that the photograph was taken in California and can infer that the woman was a migrant worker there.

Study the Visual Elements   When you look at a painting the first time, you may notice only a face, or when you study a sculpture, you may notice only its shape. Broaden your study to include the common visual elements. They are line, shape, mass, time, motion, light, color, and texture. Not every element exists within every work of art, but some are important in each.

These elements, sometimes referred to as the form, contribute to the meaning. Small details are important. For example, the grain of marble in a sculpture or the kinds of brush strokes in a painting are meaningful. A painting with deep, heavy, sharply angular lines creates a different impression from one with softly flowing lines.

In Lange's photograph, light seems to be shining on the woman's face and hand. You see harsh, strong lines in her face. Her arm is angular, not graceful. The children seem less sharp.

Write Your Reactions   As you study a work of art, jot down your responses. Write questions, initial reactions, your emotions, and so forth. Do not worry about the order of your ideas or about expressing them in grammatically correct sentences. Just record your impressions. Together, these may help you develop an interpretation of the work. While studying Lange's photograph, one student wrote the following:

- The photo is disturbing—not pleasing.
- The children's faces are hidden—are they ashamed? or perhaps crying? or afraid?
- The woman seems worried. Her hand is at her mouth.

- The children seem highly dependent on her; they seem emotionally close.
- The woman seems to be thinking, but there is no action or movement in the photograph.
- The family seems poor and disheveled.
- The mother seems in control.
- Are they homeless?

Analyze the Work   Analyzing means dividing something into parts in order to understand it. If you are looking at a statue, for instance, you might examine the pose, size, facial expression, medium, gestures, clothing, and so forth. In Lange's photograph, you might first analyze the woman and then the children. Or you might analyze how each is holding his or her body and then how each is dressed. In Lange's photograph, the woman's facial expression is particularly striking.

Consider the Meaning of the Work   An interpretation is a description of a meaning of the work. Many art historians believe that a work of art can have more than one meaning. One meaning is the meaning that it had for the artist; another is the meaning it had for the first people who looked at it. Still another is the meaning it offers to us today. Other art historians argue that a work has no meaning in itself; its only meaning is that given to it by those who view it.

One meaning that Lange's photograph seems to be depicting is the plight of migrant workers, thus suggesting sympathy. Another meaning may be drawn from the similarity of the pose of the woman and her children to traditional paintings of the Madonna and child, perhaps suggesting that the migrant woman is a universal mother figure. Many women share her worry and concern about their place in life.

EXERCISE 15–8   *Study the work of art shown on the next page, and answer the following questions.*

1. Describe the subject.
2. Identify striking visual elements. For example, consider the size and balance of the preacher's body parts. Consider, too, the background.
3. Write your reactions.
4. Describe the meaning of the work.

READING CRITICISM

Criticism discusses, interprets, and evaluates a particular work. Some students erroneously assume that criticism is only negative, or limited to finding fault with a work. Actually, its primary purpose is to analyze and interpret; it may include both positive and negative aspects. Film and book reviews are examples of criticism. Criticism also includes scholarly works that carefully research or closely examine a particular aspect, theme, or approach in literature or art.

Charles White,
PREACHER, *1952. Ink on*
cardboard, sight;
21⅛ x 29⅜ inches.
Source: *Whitney Museum of*
American Art, New York;52.25.
Photograph © 2000. Whitney
Museum of American Art.

Often, in order to complete a term paper, you will be required to consult several critical sources. Other times, to understand a work better, you may decide to read several interpretations by critical authorities.

Following is a brief excerpt from a critical work discussing Emily Dickinson's poem "Because I Could Not Stop for Death," which appears on page 000 in this chapter. Read the excerpt, and note that it offers an interpretation of the poem's meaning: the poet fears life and escapes this fear through a journey to death.

Naive, blank-faced, repelling thought and emotion, the speaker permits herself to be transported to worlds unknown. The first step is easy. The gentleman-caller she calls Death is kindly, civil. The threesome is cozy, he does what she cannot do, the unexamined space of the carriage arouses no anxiety in her, the journey is a leisured one. . . . She has all the time in the world, and in other worlds besides. Remarking on the presence of a third figure, Immortality, she cannot stop to ask herself what this barely personified abstraction, the shard of a disintegrated religious tradition, signifies. Wholly engrossed as she is by her deceptive double, she cannot afford to question whether beneath the smooth, seductive surface his intentions are equally decorous. What she has done is to yield herself up to the power of a dominant obsession. What this obsession is we do not know absolutely. The poem invokes a reason only to dismiss it: "Because I could not . . . He." Thus, although the idea of suicide is implicit in its denial, so too is the idea of controlling this death-wish by displacing it onto another character who is initially capable of masking the deception motif the poem is designed to reveal. In limited terms, perhaps this obsession may be described as the compulsion to repress the anxiety that the circumstances of her life have aroused in her. In its broadest terms, perhaps this obsession may be described as her fear of mortality itself.

—Pollak, *Dickinson: The Anxiety of Gender,* p. 191

In using critical sources, follow these guidelines.

1. *Read the original work carefully and thoroughly before you consult critical sources.*

2. *Make a preliminary interpretation of the work before reading criticism.* Decide what *you* think the work means and why it was produced. Record these ideas in note form. If you consult sources before forming your own impressions, your judgment will be colored by what you read and you will have difficulty separating your ideas from those you encounter as you read.

3. Recognize that not all critics agree; you may encounter three critics who present three different interpretations of Shakespeare's *Hamlet* or Renoir's "The Luncheon of the Boating Party."

4. Make certain that the interpretations you read are substantiated with references to the original work.

5. Although it is perfectly acceptable to revise your own interpretations on the basis of your reading, do not discard your own interpretation as soon as you encounter one that differs. Look to the original work to develop support for your interpretations.

6. Make notes on your readings, recording only key points.

To locate criticism on a particular literary or artistic work, consult one of several reference sources.

The Reader's Guide to Periodical Literature

Essay and General Literature Index

The MLA Bibliography

In many libraries, computerized versions are available.

EXERCISE 15–9

The following excerpt provides another critical interpretation of Dickinson's poem "Because I Could Not Stop for Death." Read the excerpt, and answer the questions that follow.

At first reading, the orthodox reassurance against the fear of death appears to be invoked, though with the novelty of a suitor replacing the traditional angel, by emphasizing his compassionate mission in taking her out of the woes of this world into the bliss of the next. 'Death,' usually rude, sudden, and impersonal, has been transformed into a kindly and leisurely gentleman. Although she was aware this is a last ride, since his 'Carriage' can only be a hearse, its terror is subdued by the 'Civility' of the driver who is merely serving the end of 'Immortality.' The loneliness of the journey, with Death on the driver's seat and her body laid out in the coach behind, is dispelled by the presence of her immortal part that rides with her as a co-passenger, this slight personification being justified by the separable concept of the soul. Too occupied with life herself to stop, like all busy mortals, Death 'kindly stopped' for her. But this figure of a gentleman taking a lady for a carriage ride is carefully underplayed and then dropped after two stanzas.

The balanced parallelism of the first stanza is slightly quickened by the alliterating 'labor' and 'leisure' of the second, which encompass vividly all that must be renounced in order to ride 'toward Eternity.' So the deliberate slow-paced action that lies suspended behind the poem is charged with a forward movement by the sound pattern, taking on a kind of inevitability in the insistent reiteration of the following stanza:

> We passed the School, where Children strove
> At Recess—in the Ring—
> We passed the Fields of Gazing Grain—
> We passed the Setting Sun—

Here her intensely conscious leave-taking of the world is rendered with fine economy, and instead of the sentimental grief of parting there is an objectively presented scene. The seemingly disparate parts of this are fused into a vivid re-enactment of the mortal experience. It includes the three stages of youth, maturity, and age, the cycle of day from morning to evening, and even a suggestion of seasonal progression from the year's upspring through ripening to decline. The labor and leisure of life are made concrete in the joyous activity of children contrasted with the passivity of nature and again, by the optical illusion of the sun's setting, in the image of motion that has come to rest. Also the whole range of the earthly life is symbolized, first human nature, then animate, and finally inanimate nature. But, absorbed 'in the Ring' of childhood's games, the players at life do not even stop to look up at the passing carriage of death. And the indifference of nature is given a kind of cold vitality by transferring the stare in the dead traveler's eyes to the 'Gazing Grain.' This simple maneuver in grammar creates an involute paradox, giving the fixity of death to the living corn while the corpse itself passes by on its journey to immortality. Then with the westering sun, traditional symbol of the soul's passing, comes the obliterating darkness of eternity. Finally, the sequence follows the natural route of a funeral train, past the schoolhouse in the village, then the outlying fields, and on to the remote burying ground.

—Anderson, *Emily Dickinson's Poetry: Stairway to Surprise*, pp. 245–46

1. According to this critic, what is the speaker's attitude toward death?
2. Does the criticism enhance your understanding of the poem? If so, how?
3. How does this critic's interpretation compare with that of the earlier interpretation on page 447? Discuss the similarities and differences.
4. Compare this critic's interpretation with your own interpretation.

THOUGHT PATTERNS IN THE HUMANITIES AND ARTS

Common thought patterns in the humanities and arts include process, chronological order, cause and effect, and comparison and contrast. Table 15–1 on page 450 describes the uses of these patterns and offers examples.

TABLE 15–1   THOUGHT PATTERNS IN THE HUMANITIES AND ARTS

Patterns	Uses	Examples
Process	Examining the process through which the writer achieved his or her effect	Studying e.e. cummings' use of space and print size
Chronological order	Sequence of events in fictional works; noting the development of various artists or historical or literary periods	Noting development of Impressionist style of painting
Cause and effect	Examining character motivation, studying effects of various literary and artistic techniques	Evaluating the effect of harsh brush strokes in a painting
Comparison and contrast	Studying two or more artists, works, writers, or schools of thought	Comparing the works of Wordsworth and Coleridge

LEARNING STRATEGIES FOR HUMANITIES AND ART COURSES

Humanities and art courses are unique. Grades are often based on papers or essay exams rather than on objective tests or quizzes. Frequently, the focus is on ideas and your interpretation and evaluation of them. Here are several suggestions to help you get the most from these courses.

1. *Learn appropriate terminology.* Learn the names and meanings of literary devices (stream of consciousness, pathos, persona, intrigue). Consult M. L. Abrams's *A Glossary of Literary Terms.*

2. *Learn classifications.* In literature and art history, works and authors are often grouped or classified, and groupings may be chronological (the Romantic period, 1789–1832; the Victorian period, 1832–1901 in literature, for example). Learn these periods (names, inclusive dates, and characteristics) so that you will understand the historical context of a particular work.

3. *Focus on themes and patterns.* Always analyze and evaluate. Focus on a work's significance and literary merit.

4. *Highlight and annotate as you read.* Mark key figures of speech, global statements by characters, and words and phrases that suggest the theme. Mark confusing sections or unknown references as well.

5. *Write for review.* Write plot summaries of short stories. Make brief outlines of essays. Write a statement of your interpretation of a poem or work or art. These statements will be useful as you prepare for exams or select topics for papers.

6. *Predict exam questions.* Exams are usually in essay form or call for short answers. Prepare for this by predicting the questions and drafting outline answers.

7. *Discuss the work with a classmate.* If you are having difficulty with a particular work, consult with your instructor.

Test-Taking Tips
Preparing for Exams in the Humanities and Arts

In many literature classes, you write papers instead of taking exams, although some instructors do give brief objective tests based on the assigned readings. Most final essay assignments require you to analyze and write about a work or works you have read or viewed.

You may be given several types of writing assignments. It is important to know what is expected in each.

1. *Explication.* An explication is a full, detailed explanation of the meaning of the work. It proceeds through the work line by line or even word by word, explaining meanings and examining word choices, figures of speech, and so forth. Although it is detailed, it is not limited to a discussion of specifics. Larger concerns such as theme and plot are also discussed.

2. *Analysis.* Analysis involves separating the work into components and then examining and explaining closely one or more of the parts. Usually, analyses are limited to one aspect or element, such as Hawthorne's use of symbolism in *The Scarlet Letter* or an analysis of the point of view in Poe's "The Tell-Tale Heart."

3. *Comparison and Contrast.* Writing assignments may ask you to compare two or more works or two or more authors. To do this, you must examine similarities and differences. If you are given a choice of works or authors, choose two that have much in common; you will find you have more to say than if the two are widely divergent. For suggestions on how to compare two works, refer to Chapter 4. When writing a comparison paper, you should generally integrate your discussion of the works rather than discuss each separately. Select several points or aspects that you will discuss for each work, and then organize your paper to proceed from aspect to aspect.

4. *Synopsis.* Some instructors ask students to write a synopsis or summary of a work. This assignment demands a concise description of major features of the work, such as plot, setting, and characterization. Others ask for a card report (a point-by-point description of various elements, usually on an index card). Generally, some form of evaluation of the work is also expected. If you are not certain what aspects to include or what format to use, ask your instructor.

SUMMARY

Literature focuses on the search for reasons, values, and interpretations in all areas of human interest and experience.

Understanding the language of literature involves working with descriptive, connotative, and figurative language. Specific suggestions are given for reading and analyzing each genre.

- Poetry: Reread frequently. Note the poem's action, audience, and tone. Analyze the poem's intent, and search for its theme.
- Short stories and novels: Focus on plot, characterization, setting, point of view, tone, and theme.

The visual arts focus on the expression of an idea through a medium, such as canvas, clay, or fiber. Studying art requires visual thinking and analysis. Interpretation and meaning are important.

Strategies for reading literary criticism are given. Predominant thought patterns include

- process
- chronological order
- cause and effect
- comparison and contrast

Literature

PREREADING QUESTIONS

(Answer after reading the entire poem once.)
1. What is the subject of the poem?
2. Summarize the literal action.

Leaves

Lloyd Schwartz

1.

1   Every October it becomes important, no, *necessary*
     to see the leaves turning, to be surrounded
     by leaves turning: it's not just the symbolism,
     to confront in the death of the year your death,
5   one blazing farewell appearance, though the irony
     isn't lost on you that nature is most seductive
     when it's about to die, flaunting the dazzle of its
     incipient exit, an ending that at least so far
     the effects of human progress (pollution, acid rain)
10   have not yet frightened you enough to make you believe
     is real; that is, you know this ending is a deception
     because of course nature is always renewing itself—
          the trees don't *die,* they just pretend,
            go out in style, and return in style: a new style.

2.

15   It is deliberate how far they make you go
     especially if you live in the city to get far
     enough away from home to see not just trees
     but only trees. The boring highways, roadsigns, high
     speeds, 10-axle trucks passing you as if they were
20   in an even greater hurry than you to look at leaves:
     so you drive in terror for literal hours and it looks
     like rain, or *snow,* but it's probably just clouds
     (too cloudy to see any color?) and you wonder,
     given the poverty of your memory, which road had the
25   most color last year, but it doesn't matter since
     you're probably too late anyway, or too early—
          whichever road you take will be the wrong one
            and you've probably come all this way for nothing.

3.

You'll be driving along depressed when suddenly
30 a cloud will move and the sun will muscle through
and ignite the hills. It may not last. Probably
won't last. But for a moment the whole world
comes to. Wakes up. Proves it lives. It lives—
red, yellow, orange, brown, russet, ocher, vermillion,
35 *gold.* Flame and rust. Flame and rust, the permutations
of burning. You're on fire. Your eyes are on fire.
It won't last, you don't want it to last. You
can't stand any more. But you don't want it to stop.
It's what you've come for. It's what you'll
40 come back for. It won't stay with you, but you'll
remember that it felt like nothing else you've felt
or something you've felt that also didn't last.

—Schwartz, "Leaves," *Goodnight, Gracie*

VOCABULARY REVIEW

1. For each of the words listed below, use context; prefixes, roots, and suffixes; and/or a dictionary to write a brief definition or synonym of the word as it is used in the reading.

a. irony (line 5) _____

b. seductive (line 6) _____

c. incipient (line 8) _____

d. vermillion (line 34) _____

e. permutations (line 35) _____

COMPREHENSION QUESTIONS

1. In line 3, Schwartz mentions symbolism. To what symbolism is he referring?
2. What is the poet's attitude toward human progress (line 9)?
3. To whom does the word *they* refer in line 15?
4. Describe the poem's tone.
5. What is the poem's theme?

THINKING CRITICALLY

Why does the author mention pollution and acid rain in line 9?

LEARNING/STUDY STRATEGY

Annotate the poem using the suggestions on page 432.

ONLINE RESEARCH: POETRY*

Poetry, like other creative arts, depends on the reader, viewer, or listener for interpretation. How would your interpretation of a poem change if you could hear the poet reading the poem, instead of only seeing it on the page? You can hear poets reading their own poems at the following World Wide Web sites. Go to one of the sites, and then follow the directions below. (*Note:* You need a program called RealAudio to hear the poems. It can be downloaded from these sites.)

- *The Atlantic Monthly Unbound* includes an "audible anthology of poetry" at http://www.theatlantic.com/unbound/poetry/antholog/schwartz/airport.htm. Here you can find Lloyd Schwartz reading another one of his poems, "Small Airport in Brazil."
- The Academy of American Poets Web site includes a "Listening Booth" at http://www.poets.org/booth/booth.cfm. Here you can choose whether to only listen to the poem or to read it yourself while it is being read by the poet.

1. Choose a poem from one of the anthologies. Depending on which site you have chosen, either listen to the poem first and then read it yourself; or read it yourself and then listen to the poet read it.
2. How does the author's rendering of the poem affect your interpretation? Why?

---

*If either of these sites is unavailable, use a search engine to locate a new Web site on the same topic.

The HUMANITIES and ARTS on the Internet

The Internet has numerous resources available for research in the humanities and arts, including directories and Web guides to help you find material relevant to your studies, journals and databases, references works, and government resources. Here is a list of useful Web sites to get you started.

Directories/Web Guides

Voice of the Shuttle
> http://vos.ucsb.edu/

Yahoo! Arts and Humanities
> http://dir.yahoo.com/Arts/

ADAM
> http://adam.ac.uk/

Journals/Indexes/Databases

The Internet Public Library:
Arts and Humanities Serials
> http://www.ipl.org/cgi-bin/reading/
> serials.out.pl?ty=long&id=hum00.00.00

Online Books Page
> http://onlinebooks.library.upenn.edu/

Humanities Directories
> http://www.lib.washington.edu/subject/
> Humanities/dr/eldir.html

References

Reference Tools: Arts and Humanities
> http://aok.lib.umbc.edu/MenuGen.php3?
> MenuID=24

Words of Art
> http://www.okanagan.bc.ca/fiar/glossary/
> gloshome.html

Government Resources

National Endowment for the Arts : Explore!
> http://arts.endow.gov/explore/index.html

National Endowment for the Humanities
Supported Projects
> http://www.neh.fed.us/projects/index.html

Multimedia Activities

Practice your reading and research skills on the Web.

1. **Imagination Gallery B: American Treasures of the Library of Congress**
    http://www.loc.gov/exhibits/treasures/tr33b.html#lit
    View these special items from art and literature held by the Library of Congress. Read about their history and significance. Why is it important to preserve these items? Pick one that interests you the most. Teach a friend about it.

2. **Sounds of Harpsichords and Related Instruments**
    http://www-personal.umich.edu/~bpl/hpsi.html#sounds
    Listen to snippets of music played on various instruments. Scroll down to the builder sites and visit some manufacturers' Web sites. What connections can you make between music and other disciplines?

CHAPTER 16

READING MATHEMATICS

LEARNING OBJECTIVES
- ✦ To understand the sequential nature of mathematics
- ✦ To develop a systematic approach for reading mathematics textbooks
- ✦ To solve word problems in mathematics
- ✦ To learn common thought patterns used in mathematics
- ✦ To develop study techniques for mathematics

Although mathematics uses its own language, it is concerned with ideas, concepts, relationships, and problems—just like other disciplines. Mathematics demands logical and critical thinking and the ability to deal with abstractions, relationships, and theoretical ideas. This subject is extremely rewarding because you *see* yourself learning and making progress; you can solve a problem today that you could not solve yesterday.

MATHEMATICS: A SEQUENTIAL THINKING PROCESS

Learning mathematics is a sequential process. You solve problems by estimating answers, trying a variety of special techniques, and verifying the results. In mathematics, much of what you learn is based on skills you have learned earlier; it is cumulative. In algebra, you have to understand radicals before you can solve quadratic equations, whose solutions involve radicals. In business math, to use a compound interest schedule, you must understand simple interest.

Because mathematics is sequential and cumulative, it is most important that you begin with a course at the proper level. For example, a calculus course often is required for accounting majors. However, if you have not studied trigonometry, you lack the necessary background for calculus and should take a trigonometry course first. Check the course description in your college catalog for prerequisites, or consult your academic advisor for information on appropriate course placement. If it has been several years since your last math course, your college learning center may offer a placement test to assess your present level of skill.

Mathematics is a process of solving problems—a process of reasoning about situations and understanding the relationships between variables. Too many students learn steps, memorize procedures, and follow rules to solve problems without understanding why they are performing the operations. In mathematics, understanding the meaning of the various operations is essential. Make your learning practical and useful by understanding *how* and *why* the operations work.

Why Study Mathematics?

Mathematics is a required course in many fields of study. It is essential for majors in nursing, accounting, business and finance, technologies, and the natural sciences, for example. Mathematics provides the tools with which to explore relationships and solve problems. In nursing, mathematics allows you to compute and measure dosages of drugs. In accounting, it is mathematics that enables you to calculate profits and losses, for instance.

Besides fulfilling degree requirements, however, mathematics trains you to think logically, quantitatively, and analytically. Mathematics is fun because it is exact and precise; you are either right or wrong in solving a problem. Mathematics can provide the same satisfying, deep concentration that solving a crossword puzzle or playing a game of chess does.

READING MATHEMATICS TEXTBOOKS

To learn from mathematics texts, you must allow plenty of time and work at peak concentration. Mathematics texts are concise and to the point; nearly everything is important. Use the following suggestions to develop a systematic approach for reading in mathematics.

Preview Before Reading

Previewing before reading is as important in mathematics as it is in every other discipline. For mathematics texts, however, your preview should include a brief review of your previous chapter assignment. Because learning new skills hinges on remembering what you have learned before, a brief review of previously learned material is valuable.

Understand Mathematical Language

One of the first steps to success with mathematics is learning to understand its language. Mathematics uses a symbolic language in which notations, symbols, numbers, and formulas are used to express ideas and relationships. Working with mathematics requires that you be able to convert mathematical language to everyday language. To understand a formula, for example, $I = prt$, you must translate mathematical language into everyday language: "Interest equals principal times rate times time." To solve a word problem expressed in everyday language, first you must convert it into mathematical language. You might think of equations as mathematical sentences. Just as an English sentence expresses a complete idea, an equation describes a mathematical relationship. Here are a few examples.

Sentence	Equation
The speed of train *A* is four times the speed of train *B*.	$A = 4B$
When I am as old as my mother (*m*), I shall be five times as old as my daughter (*d*) is now.	$5d = m$
In a sewing box, there are three times as many pins as needles, and one-third as many buttons as needles; the total number of pins, needles, and buttons is 1,872.	$3n + n + \frac{1}{3}n = 1872$

When you learn a foreign language, it is not sufficient only to learn the new vocabulary; you also must learn the rules of word order, grammar, punctuation, and so forth. To read and understand mathematics, then, you must know not only the signs and symbols (the vocabulary) but also the basic rules for expressing relationships in mathematical form. Figure 16–1 shows five important types of symbols and mathematical language and gives examples of each, taken from introductory algebra.

Figure 16–2 (p. 460) shows a sample page from an introductory algebra textbook. It has been marked to indicate the types of mathematical language used.

Figure 16–1 Aspects of Mathematical Language

Type	Function	Example
Punctuation marks	Make clear what parts of a statement are or are not separable; distinguish groups within groups	$(0, 1, 2, ...)$ $[3 - (a + b)^2]$
Models (graphs, charts, drawings)	Present a pictorial representation of a relationship or situation	
Numbers	Indicate size, order	3, 7, 9, 11
Variables	Represent a number that is unknown or may vary	x, y
Signs for relations	Indicate relationships	$a = b$ (*a* equals *b*) $c > d$ (*c* is greater than *b*)
Signs for operations	Give instructions	$15 \div 3$ (divide 15 by 3) $a - b$ (subtract *b* from *a*)

Figure 16–2   Sample Textbook Page

OBJECTIVE ▶ Inequalities can be used to solve applied problems involving phrases that suggest inequality. The chart below gives some of the more common such phrases, along with examples and translations.

Phrase	*Example*	*Inequality*
Is more than	A number *is more than* 4	$x > 4$
Is less than	A number *is less than* –12	$x < -12$
Is at least	A number *is at least* 6	$x \geq 6$
Is at most	A number *is at most* 8	$x \leq 8$

Caution
Do not confuse phrases like "5 more than a number" and statements like "5 *is* more than a number." The first of these is expressed as "x + 5" while the second is expressed as "5 > x."

E X A M P L E   8   Finding an Average Test Score
Brent has test grades of 86, 88, and 78 on his first three tests in geometry. If he wants an average of at least 80 after his fourth test, what score must he make on his fourth test?
　　Let *x* represent Brent's score on his fourth test. To find the average of the four scores, add them and find $\frac{1}{4}$ of the sum.

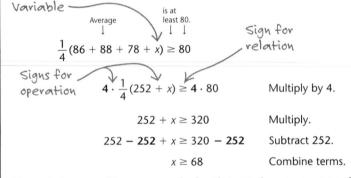

$$\frac{1}{4}(86 + 88 + 78 + x) \geq 80$$

$4 \cdot \frac{1}{4}(252 + x) \geq 4 \cdot 80$	Multiply by 4.
$252 + x \geq 320$	Multiply.
$252 - 252 + x \geq 320 - 252$	Subtract 252.
$x \geq 68$	Combine terms.

He must also score 68 or more on the fourth test to have an average of *at least* 80.

Source: Lial et al., *Introductory Algebra*, pp. 163–64

　　Much information is packed into small units of mathematical language. Some students find it helpful to translate formulas into words as they read, as is shown in the following equation for a right triangle:

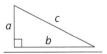

$c^2 = a^2 + b^2$ means the square of the hypotenuse of a right triangle is equal to the sum of the squares of the two remaining sides.

Figure 16–3 Sample Index Cards

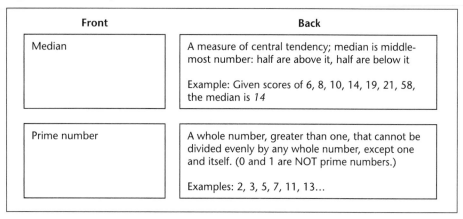

Front	Back
Median	A measure of central tendency; median is middle-most number: half are above it, half are below it Example: Given scores of 6, 8, 10, 14, 19, 21, 58, the median is *14*
Prime number	A whole number, greater than one, that cannot be divided evenly by any whole number, except one and itself. (0 and 1 are NOT prime numbers.) Examples: 2, 3, 5, 7, 11, 13...

In mathematics, you must know the *exact* meaning of both words and symbols. There are several places to find the definition of a new term. If it is from the current chapter, look at the end-of-chapter material, which often includes key vocabulary. You might also check the index to find page numbers or use the glossary to read a brief definition, if one is included. Use the index card system described in Chapter 3 to help you learn the language of mathematics. Record the term or symbol, its meaning, an example, and a diagram, if possible. Also include a page reference to where the term is used in your textbook. Two sample index cards are shown above in Figure 16–3.

EXERCISE 16–1

Read the excerpt from an algebra text shown in Figure 16–4 on page 462, and underline five examples of mathematical language that the author assumes you know.

1. Write a definition of each term you have underlined.
2. Write your own definition of the phrase, "evaluating an expression." Include an example to illustrate your definition.

Follow the Chapter Organization

Chapters in most mathematics textbooks contain four essential elements: the presentation or explanation, sample problems, graphs and diagrams, and exercises. Mathematics textbook chapters often use a decimal system for dividing the chapter into sections. For example, Chapter 3 might be numbered 3.1, 3.2, 3.3, and so on. Each number with a decimal is a new section of the chapter.

Reading Chapter Explanations Each new operation, process, or term is explained in the text. As you read this explanation, focus on *how* and *why* the process works. Discover the reasoning behind the process. If the author refers to a sample problem in the explanation, it is necessary to move back and forth

Figure 16–4   Excerpt from an Algebra Text

Evaluating an Expression   If you like to fish, you can use an expression (rule) like the one below to find the approximate weight (in pounds) of a fish you catch. Measure the length (in inches) of the fish and then use the correct expression for that type of fish. For a northern pike, the weight expression is shown.

Variable (length of fish) $\dfrac{l^3}{3600}$

where l is the length of the fish in inches.
    To evaluate this expression for a fish that is 43 inches long, follow the rule by calculating

$$\frac{43^3}{3600}$$ Replace l with 43, the length of the fish in inches.

In the numerator, you can multiply $43 \cdot 43 \cdot 43$ or use the $\boxed{y^x}$ key on your calculator. Then divide by 3600.

Enter 43 $\boxed{y^x}$ 3 $\boxed{\div}$ 3600 $\boxed{=}$ **Calculator shows 22.08527778**
        | |
      Base   Exponent

The fish weighs about 22 pounds.

    Now evaluate the expression to find the approximate weight of a northern pike that is 37 inches long. (Answer: about 14 pounds.)
    Notice that variables are used on your calculator keys. On the $\boxed{y^x}$ key, y represents the base and x represents the exponent. You evaluated y^x by entering 43 as the base and 3 as the exponent for the first fish. Then you evaluated y^x by entering 37 as the base and 3 as the exponent for the second fish.

Source: Lial and Hestwood, *Prealgebra,* p. 87

between the explanation and the sample problem. Read a sentence or two and then refer to the sample problem to see how the information is applied. Your purpose is to see how the sample problem illustrates the process being described. The steps to follow in computing the total installment cost and finance charge on a credit card are given in Figure 16–5. Then the authors give a sample problem and show how it is solved using the steps they have listed.

    As you read, refer to previous chapters if an operation is unclear or if unfamiliar terms are used. In mathematics, you should expect to look back frequently because much of the material is sequential.

Reading Sample Problems   Sample problems demonstrate how an operation or process works. It may be tempting to skip over sample problems because they require time to work through or because they lack an accompanying verbal explanation. However, careful study of the sample problems is an essential part of learning in mathematics. Follow these steps in reading sample problems.

Figure 16–5 Problem Solving Step by Step

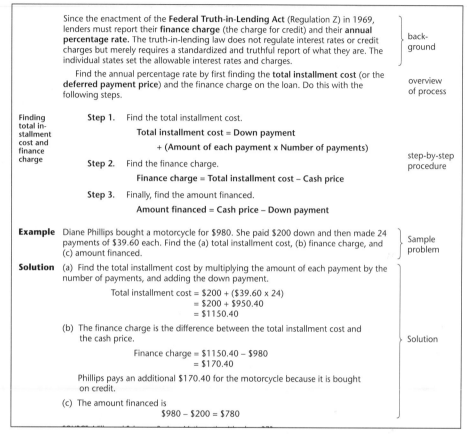

Since the enactment of the **Federal Truth-in-Lending Act** (Regulation Z) in 1969, lenders must report their **finance charge** (the charge for credit) and their **annual percentage rate.** The truth-in-lending law does not regulate interest rates or credit charges but merely requires a standardized and truthful report of what they are. The individual states set the allowable interest rates and charges. *} background*

Find the annual percentage rate by first finding the **total installment cost** (or the **deferred payment price**) and the finance charge on the loan. Do this with the following steps. *overview of process*

Finding total installment cost and finance charge

Step 1. Find the total installment cost.

Total installment cost = Down payment
+ (Amount of each payment x Number of payments)

Step 2. Find the finance charge.

Finance charge = Total installment cost – Cash price

Step 3. Finally, find the amount financed.

Amount financed = Cash price – Down payment

step-by-step procedure

Example Diane Phillips bought a motorcycle for $980. She paid $200 down and then made 24 payments of $39.60 each. Find the (a) total installment cost, (b) finance charge, and (c) amount financed. *} Sample problem*

Solution (a) Find the total installment cost by multiplying the amount of each payment by the number of payments, and adding the down payment.

Total installment cost = $200 + ($39.60 x 24)
= $200 + $950.40
= $1150.40

(b) The finance charge is the difference between the total installment cost and the cash price.

Finance charge = $1150.40 – $980
= $170.40

Phillips pays an additional $170.40 for the motorcycle because it is bought on credit.

(c) The amount financed is
$980 – $200 = $780

} Solution

Source: Miller and Salzman, *Business Mathematics,* p. 373

1. *Before you read the solution, think of how you would solve the problem, choose a method, and solve the problem.* More than one approach may be possible.

2. *Read the solution and compare your answer with the textbook's.*

3. *Be sure you understand each step; you should know exactly what calculations were performed and why they were done.*

4. *When you have finished reading the sample problem, explain the steps in your own words. This will help you remember the method later.* The best way to verbalize is to write the process down; this forces you to be clear and precise. Figure 16–6 on page 464 presents two sample problems and shows how a student verbalized each process.

5. *Test your understanding by covering up the text's solution and solving the problem yourself.* Finally, look over the solution, verifying its reasonableness and reviewing the process once again.

Figure 16–6 Verbalizing a Process

Problem 1: Find the principal of a loan that gives an interest of $30 at 10% per year for 91 days.

Solution	Verbalization
1. $P = \dfrac{I}{RT}$	1. The formula for computing principal is interest divided by the product of the rate multiplied by the time.
2. $P = \dfrac{30}{.10 \times \dfrac{91}{365}}$	2. The interest is $30. The rate, 10% per year, is converted to a decimal, .10, and the time is expressed as a fraction of a year.
3. $P = \dfrac{30}{.025}$	3. The denominator is simplified.
4. $P = \$1200$	4. The principal is $1200.

Problem 2: $\sqrt{3x+1} - \sqrt{x+9} = 2$

Solution	Verbalization
1. $\sqrt{3x+1} = 2 + \sqrt{x+9}$	Isolate one radical on one side of the equation.
2. $(-\sqrt{3x+1})^2 = (2 + \sqrt{x+9})^2$	Square both sides.
3. $3x + 1 = 4 + 4\sqrt{x+9} + x + 9$	Use formula $(a + b)^2 = a^2 + 2ab + b^2$.
4. $2x - 12 = 4\sqrt{x+9}$	Isolate the radical.
5. $x - 6 = 2\sqrt{x+9}$	Factor out 2 on the left side. Divide the equation by 2.
6. $(x - 6)^2 = (2\sqrt{x+9})^2$ $x^2 - 12x + 36 = 4(x + 9)$	Square both sides.
7. $x^2 - 12x + 36 = 4x + 36$ $x^2 - 16x = 0$ $x(x - 16) = 0$ $x = 16$	Solve for x.

Ignore the solution $x = 0$ because it will not check in the original equation. Extraneous roots can occur when you square both sides of an equation.

Source: Johnson and Steffensen, *Elementary Algebra,* p. 178

EXERCISE 16–2

For each of the following problems and solutions, verbalize the process and write each step in your own words. Compare your verbalization with that of another student.

1. Problem: The sum of two numbers is 21 and their difference is 9. Find the numbers.

   Solution: Let x, y be the two numbers.

   $$x + y = 21$$
   $$x - y = 9$$
   $$2x = 30$$
   $$x = 15$$
   $$\text{Then, } 15 + y = 21$$
   $$\text{so, } y = 21 - 15$$
   $$y = 6$$

2. Problem: Solve $x^2 - 6x + 8 = 0$ using the quadratic formula.

Solution: $a = 1, b = -6, c = 8$

$$x = \frac{-b \pm \sqrt{b^2 - 4ac}}{2a}$$

$$= \frac{-(-6) \pm \sqrt{(-6)^2 - 4(1)(8)}}{2(1)}$$

$$= \frac{6 \pm \sqrt{36 - 32}}{2}$$

$$= \frac{6 \pm \sqrt{4}}{2} = \frac{6 \pm 2}{2}$$

$$x = \frac{6 + 2}{2} = \frac{8}{2} = 4$$

or

$$x = \frac{6 - 2}{2} = \frac{4}{2} = 2$$

$$x = 4, 2$$

Reading and Drawing Graphs, Tables, and Diagrams   Graphs, tables, and diagrams are often included in textbook chapters. These are intended to help you understand processes and concepts by providing a visual representation. Treat these drawings as essential parts of the chapter. Here are a few suggestions on how to use them:

1. *Study each drawing closely, frequently referring to the text that accompanies it.* Test your understanding of the drawing by reconstructing and labeling it without reference to the text drawing; then compare drawings.

2. *Use the drawings in the text as models on which to base your own drawings.* As you solve end-of-chapter problems, create drawings similar to those included in the text. These may be useful as you decide how to solve the problem.

3. *Draw your own diagrams to clarify or explore relationships.* For example, an algebra student drew the following diagram of the trinomial equation.

$x^2 + 2xy + y$
obtained by squaring $(x + y)$

	x	y
x	x^2	xy
y	xy	y^2

$(x + y)^2 = (10 + 5)^2$
$x = 10$
$y = 5$

	10	5
10	$10^2 = 100$	$10 \cdot 5 = 50$
5	$10 \cdot 5 = 50$	$5^2 = 25$

$10^2 + 2(10 \cdot 5) + 5^2 = 225$

Another student drew the following diagram to explain why the formula for finding the area of a parallelogram is $A = bh$.

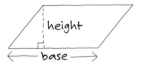

Cut off the triangle on left side of parallelogram.

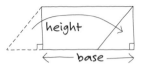

Move the triangle to create a rectangle.
Area of rectangle = base • height
so Area of parallelogram also = base • height
$A = bh$

4. *Use tables to organize and categorize large amounts of complicated data.* For example, a student made the following table to solve a frequency distribution problem in statistics, in which she was asked to identify the frequency of female Democrats and male Republicans. She was provided with the following information: Of a sample of 150 people, 62 males and 31 females are Democrats. Thirty-eight males and 19 females are Republicans.

	Democrat	**Republican**	**Totals**
Male	62	38	100
Female	31	19	50
Totals	93	57	150

Solving Word Problems   Most textbook chapters have numerous problem-solving exercises; quizzes and exams also consist primarily of problems. Often, the problems are expressed in words and are not conveniently set up for you in formulas or equations. Solving word problems is a seven-step process. In your textbook, be sure to work through exercises as they occur in the chapter. Do not wait until the end and try to work them all at once. Read the problem once to get an overview of the situation; then use the following steps:

1. *Identify what is asked for.* What are you supposed to find?

2. *Locate the information that is provided to solve the problem.* (Some math problems may include irrelevant information; if so, underline or circle pertinent data.)

3. *Draw a diagram, if possible. Label the diagram.*

4. *Estimate your answer.* If possible, make a reasonable guess about what the answer should be.

5. *Decide on a procedure to solve the problem.* Recall formulas you have learned that are related to the problem, and look for clue words that indicate a particular process. For example, the phrase "how fast" means *rate;* you may be able to use the formula $r = d/t$. If you do not know how to solve a problem, look for similarities between it and sample problems you have studied.

6. *Solve the problem.* Begin by choosing variables to represent the unknown quantities. Then set up an equation.

7. *Verify your answer.* Compare your answer with your estimate. If there is a large discrepancy, this is a signal that you have made an error. Be sure to check your arithmetic.

Figure 16–7 gives an example of how this problem-solving process works.

Figure 16–7   Sample Word Problem

Problem: A four-ton passenger paddleboat goes 210 miles down the Mississippi River in the same time it can go 140 miles upriver. The speed of the current is five miles per hour. Find the speed of the boat in still water.

Steps	*Solution*
1. Identify what is asked for.	speed in still water
2. Locate given quantities.	210 miles down 140 miles up
3. Draw a diagram.	

4. Estimate the answer.	Estimate: 20 mph
5. Decide on a procedure; recall formulas.	$d = rt$ (distance = rate x time)
6. Solve the problem.	x = speed in still water time up = time down $d = r \times t$ downstream $210 = (x + 5)t$ upstream $140 = (x - 5)t$
(a) Solve for t.	$d = rt$ $t = d/r$
(b) Determine t values.	t (downstream) $= \dfrac{210}{(x + 5)}$ t (upstream) $= \dfrac{140}{(x - 5)}$
(c) $t = t$	$\dfrac{210}{(x + 5)} = \dfrac{140}{(x - 5)}$
(d) Multiply both sides by $(x + 5)(x - 5)$.	$(x + 5)(x - 5)\dfrac{210}{(x + 5)} = (x + 5)(x - 5)\dfrac{140}{(x - 5)}$
(e) Solve the equation.	$210(x - 5) = 140(x + 5)$ $210x - 1050 = 140x + 700$ $70x = 1750$ $x = 25$
7. Compare with estimate and check arithmetic.	answer 25 mph (estimate was 20 mph)

EXERCISE 16–3   *Complete each of the following problems using the procedure outlined above. Label each step.*

1. Samantha receives an 11% commission on her sales of cosmetics. During one week, her daily sales were $482.10, $379.80, $729.62, $524.24, and $310.40. Find her gross earnings for the week.
2. If a microwave oven costs the retailer $325 and the markup is 35%, find the selling price.
3. Two joggers start jogging from the same point on a highway. One is running north, and the other is running south. One jogs 2 miles per hour faster than the other. They are 24 miles apart after 3 hours. At what rate is each jogging?
4. A collection of nickels and dimes is worth $2.85. If there are 34 coins in the collection, how many of each type of coin are there?
5. One number is 6 larger than another. The square of the larger is 96 more than the square of the smaller. Find the numbers.

EXERCISE 16–4   *Write three sample word problems. Exchange your problems with another student, and solve each other's problems.*

Using End-of-Chapter Material   Many mathematics texts include useful review material at the end of the chapter. Typically, there is a summary of key ideas from the chapter, often with sample worked examples; key terms; review exercises; and a chapter test. Use these materials to test yourself.

Use Writing to Learn

As in most disciplines, reading is not sufficient for learning mathematics. Highlighting and marking are the strategies students generally use to enhance learning; however, these techniques do not work well in mathematics. Mathematics texts are concise; everything is important. Writing, instead of highlighting, is a useful reading and learning strategy in mathematics. Writing in your own words will force you to convert mathematical language to everyday language. It will also demonstrate what you understand and what you do not. The following list suggests a few ways to use writing to increase your understanding and learning in mathematics.

1. *Definitions.* Read the textbook definition; then close the book and write your own. Compare it with the textbook definition, noticing and correcting discrepancies. Rewrite your definition until it is correct and complete.

2. *Class notes.* Rewrite your notes, including more detail and explanation. Focus on process; include reasons and explanations. Include information from the corresponding textbook section.

3. *Questions.* Write lists of questions based on chapter assignments, homework assignments, and your class notes. Seek answers from classmates, your instructor, a review book, or the learning lab or tutorial services.

4. *Problems.* Once you think you understand a particular problem or process, write down what you understand. To test your recall, write several questions based on your written explanation. Put aside both your explanation and your questions for several days. Then take out the question sheet and, without reference to your explanation, try to answer your questions. Compare your answers with your original explanation.

5. *Tests.* When preparing for an exam, construct and answer sample questions and problems. It is also effective to exchange self-constructed problems with a classmate and solve them.

6. *Diagrams.* Draw diagrams of sample problems as you read, and diagram actual problems before you attempt a solution. Describing the situation in visual terms often makes it more understandable.

7. *Review.* Review your course weekly. Write a description of what you have learned in the past week. You might compare your description with those of your classmates. Keep your weekly descriptions; they will be useful as you review for tests and final exams.

| **EXERCISE 16–5** | *Read Figure 16–8 (p. 470), an excerpt from a basic college mathematics textbook on the Pythagorean Theorem. Then complete each of the following steps.* |

1. List the terminology that is essential to understand when reading this excerpt.
2. Without referring to the text, write a definition of *hypotenuse*. Make a diagram to illustrate your definition. Compare your definition and diagram with the text excerpt. Revise your definition and diagram, if necessary.
3. Without referring to the text, describe how to use the Pythagorean Theorem to find the unknown length of the hypotenuse in a right triangle. Compare your description with the text excerpt. Revise your description if necessary.
4. Find the unknown length in the following right triangles.

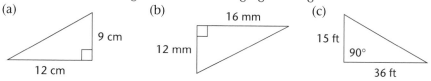

(a) 9 cm, 12 cm   (b) 16 mm, 12 mm   (c) 15 ft, 90°, 36 ft

Expect Gradual Understanding

Mathematics is a reasoning process: a process of understanding relationships and seeing similarities and differences. Consequently, mathematics is not an "either you understand it or you don't" discipline. Your understanding will develop by

Figure 16–8   Pythagorean Theorem

Objective ▶   One place you will use square roots is when working with the *Pythagorean Theorem*. This theorem applies only to *right* triangles (triangles with a 90° angle). The longest side of a right triangle is called the **hypotenuse** (hy-POT-en-oos). It is opposite the right angle. The other two sides are called *legs*. The legs form the right angle.

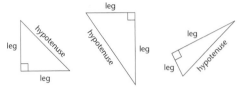

Examples of right triangles

Pythagorean Theorem

$$(\text{hypotenuse})^2 = (\text{leg})^2 + (\text{leg})^2$$

In other words, square the length of each side. After you have squared all the sides, the sum of the squares of the two legs will equal the square of the hypotenuse.

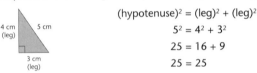

$$(\text{hypotenuse})^2 = (\text{leg})^2 + (\text{leg})^2$$
$$5^2 = 4^2 + 3^2$$
$$25 = 16 + 9$$
$$25 = 25$$

If you know the lengths of any two sides in a right triangle, you can use the Pythagorean Theorem to find the length of the third side.

Pythagorean Theorem

To find the hypotenuse, use this formula:

$$\text{hypotenuse} = \sqrt{(\text{leg})^2 + (\text{leg})^2}$$

EXAMPLE 2   Finding the Unknown Length in a Right Triangle

Find the unknown length in this right triangle.

The length of the side opposite the right angle is unknown. That side is the hypotenuse, so use this formula.

$$\text{hypotenuse} = \sqrt{(\text{leg})^2 + (\text{leg})^2} \qquad \text{Find the hypotenuse.}$$
$$\text{hypotenuse} = \sqrt{(3)^2 + (4)^2} \qquad \text{Legs are 3 and 4.}$$
$$= \sqrt{9 + 16} \qquad 3 \cdot 3 \text{ is } 9 \quad \text{and} \quad 4 \cdot 4 \text{ is } 16$$
$$= \sqrt{25}$$
$$= 5$$

The hypotenuse is 5 ft. long.

Note: You use the Pythagorean Theorem to find the *length* of one side, *not* the area of the triangle. Your answer will be in linear units, such as ft, yd, cm, m, and so on (*not* ft², cm², m²).

Source: Lial et al., *Basic College Mathematics*, pp. 548–49

degrees; it grows as you work or "play with" problems. Here is how you can work toward developing your understanding as you read.

1. *Plan on reading, and then reading and solving, and finally re-solving, problems.* As you reread and re-solve problems, you often will come to a new understanding of the process involved. (This is similar to seeing a film or reading a novel a second time; you will notice and discover things you did not see the first time.)

2. *Experiment with the chapter's content.* The style of most textbooks is concise, but this does not mean that there is no room for creativity or experimentation. Try various solutions to problems. As you experiment, you will come to a new understanding of the problems and solutions.

3. *Take risks.* Attempt a solution to a problem even if you do not fully understand it. As you work, you may discover more about how to arrive at the correct answer.

4. *Be active.* Active reading (see Chapter 1) is essential in mathematics. Get involved with the ideas, ask questions, and search for applications.

THOUGHT PATTERNS IN MATHEMATICS

Many students think that memorizing formulas, entire problems, and complete theories is the key to success in mathematics. This does not usually work because one predominant thought pattern in mathematics is *process*. Your goal in many situations is to see *how* a problem is solved or *how* a theory applies. As you make notes on chapters and as you rewrite class notes, explain, in your own words, how and why things work. Include reasons, explain relationships, and state why a particular operation was selected or why one problem-solving strategy was chosen over another.

Problem solving is also a primary pattern in most mathematics courses. Class activities, homework, and exams all require problem solving. Problem solving in mathematics involves creativity and even playfulness. It is not, as many students think, a matter of merely plugging numbers into a preselected formula and completing the necessary computations. Instead, problem solving is the process of assessing a situation (problem) and assembling and applying what you have learned that fits the problem. As you attempt to solve problems, do not immediately reach for a formula. Instead, analyze, think, and experiment while you work. Try several approaches and decide which one works best.

A third common thought pattern evident in many mathematics courses is comparison and contrast. Understanding and solving problems often requires you to see the similarities and differences among problem types and to study variations of sample problems. Often, you must look at a series of examples and detect a pattern (similarities) and then find a way to state this pattern as an equation or formula or rule. As you read and study, then, make notes about similarities and differences as they occur to you. Write, in your own words, how one problem differs from, or is a variation of, a type of problem you have previously learned about.

STUDYING MATHEMATICS

Be certain to attend all classes. Because mathematics is sequential, if you miss one specific skill, that gap in your understanding may cause you trouble all term. Expect regular homework assignments and complete them on time, even if your instructor does not require you to turn them in. Practice is an essential element in all mathematics courses. Never let yourself get behind or skip assignments. Try to study mathematics at least three times a week—more often, if possible. Use the following suggestions to learn mathematics more effectively.

Preparing for Class

1. *Emphasize accuracy and precision.* In mathematics, knowing how to solve the problem is not enough; you must produce the right answer. A small error in arithmetic can produce a wrong answer, even when you know how to solve the problem. Use a calculator if your instructor allows it.

2. *Read the chapter carefully before working on exercises.* Do not worry if you do not understand everything right away. Then, as you work on the problems, refer to the chapter frequently.

3. *Before you begin a new chapter or assignment, always review the preceding one.* If you take a break while working on an assignment, do a brief one-minute review when you resume study.

4. *Read the portion of your textbook that covers the next day's lecture before attending class.* The lecture will be more meaningful if you have some idea of what it is about beforehand.

5. *In your class notes, be sure to record sample problems that your instructor solves in class.* If you get behind in taking notes, leave some blank space; then fill in what is missing later by working with a classmate or asking your instructor. After class, review and organize your notes, rewriting them if necessary. Add your own observations and ideas from your textbook as well.

6. *Rework sample problems solved in class.* This is an excellent means of review.

7. *Find a study group and work together to solve problems immediately after class.* Get the phone numbers of a few people in class whom you can call if you have missed an assignment or are stuck on a problem.

8. *Keep your homework in a special notebook.* Star the problems you have trouble with. Bring this notebook with you when you ask your instructor for help so that you can go immediately to those problems. When you review for a test, study the starred problems.

Preparing Sample Tests

One of the best ways to learn mathematics is to create your own sample tests. Use index cards to write your questions. Try to create three or four test question cards for each section of the chapter as you go along. Write the problem, including the directions, on the front of the card; write the solution and a page number reference to your text on the back. When preparing for a test, shuffle the cards so you are forced to work the problems out of order. Try to simulate test conditions; give yourself a time limit, allow yourself the same equipment (such as a calculator), and so forth.

Building Your Confidence

1. Approach mathematics confidently. Both men and women can suffer what has come to be known as "math anxiety." Math anxiety often reflects a negative self-concept: "I'm not good at math." Some students think, incorrectly, that one either has or does not have a mathematical mind. This is a myth. Some people may find the subject easier than others, but the average student can learn mathematics.

2. If you feel uncomfortable about taking your first math course, consider taking a basic refresher course in which you are likely to be successful. You may not earn college credit, but you will build your confidence and prove to yourself that you can handle math. Other students find working with computerized review programs helpful when catching up on fundamentals. The machine is nonthreatening, offers no time pressures, and allows you to review a lesson as many times as you want. Many campuses offer workshops on overcoming math anxiety. To find out what help is available, check with your instructor, the learning lab, or the counseling center. A particularly useful book is *Conquering Math Anxiety,* by Cynthia Arem.

Test-Taking Tips
Preparing for Exams in Mathematics

Exams in mathematics usually consist of problems to solve. Use the following tips to prepare for exams in mathematics.

1. *When studying for exams, pay attention to what your instructor has emphasized.* Predict what will be on the exam, and make a sample test that includes all the important topics, and practice completing it.

2. *When studying for an exam, review as many sample problems as possible.* Do not just read the problems; practice solving them. Try to anticipate the variations that may appear. For example, a variation of the paddleboat problem shown in Figure 16–7 may give you the rate but ask you to compute the distance.

3. *Identify problems that are most character-istic of the techniques presented in the chapter you are studying.* Record these on a study sheet, and summarize in your own words how you worked them. Compare your study sheet with that of a friend.

4. *As you solve homework problems and review returned exams and quizzes, search for a pattern of errors.* Is there one type of problem you frequently have trouble with? Do you make mistakes when setting up the equation, in factoring, or in computation? If you identify such a pattern, pay special attention to correcting these errors.

5. *If you are having trouble with your course, get help immediately;* once you get behind, it is difficult to catch up. Consult with your instructor during his or her office hours. Check with the learning lab for tutoring or computer-assisted review programs.

6. *If you find you are weak in a particular fundamental such as fractions, correct the problem as soon as possible.* If you do not, it will interfere with your performance.

7. *Obtain additional study aids.* Schaum's *College Outline Series* offers excellent study guides. Check with your instructor for additional references.

8. *When a test is returned, rework the prob-lems on which you lost points to find out exactly what you did wrong.*

SUMMARY

This chapter discusses reading strategies for mathematics. Mathematics is largely sequential and cumulative; each skill builds on—and hinges on—previously learned skills.

Techniques for reading mathematics are

- learning mathematical language
- following chapter organization (including explanations, sample problems, diagrams, and graphs)
- dealing with word problems
- using writing to learn

Thought patterns that are among the most common in mathematics are

- process
- problem/solution
- comparison and contrast

Suggestions are offered for adapting study techniques to mathematics.

Mathematics

PREREADING QUESTIONS

1. Preview this selection. On the basis of your preview, write a sentence describing its contents.
2. How difficult do you predict it will be to complete the exercises at the end of this selection?

Introduction to Statistics: Mean, Median, and Mode

Margaret L. Lial and Diana L. Hestwood

1   The word *statistics* originally came from words that mean *state numbers.* State numbers refer to numerical information, or *data,* gathered by the government such as the number of births, deaths, or marriages in a population. Today the word *statistics* has a much broader meaning; data from the fields of economics, social science, science, and business can all be organized and studied under the branch of mathematics called *statistics.*

2   **Objective ▶** Making sense of a long list of numbers can be hard. So when you analyze data, one of the first things to look for is a *measure of central tendency*—a single number that you can use to represent the entire list of numbers. One such measure is the *average* or **mean.** The mean can be found with the following formula.

Finding the Mean (Average)

3
$$\text{mean} = \frac{\text{sum of all values}}{\text{number of all values}}$$

EXAMPLE 1   Finding the Mean

4   David had test scores of 84, 90, 95, 98, and 88. Find his average or mean score. Use the formula for finding mean. Add up all the test scores and then divide by the number of tests.

$$\text{mean} = \frac{84 + 90 + 95 + 98 + 88}{5} \qquad \begin{array}{l} \leftarrow \text{Sum of test scores} \\ \leftarrow \text{Number of tests} \end{array}$$

$$= \frac{455}{5} \quad \text{Divide}$$

$$= 91$$

David has a mean score of 91.

5   **Objective** ▶ Some items in a list of data might appear more than once. In this case, we find a **weighted mean,** in which each value is "weighted" by multiplying it by the number of times it occurs.

EXAMPLE 2   Understanding the Weighted Mean

6   The following table shows the amount of contribution and the number of times the amount was given (frequency) to a food pantry. Find the weighted mean.

Contribution Value	Frequency
$ 3	4
$ 5	2
$ 7	1
$ 8	5
$ 9	3
$10	2
$12	1
$13	2

7   The same amount was given by more than one person: for example, $5 was given twice and $8 was given five times. Other amounts, such as $12, were given once. To find the mean, multiply each contribution value by its frequency. Then add the products. Next, add the numbers in the *frequency* column to find the total number of values.

Value	Frequency	Product
$ 3	4	$(3 \cdot 4) = \$12$
$ 5	2	$(5 \cdot 2) = \$10$
$ 7	1	$(7 \cdot 1) = \$ 7$
$ 8	5	$(8 \cdot 5) = \$40$
$ 9	3	$(9 \cdot 3) = \$27$
$10	2	$(10 \cdot 2) = \$20$
$12	1	$(12 \cdot 1) = \$12$
$13	2	$(13 \cdot 2) = \$26$
Totals	**20**	**$154**

Finally, divide the totals.

$$\text{mean} = \frac{\$154}{20} = \$7.70$$

The mean contribution to the food pantry was $7.70.

8   A common use of the weighted mean is to find a student's *grade point average,* as shown by the next example.

EXAMPLE 3   Applying the Weighted Mean

9   Find the grade point average for a student earning the following grades. Assume A = 4, B = 3, C = 2, D = 1, and F = 0. The number of credits determines how many times the grade is counted (the frequency).

Course	Credits	Grade	Credits · Grade
Mathematics	3	A (= 4)	$3 \cdot 4 = 12$
Speech	3	C (= 2)	$3 \cdot 2 = 6$
English	3	B (= 3)	$3 \cdot 3 = 9$
Computer Science	3	A (= 4)	$3 \cdot 4 = 12$
Lab for Computer Science	2	D (= 1)	$2 \cdot 1 = 2$
Totals	**14**		**41**

It is common to round grade point averages to the nearest hundredth. So the grade point average for this student is shown below.

$$\frac{41}{14} \approx 2.93$$

10   **Objective ▶** Because it can be affected by extremely high or low numbers, the mean is often a poor indicator of central tendency for a list of numbers. In cases like this, another measure of central tendency, called the **median** (MEE-dee-un), can be used. The *median* divides a group of numbers in half; half the numbers lie above the median, and half lie below the median.

11   Find the median by listing the numbers *in order* from *smallest* to *largest.* If the list contains an *odd* number of items, the median is the *middle number.*

EXAMPLE 4   Using the Median

12   Find the median for the following list of prices.

$7, $23, $15, $6, $18, $12, $24

First arrange the numbers in numerical order from smallest to largest.

Smallest → 6, 7, 12, 15, 18, 23, 24 ← Largest

Next, find the middle number in the list.

6, 7, 12, 15, 18, 23, 24

Three are below   Three are above
Middle number

The median price is $15.

13   If a list contains an *even* number of items, there is no single middle number. In this case, the median is defined as the mean (average) of the *middle two* numbers.

EXAMPLE 5   Finding the Median

14   Find the median for the following list of ages.

$$74, 7, 15, 13, 25, 28, 47, 59, 32, 68$$

First arrange the numbers in numerical order. Then find the middle two numbers.

Smallest → 7, 13, 15, 25, 28, 32, 47, 59, 68, 74 ← Largest

Middle two numbers

The median age is the mean of these two numbers.

$$\text{median} = \frac{\mathbf{28 + 32}}{2} = \frac{60}{2} = 30 \text{ years}$$

15   **Objective ▶** The last important statistical measure is the **mode,** the number that occurs most often in a list of numbers. For example, if the test scores for 10 students were

↓   ↓   ↓

74, 81, 39, 74, 82, 80, 100, 92, 74, and 85

then the mode is 74. Three students earned a score of 74, so 74 appears more times on the list than any other score.

16   A list can have two modes; such a list is sometimes called *bimodal.* If no number occurs more frequently than any other number in a list, the list has *no mode.*

MEASURES OF CENTRAL TENDENCY

17   The **mean** is the sum of all the values divided by the number of values. It is the mathematical average.

The **median** is the middle number in a group of values that are listed from smallest to largest. It divides a group of numbers in half.

The **mode** is the value that occurs most often in a group of values.

—Lial and Hestwood, *Prealgebra,* pp. 347–50

VOCABULARY REVIEW

1. For each of the words listed below, use context; prefixes, roots, and suffixes; and/or a dictionary to write a brief definition of the word as it used in the reading.

   a. state numbers (para. 1) _____

   b. data (para. 2) _____

   c. values (para. 3) _____

   d. frequency (para. 6) _____

2. Underline new specialized terms introduced in the reading.

COMPREHENSION QUESTIONS

1. To assess your comprehension, define each of the following terms in your own words without reference to the reading: *statistics, measure of central tendency, mean, median, mode.* Verify your definitions by comparing them with the definitions in the reading.
2. What is the difference between a mean and a mode?
3. What is the difference between a mean and a median?

THINKING CRITICALLY

1. List the names and ages of 15 friends or classmates. (Estimate the ages, if necessary.)
   a. Find the mean age and the median age.
   b. Are the mean and median ages similar or different? Why did that happen?
2. List the names and ages of 10 family members or relatives. Try to include one very young person or one very old person (but not both). Estimate the ages, if necessary.
   a. Find the mean age and the median age.
   b. Are the mean age and median ages similar or different? Why did that happen?
3. List the courses you are taking at this time and the number of credits for each course.
   a. List the highest grade you think you will earn in each course. Then find your grade point average.
   b. List the lowest grade you think you will earn in each course. Then find your grade point average.
4. Suppose you own a gift shop. Last summer, you stocked T-shirts in five different sizes, but they took up too much shelf space. This summer, you want to order only one size. Using last summer's sales, should you find the mean size, median size, or mode size? Explain your answer.

LEARNING/STUDY STRATEGIES

1. Write a summary of the process involved in finding
   a. the mean
   b. the median
   c. the mode
2. What overall thought pattern(s) is or are used in the reading?

ONLINE RESEARCH: STATISTICS*

Statistics are used to describe the results of surveys and other research in many different fields. Often, the "raw" data are not given in reports; instead, the researcher has already analyzed the data before presenting it to the public.

The sites listed below include instances of both raw data and data that have already been analyzed. The questions, however, focus on raw data that you can analyze yourself.

1. The Media Awareness Network maintains statistics about television and other media. Visit their "Media Content: Television" page at http://www.media-awareness.ca/eng/issues/stats/contv.htm#unreal. Find the summary titled "T.V. 'Clutter' On The Rise." Read the summary to find out how much TV broadcasting time is taken up by commercials and other non-programming content. List the four time slots mentioned and the amount of time taken in each hour (given in minutes and seconds) for nonprogramming content. What is the mean amount of time for nonprogramming content per hour of TV content overall?

2. The Center for Science in the Public Interest, an organization that seeks to improve the safety and nutritional quality of food, includes an article about soft drinks titled "Liquid Candy" at http://www.cspinet.org/sodapop/liquid_candy.htm. Scan the article to find Table 2. From the table data, determine the mean ounces per day of soda pop drunk by all teens (boys and girls together). Then find the median number of ounces per day. Finally, does the list include a mode? If so, what is it?

*If either of these sites is unavailable, use a search engine to locate a new Web site on the same topic.

MATHEMATICS on the Internet

The Internet has numerous resources available for research in mathematics, including directories and Web guides to help you find material relevant to your studies, journals and databases, references works, and government resources. Here is a list of useful Web sites to get you started.

Directories/Web Guides

Yahoo! Mathematics

http://dir.yahoo.com/Science/Mathematics/

Mathematics WWW Virtual Library

http://www.math.fsu.edu/Science/math.html

Journals/Indexes/Databases

Math on the Web: Mathematical Journals

http://www.ams.org/mathweb/
mi-journals.html

Mathematics Journals

http://www.math.psu.edu/MathLists/
Journals.html

References

Women Mathematicians

http://www.agnesscott.edu/lriddle/women/
women.htm

20,000 Problems Under the Sea

http://problems.math.umr.edu/index.htm

Government Resources

MCS Research

http://www-fp.mcs.anl.gov/division/research/

Toward a Metric America

http://www.pueblo.gsa.gov/cic_text/misc/
usmetric/metric.htm

Multimedia Activities

Practice your reading and research skills on the Web.

1. **Math in Daily Life**

    http://www.learner.org/exhibits/dailymath/index.html

    Make a list of all the ways you apply math in your daily life. Then compare your list with the situations presented on this site. Do you use more math than you realized?

2. **Math Formula Sheets**

    http://faculty.prairiestate.edu/skifowit/htdocs/sheets/sheets.htm

    Print out these clear formula study sheets. Use memory building techniques to help you memorize them. Make copies and post them where you can see them easily. Try gluing them to index cards and quizzing yourself or a classmate.

CHAPTER 17

READING IN THE NATURAL SCIENCES

LEARNING OBJECTIVES

✦ To understand the scientific approach
✦ To develop specialized reading techniques for the sciences
✦ To learn to work with process, cause-and-effect, classification, and problem/solution patterns
✦ To adapt study strategies for the sciences

The natural sciences are divided into two categories: life sciences and physical sciences. The life sciences—biology, botany, zoology, and physiology—are concerned with the study of living organisms: how they grow, develop, function, and reproduce. The physical sciences are concerned with the properties, functions, structure, and composition of matter, substances, and energy. They include physics, chemistry, astronomy, and physical geography and geology.

THE SCIENCES: EXPLAINING NATURAL PHENOMENA

Science is built on knowledge resulting from scientific investigation. Through a process of asking well-defined, specific questions and searching for answers, science has accumulated a body of knowledge about how our physical and biological worlds function. The goal of science is to explain natural phenomena that affect our daily lives. Scientists ask questions and search for answers about any unexplained event. Consider, for example, the disease called AIDS. In scientific research that is still continuing, scientists have asked questions such as:

What causes it?

Why does it occur?

How is it transmitted?

What is its incubation period?

What are its precise effects on the immune system?

To study a problem, scientists use the scientific method. This method is also used to continually reevaluate what is known, in light of new research findings and discoveries. The operation of the scientific method was introduced in Chapter 13. In science courses, you will be reading about research findings as well as conducting your own experiments.

Because the emphasis is on observation and experimentation, most science courses have a required weekly lab in which you are given the opportunity to observe and experiment. The lab gives you direct experience with the scientific method while reinforcing, explaining, or demonstrating theories and principles presented in the course lectures.

Why Study the Sciences?

The field of natural science investigates the physical world around us. Science addresses and attempts to answer many important questions:

Is there extraterrestrial life?

Why do leaves change color in the fall?

Why do I have blue eyes when my parents' eyes are brown?

Science also explores questions essential to our well-being:

How can cancer be cured or prevented?

What synthetic substitutes can prevent depletion of our natural resources?

How can water pollution be prevented?

The study of science is fun and rewarding because you come to understand more about yourself and how you interact with the physical world around you.

SPECIALIZED READING TECHNIQUES

Although most college courses present new concepts and principles, they often cover subjects in the realm of your experience. The social sciences, for example, deal with social groups and physical and emotional needs—all concerns familiar to you. Science courses, on the other hand, sometimes deal with less familiar topics—molecular structure, mutant genes, or radioactive isotopes, for instance. Treatment of these topics may also be detailed and technical, involving a new and extensive vocabulary.

Because of the detailed nature of scientific material, plan to commit more time to reading and studying it than you would to studying other material—generally twice as much. Many students find that scientific study requires much greater time and effort than their other courses. Taking a science course is like taking three courses in one. You are, in a sense, taking a language course, since there is much new terminology to learn. A science course is also like a logic or philosophy course, since you must learn to work flexibly and logically with new ideas. Finally, a science course is like a graphic arts course in which you learn to draw and understand visual representations.

Reading scientific material requires specialized techniques, as does each of your other courses, but once you develop an effective approach, you will find science courses to be interesting and challenging, as well as manageable.

Use the following strategies to strengthen your approach to scientific reading.

Preview Before Reading

Because scientific material is often detailed and unfamiliar, previewing is even more important than in other courses. (Refer to Chapter 1 for a review of previewing techniques.) Your preview should include looking at problems at the end of the chapter and the chapter summary because they will provide clues about principles and formulas emphasized in the chapter.

Adopt a Scientific Mind-Set

To read effectively in a science course, it is essential to adopt a scientific way of thinking. The usual concerns (such as "What is important to learn?" and "How much supporting information do I need to learn?") may be of only secondary importance. Instead, to be successful, you must adopt the scientific mind-set of asking questions and seeking answers, analyzing problems, and looking for solutions or explanations. As you read, continually ask questions such as:

What does this mean? What does it *not* mean?

Does this make sense to me?

Why is this so?

How do we know this?

How does this happen?

What does this show?

Are alternative explanations plausible?

What laws govern or affect this?

To illustrate this process, Figure 17–1 shows the questions a student asked as she read a page of her chemistry textbook.

Sometimes, the questions you ask will be answered as you continue reading. Other times, you may need to seek answers yourself by referring to another chapter, by asking your instructor, or by talking with classmates. Asking and answering these questions will get you involved with the material and direct you toward scientific critical thinking.

Figure 17–1   Scientific Thinking

MARS

How far away is it?

Why?

Mars is the only planet whose surface features can be seen through Earth-based telescopes. Its distinctive rust-colored hue makes it stand out in the night sky. When Mars is near opposition, even telescopes for home use reveal its seasonal changes. Dark markings on the Martian surface can be seen to vary, and prominent polar caps shrink noticeably during the spring and summer months.

6-7   Earth-based observations originally suggested that Mars might harbor extraterrestrial life

Is it similar in other ways, as well?

The Dutch physicist Christian Huygens made the first reliable observations of Mars in 1659. Using a telescope of his own design, Huygens identified a prominent, dark surface feature that re-emerged roughly every 24 hours, suggesting a rate of rotation very much like the Earth's. Huygens' observations soon led to speculation about life on Mars because the planet seemed so similar to Earth.

What evidence did he offer?

In 1877 Giovanni Virginio Schiaparelli, an Italian astronomer, reported seeing 40 lines criss-crossing the Martian surface. He called these dark features *canali,* an Italian term meaning "water channels." It was soon mistranslated into English as *canals,* implying the existence on Mars of intelligent creatures capable of substantial engineering feats. This speculation led Percival Lowell, who came from a wealthy Boston family, to finance a major new observatory near Flagstaff, Arizona. By the end of the nineteenth century, Lowell had allegedly observed 160 Martian canals.

Why was it fashionable? Who did this?

What causes them?

It soon became fashionable to speculate that the Martian canals formed an enormous planetwide irrigation network to transport water from melting polar caps to vegetation near the equator. (The seasonal changes in Mars' dark surface markings can be mistaken for vegetation.) In view of the planet's reddish, desertlike appearance, Mars was thought to be a dying planet whose inhabitants must go to great lengths to irrigate their farmlands. No doubt the Martians would readily abandon their arid ancestral homeland and invade the Earth for its abundant resources. Hundreds of science fiction stories and dozens of monster movies owe their existence to the canali of Schiaparelli.

Source: Kaufmann and Comins, *Discovering the Universe,* pp. 144–45

EXERCISE 17–1

Read the following excerpt from a human physiology textbook. What questions could you ask about the excerpt? Write them in the margin.

COLLOIDS IN THE CAFETERIA

The next time you are in a cafeteria, look closely at the colorful gelatin dessert. It appears to be a transparent, wobbly solid, yet it consists primarily of water. The chocolate pudding nearby is also mainly water. Is it a solid or a liquid? When you fill your glass with milk, can you determine whether it is a solution or a mixture? Like most foods, these are *colloids,* suspensions of particles ranging from 20 μm to 100 μm in diameter, in a solvent. Colloidal particles are much larger than most molecules but are too small to be seen with a microscope. Colloids thus are often classified between homogeneous solutions and heterogeneous mixtures. The small particles give the colloid a homogeneous appearance but are large enough to scatter light. The light scattering explains why milk is white, not transparent.

A colloid that is a suspension of solids in a liquid is called a *sol,* and a suspension of one liquid in another is called an *emulsion.* For example, skim milk is a suspension of solids, mainly proteins, in water, so it is a sol; mayonnaise has small droplets of water suspended in oil, so it is an emulsion. When we whip cream, milk rich in butterfat, or beat egg whites to form meringues, we make *foams,* suspensions of a gas in a liquid or solid. When we separate the fat from milk and churn it into butter, we create a *solid emulsion,* a suspension of a liquid, in this case, milk, in a solid, butterfat. Gelatin desserts are a type of solid emulsion called a *gel,* which is soft, but holds its shape.

Aqueous colloids can be classified as hydrophilic or hydrophobic. Suspensions of fat in water, such as milk and mayonnaise, are hydrophobic colloids, because fat molecules have little attraction for water molecules. Gels and puddings are examples of hydrophilic colloids. The macromolecules of the proteins in gelatin and the starch in pudding have many hydrophilic groups that attract water. The giant protein molecules in gelatin uncoil in hot water. Their abundant amide groups form hydrogen bonds with water. When the mixture cools, the protein chains link together again, but now they enclose many water molecules within themselves, as well as molecules of sugar, dye, and flavoring agents. The result is an open network of protein chains that hold the water in a flexible solid structure.

—Atkins and Jones, *Chemistry: Molecules, Matter, and Change,* p. 444

Learn Terminology and Notation

Physics: wave-particle duality, torque, tangential acceleration, $v = dx/dt$

Physiology: hemagglutination, ventricular diastole, myocardial infarction, DNA

Chemistry: NaCl

Astronomy: mass-luminosity relation, eclipsing binaries, bok globules

How many of these terms are familiar? They are only a few of the new terms and notations encountered in each of these courses. As you can see, you will need to spend considerable time and effort learning terminology. You must understand the meaning of specialized and technical words in order to understand the ideas and concepts being presented.

In some courses, such as physics and chemistry, formulas and notation are important as well. Symbols, abbreviations, and formulas are used to represent objects and concepts in abbreviated form. You might think of these as shorthand systems for naming elements and quantities and describing their interaction. As you read and study, avoid memorizing formulas; instead, focus on understanding what they mean and how to apply them.

A course master file, described in Chapter 3, is extremely valuable in science courses. Mapping also works well, especially in the life sciences. Finally, as you learn the meaning of each new term, also learn its correct pronunciation and spelling.

Learn Symbols and Abbreviations

Symbols and abbreviations are frequently used in the sciences. The abbreviation "g" is a shortcut expression for a unit of mass, called a gram. The symbol "g" can also stand for the gravitational constant, 9.8N/kg, for the surface of the Earth. Textbooks use different kinds of type to distinguish types of quantities. For instance, "*v*" (in italics) means speed while "**v**" (in boldface) means velocity. Watch for clues your textbook provides.

Special Meanings of Everyday Words

Scientists sometimes attach specialized meanings to ordinary words. For example, *power, pressure, force,* and *impulse* are everyday words, but they have very specific meanings to a physicist. Power, for instance, is a measure of how fast work is done or energy is transformed and is represented by the formula:

$$Power = work \div time$$

Note that its meaning in science is different from its meaning in mathematics, too, where *power* refers to a number multiplied by itself. *Pressure,* another everyday term, in physics means the amount of force per area over which the force is distributed.

Because you are familiar with these words, it is easy to overlook them when studying or to assume you already know them. Be sure to include these terms in your course master file, along with the other specialized terminology and notations.

Learn Common Prefixes, Roots, and Suffixes

As you discovered in Chapter 3, many words in our language contain prefixes, roots, and suffixes. In most science courses, you will discover a common core of these word parts that are used as the basic building blocks of a specialized terminology. In physics, for example, units of measurement take prefixes.

Prefix	Meaning
micro-	millionth
milli-	thousandth
centi-	hundredth
deci-	tenth
deka-	ten
hecto-	hundred
kilo-	thousand
mega-	million
giga-	billion

In physiology, roots and suffixes unlock the meaning of numerous frequently used terms.

Root	Suffix	Word
hem(a)—blood	-logy (study of)	hematology
	-oma (growth, tumor)	hematoma
	-thermal (heat)	hemathermal

Similarly, in chemistry, astronomy, and biology you will find sets of core prefixes, roots, and suffixes. Include these in your master file, as suggested in Chapter 3.

Read Section by Section

Chapters in science texts are usually lengthy. Because the material is so complex, try not to read an entire chapter in one sitting. Instead, divide the chapter into sections and read one portion at a time. Look for end-of-chapter problems or questions that apply to the sections you are reading. Mark them and remember to work them out after you have read the section. Be sure to make connections between sections.

Study Sample Problems

In the physical sciences, sample problems are often included in the text to demonstrate a problem-solving process. Read the sample problems carefully, alternating between the text explanation and the mathematical solution. Next, explain the process in your own words. Doing so will solidify it in your memory. If you are unable to express the process in your own words or if you must refer back frequently to the text, this indicates that you do not fully understand the process. Do not expect to get it all the first time. These are difficult subjects, and understanding may come gradually.

Study and Draw Diagrams

Science texts contain numerous diagrams and drawings of structures and processes. These drawings often clarify a principle or concept; a diagram of a gun firing and recoiling, for example, makes the concept of conservation of momentum clear. Diagrams also are used to show forces, conditions, shapes, directions, processes, or positions. Diagrams provide a visual representation of an object or occurrence, and they increase your ability both to understand and to retain information. Diagrams are also important in answering questions and solving problems.

Many students do not pay enough attention to the diagrams included in their texts. Take time to study each drawing as you read. As you review, use the drawings to refresh your recall of key concepts and processes. Test your recall by closing the book and drawing the diagram from memory. Compare your drawing with the one in the text, noting errors, missing parts, or discrepancies. Do not be concerned if your drawings seem poor in comparison to the text; your ability to draw will improve as you practice.

You will also find diagrams useful in laboratory situations. Draw brief sketches of your equipment setup, techniques, and observations. These will help as you write your lab reports.

Brush Up on Math Skills

Mathematics is an integral part of many science courses, especially chemistry and physics. Many instructors assume you have taken algebra, which is often needed to solve equations and problems. If your math background is weak or if it has been a number of years since you studied algebra, you may need to brush up on your skills. You might consider taking a review course, purchasing a skills practice book, or using computer-assisted instructional programs in the learning lab. Talk with your instructor, and ask for recommendations.

THOUGHT PATTERNS IN THE NATURAL SCIENCES

Four thought patterns are common in the sciences: process, cause and effect, classification, and problem/solution.

The Process and Cause-and-Effect Patterns

Many of the sciences are concerned with how and why things happen: how a tadpole turns into a frog, what makes light reflect, how the tides work, how our metabolism functions, and so forth. Process and cause-and-effect patterns are often used to explain natural phenomena. Process and cause-and-effect patterns are logically linked to each other. In a process, the steps may be linked in a cause-and-effect chain. You may find that you need to read process descriptions more than once. Read the description the first time to get an overview; then read it at least once more to understand the steps and the connections between them.

Use the following strategies to read process material:

1. *List the steps.* Either in the text margin or in your notebook, write a step-by-step summary of the process in your own words. Figure 17–2 (p. 490) shows the notes a student wrote for a physics textbook chapter on plate tectonics, explaining how islands and mountains are formed.

2. *Draw diagrams or maps.* Diagrams, maps, or flowcharts help you visualize the process and will enhance your recall as well. Chapter 11 describes several types of mapping. Figure 17–3 (p. 491) shows a diagram a biology student drew to describe how convection currents stir the air and create winds.

Figure 17–2   Sample Summary

PLATE TECTONICS

Summary:

1. Earth's crust has approx. 12 large plates = lithosphere. These rest on the asthenosphere.

2. These plates spread and sink (subduction).

3. When a continental plate and an ocean plate collide, a trench and island arc will form.

4. When ocean plates collide, they create a marginal or inland sea.

5. When continental plates collide, folding and faulting of sediment and rock occurs, creating mountain ranges.

Recent ideas concerning seafloor spreading and the origin and evolution of the ocean basins are incorporated into an even more encompassing concept called **plate tectonics.** In plate tectonics theory, Earth's entire crust is composed of about a dozen large plates, up to 160 km (100 miles) thick. These plates make up the lithosphere. Each moves essentially as a rigid block over Earth's surface. The lithosphere rests upon the less rigid part of Earth called the **asthenosphere.**

The plates can be visualized as curved caps covering a large ball, or perhaps as sections of peel on an orange. Boundaries of the individual plates are usually areas of high seismic (earthquake) activity. Deformation, such as faulting, folding, or shearing mainly occurs at the boundaries between the plates. Because the surface area of Earth is essentially constant, spreading in one place must be balanced by sinking or **subduction** somewhere else.

The appearance of the edge of a continent is often influenced by its relation to areas of seafloor spreading or subduction. If a continent's edge is at the boundary

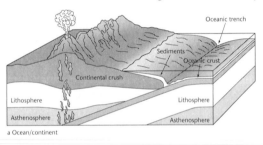

of a subducting oceanic plate, a trench will form, and sometimes an **island arc** or coastal mountain range (Figure a). A **trench** is a deep, long narrow depression in the seafloor, with very steep slopes. An island arc is a curved pattern of mainly volcanic islands and a trench. It is

a Ocean/continent

generally curved in a convex direction (bows out) toward the ocean, with the trench on the seaward side. The Aleutian Islands and Aleutian Trench in the north Pacific is a good example of a trench-island arc system.

The subducting plate forms the trench. In the process of submerging beneath the

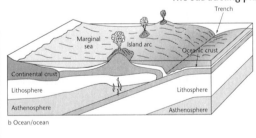

other plate, much of its sediment is scraped off onto the landward side of the trench. This material and the subducting plate may be reheated, perhaps even melted, eventually becoming part of the continental plate and forming a coastal mountain range. These are events that occur when oceanic crust is subducted beneath lighter continental crust. A similar sequence occurs during the collision of two ocean plates. The main difference is that an inland or marginal sea may form behind an island arc (Figure b).

b Ocean/ocean

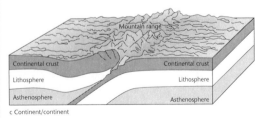

Results can be quite different when two plates of continental composition collide. In this case, both plates are of similar density, so neither easily overrides the other. The result is unusually intense folding and faulting of the sediments and rocks, often leading to the formation of a major mountain range (Figure c). The Himalayan Mountains are still being formed in this manner by the collision of India (continental crust) with Asia (continental crust).

c Continent/continent

Source: Ross, *Introduction to Oceanography*, pp. 51–52

Figure 17–3   Sample Diagram

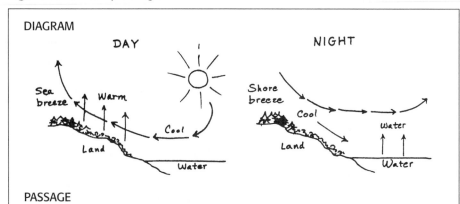

DIAGRAM

PASSAGE

Convection currents stirring the atmosphere result in winds. Some parts of the earth's surface absorb heat from the sun more readily than others, and as a result the air near the surface is heated unevenly and convection currents form. This is evident at the seashore. In the daytime the shore warms more easily than the water; air over the shore is pushed up (we say it rises) by cooler air from above the water taking its place. The result is a sea breeze. At night the process reverses because the shore cools off more quickly than the water, and then the warmer air is over the sea. Build a fire on the beach and you'll notice that the smoke sweeps inward during the day and seaward at night.

Source: Hewitt, *Conceptual Physics,* pp. 274–75

3. *Describe the process aloud.* Assume you are explaining the process to a friend who is not taking the course, or better yet, actually study with a friend. By forcing yourself to explain the process in a nontechnical way, you can test whether you really understand it and are not simply rephrasing the technical language used by the author.

EXERCISE 17–2

Read the following excerpt from a biology textbook. Working with a classmate, one student should write a summary of the transpiration process while the other draws a diagram. Exchange your work, and draw a diagram based only on your partner's summary, or write a summary based only on his or her diagram. Then compare the results with the whole excerpt.

CARBON DIOXIDE AND THE GREENHOUSE EFFECT

The possible relationship between carbon dioxide in the atmosphere and climate warming was proposed by Svante Arrhenius, one of the early winners of the Nobel Prize in chemistry (1903). Arrhenius knew a great deal about geology as well as chemistry, and he was familiar with the effects of glaciation on the terrain of his native Sweden. He was also aware of the growing discussion of the causes of glaciations that enlivened many geologists' meetings at the end of the nineteenth century. He reasoned that the small amount of carbon dioxide in the atmosphere (now about 345 ppm) could affect climate because the carbon dioxide molecules strongly absorb heat rays from the Earth.

Here is how it works. The atmosphere is relatively transparent to the incoming visible rays of the Sun. Much of this radiant energy from the Sun is absorbed by the Earth's surface and then reemitted as invisible infrared heat rays. Just as a hot pavement radiates heat as it is warmed by the Sun, the Earth's surface radiates heat back to the atmosphere. The atmosphere, however, is not transparent to these infrared rays, because carbon dioxide and water molecules strongly absorb the infrared instead of allowing it to escape to space. As a result, the atmosphere is heated and radiates heat back to the surface. this is called the *greenhouse effect,* by analogy to the warming of a greenhouse, whose glass lets in visible light but lets little heat escape.

The more carbon dioxide, the warmer the atmosphere; the less carbon dioxide, the colder. Without any greenhouse effect, Earth's surface temperature would be well below freezing and the oceans would be a solid mass of ice. Geologists now have evidence that, aside from glaciations, climates ranged from warm to cool in the geological past. It is likely that some of these changes were related to changes in the amount of carbon dioxide in the atmosphere.

—Press and Siever, *Understanding Earth,* p. 348

The Classification Pattern

In the life sciences, classification is an important pattern. As a means of studying life forms or species, biologists classify them into groups or types based on shared or similar characteristics. In fact, there are seven levels of groupings altogether. Organisms are first divided into five kingdoms. Those kingdoms are subdivided into divisions called phyla, and then into classes, orders, families, genera, and species. For example, humans are classified as follows:

Category	Classification
kingdom	animalia
phylum	chordata
class	mammalia
order	primates
family	hominidae
genus	*Homo*
species	*sapiens*

Other examples of classification include types of cells, methods of reproduction, and types of tissues.

Classification is also used in the physical sciences. In chemistry, elements are grouped and listed by groupings on the periodic table. In physics, matter is classified into gases, liquids, plasmas, and solids.

When reading material written in this pattern, first determine what is being classified and what the types or groups are. Look for a topic or summary sentence that states what is being classified. Next, discover why or on what basis the classification was made. That is, determine what characteristics members of the group share. For example, the following excerpt from a biology textbook describes the classification of animal eggs.

TYPES OF EGGS

The three basic types of animal eggs are roughly categorized according to the amount of *yolk* they have. The amount of yolk is critical since it is the embryo's food supply, at least for a time. In some species, the embryo needs only a small supply of yolk since it soon switches to nutrients derived from the mother's blood, as is the case with humans. We only need enough to last until the embryo has implanted in the wall of the uterus. In contrast, birds leave their mother's body at a very early developmental stage, and they must carry their entire embryonic food supply with them. So, whereas a human egg is smaller than the period at the end of this sentence, it would be hard to hide an ostrich egg with this whole book. Interestingly, both the young and the adults of these two species are about the same size.

Other kinds of animals have a moderate yolk supply. In these, the young must begin to find its own food long before it has reached its final body organization. The frog is an example. The frog egg has just enough yolk to get the developing embryo to the tadpole stage; after that, the tadpole can survive on food stored in its tail for a time, but it must soon begin to eat on its own.

—Wallace, *Biology: The World of Life,* pp. 446–47

In this excerpt, the basis of classification is directly stated in the first sentence: eggs are classified according to the size of the yolk.

EXERCISE 17–3 | *Read this excerpt from a physiology textbook, and answer the questions that follow.*

TYPES OF SMOOTH MUSCLE

The smooth muscle in different body organs varies substantially in its (1) fiber arrangement and organization, (2) responsiveness to various stimuli, and (3) innervation. However, for simplicity, smooth muscle is usually categorized into two major types: *single-unit* and *multiunit smooth muscle.*

Single-Unit Smooth Muscle

Single-unit smooth muscle, commonly called **visceral muscle,** is far more common. Its cells (1) contract as a unit and rhythmically, (2) are electrically coupled to one another by *gap junctions,* and (3) often exhibit spontaneous action potentials. All the smooth muscle characteristics described so far pertain to single-unit smooth muscle. Thus, the cells of single-unit smooth muscle are arranged in sheets, exhibit the stress-relaxation response, and so on.

Multiunit Smooth Muscle

The smooth muscles in the large airways to the lungs and in large arteries, the arrector pili muscles attached to hair follicles, and the internal eye muscles that adjust your pupil size and allow you to focus visually are all examples of **multiunit smooth muscle.**

In contrast to what we see in single-unit muscle, gap junctions are rare and spontaneous and synchronous depolarizations infrequent. Multiunit smooth muscle, like skeletal muscle, (1) consists of muscle fibers that are structurally independent of each other; (2) is richly supplied with nerve endings, each of which forms a motor unit with a number of muscle fibers; and (3) responds to neural stimulation with graded contractions. However, while skeletal muscle is served by the somatic (voluntary) division of the nervous system, multiunit smooth muscle (like single-unit smooth muscle) is innervated by the autonomic (involuntary) division and is also responsive to hormonal controls.

—Marieb, *Human Anatomy and Physiology*, p. 294

1. What does this excerpt classify?
2. Describe each type of smooth muscle.
3. On what basis is the classification made?

The Problem/Solution Pattern

Textbook chapters, homework, and exams in the physical sciences often contain problems. To solve these problems, you must apply the concepts, laws, and formulas presented in the chapter. Use the following steps to solve problems.

1. *Read the problem and identify what is given and what is asked for.* In word problems, mark or underline critical information. Next, restate the information using the symbols you will use as you solve the problem. Be certain not to use the same symbol to represent different quantities. For example, if there are two objects in a situation with different masses, do not use m for both masses. Use m_1 and m_2 to distinguish between the two masses.

2. *If possible, make a drawing of the problem.* Label known quantities with the correct symbols; using the symbols may suggest which equation to use in solving the problem, if you are not certain.

3. *State the principle that is related to the problem, and write the general equation that embodies the principle.*

4. *Calculate the solution.* Always write the units after each number (seconds, moles, liters, etc.).

5. *Analyze your answer.* Does it make sense? Compare your solution with similar sample problems and determine whether you followed the correct procedure. Check the units as well as the numerical values.

6. *Review your solution process.* Especially if you had difficulty with the problem, pause after you solve it to figure out what you should have done or known in order to solve it more easily. Did you overlook a step or ignore a key concept? Analyzing your solution process will help you solve similar problems more easily in the future.

Here is an example of the use of this problem-solving procedure:

PROBLEM: A cat steps off a ledge and drops to the ground in ½ second. What is the cat's speed on striking the ground? What is the cat's average speed during the ½ second? How high is the ledge from the ground?

Steps	**Example**
1. Identify what is given and what is asked for	Given: drops in ½ sec, t = ½ sec Asked for: 1. speed (velocity) (v) 2. average speed (average velocity) ($\bar{v}$) 3. height (distance) (d)
2. Draw a diagram	t = ½ sec
3. Determine the principle and formula	Principle: acceleration and motion of free falling bodies Formulae: $v = gt$, $d = \bar{v}t$ $g = 10$ m/s² $\bar{v} = \dfrac{\text{beginning } v + \text{final } v}{2}$
4. Calculate the solution	$v = gt$ $v = 10$ m/s² $\times$ ½ s = 5 m/s $\bar{v} = \dfrac{0 \text{m/s} + 5 \text{ m/s}}{2} = 2.5$ m/s
5. Analyze the answer	$d = \bar{v}t = 2.5$ m/s² $\times$ ½ s = 1.25 m
6. Review the solution process	Had to know acceleration of free-falling bodies is 10 m/s²

—Hewitt, *Conceptual Physics,* p. 21

ADAPTING YOUR STUDY TECHNIQUES

Because of the unique content of science courses, it is especially important to adapt your study habits. Use the following suggestions for studying in the sciences.

1. *Complete reading assignments before attending lectures.* Because of the unfamiliar subject matter, you can understand lectures better if you know something about the topic. You may not understand everything you read (and it will be necessary to reread after the lecture), but you will have an advantage during the lecture because the terms, concepts, and principles will be more familiar.

2. *Highlight your textbook selectively.* Everything looks important in scientific texts, and it is easy to fall into the habit of over-highlighting. Avoid this pitfall by reading a paragraph or section before highlighting. Then go back and mark only key terms and concepts. Do not try to highlight all useful facts. Refer to Chapter 11 for suggestions on how to highlight effectively.

3. *Use outlining.* Especially in the life sciences, many students find outlining to be an effective study and review technique. Some texts in the life sciences include chapter outlines; even though your text may have one, make your own. It is the process of making the outline that is important. Outlining forces you to decide what information is important and how it is related and then to express the ideas in your own words. Refer to Chapter 11 for specific suggestions on taking outline notes.

4. *Integrate your lab work with the text and lectures.* Most science courses have a required lab. Because the lab is scheduled separately from the lecture and has its own manual, you may fail to see the lab as an integral part of the course. The lab is intended to help you understand and apply principles and research techniques used in your course and provides you with an opportunity to ask pertinent questions. Use the following tips for handling lab work:
   - Be prepared before going to lab. Read the experiment once to understand its overall purpose and a second time to understand the specific procedures. Make notes or underline key information.
   - Ask questions before you make a mistake. Lab procedures can be time-consuming to repeat, so ask questions first.
   - Be sure you understand the purpose of each step before you perform it.
   - Analyze your results and do the lab report as soon as possible. The best time to study your results is while the experiment and procedures are still fresh in your mind. If you finish the lab work early, stay and discuss results and interpretations with other students or your lab instructor.
   - Follow the required format closely when writing your report.

5. *Use chapter problems as guides.* The end-of-chapter problems in your textbook help you determine what it is important to learn. Do the problems even if they have not been assigned by your instructor. As you read the problems, note the variables (temperature, pressure, volume, etc.) that appear in the problems. Then be certain to learn definitions, concepts, principles, and formulas pertaining to these variables.

6. *Develop a weekly study plan.* Science is best studied on a daily basis. Devise a weekly plan that includes time every day for previewing text assignments, reviewing lecture notes, reading text assignments, preparing for and writing up labs, and—most important—reviewing in such a way as to integrate lectures, the text, and lab sessions.

7. *Prepare for exams.* Exams and quizzes in the sciences require you to learn factual information as well as develop problem-solving ability and apply your learning to practical situations. To be prepared for exams,

- Make lists of types of problems you have studied and key facts about their solution.
- Identify key laws, principles, and concepts.
- Determine where your instructor placed her or his emphasis.
- Prepare a practice test, using problems from your text, and take it as though it were an actual exam.
- Consider forming a study group with classmates.

IF YOU ARE HAVING DIFFICULTY

If the sciences are typically a difficult field of study for you, or if you suddenly find yourself not doing well in a science course, try the following survival tactics.

Use available resources. Visit your instructor during office hours to discuss your performance or to get help with particular problems. Check to see whether tutoring is available through the department office or the college's learning center.

Make changes in your learning strategies. If you are a non-science major taking your one or two required science courses, you may feel as strange as if you were in a foreign country. First, you must revise your approaches and strategies. Plan on making the changes already described in this section.

Learn from classmates. Talk with and observe the strategies of students who are doing well in the course. You are likely to pick up new and useful procedures.

Double your study time. If you are having trouble with a course, make a commitment to spend more time on it and to work harder. Use this added time to revise and try out new study strategies. Never spend time using a strategy that is not working.

Purchase a review book. Find a student practice manual or other learning aid and work with it regularly. Many major science texts have study guides or problem-solving guides to accompany them. Your instructor may be able to recommend specific titles. If the book you purchase does not use the same notation system as your text, be sure to note any differences.

Finally, here are some specific tips to help you "pull the course together":

1. Review your lecture notes and text assignments frequently; discover how they work together and where they seem to be headed.

2. As you review, make a list of topics you do understand and a list of those you do not.

3. Decide whether you are experiencing difficulty as a result of gaps in your scientific background. Ask yourself whether the instructor assumes you know things when you do not. If so, consider finding a tutor.

4. Make a list of specific questions and ask for help from both your classmates and your instructor.

Test-Taking Tips

Preparing for Exams in the Natural Sciences

Exams in the sciences require you to learn factual information as well as to develop problem-solving ability and apply your learning to practical situations. To be prepared for exams,

1. *Identify key laws, principles, and concepts.* Prepare review sheets on which you summarize important information.

2. *Make lists of types of problems you have studied.* For example, in chemistry, for a chapter on gases, you might identify problem types such as pressure and volume, temperature and pressure, and temperature and volume. For each problem type, list steps in the solution. Practice solving each problem type by using exercises in the text or by constructing your own problems.

3. *Consider forming a study group with classmates.* Quiz each other, and work through sample problems.

4. *Prepare a practice exam using problems or review questions from your text, and take it as though it were an actual exam.*

5. *Do not review by simply rereading your text and notes.* The material will look familiar, and you will think you have learned it. Instead, test yourself: Ask yourself questions and answer them. Use guide questions (see Chapter 1).

SUMMARY

This chapter describes reading strategies for the sciences. The sciences focus on asking questions about our physical and biological world and seeking answers to those questions.

Specialized techniques for reading the sciences are

- previewing before reading
- adopting a scientific mind-set
- learning terminology and notation
- reading section by section
- studying sample problems
- brushing up on math skills

Four thought patterns predominate in the sciences:

- process
- cause and effect
- classification
- problem/solution

Suggestions are offered for adapting study techniques to the sciences.

Biology

PREREADING QUESTIONS

1. How did dinosaurs become extinct?
2. Why did other animals become extinct at this same time?

Death Stars and Dinosaurs: The Great Extinctions

Robert Wallace

1   It may be quite difficult to account for the beginnings of new species, but it is often easy to see how some species died out. We have built dams and knowingly doomed small pockets of isolated species. We have hunted other animals to extinction, as we did the dodo, the carrier pigeon, and the last common ancestor of the horse and zebra. However, other species have passed into extinction for reasons that continue to puzzle us. In particular, it is difficult to account for the massive, large-scale extinctions in which many species passed from the Earth at once. For example, why did so many species die out with the great dinosaurs at the end of the Cretaceous period?[1]

2   One hypothesis advanced to account for the die-off at the end of the Cretaceous is based on data suggesting that the temperature of the Earth dropped drastically about that time. The dinosaurs and the others, some say, simply died of the chilling effects of hypothermia. However, others have urged that the cooling of the Earth unbalanced the sex ratios of many species. They note that the sexes of many kinds of animals, such as alligators, amphibians, and some fish, are temperature dependent. That is, eggs raised in environments below a certain temperature will give rise to animals of one sex, and above that temperature, to the other sex. The argument is that as the Earth cooled below a certain critical point, all the hatchlings of some species would have been of one sex and doomed to roam the Earth without ever knowing the joys of parenthood. . . .

3   Another explanation of the great extinctions of the Cretaceous also involves a cooling episode, but this one accounts for its origins. According to the **Alvarez hypothesis,** the Earth was struck by a great asteroid that raised a cloud of dust that blocked the sun for many months and effectively impeded photosynthesis. Any such disruption of the food chain would have led to the demise of a great many species. The evidence here is circumstantial but solid. The best line of evidence is the discovery that a rare element called iridium was deposited in a fine layer over the Earth at about the end of the Cretaceous. Iridium is uncommon in the Earth's crust, but quite common in asteroids. . . .

---

[1]A period of time 65 million years ago.

4   Other researchers have suggested that the Earth was struck by some heavenly body that was not an asteroid, but perhaps three or four comets. . . . The comets, they say, were from the great belt of 100 million or so comets that lazily circle the sun far beyond the reaches of the solar system. Occasionally, though, about every 26 to 30 million years, great numbers of the comets are jerked toward our sun by the passage of a companion star to the sun. The companion star has not been located or identified, but it has been named Nemesis. Journalists, with their flair for high drama, have taken to calling it the Death Star.

5   Any such companion star, if it exists, could be any of the hefty little "black stars," dense bodies with a gravitational pull so strong that not even light can escape. It has been suggested that the star has an extremely elliptical orbit that takes it far into the celestial realm—until its next deadly loop through the belt of comets. Geologists have found that the Earth has indeed been peppered every 30 million years or so by celestial objects big enough to form craters, and that the cycles roughly match the great extinctions that paleontologists tell us have taken place on our planet. Again, there is great disagreement about the existence of Nemesis and, in fact, about the periodic extinctions themselves.

6   Finally, there are those who say that about every 20 to 30 million years, the Earth passes through severe galactic storms of dark clouds and gas as the sun takes us through the plane of the Milky Way, and that these storms are responsible for the great surges of death on the planet.

7   However, on a brighter note, the sun is now passing through a clear zone, the pristine aftermath of an exploded star. So all should be clear sailing for a while . . . or so they say.

8   In summary, we have seen that, as Darwin suggested, variation in natural populations results in some organisms being better reproducers than others and that their kinds of alleles tend to increase in populations. The best reproducers, of course, will tend to be those most in harmony with the environment. Thus, populations tend to track their environment through adaptation. Evolution, then, as we understand it today, is simply a function of basic arithmetic. Those alleles that promote successful reproduction will increase in frequency.

9   Life on Earth is subject to countless pressures as it continues striving for its very existence. It must constantly react to the nature of its situation (or its predicament) and it must change. The world is a variable and changeable place, and different life forms have evolved that are uniquely able to utilize one aspect of the Earth or another in their own ways. Put simply, life must change in order to take advantage of that part of the world available to it. In the next chapter, we will begin to explore this vast array of life and see just what the processes of natural selection have wrought.

—Wallace, *Biology: The World of Life*, pp. 191, 193–94

VOCABULARY REVIEW

1. For each of the words listed below, use context; prefixes, roots, and suffixes; and/or a dictionary to write a definition or synonym of the word as it is used in the reading.

a. doomed (para. 1) _____

b. extinction (para. 1) _____

c. asteroid (para. 3) _____

d. demise (para. 3) _____

e. comets (para. 4) _____

f. elliptical (para. 5) _____

g. celestial (para. 5) _____

h. craters (para. 5) _____

i. paleontologists (para. 5) _____

j. pristine (para. 7) _____

k. alleles (para. 8) _____

l. utilize (para. 9) _____

2. Underline new specialized terms introduced in the reading.

COMPREHENSION QUESTIONS

1. In what two ways have humans caused extinctions?
2. How could the cooling of the Earth have caused extinctions?
3. Describe one theory for the Earth's cooling at the end of the Cretaceous period.
4. Explain the "Alvarez hypothesis."
5. What is the "Death Star"?

CRITICAL THINKING QUESTIONS

1. Which theory of dinosaur extinction do you think is most likely to be true? Why?
2. Can you think of other animals (mammals? amphibians?) not mentioned in the reading that have become extinct?
3. Do you think the writer of this selection believes in the "Death Star" theory? Why or why not?
4. Choose one of the explanations. What other evidence would you look for to confirm or refute this explanation?
5. Do you think the Earth as we know it will end? Why or why not?

LEARNING/STUDY STRATEGIES

1. Prepare a chart that summarizes the different theories that account for the extinction of dinosaurs. Use the format shown on the next page.

THEORY	DESCRIPTION

2. What is the overall thought pattern used throughout this reading?

ONLINE RESEARCH: DEATH STARS AND DINOSAURS*

The study of the evolution of species is part of many scientific fields including biology, paleontology, and geology, among others. Research some of the findings of these fields at the University of California's Museum of Paleontology (UCMP).

1. The UCMP offers an exhibit on dinosaurs, which includes a section on "What Killed the Dinosaurs? The Great Mystery." Access this part of the site by going to http://www.ucmp.berkeley.edu/diapsids/extinction.html. Scan the opening to enrich your understanding of the textbook reading: What is the technical definition of "mass extinction"? What other species died out at the same time as the great dinosaurs? Then move on to the section "Current Arguments" to get further details about the Alvarez hypothesis. What evidence is presented in support of the Alvarez hypothesis?

2. The textbook reading notes that the great dinosaurs and other species died out at the end of the Cretaceous period. Researching the Cretaceous period will help you put this mass extinction in context. For example, you can consult the UCMP's geological Web Time Machine at http://www.ucmp.berkeley.edu/help/timeform.html to find out what time period the Cretaceous covers and what era the Cretaceous period is part of. To find out what life forms were developing at about the same time that the dinosaurs were becoming extinct, go to the section on "Ancient Life." To discover where various Cretaceous fossils have been found, go to the section on "Localities." Explore the aspects of the period that interest you the most.

*If either of these sites is unavailable, use a search engine to locate a new Web site on the same topic.

The NATURAL SCIENCES on the Internet

The Internet has numerous resources available for research in the natural sciences, including directories and Web guides to help you find material relevant to your studies, journals and databases, references works, and government resources. Here is a list of useful Web sites to get you started.

Directories/Web Guides

The Academy of Natural Sciences Internet Resources
> http://www.acnatsci.org/library/link.html

Internet Public Library: Life Sciences
> http://www.ipl.org/ref/RR/static/
> sci36.00.00.html

Journals/Indexes/Databases

Agricola
> http://www.nal.usda.gov/ag98/

PubMed
> http://www.ncbi.nlm.nih.gov/entrez/query.fcgi

References

FishBase
> http://ibs.uel.ac.uk/fishbase/

MEDLINEplus Medical Encyclopedia
> http://www.nlm.nih.gov/medlineplus/
> encyclopedia.html

Government Resources

Earth Science Enterprise
> http://www.earth.nasa.gov/

LLNL Biology and Biotechnology Research Program
> http://www-bio.llnl.gov/bbrp/
> bbrp.homepage.html

Multimedia Activities

Practice your reading and research skills on the Web.

1. **Astronomy Magazine**
    http://www.astronomy.com/home.asp
    Explore the "final frontier" with the online version of this classic magazine. Find out what is in the sky tonight or read up on the latest discoveries. Be sure to visit the photo gallery. Write a list of words describing how you feel about the universe and your place in it.

2. **Current Earthquake Information**
    http://www.neic.cr.usgs.gov/current seismicity.shtml
    Research the movement of the Earth at this site from the U.S. Geological Survey. Have there been any earthquakes near you lately? You may be surprised.

CHAPTER 18

READING IN TECHNICAL AND APPLIED FIELDS

LEARNING OBJECTIVES

◆ To learn what to expect in technical courses
◆ To develop specialized reading techniques for technical material
◆ To learn processes and develop problem-solving strategies
◆ To adapt your study strategies for technical material

Our society has become a technological one, in which there is a heavy reliance on automation and computerization. Consequently, more technical knowledge and expertise are required. More students are pursuing degrees in a variety of technical fields, including computer information systems, environmental technology, mechanical and electrical technology, and computer-assisted drafting. Applied fields such as EKG and X-ray technology, air conditioning and refrigeration, food service, and horticulture are other examples.

TECHNICAL FIELDS: WHAT TO EXPECT

If you are earning a degree in a technical field, you will take two basic types of courses: the technical courses in your major and required courses in related disciplines. For example, if you are earning an associate's degree in information technology, you will take numerous technical courses in programming, logic, and systems design, but you are also required to complete courses such as English composition, business communication, and physical education. Here is what to expect in each of these categories.

Technical Courses

The goal of many technical courses is to teach specific procedures and techniques that you will use on the job. These courses often present the theory and principles that govern the procedure, as well.

Grading and evaluation in technical courses is often performance-based. In addition to traditional exams and quizzes, instructors use "hands-on" exercises to evaluate your performance. In an air conditioning and refrigeration course, for example, you may be given a broken air conditioner to repair.

Work in technical fields often involves situations that require problem solving: a computer program has a "bug," a lab test produces inconsistent results, a number of landscape plantings die. Consequently, many instructors are careful to include problem-solving tasks in class, during labs, or on exams.

Many fields involve the use of instruments and equipment; others require measurement and recording of data. In either case, procedures must be followed exactly; measurements must be precise.

Although classroom lectures usually are a part of technical courses, most include some practical forms of instruction as well. Their purpose is to provide you with hands-on experience working with the procedures you are learning. As you work through lab assignments, remember that your skills are on display to your instructor just as they will be later to an employer. Develop systematic, organized routines to handle frequently used procedures and processes. Concentrate on following directions carefully. Always check and double-check your work. (Refer to Chapter 17 for additional suggestions on how to prepare and conduct lab work.) Labs also give you an opportunity to find out whether you actually understood the lecture on which the lab is based. Labs will also help you discover whether you like the career you have chosen. If you dislike labs or find them extremely difficult or too routine, you should question the appropriateness of your career choice.

Nontechnical Required Courses

Make a genuine effort to benefit from courses outside your technical field. If you are taking a required introductory psychology course, you may be the only student in the class majoring in nursing; in this case, your psychology professor can do little or nothing to relate the course to your field. As your instructor discusses various topics, you should consider how they can be applied in your field. As you learn about defense mechanisms, for example, you might consider how they might be exhibited by patients. As you study nontechnical courses, be sure to make connections and applications to your field.

READING TECHNICAL MATERIAL

Textbooks in technical fields are highly factual and packed with information. Compared to other textbooks, technical writing may seem "crowded" and difficult to read. In many technical courses, your instructor requires you to read manuals as well as textbooks. These are even more dense and, on occasion, poorly written. Use the following suggestions to help you read and learn from technical writing.

Read Slowly

Because technical writing is factual and contains numerous illustrations, diagrams, and sample problems, adjust your reading rate accordingly. Plan on spending twice as long reading a technical textbook as you spend on reading other, nontechnical texts.

Reread When Necessary

Do not expect to understand everything the first time you read the assignment. It is helpful to read an assignment once rather quickly to get an overview of the processes and procedures it presents. Reread it to learn the exact steps or details.

Have a Specific Purpose

Reading technical material requires that you have a carefully defined purpose. Unless you know why you are reading and what you are looking for, it is easy to become lost or to lose your concentration. Previewing is particularly helpful in establishing purposes for reading.

Pay Attention to Illustrations and Drawings

Most technical books contain illustrations, diagrams, and drawings, as well as more common graphical aids such as tables, graphs, and charts. (Refer to Chapter 9 for suggestions on reading graphics). Although graphics can make the text appear more complicated than it really is, they actually are a form of visual explanation designed to make the text easier to understand. Read the following excerpt from a building design and construction textbook describing the framing of roof rafters.

ROOF RAFTERS

Once the ceiling joists are nailed in place, the **roof rafters** can be installed. Common sizes or roof rafters include 2 in. x 6 in., 2 in. x 8 in., or 2 in. x 10 in. members spaced 12 in., 16 in., or 24 in. o.c., depending upon the width of the house and the magnitude of the dead and live loads imposed on the roof.

The rafters from both sides are usually connected at the top to a ridge board (Fig. A). Due to the angle cut in the rafters, the ridge board must be a larger size than the rafter. The ridge board runs the entire length of the roof and helps to distribute the roof load among several rafters. The location where the rafter bears on the exterior wall is notched to form a snug fit. The notch is commonly known as a "bird's mouth." The end of the roof is known as the gable and is the location where the roof and wall join.

Collar beams (i.e., collar ties) are often required when roof spans are long and the slopes are flat. Steeper slopes and shorter spans also may require collar beams, but only between every third rafter pair. Collar beams are usually 1 in. x 6 in. or 2 in. x 4 in. members.

—Willenbrock et al., *Residential Building Design and Construction,* pp. 171–72

Figure A
Roof Rafter/Ceiling Joist
Roof Framing System
Source: Gerald E. Sherwood
and Robert C. Stroh, *Wood
Frame House Construction*,
p. 81 (Mineola, NY: Dover
Publications, Inc. 1989).

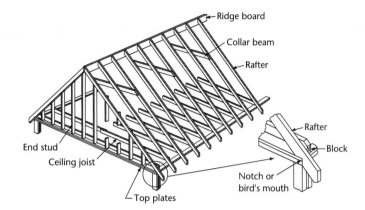

Now, study the diagram and reread the passage above. Does the diagram make the passage easier to understand?

Here are a few suggestions on how to read illustrations and diagrams.

1. *Note the type of illustrations or diagrams included in the assignment when you preview the chapter.*

2. *Look over each illustration, and determine its purpose.* The title or caption usually indicates what it is intended to show.

3. *Examine the illustration first.* Alternate between the text and the illustrations; illustrations are intended to be used with the paragraphs that refer to them. You may have to stop reading several times to refer to an illustration. For instance, when collar beams are mentioned in the preceding example, stop reading and find where they are placed in the diagram. You may also have to reread parts of the explanation several times.

4. *Look at each part of the illustration and note how the parts are connected.* Notice any abbreviations, symbols, arrows, or labels.

5. *Test your understanding of illustrations by drawing and labeling an illustration of your own without looking at the one in the text.* Then compare your drawing with the text. Note whether anything is left out. If so, continue drawing and checking until your drawing is complete and correct. Include these drawings in your notebook and use them for review and study.

EXERCISE 18–1 *Read the following excerpt on ignition coils from an automotive technology textbook, and answer the questions that follow.*

IGNITION COILS

The heart of any ignition system is the **ignition coil.** The coil creates a high-voltage spark by electromagnetic induction. Many ignition coils contain two separate but electrically connected windings of copper wire. Other coils are true transformers in which the primary and secondary windings are not electrically connected. See Figure A.

The center of an ignition coil contains a core of laminated soft iron (thin strips of soft iron). This core increases the magnetic strength of the coil. Surrounding the laminated core are approximately 20,000 turns of fine wire (approximately 42-gauge). These windings are called the **secondary** coil windings. Surrounding the secondary winding are approximately 150 turns of heavy wire (approximately 21-gauge). These windings are called the **primary** coil windings. In many coils, these windings are surrounded with a thin metal shield and insulating paper and placed in a metal container. Many coils contain oil to help cool the ignition coil. Other coil designs, such as those used on GM's **high energy ignition** (**HEI**) systems, use an air-cooled, epoxy-sealed **E coil** named for the *E* shape of the metal laminations inside the coil.

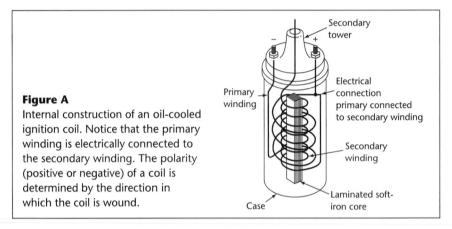

Figure A
Internal construction of an oil-cooled ignition coil. Notice that the primary winding is electrically connected to the secondary winding. The polarity (positive or negative) of a coil is determined by the direction in which the coil is wound.

—Halderman and Mitchell, *Automotive Technology: Principles, Diagnosis, and Service,* pp. 382–83

1. What is the purpose of the illustration?
2. Does the diagram make the text easier to understand? Briefly describe how.
3. Sketch a diagram of an ignition coil without referring to the above drawing.

Use Visualization

Visualization is a process of creating mental pictures or images. As you read, try to visualize the process or procedure that is being described. Make your image as specific and detailed as possible. Visualization will make reading these descriptions easier, as well as improving your ability to recall details. Here are a few examples of how students use visualization.

A nursing student learned the eight family life cycles by visualizing her sister's family at each stage.

A student taking a computer course was studying the two basic methods of organizing data on a magnetic disk: the sector method and the cylinder method. She visualized the sector method as slices of pie and the cylinder method as a stack of dinner plates.

Now read the following description of an optical disk system from a computer science textbook, and try to visualize as you read.

OPTICAL DISKS

Optical technology used with laser disk systems is providing a very high capacity storage medium with the **optical disk,** also called a **videodisk.** Videodisks will open new applications, since they can be used to store data, text, audio, and video images.

Optical disk systems look like magnetic disk systems. Each has a rotating platter and a head mechanism to record information. However, optical systems differ because they use light energy rather than magnetic fields to store data. A high-powered laser beam records data by one of two methods. With the **ablative method,** a hole is burned in the disk surface. With the **bubble method,** the disk surface is heated until a bubble forms.

The laser beam, in a lower power mode, reads the data by sensing the presence or absence of holes or bumps. The light beam will be reflected at different angles from a flat or disfigured surface. A series of mirrors is used to reflect the light beam to a photodiode, which transforms the light energy into an electric signal. The photodiode process works like the automatic doors at your local supermarket. As you walk toward the door, you deflect a light beam, which signals the doors to open.

—Athey et al., *Computers and End-User Software,* pp. 122–23

Did you visualize the disks with tiny holes or bumps?

EXERCISE 18–2

Read the following passage describing a standard bumper jack. As you read, try to visualize the jack. After you have finished, draw a sketch of the jack as it is described in the passage. After you have completed your sketch, compare it with Figure 18–1 on page 510.

DESCRIPTION OF A STANDARD BUMPER JACK

Introduction—General Description

The standard bumper jack is a portable mechanism for raising the front or rear of a car through force applied with a lever. This jack enables even a frail person to lift one corner of a 2-ton automobile.

The jack consists of a molded steel base supporting a free-standing, perpendicular notched shaft. Attached to the shaft are a leverage mechanism, a bumper catch, and a cylinder for insertion of the jack handle. Except for the main shaft and leverage mechanism, the jack is made to be dismantled and to fit neatly in the car's trunk.

The jack operates on a leverage principle, with the human hand traveling 18 inches and the car only $\frac{3}{8}$ of an inch during a normal jacking stroke. Such a device requires many strokes to raise the car off the ground, but may prove a life-saver to a motorist on some deserted road.

Five main parts make up the jack: base, notched shaft, leverage mechanism, bumper catch, and handle.

Description of Parts and Their Function

Base

The rectangular base is a molded steel plate that provides support and a point of insertion for the shaft. The base slopes upward to form a platform containing a 1-inch depression that provides a stabilizing well for the shaft. Stability is increased by a 1-inch cuff around the well. As the base rests on its flat surface, the bottom end of the shaft is inserted into its stabilizing well.

Shaft

The notched shaft is a steel bar (32 inches long) that provides a vertical track for the leverage mechanism. The notches, which hold the mechanism in its position on the shaft, face the operator.

The shaft vertically supports the raised automobile, and attached to it is the leverage mechanism, which rests on individual notches.

Leverage Mechanism

The leverage mechanism provides the mechanical advantage needed for the operator to raise the car. It is made to slide up and down the notched shaft. The main body of this pressed-steel mechanism contains two units: one for transferring the leverage and one for holding the bumper catch.

The leverage unit has four major parts: the cylinder, connecting the handle and a pivot point; a lower pawl (a device that fits into the notches to allow forward and prevent backward motion), connected directly to the cylinder; an upper pawl, connected at the pivot point; and an "up-down" lever, which applies or releases pressure on the upper pawl by means of a spring. Moving the cylinder up and down with the handle causes the alternate release of the pawls, and thus movement up or down the shaft—depending on the setting of the "up-down" lever. The movement is transferred by the metal body of the unit to the bumper-catch holder.

The holder consists of a downsloping groove, partially blocked by a wire spring. The spring is mounted in such a way as to keep the bumper catch in place during operation.

Bumper Catch

The bumper catch is a steel device that attaches the leverage mechanism to the bumper. This 9-inch molded plate is bent to fit the shape of the bumper. Its outer ½ inch is bent up to form a lip, which hooks behind the bumper to hold the catch in place. The two sides of the plate are bent back 90 degrees to leave a 2-inch bumper-contact surface, and a bolt is riveted between them. This bolt slips into the groove in the leverage mechanism and provides the attachment between the leverage unit and the car.

Figure 18–1 Sample Diagram

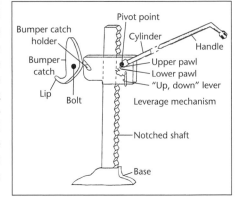

Jack Handle

The jack handle is a steel bar that serves both as lever and lug-bolt remover. This round bar is 22 inches long, ⅝ inch in diameter, and is bent 135 degrees roughly 5 inches from its outer end. Its outer end is a wrench made to fit the wheel's lug bolts. Its inner end is beveled to form a blade-like point for prying the wheel covers and for insertion into the cylinder on the leverage mechanism.

Conclusion and Operating Description

One quickly assembles the jack by inserting the bottom of the notched shaft into the stabilizing well in the base, the bumper catch into the groove on the leverage mechanism, and the beveled end of the jack handle into the cylinder. The bumper catch is then attached to the bumper, with the lever set in the "up" position.

As the operator exerts an up-down pumping motion on the jack handle, the leverage mechanism gradually climbs the vertical notched shaft until the car's wheel is raised above the ground. When the lever is in the "down" position, the same pumping motion causes the leverage mechanism to descend the shaft.

—Lannon, *Technical Writing,* pp. 419–21

Mark and Highlight

You may find your textbooks to be valuable reference sources for lab or on-site experiences; you may also use them when you are employed in your field. Take special care, then, to mark and highlight your textbooks for future reference. Marking will also make previewing for exams easier. Develop a marking system that uses particular symbols or colors of ink to indicate procedures, important formulas, troubleshooting charts, and so forth. Refer to Chapter 11 for additional suggestions on how to highlight effectively.

Learn to Read Technical Manuals

Many technical courses require students to operate equipment or become familiar with computer software. Study of and frequent reference to a specific manual are additional requirements in some technical courses. Unfortunately, many technical manuals are poorly written and organized, so you need to approach them differently from textbooks. Use the following suggestions when reading technical manuals.

1. *Preview the manual to establish how it is arranged and exactly what it contains.* Does it have an index, a troubleshooting section, a section with specific operating instructions? Study the table of contents carefully and mark sections that will be particularly useful.

2. *Do not read the manual from cover to cover.* First, locate and review those sections you identified as particularly useful. Concentrate on the parts that describe the overall operation of the machine: its purpose, capabilities, and functions.

3. *Next, learn the codes, symbols, commands, or terminology used in the manual.* Check to see if the manual provides a list of special terms. Many computer software manuals, for instance, contain a list of symbols, commands, or procedures used throughout the manual. If such a list is not included, begin making your own list on a separate sheet or on the inside cover of the manual.

4. *Begin working with the manual and the equipment simultaneously, applying each step as you read it.*

5. *If the manual does not contain a useful index, make your own by jotting down page numbers of sections you know you will need to refer to frequently.*

6. *If the manual is overly complicated or difficult to read, simplify it by writing your own step-by-step directions in the margin or on a separate sheet.*

THOUGHT PATTERNS IN TECHNICAL FIELDS

The two thought patterns most commonly used in technical fields are process and problem/solution. Each is used in textbooks and manuals as well as in practical, hands-on situations.

Reading Process Descriptions

Testing procedures, directions, installations, repairs, instructions, and diagnostic checking procedures all follow the process pattern. To read materials written in this pattern, you must not only learn the steps but also learn them in the correct order. To study process material, use the following tips.

1. *Prepare study sheets that summarize each process.* For example, a nursing student learning the steps in venipuncture (taking a blood sample) wrote the summary sheet shown in Figure 18–2.

Figure 18–2   Sample Summary Sheet

Venipuncture

1. Wash hands, explain procedure to patient; assess patient status
2. Assemble equipment
3. Locate puncture site
4. Apply tourniquet, cleanse site
5. Place thumb distal to puncture site
6. Insert needle 30° angle, aspirate desired amount
7. Remove tourniquet, place dry compress on needle tip & withdraw
8. Remove needle from syringe and place specimen in container; label

2. *Test your recall by writing out the steps from memory.* Recheck periodically by mentally reviewing each step.

3. *For difficult or lengthy procedures, write each step on a separate index card.* Shuffle the pack and practice putting the cards in the correct order.

4. *Be certain you understand the logic behind the process.* Figure out why each step is performed in the specified order.

EXERCISE 18–3

Read the following excerpt describing acid rain. After you have read it, write a process summary of each stage of the acid rain process. Compare your process summary with that of a classmate.

HOW ACID RAIN DEVELOPS, SPREADS, AND DESTROYS

Introduction

Acid rain is environmentally damaging rainfall that occurs after fossil fuels burn, releasing nitrogen and sulfur oxides into the atmosphere. Acid rain, simply stated, increases the acidity level of waterways because these nitrogen and sulfur oxides combine with the air's normal moisture. The resulting rainfall is far more acidic than normal rainfall. Acid rain is a silent threat because its effects, although slow, are cumulative. This report explains the cause, the distribution cycle, and the effects of acid rain.

Most research shows that power plants burning oil or coal are the primary cause of acid rain. The burnt fuel is not completely expended, and some residue enters the atmosphere. Although this residue contains several potentially toxic elements, sulfur oxide and, to a lesser extent, nitrogen oxide are the major problem, because they are transformed when they combine with moisture. This chemical reaction forms sulfur dioxide and nitric acid, which then rain down to earth.

The major steps explained here are (1) how acid rain develops, (2) how acid rain spreads, and (3) how acid rain destroys.

The Process

How Acid Rain Develops

Once fossil fuels have been burned, their usefulness is over. Unfortunately, it is here that the acid rain problem begins.

Fossil fuels contain a number of elements that are released during combustion. Two of these, sulfur oxide and nitrogen oxide, combine with normal moisture to produce sulfuric acid and nitric acid. (Figure A illustrates how acid rain develops.) The released gases undergo a chemical change as they combine with atmospheric ozone and water vapor. The resulting rain or snowfall is more acid than normal precipitation.

Acid level is measured by pH readings. The pH scale runs from 0 through 14—a pH of 7 is considered neutral. (Distilled water has a pH of 7.) Numbers above 7 indicate increasing degrees of alkalinity. (Household ammonia has a pH of 11.) Numbers below 7 indicate increasing acidity. Movement in either direction on the pH scale, however, means multiplying by 10. Lemon juice, which has a pH value of 2, is 10 times more acidic than apples, which have a pH of 3, and is 1,000 times more acidic than carrots, which have a pH of 5.

Figure A   How Acid Rain Develops

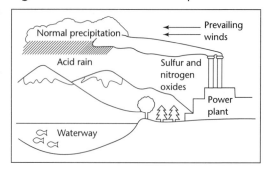

Because of carbon dioxide (an acid substance) normally present in air, unaffected rainfall has a pH of 5.6. At this time, the pH of precipitation in the northeastern United States and Canada is between 4.5 and 4. In Massachusetts, rain and snowfall have an average pH reading of 4.1. A pH reading below 5 is considered to be abnormally acidic, and therefore a threat to aquatic populations.

How Acid Rain Spreads

Although it might seem that areas containing power plants would be most severely affected, acid rain can in fact travel thousands of miles from its source. Stack gases escape and drift with the wind currents. The sulfur and nitrogen oxides are thus able to travel great distances before they return to earth as acid rain.

For an average of two to five days, the gases follow the prevailing winds far from the point of origin. For example, estimates show that about 50 percent of the acid rain that affects Canada originates in the United States; at the same time, 15 to 25 percent of the U.S. acid rain problem originates in Canada.

The tendency of stack gases to drift makes acid rain such a widespread menace. More than 200 lakes in the Adirondacks, hundreds of miles from any industrial center, are unable to support life because their water has become so acidic.

How Acid Rain Destroys

Acid rain causes damage wherever it falls. It erodes various types of building rock such as limestone, marble, and mortar, which are gradually eaten away by the constant bathing in acid. Damage to buildings, houses, monuments, statues, and cars is widespread. Some priceless monuments and carvings already have been destroyed, and even trees of some varieties are dying in large numbers.

Figure B   How Acid Rain Destroys

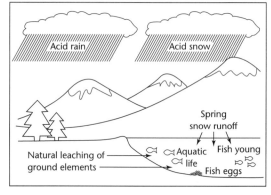

More important, however, is acid rain damage to waterways in the affected areas. (Figure B illustrates how a typical waterway is infiltrated.) Because of its high acidity, acid rain dramatically lowers the pH of lakes and streams.

Although its effect is not immediate, acid rain can eventually make a waterway so acidic it dies. In areas with natural acid-buffering elements such as limestone, the dilute acid has less effect. The northeastern United States and Canada, however, lack this natural protection, and so are continually vulnerable.

The pH level in an affected waterway drops so low that some species cease to reproduce. In fact, a pH level of 5.1 to 5.4 means that fisheries are threatened; once a waterway reaches a pH level of 4.5, no fish reproduction occurs. Because each creature is part of the overall food chain, loss of one element in the chain disrupts the whole cycle.

In the northeastern United States and Canada, the acidity problem is compounded by the runoff from acid snow. During the cold winter months, acid snow sits with little melting, so that by spring thaw, the acid released is greatly concentrated. Aluminum and other heavy metals normally present in soil are released by acid rain and runoff. These toxic substances leach into waterways in heavy concentrations, affecting fish in all stages of development.

Summary

Acid rain develops from nitrogen and sulfur oxides emitted by industrial and power plants burning fossil fuels. In the atmosphere, these oxides combine with ozone and water to form acid rain: precipitation with a lower-than-average pH. This acid precipitation returns to earth many miles from its source, severely damaging waterways that lack natural buffering agents. The northeastern United States and Canada are the most severely affected areas in North America.

—Lannon, *Technical Writing*, pp. 452–55

Problem-Solving Strategies

In technical fields, you will encounter hypothetical problems to solve that require you to apply formulas and work with procedures. More important, you will face simulated problems in labs and actual problems throughout your career. A systematic approach is helpful to improve your problem-solving abilities.

It is easy to panic when a piece of equipment fails or a procedure does not produce the expected results. Using a systematic approach to solving problems will help you in these situations. A problem is basically a conflict between "what is" (the present state) and "what should be" or "what is desired" (the goal state). For example, a medical office assistant has a problem when she cannot calm a frightened child in order to take her blood pressure. The following steps can help you attack problem situations.

Step 1: Specify the problem. Do this by evaluating the present state and determining how it differs from what is desired. The more specific you can be, the more likely that you will be able to identify working solutions. For example, if you are faced with a machine that does not function properly, decide what part or feature is malfunctioning. Do not simply say the machine does not work; instead, decide that the robot arm does not remain in position to complete the task. If your patient will not cooperate when you need to take her blood pressure, try to discover why she is unwilling.

Step 2: Analyze the problem. Analysis is a complex critical thinking skill. Begin by learning as much as you can about the problem. For instance, it may be necessary to find out why your young patient is frightened in order to be able to calm her down. To analyze a problem, it may be necessary to look beyond the obvious solution—to stretch your imagination and reach for creative options. For example, you may discover the child is frightened because you are wearing white and the child's dentist, of whom she is frightened, also wears white. When analyzing a problem, use the following suggestions.

Be flexible in your analysis. Do not eliminate possibilities because they seem unlikely or never have happened in the past.

Brainstorm about all the possibilities. Except for problems that must be solved immediately, spend a few minutes listing anything you can think of that is remotely related to your problem. Sort through the list later, preferably the next day. You probably will discover the seeds of a solution.

Talk with others about the problem. By putting the problem into words (to a classmate or your instructor), you may hear yourself say things that will lead to further understanding.

Research problems for which you lack complete information.

Step 3: Formulate a solution path. Identify a possible solution to the problem. For some problems, such as a machine malfunction, there is only one correct solution. For others, such as an uncooperative patient, various solutions may be feasible.

Step 4: Evaluate possible solution paths. If you have identified more than one solution path, the next step is to weigh the advantages and disadvantages of each one. You will need to think through each solution path in detail, considering how, when, and where you could accomplish each. Consider the likelihood of success with each solution, and weigh both short- and long-term effects. Thinking aloud may help you realize why various solutions will not work.

Step 5: Implement the solution. If your solution does not solve the problem, analyze what went wrong and repeat the problem-solving process. A trial-and-error process may be necessary. Be sure to use a logical, systematic approach and keep track of your results for each trial.

EXERCISE 18–4

Form groups of four to five students and discuss and develop a strategy for solving each of the following problems.

1. A microcomputer will not boot the program when the disk is inserted in the second disk drive.
2. A student in a science laboratory technology course gets a different result for his lab experiment than other students conducting the same experiment.

STUDY TECHNIQUES FOR TECHNICAL COURSES

Use the following suggestions to adapt your study skills to technical courses.

Pronounce and Use Technical Vocabulary

Understanding the technical vocabulary in your discipline is essential. For technical and applied fields, it is especially important to learn to pronounce technical terms and to use them in your speech. To establish yourself as a professional in the field and to communicate effectively with other professionals, it is essential to speak the language. Use the suggestions in Chapter 3 for learning specialized terminology.

Draw Diagrams and Pictures

Although your textbook may include numerous drawings and illustrations, there is not enough space to include drawings for every process. An effective learning strategy is to draw diagrams and pictures whenever possible. These should be fast sketches; be concerned with describing parts or processes, and do not worry about artwork or scale drawings. For example, a student studying air conditioning and refrigeration repair drew a quick sketch of a unit he was to repair in his lab before he began to disassemble it. He then referred to sketches he had drawn in his notebook as he diagnosed the problem.

Reserve Blocks of Time Each Day for Study

Daily study and review are important in technical courses. Many technical courses require large blocks of time (two to three hours) to complete projects, problems, or drawings. Technical students find that taking less time is inefficient because if they leave a project unfinished, they have to spend time rethinking it and reviewing what they have already done when they return to the project.

Focus on Concepts and Principles

Because technical subjects are so detailed, many students focus on these details rather than on the concepts and principles to which they relate. Keep a sheet in the front of your notebook on which you record information to which you need to refer frequently. Include constants, conversions, formulas, metric equivalents, and commonly used abbreviations. Refer to this sheet so you will not interrupt your train of thought in order to search for these pieces of information. Then you can focus on ideas rather than specific details.

Make Use of the Glossary and Index

Because of the large number of technical terms, formulas, and notations you will encounter, often it is necessary to refer to definitions and explanations. Place a paper clip at the beginning of the glossary and a second at the index so you can find them easily.

Test-Taking Tips
Preparing for Exams in Technical Courses

Exams in technical courses may consist of objective questions or of problems to solve. (For suggestions on preparing for and taking these types of exams, see the test-taking tips in Chapters 13, 14, and 16.) Other times, exams may take the form of a practicum. A practicum is a simulation, or a rehearsal, of some problem or task you may face on the job. For example, a nursing student may be asked to perform a procedure while a supervisor observes. Or an EKG technologist may be evaluated in administering an EKG to a patient. Use these suggestions to prepare for practicum exams.

1. *Identify possible tasks you may be asked to perform.*

2. *Learn the steps each task involves.* Write summary notes, and test your recall by writing or mentally rehearsing them without reference to your notes. Visualize yourself performing the task.

3. *If possible, practice performing the task, mentally reviewing the steps you learned as you proceed.*

4. *Study with another student; test and evaluate each other.*

SUMMARY

Students in technical or applied fields of study face two types of courses: technical courses and related courses in other disciplines. Specified techniques for reading in the sciences are

- reading slowly (and rereading)
- setting a specific reading purpose
- studying illustrations and drawings
- using visualization
- marking and highlighting
- reading technical manuals

Two thought patterns predominate in technical and applied fields:

- process
- problem/solution

Suggestions are offered for adapting studying strategies to technical and applied courses.

Information Systems

PREREADING QUESTIONS

1. How is data transmitted between computers?
2. Write guide questions indicating what you need to find out about each of these methods of transmitting data.

Data Transmission

H. L. Capron

1   A terminal or computer produces digital signals, which are simply the presence or absence of an electric pulse. The state of being on or off represents the *binary* number 1 or 0, respectively. Some communications lines accept digital transmission directly, and the trend in the communications industry is toward digital signals. However, most telephone lines through which these digital signals are sent were originally built for voice transmission, and voice transmission requires *analog* signals. The next section describes these two types of transmission and then discusses modems, which translate between them.

DIGITAL AND ANALOG TRANSMISSION

2   **Digital transmission** sends data as distinct pulses, either on or off, in much the same way that data travels through the computer. However, most communications media are not digital. Communications devices such as telephone lines, *coaxial* cables, and microwave circuits are already in place for voice (analog) transmission. The easiest choice for most users is to piggyback on one of these. Thus, the most common communications devices all use **analog transmission,** a continuous electrical signal in the form of a wave.

3   To be sent over analog lines, a digital signal must first be converted to an analog form. It is converted by altering an analog signal, called a **carrier wave,** which has alterable characteristics (Figure A1). One such characteristic is the **amplitude,** or height of the wave, which can be increased to represent the binary number 1 (Figure A2). Another characteristic that can be altered is the **frequency,** or number of times a wave repeats during a specific time interval; frequency can be increased to represent a 1 (Figure A3).

4   Conversion from digital to analog signals is called **modulation,** and the reverse process—reconstructing the original digital message at the other end of the transmission—is called **demodulation.** (You probably know amplitude and frequency modulation by their abbreviations, AM and FM, the methods used for radio transmission.) An extra device is needed to make the conversions: a modem.

Figure A   Analog signals.   (1) An analog carrier wave moves up and down in a continuous cycle. (2) The analog waveform can be converted to digital form through amplitude modulation. As shown, the wave height is increased to represent a 1 or left the same to represent a 0. (3) In frequency modulation the amplitude of the wave stays the same but the frequency increases to indicate a 1 or stays the same to indicate a 0.

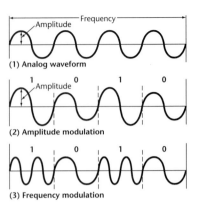

(1) Analog waveform

(2) Amplitude modulation

(3) Frequency modulation

MODEMS

5   A **modem** is a device that converts a digital signal to an analog signal and vice versa (Figure B). Modem is short for *mo*dulate/*dem*odulate.

Types of Modems

6   Modems vary in the way they connect to the telephone line. There are two main types: acoustic coupler modems and direct-connect modems. **Acoustic coupler modems** include a cradle to hold the telephone handset. Most modems today, however, are directly connected to the phone system by a cable that runs from the modem to the wall jack.

7   A **direct-connect modem** is directly connected to the telephone line by means of a telephone jack. An **external modem** is separate from the computer (Figure C). Its main advantage is that it can be used with a variety of computers. If you buy a new personal computer, for example, you can probably keep the same external modem. For those personal computer users who regard an external modem as one more item taking up desk space, new modem-on-a-chip designs have produced a modem that is so small you will hardly notice it. For a modem that is out of sight—literally—an **internal modem** board can be inserted into the computer by the user;

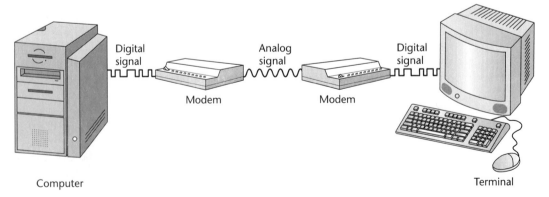

Figure B   Modems.   Modems convert—modulate—digital data signals to analog signals for sending over communications links, then reverse the process—demodulate—at the other end.

Figure C An external modem.

Source: Courtesy of 3Com Corporation

Figure D **A PC card modem.** This PC card modem, although only the size of a credit card, packs a lot of power: transmission at 56,000 bytes-per-second. The card is slipped into a slot on the side of the laptop keyboard. Look closely at the right end of the modem and you can see the pop-out jack. So, in this order: slide in the card, pop out the jack, and snap in the phone card.

Source: Courtesy of 3Com Corporation

8 in fact, most personal computers today come with an internal modem as standard equipment. As we will discuss shortly, most modems today also have *fax* capability.

Notebook and laptop computers often use modems that come in the form of **PC cards,** originally known as PCMCIA cards, named for the Personal Computer Memory Card International Association. The credit card-sized PC card slides into a slot in the computer (Figure D). A cable runs from the PC card to the phone jack in the wall. PC cards have given portable computers full connectivity capability outside the constraints of an office.

Modem Data Speeds

9 The World Wide Web has given users an insatiable appetite for fast communications. This, and costs based on time use of services, provide strong incentives to transmit as quickly as possible. The old—some *very* old—standard modem speeds of 1200, 2400, 9600, 14,400, and 28,800 **bits per second (bps)** have now been superseded by modems that transmit 33,600 bps. Most people today measure modem speed by bits per second, but another measure is **baud rate,** the number of times that the signal being used to transmit data changes. At lower modem speeds, each signal change represents one bit being sent, so bits per second and baud are the same. At higher speeds, more than one bit may be sent per signal change, so bits per second will be greater than the baud rate.

10 Since modems work over the phone lines, which are designed to carry tones of different pitches, the limited number of pitches holds the top modem speed to about 30,000 bps—or so it was thought. Now, using compression techniques, modems can send data at an astonishing 56,000 bps. This speed is limited to one direction, from the Internet to the user, but that fits perfectly with what users usually do—download files from the Internet. Note the transmission time comparisons in Table A.

Table A Data transfer rates compared	
Rate (bps)	**Time to transmit a 20-page single-spaced report**
1,200	10 minutes
2,400	5 minutes
9,600	1.25 minutes
14,400	50 seconds
28,800	25 seconds
33,600	30 seconds
56,000	12.5 seconds

ISDN

11   As noted earlier, communication via phone lines requires a modem to convert between the computer's digital signals and the analog signals used by phone lines. But what if another type of line could be used directly for digital transmission? That technology is called **Integrated Services Digital Network,** but it is usually known by its acronym, **ISDN.** The attraction is that an **ISDN adapter** can move data at 128,000 bps, a vast speed improvement over any modem. Another advantage is that an ISDN circuit includes two phone lines, so a user can use one line to connect to the Internet and the other to talk on the phone at the same time. Still, ISDN is not a panacea. Although prices are coming down, initial costs are not inexpensive. You need both the adapter and phone service and possibly even a new line, depending on your current service. Also, ongoing monthly fees may be significant. Furthermore, ISDN is unavailable in some geographic areas.

—Capron, *Computers: Tools for an Information Age,* pp. 164–65

VOCABULARY REVIEW

1. For each of the words listed below, use context; prefixes, roots, and suffixes; and/or a dictionary to write a brief definition or synonym of the word as it is used in the reading.

   a. binary (para. 1) _____

   b. analog (para. 1) _____

   c. coaxial (para. 2) _____

   d. modulation (para. 4) _____

   e. connectivity (para. 8) _____

   f. constraints (para. 8) _____

   g. insatiable (para. 9) _____

   h. superseded (para. 9) _____

   i. compression (para. 10) _____

   j. download (para. 10) _____

2. Underline new specialized terminology introduced in the reading.

COMPREHENSION QUESTIONS

1. Is digital or analog transmission the more commonly used type of transmission? Why?
2. How can a carrier wave be altered to produce a digital signal?
3. What does a modem do?

4. What are the two ways that a modem can connect to a telephone line? Which type is used more today?
5. Explain the difference between an external and an internal modem. Why do some users prefer external modems?
6. Describe two ways in which modem speeds can be measured.
7. How fast are the highest-speed modems? How is this accomplished?
8. Explain what an ISDN is, and name two advantages it has over modems.

THINKING CRITICALLY

1. Give three examples of digital and/or analog signals that are common in everyday life. Why are these signals incompatible with each other? What method(s) can be used to overcome these incompatibilities?
2. If cost were no object, what electronic device(s) would you employ to access outside information with a computer? Explain the advantage(s) these devices would offer over cheaper solutions.
3. Why is the baud rate of a modem sometimes equal to and sometimes not equal to the bits per second of the same modem?

LEARNING/STUDY STRATEGY

Draw a conceptual map showing the various methods of data transmission.

ONLINE RESEARCH: DATA TRANSMISSION*

In technical and technological fields of study, the ability to locate and apply information is important. The Internet may prove to be one of your most important resources for finding information, and your course work will teach you how to apply what you find.

1. Suppose you have connected a new 56K modem and you want to find out how quickly you are downloading data. Consult Modem Central's "56K Modem Troubleshooting Guide" at http://www.56k.com/trouble/#known, and then write a brief description of the process.
2. Go to http://www.pcworld.com/news/article/0,aid,94985,00.asp. Read this article from PC World online about boosting your modem's speed. Discuss the pros and cons of using the product described. Would you recommend it? To whom?

*If either of these sites is unavailable, use a search engine to locate a new Web site on the same topic.

TECHNICAL and APPLIED FIELDS on the Internet

The Internet has numerous resources available for research in the technical and applied fields, including directories and Web guides to help you find material relevant to your studies, journals and databases, references works, and government resources. Here is a list of useful Web sites to get you started.

Directories/Web Guides

Internet Public Library: Engineering
> http://www.ipl.org/ref/RR/static/
> sci15.00.00.html

Yahoo! Computer and the Internet
> http://dir.yahoo.com/Computers_
> and_Internet/

Journals/Indexes/Databases

Engineering E-journal Search Engine
> http://www.eevl.ac.uk/eese/

NIST Virtual Library Electronic Journals
> http://srdata.nist.gov/gateway/
> gateway?dblist=0

References

TechWeb Encyclopedia
> http://www.techweb.com/encyclopedia/

Academic Press Dictionary of Science and Technology
> http://www.onelook.com/
> ?d=all_tech&v=&sort=&langdf=all

Government Resources

Scientific and Technical Information Network
> http://stinet.dtic.mil/

National Science Foundation
> http://www.nsf.gov/

Multimedia Activities

Practice your reading and research skills on the Web.

1. **How Things Work**

    http://www.howstuffworks.com/index.htm

    http://howthingswork.virginia.edu/

    Pick some objects you use every day and find how they do what they do. Then learn about something completely new. As you use these two sites, compare their design, approach, and usability. Do you prefer one site over the other?

2. **F-Secure: Security Information Center**

    http://www.data-fellows.com/virus-info/hoax/

    Find out if that latest virus warning you received is a hoax at this comprehensive computer security site. Refer your e-mail do-gooders to this site when they forward something bogus to you. What tone does this site take toward Internet security? Write a list of the specific ways you use e-mail. Then place these into broader categories. Also record the amount of time you spend on each type of message. Evaluate your usage. How does it fit in with your overall time management plan?

ACADEMIC SUCCESS

Studying and applying the following tips will help you be successful in college.

PLANNING AND ORGANIZATION

Becoming a successful student requires planning and organization. Here are a few suggestions for ensuring your success.

1. *Organize a place to study.* Select a quiet, comfortable location and study in the same place each day. Be sure to have all your materials (paper, pens, etc.) at hand.

2. *Use a pocket calendar to record exams and due dates for papers.*

3. *Carry a small notebook for recording daily assignments for each course.* Check it each evening before you begin to study.

4. *Get to know someone in each class.* You might enjoy having someone to talk to. Also, in case you miss a class, you will have someone from whom you can get the assignment and borrow notes.

5. *Attend all classes, whether or not the instructor takes attendance.* Studies show that successful students attend class regularly, whereas students who do not are unsuccessful.

6. *Get to know your instructors.* Use your instructors' office hours to talk about exams or assignments, ask questions, and discuss ideas for papers.

KEEPING A LEARNING JOURNAL

As you begin college, you will encounter many new ideas and meet many new people from whom you will discover new ways of looking at and doing things. You also will begin to explore many new academic fields. A learning journal can be helpful in sorting out your thoughts, ideas, impressions, and reactions. Here are some suggestions for a learning journal.

1. *Keep a journal for each of your most challenging courses.* Many students use a separate spiral or steno notebook or notebook section for each course.

2. *Date your entries, and reference them to particular chapters or assignments.* Some students find it helpful to record the amount of time spent on each assignment, as well.

3. *Express your reactions to the course in general.* Record your feelings about the overall course content and what you like and do not like about the course. Include ideas that interest you and that you would like to explore further.

4. *Record your impressions about specific assignments. Include problems you encountered with particular assignments or unique features of them.*

5. *Analyze reading and study techniques you have tried.* Include both those that worked and those that did not work (and why).

6. *Include new ideas for learning.* Write down changes you made in using various study approaches, and record any new ideas you have encountered for studying the course material.

7. *Enter your reactions to and analysis of exams.* Right after you take an exam, you may have a different impression than when it is returned to you. Comparing these impressions can be useful in improving your exam-taking skills.

8. *Use your journal entries as sources for writing assignments.* They offer excellent starting points for choosing topics of papers and contain information for developing those topics.

PROCRASTINATION

When your work load increases, it is tempting to put things off. Here are some suggestions to help you overcome or control procrastination.

1. *Clear your desk.* Move everything from your desk except materials for the task at hand. With nothing else in front of you, you are more likely to start working and less likely to be distracted from your task while working.

2. *Give yourself five minutes to start.* If you are having difficulty beginning a task, tell yourself that you will work on it for just five minutes. Often, once you start working, your motivation and interest will build, and you will want to continue working.

3. *Divide the task into manageable parts.* Complicated tasks are often difficult to start because they seem so long and unmanageable. Before beginning such tasks, spend a few minutes organizing and planning. Divide each task into parts, and list what you need to do and in what order.

4. *Start somewhere, no matter where.* If you are having difficulty getting started, do something rather than sit and stare, regardless of how trivial it may seem. If you are having trouble writing a paper from rough draft notes, for example, start by recopying the notes. Suddenly, you will find yourself rearranging and rephrasing them, and you will be well on your way toward writing a draft.

5. *Recognize when you need more information.* Sometimes, procrastination is a signal that you lack skills or information. You may be avoiding a task because you are not sure how to do it. You may not understand why you use a certain procedure to solve a type of math problem, for example, so you feel reluctant to do math homework. Or selecting a term paper topic may be difficult if you are not certain of the purpose or expected length of the paper. Overcome such stumbling blocks by discussing them with classmates or with your professor.

MANAGING YOUR STUDY TIME

As college students, many of you struggle to divide your time among classes, study, job responsibilities, and friends and family. Effective planning and time management are essential for you to maintain a workable balance. Here are a few suggestions for managing your study time effectively.

1. *Develop a weekly study plan.* Allocate time for reading, reviewing, doing homework, and studying for exams. Select several specific times each week for working on each of your courses.

2. *As a rule of thumb, reserve two study hours for each hour you spend in class.*

3. *Use peak periods of concentration.* Everyone has high and low periods of concentration and attention. First, determine when these occur for you; then reserve peak times for intensive study and use less efficient times for more routine tasks such as recopying an assignment or collecting information in the library.

4. *Study difficult subjects first.* While it is tempting to get easy tasks and short little assignments out of the way first, do not give in to this approach. When you start studying, your mind is fresh and alert and you are at your peak of concentration. This is the time you are best equipped to handle difficult subjects.

5. *Schedule study for a particular course close to the time when you attend class.* Plan to study the evening before the class meets and soon after the class meeting. For example, if a class meets on Tuesday morning, plan to study Monday evening and Tuesday afternoon or evening. By studying close to class time, you will find it easier to relate class lectures and discussions to what you are reading and studying, to see connections, and to reinforce your learning.

6. *Include short breaks in your study time.* Take a break before you begin studying each new subject. Your mind needs time to refocus so that you can switch from one set of facts, problems, and issues to another. You should also take short breaks when you are working on just one assignment for a long period of time. A 10-minute break after 50 to 60 minutes of study is reasonable.

WORKING WITH CLASSMATES: GROUP PROJECTS

Many assignments and class activities involve working with a small group of classmates. For example, a sociology instructor might divide the class into groups and ask each group to brainstorm solutions to the economic or social problems of the elderly. Group presentations may be required in a business course, or groups in your American history class might be asked to research a topic.

Group projects are intended to enable students to learn from one another by viewing each other's thinking processes and by evaluating each other's ideas and approaches. Use the following suggestions to help your group function effectively:

1. *Select alert, energetic classmates if you are permitted to choose group members.*

2. *Be an active, responsible participant.* Accept your share of the work and expect others to do the same. Approach the activity with a serious attitude, rather than joking or

complaining about the assignment. This will establish a serious tone and cut down on wasted time.

3. *Make sure your group has a leader.* Because organization and direction are essential for productivity, every group needs a leader. Unless some other competent group member immediately assumes leadership, take a leadership role. While leadership may require more work, you will be in control. As the group's leader, you will need to direct the group in analyzing the assignment, organizing a plan of action, distributing work assignments, planning, and if the project is long term, establishing deadlines.

4. *Suggest that specific tasks be assigned to each group member and that the group agree upon task deadlines.*

5. *Take advantage of individual strengths and weaknesses.* For instance, a person who seems indifferent or is easily distracted should not be assigned the task of recording the group's findings. The most organized, outgoing member might be assigned the task of making an oral report to the class.

If your group is not functioning effectively or if one or more members are not doing their share, take action. Communicate directly, but try not to alienate or anger group members.

TAKING LECTURE NOTES

In many courses, your instructor will lecture, and you will need to take accurate notes for study and review. Use the following suggestions to take effective notes.

1. *Read the textbook material on which the lecture will be based* before *attending the lecture.*

2. *Listen carefully to the lecturer's opening comments;* they often reveal the purpose, focus, or organization of the lecture.

3. *Focus on ideas, not facts.* Do not try to record everything the lecturer says.

4. *Discover the thought pattern(s) on which the lecture is based.*

5. *Record the main ideas and enough details and examples so that the ideas will make sense later.*

6. *Record the organization of the lecture.* Use an indentation system to show the relative importance of ideas.

7. *Leave plenty of blank space as you take notes;* you may want to fill in missed or additional information later.

8. *Use an abbreviation system* for commonly used words (psy = psychology, w/ = with, etc.) to save time.

9. *Review your notes as soon as possible* after the lecture, filling in missing or additional information. This review will also help you remember the lecture.

LEARNING STRATEGIES

For each of your courses, you will need to learn many facts, ideas, and concepts. Use the following suggestions to learn most efficiently.

1. *Apply the principle of spaced study.* It is more effective to space, or spread out, study sessions than to study in one or two large blocks of time.

2. *Use immediate review.* As soon as you finish reading or studying, take a few minutes to look back through the material, recalling key points and rereading notes or summaries. If you review immediately after study, you will increase the amount you remember.

3. *Review frequently.* In order to retain information over time, it is necessary to review periodically. Although you are learning new material each week, reserve time to reread notes, underlining, and chapter summaries of previously covered material.

4. *Associate new information with previously learned information.* Call to mind what you already know about a topic before you begin to read or study.

5. *Use numerous sensory channels by incorporating writing, speaking, and listening into your study.* For example, consider tape recording and playing back your history notes or writing a summary sheet of key formulas for a math course.

MANAGING STRESS

College is a new and challenging experience, and new and challenging experiences tend to produce stress. Consequently, stress is a common problem that many college students face.

Common Symptoms

worn-out feeling	queasiness, indigestion
short-temperedness	listlessness
headaches	feeling rushed
difficulty concentrating	weight loss

How to Reduce Stress

1. *Eliminate stressors.* Identify possible sources of stress, and work toward eliminating them. If a part-time job is stressful, for instance, quit or find another that is less stressful. If a math course is creating stress, take action: go to the learning lab or math lab for assistance, or inquire about tutoring.

2. *Establish a daily routine.* To eliminate daily hassles and make daily tasks as simple as possible, establish a daily routine. A routine eliminates the need to make numerous small decisions, thereby giving you a sense of "smooth sailing."

3. *Accentuate your accomplishments.* When you feel pressured, stop and review what you have already accomplished that day and that week. This review will give you confidence that you can handle the work load. A positive attitude goes a long way in overcoming stress.

4. *Eat nutritious meals.*

5. *Get physical exercise.* Exercise often releases tension, promotes a general feeling of wellness, and improves self-concept. Many students report that as little as 30 minutes of exercise produces immediate relaxation and helps them to place daily events in perspective.

6. *Get adequate amounts of sleep.*

7. *Seek knowledgeable advice.* If stress becomes an insurmountable problem, seek assistance from the student counseling center. The office may offer workshops in stress-reduction techniques such as relaxation or biofeedback training.

8. *Get involved with campus activities.* Some students become so involved with their course work that they do little else but study or worry about studying. In fact, they feel guilty or stressed when they are not studying. Be sure to allow some time in each day to relax and have fun. Campus activities provide a valuable means of releasing tension and taking your mind off your work.

USING A COMPUTER AS A STUDY AND LEARNING AID

A computer's word processing capability makes it a useful study and learning aid. The following are suggestions for using the computer to organize your study. To make the most of the suggestions, you will need access to a computer on a daily basis.

1. *Use a computer to organize notes from textbook reading.* As you take notes on a reading, your notes tend to follow the organization of the text. At times it is useful to reorganize and rearrange your notes. For example, you may want to pull together information on a certain topic that is spread throughout one or more chapters. Once your notes are entered into a computer file, you can use the cut and paste function to rearrange and reorganize your notes or outlines easily without rewriting.

2. *Use a computer to organize lecture notes.* Lecture notes are, of course, recorded by hand as you listen to the lecture, unless you are using a laptop. Typing your notes into a computer file is a means of editing and reviewing, as well as reorganizing.

3. *Use a computer to integrate text and lecture notes.* The computer offers an ideal solution to the problem of how to integrate notes you have taken from your textbook and those you have taken in class. The cut and paste function allows you to move sections of your lecture notes to corresponding sections in your notes from your text.

4. *Use a computer to create lists of new terminology for each of your courses.* The computer's word processing capabilities allow you to group similar terms, organize them by chapter, or sort them into "know" and "don't know" files. A biology student, for example, grouped terms together into the following categories: energy and life, cells, biological processes, reproduction, biological systems, brain and behavior, and environmental issues.

CREDITS

Photo Credits

Page 28: Mary Kate Denny/PhotoEdit, Inc.; **49:** *The Social Mirror* by Mierle Laderman Ukeles, 1983. Mirror covered sanitation truck. Photo by D. James Dee. Courtesy Ronald Feldman Fine Arts, New York; **50 (top right):** *Landfill Cross Section (in a marble staircase)* by Mierle Laderman Ukelesn, 1990, with New York City Department of Sanitation, *Garbage Out Front: A New Era of Public Design*, Municipal Art. Layers of clays, soils, geosynthetic materials, methane venting system. Photo by D. James Dee. Courtesy Ronald Feldman Fine Arts, New York. **50 (bottom left):** *Submerged Lamppost, Salton Sea* by R. Misrach, 1985. Copyright Richard Misrach 1985. Courtesy Fraenkel Gallery; **50 (bottom right):** "Untitled" (I shop therefore I am) by Barbara Kruger, 1987. Photographic silkscreen/vinyl, 111 x 113 inches. Collection of The Broad Art Foundation, Santa Monica. Courtesy Mary Boone Gallery, New York; **51 (top):** *Mining the Museum* by Fred Wilson, 1992. Detail of installation, Cigar Store Indians facing photographs of Native American Marylanders. Photo by Jeff Goldman. The Maryland Historical Society, Baltimore, Maryland; **51 (bottom):** *Olvido (Oblivion)*, 1987–89 by Cildo Meireles. Native American tent, banknotes, bones, candles, soundtrack, 157 1/2 by 315 inches. Courtesy of the artist and Galerie Lelong, New York; **84:** Tony Savino/The Image Works; **98:** Andrew Lichtenstein/The Image Works; **251 (left, right):** ©Michael Mix; **274:** Peter Weit/CORBIS Sygma; **275:** Charles Caratini/CORBIS Sygma; **284:** Tribune Media Services, Inc. All Rights Reserved. Reprinted with Permission; **334:** © Charles D. Miller, III; **399:** Flip Schulke/Black Star; **444:** *Migrant Mother, Nipomo, California* by Dorothea Lange, 1936. Copyright the Dorothea Lange Collection, The Oakland Museum of California, City of Oakland. Gift of Paul S. Taylor; **447:** *Preacher* by Charles White, 1952. Ink on cardboard, Sight: 21 3/8 x 29 3/8 inches. Whitney Museum of American Art, New York; purchase 52.25. Photograph ©2000: Whitney Museum of American Art; **522 (top, bottom):** Courtesy of 3Com Corporation

Text Credits

Chapter 1   13: Josh R. Gerow, from *Psychology: An Introduction*, Fifth Edition, pp. 217–219. Copyright © 1997 by Addison-Wesley Educational Publishers, Inc. Reprinted by permission. **14:** Richard L. Weaver II, from *Understanding Interpersonal Communication*, Seventh Edition, pp. 423–426. Copyright © 1996 by HarperCollins College Publishers, Inc. Reprinted by permission of Addison-Wesley Educational Publishers, Inc. **17:** Bruce E. Gronbeck, Kathleen German, Douglas Ehninger, and Alan H. Monroe, from *Principles of Speech Communication*, Twelfth Brief Edition, pp. 38–39. Copyright © 1995 by HarperCollins College Publishers, Inc.

Reprinted by permission of Addison-Wesley Educational Publishers, Inc. **23:** Frank Schmalleger, from *Criminal Justice Today: An Introductory Text for the Twenty-First Century*, Fifth Edition, p. xviii. Copyright © 1999. Reprinted by permission of Prentice-Hall, Inc., Upper Saddle River, NJ. **24:** Weaver II, *Understanding Interpersonal Communication*, Seventh Edition, pp. 226–227. **24:** Jerry A. Nathanson, P. E., *Basic Environmental Technology*, Third Edition, p. 351. Upper Saddle River, NJ: Prentice-Hall, 2000. **28:** Josh R. Gerow, from *Psychology: An Introduction*, Third Edition, pp. 654–656. Copyright © 1992 by HarperCollins College Publishers, Inc. Reprinted by permission of Addison-Wesley Educational Publishers, Inc.

Chapter 2   34: Leon Baradat, from *Understanding American Democracy*, p. 163. Copyright © 1992 by HarperCollins Publishers, Inc. Reprinted by permission of Addison-Wesley Educational Publishers, Inc. **35:** Josh R. Gerow, from *Psychology: An Introduction*, Fifth Edition, p. 553. Copyright 1997 by Addison-Wesley Educational Publishers, Inc. Reprinted by permission. **35:** Joseph A. DeVito, from *Human Communication: The Basic Course*, Seventh Edition, p. 182. New York: Addison-Wesley Educational Publishers, Inc., 1997. **35:** Josh R. Gerow, from *Psychology: An Introduction*, Third Edition, p. 700. Copyright © 1992 by HarperCollins College Publishers, Inc. Reprinted by permission of Addison-Wesley Educational Publishers, Inc. **36:** Robert A. Wallace, from *Biology: The World of Life*, Sixth Edition, p. 283. Copyright © 1992 by HarperCollins Publishers, Inc. Reprinted by permission of Addison-Wesley Educational Publishers, Inc. **36:** James William Coleman and Donald R. Cressey, from *Social Problems*, Sixth Edition, p. 277. New York: HarperCollins College Publishers, Inc., 1996. **37:** Jeffrey Bennett et al., *The Cosmic Perspective*, Brief Edition, p. 28. San Francisco: Addison Wesley Longman, 2000. **37:** Gerow, *Psychology: An Introduction*, Third Edition, p. 250. **37:** Karen C. Timberlake, from *Chemistry: An Introduction to General, Organic, and Biological Chemistry*, Sixth Edition, p. 30. Copyright © 1996 by HarperCollins College Publishers, Inc. Reprinted by permission of Addison-Wesley Educational Publishers, Inc. **37:** Michael C. Mix, Paul Farber, and Keith I. King, from *Biology: The Network of Life*, Second Edition, p. 532. © 1992 by Michael C. Mix, Paul Farber, and Keith I. King. Reprinted by permission of Addison-Wesley Educational Publishers, Inc. **38:** William Keefe et al., from *American Democracy*, Third Edition, p. 186. Copyright © 1990 Harper & Row Publishers, Inc. Reprinted by permission of Addison-Wesley Educational Publishers, Inc. **38:** Gerow, *Psychology: An Introduction*, Third Edition, p. 319. **39:** Mark B. Bush, from *Ecology of a Changing Planet*, Second Edition, pp. 357–358. © 2000 by Prentice Hall, Inc. Reprinted by permission of Pearson Education, Inc., Upper Saddle River, NJ. **40:** Samuel L. Becker, from *Discovering Mass Communication*, Third Edition, p. 159. Copyright © 1992 by HarperCollins College Publishers, Inc. Reprinted by permission of Addison-Wesley Educational Publishers, Inc. **41:** Gerow, *Psychology: An Introduction*, Third

531

Chapter 6 **145:** "National Pastime Strikes Out on Drug Testing," *USA Today*, June 4, 2002. Copyright © 2002, USA Today. Reprinted with permission. **151:** "Poor Accountability Mars National Guard's Reputation," *USA Today*, December 21, 2001. Copyright © 2001, USA Today. Reprinted with permission. **157:** Barry W. Lynn, from "Pornography's Many Forms: Not All Bad," *Los Angeles Times*, May 23, 1985. **157:** Jane Rule, from "Pornography is a Social Disease," *The Body Politic*, January/February 1984. **161:** "Human-Cloning Try Nears As Company Spurns Rules," *USA Today*, April 5, 2001. Copyright © 2001, USA Today. Reprinted with permission. **165:** Paula Abend, "Arctic Oil: Black Gold or Fool's Gold," *Animals*, Winter 2001, Vol. 1, Issue 1, p. 4. Reprinted by permission. **168:** Walter J. Hickel, "ANWR Oil: An Alternative to War Over Oil," *The American Enterprise*, June 2002, Vol. 13, Issue 4. Reprinted by permission.

Chapter 7 **176:** Michael C. Mix, Paul Farber, and Keith I. King, from *Biology: The Network of Life*, Second Edition, p. 262. Copyright © 1996 by Michael C. Mix, Paul Farber, and Keith I. King. Reprinted by permission of Addison-Wesley Educational Publishers, Inc. **176:** Richard Paul Janaro and Thelma C. Altshuler, from *The Art of Being Human*, Fourth Edition, pp. 334–335. Copyright ©1993 by Paul Janaro and Thelma Altshuler. Reprinted by permission of Addison-Wesley Educational Publishers, Inc. **177:** Elaine Marieb, *Essentials of Human Anatomy and Physiology*, Sixth Edition, p. 3. San Francisco: Benjamin Cummings, 2000. **177:** Stephen Davis and Joseph Palladino, from *Psychology*, Third Edition, p. 40. Copyright © 2000 by Prentice-Hall, Inc. Reprinted by permission of Pearson Education, Inc., Upper Saddle River, NJ. **177:** Joseph A. DeVito, *Human Communication: The Basic Course*, Eighth Edition, p. 124. New York: Longman, 2000. **178:** Gerard J. Tortora, from *Introduction to the Human Body: The Essentials of Anatomy and Physiology*, Second Edition, p. 56. Copyright ©1991 by Biological Sciences Textbooks, Inc. and A and P Textbooks, Inc. Reprinted by permission of Addison-Wesley Educational Publishers, Inc. **179:** Edward Tarbuck and Frederick Lutgens, from *Earth Science*, Ninth Edition, p. 309. © 2000 by Prentice-Hall, Inc. Reprinted by permission of Pearson Education, Inc., Upper Saddle River, NJ. **179:** Tarbuck and Lutgens, *Earth Science*, Ninth Edition, pp. 620–621. **180:** Gerard J. Tortora, from *Introduction to the Human Body: The Essentials of Anatomy and Physiology*, Third Edition, p. 100. © 1994 by Biological Sciences Textbooks, Inc. and A and P Textbooks, Inc. Reprinted by permission of Addison-Wesley Educational Publishers, Inc. **181:** Tarbuck and Lutgens, *Earth Science*, Ninth Edition, pp. 278–279. **182:** R. Jackson Wilson et al., from *The Pursuit of Liberty: A History of the American People*, Vol. 2, Third Edition, pp. 492–493. Copyright © 1996 by HarperCollins College Publishers. Reprinted by permission of Addison-Wesley Educational Publishers, Inc. **183:** Philip G. Zimbardo and Richard J. Gerrig, from *Psychology and Life*, Fourthteenth Edition, p. 115. ©1996 by Philip G. Zimbardo and Richard J. Gerrig. Reprinted by permission of Addison-Wesley Educational Publishers, Inc. **183:** Alex Thio, from *Sociology*, Fourth Edition, p. 255. Copyright © 1996 by HarperCollins College Publishers. Reprinted by permission of Addison-Wesley Educational Publishers, Inc. **184:** Mix, Farber, and King, *Biology: The Network of Life*, Second Edition, pp. 663–664. **185:** Tortora, *Introduction to the Human Body: The Essentials of Anatomy and Physiology*, Second Edition, p. 77. **185:** George C. Edwards, Martin Wattenberg, and Robert Lineberry, from *Government in America*, Ninth Edition, p. 416. Copyright © 2000 by Addison-Wesley Educational Publishers,

Inc. Reprinted by permission of Pearson Education, Inc. **185:** Rebecca Donatelle, from *Access to Health*, Seventh Edition, p. 264. Copyright © 2002 Pearson Education, publishing as Benjamin Cummings. Reprinted by permission of Pearson Education, Inc. **186:** Marieb, *Essentials of Human Anatomy and Physiology*, Sixth Edition, p. 55. **186:** Wilson Dizard, *Old Media, New Media*, Third Edition, p. 179. New York: Longman, 2000. **187:** Edward Bergman and William Renwick, from *Introduction to Geography*, Updated Second Edition, pp. 442–443. Copyright © 2003 by Pearson Education, Inc. Reprinted by permission of Pearson Education, Inc., Upper Saddle River, NJ. **188:** Edwards et al., *Government in America*, Ninth Edition, pp. 223–224. **188:** Bergman and Renwick, *Introduction to Geography*, Updated Second Edition, pp. 182–183. **189:** Donatelle, *Access to Health*, Seventh Edition, pp. 223–224. **190, Note 1:** Neil A. Campbell, Lawrence G. Mitchell, Jane B. Reece, from *Biology: Concepts and Connections*, Second Edition, p. 478. Copyright © 1997 by The Benjamin/Cummings Publishing Company. Reprinted by permission of Addison-Wesley Educational Publishers, Inc. **190, Note 2:** Robert A. Wallace, from *Biology: The World of Life*, Seventh Edition, p. 524. Copyright © 1997 by Addison-Wesley Educational Publishers, Inc. Reprinted by permission. **190, Note 3:** Josh R. Gerow, from *Psychology: An Introduction*, Fifth Edition, p. 276. Copyright © 1997 by Addison-Wesley Educational Publishers. Reprinted by permission. **191, Note 4:** Wallace, *Biology: The World of Life*, Seventh Edition, p. 378. **191, Note 5:** Elaine Marieb, *Human Anatomy and Physiology*, Fourth Edition, p. 663. Menlo Park, CA: The Benjamin Cummings Publishing Company, Inc., 1998. **37:** Thio, *Sociology*, Fourth Edition, p. 534. **192, Note 6:** Wallace, *Biology: The World of Life*, Seventh Edition, p. 382. **192, Note 7:** James A. Glynn, C.F. Hohm, E.W. Stewart, *Global Social Problems*, p. 449. New York: HarperCollins College Publishers, 1996. **193, Note 8:** Gerow, *Psychology: An Introduction*, Fifth Edition, p. 278. **193, Note 9:** Richard G. Lipsey, Paul N. Courant, and Christopher Ragan, *Economics*, Twelfth Edition, p. 129. Reading, MA: Addison-Wesley Publishing Company, 1999. **193, Note 10:** Marieb, *Human Anatomy & Physiology*, Fourth Edition, p. 614. **193:** Paul G. Hewitt, from *Conceptual Physics*, Seventh Edition, p. 272. © 1993 by Paul G. Hewitt. Reprinted by permission of Addison-Wesley Educational Publishers, Inc. **194:** Donatelle, *Access to Health*, Seventh Edition, p. 516. **194:** Donatelle, *Access to Health*, Seventh Edition, p. 300. **195:** Donatelle, *Access to Health*, Seventh Edition, pp. 337–338. **196:** Thomas C. Kinnear, Kenneth L. Bernhardt, and Kathleen A. Krentler, from *Principles of Marketing*, Fourth Edition, p. 218. Copyright © 1995 by HarperCollins College Publishers. Reprinted by permission of Addison-Wesley Educational Publishers, Inc. **197:** Leon Baradat, from *Understanding American Democracy*, p. 300. Copyright © 1992 by HarperCollins Publishers, Inc. Reprinted by permission of Addison-Wesley Educational Publishers, Inc. **197:** James M. Henslin, from *Social Problems*, Fifth Edition, p. 154. Copyright © 2000 by James M. Henslin. Reprinted by permission of Pearson Education, Inc., Upper Saddle River, NJ. **198:** Henslin, *Social Problems*, Fifth Edition, p. 74. **198:** Davis and Palladino, *Psychology*, Third Edition, pp. 535–536. **200, Note 11:** Duane Preble, Sarah Preble, and Patrick Frank, *Artforms: An Introduction to the Visual Arts*, Sixth Edition, p. 136. New York: Addison-Wesley Educational Publishers, Inc., 1999. **200, Note 12:** Duane Preble et al., *Artforms: An Introduction to the Visual Arts*, Sixth Edition, p. 380. **200, Note 13:** Joseph A. DeVito, *Human Communication: The Basic Course*, Seventh Edition. New York: Addison-Wesley Educational Publishers, Inc., 1997. **200, Note 14:** George Beekman, from *Computer Confluence:*

Published by Allyn and Bacon, Boston, MA. Copyright © 2003 by Pearson Education. Reprinted by permission of the publisher. **283:** James N. Danziger, from *Understanding the Political World*, Fifth Edition, pp. 51–54. Copyright © 2001 by Addison Wesley Longman, Inc. Reprinted by permission of Pearson Education, Inc.

Chapter 10 298: The National Library of Medicine, <http://www.nlm.nih.gov>. **301:** Justine Cassell, screen shot from "Embodied Conversational Agents" found at <http://web.media.mit.edu>. Reprinted by permission of Justine Cassell. **302:** Screen shot from NAIFA Site map, <http://www.naifa.com/sitemap.html>. Used by permission of the National Association of Independent Fee Appraisers. **305:** Alan Hall, "Slices of the Past" from *Scientific American: Exhibit: Radar Archaeology:* June 22, 1998, <http://www. sciam.com/ exhibit/062298radar/index.html>. Copyright © Scientific American, Inc. <www.sciam.com>. Reprinted by permission. **307:** "Burial Mound" from *Scientific American: Exhibit: Radar Archaeology:* June 22, 1998, <http://www. sciam.com/exhibit/ 062298radar/japan.html>. Copyright © Scientific American, Inc. <www.sciam.com>. Reprinted by permission. **309:** "Remote Sensing Archeology Research at NASA," <http://www. ghcc.msfc.nasa.gov/archeology> Global Hydrology and Climate Center in partnership with NASA, Marshall Space Flight Center, Huntsville Alabama, 1998.

Chapter 11 319: Robert A. Wallace, from *Biology: The World of Life*, Sixth Edition, pp. 708, 710. Copyright © 1992 by HarperCollins Publishers, Inc. Reprinted by permission of Addison-Wesley Educational Publishers, Inc. **321:** Wallace, *Biology: The World of Life*, Sixth Edition, pp. 712–713. **327:** Wallace, *Biology: The World of Life*, Sixth Edition, pp. 632–633. **328:** Louis Berman and J.C. Evans, from *Exploring the Cosmos*, Fifth Edition, p. 145. Copyright © 1986 by Louis Berman and J.C. Evans. Reprinted by permission of Addison-Wesley Educational Publishers, Inc. **328:** Robert Divine, T. H. Breen, George M. Fredericks, and R. Hal Williams, from *America Past and Present*, Fourth Edition, pp. 890–891. Copyright © 1996 by HarperCollins College Publishers. Reprinted by permission of Addison-Wesley Educational Publishers, Inc. **334:** David Hicks and Margaret A. Gwynne, from *Cultural Anthropology*, Second Edition, pp. 378–380. Copyright © 1996 by HarperCollins College Publishers. Reprinted by permission of Addison-Wesley Educational Publishers, Inc. **338:** France Borel, "The Decorated Body" from *Le Vetement Incarne - Les Metamorphoses du Corps*. Copyright © Calman-Levy, 1992. Reprinted by permission of Calmann-Levy, Paris. English Translation © by Ellen Dooling Draper as appeared in *Parabola*, Fall 1994, V. 19, No. 3, p. 74. By permission of Ellen Dooling Draper.

Chapter 12 350: "Overview: The Issue at a Glance" from Public Agenda Online, June 2002. Copyright © Public Agenda 2002. No reproduction/distribution without permission. <www.publicagenda.org>. By permission of Public Agenda. **353:** Gerard J. Tortora, from *Introduction to the Human Body: The Essentials of Anatomy and Physiology*, Second Edition, pp. 407–08. Copyright © 1991 by Biological Sciences Textbooks, Inc. and A and P Textbooks, Inc. Reprinted by permission of Addison-Wesley Educational Publishers, Inc. **358:** W. Stephen Damron, from *Introduction to Animal Science: Global, Biological, Social, and Industry Perspectives*, pp. 202–203. Copyright © 2000 by Prentice-Hall, Inc. Reprinted by permission of Prentice-Hall, Inc., Upper Saddle River, NJ. **360:** From

Environmental Resource Handbook, p. 372. Copyright © 2001 Grey House Publishing. Reprinted with permission by Grey House Publishing, Millerton, NY. **362:** From *A to Zoo: Subject Access to Children's Picture Books*, Sixth Edition, by Carolyn Lima and John Lima. Copyright © 2001 by Bowker-Greenwood. Reproduced with permission of Greenwood Publishing Group, Inc., Westport, CT. **370:** Jared Sandberg, "Losing Your Good Name Online" from *Newsweek*, September 20, 1999, p. 57. Copyright © 1999 Newsweek, Inc. All rights reserved. Reprinted by permission. **371:** George Beekman, from *Computer Confluence: Exploring Tomorrow's Technology*, Third Edition, p. 204. Copyright © 1999 Addison Wesley Longman, Inc. Reprinted by permission of Addison-Wesley Educational Publishers, Inc. **371:** "Media Profiles: Jeff Bezos" from the December 2001 issue of *Adweek's Marketing Week* by Buck, Rinker. Copyright 2001 by BPI Communications Inc. Reproduced with permission of BPI Communications Inc. in the format Textbook via Copyright Clearance Center. **372:** Stan Gibson, "In E-Biz, Most Are Bezos Wannabes." Reprinted from *eWeek*, July 10, 2000, with permission. Copyright © 2000 Ziff Davis Media Inc. All rights reserved. **374:** Katie Hafner, "Lessons in the School of Cut and Paste," *New York Times*, June 28, 2001. Copyright © 2001 by the New York Times Co. Reprinted with permission. **378:** Frank Saxe, "Bolton Loses Court Fight with Isleys" from *Billboard*, February 3, 2001. Copyright 2001 by BPI Communications Inc. Reproduced with permission of BPI Communications Inc. in the format Textbook via Copyright Clearance Center.

Chapter 13 387: J.Ross Eshleman, Barbara G. Cashion, and Laurence A. Basirico, from *Sociology: An Introduction*, Fourth Edition, p. 46. Copyright © 1993 by HarperCollins College Publishers. Reprinted by permission of Addison-Wesley Educational Publishers, Inc. **388:** Josh R. Gerow, from *Psychology: An Introduction*, Fifth Edition, p. 290. Copyright © 1997 by Addison-Wesley Educational Publishers, Inc. Reprinted by permission. **390:** Arlene S. Skolnick, from *The Intimate Environment: Exploring Marriage and the Family*, Fifth Edition, pp. 193–194. Copyright © 1992 by Arlene S. Skolnick. Reprinted by permission of Addison-Wesley Educational Publishers, Inc. **390:** Gerow, *Psychology: An Introduction*, Fifth Edition, pp. 305–306. **392:** Eshleman et al., *Sociology: An Introduction*, Fourth Edition, pp. 356–358. **397:** William E. Thompson and Joseph V. Hickey, from *Society in Focus: An Introduction to Sociology*, Second Edition, p. 81. Copyright ©1996 by William E. Thompson and Joseph V. Hickey. Reprinted by permission of Addison-Wesley Educational Publishers, Inc. **399:** Eshleman et al., *Sociology: An Introduction*, Fourth Edition, pp. 487–490.

Chapter 14 408: Lawrence J. Gitman, from *Principles of Managerial Finance*, Ninth Edition, pp. 581–82. © 2000 by Lawrence J. Gitman. Reprinted by permission of Pearson Education, Inc. **409:** Robert C. Nickerson, from *Business and Information Systems*, pp. 263–265. Copyright © 1998 by Addison-Wesley Educational Publishers, Inc. Reprinted by permission of Prentice-Hall, Inc., Upper Saddle River, NJ. **412:** Ronald Ebert and Ricky Griffin, from *Business Essentials*, Fourth Edition, pp. 114-115, 134–135. Copyright © 2003 by Pearson Education, Inc. Reprinted by permission of Pearson Education, Inc., Upper Saddle River, NJ. **414:** William M. Pride, Robert J. Hughes, and Jack R. Kapoor, from *Business*, Fifth Edition, pp. 386–387. Copyright © 1996 by Houghton Mifflin Company. Reprinted with permission. **416:** Gitman, *Principles of Managerial Finance*, Ninth Edition, p. 8. **416:** David Van

INDEX